This book explores and analyses the political, economic and religious relations between the royal monastic institutions in tenth- and eleventh-century Germany and the Ottonian and early Salian monarchs.

In its broadest sense, the book examines the structures of power, the problems of rulership, and the realities of power and control in a pre-modern society. Specifically, it focuses on practical aspects of itinerant kingship – governing while constantly in motion – and on the *servitium regis*, those payments and services that churches and monasteries specially allied to the king were obliged to provide to him in return for royal patronage and protection, as a crucial economic underpinning of the kings' itinerary. In addition the book investigates royal–monastic relations in an effort to determine how the relationship functioned in practice. In the process, it re-evaluates the economic support that the monasteries provided, and it examines how the demands of this support affected both the monastic ideal and the institutional development of monasticism in Germany. The study concludes that German rulers of the period made much greater use of their royal monasteries than has hitherto been supposed, and that this use resulted at least in part from plan and policy.

Cambridge studies in medieval life and thought

ITINERANT KINGSHIP AND ROYAL MONASTERIES IN EARLY MEDIEVAL GERMANY, c. 936–1075

Cambridge Studies in Medieval Life and Thought
Fourth series

General Editor:

D. E. LUSCOMBE

Professor of Medieval History, University of Sheffield

Advisory Editors:

R. B. DOBSON

Professor of Medieval History, University of Cambridge, and Fellow of Christ's College

ROSAMOND MCKITTERICK

Reader in Early Medieval European History, University of Cambridge, and Fellow of Newnham College

The series Cambridge Studies in Medieval Life and Thought was inaugurated by G. G. Coulton in 1921. Professor D. E. Luscombe now acts as General Editor of the Fourth Series, with Professor R. B. Dobson and Dr Rosamond McKitterick as Advisory Editors. The series brings together outstanding work by medieval scholars over a wide range of human endeavour extending from political economy to the history of ideas.

For a list of titles in the series, see end of book.

ITINERANT KINGSHIP AND ROYAL MONASTERIES IN EARLY MEDIEVAL GERMANY, *c.* 936–1075

JOHN W. BERNHARDT

San José State University

Published by the Press Syndicate of the University of Cambridge
The Pitt Building, Trumpington Street, Cambridge CB2 IRP
40 West 20th Street, New York, NY 10011–4211, USA
10 Stamford Road, Oakleigh, Melbourne 3166, Australia

First published 1993

Printed in Great Britain at the University Press, Cambridge

A catalogue record for this book is available from the British Library

Library of Congress cataloguing in publication data
Bernhardt, John William, 1949–
Itinerant kingship and royal monasteries in early medieval Germany
c. 936–1075/John W. Bernhardt.
p.   cm. – (Cambridge studies in medieval life and thought;
4th ser.)
Includes bibliographical references and index.
ISBN 0 521 39489 9
1. Germany – History – Saxon House, 919–1024.   2. Germany – History –
Franconian House, 1024–1125.   3. Church and state – Germany –
History.   4. Germany – Church history – Middle Ages, 843–1517.
5. Monasticism and religious order – History – Middle Ages, 600–1500.
I. Title. II. Series.
DD137.5.B39   1993
943'.022 – dc20   92-34399CIP

ISBN 0 521 39489 9 hardback

For my mother, father and sister

CONTENTS

List of illustrations   *page* xi
Acknowledgements   xii
List of abbreviations   xv

INTRODUCTION   I

I   GERMAN KINGSHIP AND ROYAL MONASTERIES:
    THE HISTORICAL AND HISTORIOGRAPHICAL
    CONTEXT   3
    Ottonian history and government   3
    The Ottonians and the church   27
    Ottonian foreign policy   35

2   ITINERANT KINGSHIP, ROYAL MONASTERIES AND
    THE *SERVITIUM REGIS*   45
    Itinerant kingship and the structure of the realm   45
    Royal monasteries: problems of definition   70
    Servitium regis: the historiographical problem   75

3   *SERVITIUM REGIS* AND MONASTIC PROPERTY   85
    Charters and monastic property division   94
    Development of monastic property divisions   106
        The west Frankish realm   106
        The east Frankish and German experience   110
    Servitium regis and abbatial property   127

4   MONASTERIES IN THE SAXON HEARTLAND   136
    Definition and delineation   136
    Quedlinburg (Walbeck)   138
    Gandersheim (Eschwege)   149
    St Maurice at Magdeburg   162
    Minor royal monasteries and convents of Saxony:
        Berge, Nienburg, Alsleben, Drübeck, Gernrode
        (Frose) and Nordhausen   170

Contents

5 MONASTERIES IN WESTPHALIA 177
   Westphalia as a transit zone – the 'Hellweg' 177
   Werden 181
   Essen 190
   Corvey 195
   Royal convents in Westphalia and Engern 203

6 MONASTERIES IN THE SAXON–HESSIAN BORDER
   REGION 211
   River basins as a geopolitical setting 211
   Helmarshausen 212
   Hilwartshausen 216
   Kaufungen 222

7 MONASTERIES IN HESSE AND THURINGIA 235
   Geopolitical structure of Hesse and Thuringia 235
   Hersfeld and Fulda: background and development 241
   Hersfeld and Fulda 252
   Hersfeld (Memleben) 254
   Fulda 265
   Hersfeld and Fulda: grants of sovereign rights 282

   CONCLUSION 290

   Bibliography 330
   Index 363

ILLUSTRATIONS

GENEALOGIES

1 The Ottonians   *page* 310
2 The Salians   311

MAPS

1 Ottonian–Salian Germany: political   313
2 Northeastern frontier: Slavic peoples and territories   315
3 Ottonian–Salian Germany: physical   317
4 Main royal routes and transit zones   318
5 Royal convents and monasteries in Saxony,
   Westphalia, Hesse and Thuringia   319
6 Saxony: roads and centres   321
7 Westphalian transit zone: the Hellweg   322
8 Saxon–Hessian river basins   325
9 Central transit zone: main routes and Hersfeld's
   properties   326
10 Fulda: pertinent roads   328
11. Itinerary stations in the central transit zone   329

ACKNOWLEDGEMENTS

Throughout my studies and during the writing of this book, I have benefited greatly from the learning, advice and encouragement of many teachers, colleagues and friends, as well as from the generous support of several fellowships and grants. Robert L. Benson, at the University of California at Los Angeles, my mentor and my friend, who has spent a lifetime studying the exercise of power and the relationships between church and state in the middle ages, taught me most of what I know and suggested the initial direction of the research. He offered valuable criticism and advice throughout and his encouragement never waned. Timothy Reuter at the Monumenta Germaniae Historica read and commented upon several drafts of the manuscript and offered highly constructive criticisms and many fruitful suggestions. Also, in many pleasant conversations, he shared his insights, knowledge and intuitions about the murky world of Ottonian Germany. Sadly, this book lost an ideal reader and critic, the late Professor Karl Leyser, whose ideas and research greatly advanced the knowledge and understanding of early medieval Germany. Professor Leyser's written comments on my work at an early stage and my subsequent conversations with him gave me a greater understanding of some aspects of this topic and helped me avoid errors and pitfalls in others. Professor Leyser will be sorely missed. I owe an enormous debt of gratitude to David A. Warner at the Rhode Island School of Design. In countless conversations on every conceivable question about Ottonian and Salian Germany, he constantly offered fresh insights, bolstered with much good humour and unfailing support and friendship. I should also like to thank Professors Richard H. Rouse, Dale V. Kent and David Luscombe for their advice and helpful comments, William Davies at Cambridge University Press, who facilitated the publishing of this work and showed enormous patience in the process, and finally Mrs Virginia Catmur, who scrupulously read the final copy and made many helpful suggestions. Thanks are also due to Tomás Hulick, who assisted me with revising the bibliography. Financial support for the research of this work has come from several sources. The Deutscher Akademischer Austauschdienst in Bonn, Germany generously provided me with a research fellowship for two years in Germany, and the National Endowment for the Humanities funded the travel for an additional summer of research abroad. I should also like to thank the History Department at San José State University for the Wharburton Condon Award, which supported my last stay abroad, and for funding a graduate student to assist me.

Often in the process of scholarship personal patronage and support rank as important as financial patronage. Therefore, I want to express my appreciation to Professor Horst Fuhrmann, president of the Monumenta Germaniae Historica, for graciously allowing me to research in the marvellous library of the MGH and to participate in the intellectual community at the Institute. I also wish to express my sincere gratitude to Christa and Helmut Becker and to Ann Petersen for the hospitality and friendship they offered during long summers of research.

I thank the Regents of the University of California for their permission to publish a revised version of an article which appeared in *Viator*.

Two enormous debts incurred in the writing of this book have yet to be recognized. Rosamond McKitterick, the editor for the Cambridge Studies in Medieval Life and Thought, has been an invaluable help, a sharp critic, and constant support. She has read this work several times with great insight and has offered countless suggestions that have made it a better book. Where I have not followed her suggestions, I have done so in my own folly. My correspondence with her has been a pleasure and her patience and good cheer have been remarkable. Likewise, I want to thank Ms Jan Phillips sincerely and graciously. She painstakingly assisted me during the final stages of this work – reformatting the bibliography, checking citations, and meticulously proof-reading the entire text several times. Her suggestions have improved the book and her encouragement in the lowest of times always provided me with a welcome lift. Whatever errors remain after the scrutiny of these two women, or indeed after the comments and suggestions of all those who read the work, fall at my feet alone.

Finally, I want to acknowledge the love and constant support of my wonderful family, who patiently accepted shortened holidays and visits, and long working hours. With love, I offer this to them.

ABBREVIATIONS

a.	*anno; annis*
AD	*Archiv für Diplomatik*
AKG	*Archiv für Kulturgeschichte*
AMRKG	*Archiv für mittelrheinische Kirchengeschichte*
Ann.	*Annales*
AUF	*Archiv für Urkundenforschung*
BA	Böhmer/Appelt, *Regesta Imperii 3.1.1*
BDLG	*Blätter für deutsches Landesgeschichte*
Berichte	Berichte of the learned society indicated by the name of a city following, such as: *Berichte Leipzig = Berichte über die Verhandlungen der Sächsischen Akademie der Wissenschaften zu Leipzig,* philosophisch-historische Klasse
BF	Böhmer/Ficker, *Regesta Imperii 5*
BG	Böhmer/Graff, *Regesta Imperii 2.4*
BM^2	Böhmer/Mühlbacher, *Regesta Imperii 1*
BMik	Böhmer/Mikoletzky, *Regesta Imperii 2.2*
BO	Böhmer/Ottenthal, *Regesta Imperii 2.1*
Bouq.	Bouquet, ed., *Recueil des historiens des Gaules et de la France*
BS	Böhmer/Struve, *Regesta Imperii 3.2.3*
BU	Böhmer/Uhlirz, *Regesta Imperii 2.3*
BZ	Böhmer/Zimmermann, *Regesta Imperii 2.5*
c.; cc.	capitulum (chapter); capitula (chapters)
CCM	*Corpus Consuetudinum Monasticarum*
CDA	*Codex Diplomaticus Anhaltinus*
CDF	*Codex Diplomaticus Fuldensis*
CL	*Codex Laureshamensis,* ed. Glöckner
Cont. Reg.	Adalbert, *Continuatio Reginonis* (see under Regino, *Chronicon,* in Bibliography)

D; DD	*Diploma; Diplomata*	
	DKE	*Diploma Karls des Einfaltigen = Recueil ... Charles III le Simple*
	DKK	*Diploma Karls des Kahlen = Recueil ... Charles II le Chauve*
	DLF	*Diploma Ludwigs des Frommer*, in Bouquet, ed., *Recueil*
	[MGH] DPep III	MGH, *Pippini diploma*
	DKar	*Caroli Magni diploma*
	DLoth I	*Lotharii I. diploma*
	DLD	*Ludowici Germanici diploma*
	DLJ	*Ludowici Iunioris diploma*
	DKD	*Karoli III. diploma*
	DArn	*Arnolfi diploma*
	DZ	*Zwentiboldi diploma*
	DLK	*Ludowici Infantis diploma*
	DKo	*Conradi Burgundiae diploma*
	DK I	*Conradi I. diploma*
	DH I	*Heinrici I. diploma*
	DO I	*Ottonis I. diploma*
	DO II	*Ottonis II. diploma*
	DO III	*Ottonis III. diploma*
	DH II	*Heinrici II. diploma*
	DKunig	*Kunigundae diploma* (in *MGH Diplomata ... 3*)
	DK II	*Conradi II. diploma*
	DH III	*Heinrici III. diploma*
	DH IV	*Heinrici IV. diploma*
	DK III	*Conradi III. diploma*
	DF I	*Friderici I. diploma*
DA	*Deutsches Archiv*	
DKP Rep.	Die Deutschen Königspfalzen: Repertorium ...	
EB	*Beiträge zur Geschichte von Stadt und Stift Essen*	
EHR	*English Historical Review*	
FGB	*Fuldaer Geschichtsblätter*	
FMS	*Frühmittelalterliche Studien*	

FS	Festschrift
FUB	*Urkundenbuch des Klosters Fulda*
GWU	*Geschichte in Wissenschaft und Unterricht*
HHSD	Handbuch der historischen Stätten Deutschlands
HJB	*Historisches Jahrbuch*
HJBLG	*Hessisches Jahrbuch für Landesgeschichte*
HUB	*Urkundenbuch der Reichsabtei Hersfeld*
HZ	*Historische Zeitschrift*
JB	Jahrbuch (Jahrbücher)
JBNG	*Jahrbuch für Numismatik und Geldgeschichte*
JEH	*Journal of Ecclesiastical History*
JL	Jaffé/Loewenfeld *et al.*, *Regesta pontificum Romanorum*
Kehr	Kehr, Paul, 'Die älteren Urkunden für Helmarshausen', *NA* 49 (1932) 86–114 (name followed by a no. = number of the charter)
MGH	Monumenta Germaniae Historica

	Capit.	*Capitularia regum Francorum*
	Conc.	*Concilia*
	Const.	*Constitutiones et acta publica imperatorum et regum*
	D; DD	*Diplomata*
	Epis.	Epistolae (in quarto)
	Epis. Select.	Epistolae selectae
	SRG	Scriptores Rerum Germanicarum in usum scholarum … separatim editi
	NS	Nova Series
	SS	Scriptores (folio)

MIÖG	*Mitteilungen des Instituts für österreichische Geschichtsforschung*
MRUB	*Urkundenbuch zur Geschichte der … mittelrheinischen Territorien*, ed. Beyer
n.	note
NA	*Neues Archiv*
NF	Neue Folge
nn.	notes

List of abbreviations

NSJBLG	*Niedersächsisches Jahrbuch für Landesgeschichte*
PU	*Papsturkunden, 896–1046*, ed. Zimmermann [= Veröffentlichungen der Historische Kommission 3–4] (Vienna 1984–5)
QEBG	Quellen und Erörterungen zur bayerischen und deutschen Geschichte
RB	*Revue Bénédictine*
RE	*Registrum Erkenberti Corbeiensis Abbatis*
REK	*Regesten der Erzbischöfe von Köln*
RHEF	*Revue d'histoire de l'église de France*
RU	*Rheinische Urbare*, ed. Kötzschke
RVJB	*Rheinische Vierteljahrsblätter*
SA	*Sachsen und Anhalt*
s.a.	*sub anno; sub annis*
SB	*Sitzungsberichte* of the learned society indicated by the name of a city following, such as: *SB Vienna = Sitzungsberichte der kaiserlichen Akademie der Wissenschaften zu Wien*, philosophisch-historische Klasse
Settimane	Del Centro Italiano di Studi Sull'Alto Medioevo: Settimane di Studio
Stumpf	Stumpf, Karl Friedrich, *Die Reichskanzler vornehmlich des X., XI. und XII. Jahrhunderts 2: Die Kaiserurkunden des X., XI. und XII. Jahrhunderts* (Innsbruck 1865–83 repr. Aalen 1960)
SZ	*Soester Zeitschrift*
TAF	*Traditiones et Antiquitates Fuldenses*
UB Westfalen	*Urkundenbuch ... Westfalen*, ed. Seibertz
UBGNR	*Urkundenbuch für die Geschichte des Niederrheins*, ed. Lacomblet
UBM	*Urkundenbuch des Erzstiftes Magdeburg 1 (937–1192)*
UBSG	*Urkundenbuch der Abtei Sanct Gallen*, ed. Wartmann
VF	Vorträge und Forschungen
VMPIG	Veröffentlichungen des Max-Planck-Instituts für Geschichte
VSWG	*Vierteljahrschrift für Sozial- und Wirtschaftsgeschichte*

WdF	Wege der Forschung
WZ	*Westfälische Zeitschrift*
ZBLG	*Zeitschrift für bayerische Landesgeschichte*
ZGOR	*Zeitschrift für die Geschichte des Oberrheins*
ZHG	*Zeitschrift des Vereins für hessische Geschichte und Landeskunde*
ZKG	*Zeitschrift für Kirchengeschichte*
ZRG	*Zeitschrift der Savigny-Stiftung für Rechtsgeschichte*
	GA germanistische Abteilung
	KA kanonistische Abteilung

INTRODUCTION

This book explores and analyses the political, economic and religious relations between the royal monastic institutions in tenth- and eleventh-century Germany and the Ottonian and early Salian monarchs. In its broadest sense, it examines the structures of power, the problems of rulership and the realities of power and control in a pre-modern society. Specifically, the study focuses on practical aspects of itinerant kingship – that is, governing while constantly in motion – and on the *servitium regis* – those payments and services that churches and monasteries specially allied with the king were obliged to provide to him in return for royal patronage and protection – as a crucial economic underpinning of the German kings' itinerary. In regard to itinerant kingship and the *servitium regis*, far less research has been devoted to the role of royal monasteries and convents than to the role of the bishoprics and the royal residences or *Pfalzen*. Consequently, I investigated royal–monastic relations in this context to determine how this relationship functioned in actual practice. In the process, I re-evaluated the economic support that the royal monasteries provided to the king and his itinerant court, and examined how the demands of this support affected both the monastic ideal and the institutional development of monasticism in Germany.

I argue that the size and the political structure of the realm over which the Ottonian and Salian kings came to rule forced them to govern in a highly itinerant mode. The itinerant governance of the Ottonian and early Salian monarchs, in turn, necessitated that strategically placed royal monasteries were called upon to play a substantial role in accommodating, feeding and supplying the royal court while under way, as well as in securing and maintaining crucial corridors of transit. Consequently, a much closer and more important relationship existed between the royal monasteries and the early German kings than previous scholarship has acknowledged. I show how this relationship functioned in the realm of

I

practical politics: that is, it varied widely in the specific relationship between individual institutions and monarchs, yet overall a coherent set of responses to problems and situations emerged – in sum, a royal monastic policy.

Before discussing the royal *iter* and its importance, the structure of the German realm and the *servitium regis* in detail, however, it is necessary to provide the historical context of the study and outline the methods and structure of Ottonian government.

Chapter 1

GERMAN KINGSHIP AND ROYAL MONASTERIES: THE HISTORICAL AND HISTORIOGRAPHICAL CONTEXT

OTTONIAN HISTORY AND GOVERNMENT

On 2 July 936 Henry I, a member of the Liudolfing family of Saxony (later known as the Ottonians) and king of the east Frankish/German realm, died in Memleben near the border of southern Saxony (see Map 1 and Genealogical Table 1).[1] Almost seven years previously, however, in 929, he had set his house in order and arranged the royal succession.[2] Then shortly before his death Henry had the arrangements of 929 formally ratified by an assembly of the realm at Erfurt.[3] Through these arrangements Henry designated his eldest son, Otto, to succeed him in the kingship. Thus, although he left to his other sons, Thankmar, Henry and Brun, their inheritance in properties and treasures, he placed Otto alone in authority over his brothers and over the kingdom of the Franks.[4]

---

[1] Liudprand 4.15. The historical narrative for the late Carolingian, Ottonian and early Salian periods can be found in several general histories, which have been published in the last ten years and largely replace older works on the same topics. The most important and accessible general studies of these periods include: Beumann (1991); Reuter (1991a); Schulze (1991); Keller (1986); Fuhrmann (1986); Hlawitschka (1986); Althoff and Keller (1985); F. Prinz (1985); Herrmann (1982); and the earlier work of Holtzmann (1955), which remains unsurpassed in its detail. See Fried (1987) for a review and critique of several of these recent works. In this overview I follow the general narrative presented in these works and cite them only in regard to specific or unique points of view.

[2] On the ordering of the royal house and Otto's marriage to Edith of England in 929, see Schmid (1960/1971a), (1964/1971b), and recently Leyser (1983b) esp. 75–85.

[3] Widukind 1.41; *Vita Math. antiq.* c. 7 p. 577; *Vita Math. post.* cc. 7, 8 pp. 288–9. For the events of 929 see Schmid (1960/1971a, 1964/1971b), who cites the older literature. In spite of the objections of Hoffmann (1972), Schmid (1960/1971a, 1964/1971b), now bolstered by Leyser (1983b) esp. 79–80, remains convincing regarding Henry I's designation of Otto as king already in 929.

[4] Widukind 1.41: 'Cumque se iam gravari morbo sensisset, convocato omni populo designavit filium suum Oddonem regem,(;) caeteris quoque filiis predia cum thesauris distribuens;(,) ipsum vero Oddonem, qui maximus et optimus fuit, fratribus et omni Francorum imperio prefecit.' Keller (1982) 113–14 makes the astute suggestion that a

3

Three events within the first fourteen months of Otto's reign can be used as symbols of the continuity and the change that were to characterize the new king's practice and structure of government, both in relation to his father's reign and to the traditions of the east Frankish kingdom of the Carolingians. These events were his coronation at Aachen in August of 936, his consent to the establishment of a royal convent of canonesses on his father's burial site at Quedlinburg in Saxony, and the foundation of a new royal monastery and centre of royal power at Magdeburg on the Elbe River, which in 937 was the easternmost border of the realm.

At the beginning of Chapter 2 of his *Saxon History*, Widukind of Corvey provides us with a detailed account of Otto I's accession to the throne.[5] Here for the first time we see elements of continuity and change. Widukind tells us that like his father before him, Otto was elected king by 'all the people of the Franks and the Saxons'.[6] Otto, hearkening back to Charlemagne and Frankish models of kingship, chose the church, which Charlemagne built at his favourite residence in Aachen and in which he was buried, as the theatre for the drama of his formal coronation ceremony, to which he came dressed in Frankish garb. After being formally constituted or made king by the magnates, receiving the regalia and the sacral anointment from the leading prelates, and being acclaimed king by the assembled 'people', Otto ascended to Charlemagne's throne. Widukind's account of this event, written in the 960s, provides us with some insights to Otto's reign and method of governing. Both Otto's choice of Aachen and the ceremony itself sent distinct signals. Not only was Otto evoking the memory of Charlemagne and recognizing the fact that his kingdom was still largely rooted in Frankish tradition,[7] but he also thereby demonstrated control of Lotharingia (Lorraine), which his father

---

minor alteration of the punctuation of text in the standard edition – that is, replacing the comma after *regem* with a semicolon and the semicolon after *distribuens* with a comma (as above in parentheses) – would display Henry's actions here with a clearer emphasis.   [5] Widukind 2.1.

[6] Widukind 2.1: 'omnis populus Francorum et Saxonum'. Concerning Widukind's use of this terminology, see Schlesinger (1948) 405 n. 102 and regarding this 'election' at an unnamed location see Lintzel (1953/1971) 378–81.

[7] Holtzmann (1955) 112 and Reuter (1991a) 148 both point out that the choice of Aachen and its Carolingian tradition was also aimed at the recent coronation of Louis IV as king of the west Frankish realm in Laon, the first Carolingian ruler in the west in thirteen years. Otto appears to have wanted to use his coronation in Aachen to symbolize his pre-eminence as successor to Charlemagne.

had won back in 925.[8] Perhaps too, he wanted to indicate his intention to govern more in the fashion of Charlemagne than in that of his father.

Otto, the son of a strong and successful king, began his reign more from a position of strength than had his father. In 919, Henry I had accepted the designation and the transfer of kingship from a beleaguered king of another family, which resulted in a double election.[9] At his king-making ceremony he declined the ecclesiastical anointing and soon thereafter had to win the recognition of the other dukes and overcome the double election on the battlefield.[10] In 936, on the other hand, Otto received a dynastic designation from his own father and accepted the sacral anointing at his coronation. Moreover, the leading magnates from the other duchies of the realm, Lotharingia, Franconia, Swabia and Bavaria, peacefully assented to Otto's election and symbolically demonstrated their subordination to his overlordship by waiting on him at a ritual banquet following the coronation (see Map 1).[11] This does not mean that no dissent existed. Several sources provide us with information indicating that Henry I's act of designating a single son as sole successor to the kingship – that is, the attempt to move from a kingship dominated by the entire royal 'Sippe' or kindred to the creation of a royal dynasty[12] – met with resistance not only from Henry's other sons, especially Otto's younger brother Henry, but also from numerous factions within the Saxon

---

[8] In 911, when the east Frankish peoples had elected Conrad I, the duke of Franconia, as their king, the Lotharingians had given their allegiance to the west Frankish king, Charles the Simple. Through alliances, negotiation and warfare, Otto's father, Henry I, had won Lotharingia back under east Frankish overlordship. See *Ann. Alam. s.a.* 912 p. 55; Flodoard *s.a.* 922–5; *Cont. Reg. s.a.* 925; and Holtzmann (1955) 73–83.

[9] For a discussion of the double election of 919 see, most recently, Beumann (1973) and (1978); Thomas (1976); and Wolf (1983).

[10] On sacral anointment and Henry's refusal of it in 919, see Erdmann (1938) and Lintzel (1955/1961b) for the two seminal articles, and now Karpf (1984), who reviews all of the older literature. [11] Widukind 2.2.

[12] The period from the late ninth century to the early eleventh century appears as a general period of transition from the Carolingian successor kingdoms to the various medieval political entities of Germany, France, Italy and Burgundy. The creation of a royal dynasty in the German realm marked a stage in this period of 'becoming' that signified a growing stabilization of the concept of dynasty. See Brühl (1972) for a summary of this development. Brühl (1990) documents and analyses this period of 'becoming' of the early medieval polities in a massive monograph, which he then briefly summarizes in Brühl (1991). German scholars name this the problem of 'indivisibility of the realm' or the *Unteilbarkeitsprinzip*, and it has spawned a vast literature, which Hlawitschka (1986) conveniently summarizes and to which Schmid (1985b) and Hlawitschka (1988) have added recent discussions.

nobility, including Henry I's wife, Queen Mathilda.[13] In fact, Widukind specifically mentioned the young Henry's absence during the coronation festivities: it appears that Otto had entrusted Henry to Count Siegfried's 'protective' custody far away in Saxony.[14] This dissension within the royal house was to provide some of the tinder that fuelled the early revolts and crises of Otto's reign.[15]

Within five weeks of his coronation in Aachen, Otto I travelled east to his homeland of Saxony. It should not be overlooked that immediately after his coronation in the famous Carolingian centre of power Otto proceeded first to Quedlinburg, a fortified residence of his family which belonged to mother's dower; then to Magdeburg, a complex of old Carolingian and Liudolfing family properties, which Otto had given to his wife Edith as her wedding gift (*dos*); and shortly thereafter to nearby Werla, the traditional site for assemblies of the Saxon nobility. Nothing more clearly demonstrates the creation of a new region of royal power in Saxony than this initial perambulation of the power centres in the Saxon heartlands of the new king. At Quedlinburg, on 13 September 936, Otto I issued a charter that gave royal consent to the foundation of a convent at his father's burial site, where the resident canonesses would offer continuous prayers for the members of his family, both living and dead, and thereby promote the cult of the royal family.[16] Otto granted the congregation extensive properties and incomes, royal protection, the right to an

---

[13] Flodoard *s.a.* 936 (the most contemporary of our sources); *Vita Math. post.* cc. 6, 9; and Thietmar 1.21. Leyser (1983b) esp. 75–85, in an important article that further illuminates the events of 929 and their long-range effects, indicates that although Otto's position within the realm may have remained strong since 929, his position within his own house and within the Saxon nobility had worsened and become weaker since the coming of age of his younger brother. He sees much of this dissent being fuelled by a growing rivalry and tension between the queen dowager, Mathilda, and Otto's wife and queen, Edith, who was descended from the Anglo-Saxon royal house. See also Schmid (1960/1971a) esp. 412–14 with n. 71, who previously discussed the tensions caused by a new queen in Saxony and made suggestions as to the differing positions of Henry and Mathilda in regard to the arrangements of 929.   [14] Widukind 2.2.

[15] In addition to the general histories of this period, see Leyser (1979) 9–22, 32–42; Althoff (1982b); and Erkens (1982). Leyser has shown that these revolts from the side of the nobility fell into the accepted category of a feud, but that the Saxon and Frankish nobility needed a focal point within the royal family, a member around whom to unify in order to carry forth their feud against a powerful king with any hope of success.

[16] *DO I* 1. Widukind 1.41 reports that Henry's sons brought his body from Memleben, where he died, to its burial site before the altar of St Peter's basilica at Quedlinburg. On Quedlinburg as an Ottonian cult site, that is, a centre of the *memoria* of the Ottonian family, see Althoff (1984) 22, 166–93.

advocate from the Liudolfing family or its collateral relatives, and the prerogative to elect their abbess without outside interference.[17] Thietmar of Merseburg tells us in his *Chronicon* that Mathilda, the queen-mother, on the thirtieth day after Henry's death, established the congregation with all necessary provisions on her own property (part of her dower) and had her foundation confirmed in writing.[18] Thus, Otto's charter was a royal confirmation of this action.[19] This new foundation at the start of Otto's reign held manifold significance for the future. It marked the inception of an Ottonian familial cult site, which became one of the main centres of royal power in Saxony and the Ottonians' favourite residence in which to celebrate the high feast of Easter.[20] Thereby, it signalled dramatically the shift in royal power to the east in the Harz region and the creation of a new centre of royal dominion outside the traditional Carolingian centre of government in the Rhineland. Quedlinburg later became one of the main bastions of control for the Salians when they came to the throne. Apart from the royal properties which they inherited from the Ottonians, they were landless in Saxony. In addition, the foundation of Quedlinburg pointed to another future characteristic of Ottonian rule: a predominance in Saxony of religious institutions for women, which were founded or actively supported by the Ottonians, often under the headship of royal women.[21] Female religious institutions in Saxony and a few other areas of the realm came to play a vital role in the context of Ottonian government and for a short period in the tenth and eleventh centuries this helped to empower the women founding and ruling these institutions.

About thirteen months later, on his second long stay in Saxony,

---

[17] In the delineation of Quedlinburg's legal status, this charter (*DO I* 1) contains a now famous statement about the nature of Otto's kingship, especially in regard to the notion of 'indivisibility of the realm', the creation of a royal dynasty and the elective element in German kingship. For the constitutional significance of this charter, see Schmid (1964/1971b) 466–76.

[18] Thietmar 1.21. Quedlinburg and several other properties were granted to her by Henry I in 929 with *DH I* 20, which set up her dower. On the role of royal women, especially dowager queens, in establishing dynastic burial sites and making provisions for a family prayer cult, and other noblewomen and widows doing the same for their families, see Leyser (1979) 63–73 and Schulenburg (1988).

[19] Leyser (1983b) 82 points out that the curious failure to mention Otto's mother, Mathilda, in Otto's charter indicates the rift that existed within the royal family.

[20] Concerning crown-wearings and favoured residences of the German kings for the great liturgical feasts, see Klewitz (1939a) esp. 75–96 concerning the residences.

[21] On the German and Saxon convents, see Leyser (1979) 63–73 and Parisse (1978), (1990), and (1991). For a comparable situation in Anglo-Saxon England, see Meyer (1981).

Otto instituted another monastic foundation at Magdeburg, on the Elbe River. It was dedicated to the warrior saint Maurice, and he recruited its first monks from the recently reformed monastery of St Maximin in Trier.[22] Once again, Otto did not establish this new foundation totally alone. He founded the royal monastery of St Maurice with the assistance and at the request of his wife, Edith, who provided the properties for the initial foundation out of her wedding gift from Otto in 929, which included a fortified royal residence and its appurtenances.[23] Edith also appears to have assisted in obtaining relics of St Innocent for the monastery from Rudolf, king of Burgundy.[24] Even so, the new monastery still was founded on old Liudolfing family property in memory of Henry I and for his salvation as well as for the salvation of the new royal couple. As with the convent at Quedlinburg, this foundation of St Maurice held significance for the future. Thus already early in his reign, Otto had begun to create and institutionalize a second centre of power in Saxony, which he nurtured throughout his reign until he could finally found a 'family' metropolitan see there in 968. The monastery and later archbishopric became a main political centre in Saxony, Otto's favourite residence there, and eventually his own royal mausoleum. From the beginning, Otto appears to have envisaged political and possibly missionary tasks for his new foundation.[25] It was the central fortress of a network of dependent military settlements west of the Elbe; already under the Carolingians Magdeburg had been a significant trading post with the Slavic lands to the east. Its fortified location on the eastern frontier, at an important crossing point of the Elbe, destined it as

[22] *DO I* 14 (= *UBM* 1); *Gesta archiepiscoporum Magdeburgensium* c. 4 p. 378; *Ann. St Max.* s.a. 934 p. 6; *Cont. Reg.* s.a. 934.

[23] *DO I* 14 (= *UBM* 1): 'coniugis nostrae, et praedictus locus dos fuit'; *Ann. Magd.* s.a. 929 p. 142: 'Otto magnus Edith...matrimonio sibi iungendam Saxoniae advexit, eique urbem Magdeburg, quae nunc metropolis est Saxoniae, tunc vero Halberstadensi diocesi subiecta fuit, inter ceteras opes pro dote optulit.' Concerning this marriage settlement, see Schmid (1964/1971b) 441–7 with nn. 94–107 and now Leyser (1983b) esp. 80–9. The provisions in the foundation charter concerning the legal status of the new monastery and the report contained in the Magdeburg Annals (p. 143 s.a. 938: 'Eodem tempore praedictus rex instinctu et peticione pie coniugis suae Edith regine abbaciam regalem intra urbem Magdeburg fundavit.') confirm that St Maurice was a royal monastery from its foundation.

[24] *Ann. Magd.* s.a. 938 p. 143: 'Cuius corpus Rodoulfus rex Burgundionum ei ac reginae transmissum, regium immo divinum munus donavit.'

[25] The part, if any, that the monks of Magdeburg played in missionary work in newly conquered lands prior to the establishment of the archbishopric remains hotly debated and difficult if not impossible to determine from contemporary sources. See Claude (1972–5) 1.33 – 5 for the literature on both sides of the debate.

a staging point for Otto's expansion to the east against the Baltic and Elbian Slavs. In addition, its original foundation grant began the process of providing the monastery and later archbishopric with the economic base necessary to begin the missionary activity associated with the Christianization of the newly conquered areas east of the Elbe.[26]

These three events early in Otto's reign – the coronation of 936, the establishment of a convent at Quedlinburg, and the foundation of St Maurice at Magdeburg – help us understand better the practice and structure of government under Otto I and his successors. The Frankish Carolingians and the Saxon Liudolfings had had strong connections since the late ninth century when successive generations of Liudolfing daughters married into the Carolingian royal family. Thus, the coronation in Aachen represented not only a conscious imitation of Charlemagne, but also a continuation of long-standing Liudolfing connections with the Carolingians and with Aachen.[27] Moreover, since the death of Louis the Child, the last Carolingian king in the east, Franks and then Saxons consecutively had ruled the east Frankish kingdom; even Widukind and Otto himself saw the realm as a kingdom of Franks and Saxons.[28] With Otto's designation and election, however, we see the creation of a Saxon dynasty ruling the former east Frankish kingdom. Shortly thereafter, with the foundation of monasteries and cult sites at Quedlinburg and Magdeburg, Otto had created in Saxony a third centre of royal power for this kingdom by incorporating the Liudolfing patrimony in Saxony with the remnants of the Carolingian fisc there. As Karl Leyser has stated, 'the northeastwards shift in the centre of gravity of the east Frankish kingdom ... was the very essence of Ottonian rule'.[29] Otto ruled his kingdom like a late Carolingian king, but with a new centre of power and a new royal dynasty, which in turn dictated the nature of kingship, the structure of the realm and the cycle of the royal itinerary until the first quarter of the eleventh

---

[26] In general, see Claude (1972–5) I.1–57. In addition I would like to thank Amnon Carr, who generously allowed me to read his BA dissertation, 'Otto I and the church of S. Mauricius at Magdeburg: A survey of the evidence of the charters' (Cambridge 1986), which cast much of the material on Magdeburg and the monastery of St Maurice in a particular light which was very enlightening and helpful.

[27] Concerning the Liudolfing/Ottonian connections to Aachen, see K. Hauck (1967).

[28] Widukind 2.1, 3.63; *DO I* 1: 'Et si aliquis generationis nostrae in Francia et Saxonia regalem potestativa manu possideat sedem.' On this concept see Pätzold (1979) and Beumann (1981).   [29] Leyser (1979) 5.

century.[30] By then, the Ottonians had merged the Frankish and Saxon traditions of kingship successfully into a new German realm. Perhaps it is indeed appropriate that Karl Bosl referred to this period of transition or 'becoming', under the Ottonian rulers, as 'the late antiquity of Frankish history'.[31]

How did Henry I come to hold power in the east Frankish kingdom and how was he able to pass this on successfully to his son, Otto? How did both of these rulers stamp their reigns with their own characters and yet manage to develop methods of government which met the particular needs of their day and from which the nascent German realm would emerge? Let us briefly look back for the answers.

When one considers that the first two Saxon kings, Henry I and Otto I, successively ruled this 'kingdom of the Franks and Saxons' for fifty-four years, it should not be surprising that the force of their personalities and their experiments in governing established the foundation for the early German realm.[32] Similar to other prominent noble families in the east Frankish kingdom, the family of Henry and Otto, the Liudolfings of Saxony, had achieved their position and power, both within their duchy and within the kingdom itself, by exercising successfully the military commands bestowed on them by the Carolingian kings, that is, by defending their territories against external foes. Moreover, the Carolingians often forged marriage connections with these successful families, raising their status still higher. Already in the late ninth century, the most powerful of these military leaders (*duces*), the Liudolfing dukes in Saxony and the Liutpolding dukes in Bavaria, had achieved great prestige and had been granted a kind of quasi-royal status. Thereby, they largely dominated the churches and controlled the royal properties in their territories. By the early tenth century, the Conradines in Franconia and the Hunfridings in Swabia had established similar power concentrations in their areas

---

[30] Müller-Mertens (1980), (1990), (1991) and Keller (1982) have provided significant research containing important findings and suggestions on the nature of Ottonian kingship, the structure of the realm and the cycle of the royal itinerary into the early eleventh century. In addition, two of Eckhard Müller-Mertens's students, W. Huschner (unpub. diss. 1986) and G. Beyreuther (work in progress), have completed studies of the structure of the realm and rulership practice under Conrad II and Henry II respectively which they are currently preparing for publication.

[31] Bosl (1980) 14.

[32] Althoff and Keller (1985) 55, who formulate this theme as a central thesis of their work.

and had established themselves as the other leading families in the east Frankish kingdom. Upon the death of Louis the Child in 911, the leading magnates of the east Frankish realm elected Conrad of Franconia as their king instead of recognizing the west Frankish Carolingian king, Charles the Simple.[33] The magnates of Lotharingia led by the Reginarids, however, gave their allegiance to Charles the Simple. During a contentious reign of eight years, Conrad was not particularly effective in waging war against external foes and he succeeded in alienating the dukes of Swabia and Bavaria by attempting to subdue them in alliance with leading prelates of the church. On his deathbed in 918, Conrad I made a famous and fateful decision. With his brother Eberhard at his side, Conrad designated one of the two most powerful men in the realm, Duke Henry of Saxony, as his successor in the kingship. Claiming that the Conradine family had all the necessary attributes to be kings, but lacked the indispensable 'fortuna atque mores', Conrad passed over Eberhard and instructed him to take the regalia to Henry and to make peace and friendship with him. Eberhard dutifully obeyed his brother.[34] These events therefore provide the background for Conrad's 'transfer of the renowned realm of the Franks to the celebrated people of the Saxons',[35] and for the resulting double election of 919, in which Henry was elected king by the Franks and the Saxons; Duke Arnulf of Bavaria was made king by the Bavarian magnates. The Swabians remained curiously absent from the process.

The events surrounding Henry I's accession to the throne dictated his policy of governing in the early years of his reign. He took the field against Duke Burchard of Swabia and then Duke Arnulf of Bavaria and quickly gained their recognition of his overlordship, but not without paying a price. In return for their recognition that their ducal rights derived from the king, that is, their feudal recognition, Henry granted both dukes a vice-regal status, guaranteeing them control over royal properties and churches in their principalities.[36] Thus, to overcome an initial

---

[33] On Conrad I's election in general, see Hlawitschka (1986) 96–8. For more detailed information on this election, see Lintzel (1953/1971) 311–37 and Schlesinger (1948) 398–402.

[34] Widukind 1.25–6. Henry's initial relationship with Eberhard was thus based on an *amicitia* bond, which Henry continued to use with the other dukes.

[35] Hrotsvitha, *Gesta Ottonis* p. 204.

[36] In the case of Arnulf of Bavaria, this certainly included the right to make episcopal appointments (Liudprand 2.23 and Thietmar 1.26), but sources say nothing specific in

regional particularism and hold the realm together, Henry recognized the kind of local autonomy that had brought his own family to power, and began his reign in a 'dualism' or shared authority with the southern dukes. His early relations with the southern duchies showed a strong continuity with the late Carolingian tradition of the *dux regni*, a vice-regal type of position, as well as a recognition of the earlier position of these areas of sub-kingdoms within the Carolingian realm.[37] Moreover, in his negotiations and alliances with the southern dukes, Henry employed a Carolingian diplomatic method, the sworn bond of friendship or *amicitia*. Whereas the late Carolingians used *amicitia* bonds within the kindred, that is, among the kings of the various sub-kingdoms throughout the greater Frankish empire, Henry employed it in his diplomatic interactions with the most powerful magnates of his realm. Gradually, it became one of the characteristic elements of his relations with dukes, with foreign kings, and also with certain nobles in his realm, especially those in Saxony.[38]

Throughout most of his reign, Henry remained on good terms with the dukes, but as his strength and prestige grew, the bonds of *amicitia* upon which he based his relationship to the duchies began to alter slightly. One first sees evidence of this change, for instance, after Henry had initiated a successful 'western' policy in 920. This policy resulted in the acknowledgement of his kingship by Charles the Simple in 921; the incorporation of Lotharingia, along with the tradition-rich royal city of Aachen, into his realm in 925; and the recognition of Henry's seniority in 926 by King Rudolf II of Burgundy during an assembly of the realm held in Worms.[39] At

---

this regard about Burchard. Karpf (1984) 15–22 discusses the power of the southern dukes over the churches in their duchies and its connection with Henry I's refusal to accept the ecclesiastical consecration in 919, and at p. 19 n. 90 he cites the older literature dealing with the extent of Burchard's power.

[37] Keller (1982) 103–5.

[38] For an overview of *amicitia* bonds, see Althoff (1990) 88–119. On the Merovingian and Carolingian tradition and use of bonds of *amicitia*, see Fritze (1954) and (1973) and Schneider (1964). On Henry I's varied use of *amicitia* bonds, see Schmid (1960/1971a), Althoff and Keller (1985) 62–5, Althoff (1986) and Reuter (1991a) 137–47. Gerd Althoff and Karl Schmid have announced a forthcoming complete study of *amicitia* relationships in the ninth and early tenth centuries.

[39] On Henry's 'western' policy and relations with Lotharingia and the kingdom of Burgundy, see Büttner (1964) here esp. 49–50 and Hlawitschka (1968). For the sources concerning the assembly at Worms in 926, see BO 13a. While it is clear from *DH I* 14 that Rudolf II of Burgundy attended this assembly, some scholars have suggested that he paid feudal homage to Henry there, but the nature of his 'recognition' of Henry is

the same assembly, Henry appointed a new duke to the duchy of Swabia to fill the vacancy left by the death of Duke Burchard II, who had been killed while on campaign in Italy. Henry did not appoint a Swabian as the new duke, however, but a Conradine named Hermann, the cousin of Conrad I and Eberhard.[40] Not only did the king treat the duchy as a royal office but, moreover, he reinstated royal control of the churches in Swabia.[41] Thus, increased control of the ducal office and over royal churches began to emerge as the foundations of Henry's governance. If the position of duke now began to assume the character of a royal office that could be granted by the king, this did not apply, however, to the ranks of the lower nobility. Unlike the Carolingians, Henry made no attempt to supplant the local nobility in the duchies with Saxons or other nobles of his choosing, but instead recognized dynastic succession, except at the highest level of the dukedom.[42] This guaranteed the position of the local noble families within their duchy, but at the same time institutionalized the ducal office as one near to the king, so that peoples in all regions would have a voice at, or an access to, the royal court.[43] Later, in 928, when Henry formally recognized Giselbert as duke of Lotharingia, he not only entered into an *amicitia* bond with him, but he further cemented the relationship through a marriage alliance, in that Giselbert married his daughter Gerberga.[44]

Events of the years 929 and 930 demonstrate a momentary high point in Henry's power and prestige. These mark the culmination of his successful relations with the dukes and reveal his initial steps toward a new concept of ruling. This new concept, the idea of indivisibility of the realm, which broke with the Carolingian

vague at best. It is also possible that this assembly may have been the occasion when Henry acquired the 'Holy Lance' (Liudprand 4.25) from Rudolf.

[40] *Cont. Reg. s.a.* 926; BO 13a. Keller (1982) 106 makes the important observation that Henry's appointment of Hermann as duke of Swabia in 926 indicated not only the power of the king, but also the status and importance of the Conradine family in Henry's realm. In the final analysis this was still a realm of the 'Franks and the Saxons' and Henry needed the support of the Conradines for his policies.

[41] *DDH I* 11 (Chur), 12 (St Gall), and *DDH I* 10 and 15, which both deal in some measure with the monastery of Kempten located on the Swabian–Bavarian border.

[42] Althoff and Keller (1985) 80–1, 223. Reuter (1991a) 93–4 points out that this development had parallels in the east Frankish kingdom, where already the late Carolingian kings could not supplant the local nobility without difficulty and thus an element of continuity did exist.

[43] Althoff and Keller (1985) 80–1.   [44] Widukind 1.30.

tradition of dividing the realm between the sons, evolved during the tenth century in most of the successor states to the Carolingian empire. Henry adopted it at a time when he could begin to consolidate the power of the Saxon kingship within the realm. He enjoyed a strong working relationship with the dukes and had pursued a successful western policy. In the east, he likewise pursued a prudent and fruitful course of action. In 926, he had concluded a peace treaty with the Magyars, which guaranteed him nine years of peace in return for his payment of tribute to them. He used this time wisely to strengthen his defences and improve his fighting machine. He had also enjoyed some success in securing his northeastern borders against the Slavs, and had subjugated the Bohemians to a tributary status.[45] With these successes behind him, Henry inaugurated, in September of 929, an ordering of the royal house and the realm which lasted into the spring of 930.

He established a dower – that is, a widow's endowment – for his wife, Mathilda, decided upon an ecclesiastical future for his youngest son, Brun and, most significantly, arranged for the marriage of his eldest son, Otto, to an Anglo-Saxon princess.[46] In so ordering the royal house, Henry simultaneously made known his wishes for the future succession. Otto's marriage and the events surrounding it held great significance. By having his son marry the daughter of an Anglo-Saxon king, Henry consciously broke with the Carolingian tradition of marrying sons of the royal family to daughters of the high nobility in the realm. Thereby, Henry bound his house with an older Saxon kingship and further legitimated it, both outside Saxony and within the Saxon nobility at large. At the same time, this marriage raised the position of his eldest son above that of the dukes and above that of his own brothers. Henry obviously intended that the kingdom would remain undivided and its rulership would pass solely to his eldest son Otto, newly married to Edith, the daughter of King Edward the Elder and half-sister to reigning King Aethelstan.[47] In character with Henry's general method of ruling, however, these were not

---

[45] Although Leyser (1983b) 79–80 criticized Schmid (1964/1971b) 454–63 for over-stressing Henry's successes in these years, Reuter (1991a) 142–5 makes the point that, while Henry's later successes against the Magyars and the Danes may have enhanced his reputation greatly, they certainly did not make it.

[46] Schmid (1960/1971a) and (1964/1971b) did the seminal research on the events of 929–30, but see Leyser (1983b) 75–85 for some sharpening and refinements in the argument and Althoff and Keller (1985) 101–12 for a convenient summary of the events and their significance.   [47] Leyser (1983b) 77–8.

unilateral acts, but ones accomplished through close co-operation and negotiation with the leading magnates of the realm and of Saxony. It is in this light that one must view and understand why the charter establishing Mathilda's dower (*DH I* 20) specifically mentions Otto's consent as well as the petitions of the princes; why Henry made a progress through all areas of the realm in 929–30 visiting and feasting in each duchy in turn; and why entries of the entire royal family and leading magnates of Saxony appeared at this time in memorial and confraternal prayerbooks of the monasteries of St Gall and Reichenau, where the wedding negotiations may have occurred.[48] One of these entries entitles Otto as king (*rex*) already in 929 and the Annals of Lausanne (although admittedly corrupt!) claim that Otto was actually consecrated king in 930 at Mainz, where his marriage also may have taken place.[49] Since all of these events had significance for the entire realm – still essentially an east Frankish realm – they had to occur in Frankish territory, and Henry had to procure the assent of the leading magnates and nobles of the realm for his plans.

Further moves toward internal consolidation and some dramatic successes in the realm of foreign policy marked the last six years of Henry I's reign. Already in the late 920s, Henry had begun to build a stronger relationship with the church, as seen not only by his retaking control over royal churches in Swabia, but also by officially reviving the institution of the royal chapel. In accordance with Carolingian tradition, Henry called and presided over a synod of the realm at Erfurt in 932 to deal with sundry ecclesiastical matters.[50] One of the decisions made at this synod had particular significance for Henry's foreign policy, that is, the decision no longer to pay annual tribute to the Magyars. This led shortly thereafter, in 933, to a confrontation with the Magyars at Riade (an unknown location near the Unstrut River in northern Thuringia). The battle at Riade resulted in a great moral and status-building victory for Henry. He levied troops from all parts

---

[48] Schmid (1960/1971a) 400–2.
[49] Schmid (1960/1971a) 392 with n. 11 and 410 with n. 60. We do not know exactly where Otto's marriage took place. Schmid (1960/1971a) 403, 410–11 and (1964/1971b) 447 suggests Frankfurt as well as possibly Mainz, whereas Althoff and Keller (1985) 107–8 seem to prefer Mainz.
[50] *MGH Conc. 6.1* no. 8. This synod was attended by prelates from all areas of the realm, except Bavaria, where Duke Arnulf still retained firm control over the Bavarian churches and held a separate synod in Dingolfing. For this synod, see *MGH Conc. 6.1* no. 9.

of the realm and, faced with Henry's mounted contingents, the Magyar forces fled.[51] The time Henry had bought with his treaty in 926 had paid off by allowing him to restructure his army as well as to test it in wars against the Slavs. Thus, the time bought yielded the added benefit of allowing Henry to break the Slavic alliance with the Magyars. Although the Magyar invasions did not cease completely until 955, when Henry's son Otto won his famous battle at the Lech River, Henry had shown a unified front at Riade and had broken the Magyar yoke of tribute. He followed this victory in the next year, moreover, by subduing the Danes and reducing them to a tributary status. Thus, by 935 when Henry fell ill, he had consolidated the realm internally by judiciously using the forces at his disposal and by means of effective diplomacy based on bonds of *amicitia*. He had also secured the external borders of the realm using the might of his restructured army. Before he died, Henry called an assembly at Erfurt to assure the assent of the Franks and the Saxons to the agreements of 929–30, that is, to the accession of his son Otto to the throne.

In spite of the smooth transition of power upon Henry's death, the apparent harmony reigning at the Aachen coronation in 936 and the establishment of new centres of royal power in Saxony soon thereafter, Otto's honeymoon period did not last long. Numerous tensions lay just below the surface calm. These tensions quickly mounted, compounded, and brought about a series of early crises to the new king and his rulership. The seeds of discontent included the reaction of the dukes and the Saxon nobility to the gradual advance of royal power and Otto's methods of ruling, a common instinct, both on the part of external as well as internal powers, to test a new, young and untried king, and the friction within the royal house due to the succession of a single son to the kingship. Otto's success and methods in dealing with these early crises determined much about his later practice of government.

Otto's initial relations with the nobility and the dukes were much more contentious than those of his father. In fact, according to Widukind, the crises beginning in 937 and lasting until 941 almost brought Saxon kingship to an early demise.[52] Problems began in 937–8 surrounding the succession to the dukedom of Bavaria. Eberhard, the son and designated successor to Duke

---

[51] Widukind 1.38; Flodoard *s.a.* 933.   [52] Widukind 2.24.

Arnulf, who died in 937, challenged Otto's authority by ignoring a royal summons to appear before the king. Otto dealt quickly and decisively with the situation, deposing Eberhard and appointing Arnulf's brother Berthold as duke.[53] As had happened with the Swabian dukedom in 926, the Bavarian ducal office lost much of the independence that the powerful Duke Arnulf had exercised, probably including the loss of full ducal control of the churches. Thus, it also began to assume the character of a royal office that could be granted by the king. Soon thereafter, serious discontent and a progression of rebellions arose in Saxony, which spread quickly to Franconia and Lotharingia. Before Otto emerged victorious in 939, the dukes of Franconia and Lotharingia, two brothers of the king, many powerful Saxon nobles, several high prelates of the church, and even the west Frankish king numbered among those in open opposition to him. These new rebellions arose primarily from: displeasure, especially on the part of Otto's half-brother Thankmar and another Saxon noble, Wichmann Billung, over Otto's disposition of *honores* and *legationes*, that is, of high offices and permanent military commands on the frontier; Eberhard of Franconia's opposition to a royal court decision against him and his general feeling of loss of power; and from the lingering tensions between Otto and his younger brother Henry resulting from the new indivisibility of the kingdom and Henry's own desire to be king, which lured him into the rebel camp.[54] From the point of view of the monarch and in the words of Widukind, these rebellions were 'civil wars'; but from the side of the rebels, they were legitimate feuds engendered by offences or dishonourable treatment by the king.

Both the causes and the results of these early rebellions allow us to make some initial observations about elements of continuity or of change in Otto's early practice of government. From the beginning, Otto appears to have avoided, if not actually rejected, the *amicitiae* and *pacta mutua* relationships, which had been so successful for his father.[55] His actions in regard to the Bavarian

---

[53] Widukind 2.8; *Cont. Reg. s.a.* 937, 938.

[54] For a thorough account of these and later crises of Otto I, see Leyser (1979) 9–47. Reuter (1991a) 150–4 provides an excellent overview containing interesting and important insights.

[55] Althoff and Keller (1985) 120–4, 235–8. Zotz (1989) 170–1 makes the point that relationships of *amicitia* do not totally disappear under Otto I and that perhaps the polarity set up from the sources by Althoff and Keller (p. 121), that is, Henry (*pax* and *concordia*) and Otto (*contentio, discordia, rebellio*), does not account enough for the

succession as well as to Duke Eberhard of Franconia's dispute with his Saxon vassal, Bruning, demonstrate an early effort to exert stronger royal control over the ducal office and to regain control over the granting of other royal offices or ranks such as countships, a prerogative which the dukes of Franconia, Swabia and Bavaria had enjoyed under his father.[56] On the other hand, he fell foul of Thankmar and Wichmann Billung by a clear demonstration of the royal will while furthering a policy practised by his father concerning the nobility. In both cases, when Otto granted Margrave Siegfried's march to Siegfried's brother Gero, over his own half-brother Thankmar, and when he conferred the military command in northern Saxony on Hermann Billung, in preference to Hermann's older brother, Wichmann, the king recognized hereditary right to positions below the dukedom as his father had but, at the same time, he vigorously asserted the royal prerogative to determine the specific candidate on the basis of his suitability or dependability as judged by the king. Thereby, Otto rejected the claims made by Thankmar and Wichmann that they had higher suitability and right to the positions than the other candidates on the basis of their *Königsnähe*, that is, their closer relationship to the royal family.[57]

The conflict between Otto and his younger brother Henry arose out of the gradual transition toward the principle of indivisibility of the realm. While the designations of 929 and 935 and election(s)

radically different situations of the two kings upon coming to the throne. On Otto's rejection of negotiated *pacta*, see Widukind 2.25, 3.15 and 3.37.

[56] According to Widukind 2.8 ('et filius eius in superbiam elati regis iussu contempserunt ire in comitatum'), Duke Arnulf's sons, out of arrogance, refused a royal command to come to the royal residence. Under Otto I the obligation to come to court symbolized the vassalic bond of the duke as an official of the king. See Keller (1982) 92 with n. 87. On the feud between Bruning and Eberhard, see Widukind 2.6, 2.10. In his review of Althoff and Keller (1985), Zotz (1989) 173–5 greatly clarifies the conflict between Duke Eberhard and the Saxon Bruning and the significance of Otto's interference. By translating *quaestura* in the Widukind passage (Widukind 2.6) as a comital office and not as a feudal *beneficium* or tenure as most scholars have, Zotz demonstrates that Otto was not blatantly interfering in a feudal relationship, but rather reasserting control over the granting of a royal office, which Henry I had probably alienated to Eberhard in the succession agreements of 919. This interpretation further strengthens the arguments of Althoff and Keller (1985) 120–4, 235–8 that Otto I began a systematic change in his concepts and practice of rulership back to Carolingian models, which he imitated at his coronation.

[57] Keller (1982) 112–13. As well as being a distant relative of Margrave Siegfried through his mother, Thankmar of course was Otto's half-brother; and Wichmann claimed a superior claim to that of Hermann because he was related by marriage to the queen dowager, Mathilda.

of 936 favoured Otto, various sources attest that young Henry wanted and felt entitled to be king.[58] Most scholars now agree that the question in 936 and the years immediately following was not whether the realm would remain unified under a Saxon king, but which son of Henry I, Otto or Henry, would be able to assert the better claim to the position and maintain himself in it.[59] The rebellions in which the young Henry participated or which he led during the first years of Otto's kingship demonstrate clearly that the issue was not decided until 941. In the first rebellion of Thankmar, Wichmann and Eberhard, Henry stood on the side of his brother and only in the following year did Henry revolt along with dukes Eberhard of Franconia and Giselbert of Lotharingia. What we cannot determine with any degree of certainty, however, is the degree to which his rebellions against his brother were fuelled solely by his own desire to be king, or alternatively, by the encouragement of his mother, or of nobles, who saw in Henry a member of the royal family around whom they could rally in order to better the chances of their own feuds succeeding against Otto in terms of victory or an advantageous negotiated settlement.[60] Finally, in 941, Otto thwarted the most serious aristocratic conspiracy waged against him. With Henry as their leader, a large group of east Saxon warrior nobles, disgruntled over the breakdown of tribute payments, plotted to kill the king during the Easter solemnities at Quedlinburg. Someone disclosed the plot to the king, who foiled it by holding the Easter court in full pomp, but under heavy guard. Henry was captured or surrendered shortly thereafter. Following a brief imprisonment at Ingelheim, he made a reconciliation with his brother during the Christmas court at Frankfurt in 941 and was received back into royal grace.[61]

In the course of these conflicts, Otto's half-brother Thankmar had been killed in 938, Duke Eberhard of Franconia and Duke Giselbert of Lotharingia had died at the battle of Andernach in 939, the Conradine family of Franconia and the Liutpoldings of Bavaria had both split their allegiance between the warring factions, and Otto's younger brother Henry had managed to stay alive and to regain royal favour in 939 and again in 941. Thus, the rebellions left Franconia and Lotharingia without a duke, internal

---

[58] Widukind 2.12, 15; *Vita Math. post.* cc. 6, 9; Liudprand 4.18; Thietmar 1.21.
[59] E.g. Hlawitschka (1986) 116–17 and Reuter (1991a) 149–50.
[60] See Leyser (1979) 9–22 and n. 15 above.
[61] Widukind 2.30–1; Leyser (1979) 32–42.

pressures within the Ottonian house arising out of the move to indivisibility of the realm for which a solution would have to be found, and a need to reward Otto's supporters. In the years during and immediately following these early crises, Otto forged new relationships with the nobles and his family members, and he instituted rulership practices that reflected to a degree the outcome of the rebellions and addressed some of their inherent causes.

Otto began by suppressing the duchy of Franconia, that is, not appointing a duke to replace Eberhard, but making Franconia part of the royal domain and placing it directly under royal jurisdiction.[62] This action had great practical and symbolic significance for Otto's practice of government. He thereby ensured that the powerful ecclesiastical centres, the royal fisc and the royal palaces inherited from the Carolingians in the middle Rhine region – and the centre of his realm – would remain firmly under royal control. We must remember that Otto and his father had initially been elected by the Franks and the Saxons, and Otto's main supporters in his early crises had been Franks and Saxons. These two peoples and regions were the core and focus of royal power and, hence, the king retained direct lordship over them without allowing any strong intermediary power to emerge.[63] Otto's practice of government clearly demonstrates this change. The amount of time spent by the king in the political centres of Franconia, such as Frankfurt, Ingelheim, Worms and Mainz increased dramatically over that spent by his father. In addition, in continuity with Carolingian tradition, Otto ruled the entire kingdom predominantly from the political centres located in these two areas and he required the dukes and other nobles from bordering duchies to come to him in these centres to carry out the

---

[62] Ekkehard of St Gall refers to this new status of Franconia when comparing Swabia in the very early tenth century to it. Ekkehard IV, *Casus Sancti Galli* c. 11 p. 36: 'Nondum adhuc illo tempore Suevia in ducatum erat redacta; sed fisco regio peculialiter parebat, sicut hodie et Francia.'

[63] Keller (1982) 113–14, who cites the famous example in 972 of Duke Hermann Billung who, perhaps owing to his strengthened position in Saxony and the king's long absence, usurped the king's prerogative to a royal *adventus* in Magdeburg and thereby excited a quick and angry reaction from Otto. Cf. Reuter (1991a) 160, who sees the same event from a quite different perspective. While some members of the Conradine family after Eberhard's death are called duke, it appears to have been used merely as an honorary title rather than to designate the holder of the office of duke. Likewise, the Ottonians retained their own dukedom in Saxony. Only in the course of the tenth century did the Billungs transform their office of margrave into duke, and even then they 'were not dukes "of" Saxony, but "in" Saxony'. See Fuhrmann (1986) 42 and Reuter (1991a) 154, 159–60.

business of government.[64] On the basis of the documented whereabouts of the king and a calculation of the duration of his stays, it appears that Otto I spent approximately sixty-five per cent of his time in these two duchies, and when one adds the royal fisc and palaces in Lower Lotharingia centred on Aachen, he spent eighty-three per cent of his total time in the realm in areas inhabited by peoples who were considered Franks or Saxons.[65] Thus, by taking control of Franconia and the former Carolingian fisc there, by attempting to dominate the remnants of the Carolingian fisc in Lotharingia,[66] and by establishing new political centres in Saxony, Otto created a huge area of royal power and influence.

An obvious disadvantage of this policy lay in the possibility of seriously offending those members of the Conradine family who had been his loyal supporters. Otto averted this possibility in two ways. He did not make a blanket confiscation of all Conradine lands in Franconia, and just as he had merged the areas of the Franks and the Saxons, so he bound the two dominant families of each people by marriage. In 939, he betrothed his son Liudolf (still only nine years old) to Ida, the daughter of the Conradine Duke Hermann of Swabia, whose support, along with that of his brother Udo and other Conradine relatives, had saved Otto's kingship. Liudolf and Ida were married probably in 947, the year after his mother, Queen Edith, had died and the year before his father designated him as successor to the throne. Through this marriage alliance, Otto rewarded the Conradines for their support, compensated them for their loss of the duchy of Franconia, and connected the two families which had ruled the east Frankish realm since the Carolingians.[67] Upon Duke Hermann's death in 949, Otto's son and heir apparent became Duke of Swabia.

Otto also used his family and marriage connections to the royal family to reward fidelity or effect solutions in the duchies of Bavaria and Lotharingia. Soon after the battle of Andernach in 939, the king offered a marriage alliance to Duke Berthold of Bavaria, who had remained loyal to Otto and had not used the crises in the north and west to launch another Bavarian revolt.

---

[64] Müller-Mertens (1980) 133–65, 224–34, did the ground-breaking research on this characteristic of Otto's governing practice. See also Keller (1982) 90–9, who largely follows him, but adds some additional insights.

[65] For these percentages see the statistical data compiled by Müller-Mertens (1980) 269 Table 3.   [66] F. Prinz (1985) 246.   [67] Keller (1982) 106–7.

Liudprand tells us that Otto offered the Bavarian duke the opportunity to marry his sister, Gerberga, the widow of Giselbert, or their daughter, Alberada; but neither marriage ever took place.[68] Otto invoked a similar 'family' strategy in regard to Lotharingia. Initially, in 940, after Giselbert drowned in the Rhine while resisting royal forces, Otto granted the duchy of Lotharingia to his rebellious, but forgiven, brother Henry, in an attempt to quell resentment within the royal family by giving his brother a share of governing power. Owing to indigenous resistance to this appointment, however, Henry was not able to establish himself in Lotharingia and soon returned to Saxony, from where he launched his final challenge to Otto.[69] The king then appointed a former ally of his father, also named Otto, as the new duke. When Duke Otto died in 944, however, the king once again used the opportunity not only to strengthen the royal position in Lotharingia, which was rich in fiscal property, but also to reward and assuage his Conradine vassals. Otto appointed Conrad the Red, a Conradine and ally from the Worms area, as duke and furthered his Frankish–Saxon alliance by arranging Conrad's marriage to his daughter, Liutgard, three years later in 947. In the same year, Otto had another opportunity to consolidate Saxon rulership in the realm and, at the same time, allay any lingering discontent and potential discord in the royal house. When Duke Berthold of Bavaria died in 947, Otto made his final reconciliation with his brother Henry, who had remained loyal and in Saxony since 942. He appointed, as the new duke of Bavaria, Henry, who earlier had married Duke Arnulf's daughter, Judith.[70]

A number of observations should be made concerning Otto's policies in the years between 940 and 949. The period after 941 was one of relative calm and consolidation. In this period Otto continued to build up his new centres of power in Saxony; he effectively took control of one of the two main areas of the former Carolingian fisc in his realm; and he attempted to monitor the other areas through his power of ducal appointment and by building ties to the royal family. This firmly established the tripolar structure of the realm (Magdeburg–Frankfurt–Aachen), which remained fully intact until the 990s, and began to alter significantly only in the first half of the eleventh century. He also

[68] Liudprand 4.31. See Leyser (1979) 54.
[69] Widukind 2.29, 31; *Cont. Reg. s.a.* 940, 941.   [70] Widukind 2.36.

tried to solve the tensions and problems that the principle of indivisibility had caused in the royal family by offering members of his family opportunities to participate in royal government, that is, to rule in the duchies of Swabia, Bavaria and Lotharingia. Thus, whereas the duchies under Henry I had the same function as sub-kingdoms did for the Carolingians, Otto I used them in an undivided realm in a similar fashion, but in somewhat changed circumstances to placate members of the royal family not wearing the crown. This policy had several additional advantages. It bound the Franks (through the Conradine family) and the Saxons together as the ruling people. It created a personal relationship between the royal kindred and the rest of the realm, and spread the charisma of the royal family without transplanting Franks and Saxons throughout the ranks of the nobility to other parts of the realm. Finally, although members of the royal family, such as Otto's brother Henry and his son Liudolf, still held patrimony in Saxony, it removed them physically from Saxony. This prevented them from providing too easily the focus for any discontent among the Saxon nobility, who were still adapting to the Liudolfings' or Ottonians' rise in stature above them, just as Otto's brothers were adapting to his heightened position within the Liudolfing family. Thus, while instituting a family policy by which all the duchies surrounding the core areas of Franconia and Saxony were held by his blood or marital relatives, Otto carefully protected royal interests in two ways. He did not grant power to members of the royal family in the areas containing the crucial centres of royal power, that is, Saxony and Franconia, and he did not allow them to establish large numbers of the Saxon and Frankish nobility, on whom he depended for his power, in their new territories. These practices of Otto's rulership continued to reflect the Frankish–Saxon gentile concept of the realm and at the same time demonstrate that Otto was simultaneously expanding Ottonian governmental control while also making a settlement within his own family.[71]

If peaceful relations with the dukes and the nobility, conciliation within the royal family and a brief consolidation of royal power had marked the years since 941, the first years of the next decade brought mounting tension and pressure, which in 953 burst into the last major rebellion of Otto's reign. The key *dramatis personae*

---

[71] Keller (1982) 109–16. Cf. Reuter (1991a) 153–4, who sees this a bit differently.

of the revolt comprised, on one side, Otto's son, Duke Liudolf, his son-in-law, Duke Conrad the Red of Lotharingia, and their Saxon and Bavarian adherents, particularly Wichmann Billung's son and namesake. On the other side stood Otto himself, his brother and Liudolf's uncle, Duke Henry of Bavaria, and Hermann Billung, the young Wichmann's uncle. 'It was a war between generations' fought over rising, 'sometimes unfulfilled' expectations, status and influence at the royal court, inheritances, honour and growing royal power.[72] Although the rebellion was fuelled and even decided to some extent by affairs beyond the borders of the realm, it once again coalesced around a member of the royal family, Liudolf. This time, however, it was waged more against the king's brother Henry than the king himself. This, and the fact that the revolt became associated in 954 with a Magyar invasion of the realm, made it difficult if not impossible to sustain.[73]

The events fuelling this new rebellion began in Italy. In 951, on an appeal from Adelheid, the recent widow of King Lothar of Italy, Otto intervened south of the Alps as had the Carolingians before him. He marched to Italy and with little resistance took the kingdom from the usurper, Berengar, who had taken Adelheid captive as part of his claim to the realm. In September 951, five years after the death of his first wife, Edith, Otto married Adelheid and received the commendation of the northern Italian nobility at Pavia to complete his claim to Italy. Otto had not acted first, nor alone, and the mop-up action extended into 952. In fact, his move to Italy was preceded by independent actions on the part of both southern dukes, his brother Henry of Bavaria and his son Liudolf. They both assisted him in 951, and after returning to Saxony, Otto left behind his son-in-law, Conrad the Red, to bring Berengar to heel and to negotiate with him. The Italian campaigns and their aftermath provided much of the impetus for Liudolf and Conrad to revolt. During the campaigns Liudolf was upstaged twice by his uncle, who gained in real power (control of the marches of Verona and Aquileia) and in increased influence with Otto and his new wife. Liudolf, on the other hand, the designated successor to the throne, came away empty handed and apparently felt that his

[72] Leyser (1979) 23.

[73] See Erkens (1982) 315–38 for the most detailed examination of the rebellion of 953–4 and its far-ranging causes, but also see Leyser (1979) 18–23 and Althoff and Keller (1985) 144–58, who offer some differing and important insights, especially in regard to the confraternal grouping of the dissidents, and Reuter (1991a) 155–60, who conveniently summarizes the salient points.

influence at court had been threatened if not diminished. The birth of a son to Otto and Adelheid a year later must have increased anxiety in Liudolf, who since the death of his mother, Edith, in 946 no longer had an advocate at court. Similarly, Duke Henry's influence apparently played a role in persuading Otto to make Berengar wait for three days before receiving the royal advent during Easter at Magdeburg in 952 by which Otto recognized him as a sub-king in Italy. This offended the honour of Duke Conrad the Red, who had negotiated the settlement between Otto and Berengar, and drove him into Liudolf's camp. Finally, to this constellation came Wichmann the Young, who, concerned about his inheritance, revived the old feud of his father against Otto and Hermann, and the Liutpolding Count Palatine, Arnulf of Bavaria, who took up the former rebellion of his brother Eberhard, but directed now at Duke Henry.

Aside from trying to diminish the influence of Duke Henry at court and with the king – which Otto apparently had no intention of allowing – the objectives of the frondeurs never became sufficiently focused for success. Moreover, whether or not they were in alliance with the Magyars or had called them into the realm, the invasion in 954 rallied disparate elements in the realm together around Otto, even Conrad the Red, and doomed the revolt. First Conrad and then Liudolf and his followers capitulated. Both lost their duchies, but not their hereditary properties. Thus ended the last major revolt during Otto's reign.[74] In the following year, Otto managed to recruit an impressive army from all the duchies of the realm – in itself a demonstration of royal authority – which decisively defeated the Magyars at the Lech River and finally put an end to their invasions.[75] The heroes of the battle were Bishop Udalrich of Augsburg, who gamely led the defence of his city, Conrad the Red, who fell in battle, and Otto himself, who after victory on the battlefield was acclaimed by his army as 'pater patriae imperatorque'.[76] The battlefield acclamation and the renown won by Otto for this great victory foreshadowed the renewal of the emperorship and Otto's acquisition of the imperial dignity at Rome in 962.

---

[74] For an overview of the tensions and rebellions during the later reigns of Henry II, Conrad II and Henry III, which were qualitatively different from those during Otto I's reign, see Reuter (1991a) 200–1.   [75] Reuter (1991a) 160–2.

[76] Widukind 3.49. For the account of the battle, see Widukind 3.44–50 and *Vita s. Oudalrici* c. 12.

Contrary to much historical writing of an earlier era, Liudolf's revolt neither turned Otto against the idea of granting duchies to family members or marital relatives, nor did it make him turn suddenly to empowering bishops and the church in general as a hedge against the power of the dukes.[77] Ottonian family members and nobles related by marriage to the Ottonians continued to be appointed dukes, and Otto, building on Carolingian precedents, had begun to empower the prelates and ecclesiastical institutions in his realm long before the crisis of 953–4. In both areas, however, we see some significant changes and evolution in terms of Ottonian government.

Let us look first at ducal government. In 953, when Otto deposed Duke Conrad for his participation in the insurrection, he appointed as the new duke of Lotharingia his brother Brun, whom he had recently made archbishop of Cologne. In the following year Otto ousted Liudolf from the Swabian ducal office and appointed Burchard III, who possibly was the son of a former Swabian duke, Burchard II (but definitely a relative). Burchard III also was related by marriage to Otto's new wife, Adelheid, and married Duke Henry's daughter, Hadwig. Later, in 955, Duke Henry died and was followed in his office by his four-year old son and namesake under the regency of Henry's wife Judith. Thus, family members and relations did retain their claim to leadership of the duchies. However, after the death of Brun in 965, none of the Ottonian relatives holding ducal offices was a brother or son of a king until the advent of the Salian dynasty. Moreover, the southern dukes and their duchies lost their semi-regal status and thus were weakened (even if imperceptibly at first) in respect to the growing power of the king. By regaining nominal control of the bishoprics and royal monasteries in these southern duchies, the king had interjected a strong royal influence and thereby created a barrier to the rise of an independent ducal power.[78] On the other hand, as with other noble offices and tenures during the tenth century, the ducal office gradually evolved into a hereditary office. The king could still depose a duke for cause (infidelity), however, or appoint a new duke when no direct heir was at hand. Whereas in the southern duchies ducal power was slowly declining from a

---

[77] Santifaller (1964) contains the classic statement of this position as well as the complete formulation of the so-called 'Ottonian–Salian Imperial Church System', which has frequently been followed to one degree or another in subsequent general works.

[78] F. Prinz (1985) 246–7.

highly independent and semi-regal nature, in Lotharingia and Saxony princely power was on the advance, albeit from a far weaker starting point. Beginning in 958 Lotharingia split into two political entities, Upper and Lower Lotharingia, and in these, as well as in Saxony, strong margraviates slowly evolved into ducal offices which had a hereditary character from the beginning.[79]

THE OTTONIANS AND THE CHURCH

Lotharingia also provides a point of reference to make some general comments about Otto I and his relations to the churches and monasteries of the realm. On the basis of Brun's position in Lotharingia – simultaneously duke and archbishop of Cologne, or *archidux*, to use Ruotger's word – he was able to combine, for a short period of time, secular and ecclesiastical rulership functions in one person.[80] In the process he broke the power of the Reginarid family in Lotharingia, managed to man a number of Lotharingian bishoprics with candidates selected from his episcopal school at Cologne, and supported reform movements in a number of monasteries. An earlier generation of historians claimed that Otto, looking to Brun as a model 'royal official', embraced this idea of a prelate performing secular functions and began, after Brun's death in 965, systematically to draw promising clerics from the cathedral schools to the court chapel.[81] There they would learn the problems and methods of royal government and be trained from a royal perspective to become competent and loyal bishops. The king thereby created a pool of candidates to fill vacancies in bishoprics (and sometimes in important royal monasteries) and placed these men in the high ecclesiastical offices of the realm.[82] The king then enriched their institutions and empowered them with secular governing duties to counter the unreliability of the dukes and the nobility. While the neatness of this argument is

---

[79] On the developments in the southern duchies, see Keller (1982) 100–21, who also cites the most pertinent findings from Maurer (1978). F. Prinz (1985) 243–9 provides a convenient summary of developments in the duchies of the realm.

[80] Ruotger c. 20. Reuter (1991a) 157 rightly stresses that Brun's unusual position in Lotharingia hinged primarily on the fact that he was the king's brother, not just any bishop.

[81] Fleckenstein (1956) has indicated the connection between the resurgence of the cathedral schools under Brun and Otto I and the modification of the court chapel.

[82] On the developments of the royal chapel under the Ottonians and Salians, see Fleckenstein's monumental work, Fleckenstein (1966), which built and expanded upon the earlier studies of Görlitz (1936) and Klewitz (1939b).

attractive and it has not been shaken in its entirety (nor perhaps should it be completely), recent scholarship has pierced its armour significantly.[83]

In order to understand some of the objections to this traditional theme as well as the significant changes that did take place in relations between the monarch and the prelates of his realm – that is, how they came to play a supportive role in governing – it is useful to outline the origins and the nature of the relationship that existed between the Ottonian, and later, the Salian kings and the churches and monasteries in their realm. Close co-operation between Christian rulers and ecclesiastics in governing, both in the secular and in the ecclesiastical spheres, had a long history. In early medieval Europe it was the rule rather than the exception in most Christian polities. Extending back at least to Constantine in late antiquity and being greatly expanded under the Carolingians, especially Charlemagne and Louis the Pious, this method of governing was a durable structure of long standing. Thus, the relationship of the Ottonian and Salian monarchs to the prelates and ecclesiastical institutions of their realm was rooted in the general tradition of Christian kingship and shared many of the basic characteristics of Carolingian governmental structure.[84] The king, on the basis of his sacral anointing and because of his duty to protect churches, which was one of the obligations contained in the office or *ministerium* bestowed on him by God to act as His 'vicar on earth',[85] came to have considerable influence on the election of bishops, despite the fact that, under strict canon law, this task fell to the clergy and the people in episcopal elections, and, theoretically, to the community in abbatial elections. Further-

---

[83] Reuter (1982) called for a reappraisal of the traditional canon, questioned just how systematic the relationship between monarchs and bishops was, and called the whole 'system' into question. Fleckenstein (1985) refuted a portion of Reuter's reassessment on technical grounds, but by no means his entire thesis. Hlawitschka (1986) 212–15 adds some criticisms to the traditional view and provides a recent review of the scholarship.

[84] The best overviews of the origin and nature of this relationship are: Santifaller (1964); Köhler (1968); Hlawitschka (1986) 53–8, 129–30, 154–5, 212–15; and Fleckenstein (1985). On the Carolingian governing structure, see Fried (1982).

[85] A charter of Henry III from 1048 (*DH III* 225) restoring the 'royal' status to the monastery of Disentis in the Alps, clearly formulates the general nature of the king's obligation to protect churches in his realm: 'Quoniam ex iure suscepti regni omnibus ecclesiis Romani imperii debitam sollicitudinem debemus impendere, volumus unamquamque quantum ex divinae gratiae nobis conceditur munere impense procurare et ad dei laudem servitii reformare.' See Fleckenstein (1974) 69, who drew attention to this passage.

more, according to proprietary concepts contained in early medieval law, the king as lord (*seigneur* or *Grundherr*) assumed the right to appoint the ecclesiastical heads to lower churches and monasteries founded on royal property.[86] Additionally, in their position as sovereign, the Merovingian and Carolingian kings had granted rights of immunity (*immunitas*) to many of the higher churches in the realm and to numerous monasteries. This freed these institutions, their lands and any dependent populations from public taxation and from the jurisdiction of local counts. An immunity essentially was an *introitus* prohibition, that is, it forbade public officials from entering the immune area of the monastery to exercise their fiscal and judicial functions, and it gave all public dues and fining rights for lesser offences to the immunist: that is, the immunist could exercise low justice.[87] At least since 802, all churches had to choose a layman called an advocate,[88] who would represent the church in its secular affairs (court cases, property transactions, etc.) and would administer its immunity in cases involving high jurisdiction, that is, corporal or capital punishment. Early in the ninth century, Louis the Pious linked all future grants of immunity, as well as confirmations of previous grants, to the simultaneous entry into an elevated status of royal protection (*mundiburdium*). In this way all of the higher churches of the realm, the bishoprics, royal monasteries and all other ecclesiastical institutions acquiring this status, whether or not they were founded on royal property, were gradually drawn into a special and closer legal relationship to the monarch, who thereby became their overlord. Thus, notions of proprietary law and governmental right merged or became unclear at best.[89] This new relationship had benefits and obligations. Ecclesiastical institutions with this legal status fell directly under the royal jurisdiction. Thereby, they had the king as the ultimate protector of their rights and property, but thereafter the king exercised a more active influence on episcopal and abbatial elections, with royal wishes usually prevailing. They also benefited from royal munificence and

---

[86] On the proprietary church, see Stutz (1894/1938), which remains the starting point, but also Feine (1972) 160–82, 205–13, and Kempf (1969), who broaden the concept and summarize the scholarship since Stutz, much of which has refuted parts of his thesis.

[87] In the case of monasteries, the *introitus* prohibition of an immunity sometimes extended to diocesan bishops and kept them from exercising their ecclesiastical jurisdiction in a monastic 'immune' area.   [88] *MGH Capit.* I no. 33 c. 13 p. 93.

[89] On the merging of immunity and royal protection, see Fleckenstein (1974), who conveniently reviews the older scholarship and, most recently, Semmler (1982).

thereby acquired new properties, exemptions from tolls, and valuable income-producing rights, such as fines and fees accruing from local jurisdiction or from administering royal forests. With increased benefits, however, came increased obligations to the king and realm. Churches, monasteries and their prelates so favoured could be asked to perform numerous services for the king, the *servitium regis*.[90] The communities of all such institutions were required to pray for the general well-being of the realm, and their prelates to attend court to advise the king, or undertake diplomatic missions when requested. Depending on the size and wealth of the communities, they might also be asked to give annual gifts to the king, provide hospitality or renders of food and drink for the royal retinue when it travelled, or supply a military contingent to the royal host drawn from the vassals and freemen inhabiting their domains.

When the Carolingian empire was divided in the ninth century among the sons of Louis the Pious, the working relationship between the kingship and the royal churches and monasteries remained largely intact, but they now allied with their respective kingdoms. At the end of the ninth century and the beginning of the tenth, a significant difference arose between the west and east Frankish kingdoms due largely to the different conditions affecting the two areas and the varying levels of political and social development existing in each. In the west, as the power of the Carolingian rulers progressively diminished, the area gradually broke up into numerous principalities. In this process, royal control over the bishoprics and royal churches was mediatized and passed largely to the feudal princes in each principality. In the east, however, the dissolution of the royal fisc and of royal power over churches was not as extensive. Except for a short period when various dukes controlled the bishoprics and royal monasteries in their territories, the church remained essentially regnal in character.[91] Thus, after the kings from Saxony had come to the throne, and Henry I and Otto I had retaken control of the royal churches

---

[90] The standard works on the *servitium regis* are: Heusinger (1922); Brühl (1968); and Metz (1978b). For a more detailed discussion see Chapter 2.

[91] Thietmar 1.26, in a passage famous for its theocratic implications and for documenting the Ottonian kings' right to appoint bishops, mentioned Otto's regaining control over the episcopal churches in Bavaria at the beginning of the passage; further on, he implied that royal control over bishoprics did not always exist elsewhere (from the context, presumably in other parts of Europe) because he had heard that dukes and even counts controlled bishoprics.

respectively in Swabia and Bavaria, the Carolingian model was still at hand and the old structures were still in place to revive and modify. As mentioned earlier, Henry I, late in his reign, had begun to forge a closer relationship with the church and revived the institution of the royal chapel. This institution, founded by the Merovingian kings and further developed by the Carolingians, comprised a group of clerics at the royal court who had sundry duties. They were charged with the care of the most precious royal relics and other treasures, they performed religious services and other liturgical functions for the king, and eventually they took over the royal writing office or chancery.[92] Since it was in the royal chapel that Otto I had his prospective episcopal (and less often abbatial) candidates 'trained', this brings us back to the claim that Otto, as a result of the rebellion of 953–4, turned to empowering the church and its prelates and governing jointly with them as an insurance policy against the unreliability of the dukes and family members.

There are numerous problems with this thesis as traditionally formulated. Although one cannot deny that, from the time of Otto I onward, royal churches and monasteries were incorporated into royal government at an increasing rate, the sources just do not support it happening as a result of Liudolf's rebellion. Already prior to the conclusion of this last major crisis in 954 (or 955, if one thinks of the Battle of the Lech), Otto had begun to build up royal churches and monasteries, not only with property grants (some of it confiscated from rebellious nobility), but also with significant income-producing rights derived from the exercise of power. These normally came with grants of the royal ban, that is, the king's right to command, prohibit and punish, and could include tolls, fishing and forest rights, coining privileges, fiscal incomes, rights to hold markets, and fines accruing from grants of immunity.[93] Rather than seeing Otto's growing co-operation with royal churches as a response to a specific event, it should be seen in the light of its continuity with Carolingian precedents, which Otto liked to emulate. It was a gradual re-introduction of an older, successful structure to a new government during a period of great transition as well as a means to create the personal bonds

---

[92] On the early development of the royal chapel, see Klewitz (1937) and Fleckenstein (1959).

[93] A quick review of Otto I's charters for the period up until 955 confirms this observation.

necessary for an additional political alliance. The old structure was adapted, modified and extended to meet the needs of a newly emerging political entity.

This can be seen best, although not exclusively, through the example of the royal chapel. Here, Otto I made significant innovations to the old institution in an attempt to expand his power of governing. The court chapel retained its former functions, but in addition became a kind of clerical academy sponsored by the king for the training of prospective candidates to high church office. Increasingly, these men received their initial schooling in royally supported cathedral schools such as Cologne, Magdeburg and Hildesheim from where they were selected to come to the royal court as *capellani* or chaplains to learn the ways of royal government, form a camaraderie of office, or so it was to be hoped, and through royal influence win high ecclesiastical office.[94] Although a significant innovation, Otto I's royal chapel had definite limitations. It did not change the fact that most bishops and abbots came from the nobility, and they did not give up their allegiance to family and kindred overnight. In fact, family connections and influence often played a role in their being called to the court in the first place. Moreover, this was a developing institution, and although serving as a royal chaplain was one way to become a bishop, it never became the only way, neither under Otto I nor his successors, who used it much more extensively to that end. Although Otto's previous successes and increased prestige after 955 may have given him added influence on episcopal elections, his control over the electoral process was by no means total. Custom, familial rights and political alliances all played a role. Even when the king did manage to secure the election of a 'royal' candidate from the court chapel, this was no automatic guarantee that the new bishop always would support the royal 'programme'. Family allegiances, noble alliances and local political realities still influenced bishops a great deal. Thus, in one sense, the king's attempt to expand royal power using the chapel still came up against noble families and their claims to local influence. Moreover, once in office, a new prelate's main responsibility was to his diocese or congregation and often he had to protect these interests against both the king and the nobility.[95]

---

[94] Fleckenstein (1956), (1966) 17–63, and Klewitz (1939b).
[95] Reuter (1982) 350–8, (1991a) 156–8; Althoff and Keller (1985) 48–51, 217–22; and Keller (1985a) 26–7.

The king also faced a very real limitation by the fact that – unlike a count or a duke – a bishop, once consecrated, could not customarily be removed for cause. This was not the case, however, with royal abbots and abbesses over whom the king had much greater control owing to his stronger proprietary relationship to the monasteries.[96]

However, limitations on the king's ability positively to control all aspects of his co-operative relationship with royal churches and monasteries do not nullify its successes and positive effects. For all of its limitations, the expansion of the royal chapel provided essential links between the bishoprics, with their cathedral chapters and schools, and the royal court. Over time this increased contact allowed the king to build up a transregional communication network among the higher clergy and royal chaplains, which gave the king some latitude in extending royal influence into the duchies and created an element of continuity in royal government.

A similar network arose within the royal monastic ranks also, as is witnessed by the transregional spread of royally supported monastic reform by reforming monks.[97] This also began under Otto I and reached a high point under Henry II and Conrad II. Both examples show an ability of using the relationship with the church to overstep the internal political boundaries of a multi-national or 'imperial' kingship.[98] The creation and extension of these networks coincided with the evolution of the monarchy and the structure of the realm. Whereas Otto I promoted candidates from the royal chapel primarily to bishoprics in Saxony, Franconia and Lotharingia (the traditional centres of the German kings' power), when Otto III and Henry II expanded their power in the beginning of the eleventh century to assume more direct control in Swabia and Bavaria, royal chaplains became prelates in those areas also.[99]

Moreover, royal grants of property, incomes and sovereign or income-producing rights to bishoprics and royal monasteries

---

[96] Reuter (1982) 356–8.

[97] F. Prinz (1985) 229–32; Althoff and Keller (1985) 221–2; and Reuter (1991a) 210–12. On contacts among reform monasteries, especially through necrological prayer communities, see Althoff (1978) esp. 925–8; Jakobi (1978) esp. 820–8; Wollasch (1978); and Freise (1983).

[98] On the concept of an 'imperial' kingship, see Keller (1982) 114–21, who cites the earlier literature.

[99] Fleckenstein (1966) documents this in great detail in the chapters devoted to these two rulers.

continued to increase under Otto I and his successors. Gradually, sovereign rights came to include grants of high jurisdiction, exercised through the appointed advocates of the bishop, abbot or abbess, making ecclesiastical advocates into private counts of the immunist; and eventually even comital rights over areas independent of land ownership, called ban immunities, were granted to bishoprics and royal monasteries, in effect making the immunist a count.[100] With these grants came increased wealth and power, and the expectation of greater service. Thus, beginning with Otto I and expanding, especially under Henry II and the first Salian kings, the German kings began economically and governmentally to utilize bishoprics and royal monasteries more systematically than had their Carolingian predecessors.[101] This further integration of the high churches of the realm as a major economic and governmental support of the monarchy manifested itself most clearly in the economic underpinning of the royal itinerary, the growth of ecclesiastical markets and mints, the administration of royal forests and the provision of large military contingents to the royal army. In all of these areas the role played by royal churches became predominant. For example, in addition to the traditional use of royal residences or *Pfalzen* (many of which were gradually granted totally or in part to royal churches), bishoprics and royal monasteries increasingly acted as the primary stopping-places on the royal itinerary and as economic providers for the royal court. Likewise, when the royal army shifted from a host drawn from the duchies, as at the battles of Riade and of the Lech, to one of vassalic contingents, royal churches provided from two-thirds to three-quarters of the military contingents to the royal host from warriors supported on their landed estates. For instance, Otto II's troop levy of 981/2, the *Indiculus Loricatorum*, called the great majority of the troops from royal churches, and contingents sent to help Otto III in 1001 or 1002 also mention royal churches as the suppliers of the troops.[102] Overall, then, the increasing incor-

---

[100] For a general discussion of immunities, see Reuter (1991a) 218–19 and (1982) 363–4, 367. For the technical studies of this development, see Stengel (1910) 588–98; Waas (1919) 99–118, 119–44, 158–73; Otto (1933) 80–129, 141–2; Mayer, T. (1950) 1–49; Scheyhing (1960) 202–3, 313–17; and recently, Hoffmann (1990) 456–80.

[101] T. Schieffer (1951) 393–404 and Brühl (1968) 126–33.

[102] See *MGH Const.* 1 no. 436 pp. 632–3. On the transformation of the royal army into a vassalic army, see Werner (1968). While the *Indiculus Loricatorum* indicates that the number of knights in the specific contingents was fixed already in the Ottonian period, Keller (1985a) 21 n. 14 points out that these levies most likely represent the lowest amount to be sent and would not exhaust the full potential of warriors available to

poration of the royal churches and monasteries into royal
government neither enabled the German monarchs to 'control'
the secular princes nor poised the church as a 'counterweight' to
them, but it did create an additional basis of royal support. It gave
the king another method of influencing the government of the
realm and of increasing and expanding royal power. For within
definite limitations, royal bishops, abbots and chaplains allowed
the king to extend his influence into areas outside direct royal
jurisdiction and to bind the realm more closely to the central
power; royal churches became the main bastions of economic and
military support for the king on the basis of their large landed
estates. Thus, it is not surprising that the Ottonian and Salian kings
granted extensive properties and wide-ranging rights to bishoprics
and royal monasteries, and encouraged the foundation of new sees
as they expanded into new territories in the east.

OTTONIAN FOREIGN POLICY

For the purposes of this work, it is necessary only to provide the
most general overview of Ottonian foreign policy; more specific
information is required only in regard to policy on the Saxon
eastern frontier, where the Ottonians built a concentrated centre
of royal power and several royal monasteries played key roles.[103]
Let us first look briefly to the west and the south.

Building on his father's successes in the southwest and west,
Otto I managed even during his crisis years to expand his influence
and authority on the western frontier. In 939 Otto took the young
king of Burgundy, Conrad, under his protection and thereby
continued the east Frankish tradition of overlordship in Burgundy.
Both Conrad of Burgundy, who ruled until 993, and his son
Rudolf III remained solidly under Ottonian influence. In fact,

various religious institutions should the king need more. For the contingents sent to
help Otto III, see Thietmar 4.48; and *Vita Burchardi Episcopi* c. 8 p. 836, where it states:
'Postea vero sedatis seditionibus et pace inter illos vix firmata, iussu imperatoris
episcopus cum apparatu magno et milites Moguntinenses necnon et abbas Fuldensis
atque episcopus Wirtzburgensis cum non modica multitudine in Italiam profeci sunt.'
I thank Timothy Reuter for directing me to the information about the troops sent to
Otto III in 1001 or 1002.

[103] Reuter (1991a) 160–74, 253–74, whom I follow to a large extent, provides the most
concise and convenient, yet synthetic and intellectually stimulating treatment of
Ottonian foreign policy, especially in regard to 'eastern' policy. However, see also the
pertinent sections in Reuter (1991b), Hlawitschka (1986), F. Prinz (1985) and Herrmann
(1982) for other overviews.

Rudolf III, who had no heir and was related to Henry II, made the Saxon king his successor, but Rudolf outlived him. Later, when Rudolf died, Conrad II, the first Salian ruler and Henry II's successor, made good Henry's claim and incorporated Burgundy into the Salian Empire. Relations between the Ottonian rulers and the west Frankish realm were similar, but not as one-sided. Otto I intervened as had his father in west Frankish affairs, often receiving the commendation of west Frankish nobles and mediating in the rivalries between the Carolingian and the Robertine families. Gradually Otto achieved a loose hegemonic position over the west Frankish realm, which he exercised primarily through the dukes of Lotharingia, marriage alliances and personal relationships. The synod of Ingelheim in 948, called by Otto and presided over by a papal legate, which discussed and made decisions on west Frankish affairs, provides a manifestation of this hegemony.[104] This synod and Otto's subsequent victory over the Hungarians at the Lech in 955 both served to enhance his prestige and authority. However, while Ottonian hegemony reached its peak from about 940 until 965, it never became institutionalized and there never was a question of incorporating the west Frankish realm into the Ottonian empire. In fact, Ottonian influence and hegemony had already begun to weaken under Otto II and during the minority of Otto III, and the accession of the Capetians to the west Frankish throne in 987, after the last Carolingians, Lothar and Louis V, had died in quick succession, brought an end to Ottonian hegemony.

Otto I's power and authority, his adherence to Frankish traditions and the political situation south of the Alps all worked to draw him south to Italy also. There, as has been mentioned, he defeated Berengar in 951 and was crowned king of Italy in Pavia. Later, in 952, he received Berengar as a sub-king, and once again created an overlordship. But as Otto and his successors were to discover, controlling Italy from the north would never be an easy task. Otto returned in 961 at the request of the Pope in the face of continued incursions on the part of Berengar. On this occasion Otto not only drove Berengar into exile, but more importantly received the imperial coronation on 2 February 962, renewing the western emperorship in the spirit of Charlemagne. Thereafter, the Ottonians and their successors, the Salians, also ruled Italy. However, they ruled it from afar, spending only intermittent

---

[104] On this synod, see Fuhrmann (1964).

periods there (with the exception of Otto I late in his reign and Otto II late in his), and they only rarely controlled more than Lombardy and Tuscany and the roads south to Rome, where they customarily received the imperial coronation. Each trip to Italy was an expedition with a full army and, in a sense, a reconquest.[105] Nevertheless, they did manage a certain level of control in the north and regarded Italy as a key element of their empire.[106]

Some of the turmoil of Otto I's early years arose on the eastern frontier, where, as related earlier, his father had won a significant victory over the Magyars at Riade, had led a successful policy of military expansion against the Abodrites and the Elbian Slavs to the north and east of Saxony, and had subjected the Bohemians to the southeast to his rule. Immediately upon Otto I's succession, various eastern peoples tested the new king. The Magyars staged new incursions into Saxony and Franconia, the Bohemians successfully revolted from their previous tributary status, and both the Abodrites and the Elbian Slavs withheld payments of tribute. These external problems indeed contributed to the early crises of Otto's reign because the curtailment of tribute payments caused disaffection among a portion of the east Saxon nobility. As we have seen, however, Otto began to address these problems as early as 937. He established two large border marches on the eastern frontier – Hermann Billung's margraviate positioned against the northern and eastern Slavs, and Gero's against the Sorbian Slavs of the middle Elbe and Saale rivers – to protect Saxony from attack, to regain control over the Slavic peoples, and to consolidate Saxon overlordship (see Map 2). At the same time, as we have seen, Otto began to build up and strengthen the eastern frontier with the foundation of the monastery of St Maurice at Magdeburg. Whereas Henry I's engagements with the Slavs on the eastern frontier were connected primarily with the expansion of Saxon political and military influence, his son Otto appears early in his reign to have added the conscious goal of missionary activity and Christianization of the subjected peoples. Thus, eventually the new margraviates would safeguard missionary activity and new ecclesiastical foundations in the area.

Beginning in the late 940s, Ottonian domination and missionary activity in the northern and eastern border regions began to intensify. Gradually overlordship was replaced with lordship, and

---

[105] Reuter (1991a) 269–71.   [106] Pauler (1982).

'tribute-paying peoples' were transformed into 'census-paying peasants'.[107] The establishment of a network of burgwards in Gero's margraviate provides good evidence of this intensification of dominion. These consisted of a fortified centre which was economically supported by a group of nearby dependent villages and manned with garrisons of mounted troops, mostly of Slavic origin. Missionary activity also increased dramatically. In the years 947–8, Otto established five new missionary bishoprics, three (Schleswig, Ripen and Aarhus) set up for the Danish mission and linked to the archbishopric of Hamburg–Bremen, and two (Brandenburg and Havelberg) designated for the Wilzes and the Hevelli (later the Liutizi), and subject to the archbishopric of Mainz on the Rhine.

During the 950s and 960s pressure on the Slavs increased. Bohemia was reduced once again to tributary status by 950 and, in 955, after a Saxon army had suffered a defeat at the hands of the Slavs, Otto I, coming fresh from victory over the Magyars at the Lechfeld, won another on 16 October over the Abodrites at the Recknitz in Mecklenburg. From about 955, Otto appears to have planned, and to have received papal approval for, the trans-formation of the royal monastery of St Maurice into a new archbishopric at Magdeburg, which would act not only as an archbishopric and centre of Ottonian power in the Saxon heartland, but would also co-ordinate missionary activity in the east. This plan, however, met with tenacious resistance from the bishop of Halberstadt, Bernard, whose bishopric was originally to have been transferred to Magdeburg, and from the archbishop of Mainz, Otto's illegitimate son William, who saw the plan as a threat to the primatial position of Mainz, as well as to its traditional missionary mandate on the eastern frontier. Therefore Otto was not able to implement his plan until 968, after the deaths of these two prelates. In the meantime, Margrave Gero had managed to reduce not only the Lausitzi to tributary status, but also Miesco I of Poland, with whom the Saxons now came into contact owing to their relentless campaigning against the Elbian Slavs.[108] Miesco, however, was not merely a tribute-payer; he also appears to have entered into an *amicitia* relationship with Otto.[109] Later, in 966, he accepted Christianity and was baptized after his marriage to a Christian princess, Dobrava of Bohemia. In the north, Harald

[107] Reuter (1991a) 162, 166.   [108] Widukind 3.67–8.   [109] Widukind 3.69.

Bluetooth of Denmark accepted Christianity in 965, after a Christian bishop willingly and successfully underwent the ordeal of glowing iron to prove to the king the pre-eminent power of the Christian God. But Widukind also ascribed his conversion to the effects of Otto's missionary efforts in this area.[110]

The year 968 provides a pinnacle and a turning point in Otto I's 'eastern' policy. In this year, Otto finally transformed the monastery of St Maurice into a Saxon archbishopric at Magdeburg. At the same time he created three new suffragan bishoprics for the archdiocese at Merseburg, Meißen and Zeitz (later moved to Naumburg), and the bishoprics of Brandenburg and Havelberg were taken from Mainz and added to Magdeburg's archdiocese. With the establishment of this Saxon archbishopric to co-ordinate the eastern mission, Otto once again followed in the Carolingian tradition. As befitted his recent imperial dignity (962), he ruled as a missionary king. The foundation of the archbishopric of Magdeburg also marked the culmination of Otto's efforts to create a Saxon centre of power in the realm, which he had begun in 936–7. In fact, it has been compared to Charlemagne's building up of Aachen as his favoured residence.[111] Although Otto followed some Carolingian precedents, his actions can also be seen as a manifestation of a new Saxon consciousness, which gradually freed itself from the old Carolingian centres of power. Thus, with the foundation of a Saxon archbishopric, it became the primary centre for the mission to the east instead of the Carolingian Mainz on the Rhine, which had traditionally borne that mandate. In the same year, the bishopric of Oldenburg (archdiocese Hamburg–Bremen) was created for the Wagrians in the north and a bishopric was established at Poznań to aid in the Christianization of Poland. Officially in 973, but in actuality first in 976, a bishopric was established at Prague for the Bohemian Slavs, which, apparently in a concession to the archbishopric of Mainz, fell within its ecclesiastical jurisdiction. With increased Saxon influence in Bohemia, the royal monastery of Corvey on the Weser River took an active role in this missionary field, which had previously fallen within the missionary sphere of the bishop of Regensburg. The facts that two of the first three bishops of Prague came from Corvey and that the Bohemian prince's chapel was dedicated to Corvey's patron saint, St Vitus, indicate Corvey's activity in the

---

[110] Thietmar 4.55–6, 2.14; Widukind 3.65.   [111] E.g. Schlesinger (1968) 28–31.

Bohemian mission.[112] Thus, in 968 Saxon missionary activity became institutionalized and by 973 the majority of the ethnic groups on the eastern frontier had their own bishopric. Ottonian conquests and missionary activity among the Slavic peoples east of the Elbe, moreover, had brought the Saxon rulers into contact with formidable princes in Bohemia and Poland, who also commanded large bands of warrior nobles. Although these princes paid tribute to the Ottonians, they also forged connections with the Saxon nobility and increasingly took part in Saxon politics, such as the disputed successions of Otto III and Henry II.

Through the establishment of the royal monastery of St Maurice and later archbishopric of Magdeburg, Otto I dramatically created a new focal point and centre of political power on the Elbe River. The additional creation of the bishopric of Merseburg (968), which was dissolved in 981 and reinstated in 1004 and, later, Otto II's foundation in 979 of the royal monastery and Ottonian cult site at Memleben, the place where both Henry I and Otto I died, further stabilized the eastern frontier along the Saale River. With the foundation of these three ecclesiastical centres, the Ottonian rulers had established the launching points from which would proceed the continued conquest to the east, the Christianization and organization of the Slavic peoples and lands and their final integration into the realm. The summer of 983, however, brought a serious setback in the newly won and organized lands east of the Elbe–Saale line. In that year, the Danes and the Slavic Abodrites revolted in the north, and the Liutizi, a coalition of Elbian Slavs united by a militant paganism, revolted along the middle Elbe and endeavoured to destroy the Saxon overlordship as well as to wipe out Christianity. During the revolt, the episcopal cities of Havelberg and Brandenburg were burned down, Christians were slain, and most of the territorial gains of the last fifty years were lost, many of which had been granted to the archbishopric of Magdeburg and some to the royal monastery of Memleben. Subsequently, in the decades of the 980s and 990s, a coalition of Christian princes and their followers, including the Ottonians, the Piasts of Poland and sometimes the Przemyslids of Bohemia (although the Piasts and Ottonians often stood together in conflict with the Przemyslids), managed to stem this revolt and other Slavic incursions by campaigning in the region against the Elbian

[112] Hilsch (1972).

Slavs. Nevertheless, the former tributary status of these areas was never reinstated totally and, thereafter, the Elbe–Saale line was gradually accepted as the political frontier in the east.[113] The acceptance of this new boundary for the realm, of diminished influence beyond the Elbe and of reduced or lost tributary payments demanded that the Saxon nobility reassess their situation and decide how to adapt to new circumstances. This process took a long time and much energy, but for the Ottonian kings, the discovery of silver in 968 at Rammelsberg near Goslar reduced their dependence on tribute payments and greatly eased the situation. The rest of the east Saxon nobility, who had little to show for many years of campaigning, were not so fortunate.[114]

The culmination of this Christian coalition occurred with Otto III's pilgrimage in 1000 to the shrine of Adalbert of Prague, which the Polish prince, Boleslav Chrobry, had set up at Gniezno. On this trip Otto III created a new archbishopric for Poland, presented the Polish prince with a copy of the Ottonians' Holy Lance, and reaffirmed an *amicitia* relationship with Boleslav with the promise of a marriage alliance. These acts established the ecclesiastical independence of Poland, as well as symbolically and effectually elevating Boleslav's status while not, however, making him a king.[115] However, this new relationship between the Ottonian and Piast families did not last long. Boleslav Chrobry's initial support of Ekkehard of Meißen, instead of Henry II, for king during the contested election of 1002 and related disputes thereafter sparked a bitter feud between the two rulers. Henry reversed the prevailing alliance of the last two decades and made a new alliance with the pagan Liutizi against the Piast ruler.[116] The feud between Boleslav and Henry and its resultant hostilities found a compromise solution finally in 1018, but enmity continued throughout Henry's reign and not truly until 1032 did Conrad II re-establish German hegemony over Poland.[117]

[113] On the Slavic uprising of 983 and its aftermath, see Fritze (1984); Ludat (1971); and Brüske (1955).

[114] On the discovery of silver in 968, see Hillebrand (1967). Leyser (1981) 742–5, 752–3 discusses the impact that this discovery had on the Ottonian rulers, on their ability to maintain power and on their governing ability in the face of serious setbacks.

[115] On the events at Gniezno, see Ludat (1971) 67–93 and Fried (1989).

[116] On this new alliance with the pagan Liutizi, see Thietmar 5.32 and Brüske (1955). For contemporary criticism of Henry for the alliance with the Liutizi, see Thietmar 6.25 and Brun of Querfurt's letter of 1009 in Giesebrecht (1885) 702–5.

[117] Reuter (1991a) 257–64 and (1991b) discusses relations between Henry II, Duke Boleslav Chrobry and their respective retainers and relatives as an extended feud. On the

After the great territorial losses east of the Elbe River in the Slavic rebellion of 983 and the continuing incursions thereafter, and with the conflicts around Meißen with Boleslav Chrobry, now the head of an emerging and powerful Polish polity early in the eleventh century, Henry II decided to abandon the imperial designs of his predecessors toward the Slavic peoples on the eastern frontier, as well as toward Poland. He began to return to an earlier Carolingian conception of the realm, which was more defensive in character and which he then adapted to correspond to the political realities of his day. Henry II's new policies formed part of a long-range political programme, which he appears to have formulated early in his reign, and which he referred to as a *Renovatio regni Francorum*,[118] that is, a 'renewal of the Frankish realm'.[119] Henry's overall programme was to retreat from the ambitious hegemonic designs of the three Ottos, accept the Elbe–Saale line as the eastern frontier, and shift the focus of royal power from the frontier to the centre of the kingdom. In essence Henry strove to strengthen significantly the basis of royal power by establishing a closed complex of royal properties and royally aligned church properties in the centre of the realm. Theoretically, from this power-centre any king could effectively rule the surrounding regions of his kingdom as well as secure the realm against external incursions or internal rebellions. Thus, Henry abandoned the Ottonian notion of a realm incorporating vast eastern lands administered from centres established at Magdeburg and Merseburg (and, after its dissolution in 981, at Memleben) and returned to an earlier Carolingian concept of the realm, which emphasized the centre. This consisted of retreating to a stable, established frontier and centralizing royal power in the middle of the kingdom through a consolidation and enlargement of the royal domain in eastern Franconia, Hesse and Thuringia. Henry re-established a frontier in the east along the Elbe–Saale line,

---

breakdown of Otto III's Polish alliance, see also Beumann and Schlesinger (1955) 226–36.

[118] This legend, which first appeared on 15 January 1003 as the legend on a royal *bulla*, stands in stark contrast to Otto III's formula, *Renovatio imperii Romanorum*, that is, a renewal of the Roman Empire, and represents the renunciation of Otto III's policies in the east. See Foltz (1877–8) 39–45; Schramm (1928) 196; and Folz (1950) 95–8. Weinfurter (1986) 295 offers an alternative interpretation.

[119] Especially on the ecclesiastical elements of Henry's programme, see Diefenbach (unpub. diss. 1952). Concerning the political parts of Henry II's programme, see Weinfurter (1986). See Keller (1982) 99 on the related changes in Henry's practice of issuing charters and his expanded royal itinerary.

which was supported by royal churches both along this line and in the centre of the realm, but whose main estates lay west of the Elbe–Saale line as well as in the centre of the realm. This had the effect of anchoring the frontier to the centre.

Henry effected his revisions to his predecessors' eastern policy in various stages over a fifteen-year period.[120] He did this in conjunction with an overall programme, which included intensifying royal claims to governmental rights over bishoprics and royal monasteries, and systematically augmenting their ability to serve the realm politically and economically.[121] Henry consciously and systematically emphasized some of his own bases of support in eastern Saxony, such as Merseburg, and raised others, such as Walbeck, to new prominence. He re-established Merseburg as a bishopric in 1004 and eventually made this episcopal city the main site in Saxony, where he customarily celebrated Easter, thus altering the former Ottonian custom of holding Easter in Quedlinburg. The monastery of Walbeck became the Palm Sunday feast-site, replacing Magdeburg where, however, he celebrated Easter in 1024.[122] At the same time, Henry showed less royal favour in terms of visits and/or grants to some of the main centres of the Ottonians such as Quedlinburg, Memleben and, to a smaller degree, Magdeburg. Henry also founded a strategic new bishopric in 1007 located at Bamberg, near the southeastern frontier and midway between the northern and southern regions of the realm.[123] Moreover, the last Ottonian king attempted to strengthen and build up the central regions of the realm with the support of old royal monasteries such as Hersfeld, Fulda, Corvey and Lorsch, as well as the more recent foundations at Hilwartshausen and Kaufungen, the bishoprics of Halberstadt, Paderborn, Würzburg and Mainz, and the newly founded bishopric of Bamberg. Henry II died without completing all of the

---

[120] It is certainly no accident that the king's alterations in eastern policy occurred during approximately the same period of his reign as when he undertook numerous campaigns against Boleslav Chrobry of Poland, which necessitated frequent sojourns in the eastern regions.   [121] T. Schieffer (1951) 397–402.

[122] Although Merseburg was officially re-established in 1004, re-endowment of the bishopric with new and former properties lasted approximately until 1017. See BG 1680a, 1861, 1944b, 2037c and 2059d for Henry II's celebrations of Easter in Saxony. On the new importance of Merseburg and Walbeck as feast-sites, see Rieckenberg (1941/1965) 76–7 nn. 8, 9 and Benz (1975).

[123] Similarly, even though Bamberg received a huge endowment upon its foundation in 1007 (twenty-seven separate charters on the same day!), Henry II, throughout his reign, continued to favour the new bishopric and to help it consolidate its holdings.

various and interconnected components of his overall concept, but his successors from the Salian house continued and, in some aspects, completed the general direction of his ideas, although different times and circumstances caused some significant changes in their policies.

Chapter 2

ITINERANT KINGSHIP, ROYAL MONASTERIES AND THE *SERVITIUM REGIS*

ITINERANT KINGSHIP AND THE STRUCTURE OF THE REALM

Itinerant kingship refers to government in which a king carries out all the functions and symbolic representations of governing by periodically or constantly travelling throughout the areas of his dominion. Although especially well documented and most studied for the Frankish–Carolingian and the German realms of early medieval Europe, itinerant kingship existed throughout all of Europe during most of the middle ages.[1] In fact, in the middle ages whoever exercised any kind of dominion – kings, dukes and counts; popes, bishops and abbots – all found themselves constantly under way to carry out the manifold functions of their office.[2] Moreover, while particularly prevalent in medieval Europe, this method of governing existed beyond the geographical and cultural boundaries of Europe and lasted in some places beyond the end of the European middle ages.[3]

One finds itinerant rulership in Indonesia, in the South Sea Islands and in Africa, where it survived into the early twentieth century.[4] For example, the fourteenth-century kings of Java practised an itinerant kingship that was rooted firmly within the intensely hierarchical and mystical nature of Hinduism. The rulers of the Hawaiian and Tahitian islands made circumambulations in connection with religious cult festivals. In Morocco, from the late seventeenth century until the early twentieth, the resident kings, under the influence of Islamic concepts of theocracy and struggle, led a royal progress that was combative in nature and that focused

---

[1] In general see: Rieckenberg (1941/1965); Brühl (1968) and (1983); and Peyer (1964/1982) and (1987).

[2] Peyer (1987) 147–8. On the progressions and travels of the early medieval bishop, see Scheibelreiter (1983) 202–36.

[3] Peyer (1964/1982) 111–15.　　　　[4] Ibid. and Geertz (1977).

on the demonstration and exercise of personal power.[5] Likewise, itinerant kingships existed into the nineteenth century in Ethiopia and in the kingdoms throughout the highland lake region of East Central Africa.[6]

Itinerant kingship, therefore, is not peculiar to Europe and the middle ages, but is rather a method of government found widely in pre-modern societies and is determined by various economic, social, political, religious and cultural factors.[7] Societies having this kind of rulership displayed certain common characteristics: a largely natural economy; the dominance of peasant farmers by warriors or by a particular clan or family; governmental authority deriving from personal relationships and often from feudal relations; magical or sacred conceptions of rulership, and, in some cases at least, only marginal reliance on the written record in literature in government.[8] In such societies, kings or chiefs moved constantly throughout their territories making their presence felt and reinforcing the personal bonds of their rulership. They gathered their people around them, took part in solemnities, conferred gifts and honours, pronounced justice, fought enemies and rivals and ensured general security. In this way, the king-in-motion identified – even embodied – the society's centre of power; and the royal progress itself became the major institution of government. Through it, the king took symbolic as well as actual possession of the realm.

Roderich Schmidt has studied the importance of the initial royal progression or perambulation through the realm (*Umritt* in German) during the late Ottonian and early Salian periods for taking real and symbolic possession of the kingdom upon accession. On this initial progression, the new king gathered the assent to his election from the regional assemblies of nobles and received their homage. His election was thereby legitimized. At the same time, he demonstrated his ability to undertake a journey through the entire realm and made claim to royal properties and

---

[5] Geertz (1977) 157–67, where he briefly summarizes the particular characteristics of the royal progress in Java and Morocco and provides references to the sources and the older literature. Also concerning Morocco as well as the South Sea Islands see Peyer (1964/1982) 112–13.

[6] Bunyoro, Ankole, Rwanda and Burundi. See Peyer (1964/1982) 111–12; Beattie (1960) 33–5, 39–41; and Horvath (1969) 209–12, 218–19.

[7] Some pre-modern societies practising itinerant rulership continue to exist today in the modern period as well as some 'modern' societies which practise alternate forms of the old itinerancy. [8] Peyer (1964/1982) and (1987) 146–8.

prerogatives in the areas visited.[9] In 929–30, Henry I used a similar *Umritt* in a different context – to gain the assent of the regional powers to the designation of his son, Otto, as his sole successor.[10] Thus, the royal progress marked the limits of the ruler's domain, unified the realm through contact with other centres of power, and attempted to give legitimacy to the notion that the ruler received his sovereignty from God (or the gods).[11] Although a king could not be omnipresent like God, he could attempt to give that impression.[12] Thus, the royal itinerary dramatized in concrete terms the fact that the king was ruling, and consequently it formed a central element of his power.

The frequency and the pace of the royal *iter* or progress varied greatly. In some societies rulers resided in permanent capitals from which the royal progress always began and to which it always returned.[13] Rulers in other societies had several semi-permanent 'capitals' or, more aptly, concentrated regions of power and favoured residences in which they spent large blocks of time – for example, winters – during the course of their travels.[14] Finally, in some societies the king and the royal court stayed almost constantly in motion, although the frequency, if not the duration, of visits to particular places and regions marked them as chief locations or 'centres' of royal power.[15]

In Europe between 500 and 1500, itinerant rulership emerged in virtually all of the Germanic successor kingdoms to the Roman empire and in the kingdoms deriving from them. It also evolved in areas which had never formed part of the Roman empire, such as Ireland, Scandinavia, Poland, Bohemia, Hungary and Russia.[16] The degree of itinerancy varied greatly within the geographical and chronological boundaries of medieval Europe. For instance, the Merovingian and Carolingian kings travelled extensively, although not constantly, since they resided for long periods of time in favoured residences. This became particularly evident after

---

[9] Schmidt (1961).
[10] Schmid (1964/1971b) 458–63.
[11] Geertz (1977) 163–4.
[12] Ibid. 162–3.
[13] Ibid. 157–60. Hayam Wuruk's Java provides an excellent example of an itinerancy based on a permanent capital.
[14] One finds an itinerancy of this type for example in the realms of the Merovingian and Carolingian Franks from the sixth through to the ninth centuries. See Ewig (1963) 47–72; and Brühl (1967) and (1968) 1–53.
[15] The premier and most well documented example of kings constantly in motion is the early medieval German kingdom under the Ottonian and Salian rulers. See Rieckenberg (1941/1965); Brühl (1968) 116–219, 452–576 and (1983); and Müller-Mertens (1980).
[16] Peyer (1964/1982) 98–110.

794 when Charlemagne established Aachen as the primary residence of the most 'centralized' Germanic kingdom – and, after 800, Germanic empire – in early medieval Europe.[17] The kings of Anglo-Saxon England and early Capetian France did not have to travel so far or so often owing to the smaller size of their royal domains and, in the case of Anglo-Saxon England, owing to the existence of more sophisticated and 'centralized' governmental institutions.[18] In early medieval Germany (Map 3), on the other hand, the vast size of the realm and its political structure caused the Ottonian and Salian kings, in co-operation with high church officials – that is, the great bishops, abbots and abbesses of the realm – to forge a highly mobile form of itinerant kingship. These kings spent at least half of their time on the road and they rarely stayed in one place longer than a few days or at most a few weeks. For these rulers the royal itinerary was a vital and growing institution which became increasingly complex as they transformed it into a symbolic representation of royal theocracy and a functioning system of government. Consequently, itinerancy became the fate of the Ottonian and Salian rulers of early medieval Germany, and long absences brought on the greatest evils.[19]

As with other kings in France and Anglo-Saxon England, the early German kings, by virtue of their ecclesiastical anointment with holy oil upon coronation, acquired a sacral or sacred nature.[20] The act of anointment raised the king above other laymen, and made him the vicar of Christ on earth. He became in essence both king and priest, *rex et sacerdos*,[21] or, more correctly, king and priest-like. In reality, 'the king was neither a simple layman nor an ecclesiastic; he stood between or above both spheres'.[22] The Ottonian and Salian kings used the royal itinerary to combine the symbolic and sacral nature of their kingship with the political and judicial aspects. Indeed, the king's frequent personal appearance throughout his realm formed the common link to the dual nature

---

[17] On Aachen's position as the Carolingian 'capital', see Bullough (1985) and Brühl (1967) 208–11.

[18] As Reuter (1991a) 212 points out, the area ruled effectively by the west Frankish or Anglo-Saxon rulers equalled only about the size of a single German duchy. On Anglo-Saxon governmental institutions, see Loyn (1984).   [19] Leyser (1979) 103.

[20] In general, see Beumann (1948). On the problems of terminology in using 'sacred' or 'sacral', see Nelson (1973) and Leyser (1979) 75–82, who does not agree with all of Nelson's distinctions regarding the terms.

[21] *rex et sacerdos*: generally concerning the problems with this concept, see Beumann (1948) and Angenendt (1982).

[22] Fichtenau (1984) 219 (trans. by Geary p. 161).

of his kingship. Therefore, one cannot separate the strongly personal and sacral elements of German kingship from the material and institutional; and the royal *iter* was the vehicle which bore the king's sacrality throughout the realm, as well as integrating the realm physically.[23]

For the Ottonian and Salian kings and those around them,[24] the sacrality of kingship was an earnest religious experience, and like the royal itinerary – the vehicle which physically transported it – sacral legitimization of the king was an expanding and developing practice. This explains the marked increase in liturgical representation under these kings.[25] The king, the anointed of God, needed to display, and thus enhance, his sacrality using all of the symbolic and liturgical means at his disposal. These included frequent crown-wearings or 'going under the crown', church consecrations and repeated solemn receptions of the king in the cities and monasteries of the realm with the singing of liturgical praises or *laudes* to the ruler.[26] In addition, art and architecture served and furthered the liturgical representation of the anointed king. Thus, the sacral and liturgical representation of these kings developed significantly in Ottonian and Salian art. A series of contemporary artistic representations of the Ottonian and early Salian kings as the anointed of the Lord document how the concept of ruler sacrality advanced beyond Carolingian concepts. They were elevated out of and beyond the worldly plane of the artists' rendering into the plane of Christ and the saints. From there, under divine protection, they were to fulfil their earthly mandate, even as it related to 'sacred' duties; and through their actions as Christ's vicar and through continual prayer, they could merit final integration into the higher sphere. Nothing better illustrates the curious position of the anointed king, placed both

---

[23] Keller (1985a) 29; and Althoff and Keller (1985) 240.

[24] Leyser (1979) 92–107 examines the practical aspects of how the secular nobility viewed and reacted to the king's sacral status.   [25] Althoff and Keller (1985) 240.

[26] Regarding the symbolic and liturgical manifestations of sacral kingship, see Vogel and Elze (1963–72) 226.257–8; Klewitz (1939a); Bulst (1941); Kantorowicz (1944/1965) and (1958); Schramm and Mütherich (1981); Benz (1975); Keller (1985a) 28–34; and Mayr-Harting (1991). Specifically on the *adventus*, see Willmes (1976) and Fichtenau (1984) 76–9. Although the *laudes* were normally sung or chanted by members of the ecclesiastical orders, there were instances, perhaps similar to the old Germanic acclamation of the ruler, when the *laudes* were sung by the lay persons present. See *Ann. Qued. s.a.* 984 p. 66; Thietmar 5.17; and Wipo, *Opera*, c. 3. It appears that new chants may have been written for every new royal *adventus*. See Ekkehard IV, *Casus Sancti Galli* c. 14 p. 40.

between and above earthly laymen and ecclesiastics, and between God and man.[27] Also, vigorous building programmes of bishops and royal abbots and abbesses served the needs of the royal *iter* and royal sacrality. These efforts provided not only expanded quarters for the royal entourage, but also more suitable venues for enacting the drama of the king's advent or his 'going under the crown' and for the king's participation in the religious ceremonies of the specific community.[28] Royal sacrality had secular advantages as well. The king's presence served to document his relationship with those having nearness to him (the concept of *Königsnähe*), and it thereby also legitimized the nobility. This and the sacrality of the king's person acted as a real and an ideological protection against opposition.[29] Thus, royal sacrality provided one substitute for the missing governmental institutions.[30]

On the other hand, as a secular ruler in a large, but politically and economically decentralized, realm – in which he was only one of many powerful lords – the king constantly had to exercise his prerogatives in order to maintain his dominion and his claim to royal lordship. In this aspect of his rulership, the fact that the king thought of himself as *rex et sacerdos* brought little advantage if he could not ride more quickly and travel more securely than any rivals.[31] In a realm as large as medieval Germany, the king faced a huge task. For in accordance with the highly personal nature of early medieval kingship, he had to command his vassals and subjects throughout the realm verbally and in person. The nobility expected, even demanded, the royal presence to legitimate its own position. Thus, the king had to devise a means of ruling such a large area through the creation of personal bonds.[32] Royal grants

---

[27] Hagen Keller has demonstrated convincingly the development of the sacral and liturgical representation of these kings. In general, see Keller (1985a) 30–1 and 34, where he points out that the 'liturgical' portraits characteristic of the Ottonian and early Salian kings end with the 'Investiture Struggle' and an altered concept of ruling. Thereafter, royal portraits leave the sacramental and liturgical sphere and become more worldly. On Ottonian and early Salian sacral representation in art with numerous plates, see Keller (1985b) and Mayr-Harting (1991).

[28] On the building activities of prelates, both secular and regular, and their varied motives, see Giese (1982). For the connection of building activity with the sacral and liturgical representation of kingship, especially in regard to royal monasteries and royal residences, see Metz (1984) and the exhaustive work of Streich (1984).

[29] Fichtenau (1984) 216–19.

[30] Leyser (1981) 752; and Althoff and Keller (1985) 240.

[31] Gillingham (1971) made a similar observation.

[32] Althoff and Keller (1985) 205–10 discuss the personal nature of Ottonian and Salian kingship. Keller (1985a) makes important observations concerning the ways in which

and royal jurisdiction served this end. For example, grants of property and rights, especially to bishoprics and royal monasteries, were one way of creating personal relations as well as of establishing a material basis of rulership. As we shall see when discussing individual monasteries, royal visits to monasteries, which provided the king with hospitality or religious benefits, were often followed shortly thereafter by royal grants of properties, income-producing rights, or other rights favouring the institution, especially if the visit was somehow out of the ordinary. In general, the king had to appear again and again in the various regions of his kingdom and assemble the princes of the realm around him. He had to hold court, dispense justice, reward faithful vassals, punish or take the field against enemies, and settle claims between contesting parties. As the historiographer Wipo stated about King Conrad II, 'he had to preserve the peace and make law'.[33]

Since the Ottonian and Salian kings lacked the governmental infrastructure of the Carolingian kingdom and empire at the height of its power, they governed less through their representatives or written instructions sent out from court and generally had to make their will manifest in person. There is little doubt that the Ottonian kings made less use of the written word in government than the Carolingians had at the height of their power.[34] In fact, the east Frankish kingdom of the Carolingians already used the written word in government less than did its west Frankish or Italian contemporaries.[35] On the other hand, other evidence of a diverse nature – for example, occasional royal commands in letter collections and the royal judicial 'memory' about complicated and distant property transactions – indicates that the Ottonians nevertheless used writing and written documents in government to a far greater degree than the few documents which have been transmitted to us would allow us to imagine.[36] In a kingdom lacking centralized institutions and depending still only marginally

the Ottonians tried to create institutions of government and how those nascent institutions were nonetheless ultimately effective only when tied to, and simultaneously limited by, the personal nature of the ruler.

[33] Wipo, *Gesta Chuonradi* c. 38 p. 58: 'pacem firmando, legem faciendo'.

[34] On the Carolingians' use of the written word, see Ganshof (1951); McKitterick (1989) 23–77; Nelson (1990). [35] Reuter (1991a) 89.

[36] See Leyser (1981) 749–50 and Reuter (1991a) 211–13, who make strong arguments to this end.

on written records, however, the royal itinerary was a crucial vehicle for the manifestation of the royal will. It provided another substitute for the missing institutions, and it gave the realm the best cohesion possible.[37] Since the governmental institutions themselves were weak, the personal bonds of kingship were of greater necessity for integration.[38] We have already seen that the predecessor of the Ottonian realm, the east Frankish kingdom of the ninth century, functioned with a simpler government than those mentioned above – one less dependent on the written word and increasingly itinerant. Thus, the increased importance of personality and personal presence, which was conveyed by the itinerary, corresponded somewhat to the decline of written government.[39]

For the king not to appear in a specific region for a long period of time implied a decreased intensity of royal government there. With some degree of accuracy the intensity of royal government in a certain area can be estimated by looking at the king's itinerary. If one views the royal itinerary between various points as a net covering the kingdom, those areas of fine mesh tend to designate areas of realm where royal government was personal and intense, while areas of very wide mesh or of no coverage at all indicate areas where the king had to rely almost totally on surrogates – dukes, margraves, counts and prelates or their advocates – to govern the areas for him.[40] Recently, however, it has been demonstrated that Otto I effectively exerted influence and a certain degree of control far beyond the central zones, that is, the areas of fine mesh.[41] The fact that Henry I and Otto I could muster troops from all duchies of the realm for the battles of Riade and the Lech also demonstrate royal authority and control in areas outside of the customary itinerary. In regard to royal governance and influence outside of the central regions of kingship, Timothy Reuter makes several important observations: royal charters demonstrate a recognition and knowledge of conditions outside of the intensely governed areas; the ability of the king to require lords from the infrequently visited areas of the realm to come to him in the central areas to do business, and the magnates' continued demand for charters, provide an indication of the extent of royal

---

[37] Leyser (1981) 747–8. [38] Keller (1985a) 28–9 emphasizes this fact.
[39] Reuter (1991a) 89. [40] For instance, see the itineraries in Mayer (1941/1959).
[41] Müller-Mertens (1980) 165–245, summarized on 247–54.

power; and the royal charters served as a written counterpart to ceremonial appearances.[42]

In fact, owing to the personal nature of rulership in the tenth and eleventh centuries, real problems arose when the ruler was absent from the areas of his domain, which he regularly visited, or from the realm itself for long periods of time. For instance in the far northern areas of lower Saxony powerful families like the Billung ducal family and the comital family later called Stade exercised power over relatively large areas and had to be taken into consideration. The widely cited report from Adam of Bremen concerning Henry III's visit to Adalbert of Bremen in 1047 demonstrates well the caution which the king had to display when visiting a bishopric in an area off the normal itinerary and in the area of influence of a powerful, regional lord, or of a pre-eminent and potent family.[43] The king's absence left churches and monasteries, the poor and other subjects defenceless, open to devastation by foreign enemies and to property seizures by the local nobility, some of whom were royal office holders.[44] Bishop Adalbold of Utrecht gives a contemporary voice to this sentiment in explaining Henry II's decision to travel to Upper Lotharingia in 1003: 'For he knew that the land which the king does not visit often abounds in the outcries and woes of the poor.'[45] Moreover, during long absences, the personal presence of the king could not always be replaced by written commands or instructions, and when the king did not exercise a royal prerogative, the local nobility would often be quick to usurp it.[46]

Two examples serve to illustrate this fact. Both concern the period during the last twelve years of Otto's reign, when he spent ten years in Italy, far removed and long absent from the Germanic regions of the realm. In 968, Otto sent a letter to the Dukes Hermann and Thiadrik, which was read at the assembly of the Saxon nobility at Werla. In it Otto commanded them to take the field against the Redarii and to grant them no peace on account of the frequent infidelity of that people. Nevertheless, the leaders of

---

[42] Reuter (1991a) 208–12.   [43] Adam of Bremen c. 8 p. 149.

[44] Constantine, *Vita Adalberonis II* c. 25 p. 667; Leyser (1979) 103–4.

[45] Adalbold, *Vita Heinrici II* c. 19 p. 688.

[46] Althoff and Keller (1985) 194, 206–8. Wipo, in a poem written for Henry III, warns him to travel soon to Burgundy because even subjects tend toward inconstancy when the king remains absent too long: 'Praeterea tibi, rex, mandat Burgundia, surge / Atque veni, propera; noviter subiecta vacillant / Interdum domino per tempora multa remoto.' Wipo, 'Tetralogus' ll. 202–5.

the Saxon nobility, who were closer to the situation and simultaneously engaged in a war with the Danes, disregarded Otto's command and kept the peace with the Redarii.[47] Certainly the most famous example of a usurpation of royal prerogatives occurred in 972, again during an assembly of the Saxon nobility and very possibly on Palm Sunday, which the king traditionally celebrated at Magdeburg when present in Saxony. While Otto was still in Italy, Hermann, duke in Saxony and Otto's surrogate there, took it upon himself to exercise the royal prerogatives in Magdeburg, possibly with the intention of sending a general message of discontent about the king's long absence. With the assent and co-operation of Archbishop Adalbert, he received a full royal advent into the city, took the king's seat at the banquet table, and slept in the king's bed.[48] Whether it was a symbolic message or an overt usurpation and thus a threat, the event caught Otto's attention. As a result of this offence against the king, Adalbert had to send Otto as many horses as the number of bells which had been rung and candelabra which had been lighted for Hermann. Hermann, a close relative of Otto, appears to have received a much milder rebuke, but that also is not completely certain. Reading the passages in Thietmar (which are not totally clear) in their entirety,[49] one could possibly defend the interpretation to the effect that Hermann may have had to surrender his ducal office and then received it back again from the king. Although it might be pressing the source a bit hard, Hermann is called 'duke' prior to his advent, then 'count' in the section on Otto's reaction and issuance of punishment, and then later, after receiving a golden torc (back?) from Otto, he appears once again called 'duke'. Did Otto force Hermann to relinquish momentarily his ducal office, symbolized by giving up the golden torc, and then, after he had regained favour, did Otto return the golden torc and the ducal office to Hermann? In any case, it can be no accident that one year later (973), after Otto had returned to his homeland, he celebrated the same feast, Palm Sunday, also in Magdeburg with an elaborate royal advent and liturgical spectacle, which Thietmar describes in great detail.[50] Thereby, Otto upstaged the event of the previous

---

[47] *DO I* 355; Widukind 3.70.

[48] Thietmar 2.28. On this event, see Althoff (1982a). Reuter (1991a) 163 sees this event a bit differently – as a manifestation of the 'semi-regal' position of Hermann in Saxony.

[49] Thietmar 2.28–31.

[50] Thietmar 2.30. Of all the scholars who have commented on these passages in Thietmar (2.28, 2.30), only Althoff and Keller (1985) 206–7 and Warner (unpub. diss. 1989) 55–8

year and made it totally clear that the king had returned and was ruling. These events and others poignantly demonstrate that in a kingship based largely on personal relations and presence, distance, especially for long periods of time, weakened the royal ability to impose its will, and to exercise and maintain royal prerogatives.[51] Consequently, the king had to move throughout his realm quickly, securely, and on a regular basis.

Events known to us from the monastery of Tegernsee in Bavaria provide an excellent example of the trials and tribulations of a royal monastery in a region not visited frequently by the three Ottos, and one drawn more within the orbit of the royal itinerary only by Henry II and the first two Salians, Conrad II and his son, Henry III.[52] The information comes from the monastery's tenth- and early eleventh-century letter collection and provides us with some particularly enlightening insights into the dangers facing a monastery, even one enjoying the king's protection, in an area in which the royal visits were few and far between. A letter of Otto III to a Count Thiemo of Bavaria threatened him with the loss of royal grace if he did not stop interfering with the monastery's properties, especially those situated around Munich.[53] This mandate appears to have resulted from a complaint (or several complaints) from Abbot Gozpert (982–1001) to Otto III, which implies that Otto may have warned Thiemo previously about the same or similar transgressions.[54] In any case, Otto's written mandate did not alter the situation much, for some years later Abbot Peringer (1003–13) appealed again, this time to the Bavarian duke, Henry V: he reported new harassments of the monastery by Count Thiemo and appealed for the duke's protection.[55] Obviously, Otto III's written mandate had not produced the results that his presence might have achieved, and the abbot availed himself of a local power closer at hand. Whether or not Duke Henry V solved the problem of Tegernsee remains

have seen and commented on the symbolic connection between the *adventus* granted to Hermann in 972 and Otto's Palm Sunday processional of the following year.

[51] The *Chronicon Benedictoburanum* pp. 218, 233 also reports an example of usurpation of royal prerogatives during the king's absence. Two counts, Unarc and Gamanolf, seized the little remaining of Benedictbeuren's possessions 'while the emperor [Otto I] was absent and caught up in expeditions', that is, while he was in Italy.

[52] Rieckenberg (1941/1965) 89–95, 113–17.

[53] Froumund p. 99 no. 94 possibly of year 1000.

[54] Ibid. 'Quia abbas de Tegrinseo *sepe se proclamando de tua iniuria* nos inquietavit, nobis multum displicet. *Quare iterum atque iterum, quia sepe a te neglecti sumus*, tibi pro gratia nostra precipimus...' (my emphasis).   [55] Ibid. p. 85 no. 76.

unknown. Otto III wrote another letter in response to a request from the monks of Tegernsee to a Count Otto demanding under threat of loss of royal favour that he restore to the monks some vineyards near Bolzano which the count's predecessors had illegally alienated; again we have no idea how much notice was taken of this.[56]

The continuing exchange of letters between the abbot of Tegernsee and King Henry II highlight the manifold problems and the threats facing the monastery. Praising the royal power and imperial authority, Abbot Eberhard (1002–3) made an appeal to Henry II asking him to countermand an unjust alienation of property by Count Poppo and his brother Pilgrim, and to protect the monastery from false and corrupt judges by having the case heard in his presence.[57] Once again the difficulties with Poppo and Pilgrim did not cease and we have another letter to Henry II from Eberhard's successor, Abbot Peringer, complaining of new transgressions by Poppo or Pilgrim.[58] In it the abbot explained that he had already taken his plight to Duke Henry V of Bavaria, who ordered Poppo (or Pilgrim) to desist, but to no avail. So Peringer, as did his predecessor, appealed to the highest authority in the land, the king. Finally, when Henry II was in Regensburg in 1009, he restored to the monks of Tegernsee one of the disputed properties which Count Pilgrim had held unjustly in benefice, confirmed to them the possession of all their properties, and placed them anew under royal protection.[59] The continuing struggles of Tegernsee depicted in its letter collection thus clearly demonstrate the problems and dangers facing monasteries and churches around the turn of the millennium, even those legally standing under royal protection, and especially those situated in regions infrequently visited by the king.[60]

A truly effective itinerant kingship presupposed that the king had a monopoly or near-monopoly of long-distance travel and communication. In order to execute the business of government over large expanses of territory without an established bureaucracy, the royal entourage, members of the royal family and royal

---

[56] BU 1343.   [57] Froumund p. 74 no. 68.   [58] Ibid. pp. 89–90 no. 83.
[59] *DH II* 193 (22 May 1009). It is probably no accident that Henry II finally resolved the matter when he was personally present in Bavaria.
[60] Concerning property seizures by lay nobles at nearby Benedictbeuren during the reign of Otto I, see n. 51 above. Although the source derives from an eleventh-century tradition, its report reflects a rather common experience in the tenth and eleventh centuries, as the letters from Tegernsee have shown.

emissaries had to have a reasonably safe and assured network of roads and accommodation at their disposal. Within the German realm and south through imperial Italy to Rome, only the Ottonian and early Salian kings had anything close to a monopoly of long-distance travel. Another indicator of the king's ability to travel freely was his capability to arrange passage for others. Dukes, margraves, counts, bishops, abbots or abbesses could not claim such a freedom of action outside their specific area of power and influence without undergoing great personal expense.[61] For example, on one occasion poor communication and the inability of the Augsburg clerks to travel too far to address the king set them up to be deceived by Duke Burchard of Swabia in the matter of the election of the successor to Bishop Udalrich of Augsburg.[62] Thus, as with the Tegernsee example discussed above, when you could not travel, letters had to suffice; these were rarely as effective as an audience with the king.

The kings and the royal court, on the other hand, moved throughout the realm relatively unhindered on royal roads, which were controlled, protected and often maintained by royal vassals, but more frequently by royal churches. Some evidence, indeed, indicates that counts and royal churches may have had an obligation to maintain and protect the roads or river crossings in their area or on their lands. Duties of this sort appear particularly to apply when a monastery or church received a grant of *Burgbann* or castlework as did for instance, St Maurice, Corvey and Gandersheim. The *Burgbann* consisted of the powers of enforcement over the local dependent populations who had to take refuge in and thus work on the upkeep of the local fortress. Moreover, the location of many monasteries or monastic properties by important river crossings and mountain passes may itself indicate some sort of a supervisory or protective function. Although we know little from the sources about the protection and maintenance of the royal roads and the main trade arteries, a charter issued in 903 by Louis the Child to the episcopal church at Freising contains a specific reference to dependants of the church called 'sindmannis' and 'hengstfuotris' – that is, people charged with specific services for the upkeep of the roads.[63]

---

[61] Leyser (1981) 747–51.   [62] Gerhard, *Vita s. Oudalrici* c. 28.
[63] *DLK* 28. See Boegl (1949) 94–6 and esp. Störmer (1966) 331–2. For a complete discussion of duties relating to the upkeep of roads and bridges from the late antique through to the Carolingian and Ottonian periods, see Szabo (1984). McKitterick (1979)

Thus, along these royal roads, the German kings, at the end of each day, normally had the assurance of accommodation and food for themselves, their retinue and their horses. This royal entourage numbered into the hundreds and often reached the proportions of a full-scale army. Many scholars have addressed the difficult problems regarding the size of the entourage normally accompanying the king, without coming to any real consensus. The numbers suggested vary between fifty members, in very tight circumstances, to over 1600. A highly divergent middle value of somewhere between 300 and 1000 appears to provide the best and most accurate estimate to date.[64] The accommodation of the royal retinue was supplied at one of countless royal palaces or manors, episcopal cities or royal monasteries, or episcopal or monastic manors.[65] In addition, strategically placed markets provided for the ever-present needs of the royal entourage. Wolfgang Metz has demonstrated convincingly that a certain degree of systematization and intent stood behind the market policies of the Ottonian and Salian kings, especially those of Otto III and Henry II.[66] Often bishops or abbots or their advocates possessed the dominion over these markets under the king's protection. We know from twelfth-century evidence that market incomes formed a part of the *servitium regis* and this situation most likely extends back to the early eleventh century.[67] For instance, Pope Paschal II's privilege for Henry V enumerates the *pertinentia* of bishops and abbots that traditionally belonged *ad regni servitium* and thereby comprised the *regalia*. Among these were the royal monopolies to coin money, collect tolls and hold markets.[68]

96 also has pointed to repairs and maintenance of this kind appearing in Carolingian legislation. Additionally, see Rieckenberg (1941/1965) 117–20; Stein (1922) 60–6; and Goetting (1973) 264.

[64] Brühl (1968) 168–71 esp. nn. 214, 217 lists the relevant older literature regarding this problem and Oehler (unpub. diss. 1957) makes some pertinent observations concerning the continually shifting size of the royal retinue. See also Müller-Mertens (1980) 108 and Stüllein (unpub. diss. 1971) 10–12.

[65] Leyser (1981) 745–9. Peyer (1987) 162–3 indicates that normally the ruler and his immediate retinue stayed in the palace, fortress, episcopal seat or monastery, and that the larger retinue appears to have camped in the area. Nonetheless, even the upkeep of the immediate retinue appears to have been a substantial burden.

[66] Metz (1971) 279–91 and (1972b) 50–5.　　　　[67] Metz (1978b) 19–20.

[68] *MGH Const.* 1 no. 90 p. 141. For further information about general economic development and its connection to episcopal cities, royal monasteries and supplying the material needs of the court, see: Hardt-Friedrichs (1980); Hess (1974b); Schlesinger (1973); and Keller (1985a) 27–8. Reuter (1991a) 233–4 urges caution, however, in automatically assuming that all existing markets were founded and sanctioned by the king.

Under normal circumstances the king and even individual members of the royal family planned their journeys weeks if not several months ahead. Hrotsvitha of Gandersheim, when referring to the return of Otto I's son, Duke Liudolf, from Italy, clearly indicates that Liudolf had pre-arranged his itinerary and his accommodation.[69] Widukind and Adalbert of Magdeburg also provide evidence indicating a pre-planning of the itinerary and major feast sites. Otto I's problems in finding a place to celebrate Easter in 953 illustrate the pre-arrangement of the royal *iter* particularly well. Otto intended to celebrate Easter at Ingelheim and then at Mainz, but when his counsellors advised him against those places owing to the political situation, he travelled to Aachen. There, however, he found that the necessary preparations for a royal Easter festival had not been executed and finally he had to travel east to Dortmund.[70] Further evidence also strongly supports the notion that the royal *iter* was deliberately and systematically pre-arranged.[71] A letter in 994 or 995 from Otto III's grandmother, the empress Adelheid, to a clerk in Würzburg demonstrates how such journeys were arranged. She announced the date of her arrival and expected full accommodation for herself and her retinue.[72] We have similar examples from the eleventh century. For instance, Henry II, while celebrating Christmas in Pöhlde (1014), invited Udalrich of Bohemia and Boleslav of Poland to the Easter court to be held at Merseburg in April of the following year, and Bishop Burchard of Worms was described as being greatly disturbed when Conrad II gave him only a week's notice of an impending visit to his city.[73]

Although the Ottonian and early Salian kings possessed a near-monopoly of long-distance travel, that is not to say that they could travel with equal freedom and ease in all regions of their realm. The planning and organization of the royal *iter* depended largely upon the resources and means of support along the way. These included royal and familial properties, proprietary or privately owned monasteries of the royal family, and the services or *servitia* due from the royal bishoprics and monasteries – that is, in this

---

[69] Hrotsvitha, *Gesta Ottonis* 11. 1176–80: 'Hoc quoque melliflui verbis signaverat oris, / In quis castellis, in quis voluitque locellis / Sumptus hospitalii dignos sibimet reparari.'

[70] Widukind 3.14 and *Cont. Reg. s.a.* 953.

[71] See Bresslau (1879–84) 2.426–34 Excurs 1 §1; Rieckenberg (1941/1965) 120–3; and Brühl (1968) 161–5. [72] Froumund p. 16 no. 16; Leyser (1981) 746–7.

[73] For Henry II see Thietmar 7.4, 7.8 and BG 1852b, and for Burchard and Conrad II, see *Vita Burchardi Episcopi* c. 21 p. 844; Brühl (1968) 159–65.

context, the provision of full accommodation and renders of food and drink for the retinue, and fodder for the horses, which royal churches and monasteries offered the king in return for his patronage and protection. In addition, the political structure of a region was an important factor in the planning of the itinerary. It often determined the resources available to the king, or even his ability to travel there.[74]

In order to comprehend the overall dynamic of the Ottonian–Salian royal itinerary in the period from 936 to 1075, one must understand the general structure of the early German realm. In his pioneering and brilliant, but difficult, study on the structure of the kingdom and the practice of government under Otto I in the Germanic regions of his kingdom-empire, Eckhard Müller-Mertens examines the interconnection of the royal itinerary and the structure of the realm.[75] Müller-Mertens's work revolutionized itinerary research with the introduction of an entirely new methodology for analysing the royal itineraries and the documents, charters and narrative sources on which the itinerary is established.[76] A sentence or two cannot do justice to this complex methodology and its results, but I will clarify what is necessary for understanding my arguments. The key elements of Müller-Mertens's research lay in projecting the known itinerary, rather than the individual stops, on areas and then injecting carefully calculated time elements into the equation – for instance, how long it took to move from one place or region to another along the established routes, how long the king remained at one place or in one region, and how much time the court spent travelling between the main regions. Müller-Mertens's results are important as well as astounding. Formerly we could account for Otto's whereabouts for only ten per cent of his total time spent in the Germanic regions of the realm; using his new methods, Müller-Mertens can account for Otto's general presence for sixty to eighty per cent of the time. In their Berlin dissertations, students of Müller-Mertens have developed his methods further and applied them to the itineraries of Arnulf of Carinthia, Conrad II and

---

[74] Metz (1971) 278–9. [75] Müller-Mertens (1980).

[76] For a thorough introduction to this complex methodology, see Müller-Mertens (1980) 101–24. For the uninitiated, who may find this difficult to read and understand, see: Brühl (1983) 623–30, who has conveniently summarized Müller-Mertens's revolutionary methodology; Müller-Mertens (1991) 141–3, who provides a clearer summary; or, in English, Thomas F. X. Noble's review of Müller-Mertens's book in *Speculum* 56 (1981) 634–7.

Henry II.[77] Müller-Mertens himself has recently written a preview of the research that he and Wolfgang Huschner are jointly preparing on Conrad II, in which they claim to be able to account for Conrad II's whereabouts for about ninety per cent of his reign.[78]

One can divide the realm into three types of geopolitical regions or zones in which the intensity of royal government and control, the economic support available to the king, and the frequency of the king's visits varied significantly – the core and central regions (*Kernlandschaften*), the remote regions (*Fernzonen*) and the transit zones (*Durchzugsgebiete*). For the purpose of this study I have adopted, but slightly modified, Eckhard Müller-Mertens's division of the German realm into geopolitical regions. To characterize these regions Müller-Mertens devised this technical terminology. Truly, however, the division of the Ottonian realm into three zones of kingship refers not only to geography and political control, but also to the economic function of the regions in support of the kingship.[79] Recently, Müller-Mertens has introduced a fourth type of geopolitical area, the *Nahzone*, a concept which was developed by Wolfgang Huschner.[80] According to Müller-Mertens's description, a *Nahzone* appears to have been a geopolitical area under the Salian rulers which previously had been part of a transit zone or remote region under the Ottonians. Thus, it lay outside of the traditional core areas of royal property, power and influence. Owing to a new expansion of government – but not necessarily the intensification of government – into these areas, the *Nahzonen* became more frequently and more intentionally visited than previously. These *Nahzonen* characteristically contained one or more newly favoured centres of royal patronage, which were consistently the places for a royal visit. These were predominantly, but not exclusively, bishoprics, such as Paderborn and Minden, Strasbourg and Basel, Ulm and Augsburg and Regensburg or Bamberg, or later Nuremberg. Since the research on Henry II is as yet incomplete and since visits to these *Nahzonen* included accommodation by royal monasteries only as a small fraction of the total accommodation, I have chosen not to use the category in this study.

---

[77] Eibl (unpub. diss. 1982), Huschner (unpub. diss. 1986), and Gerald Beyreuther (in preparation).   [78] Müller-Mertens (1991).

[79] See Müller-Mertens (1980) 133–48, 162.

[80] Müller-Mertens (1991) 146–8 and W. Huschner (unpub. diss. 1986), which was not available to me.

The core regions of kingship were those areas where the king spent the greatest blocks of time, where he could normally depend upon full political and economic support, and where he carried out the great business of governing in specific political centres. The concept of a political–central area, on the other hand, includes the general basis of a core zone, that is, a large amount of power, property and economic support in an area; but it goes further, in that key centres in the core areas served as the chief locations for royal political activity and had an integrating function by drawing political business from the surrounding transit and remote zones of the kingdom into the core areas. Thus, secular and ecclesiastical magnates from the transit zones and especially from the remote zones travelled to see the king in these centres when they wanted or needed to engage him to carry out political, judicial or ecclesiastical business in their respective areas.[81] Eastern and southern Saxony – the heartlands of the Ottonian kings – along with the properties which they inherited from the Carolingians in the Rhineland and Lower Lotharingia, centred around Mainz and Aachen, made up the three central regions. These core areas comprised the territory within a group of three rough triangles, Gandersheim–Magdeburg–Merseburg, Frankfurt–Ingelheim–Worms and Aachen–Nijmegen–Cologne[82] (see Map 1). Owing to the Ottonians' strong influence at Gandersheim and their numerous properties in the area, I have modified and extended Müller-Mertens' Saxony triangle. I have used Gandersheim instead of Werla as one of the points, thereby including both Werla and Goslar, the new palace centre established under Henry II to replace Werla. The remote regions of the realm comprised outlying areas where royal power and resources were limited. Consequently, visits to these areas occurred only infrequently and for specific reasons. These included large areas of Bavaria and Swabia, Upper Lotharingia and the northernmost regions of Saxony. Finally, the transit zones lay between the three central zones of kingship and between the Saxon heartlands and Bavaria and Italy. These were the main corridors of travel through Westphalia, and through Hesse and Thuringia (see Map 4).

Within this general designation of a core or central region, one can designate further the central zone in Saxony, the homeland of the Ottonian kings, as the base zone (*Basislandschaft*) or heartland

---

[81] Müller-Mertens (1980) 140–8 and (1991) 144–5.   [82] Ibid. 144.

of royal property, presence and power (see Map 1). This was the
region where the early Ottonians owned the most personal
property, stayed longest and most often, and where they
frequently celebrated the high feasts of the liturgical year.[83] Thus,
the heavy predominance of eastern and southern Saxony and
northern Thuringia in the itinerary of the Ottonian kings,
especially in the Harz region, mirrors the large conglomeration of
Liudolfing familial lands in the area, the rich episcopal and
monastic *servitia* at hand, and the large amount of patronage and
revenues at the king's disposal.[84] In this core region of the realm,
the Saxon heartland, Otto I and perhaps the succeeding two Ottos
and Henry II acted simultaneously in the capacity of king and of
duke, owing to their extensive Liudolfing family holdings and
their close connections with the local aristocracy.[85] Setting out
from the Harz region the Ottonian kings made their cyclical
journeys around the realm and then returned again to the security
they felt in Saxony.[86] Consequently, this region was not only the
most highly frequented area of the realm, but also the most
minutely or intensely governed by the king, that is, it had the most
sophisticated military, governmental and fiscal institutions in the
kingdom. Saxony remained the most frequently visited and most
intensely governed region of the realm, even after the Salians,
whose lands were primarily in the Rhineland, succeeded the
Ottonians as kings and took over their lands in Saxony. This
situation lasted until the revolts of the Saxon nobility in 1073 and
again in 1076.[87] In fact, the traditional intensity of government in
Saxony and the attempts of the Salians to further intensify and
exercise their power emerge as the main secular causes which led
to the revolts of the Saxon nobility. Karl Leyser's analysis of royal
property grants and governmental institutions in Saxony agree
with and complement Müller-Mertens's evidence from his structural analyses in terms of the intensity of government and the

---

[83] Müller-Mertens (1980) 143–8 and (1991) 145–6.   [84] Leyser (1981) 745–6.

[85] Thietmar 2.28, where he talks about the *adventus* which Hermann received in 972, gives
good evidence of the dual capacity of the king in Saxony. In reference to Otto in Italy,
Thietmar states: 'Interim Hirimannus dux Saxoniam regebat...', which subtly implies
that if Otto were there he would be ruling Saxony.

[86] Müller-Mertens (1980) 143–58, 162, (1991) 145. Otto I spent twenty per cent of his
reign in the Harz *Basislandschaft*. Even Henry II, who at times had difficulties in Saxony,
recognized the security and abundance that awaited him there. See Thietmar 6.10.

[87] Leyser (1981) 733–46.

amount and duration of royal presence in Saxony *vis-à-vis* other areas of the realm.[88]

In addition to the Saxon heartlands, a high concentration of royal palaces, fiscal properties and royal church property inherited from the Carolingians in the middle Rhineland around Frankfurt, Mainz and Worms, and in the lower Rhineland around Cologne and Aachen as well as in Lower Lotharingia, combined with a moderately successful royal policy of monitoring the political structure there, made these areas too central zones of the kingship which experienced a high frequency of royal presence.[89] Thus, under the Ottonians the central areas of kingship as well as both the symbolic perambulations of the realm (*Umritt* in German) and the primary cycle of the royal itinerary were confined to Saxony and Francia in the broad sense, that is, Franconia and Lower Lotharingia, the former Carolingian landscapes. Hagen Keller has commented on this royal progression of a limited or confined nature, showing that symbolic progressions from the middle Rhine to Aachen and to Saxony occurred in significant years, such as during the ordering of the succession in 930 and 961, following the designation of Liudolf in 948, after Otto I's death in 973, and on three important occasions during the minority and contested regency of Otto III.[90] Keller sees these perambulations as forerunners to the more extensive *Umritt* (one including Swabia and Bavaria) which began in the early eleventh century under Henry II,[91] which he ties to a basic structural change in the realm around 1000 – the extension of the royal presence over a greater area of the realm.[92] He also sees the movement from a limited to a more extensive *Umritt* as connected with the movement from the early Ottonian gentile or 'people-centred' concept of the realm, as expressed by Widukind's characterization of it as a kingdom of Franks and Saxons, to the broader concept of a German realm (*regnum Teutonicorum*), which appears to have begun in the first quarter of the eleventh century.[93]

---

[88] Leyser (1983a) esp. 433–7, a brilliant article and perhaps overlooked in regard to its important contribution to the legal understanding and political implications of royal grants *in proprietatem* (esp. pp. 426–32).

[89] Müller-Mertens (1980) 140–3.

[90] Keller (1982) 116–17 esp. n. 202.

[91] Schmidt (1961).

[92] Keller (1982) 85–100.

[93] Ibid. 117, 121–5; Widukind 2.1. The seminal work on this important and controversial conceptual change remains Müller-Mertens (1970), but see also Brühl (1972) and Beumann (1973). Müller-Mertens (1991) 146–8 points out that the conceptual change mirrored the structural changes of the early eleventh century.

When Conrad II from the Salian family acceded to the throne in 1024, a significant change took place within the central zones of kingship. A second *Basislandschaft* or heartland in the Rhine–Main area, the Salian familial lands centred around Worms and Speyer, was added to the existing structure. In addition, as successor to the throne, the new Salian king also took over the huge inheritance of the Ottonians in Saxony and the Harz region, and thereby Saxony also remained as a *Basislandschaft*. Conrad's quick progression to Saxony as the first part of his initial *Umritt*, his reception and legitimization by two Ottonian abbesses and princesses, the long initial period he spent in Saxony (three months), as well as the Salians' later policies in Saxony of land consolidation through confiscation (which occasioned much dissension on the part of the indigenous 'Saxon' nobility against the 'foreign' Salians) clearly demonstrate Saxony's importance to the Salians.[94] Even with the creation of a second royal heartland, however, the itinerary in the central areas of kingship and the transit zones connecting them barely changed. Otto I and Conrad II spent approximately the same amount of time in the central and in the transit zones. There was, however, an internal shift within the three central regions of kingship. Some palaces in the Harz declined in use (and some increased), and some in the Rhineland increased, but the huge amount of time spent by Otto in the Harz region was now reduced by about one-third and that third was spread over the two other central areas. Thus, although there were changes in some of the favoured political centres as between Otto I and Conrad II, their location nevertheless remained within the central zones of kingship.[95]

Conversely, the early Ottonians rarely visited the remote regions (*Fernzonen*) of their realm where royal resources and the prevailing political structure made visits to such areas less desirable, necessary or politically feasible. Thus, Bavaria (where relatively powerful and independent dukes and numerous strong comital families exercised political power), large parts of Swabia, Upper Lotharingia (largely under control of local families) and northern Saxony (the stronghold of the powerful Billung ducal family) remained areas largely outside the normal reach of the Ottonian

---

[94] Reuter (1991a) 188. On the later policies of the Salian kings in Saxony and their conflict with the Saxon nobility, see Leyser (1983a) and also Seibert (1991) 537–40.

[95] Müller-Mertens (1991) 145–8.

kings.[96] Consequently, visits to those areas occurred infrequently, normally only during campaigns beyond the frontiers, on the way to Italy or for specific diplomatic reasons, such as occasional meetings with the west Frankish, and later French, kings.[97] Gradually, with the structural shifts of the early eleventh century under Henry II, Conrad II and Henry III, some of these areas, particularly Swabia and Bavaria, experienced an increase in royal visits, and thereafter no entire region of the realm remained unvisited by the king: that is, the royal itinerary now encompassed the whole realm.[98] In fact, beginning with Otto III, not only were these areas visited 'periodically', but kings also began to issue charters in them instead of the Swabian and Bavarian nobility always travelling to the central regions to receive their royal grants.[99] However, it is important to note that this change merely represented an extension of the royal presence to areas which formerly were visited very infrequently. In no way did it entail an equalization of royal presence throughout the realm nor, indeed, a concentration of royal power or an intensification of royal government in these new areas of royal representation comparable to that which existed in the central regions.[100]

Situated between the central zones of the kingship lay the so-called transit zones (*Durchzugsgebiete*)[101] (see Map 4). In these areas lay the major royal roads connecting the three central zones of kingship,[102] as well as the roads linking Saxony to Italy via Bavaria.[103] The German kingdom had two main transit zones:

---

[96] Leyser (1979) 103–4 and (1981) 733–4; Müller-Mertens (1980) 138–40; Metz (1971) 278; and Rieckenberg (1941/1965) 120–30. See above n. 43 concerning Henry III's visit to lower Saxony and the power of the Billung family there.

[97] On these meetings, see Voss (1987).

[98] Rieckenberg (1941/1965) 89–95, 113–17; Brühl (1968) 126–34; and Keller (1982) 85–100.

[99] Ibid. On Müller-Mertens's 'reclassification' of these areas in the eleventh century from 'Fernzonen' to 'Nahzonen', see Müller-Mertens (1991) 146–7 and above p. 61.

[100] Müller-Mertens (1991) 145–8, esp. 147 added these refinements to the observations of Keller (1982) 85–100. He also points out convincingly that the amount of time Conrad II spent in the new *Nahzonen* encompassing Alsace, Swabia and Bavaria (10·6%) *vis-à-vis* Otto I in the *Fernzonen* (3·2%) arose not at the cost of time spent in the central regions, but because of less time spent in Italy (19·6% versus 26·4% for Otto I).

[101] Müller-Mertens (1980) 140–3 identified and defined these as 'transit zones'.

[102] Rieckenberg (1941/1965) 51, 59–61 and Metz (1971) 268–72, 284–6.

[103] Rieckenberg (1941/1965) 60–4. Especially since the creation of the archbishopric of Magdeburg and its southern suffragan bishoprics – Merseburg and Zeitz – in 968, and the foundation of Memleben in 979, Thuringia, which lay between Magdeburg and the southern and central regions of the German realm, became a crucial and highly travelled transit zone.

first, the roads and contiguous areas from the Harz region through western Saxony and Westphalia to the lower Rhine; and second, those through Thuringia, Hesse and eastern Franconia to the middle Rhine–Main area and, in the eastern sector, to Bavaria.[104] The areas traversed by these roads had several common characteristics. The Ottonian and Salian royal families did not possess much personal property in the transit corridors and royal property that had existed there had largely been granted out in benefice.[105] However, since many of these grants benefited royal churches, they did not necessarily lessen the king's power, for the king still had his right of use on demand, his usufruct. The transfer of kingship to the Liudolfings (Ottonians) in 919 and the addition of the core region of royal property and power in eastern Saxony to the two former Carolingian centres of power in the Rhineland dramatically increased the importance of the transit corridors connecting these three areas. They became the crucial links integrating the three central regions of kingship, which contained the main political and economic centres of the realm. Thus, they served a strategic function, both militarily and politically. Since Saxony provided a home base for the royal *iter*, the king and the royal entourage passed again and again through these transit zones on their travels to and from the three main centres of power. Consequently, the transit zones experienced an extensive and frequent royal presence – though rarely a visit of long duration.[106] Without a favourable political structure and a stable economic basis, these areas would lose their strategic function of integrating the realm for the king. The king had to ensure that political control of the transit zones remained in loyal hands and that ample means of provision existed there to supply the royal court on its frequent sojourns.[107] Thus, in the main transit zones of the realm, where the Ottonian and Salian kings lacked fiscal and patrimonial property, they found their major political and economic support in the royal monasteries and bishoprics situated in these areas, and in the large property holdings of these institutions strategically located on the major routes.[108] Essen, Werden, Corvey, Soest

---

[104] For the various courses of these roads, see: Rieckenberg (1941/1965) 51, 59–63; Patze (1962) 30–41 esp. nos. 25, 26, 32, 34, 37; Hörle (1960) 52 (map); Hömberg (1967a) 198–200; and Metz (1971) 284–6.

[105] Bannasch (1972) 12–22 and the literature he cites.

[106] Müller-Mertens (1980) 238 and Metz (1971) 268–71.

[107] Müller-Mertens (1980) 142.

[108] Metz (1971) 268–79, (1976) 223–8 and (1978b) 67–74.

(belonging to Cologne) and Paderborn were located along the Hellweg or Westphalian transit zone. Corvey, Helmarshausen, Hilwartshausen, Kaufungen, Hersfeld, Fulda, Mainz (property holdings) and Bamberg (after Henry II) were situated along the routes from western Saxony and from the Harz region through Thuringia and Hesse southwest to the Rhineland or through Thuringia and east Franconia to Bavaria – that is, the central transit zone. Consequently, these corridors of transit remained politically stable, providing the king with everything he needed for unimpeded and well provisioned travel.

Symbolic, political and economic considerations, therefore, compelled the Ottonian and early Salian kings to travel continually throughout their realm. They ordered and planned these journeys according to accepted custom, personal preference and with regard to prevailing economic and political conditions.[109] The total economic means at the king's disposal and the ruling political structure varied considerably from region to region. To treat the hospitality and the economic *servitium regis* of the royal monasteries as an undifferentiated kingdom-wide phenomenon, therefore, would provide a very abstract, unclear, and at times even false, picture of monastic obligations and would not show how they may have fitted into the overall schema of the royal *iter* or into a conscious or unconscious royal monastic policy. Moreover, this approach would ignore and not fully take advantage of the strong emphasis on local and regional studies in German historical scholarship begun during the last two generations by Hermann Heimpel and Theodor Mayer. These scholars and others led a shift in emphasis in German historical study from the nation-centred concept of a uniform constitutional and legal history of the late nineteenth and early twentieth century to a study of regional history, which they hoped would eventually fuse with constitutional and institutional studies.[110] Also, the prosopographical approach of Gerd Tellenbach and his student Karl Schmid entered the scene and made significant advances, as did a kind of 'structural–regional' approach availing itself of solid prosopographical research, which has been advocated and followed by the *Konstanzer Arbeitskreis*, most recently by Helmut Maurer.[111]

---

[109] Klewitz (1939a) 75–96.
[110] In particular, see T. Mayer (1958) and Schlesinger (1963).
[111] Maurer (1978). For a short critique of the German historical schools, see Reuter (1981), and for a full historiographical survey, Reuter (1991a) 1–17.

In some areas of the realm rich in fiscal and patrimonial property and with large and wealthy episcopal cities such as the Rhineland, Lower Lotharingia and gradually east Saxony, the economic *servitia* of the royal monasteries functioned in conjunction with or as complements to those of the royal and episcopal properties, unless the economic or political conditions in an area altered drastically.[112] For instance, in the eleventh century, after members of the Salian family had been elected to the kingship, Henry III and Henry IV were forced to rely more heavily upon the large royal convents of Quedlinburg, Gandersheim and Gernrode for their material and political support in the area in order to hold their position in Saxony against the growing opposition of the indigenous nobility.[113] On the other hand, in territories where little fiscal or family property existed, the *servitia* of the bishoprics and royal monasteries provided the main source of support for the king on his journeys. This situation existed primarily in Swabia on royal journeys to Italy and in the transit zones through Thuringia, Hesse and eastern Franconia and along the Hellweg through Westphalia to the lower Rhine.[114] As an example, on the infrequent occasions when the king came to Swabia prior to 1000, he was quartered at the cost of the secular nobility or, more often, at the cost of royal churches because he controlled little land there. Thus, in Swabia the hospitality of the Ottonians was 'based on feudal relations in the narrow sense'.[115] In the remote areas of the realm, visited only infrequently or not at all by the king, either the *Reichskirche* bore the entire weight of the king's upkeep, or the king exacted little or no *servitia* because he lacked adequate political control in the area or had little reason to visit it. Bavaria provides a good example of an area not regularly visited by the king where the *Reichskirche* bore the great majority of the king's upkeep when he did come there. For instance, in Regensburg, which throughout the period of this study was the Bavarian locality most consistently visited by the Ottonian and Salian kings (that is, except for Bamberg under

---

[112] Brühl (1968) 200–3.

[113] Goetting (1949) 100–1 and (1973) 94–6. As Reuter (1991a) 188 points out, Conrad II's initial *Umritt* in 1024–5 provides incipient evidence of the connection between the Salians and these convents. On this journey, Conrad was 'regally' received – and thereby legitimized – by the two surviving Ottonian princesses, Sophie and Mathilda, who were the abbesses of Gandersheim and Quedlinburg.

[114] See Metz (1971) 268–79 and (1978b) 67–74.

[115] Keller (1982) 76–85, quote on p. 82.

Henry II), the king, in addition to what was available at the royal *Pfalzen* there (one of which was located in the monastery of St Emmeram), had *servitia* at his disposal from the bishop of Regensburg and his episcopal priory headed by the abbot of St Emmeram, and from the abbesses of Ober- and Niedermünster.[116] The Billung stronghold in lower Saxony, on the other hand, was an area which the Ottonian and Salian kings almost never visited and in which the king had little or no *servitia* at his immediate disposal. I propose therefore to examine the obligation of the royal monasteries to house and feed the royal retinue as a function and as an interworking of various economic and political factors. As Josef Fleckenstein has shown for the bishoprics,[117] moreover, the king had to control the royal monasteries politically, or at least have nominal influence and control in the area in which they were situated, in order to exact service and political support from them effectively. Consequently, the royal monasteries visited most frequently by the Ottonian and Salian kings, and those most responsible for the kings' upkeep, were located in the Saxon heartlands and in the major transit zones of the realm. Thus, I have chosen to focus primarily on the numerous royal monasteries in those areas which experienced the most consistent royal presence and most intensive royal government throughout the Ottonian and early Salian periods.[118] Not surprisingly, the royal monasteries bearing the greatest burden of the *servitium regis*, especially those providing hospitality or delivery of foodstuffs to support the royal *iter*, received royal grants of immunity and protection as well as grants of property and governmental rights, with some regularity.

ROYAL MONASTERIES: PROBLEMS OF DEFINITION

Before examining the broader issue of itinerant kingship and royal monasteries, it is necessary to clarify two crucial concepts – 'royal

---

[116] Brühl (1968) 154, 160–1; Metz (1978a) 245–6 and (1984) 8–9.
[117] Fleckenstein (1966) 20–3.
[118] The research of Leyser and Müller-Mertens buttresses the selection of these areas for study. Leyser (1981) 733–4, 746 argues that the intensity of royal government in Saxony was unique to this area and continued unabated until the revolts of 1073 and 1076. Müller-Mertens (1991), in his comparative study on the structure of the realm, demonstrates that, although the royal presence extended to new areas under Henry II and Conrad II, the intensity of royal government did not increase comparatively in these areas.

monastery' and *servitium regis* – as I will use them in the context of this study, and, if only briefly, to indicate some of the controversies surrounding these concepts and to place them within their historiographical tradition. First, we must define: what was the royal church and what exactly was a royal monastery? Legal scholars and historians do not agree fully on the general concept of the 'royal church' nor on the more specific concept of the 'Ottonian–Salian royal church'.[119] As a working definition, I intend to follow closely the one suggested by Josef Fleckenstein: royal churches comprised all bishoprics, monasteries and other religious institutions which enjoyed the special, in contrast to the general, protection of the king and were, at least partially, royal proprietary churches or appurtenances of the realm. Fleckenstein demonstrates convincingly that the sources recognize this distinction between the king's general duty to protect all churches in the realm and the closer bond of protection granted for a narrower group of churches, which enjoyed special royal protection and thereby a higher legal status.[120] This definition describes the specific legal status of the individual churches, and stresses that they stood in the special protection (*ecclesias...sub nostrae tuicionis munimine defendendas*) of the king and by extension under direct jurisdiction of the king and the realm (*in ius et proprietatem nostri publici iuris aut fisci*).[121]

The royal monasteries formed a subgroup within the larger class of royal churches, which the sources refer to with numerous designations such as *monasteria regalia, ad nostrum publicum eadem abbacia ius...pertineat, precipua nostri imperii monasteria*, and *regii vel imperatorii iuris abbatiam*.[122] Theodor Mayer advanced a legal theory differentiating between royal monasteries (*Königsklöster*)

---

[119] On the constitutional and legal questions concerning the royal churches or monasteries, see Ficker (1861) vol. 1, esp. §§ 43–4, 224–8 and (1872), Hörger (1926), T. Mayer (1950), Semmler (1959 and 1982), Fleckenstein (1974) and Köhler (1968). Fleckenstein (1985) is in part a rebuttal of Reuter (1982). Finally, Minninger (1978) 54–79 touches on some constitutional issues in the context of a larger work on the feudal relationship existing between the German bishops and kings, and Seibert (1991) makes important comments about the legal situation of royal monasteries and legal developments during the Salian period.

[120] Fleckenstein (1974) 67–70. A charter of Henry II for the episcopal church at Brandenburg (*DH II* 223) made this distinction: 'Haec quidem nos sollicita consideratione pensantes dignum ducimus et salutiferum iudicamus ecclesias dei sub nostro regimine positas ac presertim eas, quae ab iniquis hominibus opprimuntur, sub nostrae tuicionis munimine defendendas suscipere...'

[121] *DH II* 223 and *DO I* 322; Fleckenstein (1974) 67–70.

[122] *DDH II* 29, 87; *DO III* 326; *DO II* 93.

and imperial monasteries (*Reichsklöster*), specifically in regard to alienability and military service.[123] Mayer claimed that all Carolingian royal monasteries were inherited *en masse* by the Ottonian kings and thereafter became part of the realm. He designated these as 'imperial monasteries' (*Reichsklöster*), and said that they could not be alienated by the king. On the other hand, he designated as 'royal monasteries' (*Königsklöster*) those monasteries which were founded by the Ottonian kings and their successors or were granted rights of immunity, protection or free election by them. These, he said, were true proprietary monasteries of the king and thus they could be alienated or given away by him. Although Mayer's legal theory has been adopted by some scholars,[124] others have voiced strong criticism of his formulation.[125] Most importantly, however, the sources and the events of the Ottonian and Salian periods do not indicate a difference between an 'imperial' and a 'royal' monastery.[126] Both Gandersheim, which was part of the Carolingian inheritance, and Quedlinburg, which was founded by Otto I and his mother, are used in Ottonian charters as the prime examples of female convents holding the highest legal status. Yet both are called alternatively 'royal' or 'imperial'.[127] Moreover, as I will show, Ottonian and Salian kings alienated several old Carolingian royal monasteries, for example, Kempten, Wissembourg (Weissenburg), Lorsch and Corvey, and thus Mayer's claim to inalienability of his 'imperial' monasteries does not hold.[128] At least in the realm of legal theory, however, specific characteristics of a royal monastery can be further clarified. According to Josef Semmler, the six fundamental characteristics of a royal monastery comprised: (1) the inalienability of these monasteries and their property from the possession of the realm; (2) the king's right to full disposition over the royal monasteries, meaning that they were required to perform various mandatory services (*servitia*) for the king and the realm; (3) royal immunity, which safeguarded these monasteries from the encroachments of public officials and gave them legal jurisdiction within their domains; (4) the sole exercise of protection over the monastery by the king, which resulted in a royal proprietary right

---

[123] T. Mayer (1950) 25–7, 36–8, 48–9, 220–34 and 306–8.
[124] With reservations by Semmler (1959) 27–8, and uncritically by Köhler (1968) 178–9 and Minninger (1978) 59–61. [125] Brühl (1968) 197–8 and Auer (1972) 60–4.
[126] Recently, Kölzer (1989) 39 made reference to this fact.
[127] *DO II* 190 and *DO III* 326. [128] This whole question needs re-evaluation.

over the protected monastery; (5) the community's right freely to elect its own abbot or abbess, conditional upon the king's right to approve and to invest the candidate with his or her office; and (6) the monastery's obligation to appoint a lay advocate, who would administer the monastery's jurisdiction, represent it in the secular world, and exercise the king's rights within the monastery.[129]

All of these characteristics did not, however, always pertain in practice. Some monasteries which did not legally possess 'royal' status – for example, St Emmeram, which was a proprietary monastery of the bishop of Regensburg – enjoyed very close royal ties and often received as much royal protection and favour as those holding the higher legal status – sometimes more.[130] On the other hand, the convent of Geseke, having received grants of royal protection, immunity and election, appears to have become a royal monastery. Yet the interests of the founding Hahold family were strong enough for the monastery to be granted by the last abbess from that family in 1014 to the archbishop of Cologne without any mention of the king.[131] Thus, at a time when custom and customary law played a predominant role, legal norms and definitions often remained vague and varied widely according to person, place and circumstance. Examples of legal practice not corresponding to legal theory occur in regard to several of the above characteristics, especially the principles of free right of election and of inalienability. A grant of free election to monasteries (and also to bishoprics) along with royal immunity and protection established them as royal monasteries and appurtenances of the realm in the Carolingian period.[132] Moreover, at Frankfurt in 951, a general legal ruling or *Weistum* 'was discovered' in the presence of King Otto I, which recognized this same principle and tied it to inalienability and royal protection. It stated that no abbey which held the right to elect its abbot or abbess could be given into the ownership (*in proprium*) of a monastery or anyone else, but that abbeys lacking the election right could be annexed to another monastery which stood under

---

[129] Semmler (1959) 27–33.

[130] Specifically on St Emmeram and its ties to the Ottonian kings, see Budde (1914).

[131] *DO I* 158 and *DO III* 29; *REK* I no. 630 and *UB Westfalen* 25 no. 23 (3 February 1014). See also Semmler (1959) 17.

[132] Semmler (1982) 115–22 designates the right of election as a key characteristic and sees a decisive shift occurring under Louis the Pious, who integrated bishoprics and royal monasteries into Carolingian government with a much firmer legal bond than had Charlemagne.

royal protection.[133] This *Weistum* nicely pulls together three general characteristics of a royal monastery – right of election, inalienability and royal protection.

The legal principle contained in the *Weistum*, however, did not translate at all times into legal practice. Ottonian and Salian kings – even Otto himself – exchanged, gave away or alienated royal monasteries which enjoyed the right of election and royal protection, especially if such a transaction met a specific need, rewarded a faithful vassal or made monastic property more serviceable to the realm. A few examples should suffice. A charter of 963 for the former Carolingian royal monastery of Kempten indicates that Otto I had given the royal monastery to Udalrich, bishop of Augsburg.[134] In 966, Otto exchanged the royal nunnery of Oeren with the archbishop of Trier for St Servatius at Maastricht, implying that St Servatius would be helpful in carrying out royal business in its area;[135] and later, in 968, he gave the old Carolingian royal monastery of Wissembourg (Weissenburg) to the archbishop of Magdeburg.[136] Because of their limited ability to serve the realm, Henry II granted the royal monasteries of Memleben and Helmarshausen to the royal monastery of Hersfeld and the bishopric of Paderborn respectively.[137] In 1026, Kempten was once again the object of a gift when Conrad II gave it in benefice to Duke Ernest II of Swabia.[138] Finally, in one of the most famous and blatant exercises of royal power, Henry IV granted two of the oldest and most powerful royal monasteries, Lorsch and Corvey, to Archbishop Adalbert of Hamburg for a short period.[139] Curiously enough these alienations engendered

---

[133] *MGH Conc. 6.1* no. 17 p. 184 (also published in *MGH Const.* 1 no. 8 p. 17): 'Inventum est etiam coram prefato rege, ut nulla abbatia, que per se electionem habet, ad monasterium nec alicui in proprium possit donari; ille vero, quae electione carent regis donatione et privilegio, ad illud monasterium, quod sub eius mundiburdio consistit, surrogari possint.' (I have altered the punctuation of the *MGH* edition, but this merely clarifies the passage and does not alter the sense.) This *Weistum* is contained within the sole capitulary or legal promulgation of the entire Ottonian period. On the concept of a *Weistum*, see Leyser (1981) 730. As Hehl points out in the new edition of the Frankfurt council of 951 (*MGH Conc. 6.1* n. 13 p. 184), the *Weistum* appears to have influenced a Burgundian ruling made in the presence of Conrad of Burgundy, Otto I and his son, Otto II, which is mentioned in Conrad's charter of 968? for Münstergranfelden (*DKo* 66 p. 166): 'quod per privilegia constructum est, per manum regiam in proprietatem dari liceret. Illis cuntis communiter iudicantibus, quod nulla tenus licitum esset.'

[134] *DO I* 255.   [135] *DDO I* 168, 322.   [136] *DO I* 365.

[137] *DDH II* 25, 47, 331, 371.   [138] Wipo, *Gesta Chuonradi* c. 11.

[139] *DDH IV* 168, 169. See Seibert (1991) 544–50 and Vogtherr (1991) 442–4.

very few outcries of injustice in the sources.[140] These instances demonstrate that often a royal monastery's 'inalienable' status conflicted with the king's proprietary right over the monasteries which he protected and his right to full disposition over royal monasteries, and to the services which that implied.

SERVITIUM REGIS: THE HISTORIOGRAPHICAL PROBLEM

Now let us examine the second crucial concept, the *servitium regis*. In return for the king's protection (*mundiburdium*) and royal immunity (*immunitas*), a royal monastery had to make obligatory payments to the king and provide sundry services for him and the court. *Servitium regis* is the most common technical term encompassing the totality of these payments and services rendered. In general, royal monasteries, and sometimes other monasteries which had not achieved direct 'royal' status, had to provide the king and the royal court with five main kinds of reciprocal service. The first of these was a general duty to feed and house the royal court during its continual peregrinations through the realm, that is, whenever the court halted at the monastery or on a monastic estate, however distant from the monastery itself. Using the itinerary and the regional studies of the last thirty years, it has been demonstrated convincingly that the king and his retinue frequently used monastic estates and vills, often quite distantly removed from the monastery itself, as places to halt overnight or stay for short durations.[141] The terms used in the sources for this general duty are *hospitium, mansio, gistum, fodrum* (for the requisition of fodder for the horses). The second was similar in that it consisted of payments in kind and/or in money (especially from the mid-eleventh century onwards), which were sent to the nearest royal palace, episcopal see or regular stopping point, in order to supply provisions for the king's table.[142] The third was an obligation to

---

[140] Only Thietmar 7.31 (in regard to Memleben being given to Hersfeld) and Wipo, *Gesta Chuonradi* c. 11 (regarding Kempten being enfeoffed to Duke Ernest II) record dismay.

[141] Metz (1978b) 67–74.

[142] Matthäi (1877) 41–4 already noticed the concept of a delivery of provisions or money payments to supply the king's table. This was particularly important for monasteries not often visited by the king. For example, see Schmitt (1974) 32–56 concerning Reichenau's delivery of *servitia* to the royal palace at Ulm, and Metz (1976) 194–7 and Flach (1976) 87–90 on the delivery of *servitia* to Aachen by Stavelot.

pray for the king, the royal family and the realm.[143] The fourth
was the obligation of abbots, and perhaps other monastic officials,
to provide advisory and messenger or diplomatic service at the
royal court.[144] Fifth and last, the richest and most powerful
monasteries, and possibly nunneries,[145] were obliged to equip and
place a military contingent at the disposal of the king for use in the
armies of the realm. Over and above these five main components
of *servitium regis*, the king often exacted additional services from
the royal monasteries, which one may also categorize loosely
under the concept of *servitium regis*. To these additional services of
the royal monasteries belong the production of books on royal
commission, the use of royal monasteries as political prisons, the
manufacture of armour and weapons within the monasteries and
on monastic property to supply the royal army or at least the
monastery's troop contingent, and the responsibility to maintain
royal roads and bridges in the vicinity of or on the property of a
royal monastery.[146]

These types of services existed already in the Carolingian realm.
Generally, the *servitium regis* of the royal monasteries during the
Carolingian period consisted of yearly payments in kind (or less
often, in money) delivered to the court of the king, specific yearly
tasks of conveyance or transportation performed for the king,
service at the court, and the obligation of hospitality for the king
and his *missi*, if they visited. The sum of these obligations were
called the *servitium* or the *obsequium debitum*, but sometimes they

---

[143] This obligation appears to have existed in a general way on all the churches and
ecclesiastical institutions of the realm. The special application of it to monasteries and
specifically to royal monasteries appears in the *Notitia de servitio monasteriorum* of 819
and in Carolingian charters, e.g. *DLD* 90, and it repeatedly occurs in Ottonian and
Salian royal charters, especially in grants for the salvation (*Seelenheil*) of the king or
royal family and ancestors, or in charters designating property for the upkeep of the
congregation. See Neuman (1978) 339.

[144] Voigt (1917) 32; Pöschl (1908–12) 1.156–9; Wehlt (1970) 76; *MGH Epis.* 6.39–41
no. 32.

[145] On military provision for the royal host from nunneries, see Auer (1972) 63–4. For the
best evidence from this period that convents also had contingents at their disposal, see
DH II 39a for Essen. A Carolingian precedent exists in a capitulary of Louis the Pious
from 919 (*MGH Capit.* 1 no. 141 c. 27 p. 291).

[146] On book production, see Hoffmann (1986) and Klein (1984). Although Leyser (1981)
745, Althoff and Keller (1985) 143, Weinfurter (1986) 250 and numerous sources
mention the use of monasteries as prisons in the Ottonian and Salian period, no one to
my knowledge has written on this topic. Likewise, although sources document the
activity, the manufacture of armour and weapons within monasteries and on monastic
property has not been addressed. On roads and their maintenance see above at n. 63.

were included under the *dona annualia* or annual gift.[147] The conceptual underpinning for the exaction of these services lay in the existing notion that all individuals or groups in the realm owed the king some kind of general performance or duty,[148] and that the king had a proprietary right or governmental right to the property of the royal monasteries.[149] A document from the reign of Louis the Pious, the *Notitia de servitio monasteriorum*, written in 819, enumerates *militia* (military service), *dona* (the yearly gift, tax or special service provided for the king from a monastery or its dependants) and the omnipresent *orationes* (prayers for the king and realm) as the services which certain monasteries in the realm had to perform for the king.[150] We also possess scattered references in the Carolingian period in charters, estate surveys or polyptychs, chronicles and Saints' Lives or *Vitae* to one or more of these obligations of the *servitium regis*. During the late Carolingian period, in response to the changing political, military and economic climate and the gradual decentralization of the realm, especially in the west, the characteristic Carolingian conception of *servitium regis* and the method and extent of the exaction began to alter and its emphasis shifted. Increasingly, powerful territorial princes appropriated the exaction of these services to their own use and they slowly became 'feudal' obligations.

The Ottonian and Salian kings and emperors revived and re-established the Carolingian bases of *servitium regis* (exclusive of the

---

[147] On the Carolingian *servitium*, see Lesne (1910–43) vol. 2.2 pp. 433–55 and Brühl (1968) 14–50, 70–4, 97–115. Concerning the *dona annua* or *dona annualia*, see Waitz (1893–6) 3.591, 4.107–10, which remains the starting point, Lesne (1910–43) vol. 2.2 pp. 411–19, and Reuter (1985) 85–7.

[148] This concept of a general obligation to the realm and correspondingly to the king finds expression in the words *publicum servitium*, which occur occasionally in Carolingian charters. See: Poupardin, *Saint-Germain-des-Prés* no. 28 p. 45 (*DLF* for St Germain): 'quantinus nullo occasione nec rei publice servitio quis quam ex successoribus suis impedimentum in futuro inferre potuisset'; Bouq. 6.611A (= BM² 961 – *DLF* for St Colombe near Sens) 'ut absque regali aut publico servitio'; *DKK* 160; *DKD* 47.

[149] The question as to whether the German king had a governmental or a proprietary right over the higher churches of the realm remains disputed and not fully answered. For the background to the dispute and some new leanings toward the idea of a governmental right, see Classen (1973) 426, 453–4 and also Semmler (1982) 120–4. For an overview of the legal basis of royal monasteries, see Metz (1978b) 64–6, and for a summary of the constitutional issues, see T. Mayer (1950) 25–49.

[150] *Notitia de servitio monasteriorum* in *CCM* 1.483–99. This document clearly represents a by-product resulting from the monastic reform councils of 816 and 817. See Lesne (1920) for a full discussion. Reuter (1991a) 44 also sees the *Notitia* in its relation to the royally sponsored reform of the monasteries, as well as to the heavy burdens placed by the king on monastic property. In regard to the omnipresent *orationes*, see also the *Supplex libellus* in *CCM* 1.321; Semmler (1963) 26–8; and Ewig (1982a) and (1982b).

dona annualia, which became merely a token charge, if assessed at all), expanded its exaction in conjunction with the increased itinerancy of their court, and attempted to institute a more systematic exploitation of the *servitium* available to the king. Accordingly, in discussing the general *servitium regis* of the Ottonian and Salian royal monasteries, I define the term as all the various services or duties performed by the royal monasteries, their abbots and their dependants on behalf of the king and the realm. More specifically, the *servitium regis* of the royal monasteries in the economic sense comprised only the accommodation of the king and the royal court at the monastery and on distant monastic estates or manors, and the delivery of foodstuffs and other necessities to specific (but not always designated) stations to support the travelling court.

The amount of food and supplies needed to provision the royal entourage could be staggering. Two twelfth-century sources provide some information about the resources necessary to supply the daily needs of the royal court during the tenth century. The Saxon Annalist, who is a dependable compiler and appears to have had a written source of an unknown date before him, provides us with some specifics concerning Otto I's court. He states that on a daily basis the king had at his disposal 1000 pigs and sheep, ten wagonloads of wine, just as much beer, 1000 measures or units of grain, eight heads of cattle and in addition chickens, pigs, fish, eggs, vegetables and other things in abundance.[151] From this one may deduce the possible daily consumption of the court, at least at its maximum extent. According to the Pöhlder Annals, the king had the equivalent of thirty pounds of silver daily to use in feeding his court.[152]

Later, in the twelfth and thirteenth centuries under the Hohenstaufen kings, the economic *servitium regis* began to change with the gradual shift toward a money economy, from payments

---

[151] *Ann. Saxo s.a.* 968 p. 622: 'Iste inperator singulis diebus habuit huiusmodi cibum, sicut scriptum invenitur: Mille porcos et oves, 10 carradas vini, 10 cervisie, frumenti maltra mille, boves 8 preter pullos et porcellos, pisces, ova, leguminia, aliaque quam plura.' Although many scholars have judged these figures as extraordinarily high, Peyer (1987) 158–9, using comparative data from Spain and England in later periods, has recently demonstrated convincingly that the quantities given by the Saxon Annalist could easily have corresponded to the daily needs of a court of approximately one thousand people.

[152] *Ann. Palid. s.a.* 935 p. 62: 'Otto rex...ad cuius mensam cotidie 30 libre argenti pertinebant'. Against Brühl (1968) 174–5, who interpreted this report and that of the Saxon Annalist in n. 151 above as the 'daily use' of the court, see Fleckenstein's review in *HZ* 212 (1971) 122–3.

in kind to specific monetary payments or yearly taxes due from the monasteries and their dependants. The *servitium regis*, however, never lost all of its non-monetary aspects. That the *servitium regis* in the Ottonian period can also be understood in terms of the five-fold nature of the services described above appears to be a justifiable extrapolation both from the Carolingian evidence[153] and from the explicit words contained in a source from the twelfth century, a letter from Wibald, abbot of Corvey and Stavelot, to Bishop Bernhard of Hildesheim: 'exhibiting royal service on campaign, as well as attending court and providing hospitality'.[154]

The first detailed study of the secular and ecclesiastical *servitium regis* in Germany from 900 to 1250 was provided by Bruno Heusinger.[155] Since the publication of his pioneering work many scholars have focused, directly or indirectly, on the *servitium regis*. Carlrichard Brühl, for example, greatly expanded the chronological, topical and geographical scope of Heusinger's work and added many valuable corrections and additions to it,[156] and, more recently, Wolfgang Metz in a series of books and articles has contributed considerably to our knowledge of *servitium regis*, and especially its connection with the itinerary of the German kings.[157] Heusinger confined his definition of *servitium regis* to the purely economic sense of the term, that is, payments in kind and money to supply the king's table. Brühl retained Heusinger's purely economic focus, although he expressly acknowledged and indicated the manifold nature of the term and the concept.[158] Metz likewise pointed to the diverse ways in which *servitium regis* can be defined.[159] In his work he has demonstrated how the investigation and the solution of new and long-standing problems regarding the *servitium regis* of the German kings must of necessity be closely linked with local studies and research on the royal residences, which have dominated German historical scholarship in the last

---

[153] See esp. Pöschl (1908–12) 1.156–9.

[154] Jaffé, *Bibl.* I.239 no. 150: '...servitium regis in expeditione quam in curia adeunda et in hospiciis procurandis exuberare'. This reference lacks only the obligation of prayer (*orationes*), either because it was common and understood, or because the *orationes* were primarily the obligation falling on the brothers (and their property) while the other three services mentioned fell due on the abbot's property. A discussion of this point appears at the end of this chapter.

[155] Heusinger (1922).   [156] Brühl (1968).

[157] Metz (1970), (1971), (1972b), (1976), (1978a), (1978b) and (1985). See also the useful comments by Leyser (1981).   [158] Brühl (1968) 97–101.

[159] Metz (1976) 188–9. Also, Pöschl (1908–12) 1.156–9, Waitz (1893–6) 8.380–1, and especially Haverkamp (1968) 770 indicate the manifold nature of this term.

thirty years.[160] This is particularly true in regard to Metz's work on royal accommodation in the Pfalz region of the Rhineland, his examination of royal roads, property holding, and *servitium regis*, and his investigation of Ottonian and Salian markets and market policy.[161]

Much research on the king's palaces (*Königspfalzen*) has emanated from the Max-Planck-Institut für Geschichte in Göttingen. Three volumes entitled *Deutsche Königspfalzen* contain numerous articles dedicated to individual royal residences.[162] Detailed individual studies examining a specific royal residence or an area of royal power, the complex of properties surrounding or comprising it, and the political and economic characteristics of the area – such as Frankfurt, Kassel, Goslar, the Ardennes forest region and Aachen – have also appeared.[163] The Institute's continuing project on royal palaces and property provides schematized and detailed descriptions of all royal properties or halting points on the royal itinerary, arranged by regions.[164]

Investigations of royal roads and of the itineraries of the German kings have also yielded important advances. Albert Hömberg and Wolf Deus have studied royal property and the itinerary through the Westphalian Hellweg.[165] Dietrich Denecke has advanced the methodology of establishing the medieval road structure in general and has largely completed the delineation of medieval and early modern roads in Saxony.[166] Wolfgang Metz has examined medieval roads especially in their connection with the royal itinerary, and Wolf-Arno Kropat has investigated the political structure and roads in the Wetterau region of lower Hesse.[167] Eckhard Müller-Mertens, on the other hand, has calculated distances along royal roads on the basis of railway lines on similar routes (which often follow old roads) and has added a time component, both for travelling between specific places and in regard to how long the court may have remained in one place, based on stops before and after a specific place.[168] Other important work concerns individual monasteries, such as Fulda, Hersfeld,

[160] Metz (1970), (1971), (1972b), (1976), (1978a), (1978b) and (1985).
[161] Metz (1970), (1971), (1972b).   [162] Deutsche Königspfalzen (1963, 1965, 1979).
[163] Schalles-Fischer (1969), K. Heinemeyer (1971), Wilke (1970), Müller-Kehlen (1973) and Flach (1976).   [164] DKP Rep. (1983, 1984, 1986 and 1988).
[165] Hömberg (1943–52), (1960) and (1965); and Deus (1960).
[166] Denecke (1969) and (1970).
[167] Metz (1971), (1972b) and (1978b); Kropat (1965).
[168] Müller-Mertens (1980) 107–24.

Corvey, St Maximin, Reichenau, Lorsch, St Emmeram, Niedermünster and Obermünster, and their political and economic relations with the monarchy.[169] New studies on the 'regalia' or royal monopolies, especially the minting of coins and holding markets, have targeted coinage and minting rights and laws,[170] and have examined markets, trade and tolls in connection with the royal itinerary and general economic development under the Ottonian and Salian kings.[171] Recent studies of the army of the German kings and of the military service of the clergy in the Ottonian realm represent further additions to our knowledge of the practical workings of Ottonian government.[172] In sum, all this research (of which I have cited only some) has shed important light on problems related to the *servitium regis* of the German kings and provided the answers to some hitherto unanswered or inadequately formulated questions.

Since the economic *servitium regis* of the royal monasteries primarily consisted of renders of food and drink and some manufactured goods, such as cloth and dishes (whether provided at the monastery or elsewhere), we must examine briefly the structure and administration of the monastic landed estates, on which agricultural production, animal husbandry and rudimentary manufacturing were practised, and the methods of exploitation of these estates.[173] In the early middle ages a lord or the holder of a large estate could farm his land and tend the herds directly using slave labour and/or he could grant out parts of his estate to free peasants, who, as tenant-farmers, in turn paid rent in kind or money to the lord. The most common form of exploitation, however (especially as it developed in the Carolingian areas west of the Rhine), was the *grande seigneurie* or *Groß-Grundherrschaft*, which has been called the 'classic demesne

---

[169] Wehlt (1970) – Fulda, Hersfeld and Lorsch; Schmitt (1974) – Reichenau and Ulm; Hess (1963) – Hersfeld and Fulda; Semmler (1973–7) – Lorsch; Kaminsky (1972) – Corvey; Wisplinghoff (1970) – St Maximin; Keller (1964) – Einsiedeln; and Bosl (1966) – St Emmeram, Niedermünster and Obermünster.

[170] Volz (unpub. diss. 1967); Wadle (1971); and Kaiser (1976) esp. 321–7.

[171] Hess (1963), (1974a) and (1974b); Metz (1971) 279–91 and (1972b); Duby (1974) 127–39; and Hardt-Friedrichs (1980).

[172] Werner (1968); F. Prinz (1971); Auer (1971) and (1972); and Scherff (unpub. diss. 1985).

[173] The literature on early medieval agriculture and the manorial system is vast. Good and accessible introductions can be found in Lütge (1963); Duby (1968) 5–58 and (1974) 77–97; and Dollinger (1982) 41–191. Reuter (1991a) 94–102 provides a concise overview of the economy of the east Frankish realm.

organization' (*le régime domanial classique*).[174] In this arrangement, people outside of the family and the immediate household of the lord had fallen into a relationship of direct dependence toward the owner, who thus had seigneurial authority over a great landed estate or over multiple estates (*Villikation* in German) and the dependent populations living there. Some of the estate was parcelled out in tenancies for which the lord received rent, and the lord's parcels, the demesne (*mansus indominicatus*), continued to be farmed directly, not primarily by slaves, however, but by his dependent tenants or serfs, who owed the lord labour services in addition to the rents paid for their tenancies.[175] This classic manorial system or bipartite domainial structure (*le domaine bipartite*) predominated most in the area between the Loire and the Rhine, but was not exclusive even there.

Slightly different conditions east of the Rhine – smaller estates, greater use of slave labour, more sparsely settled areas, a greater number of independent, peasant farmers, and large areas not conducive to cereal production – led to the development of a greater and more apparent diversity of estate structures.[176] The great landed estate itself, based on dominion over land and people (*Grundherrschaft*), did exist east of the Rhine and even in Saxony before the Frankish conquest;[177] but the classic bipartite domainial organization spread with the Carolingian rulers, especially on royal lands (which later were often granted to churches and monasteries), and thus agrarian structures based on the great landed estate increased. Consequently, in areas east of the Rhine two main types of manorial organization emerged (with countless variations in between) based on specific local conditions – the classic bipartite domainial organization previously described, and an estate structure based entirely on rent income (in kind or money) from the dependent peasants without the payment of

---

[174] Verhulst (1966) and (1983).

[175] Verhulst (1966) designates this characteristic form as 'le domaine bipartite'. See also Verhulst (1985), a valuable collection of essays devoted primarily to the core region of the Merovingian and Carolingian Franks between the Loire and the Rhine; Devroey (1984) and (1986); and Fossier (1978).

[176] In general, on the development of estate structures east of the Rhine, see Lütge (1963); Droege (1970); Dollinger (1982) 41–191; Metz (1981); Rösener (1980), (1985) and (1989); and Verhulst (1989). For the estate development of selected individual monasteries and convents, see Kötzschke (1901) and (1906–58) vol. 4.2; Weigel (1960); Kaminsky (1972), who provides a new edition of the Corvey land register (pp. 224–39); Rösener (1980); Weidinger (1989); and Goetz (1990) 146–56.

[177] Rösener (1980) and (1985) 175–81.

personal labour services. Whereas Georg Droege saw the estate structure based entirely on rent income as typical of Westphalia and Saxony,[178] Werner Rösener, using the numerous estates of the monasteries of Werden and Corvey, demonstrated that both methods of manorial organization existed side by side according to specific conditions in the immediate vicinity of the estate.[179] Similarly, Ulrich Weidinger revealed that Fulda's estates also exhibited many structural and organizational variations.[180] Both types of agrarian organization employed a multiple estate or *Villikation* system, the first organized around the lord's manors on which labour services were due, and the second around the centres established for the collection of rents in a particular area. The lord established a steward or overseer (*villicus*) in these centres who collected the rents and then, once or twice yearly, the lord or his appointed official (in the case of a monastery, the abbot or a monastic official) would travel a circuit around all of these collection centres to gather the rents.

Not surprisingly, one also finds two main types of estate surveys. The land register, or *Urbar*, which closely resembles the Carolingian polyptych in a less detailed format, lists peasant land holders, their holdings, and the dues they owe, both in rent and in labour. Conversely, a register of taxes or dues, a *Heberolle*, contains little information on land holdings, usually only the name of the dependant and the rent owed. On the basis of extant land surveys for the monasteries of Werden and Corvey, Werner Rösener demonstrates the existence and spread of both organizational methods. Werden's closed complex of estates along the Rhine at Friemersheim and those in the immediate vicinity of the monastery were organized on the classic demesne structure with labour services, but its distant and scattered estates in less arable areas north of the Lippe River were organized strictly on the basis of rent payments (although the monastery gradually expanded the classic structure). For the first type we possess an *Urbar* or true estate survey, while for the second type of organization we possess a *Heberolle* or tax roll. Corvey's estates were organized along Carolingian models, and the estate survey, although referred to as a *Heberolle*, resembles an abbreviated version of a Carolingian polyptych and includes the labour services due from dependants in addition to their rents.[181]

[178] Droege (1970).   [179] Rösener (1985) esp. 179–81.   [180] Weidinger (1989).
[181] Rösener (1985).

It is neither intended nor necessary here to provide an exhaustive examination of the sources regarding the *servitium regis* of the royal monasteries, which primarily consist of land registers of estate surveys and information on property holding and monastic *servitium* drawn from royal charters. This former gap in the scholarship on the *servitium regis* has been adequately and admirably treated by Wolfgang Metz in regard to the royal monasteries, the bishoprics and the properties of the royal domain.[182] Suffice it to say that for the Ottonian and early Salian periods the sources provide us with little information regarding the *servitium regis* in general and with even less concerning that of the royal monasteries. As indicated above, however, the sources are somewhat more favourable in the later Carolingian period (the ninth and early tenth centuries) and the vast majority of the sources for the *servitium regis* survive from the twelfth and early thirteenth centuries. Hence, one must extrapolate forward from the ninth-century sources and backward from those of the twelfth century to fill the gaps in the tenth- and eleventh-century evidence. The pitfalls of this approach are obvious, but the paucity of source material in this period forces us to make the most intelligent and thoughtful use of the sources that we have at our disposal.

[182] Metz (1976), (1978a) and (1985).

Chapter 3

SERVITIUM REGIS AND MONASTIC PROPERTY

In the Carolingian Empire, and especially in the German realm from the mid-tenth to the mid-eleventh century, as the great ecclesiastical institutions – the bishoprics and the royal monasteries – gradually became integrated into the structure of feudal government, they had to serve the realm in a secular as well as a religious capacity. This new legal relationship between the bishoprics and royal monasteries and their 'protector', the king, brought with it manifold obligations to the king, which we call the *servitium regis* described above. These services for the king generally tended to 'secularize' the royal monasteries, and seriously affected the monastic ideal as well as the development of monasticism in Germany. For instance, the monastic ideal required the relinquishment of private property and a vow of poverty. Yet in order to fulfil the *servitium regis*, the royal monasteries had to have property far beyond their needs for subsistence. Likewise, the monastic conception of the ascetic life was partially compromised by increased contact with the secular world. As father of his congregation and as the king's vassal (or royal representative), the abbot no longer stood within the congregation, but outside and above it, a prince of the realm between the monastery and the king. This progressive secularization of the abbot's position and of monastic property began to threaten the brothers' endowment and, consequently, their ability to lead the ascetic life unencumbered and to offer constant prayer for the king and the realm. In order best to protect and assure that those properties, which provided the essential needs of the community, did not suffer from increasing secular and abbatial encroachments, monastic congregations needed an internal reorganization of monastic properties and a separation of those properties between the abbot or abbess and the congregation. Thus, as this division of function between the abbot and the monks emerged, it encouraged a corresponding division of the resources supporting those functions.

The *servitium regis* of a monastery consisted of economic (*hospitium, gistum, mansio, fodrum*), military (*hostilicum* or *militia*), personal or political (*consilium et auxilium*), and spiritual (*orationes*) components. As a term for the upkeep of the king, *hospitium* does not occur in any German source for the period. Most frequently the terms *mansio* (seldom, except in immunity grants) and *servitium* or *servitium regis* or *regale* replace *hospitium* in the German sources.[1] These components, however, were not always equally assessed on the same property or members of the monastery, but a straight-forward separation of the services did exist. All material and secular services of the monastery for the king fell due on the monastic property over which the abbot or abbess had a full and free right of disposition; while the spiritual obligations of the monastery – constant prayer on behalf of the king, royal family and the realm – were primarily the responsibility of the congregation (though the abbot also participated in this obligation, either alone or by leading the congregation in prayer). Thus, those possessions assigned strictly for the use or upkeep of the congregation or the church – that is, the prebend – normally remained free of any material or secular services. An unusual charter of Zwentibold makes a special allotment of the monastery's possessions to the brothers but, at the same time, the king retains the right to extract a *servitium regis* from this separate endowment or prebend. On the other hand, the charter forbids the abbot or anyone else to impose any other *servitium* on the brothers' prebend.[2] These prescriptions by Zwentibold, however, do not appear in Arnulf's diploma for the same monastery, nor in Charles the Simple's charter confirming Arnulf's charter.[3] Diverse evidence from early in the ninth century, moreover, increasingly points to a separate allocation or separation, whether informal or formal, of monastic property into abbatial and fraternal holdings.

A few scholars have written general studies which attempt to clarify the difficult economic and judicial problems surrounding the various kinds of separate allocations or separations of the monastic possessions.[4] The excellent accounts by Arnold Pöschl and Emil Lesne, appearing almost simultaneously, complement each other nicely. Both works, however, confine themselves largely to the eighth and ninth centuries in the territories west of

---

[1] See Brühl (1968) 167 n. 208a.   [2] *DZ* 14 (13 June 897).
[3] *DArn* 114 (from which *DZ* 14 is largely derived); *DKE* 69.
[4] Matthäi (1877), Pöschl (1908–12) 1.156–9 and Lesne (1910).

the Rhine. Georg Matthäi alone has dealt exclusively with monasteries and has given substantial information regarding the east Frankish realm and the later German empire. Unfortunately, although some of Matthäi's conclusions remain valid, many of the documents on which he built his thesis have proven to be forgeries. Although no general study of the division of monastic property between abbot and brothers in the German empire has appeared since Matthäi's study, Rudolf Schieffer has devoted an essay to property division in the cathedral chapters of the empire.[5] The technical terminology referring to these property allocations, separations and finally 'divisions' varied greatly. The first chapter of Lesne's treatise contains a concise treatment of the Latin terminology – for example, *segregare*, *attribuere* or *deputare in usus fratrum*, *ad stipendia* or *a parte fratrum*, and Schieffer offers some pertinent remarks on misunderstandings of the terminology as used in the secondary literature.[6] He warns that one should be careful not to confuse separate allocations of property to specific ends (for example, to the upkeep of the congregation), which are often referred to as property divisions (*Güterteilungen*), with later actual 'divisions' or breaking-up of property into separate holdings for the monastic congregation or cathedral chapter, over which the monks or canons exercised full legal control. Since this separation of the services due to the king mirrors the assignment of property within the monasteries, it is worthwhile to review the evolution of these property allocations, which grew more distinct in German monasteries during the Ottonian and Salian periods. In particular, I shall examine the tenth- and eleventh-century evidence for the existence of such property separations and for the exaction of the material *servitium regis* primarily from the abbatial segment of a monastery's property and assets.

In general, from the ninth century through to the mid-eleventh century, an internal redistribution or restructuring of properties occurred in many monasteries. It began in the ninth-century Carolingian and west Frankish realm, first in those monasteries under the direction of a secular or lay abbot, and had extended by the eleventh century to many German royal monasteries in connection with royally initiated reforms. In order to clarify the terminology, I shall make the following general distinctions. A 'secular abbot' indicates an abbot (abbess), who was a prelate,

---

[5] R. Schieffer (1976).   [6] Lesne (1910) 1–9; R. Schieffer (1976) 262–3.

usually a bishop or archbishop, or a secular canon (canoness), who lived according to the canons; whereas a 'lay abbot' refers to an abbot (abbess) who was a layperson. Both secular and lay abbots (abbesses) stand in contrast to regular abbots (abbesses), who always were monks (nuns), living according to a monastic rule. In the literature on these topics 'lay abbot' often refers to both an abbot or abbess who was a secular cleric as well as to one who was a layperson. Initially, the totality of monastic property and assets never underwent a thoroughgoing 'division' or 'separation', and one does not encounter this in legal proceedings. Instead, within the unity of monastic possessions certain specific properties or assets were allotted to serve strictly spiritual ends, that is, the upkeep of the church or the congregation. Thus, they were removed from the abbot's arbitrary power of disposition. When such property assignments did occur, or later, when our evidence points more clearly to a separation of property (by granting the brothers a separate endowment and the independent control of that property), the abbot still retained final judicial control of the whole of the monastic possessions. This is particularly evident in precarial or exchange charters granted or contracted with third parties concerning the brothers' property (prebend), in which the abbot still appears as the juridically responsible party (although the consent of the congregation is often included). But it is not clear whether the abbot retained this jurisdiction when the congregation had the right to appoint its own provost and to procure the representation of the monastery's advocate specially for its prebend. Although it would seem that in such cases the brothers' provost and the advocate would exercise their appointed jurisdiction, I have found no documented proof of this. In any case, the consent or witness of the abbot to the transaction, as official leader and official possessor of the monastery's proprietary rights, still appears to have been required (as it appeared often in the charters).[7]

The allocation of a part of the property and assets of a monastery for the specific use of the congregation (*ad victum et potum, ad praebendam, annonam, ad mensam fratrum*),[8] or of the abbot (*potestas*

[7] Concerning some of these judicial problems, see Pöschl (1908–12) 2.37–42 and Lesne (1910) 128–38. On English monasteries and the abbot's position as legal representative of a monastery's proprietary rights, see John (1955) 154 and Howell (1982) 191–2.

[8] These examples represent a mere sampling of the numerous Latin terms with which the charters refer to the congregation's prebend. For a longer list, see Pöschl (1908–12) 2.17–22 and Lesne (1910) 5–8.

abbatis, ratio abbatiae, beneficariae),[9] and the later separation or division of monastic properties reflect historical developments in the ninth, tenth and eleventh centuries as well as changes within the monasteries that affected a unified monastic property structure.[10] This proprietary restructuring in monastic institutions proceeded to some degree as part of the general historical development of church property. It also resulted, however, because of increased demands from the state on church property. At the same time, it was in harmony with the political and ecclesiastical goals of the Carolingian reform movement and the later reform movements supported by the Ottonian and Salian emperors. This process varied temporally and spatially: it took place earlier and more clearly west of the Rhine than east of the Rhine; and it occurred more readily in those areas or centres of active monastic reform.

By and large most monasteries (especially those in the regions of the empire east of the Rhine) were not rich enough until the eighth and ninth centuries for gifts from princes and the faithful to result in an accumulation of wealth and property significantly beyond what was needed for the upkeep of the monastery and the congregation. During the late eighth century and early ninth, however, the quantity of property grants to churches and monasteries and their respective clerics or monks increased dramatically. This was due to large grants of land to monasteries from the royal fisc, especially under Charlemagne and Louis the Pious, and an increasing number of gifts from noble believers, who hoped to gain the constant prayers of the monks on their behalf or the intercession in heaven of the monastery's patron saint.[11] With this significant improvement in their economic

[9] Pöschl (1908–12) 2.22 was mistaken when he claimed that the Latin terms *abbatia* and *abbatiola* in charter sources refer to the property of the abbot as opposed to the prebend of the congregation. Only in very few instances do these Latin terms have this meaning, and only in west Frankish sources, never in an east Frankish or German source. Even in the evidence he cites, the word *abbatia* (*abbatiola*) obviously means either the spiritual institution itself or the whole of the monastic property. Concerning the historical and linguistic development of the word *abbatia* and its primary meaning, see Blume (1914) and Lesne (1914) 28–39 esp. 36.

[10] The words most frequently used when establishing a separate endowment for the congregation are *segregare, attribuere, deputare*; whereas the Latin *divisio* in this context almost always implies an impious secularization of monastic property. See: Ribbeck (unpub. diss. 1883) 103–6; Lesne (1910) 2–5; and Werner-Hasselbach (1942) 125–6, esp. nn. 28 and 30.

[11] Concerning the religious and economic development of monasticism under Charlemagne, see Semmler (1965). For the continued developments under Louis the

condition during the ninth century, monasteries often possessed property and assets far in excess of the amount necessary to support the essential needs of the church and the congregation. Thus, the abbot or rector of a monastery now had the economic freedom to alienate excess possessions, allocating them to his own table (*mensam abbatis*) or personal use, granting them to vassals in benefice or using them in service of the king.[12] Customarily, the abbot or rector of a monastery was obligated only to provide for the needs and upkeep of the church and the congregation.[13] The decision concerning how to supply these from the various monastic properties and incomes at his disposal was left entirely to the abbot's discretion.[14] In the late eighth century and early ninth and especially in the larger and richer monasteries, such as Saint-Germain-des-Prés, St Denis, Flavigny, St Bertin, St Gall, Fulda and Hersfeld, disposition of the monastic possessions by the abbot did not cause excessive problems, even though both Charlemagne and Louis the Pious made increasingly heavy demands on abbots and church property in support of the state. Beginning in the mid-ninth century and extending into the early tenth, a constellation of events, however, caused the state's demands on church property to increase even more. The civil wars between Louis the Pious and his sons caused weakened rulers to seize upon monastic and church property for support and left many churches and their lands unprotected from other nobles. Likewise, the increasing number of Viking incursions during this same period and later created a growing need on the part of some monasteries to provide for or

Pious, especially the monastic reform movement and the attempts led by Benedict of Aniane to impose the Benedictine Rule throughout Francia, see McKitterick (1983) 106–26, who summarizes the most important research and includes many important additional insights.

[12] For an excellent, brief summary of the social and political ascendancy of the office of abbot and the material rise of monasteries under the Carolingians, see Felten (1974) 422–8.

[13] This definitely applied to houses following the Benedictine Rule. See Fry (1981) cc. 22, 32, 39, 40 and 55 of the *Rule* as well as pp. 368–70 ('The abbot as administrator'). However, as Semmler (1965) 255–67 shows, Charlemagne's Francia contained monasteries of multiple observances and the emperor had only limited success in encouraging others to follow Benedictine customs.

[14] For an example of a provision where the abbot was obligated to provide the monks with a specific amount of upkeep, see Louis the Pious's charter for Saint-Germain-des-Prés: Poupardin, *Saint-Germain-des Prés* 43–7 no. 28; and Pöschl (1908–12) 2.24–5. In general, the overall size of the monastic possessions and the judiciousness of the abbot conditioned the whole early development of separate endowments for monastic congregations.

secure their own self-defence. Consequently, more and more monasteries came under the headship of powerful ecclesiastical or lay lords (secular or lay abbots) instead of regular abbots, to whom monastic lands were granted for them to organize the protection of the monastery. Thus, kings, abbots themselves and powerful laymen came to possess, and often confiscated, an increasingly large share of the monastery's property to employ it toward secular ends.

Traditionally scholars have viewed lay abbacy in a totally negative light.[15] Franz Felten, however, has thoroughly re-examined the entire question of lay abbacy. Through his examination of the concept as it existed both in the sources and in the secondary literature, he has clarified a whole series of difficulties in the general use and perception of the term 'lay abbot'. Most importantly, he has demonstrated convincingly that 'bad abbots', that is abbots who either blatantly led a lifestyle inconsistent with ascetic ideals or, more related to the topic at hand, were despoilers of monastic property to the detriment of the congregation, were referred to in the sources and the secondary literature as 'lay abbots', regardless of whether they were regular, secular or lay. Moreover, he indicates that lay abbacy has to be seen in the context of the historical situation of the period – a response to particular needs – and that it was not in itself a bad thing. In fact, many lay abbots took an active role in the welfare of their congregations and actually increased their holdings. He sees the intense reform mentality of the ninth century as placing a negative moral characterization on the institution as reflected in the sources, which has been followed in turn by much of the secondary literature.[16]

Progressive secularization of monastic property, whether in the time of Charlemagne and Louis the Pious or later in the ninth century, however, could threaten the properties upon which the existence of the monks depended. Thus, to ensure the existence of the congregation it became necessary, within the generally unified structure of monastic property, to make special assignments or actual internal divisions of property between the abbot and the congregation, especially in those institutions whose abbacy was in the hands of a layman or non-regular abbot. Not the institution of

---

[15] E.g. Voigt (1917); Lesne (1910) 44 and Lesne (1910–43) vol. 2.1 p. 260, vol. 2.2 p. 155. See Felten (1974) 397–400 for other instances.

[16] Felten (1974) and (1980). Fichtenau (1984) 309–17 also offers some interesting comments on lay abbacy.

lay abbacy itself, but the problem of alienation of church property thus became the focus of legislation and new grants attempting to address the problem.[17] This general situation, coupled with the strong ecclesiastical and monastic reform movements of the ninth century begun under Louis the Pious,[18] occasioned a gradual and successive development within many monasteries, beginning generally in the western regions of the Frankish empire under Louis the Pious and spreading out from there. Thus, the development was regionally and temporally diverse. In the course of the ninth century (primarily in the west Frankish realm) this led to a separation of the prebend (that is, those estates allotted solely for the upkeep of the monastery and the congregation) from the remaining property of an institution. For instance, as I will discuss below, Louis the Pious, under the influence of Benedict of Aniane, ruled that, in all monasteries of strict observance which did not have a regular abbot, certain properties should be reserved solely for the use of the congregation.[19] We possess scattered evidence of this development already in the time of Charlemagne; it appears in full bloom under Louis the Pious, Lothar and Charles the Bald; and east of the Rhine, it grew increasingly in the late ninth and tenth centuries. In Chapter 15 of the so-called *Supplex libellus* of 812 (817),[20] the congregation of monks at Fulda complained directly to Charlemagne (and later to Louis the Pious) about conditions in their monastery, including some grants of the monastery's property by their abbot into secular benefices.[21] Although this letter did not result in a separation of abbatial property from the brothers' prebend, it appears to have occasioned an administrative reorganization of the monastery's property for more effective use. It stands as one of the earliest examples, especially from the eastern regions of the realm, of a complaint

---

[17] Felten (1974) 406–9 and Lesne (1920) 321–38.   [18] McKitterick (1983) 106–26.

[19] See Lesne (1920) 331–5. The 'Ecclesiastical' capitulary of 819 contains a similar provision concerning churches in general (*MGH Capit.* 1 no. 138 c. 10 p. 277) and the council of Aachen in 836 warns the heads of monasteries not to subtract from the necessary needs of the monks and employ those goods to other ends (*MGH Conc.* 2.2 no. 56 c. (37) XIII p. 713). Also, legislation under Charlemagne had already forbidden laymen to be *prepositi* (*MGH Capit.* 1 no. 43 c. 15) and this prohibition was repeated frequently in reform legislation, pointed especially at monasteries where a regular abbot was lacking. For a detailed discussion of these developments, see Gast (1965) 74–138. Also see Felten (1974) 407–8.

[20] *Supplex libellus monachorum fuldensium* ... In his detailed commentary and analysis of the document, Semmler (1958) 296–8 also discusses its dating. See also Thiele (1976).

[21] *CCM* 1.325 c. 15.

about the enfeoffment of monastic property by a regular abbot.[22] Several sources from the reign of Louis the Pious, when the great ecclesiastical and monastic reform movement of the ninth century had its inception and greatest success, document a growing concern about secularization of monastic property and the need to protect the congregation's prebend. For instance, Benedict of Aniane, Louis's leading monastic reformer, perceived the need to protect the prebend from abbatial encroachments, especially in monasteries where a secular or lay abbot stood over the monks instead of a regular abbot. In those monasteries ruled by secular abbots he regularly made special assignments of property for the exclusive use of the brothers.[23] One finds support for this statement in Louis the Pious's charter for St Columbe de Sens (2 April 836), where Benedict had been sent to reform the monastery. Having found a secular abbot, he separated several properties out of the monastery's possessions as a prebend for the brothers.[24] According to Ardo, Benedict's biographer, Louis the Pious also determined those monasteries in which a regular abbot should remain. Unfortunately, this document has not come down to us, but it appears to be closely connected with the *Notitia de servitio monasteriorum* of 819.[25]

A letter written to the Emperor Louis the Pious by Frotharius, bishop of Toul, and Smaragdus, abbot of St Mihiel's at Mosen, provides interesting and illuminating evidence documenting the struggle between monks and their abbots over the necessity of instituting specially designated and separate prebends to counteract the confiscations made by abbots.[26] Written between 825 and 830 by the two men acting as *missi dominici*, it contains a report about a long-standing dispute between the abbot and the monks of the royal monastery of Moyenmoutier. The dispute centred on a special property that the monks had acquired under their abbot *in absentia*, Fortunatus, patriarch of Grado, by command of the emperor, so that they could live according to the Rule.[27]

---

[22] See Werner-Hasselbach (1942) 125–6, and Semmler (1958) 283. Cf. Pöschl (1908–12) 2.33.

[23] Ardo, *Vita Benedicti Abbatis* c. 39 p. 218: 'His vero monasteriis quae sub canonicorum relicta sunt potestate constituit eis segregatim unde vivere regulariter possent, cetera abbati concessit.' [24] See Bouq. 6.610 (BM² no. 961).

[25] See the *Notitia* in *CCM* 1.485–8 and Lesne (1920) esp. 458–9.

[26] *MGH Epis.* 5 no. 21 pp. 290–1.

[27] Ibid. p. 290: 'tempore Fortunati Mediolanensis monasterii abbatis per iussionem vestram Smaraedum ipsius monasterii monachis portionem de abbatia dedit, ut

Subsequently, their new abbot, Ismundus, confiscated the property, promising to supply all their necessities regularly. When he failed to do this, the monks complained to their bishop, Frotharius, that they could no longer live according to the Rule. Frotharius and Smaragdus went to the monastery, confirmed the situation, and received a promise from the abbot not to neglect the congregation in the future. He refused, however, to reinstitute the property separation except on direct order of the emperor. The monks, therefore, fearing a similar recurrence, implored the *missi dominici* to grant them permission to take their case directly to the emperor, saying that they would prefer to be forced out of the monastery and have to go about begging rather than trust in vain promises and serve falsely under the title of monks.[28] The *missi* granted them licence to appeal, and then sent their report and an additional letter to the emperor requesting his attention and favour as far as the monks' request was concerned.[29] This particular case study vividly depicts the alternating power struggle between monks, who sought to ensure their upkeep and existence by means of special property assignments when faced with abbatial confiscations, and abbots, who wanted to maintain, or even regain, their former and advantageous position of having unlimited power of disposition over all the monastic assets.[30]

CHARTERS AND MONASTIC PROPERTY DIVISION

The need for an internal reorganization of monastic property greatly increased as a result of continuing secularization of that

---

regulariter viverent. Et idcirco bene et secundum regulam vixerunt, quousque Fortunatus recessit.'

[28] Ibid. p. 291: 'Quod quia ipsa sine vestra iussione nullatenus se facturum dixit, ideo illi omnes pariter communi intencione communique prece postulaverunt, ut illis licentiam daremus ad vestrae pietatis praesenciam recurrendi et vestram misericordiam implorandi, dicentes se magis velle de eodem monasterio expelli et in peregrinatione et mendicitate vivere, quam falsis promissionibus ulterius credere et sub falso monachorum nomine militare.'　　[29] MGH Epis. 5 no. 22 pp. 291–2.

[30] An analogous notion appears in Chapter 10 of a capitulary of 818/819. The capitulary pertains generally to all churches, orders and ecclesiastics of the realm. Chapter 10 concerns parish priests and protects their minimum upkeep against infringements by their proprietary lord. It prescribed that every parish church must maintain one manse, free of all service, exclusively for ecclesiastic use; and only if it has additional holdings at its disposal may these be assigned as *servitium* to their lords. MGH Capit. 1 no. 138 c. 10 p. 277: 'Sanccitum est, ut unicuique ecclesiae unus mansus integer absque alio servitio adtribuatur...neque praescripto manso aliquod servitium faciant praeter ecclesiasticum. Et si aliquid amplius habuerint, inde senioribus suis debitum servitium impendant.'

property. The prelates of monasteries often oppressed the 'soldiers of God', the monks, who had to endure unfulfilled needs and sharply reduced provisions of food and clothing. As I will demonstrate, from the mid-eighth century, reaching a peak west of the Rhine in the mid-ninth, and continuing into the tenth and eleventh centuries east of the Rhine, charter evidence documents both a growing concern about secularization and abbatial usurpation of monastic property, and a gradually evolving specialization and division of property within the monasteries. In royal and private diplomas granted to monasteries, especially the *traditiones*, certain alterations in the charter *formulae* appear that indicate an attempt on the part of the grantors to limit the frequency of abbatial expropriation of monastic possessions.

The traditional style of grant comprised a transfer of personal property to a saint or saint's relics, to an altar or to a church itself. Normally such a grant contained no restrictions on the use of the gift. Consequently, the abbot, abbess or protectors (*abbas, custodes, rectores*) of the institution acquired an unhindered right of administration and disposition.[31] Side by side with the traditional *formulae*, new forms of grants appeared that bound the granted property to a specific use. Often they contained definite limitations on the abbot's power of disposition and were coupled with strong admonitions against abbatial usurpation of property bestowed for the upkeep of the brothers. This new phase in the development of separate abbatial and conventual properties occurred, although with temporal and regional variations, generally throughout the monasteries of the west and east Frankish realms and later in the German empire.[32] Whereas previously benefactors had granted the charters bestowing their gifts generally to the church or the abbot, and the brothers' use of the grant had been assumed, from the middle of the ninth century onward grantors increasingly directed their *traditiones* specifically for the sole use of the brothers.[33] They also designated their grants for special uses such

---

[31] The Latin designations *custodes* or *rectores* as synonyms for *abbas* (or *episcopus*) occur often in the charters of the ninth and tenth centuries. See especially the tenth-century private charters of the monastery of Werden, *Een Diplomatisch Oonderzoek...Werden*, pp. 156–219. Numerous examples of *custodes* or *rectores* occur in the private charters of other prominent monasteries, e.g. St Gall, Fulda and Hersfeld, and occasionally in royal charters, e.g. *DArn* 10 and a charter of Otto I, *DO I* 54. Concerning this terminology, see T. Mayer (1950) 4–17.

[32] For a specific example, see Werner-Hasselbach (1942) 129–30.

[33] *CDF* nos. 638: 'pro aeterna requie animae meae ad servitium monachorum'; 654: 'ad generales usus fratrum perpetuo conserventur'. Similarly in royal grants one finds the

as the upkeep of the lights of the church,[34] or they specified their grants as alms on behalf of their salvation (*in elemosina nostra*), obliging the congregation to pray and say masses for the grantors or their deceased family members at certain times of the year. Grants often consisted of some combination of the three elements. Coupled with these limitations we find a growing tendency in the charters, both in grants specially designated for the congregation and in memorial grants, to prevent alienation of the gift by forbidding the abbot or leader of an institution, or anyone else, to grant the property in benefice.[35] It is instructive to view this development over a span of time in both the royal and the private charters.

In January 806, Charlemagne granted a certain property to the monastery of Prüm as alms on behalf of his salvation (*in elemosina nostra*). He designated the gift for the lights (*in luminaribus*) of the church and placed it in the care of the abbot.[36] In April of 807, he bestowed a similar charter for the church lights and the general upkeep of the brothers (*seu stipendia servorum dei*).[37] His successor, Louis the Pious, gave the monastery of Fulda a *villa* in July of 820.[38] He not only stipulated the specific use of the property (the upkeep and necessities of the brothers and the support of the poor and pilgrims);[39] but he also expressly forbade the *rectores et ministri* of the monastery from secularizing the property in any way.[40] Louis the German, in bestowing a memorial gift (*in nostra elemosina*) on the monastery at Prüm in 871,[41] directly addressed the growing problem of secularization of the prebend through abbatial confiscation, saying: 'No abbot should dare to grant anything from these properties to anyone in benefice, but they should perpetually remain in the use of the brothers of Prüm,

following designations: *DLD* 131: 'perpetuum ad usus fratrum'; *DArn* 58A: 'Ad usus fratrum'; *DO I* 14: 'ad usum nutrimenque congregationis inibi'; and *DO III* 242: 'ad usum puellarum in prefato monasterio'. From both private and royal charters one could easily multiply these examples.

34 *DKar* 203: 'in luminaribus ecclesia proficiat in augmentis'. Other examples include: *DKar* 205; *CL* 1.328 no. 45 [= *DKD* 103 (11 June 884)]; and *DO I* 116.
35 Matthäi (1877) 17–19.   36 *DKar* 203.
37 *DKar* 205. Some charters of this type occur already in the eighth century: *DDPep* III 3, 21; *DDKar* 82, 83, 165, 186.   38 *CDF* no. 390.
39 Ibid.: 'ad stipendia fratrum...et ad subsidia pauperum ac receptiones hospitium vel cunctas eiusdem congregationis necessitates consolandas'.
40 Ibid.: 'ita videlicet ut quicquid de ipsis rebus rectores et ministri...disponere atque ordinare vel statuere voluerint, libero in omnibus perfruantur arbitrio preter hoc solum quod nunquam de fuldensi monasterio commutent, vel vendant, vel cuiquam laico in beneficium concedant'.   41 *DLD* 141.

without the contrary intervention of anyone, in our memory and that of our wife and for the salvation of our progeny and that of Otbert and his wife.'[42] Finally, a grant of former royal lands by a priest to the monastery of St Gall contains a clause that would countermand the bestowal and demand the restoration of the lands to the fisc should the gift become alienated from the ecclesiastical ends (*ad usus monasterii*) designated by the grantor. On 1 May 879 a certain priest, Baldiuc, gave some properties to St Gall,[43] which he had acquired five years earlier in a grant from Louis the German.[44] Baldiuc effected the *traditio* with the permission of Louis's son, Charles the Fat (obviously because the grant concerned former royal lands granted to the monastery in Louis's memory). Charles forbade the officials of the monastery from granting the property in benefice to anyone; it was to remain solely for the monastery's use in Louis's memory, and if alienated, it would revert back to the royal fisc.[45]

These five charters (and more which one could select from the ninth and tenth centuries) demonstrate clearly that the kings and emperors, in conformity with the reforming tendencies of the time or, conversely, in response to the deteriorating spiritual and economic situation of many monastic congregations resulting from increased secularization of their property, attempted in their new grants to assure the upkeep of the brothers and of the monastic churches. At the same time, they strove to limit the abbot's arbitrary power of disposition. They assigned certain gifts (especially those from the royal fisc) exclusively as a prebend for the congregation or as a special endowment for the church, appended strong admonitions against alienation to these grants, expressly forbade the abbot to grant gifts to the prebend in

---

[42] Ibid. p. 198.5–11: 'et [ut] nullus abbas quippiam de illis rebus in beneficium praestare alicui praesumat, sed in usus praescriptorum fratrum in nostra elemosina ac dilecte coniugis nostrae Hemmae carissimeque prolis salute ipsiusque Otberti ac coniugis suae ... ad praefatum monasterium Prumiae perpertualiter permaneant absque alicuius contradicentis obstaculo'. Louis the German similarly had prohibited the bishop of Regensburg from alienating a property that he had granted on 1 May 859 from the royal fisc to the monks' table (*ad mensam monachorum*) at St Emmeram (*DLD* 96).   [43] *UBSG* 3.688 no. 8.   [44] *DLD* 165 (3 October 875).

[45] *UBSG* 3.688 no. 8: 'ut praedictae res iussu domini Karoli nulli hominum a rectoribus monasterii in beneficium tradantur, sed ad usus monasterii pro memoria piissimi patris sui Hludowici perpetualiter redigantur; sin alias, in fiscum publicentur'. Although this is the only extant royal repossession formula in a charter for a royal monastery, others appear in royal grants to chapters of canons and to an episcopal proprietary monastery. See: *DDO I* 202, 203, *DH II* 56, 192 and *DK II* 138.

benefice, and, in at least one instance, inserted a repossession formula.[46]

An examination of the private charters for monasteries in the ninth and tenth centuries provides similar evidence indicating an increased incidence of secularization and abbatial alienation of the prebend and documenting benefactors' attempts to limit the abbot's arbitrary disposition of monastic property. Although significant temporal and regional variations as well as developmental differences within individual monasteries necessarily condition such an examination, certain general and instructive patterns emerge nevertheless. Increasingly during the ninth century, benefactors – hoping for the redemption of their sins and of their souls through gifts of worldly possessions – directed their private *traditiones* and memorial gifts solely to the monastic prebend as the representative of the real spiritual property of the church (as opposed to property that might have been enfeoffed to vassals and thus employed for secular ends).[47] Further limitations on the abbot's right of disposition emerge in several charters specifically emphasizing the inalienability of the prebend; first by limiting grants to the brothers' use, and then by adding admonitions against alienation of the gift, normally directed at the abbot.[48] Perhaps the best example of this type of grant is Heririch's charter of 868 for the monastery of Prüm.[49] Heririch, probably apprehensive about abbatial encroachments, expressly and resolutely conferred the sole claim to his gift upon the brothers, who were to use it for their upkeep and would receive a special additional allocation to their daily food allotment once annually in his memory. He then sharply forbade the abbot, on threat of eternal damnation, to alienate the grant in any way.[50]

---

[46] For example, one finds royal provisions against episcopal or abbatial usurpation of the prebend in the charters of almost all of the kings and emperors of the east Frankish realm and the German kingdom and empire from Louis the German through to Henry IV. A sampling of these includes: *DLD* 96; *DArn* 133; *DO I* 203; *DO II* 234; *DDH II* 441, 442, 443, 448, 503; *DH III* 128; *DH IV* 153. For the one repossession formula, see n. 45 above.

[47] Pöschl (1908–12) I.29–30; *CDF* no. 403 (29 December 822): 'in elimosinam meam et coniugis meae ... filique mei ... ad utilitatem monachorum ibidem'; no. 638: 'in elimosinam meam ... pro aeterna requie animae meae ad servitium monachorum'.

[48] *MRUB* no. 110; *CDF* nos. 534, 535 (20 May 841), 555 (27 March 847), 601 (– March 869), 654 (6 April 910).   [49] *MRUB* no. 110.

[50] Ibid.:

Nullusque rectorum vel in beneficium vel prestariam dandi aut commutandi aut vendendi aut in alium quemlibet usum tranferendi horum quippiam potestatem habeat ... Et si quis rectorum diabolica presumptione huic devotioni nostre ac

In the course of time, however, benefactors found that limiting their grants with memorial obligations, gifts stipulated for the brothers and mere exhortations against abbatial usurpation or alienation did not always achieve the intended goal. In the face of increased alienations (which seriously endangered or abrogated the grantors' religious motives for a grant!), they inserted *formulae* into their charters, rendering them null and void if anyone alienated them.[51] This ensured that they and their descendants would maintain control over their grants. Various examples of private charters containing this kind of *formula* have come down to us from several monasteries, such as St Gall, Werden, Fulda, St Maximin and Lorsch, in the ninth and tenth centuries.[52] One of the earliest *formulae* of this type appears in Count Werinhar's charter of 30 July 846 for the monastery of Lorsch.[53] Werinhar granted the monastery several possessions in Biblis, Wattenheim and Zullenstein (which he had received ten years earlier from Louis the German)[54] for his own spiritual salvation, as well as that of the king, one of his own vassals and the vassal's wife. The grant contained numerous stipulations, but eventually the properties would devolve fully to the monastery to be used specifically for the brothers' *mensa*.[55] Further, Werinhar stated that the properties could not be granted in benefice to anyone unless the monastery

deliberationi dementie ipsius domni salvatoris commisse in rebus ipsis vel elemosina nostra contrarius aut fraudator exstiterit, iusto iudicio dei omnipotentis procellatur perpetuique anathematis vinculo obligatus in iudicio magni diei coram ipso domno salvatore rationem reddens in conspectu ss. angelorum santorumque omnium alienus eorum consorcio exstet in perpetuum.

Heririch concluded by adding a more secular admonition to his family and descendants not to abrogate his charter on penalty of paying 100 pounds of gold and 50 pounds of silver to the fisc. *DLD* 131 (12 April 870) confirms Heririch's grant.

[51] Matthäi (1877) 21–4 and Kallen (unpub. diss. 1924) 7. Although benefactors normally directed their admonitions and repossession clauses at abbots or leaders of the institution, many grants also contained warnings and penalty clauses aimed at family or descendants who might abrogate or counter their wishes (n. 50 above). The penalty usually comprised a monetary fine paid either to the monastery or the fisc or half to each and, sometimes, a threat of spiritual damnation or a sin against God to be carried into the hereafter, that is, imposing the wrath of God and the saints.

[52] *UBSG* 1.179 no. 180 (29 May 806), 1.334 no. 359 (816–37), 2.4–5 no. 385 (29 August 842), 2.202–3 no. 691; and *UBGNR* 1.30 no. 65. For similar charters from Fulda, St Maximin and Lorsch, see: *CDF* 277 no. 613; *MRUB* nos. 83 (1 April 853), 206 (8 April 960) and 268 (963); and *CL* 1 nos. 27, 33, 40; *CL* 2 no. 532.

[53] *CL* 1.310–11 no. 27 (Reg. 3327).   [54] *DLD* 19 (26 May 836).

[55] *CL* 1.311 no. 27: 'Post obitum vero nostrum utreque memorate res cum omni integritate ad prenominatum venerabile monasterium absque ullius contradictione recipiantur, et in eius potestate atque domino permaneant, fratribus specialiter ad sustentaculum.'

(that is, the congregation) could make better use of the properties through a precarial grant. In the case of an illegal grant in benefice, Werinhar stipulated that his heirs had the right to revoke the grant and divide the land among themselves.[56] Finally, the count stipulated (presumably with Louis the German's consent) that anyone who violated or attempted to surmount the conditions of the charter must pay a fine of one pound of gold and twelve pounds of silver to the monastery, enforced by the fisc, that is, the king or a royal official.[57] Another *formula* of this type from Fulda stated that the properties were granted to the monastery 'on the condition that from the present day they remain fixed and unwavering for the private service of the aforementioned martyr and the brothers there serving God, and that they never be granted in benefice to any cleric, layman or any other person; and if that is ever done, we or our descendants may repossess these properties by hereditary law'.[58]

The history of a single property granted to the monastery of St Emmeram in Regensburg, seen in the context of the general history of the monastery and its relations with the bishopric between *c.* 972 and 1031, enables us to discern how individual grantors and their heirs attempted to enforce the repossession *formulae* in their grants, and sheds some light on the intended meaning of many of these clauses. Some time between 972 and 974, Judith, duchess of Bavaria (wife of Henry I of Bavaria), issued two separate charters granting a property at Aiterhofen to the common use of the monks of St Emmeram.[59] In the second charter she added a repossession clause in relation to her heirs in the event

---

[56] Ibid.: 'et nulli umquam in beneficium dentur. Quod si factum fuerit, heredes mei illud inde abstrahere licentiam habeant, atque inter se dispertiri, excepto nisi maior utilitas eidem monasterio per prestariam acquiri possit.'

[57] Ibid.: 'Et si aliquis contra hoc nostre donationis testamentum resultare voluerit, atque illud convellere atque evacuare temptaverit, primitus Christum, et sanctum martyrem eius N. nefandis ausibus suis contrarium sentiat, et insuper fisco distringente multam de rebus propriis parti predicti monasterii coactus exsolvat, auri videlicet libram I, argenti pondo XII, et nec sic quod conatur repetere possit evindicare: sed hoc donatio firma et stabilis omni tempore permaneat. Stipulatione subnixa.'

[58] *CDF* no. 613 (23 July 876): 'ea videlicet ratione ut a die praesente ratum et stabile permaneat ad privatum praedicti martyris servitium et fratrum illic deo servientium et ut nullius clerici vel laici aut alicuius personae beneficium nunquam fiat et si unquam factum fiat nos iure hereditario praedictum locum accipiamus vel successores nostri accipiant'.

[59] *Traditionen Regensburg* pp. 145–7 nos. 195, 196; no. 195: 'tradidit memorata domna ad altare sancti Emmerammi et ad commune servitium monachorum'; no. 196: 'ut monachi ibidem … ad communem utilitatem perpetualiter eandem curtem possideant'. Her son, Duke Henry II, appears as her advocate in both charters.

that any bishop usurped the property for his private *servitium* or
granted it in benefice to any of his vassals.[60] For the background
information necessary to understand fully the later history of this
property we must briefly survey the relations between the
monastery and the bishop in the late ninth and early tenth
centuries.

St Emmeram was not a royal monastery. Before Bishop
Wolfgang reformed the monastery in 975 by placing the reform
monk Ramwold of St Maximin in Trier as the independent
abbot, St Emmeram had been a monastic chapter of the
Regensburg bishopric. Afterwards St Emmeram remained a
proprietary monastery of the bishop of Regensburg, but one that
had gained a considerable amount of independence from the
bishop, and possessed very close royal connections, especially with
Otto III and Henry II.[61] Bishop Wolfgang, who had maintained a
close personal relationship with Abbot Ramwold and had a great
interest in the reform and well-being of the monks, died in 994.
Soon after that, his successor, Bishop Gebhard I, a former royal
chaplain,[62] attempted to employ the monastery's goods and
property for his own ends. He thus renewed the policies of former
bishops that had brought the monastery to the state of decline in
which Wolfgang had found it before he instituted a reform.[63]
Already when Otto III visited St Emmeram in 996, Abbot
Ramwold and the monks complained to him about large
confiscations of property made by Bishop Gebhard. Otto,
convinced and moved by Ramwold's complaint, summoned
Gebhard before the altar of St Emmeram to account for his
actions. Then he warned Gebhard not to encroach upon the
monastery's property in the future and to leave it in peace as it
stood under his (royal) protection.[64] Probably as a result of this
judgement, Gebhard I, unlike Wolfgang, no longer appears
mentioned as a recipient or co-recipient in the *traditiones* of St
Emmeram; also, his actions against the monastery appear to have

---

[60] Ibid. no. 195: 'Si vero aliquis episcoporum per futura tempora succedentium ad suum,
quod fieri non credo, privatum servitium redigere vel vassallis suis ad beneficium dare
temptaverit, heres meus sicut reliqua sibi derelicta hereditario iure et hanc curtem
possideat.'   [61] Budde (1914).

[62] Gebhard became bishop of Regensburg when Otto III passed over Tagino, the
candidate already designated by Wolfgang and duly elected by the congregation, and
arbitrarily appointed Gebhard. This led to considerable strife with the Duke of Bavaria,
who supported Tagino. See Thietmar 6.42–3 pp. 268–71 and BU 1121b, 1142a.

[63] Budde (1914) 164–5, 169–71.

[64] Arnold, *De sancto Emmeramo* bk 2 c. 33 pp. 566–7; BU 1163c.

resulted in frequent admonitions and repossession *formulae* directed against the bishops of Regensburg in subsequent *traditiones*.[65] Wolfgang's institution of an independent abbot carried with it an additional complication. Whereas before, the monastery's property had consisted merely of the brothers' prebend with no separate endowment for an abbot, the reform of the monastery noticeably raised its prestige and thus gifts increased considerably, surpassing the needs of the congregation. Obviously, as we have seen in other monasteries, the abbot could thus create his own separate endowment with the surplus and even grant property in benefice to ministerials or vassals. According to the *traditiones*, this is exactly what happened. We now find *traditiones* containing admonitions and repossession clauses directed not only at the bishops, but also at the abbots.[66]

Later information reveals, however, that the struggle between the monastery and the bishops of Regensburg had neither abated nor been fully resolved. Thietmar of Merseburg, an eyewitness, reports that in May of 1009 Abbot Richolf and the brothers of St Emmeram humbly pleaded once again, this time to King Henry II, about Bishop Gebhard.[67] Moreover, the account of Arnold, an eleventh-century monk of St Emmeram, and the evidence of royal charters provide us with other details of the struggle.[68] Apparently Aiterhofen, the property granted to the monks of St Emmeram by Duchess Judith in 972–4, was one of the properties confiscated or usurped by Bishop Gebhard. Thus, in accordance with the repossession clause in Judith's charter and as one of Judith's rightful heirs, her grandson, Bruno, bishop of Augsburg (brother of King Henry II), attempted to repossess the property on account of the bishop's illegal confiscation.[69] The monks of St Emmeram, on the

---

[65] *Traditionen Regensburg* nos. 260, 276, 291, 298, 310, 413, 469, 474, 498, 507, 516.

[66] *Traditionen Regensburg* nos. 474, 507; Budde (1914) 170–2.

[67] Thietmar 6.41. Further support of Thietmar's report and of the monks' complaints against Bishop Gebhard exist in a charter issued by Henry II at exactly this time. On 20 May 1009 Henry granted a royal *mansus* to Prühl, another proprietary monastery of the bishop of Regensburg. In this grant, Henry specifically stated that if the bishop of Regensburg abolished the monastery or attempted to impair the monastic life there the granted *mansus* would revert again to royal possession (*DH II* 192: 'si quis Ratisponensis ecclesie episcopus, quod absit, idem monasterium destruere vel monachiam vitam inibi violare presumpserit, prescriptus mansus iterum ad regales redeat mansus'). It is no accident that one of two charters of Henry II having some kind of a repossession formula occurred at precisely this time for a proprietary monastery of the bishop of Regensburg.

[68] Arnold, *De sancto Emmeramo* bk 2 c. 57 pp. 570–1; *DDH II* 441, 442, 443.

[69] Arnold, *De sancto Emmeramo* bk 2 c. 57 p. 571.

other hand, appear to have claimed that they remained rightful owners of the property because Gebhard had long since restored it to them.[70] Bruno took his case before both the district court which possessed jurisdiction over Aiterhofen and the ducal court at Regensburg, presided over by Duke Henry V of Bavaria in the presence of Queen Kunigunda, who was Duke Henry's sister. In both instances the courts rejected Bruno's claim. Eventually, King Henry II, who as co-heir also had a claim to the property, adjudicated the case.[71]

By virtue of his royal power and most probably in accordance with the true sense of Judith's repossession formula, Henry II rejected his brother's claim for a full restitution of Aiterhofen to Judith's heirs and formally adjudged the property to the monks of St Emmeram.[72] Other *traditiones* for St Emmeram, as well as the judgements of the district and the ducal courts in this case, support Henry's interpretation of the repossession clause. Numerous grants stipulate that if a bishop or anyone else usurps the property or grants it in benefice, the property reverts to the heirs of the grantor until they are able to assure its restoration to the monks.[73] This interpretation of repossession *formulae* removes the apparent injustice contained in such clauses *vis-à-vis* the monks. If interpreted literally, the monks, to whom the property was originally granted, suffered the loss of their property first at the hands of the usurper and second at the hands of their benefactor's heirs. In short, should anyone succeed in usurping or granting their property in benefice, the monks would lose the property regardless; and this does not seem to reflect or effect the original purpose of the benefactor(s). It is more likely, as in the case of Aiterhofen, that the many repossession clauses have a deterrent function *vis-à-vis* would-be aggressors and a restitutive function *vis-à-vis* monks, even when the grant does not explicitly state this. A sizeable number of royal restitutions of prebendal properties seem to support this contention. This also seems to be the intent of the repossession clause contained in Henry II's charter of 1020 issued for the nunnery of Göss, but here the founders of the monastery, who gave it over into the royal *libertas*, may have had the clause included as a hedge against Henry himself.[74]

---

[70] Hirsch (1862–75) 2.216.   [71] Arnold, *De sancto Emmeramo* bk 2 c. 57 p. 571.

[72] *DH II* 442; Matthäi (1877) 24 n. 3; Budde (1914) 174–5.

[73] *Traditionen Regensburg* nos. 291, 298, 304, 310, 413, 469, 498, 516.

[74] *DH II* 428. See Seibert (1991) 513–14 and at n. 81 below.

On 3 July 1021 Henry II issued three charters for St Emmeram, two confirming its possession of Vogtareuth and Aiterhofen and the last confirming the totality of its possessions acquired through *traditiones*.[75] All three charters contain an identical *formula* excluding the properties from all ecclesiastical and judicial power of the bishop, forbidding him to alienate any of the properties from the brothers' use, and granting the abbot full power of disposition over the properties as long as his actions proved advantageous to the needs of the brothers.[76] In short, Henry II had assured the monastery of its own properties and granted it full administrative power over those properties. The case of Aiterhofen demonstrates particularly well that private and royal *formulae* against abbatial and episcopal abuse did not merely have a deterrent function. In specific cases, they caused the actual restoration of an illegally seized property to a monastery or its brothers and facilitated the creation of a separate administration of monastic and prebendal properties.[77]

Thus, private benefactors and even kings realized that without some sort of guarantee the conditions specified in their *traditiones* remained tenuous. Therefore, they endeavoured to limit abbatial and episcopal confiscations or usurpations and other secularizations of monastic properties granted to the brothers by inserting a new type of *formula* in their charters demanding revocation of the grant should it be alienated. Often private grantors accomplished this in conjunction with the king. A royal charter of Henry I in 929 for the monastery of Kempten provides us with an example where a private benefactor had his *traditio*, which contained various conditions and provisions (including a repossession formula – 'if

---

[75] *DDH II* 441, 442, 443. *DH II* 441 confirms the possession of the manor of Vogtareuth, which Count Warmund had granted to the monks of St Emmeram *c.* 959 by means of a royal charter of Otto I. Thus *DH II* 441 is a confirmation of *DO I* 203.

[76] *DDH II* 441, 442, 443:

ea videlicet ratione ut nec episcopus eiusdem loci nullaque ecclesiastica vel iudicaria potestas aliquam habeat potestatem prenominatam curtem prefate ecclesiae auferre vel usibus fratrum ibidem sub monachia institutione deo servientium abalienare, sed predictus Richolfus eiusdem loci abbas suique successores liberam exinde habeant potestatem quicquid eis placuerit faciendi ad utilitatem tantum modo fratrum ibidem sub regula sancti Benedicti deo sanctoque Heimmerammo famulantium, omnium hominum contradictione remota.

Neither *DH II* 441 nor *DH II* 442, however, contain a repossession clause as the original grants did.

[77] In St Emmeram's land register of 1031 (ed. Dollinger [1982] 455 no. 5) Aiterhofen still remained a possession of the monastery.

they are alienated from them [the brothers], let them revert to the donors or their successors'), confirmed and validated by the king.[78] Similarly, in 959 Otto I issued two charters, one for the canons of Salzburg cathedral and the other for the monks of St Emmeram.[79] Both grants derived from Count Warmund, who had given them originally to the respective chapters for the sustenance (*annonam*) of their members; and both contained a repossession clause calling for the restitution of the properties to Duchess Judith, her son Duke Henry II, or their closest heirs should any bishop or noble attempt to seize the properties or divert them from their stipulated purpose.[80] Many of the royal restoration charters of the tenth and early eleventh centuries for monasteries, moreover, involve properties designated to the brothers' prebend. These, like Aiterhofen, may have come to the monasteries in grants originally containing repossession clauses.[81]

Although the limitations written into the royal and private charters of the ninth and tenth centuries in no way instituted monastic property divisions by themselves, they do document the gradual and successive developments that led finally to such divisions. By binding certain donations to specific and defined purposes, and by freeing certain properties and assets from the abbot's power of disposition, benefactors of this period gradually increased the conventual or brothers' endowment and as a consequence slowly eroded the unity of monastic property. In this way their charters smoothed the way for formal separation of the congregation's possessions from the remaining property of the monastery.[82] The variety of limitations with their temporal and regional variations, moreover, contributed in part to the manifold development of monastic property separations.[83]

---

[78] *DH I* 19 (30 June 929): 'si eis [fratribus] abstraherentur, ad condonatores vel successores eorum remerarent'. The repossession clause in this charter may well be a consequence of the vast confiscations made in the early tenth century by Duke Arnulf of Bavaria. See Reindel (1953) 80–92 no. 40, 147–8 no. 75.   [79] *DDO I* 202, 203.

[80] *DO I* 202: 'ea tamen ratione ut, si episcopus eiusdem monasterii hec suprascripta de annona canonicorum violenter eripiat, cunta redeant in potestatem domne Iudite et filii eius Heinrici ducis'. *DO I* 203: 'ea tamen ratione ut, si episcopus eidem monasterio presidens aut aliqua potens persona hanc traditionis firmitatem violenter infringere voluerit, cuncta que tradita fuerant, redeant in ius et potestatem domine Iudite et filii eius Heinrici ducis seu ipsorum heredis proximi'.

[81] To list a few of these charters: *DK I* 17; *DO I* 176; *DDO II* nos. 57, 97, 133; *DDH II* 193, 212; *DK II* 39, 139. See also n. 45 above.

[82] R. Schieffer (1976) 263, 269–72 has made similar observations concerning the development of property divisions in the German cathedral chapters.

[83] Pöschl (1908–12) I.29–31.

DEVELOPMENT OF MONASTIC PROPERTY DIVISIONS

The west Frankish realm

Evidence derived from other royal charters indicates at least two further stages in the evolution of monastic property divisions: first, the creation of separate special endowments for the brothers, inalienable and unburdened by a royal or an abbatial *servitium*, but remaining under the abbot's general administration, and second, the establishment of conventual prebends under the direct administrative control of the monks or their appointed provost (thus distinguishing conventual endowments or prebends even more directly from the remaining possessions of the monastery). west Frankish and German cathedral chapters exhibited a similar pattern of development. Sometimes the development of a separate prebend in the monasteries and in the cathedral chapters is exactly the same and occurs simultaneously, and at other times it is varied.[84] These same charters in turn substantiate the view that during the ninth century in the majority of the larger monasteries (predominantly in the west Frankish realm) such property divisions or special endowments were created on congregational, abbatial or royal initiative, or a combination of the three.[85] In royal charters beginning as early as the late eighth century one finds specific charters and charter *formulae* that initiate or confirm monastic property division.[86] Common to a majority of these charters is a comprehensive prohibition *formula* forbidding the abbot or leader of the monastery to diminish in any way the properties allocated to the brothers, to employ them for his personal use, to grant them in benefice, or to exact *servitium* of any kind from them.[87] Some of the charters, furthermore, state the

---

[84] See R. Schieffer (1976) 263, 269–72.

[85] Matthäi (1877) 20–5; Pöschl (1928) 26; Wehlt (1970) 78; and Lesne (1910) 2–3.

[86] DKar 97 (10 May 755), for which see below n. 90; *MGH Formulae Merowingici et Karolini aevi* p. 304 Form. Imp. 25 (for chapters of canons); *DKK* 92 (23 March 847) for St Amand in vol. 1 p. 249, 11. 10–15: 'quod propter suspectas succedentium rectorum voluntates monachis…ad eorum petitionem ex facultatibus ipsius cenobii… segregavimus villas quasdam que proprie fratribus deservirent nec per ullam occasionem valerent a quolibet deinceps abbate ad usus alios detorqueri'. *DKK* 111 (26 February 849) for St Pierre de Jumièges in vol. 1 p. 296, 11. 8–10: 'quasdam villas ex prefati monasterii abbatia secundum eorum electionem usibus et stipendis eorum deputasse et ab aliis villis eiusdem abbatie suorum usuum selegisse'.

[87] Poupardin, *Saint-Germain-des-Prés* 1.46 no. 28 (13 January 829) [= BM² no. 857]: 'ut nullas abba per successiones quod salubri egit consilio subtrahere aut minuere audent, aut ad suos usus retorqueat aut alicui in beneficio tribuat, sed neque servitia ex eis

general reason for the allocation or the division,[88] and a few designate the actual number of monks for which the conventual portion should suffice.[89]

As early as 775, Charlemagne, at the request of Abbot Hitherius of Tours, issued a royal charter confirming numerous estates that Hitherius's predecessor, Autlandus, had set aside for the brothers' *mensa* and general upkeep. Each month throughout the year these estates would supply the brothers' needs and the king expressly stipulated that the brothers' cellarer should administer this special allotment.[90] A series of charters for Saint-Germain-des-Prés[91] and St Denis[92] demonstrate especially well the successive nature of the property division. In both cases Louis the Pious, at the request of the secular abbot, established set amounts of provisions and supplies that the abbot had to provide for the brothers and the church, and he allocated some special endowments (incipient property separations) exclusively for the brothers' use. Later, Charles the Bald confirmed and strengthened his father's charters for both monasteries and in the process enacted a full division of abbatial and conventual property, thus granting the monks their own prebend.[93] In fact, many of Charles the Bald's charters for monasteries either initiate or confirm separate property allocations.[94] In 840, a diploma of Lothar I, Louis the Pious's oldest son, similarly confirmed an abbatial–fraternal property separation that Louis's emissaries had enacted some time between 829 and 836 at Flavigny.[95] These, and many similar charters, clearly record the

---

exactet, neque paraveredos aut expensas ad hospitum susceptionis recipiat, neque ullos in aliqua re exactiones inde exigat'.

[88] *DKK* 92 (23 March 847): 'quod propter suspectas succedentium rectorum voluntates monachis…ad eorum petitionem ex facultatibus ipsius cenobii…segregavimus villas quasdam'. *DKK* 177 (25 September 855): 'propter rerum diminutionem quas praeteriti praelati eiusdem monasterii inordinatius quam decuit saecularibus attribuerant'.

[89] Poupardin, *Saint-Germain-des-Prés* 1.46 no. 28: 'Hec enim, ut putamus, ad usus centum .XX. monachorum sufficiunt.' *DDKK* 247, 304, 363.

[90] *DKar* 97 (10 May 755): 'qualiter antecessor suus Autlandus abba quasdam villas instituerit, quae fratribus mensuatim per totum annum servire deberent…Similiter statuimus…ut eiusdem monasterii cellerario fratrum ministretur.' Later, in 832, Louis the Pious confirmed this charter (BM[2] 909 = Bouq. 6.582) as did Charles the Bald in 844 or 845 (*DKK* 61).

[91] Poupardin, *Saint-Germain-des-Prés* 1.43–7 no. 28; *DKK* 363 (20 April 872).

[92] *MGH Conc.* 2.2 no. 53 pp. 688–94 (22 January 832); a charter of Louis the Pious from 26 August 832 (Bouq. 6.579 = BM[2] 906), which confirmed the precepts contained in the document of 22 January 832; and *DKK* 247 (19 September 862).

[93] Pöschl (1908–12) 1.24–8 provides a detailed analysis of these two charters of Louis the Pious and Charles the Bald for Saint-Germain-des-Prés.

[94] E.g. *DDKK* 92, 197, 247, 304, 363 and 372. [95] *DLoth* I 50 (4 December 840).

development and establishment of monastic property division in the west Frankish realm.[96] In fact, ninth-century charters instituting monastic property separations occur exclusively in cases where a canon or a layman stood at the head of a regular monastic congregation.[97] One has to consider the dramatic increase in charters enacting property divisions and creating conventual prebends (especially under Charles the Bald) in the light of his heavy lodging and servitial demands on the royal monasteries as well as his tendency to enfeoff whole abbeys to his vassals. Aware of the possible deleterious effects of his policies on monastic congregations, Charles sought to safeguard the livelihood of the brothers.[98]

In Lotharingia, although most of the monasteries belonged to the east Frankish realm after the *Divisio Regni* of 870, and to the German kings and emperors in the tenth and eleventh centuries, nevertheless their development in the ninth century strongly resembled the trends of monastic development in the west Frankish realm. Thus, the proprietary holdings and rights of monks in relation to their abbots advanced significantly in Lotharingia as well. Moreover, the royal diplomas conferred on the Lotharingian monasteries exhibit the characteristic style of the west Frankish charters written for similar purposes. Several charters for Lotharingian monasteries document this process well. A diploma of Charles the Bald for the monastery of St Mihiel on the Meuse River confirmed and strengthened a lost charter of Lothar I, which had allotted special properties exclusively for the upkeep of the brothers.[99] Charles's grant not only recognized the properties set aside for the brothers, but also appended a strong prohibition *formula* directed at the abbot or any other authority, and assigned the properties to the special administration of the provost, acting with the consent of the brothers.[100] Later, in 895, a diploma of Zwentibold for the same monastery expressly recognized the existence of the prebend of the brothers, and increased it by forty-

---

[96] *DDKK* 92, 111, 156, 160, 177, 191, 197, 215, 293, 304, 306, 338, 357, 372.

[97] Lesne (1910) 64–5, 69–71 and (1910–43) 2.1.142–5 esp. 142 no. 3; and Semmler (1958) 283–4. See also Brühl (1957) 8–13.

[98] See Brühl (1968) 39–52; Felten (1974) 427–31; and Nelson (1979).

[99] *DKK* 431 (24 June 877).

[100] Ibid. p. 464, 11. 25–8: 'ut nullus abbas vel quelibet alia potestas ordinandis eorum rebus se intermittat, scilicet vel ministeriales in prefato monasterio mutare vel prebendas dare, sed tantum preposito eiusdem loci cum consensu ceterorum fratrum res eorum sine alicuius perturbatione liceat ordinare'.

five *mansi* and several chapels.[101] Moreover, it called particular attention to a property division when it stated that the properties formerly had belonged to the monastery, but not to the prebend of the monks; on the contrary, they had pertained personally to the abbot.[102]

Similarly, another charter of Zwentibold in 897 for the monastery of Nivelles[103] confirmed and renewed a diploma of Charles the Bald that had assigned the congregation specific properties as a prebend.[104] As with many other monasteries, Nivelles appears to have abandoned the stricter monastic life headed by a regular abbess, and to have become a house of canons and canonesses headed by a lay abbess, Gisela.[105] Echternach, which also had become a monastery of canons and stood under Ratbod, archbishop of Trier, received royal confirmation of ninety-seven and a half *mansi* to its prebend from Zwentibold.[106] Close by at St Maximin in Trier a diploma of King Arnulf,[107] which Zwentibold and Charles the Simple later confirmed,[108] established a prebend for the brothers on which the possessor of the monastery could exact no *servitium* except the customary payment rendered on the benediction of the abbot.[109] In addition, Arnulf granted the brothers the right to appoint (and, if necessary, remove) a special

---

[101] *DZ* 3 (14 August 895): 'ad suam prebendam concederemus'. Louis the Child confirmed this charter in 908 with *DLK* 62, and in 915, Charles the Simple confirmed the majority of these properties for the monks of St Mihiel without using Zwentibold's diploma. See *DKE* 11.

[102] *DZ* 3: 'Hocque totum quod concedimus ad predictam abbatem pertinebat antea, non tamen ad monachorum annonam, sed ad abbatem specialiter rediit.'

[103] *DZ* 16 (26 July 897).   [104] *DKK* 433 (9 July 877).

[105] Concerning Gisela and the legal status of Nivelles, see Hoebaux (1952) 109–12. On the technical differences between the life of a nun (according to a monastic rule) and that of a canoness (according to the rule of the canons), see Parisse (1978) 109–14, (1990) 319–22 and (1991) 478–83; and Fichtenau (1984) 300–5.

[106] *DZ* 5 (28 October 895): 'quatinus fratribus... quod ab antecessoribus nostris ad eorum provendam [prebendam, ms.c] habuerant concederemus... tales res quales adhuc habent ad illorum victum concedimus atque donamus'.

[107] *DArn* 114 (11 February 893).

[108] *DZ* 14 (13 June 897); *DKE* 69 (1 January 912).

[109] *DArn* 114 (11 February 893): 'nec nobis neque illi, qui hanc abbatiam tenuerit, aliquod servitium impendant, excepto hoc quod more solito benedictionem suam illi offerant, qui monasterio presit, potestatemque teneant super ipsas res suam prepositum specialiter constituere eumque pari modo, si bene officium praepositurae suae non expleat, degradere'. The confirmation charter of Zwentibold (*DZ* 14) limits this freedom of the prebend from *servitium* with the following words: 'nullique illius abbatiae dominorum quiddam servitii inpendat ex praescriptis rebus nisi solummodo nobis et successoribus nostris regibus sub nostra semper, non sub abterius [alterius, mss. C, D] ullius tuitione quiete domino serviens'.

provost for their prebend.[110] Eighty years later, Otto II recognized
the legal existence of a brothers' prebend at St Maximin in a
diploma which restored to the congregation certain prebendal
properties that previously had been granted illegally in benefice.[111]

The east Frankish and German experience

Outside Lotharingia, which shared in the west Frankish development, this specific type of charter, so characteristic of the
monasteries of the west Frankish realm, does not appear.
Nevertheless, scattered evidence from the ninth century and good
documentation from the tenth and early eleventh centuries
indicates that a similar type of monastic property division
materialized slowly in the east Frankish realm and became firmly
established during the German imperial period. The economic,
political and religious conditions that instigated and, in some
ways, presupposed the assignment of special conventual endowments and the eventual divisions of monastic property did not
exist to the same extent east of the Rhine. Thus, development was
slower there. For instance, in comparison with the west Frankish
monasteries, those in the east Frankish realm – with the possible
exception of Lorsch and St Gall and, perhaps, Fulda, Hersfeld and
Corvey – did not at this early date possess property and assets in
such abundance that the abbot had a huge excess to grant in
benefice or to secularize, and thus endanger the needs of the
monastery and the congregation. Moreover, Christianization and
the establishment of monastic communities occurred much later
east of the Rhine, especially in the areas north of the Main River.
Thus, in the ninth century and the early tenth most of the
monasteries there did not yet exhibit basic preconditions that
made reform necessary. Thus, the ninth-century monastic reform

---

[110] *DArn* 114: 'super ipsas res suum prepositum specialiter constituere eumque pari modo,
si bene officium praepositurae suae non expleat, degradare'. The existence of a brothers'
prebend at St Maximin separate from the remaining properties of the monastery is also
confirmed by a passage in Sigehard, *Ex miraculus s. Maximini*, c. 11 p. 231: 'Siquidem
post memoriatum Megingaudum potestatibus et usibus huius regni ducum haec abbatia
subiacuit, his tantum exceptis, quae fratrum sustenationi dudum sequestrata fuerant;
quae tamen ipsa, sicut et adhuc, eorum defensioni a regibus committebantur.'

[111] *DO II* 57 (27 August 973): 'qualiter venerabilis abbas Thietfridus coenobii sancti
Maximini ... piissimi genitoris nostri Ottonis imperialem Ravenne adierit clementiam,
postulans quasdam proprietates praedicti confessoris Christi iure quidem prebendarias,
sed multis retro temporibus iniuste beneficiarias eiusdem loci coenobitis restituti'.

movement was more dominant in the west than in the east.[112] Widespread monastic reform appeared east of the Rhine first during the reigns of the three Ottos, all of whom displayed a favourable disposition to reform. This movement, the Lotharingian or Gorzean reform, spread slowly eastward via St Maximin in Trier, Einsiedeln and Regensburg.[113] In addition, the internal problems of the realm and the invasions of the ninth and tenth centuries did not affect the areas east of the Rhine as severely as those west of the Rhine. Consequently, the tendencies toward secularization of church property and decentralization of power to meet the needs of defence, and toward gradual feudalization which the difficulties of the period brought in their wake, did not manifest themselves as early or to the same degree east of the Rhine.

Since the Carolingians administered much of the territory east of the Rhine with a different emphasis, that is, as a march region with larger areas concentrated under the control of stronger 'super counts', *duces* (meaning military commanders, not indigenous dukes) or margraves, these areas did not experience the same degree of decentralization during the invasions of the late ninth and early tenth centuries as the west Frankish territories, which were organized more intensely on the basis of the county. Hans K. Schulze has studied the formation of counties in the east Frankish realm and sees evidence that, even in Saxony, counties were introduced in the mid-eighth century, but never systematically and always with regional variations.[114] The greater degree of decentralization in the west also appears to have created a higher instance of lay abbacy. In the context of discussing the development of lay abbacy in the Carolingian period, Franz Felten points to some similar factors that may account for the high rate of lay abbacy in the west and in Lotharingia that was absent from in the east. To a certain extent, he sees these factors as rooted in some

[112] Concerning the ninth-century monastic reform, predominantly west of the Rhine, and its legacy in the tenth century, see Semmler (1983) and (1989). On the few indications we have for the spread of the ninth-century reform east of the Rhine, see Semmler (1970) concerning monasteries in Saxony, especially Corvey and Herford, and Semmler (1958) esp. 292–5 and (1980) 186–7 regarding the reform in Fulda.

[113] In general concerning monastic reform under the Ottonians, see A. Hauck (1952) 3.343–88 esp. 372–88 and Keller (1964) 111–18. Specifically regarding the Gorzean reform in Germany, see Wolff (1930) and Hallinger (1950) vol. 1. Hallinger (1950) received praise and approval, as well as strong criticism. See T. Schieffer (1952) for the praise and Leclercq (1957) and Wollasch (1977) for the criticism.

[114] Schulze (1973) esp. 271–3, 295, and 345–8.

basic structural differences between the west and the east, such as: (1) a greater degree of feudalization in the west caused by many factors – the end of military expansion and a decreasing amount of royal property lessened the means available to reward vassals; the great impact of the civil wars of the 930s weakened all rulers; more intense invasions gave the nobility greater opportunities to expand their power; (2) Louis the German in the east beginning his rule from an inherently more stable position than Charles the Bald in the west, who had to struggle long and hard for his portion of the realm; and (3) a reform mentality of the ecclesiastics in the west which was highly advanced compared with that in the east and thereby more divisive of the relationship between rulers and churches.[115] Thus, the demands of the state on monastic property in the east during this period (except perhaps in Bavaria under Duke Arnulf) did not present the same burden or threat to monastic congregations there.[116] One indicator of this is that fewer royal monasteries in the east appear to have had secular or lay abbots, and therefore the need to institute monastic property divisions also was not so acute. For instance, Fulda only gradually developed a property division and maintained a regular abbot throughout.[117] Unfortunately, we have no information about property separations in Hersfeld, which was the only royal monastery east of the Rhine in the early tenth century that had a lay abbot, Otto, Duke of Saxony.

Thus, on account of these differing conditions, the development of special conventual endowments and especially the strengthening of the monks' proprietary rights over their prebend progressed more slowly east of the Rhine. Here the general development in the ninth and early tenth centuries consisted of restricted private and royal grants under abbatial control, and in the Ottonian period, of a significantly increasing number of grants from the royal fisc designated solely for the brothers. In the German

---

[115] Felten (1974) 426–31. Concerning Charles the Bald and Louis the German and the differing conditions in the west and the east in relation to the church, the nobles and invasions, see McKitterick (1983) 169–99 esp. 170–7. Reuter (1991a) 90–1 points to the military superiority of the east during the ninth-century invasions, and Reuter (1990) addresses the problems connected with the ending of Carolingian military expansion as early as the reign of Charlemagne.

[116] The *Notitia de servitio monasteriorum* of 819 (*CCM* 1.494) lists only four monasteries east of the Rhine that had to provide both *militia* and *dona* – Lorsch, Schuttern, Mondsee and Tegernsee. Of these four, only Lorsch and Tegernsee had great pre-eminence during the Ottonian–Salian period.   [117] Semmler (1958).

regions, even during the Ottonian period, a conventual endowment under the brothers' administration or an official
appointed by them remained an exception.[118]

Although the establishment of monastic property divisions in
Germany is not necessarily an exclusive phenomenon of the ninth
and tenth centuries, several examples from the ninth century and
one from the tenth demonstrate that such divisions did indeed
occur or exist east of the Rhine, especially in monasteries not
having a regular abbot. These, and perhaps those in German
Lotharingia, represent harbingers of a later development. A charter
of Louis the German in 858 for the royal convent of Herford gave
the nuns there certain properties exclusively for their subsistence,
forbade them to grant these possessions in benefice, and granted
them immunity and royal protection for the properties.[119]
Moreover, the wording of the charter implies that a separate
conventual *mensa* existed at Herford, and that the nuns may have
had some degree of administrative control and disposition over
their *mensa*.[120] Likewise, a royal charter of the following year
confirms that the monks of the cathedral monastery of St
Emmeram in Regensburg also possessed their own prebend
separate from the properties of the bishop.[121] Louis granted half of
a group of royal estates at Tulla in Pannonia to the monks' *mensa*
and forbade the bishop to grant the properties in benefice or to
seize them for his own use.[122] In addition, he stated that the monks
were the sole possessors of the lands and granted them the right of
disposition over the estates.[123] Thus, by the mid-ninth century the

---

[118] R. Schieffer (1976) 269, 281, 285, noted a similar pattern of development for the
property of the cathedral chapters.   [119] *DLD* 93 (13 June 853).

[120] Ibid.:

> ea scilicet ratione ut perpetuo sanctis monialibus ibidem…in cibariis et victualibus
> reliquisque usibus earum per futura tempora…consistant et in benefitio res ipse nulli
> concedantur, sed solummodo absolute ad mensam eorum iugiter deserviant, et nullus
> successor noster hanc auctoritatem largitionis nostrae aliter immutare possit neque
> ullus publicus iudex aut aliqua iudiciaria potestas aliquam molestiam aut contrarietatem
> in his rebus illis facere praesumat; sed liceat ipsis res suas libere et absolute domino
> adiuvante et nostra munitione tuente possidere omni iudiciaria remota potestate.

[121] *DLD* 96 (1 May 859).

[122] Ibid.: 'ea ratione ut ipsa medietas ipsius fisci ad mensam monachorum ibi domino
famulantium ibi iugiter deserviat, et nullus episcopus aut quislibet praelatus easdem res
in beneficium alicui dare sive ad opus suum recipere praesumat, sed solummodo ad
opus ipsorum deserviant'.

[123] Ibid.: 'memorati monachi praefatam medietatem fisci cum omnibus supra consisten-
tibus recipiant teneant aque possideant et quicquid exinde pro utilitate sua facere
voluerint, liberam et firmissimam in omnibus habeant potestatem Christo propitio
faciendi'.

monks of St Emmeram not only possessed their own prebendal properties, separate and distinct from the remaining properties of the cathedral, but had also achieved some degree of disposition over them independent of the bishop.[124] A few years later, in 863 or 864, Louis the German granted a charter to the monks of Niederaltaich that expressly recognized a division of the monastic property between the brothers and their abbot.[125] The diploma confirmed the existing prebend of the brothers and several new properties added to it by Abbot Otgar; and it prohibited the alienation of these properties from the brothers by future rulers, the abbot or anyone else. Then, distinctly calling attention to the property division, the charter stated: 'any remaining properties of the monastery of Niederaltaich, wherever they were, should be under the dominion and administration of the abbot, whom the brothers should elect according to the Rule of St Benedict'.[126] Whether or not the monks had independent control of their prebend remains unclear. Although the diploma does not contain a specific provision granting the brothers independent admin-istrative control or the right to establish their own advocate over the prebend, the specific words employed in relation to the abbot and the remaining properties of the monastery ('relique... res...pertinentes...sub domino et gubernatione abbatis existant') may perhaps suggest that the brothers exercised control of their prebend. If the abbot maintained administrative control of the brothers' prebend, why use both 'sub domino et [sub] guber-natione' when referring to the remaining monastic properties? While *domino* and *gubernatione* together may be a normal medieval pleonasm, it might also imply that the brothers had some administrative control, independent of the abbot, over their share of the monastic property. As in so many instances in the west, this case provides one of special properties being confirmed and instituted in a monastery that did not have a regular abbot at the time.[127]

A similar example exists for the convent at Essen, which was founded in the mid–ninth century by Bishop Altfrid of

---

[124] Budde (1914) 161–2.

[125] *DLD* 116 (18 December 864). When Matthäi (1877) 26 and Werner-Hasselbach (1942) 121 stated that no charter evidence for a monastic property division existed from the east Frankish realm, they overlooked this diploma of Louis the German. Kallen (1924) 202–3, on the other hand, recognized that some monastic property divisions east of the Rhine existed already in the ninth century.   [126] *DLD* 116.

[127] Abbot Otgar was also the bishop of Eichstätt.

Hildesheim. Although scholarly opinion varies, Altfrid appears to have founded Essen as a Benedictine nunnery.[128] During the period of common life the abbess administered the sizeable properties and incomes of the convent and had the right of free disposition. She, in turn, provided the sisters with a share from the totality of the monastic possessions for their upkeep and necessities. Then, some time presumably in the first half of the tenth century, the congregation abandoned the Benedictine observance and the common life and became a house of canonesses, with a succession of Ottonian princesses as its abbesses. With this shift in observance, the unified structure of the convent's property appears to have been broken by the creation of a conventual prebend separate from the remaining properties of the abbess. Although the final division of property resulted from a series of successive acts (similar to those at Saint-Germain-des-Prés),[129] a diploma of Otto I from 966 instructs us concerning its initial stages.[130] With this charter, Otto granted the canonesses at Essen a court at Ehrenzell that he had formerly given to his granddaughter Mathilda.[131] In addition, he issued to them a royal immunity for the property and prohibited all royal judges and public tax collectors, as well as the abbess and her advocate, from entering the court at Ehrenzell or from making any exactions there. Lastly, he conferred upon the canonesses the explicit right to administer the property through their own provost. Thus, with this charter, Otto established a prebendal property exclusively for the canonesses that remained separate from the remaining properties of the monastery and

---

[128] Semmler (1970) 310–15 cites specific connections to other monasteries and various references to the veneration of St Benedict, based on a late ninth-century sacramentary from Essen and other later Essen manuscripts, as evidence that Essen was founded as a Benedictine nunnery and remained so. On manuscripts and writing activity at Essen, see McKitterick (1991) 87–90. Weigel (1960) 54–6 contends that since Essen's foundation in the mid-ninth century, the canonesses and their abbess lived the common life according to the Rule of Chrodegang of Metz and in accordance with the provisions of the Aachen Synod of 816, and Goetz (1990) 137 also views Essen as a canonry from the beginning. While Semmler builds a good argument regarding the foundation of Essen, I cannot agree with him that Essen remained a nunnery because some time before the mid-tenth century it had become an Ottonian royal canonry. See also Kohl (1980) 127–39 esp. 135 who sees the situation similarly. In general regarding Ottonian female canonries see Parisse (1978) and (1991) 465–8, where he discusses the difficulties in distinguishing between nunneries and canonries in this period, and where at n. 11 he sees many of Semmler's conclusions about Benedictines in Saxony and Westphalia as too sweeping. [129] Weigel (1960) 54–6.

[130] *DO I* 325 (1 March 966).

[131] Mathilda appears as abbess of Essen in a charter of Otto II in 973 (*DO II* 49). She died there in 1011. See *DO III* 114 (5 February 993) and *Ann. Qued. s.a.* 1011 p. 80.

independent of the abbess's powers of exaction and administration.[132] This does not mean, however, that the canonesses had their own advocate for this property.[133] The charter states only that Otto granted administrative power over Ehrenzell to the canonesses in the person of their provostess and says nothing about a separate advocate for the canonesses' property. Although the abbess and her advocate lost any administrative, taxing and servitial rights to the property, in this case it is more plausible that the advocate, though restricted by the general *introitus* prohibition, retained his legal obligation to protect the canonesses and their property and to act as their legal and judicial representative. Thus, the abbess's advocate and the canonesses' advocate for their prebendal property could (and most probably did) remain one and the same person. Upon request of the provostess he could then enter the property to execute his legal obligations. In any case, this particular property appears to have remained firmly in the possession of the convent until the beginning of the thirteenth century.[134]

Additional evidence from the royal charters of the tenth century indicates or confirms that special conventual endowments, prebends or a *mensa* (most probably internally 'separated' from the remaining properties and assets of the monastery, but still under the abbot's or abbess's general administration)[135] existed in

---

[132] *DO I* 325:

> tradidimus in comitatu Hooldi comitis in pago Borhtergo curtem praedictam scilicet Ericseli cum omnibus appenditiis...cum omni integritate praedictis monialibus donavimus et sub perpetua emunitatis nostrae tuitione esse volumus, ita ut nullus noster iudex aut publicus fisci exactor nec non ipsa abbatissa vel advocatus vel alius aliquis praenominatam curtem ingredi audeat aut fredas exigendas aut paratas faciendas vel hominibus praescripti monasterii inibi habitantibus distractionem ingerendi vel aliud quid potestatis exercendi licentiam habeat, nisi moniales et praeposita quam sibi ipsae utilem et necessariam habeant, suis ut libuerit usibus adiungat.

[133] Cf. Weigel (1960) 18, who states that the property of Ehrenzell was taken away from the power of the abbess and her advocate and placed under its own (that is, the canonesses') advocate. Although this is indeed possible, in this situation it is not likely.

[134] Weigel (1960) 18.

[135] A charter of Adalbert, bishop of Metz, restoring many properties to the newly reformed monastery at Gorze, mirrors this situation perfectly. *Cartulaire de l'Abbaye de Gorze*, no. 92 (16 December 933) esp. pp. 169–70: 'Sepedictus namque constituit presul ut quicquid ad mensam fratrum pertineret, hoc abbas previderet, absque ullius interdictione...quod si omnem teneret abbatie terram, oporteret ei satellites tenere, cum quibus publice militaret, sin autem nil amplius haberet, nisi quod ad mensam fratrum pertineret, nullum deberet servitium, nisi fratribus ministrare et religionem previdere.' Similarly, a charter of Otto II for the convent at Nordhausen, *DO II* 83 (17

---

numerous monasteries, especially those situated in territories bordering the Rhine.[136] Moreover, this trend toward some sort of internal division of a monastery's estates probably had a much greater diffusion and general acceptance than the sources can document. For instance, a private charter of 1004 recorded an earlier property transaction of a Saxon noblewoman named Helmburg and her four daughters with the convent of Hilwartshausen which had been ratified in the presence of the king and which implied the existence of separate abbatial and conventual properties as early as 965 or 966.[137] Helmburg and her daughters granted several properties to the canonesses at Hilwartshausen with the specific stipulation that the grant be used for the upkeep of the canonesses and that no abbess might assume anything from the gift for her own *servitium* nor might she alienate the property through exchange.[138] On the basis of this transaction shortly after Hilwartshausen's foundation in 960, it appears that properties of the convent were already being divided internally between the abbess and the canonesses.[139] Also early in the 960s, when Otto I sent a commission of bishops and abbots to St Gall to investigate the monastic customs and practices there,[140] its members expressed astonishment and great praise for St Gall when they discovered that the abbot and the monks shared the same wine cellar, and that the abbot supplied the monks with their prescribed allowance from the common properties and assets of the monastery;[141] that is, the property and incomes of the monastery had *not* been internally divided.

In the course of the tenth century the economic, political and religious conditions of the German monasteries altered con-

---

June 974), states: '...eo tenore ut deinceps eidem ecclesiae ac sanctimonialibus ibidem servientibus vel per aevum servituris idem predium eiusque appertinentiae in perpetuum usum abbatissa hoc semper providente permaneat'.

[136] *DDLK* 35 (Kaiserswerth), 54 (Lorsch); *DK I* 17 (Murbach); *DDO I* 70 (Gorze), 168 (Oeren), 318 (Nivelles), 427 (Echternach); *DO II* 57 (St Maximin). Echternach, Murbach, Nivelles and St Maximin all had special conventual allotments already in the ninth century (see above at nn. 103–4 and 106–11, and *DK I* 17).

[137] Goetting (1979).

[138] Goetting (1979) 56–8 provides a new edition of the charter, p. 57: '...ea scilicet pactione, ut sanctimoniales ibidem Hildiwardeshusun deo servientes necessaria unde viverent inde habuissent nec ulla abbatissa aliquid de illo predio in suum servitium assumpsisset aut pro alio aliquo transmutando aufferret, et si aliquis in posterum fecisset, in die iudicii rationem reddidisset'.

[139] Goetting (1979) 40 and (1980) 158–9; K. Heinemeyer (1974) 143–5.

[140] For the dating, see Hallinger (1950) 1.187–99 at 195–6.

[141] Ekkehard IV, *Casus Sancti Galli* cc. 102, 103.

siderably. Since the mid-tenth century, when Otto I had embarked upon a policy destined to bind the churches and monasteries of the realm more closely to the central government, royal grants of property and sovereign rights to the spiritual institutions of the realm had multiplied dramatically.[142] Thus, the possessions and the legal rights of the German royal monasteries increased significantly as did their economic power and importance. With this royal munificence and the consequent rise in the wealth and power of royal monasteries, however, came additional obligations to the king and the realm. On an ever increasing scale the Ottonians requisitioned the abbots of the realm and the property of the monasteries to support the state politically, economically and militarily. For example, in Otto II's military levy of 981–2,[143] out of a total levy of almost 2000, eleven royal monasteries provided a military contingent of 442 fully outfitted knights, the great majority of whom were led into battle by their abbots. The monasteries' new wealth also made them inviting targets for secular and ecclesiastical nobles (often in co-operation with less than scrupulous abbots) wanting to enlarge their own power base at the monastery's expense.[144] At the same time, however, the Ottonian rulers designated more and more of their private gifts, as well as a majority of grants emanating from the royal fisc, solely for the congregation's use and thereby contributed to a developing prebend or conventual *mensa*.[145]

The increasing secular demands on monastic property for *servitium* and the progressive secularization of the abbot's position, which often led to abbatial encroachments of property, began to threaten the brothers' endowment. Thus, in order to protect their prebend, the monks needed some kind of internal reorganization

---

[142] An examination of the diplomas of the Ottonian rulers easily confirms this. Several statistical compilations and comparisons survey the charters for monasteries. See: Santifaller (1964) 35, 53–67, 78–115; J. Mayer (1901/1902) 12–15; and Seelig (unpub. diss. 1919) 30–42.   [143] *MGH Const.* 1 no. 436 pp. 632–3.

[144] *Casus s. Galli continuatio II* c. 3 pp. 152–3, where the abbot appears to have given many monastic possessions in benefice and regularly took part in secular business and intrigues with noblemen, and *DO I* 169 and *DO II* 57, where Archbishop Rotbert of Trier unjustly attempted to usurp the legal possession of St Maximin. These represent only two of many examples in the chronicles, histories, hagiographical sources and charters of this type of abuse. See also Beyerle (1925) 1.112/22 (*sic!*) concerning Abbot Witigowo of Reichenau.

[145] Matthäi (1877) 29, 53, 62, first recognized this fact, although he based his assumption on partially forged charters. In his investigation of Fulda's land registers, Werner-Hasselbach (1942) 134 has validated Matthäi's findings in regard to Fulda.

and division of properties within their monasteries. Owing to the abbot's secular duties, moreover, which tended to separate him more and more from the daily life of the monastery, a basic division of function between the abbot and the monks began to emerge. For instance, the abbot, in the exercise of his service to the king, might be called upon to attend the royal court, undertake diplomatic missions, and even lead a monastery's military contingent into battle; whereas the primary function of the monks was constant praise of God and prayer on behalf of the congregation, the king and the realm. This encouraged a corresponding division of the resources supporting those functions. Increased prosperity and greater secularization also worked negatively on monastic discipline. Abbots often pursued their secular obligations as tenant-in-chief or political advisor at court, to the neglect and detriment of their spiritual obligations to monastic discipline, to their congregation and to God.[146] Likewise, monks, because of their abbot's frequent absences, their own predominantly noble background (often they were the younger sons of noble families), and the increasing comforts afforded by the monastery's new prosperity, became lax in their monastic discipline. Not surprisingly, the monastic chronicles, and especially the *Vitae* of revered reformers of the late tenth and early eleventh centuries, repeatedly make references or allusions to the general decline of monastic discipline.

On the other hand, although a general decline in monastic discipline occurred in many monasteries at this time, the particular monastic *consuetudines* followed within a monastery formed an equally and often a more important role in the process of royally supported monastic reform. Frequently the introduction of a new or different custumal (*consuetudo*) caused a full-scale revolt on the part of a congregation accustomed to or following another (and often older) monastic tradition. Thus, by the late tenth and early eleventh centuries, economic, political and religious conditions existed in Germany (especially in regard to the monasteries) that somewhat resembled those in the western regions of the Carolingian realm in the ninth century. Under this new set of circumstances, one finds that the most significant and extensive reorganization of the tenurial arrangements of the German monasteries took place.

---

[146] *Casus s. Galli continuatio II* c. 3 p. 153, ll. 1–13.

As in the ninth century, the proprietary restructuring in the German royal monasteries occurred not only in response to generally increased governmental demands on church property, but also in the wake of a powerful new surge of reform activity. The last Saxon king, Henry II (1002–24), strongly supported and furthered the monastic reform movement that emanated from Gorze in Lotharingia and came to Bavaria through Wolfgang of Regensburg via St Maximin in Trier and Einsiedeln.[147] In general, this reform initiated a stricter and different monastic custumal (*consuetudo*) and called for more orderly estate management and improved economy with monastic lands. Henry had first encountered the Gorzean reform activity while duke of Bavaria,[148] and had employed one of its adherents, Godehard, to reform the Bavarian monasteries, Niederaltaich (995) and Tegernsee (1001). Although a true proponent of ecclesiastical and monastic reform, Henry was also a politically practical monarch and recognized the necessity of strengthening the rights and powers of kingship within Germany that had been successively weakened under Otto II and Otto III. To that end he instituted a general programme, a *Renovatio regni Francorum*, that is, a renewal of the Frankish realm.[149] A major part of this programme consisted of vigorously re-establishing the royal claim to a governmental right over the higher churches of the realm, the bishoprics and the royal monasteries,[150] and systematically augmenting their service in the politics and economy of the realm.[151] Thus, in conjunction with royally initiated Gorzean reform measures, Henry II confiscated or secularized some properties of the reformed royal monas-

---

[147] In general concerning monastic reform in Germany, see A. Hauck (1952) 3.443–515. Specifically regarding the Gorzean reform in Germany, see Wolff (1930), Hallinger (1950) vol. 1, and Vogtherr (1991) 430–6 regarding Corvey, Fulda and Hersfeld. For the monastic customs characteristic of the Gorzean reform, see Hallinger (1950) vol. 2.

[148] See Wühr (1948) 370–88, who covers the Bavarian reform movement within his discussion of Montecassino's reform.

[149] See Matthäi (1877) 66–7 and T. Schieffer (1951) 385–6, 394. Dieffenbach (unpub. diss. 1952) provides a detailed analysis of all aspects of this programme with an emphasis on the ecclesiastical arrangements, and Weinfurter (1986) looks closely at the secular aspects of Henry's 'programme'.

[150] The question as to whether the German king had a governmental or a proprietary right over the higher churches of the realm has not yet been answered adequately. For the background to the dispute, see Classen (1973) 426, 453–4, who leans toward the idea of a governmental right. For a summary of the constitutional issues, see T. Mayer (1950) 25–49.

[151] Concerning the *servitium regis* in this instance, see T. Schieffer (1951) 397–402. For a summary of Henry's policies, see Seibert (1991) 507–14. Concerning monastic reform in the context of Henry's overall programme, see Franke (1987) 107–16.

teries.[152] As a consequence of these increased secularizations and of the Gorzean reform measures, and in general accordance with the slowly developing conventual endowments of the tenth century, one finds the first evidence of formal monastic property divisions within the royal monasteries of the German realm.[153] Henry II's change in policy towards the *Reichskirchen* (that is, calling upon them to serve the realm more effectively, especially concerning accommodation of the king and court), the increased secularization of property in royal monasteries, and monastic property divisions occurring just at this time, might be compared with similar developments in the west Frankish realm of the ninth century as a result of Charles the Bald's policies.[154]

In comparison with the ninth and tenth centuries, the first quarter of the eleventh century offers a rich amount of documentation from varied sources demonstrating the existence or the inauguration of property divisions in several German royal monasteries. This evidence consists primarily of land and property registers, all of which appear closely connected with Henry II's reform interventions and secularizations in the royal monasteries.[155] It is possible, for instance, that a formal division of the monastery's properties occurred when Henry II had Prüm reformed along Gorzean lines in 1003. Henry II ordered Abbot Udone (whom Abbot Immo from Gorze soon replaced) to make

---

[152] Matthäi (1877) 66–78 recognized and emphasized only the economic and political sides of Henry II's reform interventions, whereas T. Schieffer (1951) 399–404 and A. Hauck (1952) 3.454–6 made a more correct assessment of Henry's twofold personality, that is, a practical monarch coupled with a serious religious reformer.

[153] Gerhard Kallen (1924) 200–4 recognized the very close connection between secularizations for royal *servitium* and the property divisions in monasteries and cathedral chapters, but he rejected completely the idea put forth by Pöschl (1908–12) 2.14–15, 70–3 that such property divisions were also a 'work of reform'. Concerning ninth-century monastic reform, Semmler (1958) 283–4 agreed with Kallen in rejecting Pöschl's thesis. Concerning the eleventh-century canonical reform (and here the conditions most clearly resemble those affecting the German monasteries), R. Schieffer (1976) 286–9, however, disagreed convincingly with Kallen and supported Pöschl. Schieffer's argument refers equally well to the monasteries. He demonstrated the close connection between cathedral and monastic property divisions, royal service via secularizations, and the strong reform movement of this period.

[154] On Charles the Bald's systematic exploitation of church property, especially of monastic property, without wantonly despoiling it, see Nelson (1979), who also sees (p. 117 n. 78) striking similarities between Charles the Bald's use of the royal monasteries and that of Henry II. While Brühl (1958) esp. 267–74 and (1968) 39–48 esp. 42–5, 131–3 noticed these similarities, he puts too much stress on the differences [(1958) 274 n. 703 and (1968) 131], because, as I will demonstrate later, he under-emphasized the overall economic importance of the royal monasteries under Henry II.

[155] Kaminsky (1972) 52, where, in nn. 44, 45, he cites the older literature.

a list of the monastery's precious moveable goods. Henry's motives remain unknown; but as other examples show us, the making of property and goods registers often went hand in hand with reform interventions, with the introduction of a more accountable administration, and sometimes with secularizations of monastic property to serve royal needs. Since the mid-ninth century Prüm had received both royal and private grants designated solely for the brothers' prebend, and a charter of Henry II in 1016 called particular attention to the existence of this conventual prebend and forbade the abbot to diminish it when he endowed the new monastery of St Mary's at Prüm.[156] The monastery of Fulda, however, provides us with the best-documented example. After he had initiated monastic reforms in Prüm (1003), Hersfeld (1005), Lorsch (1005) and Reichenau (1006), Henry II brought the Gorzean reform to Fulda in 1013. He deposed Abbot Brantoh, naming Abbot Poppo of Lorsch the abbot of Fulda as well, and assigned him the task of reforming it along Gorzean lines. At the same time, the king confiscated a part of Fulda's property to make it more serviceable to the realm.[157] Most likely, this property had already been internally designated as abbatial.[158] The confiscation, coupled with the reform in general, appears to have effected, or at least instigated, a formal division of the monastery's properties and assets between the abbot and the brothers. For some time between 1015 and 1025, a partial land and property register was compiled at Fulda, which is the first extant witness for the existence of separate abbatial and conventual *mensae* there.[159]

An analysis of this land register indicates that it is an inventory of conventual properties (*Descriptiones villarum, que ad prebendam fratrum Fundensium pertinent*) and, furthermore, that a great majority of these properties originated out of gifts from the royal fisc.[160] In addition, two further Fulda inventories from the first

---

[156] *DH II* 358.
[157] *Vita Bardonis Maior* c. 2 pp. 323–4; *Ann. Qued. s.a.* 1013 p. 82. In general concerning Henry II's reform of Fulda, see Franke (1987) 95–107, 116–32.
[158] Matthäi (1877) 71–3 asserted that Henry confiscated a large amount of the monastery's property assigned to the brothers, that is, the conventual *mensa*, but Werner-Hasselbach (1942) 136 esp. at n. 93, who has made the most extensive study of the Fulda land and assessment registers, has demonstrated convincingly that Henry's confiscations at Fulda touched only some of the property under the abbot's full disposition.
[159] *TAF* c. 43 pp. 115–25. For the dating, see Werner-Hasselbach (1942) 9–19 esp. 14–17.
[160] 'Descriptions of the estates which pertain to the prebend of the brothers of Fulda'. Werner-Hasselbach (1942) 133–4.

half of the eleventh century confirm the property division there. Chapter 10 of the *Traditiones* contains a partial listing of properties belonging to the *mensa* of the abbot (*ad abbatis sequestrationem*), and Chapter 13 comprises an enumeration of income in kind delivered by specific places toward the sustenance of the brothers.[161] These three property registers verify the existence of separate *mensae* at Fulda in the early eleventh century.[162] They represent the formalization of an internal property arrangement which had probably been developing slowly throughout the ninth and tenth centuries and probably had a definite form already in the late tenth century.[163] Nevertheless, because of the royally sponsored Gorzean reform of Fulda in 1013, the simultaneous secularization of the abbatial property and the generally increasing demands of the state on monastic property,[164] there was a new urgency to confirm and protect the brothers' mensal properties. This supplied the catalyst to draw up Fulda's most extensive economic inventories to date and to separate those properties supplying the brothers' upkeep from those liable to abbatial or royal *servitium*.[165]

A similar process occurred throughout several of the most powerful and wealthy royal monasteries of the realm. In 1014, Henry instituted the Gorzean reform at Corvey by deposing Abbot Walh and installing the reform monk Druthmar from Lorsch as abbot.[166] The king appears to have secularized some of the monastery's property and made it available for the *servitium regis*,[167] by decreasing the size of the conventual prebend and converting some of it into abbatial property.[168] At the time Henry could do this with little difficulty, since reports from Hersfeld, Reichenau, Fulda and Corvey all indicate that upon the initial reform interventions a large number of the monks left the

---

[161] *TAF* cc. 10 and 13, pp. 54–5. Especially concerning the dating, see Werner-Hasselbach (1942) 89–93, 137–8.

[162] Whether or not there was a complete separation of all the various offices of the monastery remains unclear. As Werner-Hasselbach (1942) 138–9 has shown, there is good evidence demonstrating that the brothers had a separate cellarer. A. Hauck (1952) 3.447 n. 1, on the basis of *DH II* 507, which mentions the treasurer of the abbot, also presupposes the administrative separation of the monastery's properties.

[163] Werner-Hasselbach (1942) 136–7. This appears to correspond roughly to the development in the monastery of Werden on the Ruhr. See Kötzschke (1906–58) 4.2.234–7.   [164] See nn. 149, 151 above.

[165] Werner-Hasselbach (1942) 137.

[166] Thietmar 7 c. 13 pp. 412–13; *Ann. Qued. s.a.* 1014 p. 82, ll. 40–6. On Henry II's reform of Corvey, see Franke (1987) 102–4 and Metz (1989) 255–70.

[167] *Ann. Qued. s.a.* 1015 p. 83, ll. 18–22. Kaminsky (1972) 52.

[168] Concerning Corvey, see above n. 166.

monasteries in protest. A decrease in the amount of property at the congregation's disposal, that is, their mensal properties, could conceivably fall in line with the Gorzean reform's demand for a simpler life-style for the monks. Nevertheless, we have very little hard evidence that Henry II, in his confiscations or secularizations, depleted the *mensa* of the brothers to any great extent. In fact, in two monasteries where large secularizations from the brothers' prebend are said to have occurred, Hersfeld and Fulda, the consensus of the evidence and of the scholars who have examined that evidence indicates otherwise. The fact that Druthmar at this time held the abbatial office only at Corvey makes this more plausible. In other circumstances Henry often placed several monasteries in the hands of a single abbot, thus reducing costs for the abbot's upkeep and directly or indirectly making a greater share of abbatial property available for *servitium regis* (for example, Niederaltaich, Tegernsee and Hersfeld; Gorze, Prüm, Reichenau; Lorsch and Fulda; and Stavelot-Malmédy and St Maximin). It is no accident, therefore, that under Abbot Druthmar (1015–46) an assessment register was originated at Corvey that clearly confirms the existence of separate abbatial and conventual properties.[169] As in the case of Fulda, it appears that this new property and assessment register resulted from Henry's reform intervention, and represents a reorganization of Corvey's manorial estates in order to force the monks to greater economy and to exploit the political and economic potential of the royal monastery more effectively for service to the realm. To protect the essential upkeep and assure the existence of the monastic congregation in view of this 'secularizing' process, a division of the monastery's properties or the formalization of a pre-existing internal arrangement ensued.

Six years later, upon the death of Abbot Bertram, Henry II brought his royally initiated reform to Stavelot-Malmédy. He appointed as abbot the reform-oriented monk, Poppo, a student of Richard of St Vanne.[170] A short-lived revolt of the *ministeriales* against the new abbot suggests that the reform measures included some kind of property seizures as well as an altering of the *consuetudines*.[171] Twelfth-century evidence expressly referring

---

[169] Kaminsky (1972) 39. As an appendix (pp. 195–222) to his study, Kaminsky offers a new edition of the eleventh-century Corvey assessment register containing the source evidence for the property division at Corvey. Refer to Kaminsky's citations (p. 52) for specific references. See also Metz (1989) 255–61.

[170] Everhelm, *Vita Popponis* at c. 15 pp. 291–2.

[171] Ibid. See also Wehlt (1970) 215.

back to the time of Abbot Poppo I (1020–48) indicates that a formal separation of monastic properties existed at Stavelot-Malmédy. This evidence appears in one of several property and assessment registers that Abbot Wibald of Stavelot-Malmédy had compiled in 1130–1 in an attempt to repossess certain properties and revenues lost through the poor administration of one of his predecessors, Abbot Poppo II (1105–19), whom he named 'depopulator loci nostri'.[172] Particularly significant is the register comprising a list of specific churches and courts that belonged to the abbot of Stavelot-Malmédy at the time of Abbot Poppo I (designated 'renovator cenobii nostri') expressly to provide the abbatial or royal *servitium*.[173] The list also implies that some of the churches of the monastery and their proceeds pertained only to the upkeep of the congregation.[174] Certain churches and courts, therefore, stood at the disposal of the abbot and could be used for secular ends, but others remained exclusively as a conventual prebend. This tenurial arrangement appears to go back to the second half of the tenth century, as it corresponds so well to a charter of Otto I from 966, in which Otto restored to the brothers' prebend certain churches and their appurtenant properties that had belonged to the monks at Stavelot-Malmédy. He declared that no one could grant them in benefice, and granted them and the monastery royal protection and immunity.[175] The twelfth-century source, which refers back to a time shortly after the eleventh-century reform of Stavelot-Malmédy and the possible property secularizations accompanying it, however, first confirms a formal separation of abbatial and conventual properties of Stavelot-Malmédy, especially in regard to the obligatory services owed to the king.

---

[172] *Recueil … Stavelot-Malmédy* 1.302–14 nos. 150–4.

[173] Ibid. 1.307–8 no. 153: 'ecclesias et possessiones ad abbatis et regni servitium pertinentes'.

[174] Ibid.: 'Abbas a prima institutione monasterii numquam habuit aliquas proprias curtes suo vel regni servitio deputatas, sed tenebat ecclesias abbatie suis et regni necessitatibus servientes, exceptis quibusdam que ad usum fratrum pertinent.'

[175] *DO I* 319 (24 January 966):

ecclesias cum decimationes et mansis et mancipiis … [ad cenobia] Stabulense vel Malmundariense pertinentes monachis … munifica largitate reddidimus et usibus vel stipendiis eorum perpetualiter servituras decrevimus, et ut nulli umquam in beneficium dentur, volumus et firmiter iubemus. Ipsa vero cenobia Stabulense vel Malmundariense cum omnibus ad victualia vel stipendia monachorum deputatis sub perpetua nostre regie vel imperatorie dignitatis defensione vel emunitate esse decrevimus.

Additional evidence from the middle of the eleventh century demonstrates the existence or occurrence of property divisions in at least two more royal monasteries. Two charters of Henry III for Hersfeld, a monastery which was reformed by Godehard in 1005 at Henry II's request, suggest that some kind of property division existed there also. Nevertheless the brothers' *mensa* most likely remained under the general administration of the abbot. In one of the charters, Henry III gave the brothers at Hersfeld a vineyard for their prebend[176] and, in the other, he restored certain unjustly alienated properties to the brothers' *mensa* and seemingly acknowledged the abbot's administration of at least this part of the prebend.[177] Also in the monastery of Werden on the Ruhr a property division appears to have developed. The evidence does not allow us to establish the exact date or nature of the development, but as early as the late tenth century the brothers began to accumulate properties specifically allotted for their use.[178] For instance, Werden's extensive ninth-century estate of Friemersheim had been broken up in the course of the tenth century and divided between the abbot and the brothers. The abbot received the vills of Friemersheim and Borg, and the brothers received the vill of Asterlagen which the provost administered.[179] By the middle of the eleventh century, an assessment roll of the monastery, dating from about 1031–8,[180]

---

[176] *DH III* 274 (31 July 1051): 'vineam unam ... fratribus ad prebendam ibidem ... in proprium dedimus atque tradidimus'.

[177] *DH III* 302 (30 April 1053): 'predictae aecclesiae ... in proprium reddidimus et concessimus ad stipendium fratrum in predicto loco ... ea videlicet ratione, ut prenominatus reverendus abbas suique successores de prefato predio liberam dehinc potestatem habeant obtinendi tradendi commutandi precariandi vel quicquid illis ad usum aecclesiae et ad stipendium fratrum placuerit exinde faciendi'. See also n. 162 above.

[178] Kötzschke (1901) 114–18; Kötzschke (1906–58) 4.2 p. 236; and *RU* 2.152 *Urbar* C v2: 'predium unum in Thrire, quod venerabilis abbas Eingilbertus ad specialem fratrum utilitatem dedit'.

[179] See Kötzschke (1901) 19–25 and, following him with some clarifications, Ganshof and Verhulst (1966) 307–8 and Stüwer (1980) 250–1, 253 and 256–7.

[180] Kötzschke, in *RU* 2.cxxxii–iii, and a great number of scholars following him, have dated *Urbar* C from Werden to the end of Abbot Gerold's abbacy, that is around 1050. Leidinger (1965) 96–8 esp. 97 n. 9, however, has offered a strong argument on the basis of eleventh-century prosopography that *Urbar* C must have been written earlier in Gerold's abbacy, between his assumption of office in 1031–2 and 1038, the death of Count Liudolf of Brunswick, who is mentioned in the land register (*RU* 2.149 §21 1.4). In fact, Leidinger's argumentation supports and probably confirms the remarks of a sixteenth-century hand written on folios 1ª and 1ᵇ of *Urbar* C designating the date of the *Urbar* as 'Anno domini 1032' and 'circa annum domini MXXXII'. See *RU* 2.cxxxii and 2.139 §1 note e (ms. D): 'Conscriptus est presens liber de curtibus

unequivocally demonstrates the existence of separate abbatial and conventual *mensae*. The assessments due in various places or courts are often highly specialized, designating whether the payment goes to the brothers, the abbot, the *heriscilling* (military tax), or the *servitium regis*.[181] Although either Abbot Heitanrich (1015—29), or possibly Abbot Bardo (1029–31), reformed Werden,[182] we have no reports or documented evidence of property secularization as in the other reform interventions of Henry II. The process in Werden seems to have progressed gradually as a logical development of the administration of its manorial estates and to have corresponded to a general trend in the royal monasteries.[183] The same assessment roll which witnesses the property division, on the other hand, also contains the most detailed eleventh-century delineation of payments due on monastic properties for the *servitium regis*.[184] This close proximity of extensive secular demands on monastic property and the existence of separate mensal properties in the monastery's most complete eleventh-century assessment roll do indeed imply a degree of cause and effect. When seen together with the reform of the monastery along Gorzean lines and with similar developments in other monasteries such as Fulda, Corvey and Stavelot-Malmédy, moreover, the connection becomes even stronger.

SERVITIUM REGIS AND ABBATIAL PROPERTY

In view of the general connection between *servitium* and property and a more specific relationship between property division and the *servitium regis*, I will now examine briefly the most important evidence indicating that the abbot or abbess normally had to provide the material royal service (*servitia et militia*) from his or her portion of the monastery's property and assets and, in so doing, further demonstrate how *servitium regis* formed a motive for

monasterii circa annum domini MXXXII' (then written by a later hand) 'sub Geroldo abbate'.

[181] Although Kötzschke, in *RU* 4.2.235, also claims to have charter evidence from the end of the eleventh century documenting the existence of the abbot's *mensa*, the charter upon which he lays the heaviest burden of proof (*DH IV* 461) is a forgery. See: Bendel (1908) 67–9 no. 19; Oppermann (1922) 136–8; and *DH IV* 461.

[182] Hallinger (1950) 1.231–2 credits Bardo with the reform of Werden, whereas Stüwer (1980) 94, 308–9 indicates that the reform of Werden along Gorzean lines was carried out earlier (*c.* 1015) by Abbot Heitanrich and under the influence of Archbishop Heribert of Cologne, although he appears a bit hesitant about his assertion (pp. 308–9).

[183] Kötzschke (1901) 112–18 and *RU* 4.2.234–6.

[184] Heusinger (1922) 12, 127–8 [37, 152–3].

monastic property divisions. As mentioned above, the tenth chapter of the ecclesiastical capitulary of 818–19 demonstrates a general link between *servitium* and property by designating one *mansus* of every church free of all secular service. The remaining property of the church was liable for a debt of *servitium* to its respective secular (proprietary) lord.[185] A charter of Louis the Pious in 829 for Saint-Germain-des-Prés also provides some interesting evidence referring to the connection between monastic property divisions and *servitium regis*.[186] The abbot of St Germain, Hilduin, fearing that the monastery might suffer in the future through the neglect or frugality of future abbots, requested Louis to issue a charter establishing fixed yearly *stipendia* of food and drink for the brothers and assigning them specific properties to provide for their various needs.[187] Furthermore, in response to Hilduin's apprehension that future abbots might exact public *servitium* from these assigned properties,[188] Louis inserted a prohibition against abbatial usurpation of this endowment, stating that no future abbot could appropriate these properties for his own use, nor could he give them in benefice or exact any kind of service from them.[189] Thus, this charter, especially the reference to Hilduin's fear that a future abbot might exact public *servitium* from the brothers' prebend and Louis's prohibition *formula*, clearly demonstrates that the abbatial property bore the burden of all public service, that is the *dona, servitium regis, servitium curie* and *militia*.

A source from the mid-ninth century (*c.* 844–59), *the Breviatio villarum monachorum victus*, contained in Folcwin's *Deeds of the Abbots of St Bertin* as well as in the *Cartulary of St Bertin*, likewise affirms that the obligation of secular services was due from properties other than the conventual properties. Abbot Adalard

---

[185] See n. 30 above.   [186] Poupardin, *Saint-Germain-des-Prés* 1.43–7 no. 28.

[187] Ibid. 1.44–5: 'Hilduinus...abba...nostre suggessit serenitati quod pro Dei omnipotentis amore et futuro eiusdem congregationis cavendo periculo, ne aliqua successorum suorum negligentia aut parcitate ordo in ea futuris temporibus perturbaretur monasticus, stipendia eorum que annuatim in cibo et potu accipere debebant, nec non et quasdam villas specialiter necessitatibus illorum deserviendas constituisset ac deputasset.'

[188] Ibid. 1.45: 'quatinus nulla occasione nec rei publicae servitio quisquam ex successoribus suis impedimentum in futuro inferre potuisset'.

[189] Ibid. 1.46: 'precipientes ut nullus abba per successiones quod salubri egit concilio subtrahere aut minuere audeat, aut ad suos usus retorqueat aut alicui in beneficio tribuat, sed neque servitia ex eis exactet, neque paraveredos aut expensas ad hospitum susceptiones recipiat, neque ullas in aliqua re exactiones inde exigat absque inevitabili necessitate'.

had a general survey of the monastery's property drawn up, which enumerated those properties pertaining to the brothers' use and upkeep, and omitted those that were assigned to other monastic offices (*ministeriis*) or were granted out in benefice to military vassals.[190] Once again the properties set aside expressly for the use and upkeep of the congregation stood separated from the monastic properties designated to other offices within the monastery and from those enfeoffed and liable to secular services. Karl Voigt's interpretation of this document is different from mine – in fact, directly opposed to mine – and contrary to the evidence which I shall present demonstrating that the *servitium regis* customarily fell due only on the abbot's portion of the monastic properties.[191] Voigt rejected the idea of a distinction between conventual and abbatial property in this text and instead saw only a distinction between two classes of conventual property, those providing the brothers' upkeep and those designated to other ends. His interpretation did not fully consider the historical situation at St Bertin as reported by Folcwin and thus failed to recognize the reason behind Adalard's survey and Folcwin's reporting of it: that was, to rectify further the shameless secularizations made earlier by Fridogisus.[192] This text implies a tripartite division of the monastery's properties into those assigned for the support of the brothers, those designated to specific monastic offices, and those remaining fully at the abbot's disposal, and in this case partially granted out in military benefice.[193]

Additional and even stronger evidence from the tenth and eleventh centuries in Germany supports the suggestion that the abbatial properties of a monastery normally had to supply the *servitium* paid to the king. The clearest proof comes from Bishop Adalbert of Metz's charter of 933 for the monastery of Gorze in which he restored some properties to the brothers of the newly re-

---

[190] Folcwin, *Gesta Abbatum s. Bertini* c. 63 p. 619 and the *Cartulaire de Saint-Bertin*, p. 97, where the survey of conventual properties and payments due from those properties (pp. 97–107), which was omitted from the *MGH* edition of Folcwin's *Gesta*, directly follows the narrative: 'Abbas igitur Adalardus villas ad fratrum usus pertinentes vel quicquid exinde sub qualicumque servitio videbatur provenire, absque his quae in aliis ministeriis erant distributae vel quae militibus et cavallariis erant beneficiatae, tali iussit brevitate describere.' *Le Polyptyque ... Saint-Bertin s.a.* 856 p. 13 contains a more recent edition of this passage. See also Schwarz (1985) 32.   [191] Voigt (1917) 30 n. 3.

[192] See Folcwin, *Gesta Abbatum s. Bertini*, pp. 614–16 (= *Cartulaire de Saint-Bertin* pp. 74–5, 84) and Lesne (1910) 63, 88, 126.

[193] Kötzschke (1901) 112–18 describes a similar tripartite division that existed at Werden on the Ruhr in the late tenth and early eleventh centuries.

formed monastery.[194] The charter states unequivocally that the abbot had the obligation to hold and provide vassals for the royal host (*publica militia*) if he possessed all of the properties of the monastery. If, however, he possessed only those properties that pertained to the conventual *mensa*, then he owed no *servitium* except to minister to the brothers and oversee the monastic community.[195] Almost twenty years later, Otto I, in a charter confirming the conventual *mensa* of the nuns at Oeren,[196] prohibited his successors in the kingship as well as anyone that held a benefice from the monastery from exacting any *servitium* from the nun's prebend.[197] Thus, any *servitium* exacted had to fall on the properties of the abbess.

Earlier, during my discussion of Henry II's reform interventions in several of the German royal monasteries, I pointed out that new land and property registers, manifesting formalized monastic property divisions, arose in several monasteries in conjunction with those reforms. One of those property listings, which designates certain churches and properties owing service to the abbot of Stavelot-Malmédy, clearly indicates that the monastery's abbatial properties bore the burden of the *servitium regis*.[198] The register specifically excludes the properties of the brothers' prebend from owing service to the abbot or king and distinctly lists those abbatial properties and churches responsible for the abbot's and the king's *servitium*.[199] Likewise, in Werden, where a

---

[194] *Cartulaire de l'Abbaye de Gorze* 169–73 no. 93 (16 December 933). A comparison of conventual properties in this charter with those in *DO I* 70 (13 July 945) clearly demonstrates that the bishop of Metz returned only a portion of the conventual properties with this charter; presumably, the rest remained granted out in benefice to secular lords.

[195] *Cartulaire de l'Abbaye de Gorze* 170: 'quod si omnem teneret abbatie terram, oporteret ei satellites tenere, cum quibus publice militaret, sin autem nil amplius, haberet, nisi quid ad mensam fratrum pertineret, nullum deberet servitium, nisi fratribus ministrare et religionem previdere'.   [196] *DO I* 168.

[197] Ibid.: 'sanctimoniales in Horreensi cenobio...partem abbatiae quam modo possidere videntur, eis in perpetuos usus infestationis obstaculo tenendam...concederemus...Et ut nullus successorum nostrorum, videlicet regum, vel aliquis eorum qui reliquas abbatiae partes in beneficiis possidebunt, ullam habeat potestatem eadem loca aut in beneficium dandi aut aliquod ab eis servitium exigendi.'

[198] *Recueil...Stavelot-Malmédy* 1.307–8 no. 153; see above at nn. 171–3.

[199] *Recueil...Stavelot-Malmédy* 1.307–8 no. 153: 'Abbas a prima institutione monasterii numquam habuit aliquas proprias curtes suo vel regni servitio deputatas, sed...tenebat ecclesias abbatie suis et regni necessitatibus servientes, exceptis quibusdam que ad usum fratrum pertinent. Et sicut abbas Poppo...ipse tenuit et successoribus suis tenendas reliquit, ita ecclesias et possessiones ad abbatis et regni servitium pertinentes annotabimus.'

property division had evolved and we also have information about the *servitium regis*, those properties allotted to the abbot bore the burden of royal service. For example, after Werden's large estate of Friemersheim had been divided among the abbot and the brothers in the tenth century, the abbatial allotments, the vills of Friemersheim and Borg, appear in the eleventh-century land register owing substantial payments to the *servitium regis*, but there is no mention of payments from Asterlagen, the brothers' property.[200]

Later, Henry IV's charter of 1073 for the convent of Niedermünster at Regensburg provides an equally explicit statement about monastic property divisions and the burden of *servitium regis* weighing upon the abbatial properties.[201] When Abbess Gertrude complained to Henry IV that her yearly *servitium regis* was so large that she could not pay it without taking a large amount from the sisters' prebend, Henry reduced her *servitium regis* from sixty to forty pigs (along with all other appurtenances of the *servitium*) and granted the total reduction to the conventual *mensa* (*prebendae*).[202] This charter documents that a property division already existed in Niedermünster and that the abbess paid the *servitium regis* from her properties. Likewise, the wording of a similar charter of Henry IV reducing the debt of the *servitium regis* at the neighbouring convent in Regensburg, the Obermünster,[203] also implies that the abbess, and not the convent as a whole, bore the responsibility of providing the material services due to the king. It is not known when the property division took place in Niedermünster (or Obermünster), but it has been suggested that the size of the *servitium regis* for Obermünster might have been established during Conrad II's inquiry in 1027 concerning royal

---

[200] *RU* 2.146–7 (§ 16) esp. p. 147 n. 1; Kötzschke (1901) 19–25. Following him with some clarifications, Ganshof and Verhulst (1966) 307–8, and Stüwer (1980) 250–1, 253 and 256–7. For the extent of the payments due, see Chapter 5 below, at n. 34.

[201] *DH IV* 265 (27 October 1073).

[202] Ibid.:

Adiit namque nostrae regalis magnitudinis clementiam eiusdem monasterii abbatissa Gerdrvdis conquerens magnum et grave atque intolerabile, quod nobis annuatim deberet, esse servicium, quodque nequaquam sine magno monialium suarum prebendae defectu exsolvere quivisset. Nos autem super querela eius et petitione miserti rogatui illius facilem prebuimus effectum et de LX porcis, quos singulis annis ut supra retulimus ad nimis magnum nostrum servicium dandos procuravit, XX cum omni appendente servicio nostro usui detraximus et ad suplementum sanctimonialum inibi servientium prebendae tradidimus et perpetua stabilitate dicavimus.

[203] *DH IV* 264.

property in Bavaria.[204] It is possible that a formal property division occurred in the two convents at that time. Already under Otto I and Henry II, the sisters in these monasteries received royal grants expressly for their prebends.[205] Recently, Wolfgang Metz has indicated – without, however, providing an adequate or convincing argument – that conventual properties, especially in the cathedral chapters, but perhaps those too in collegiate chapters and regular monasteries and convents, also appear to have borne the burdens of the *servitium regis*.[206] Although this may indeed have occurred in isolated instances (for example, at Remiremount in Alsace),[207] the weight of the evidence points to constant attempts to spare the conventual properties from payments to the *servitium regis* and to exact these primarily, if not solely, from the abbatial properties. Metz even goes so far as to cite Henry IV's charter for Niedermünster as evidence that the prebendal properties were also called upon to supply the *servitium regis*,[208] a notion which a careful reading of the charter quickly dispels. In fact, the wording of the diploma makes it clear that the abbess came to the king with a complaint over the size of the *servitium* demanded from her and that her petition contained a subtle threat – unless the *servitium* were reduced she would have to seize it from the prebendal properties. Thus, the nature of her petition clearly implies that the use of conventual properties for this end was not customary, but would constitute an extreme measure as well as an abbatial usurpation. Henry's resolution of the situation supports this interpretation; he expressly granted the reduction of the abbess's *servitium* to the prebend and not to the abbess herself.

Finally, a charter from one of a series of forged charters for St Maximin offers interesting evidence on this topic.[209] Although the charter is an early twelfth-century forgery in the name of Henry II, it appears to have been composed from an authentic charter of 1023.[210] The forgery claimed that Henry II confiscated a large

---

[204] *MGH Const.* I no. 439 p. 645; Metz (1976) 214–15.

[205] *DDO I* 432, 433; *DDH II* 116, 213, 455a.

[206] Metz (1985) 296–9. Reuter (1982) 364–5 suggests that one aspect of the king's personal participation as a canon in cathedral chapters was the financial potential of exploiting the revenues of the chapter as well as those of the bishop. Cf. Fichtenau (1984) 301–4, however, who totally rejects this notion. [207] Metz (1976) 200–3.

[208] *DH IV* 265; Metz (1985) 296–9.

[209] *DH II* 500. Note especially Bresslau's introductory remarks concerning this diploma.

[210] After an extensive study of the St Maximin charters, Bresslau (1886) 45–7 first noted that *DDH II* 500, 502 and *DK II* 48 are based on authentic charters. Bresslau's opinion found general acceptance along with some reinforcement. See: T. Mayer (1950)

portion of the monastery's (abbot's) property to grant it to three of his vassals because the aged abbot could no longer perform the *militia* and the *servitium curiae*.[211] Thus, Henry freed the abbot from the obligations of *militia* and *servitium curiae*,[212] and from the monastery's customary *servitium regis* unless he reacquired the requisite land in some way.[213] He also forbade the abbot and his successors from granting any of the properties given by former kings and emperors, which were expressly delegated to the conventual prebend, to anyone as a benefice.[214] Consequently, these properties would not be liable to any noble or royal *servitium*. In essence the charter constituted a kind of division of abbatial and conventual properties,[215] and most unmistakably demonstrates the

139–40, 143–5; Wisplinghoff (1970) 36, 84–5, 154–5, who has completed a thorough and important examination of St Maximin's history and many of the problematic charters; and Metz (1976) 198. Kölzer (1989) has re-examined all of St Maximin's forgeries, including (pp. 172–80) this group of forgeries by Benzo from around 1116.

[211] *DH II* 500 p. 637, l. 44 to p. 638, l. 4: 'quasdam curtes et territoria...a prefato abbate accepimus et his fidelibus nostris...ea ratione beneficavimus, ut, quia predictus abbas iam senio confectus commode nobis domi militieque servire non poterat'. The forged charter claims that Henry II confiscated 6656 *mansi* (6670 in *DH II* 502). Although Henry II's proprietary attitude toward the higher churches of the realm, especially the royal monasteries, and the forced reform of St Maximin by Poppo of Stavelot at around the same time, indicate that he most likely made some confiscations at St Maximin in 1023–4, the number of 6656 (6670) *mansi* has to be highly exaggerated. It is most probable that the forgeries of the early twelfth century attempted to counter the gradual impoverishment of the monastery in the second half of the eleventh century. See T. Mayer (1950) 144 n. 2 and Wisplinghoff (1970) 36, 82–3. On diplomatic grounds it remains impossible to determine exactly how much of *DDH II* 500, 502 and *DK II* 48 was forged, and how much corresponded to the historical situation in 1023 or as it appeared in the authentic charter. Research continues, however on many of these problems, and Wisplinghoff (1970) 36, Metz (1976) 198, and even Kölzer (1989) 172–80 have indicated that the charters must have held elements of historical truth.

[212] *DH II* 500 p. 638, ll. 5–6: 'abbas vero suique successores a curia regia et omni expeditione...omnino sint liberi'.

[213] Ibid. ll. 12–19:

servitium, quod nobis et quibusdam predecessoribus nostris de eadem abbatia in secundo semper anno persolvebatur, pro eisdem bonis et possessionibus, que inde abstulimus...cuntisque per eos inibi abbatibus in perpetuum ignoscendo et indulgendo ignoscimus...et ne quis successorum nostrorum regum vel imperatorum idem servitium in periculo anime nostre ac sue inde ulterius exigat, nisi ea bona, que non tam in nostrum quam in eorum servitium inde distraximus, ex integro reddat aut restituat.

[214] Ibid. ll. 20–4: 'Precipimus etiam atque interdicimus prefato abbati suisque successoribus in perpetuum, ne de reliquis curtibus sive bonis, que ad prebendas fratrum a nostris predecessoribus regibus et imperatoribus et per nos etiam specialiter delegata sunt, alicui de maioribus sive liberis hominibus aut aliene familie vel alterius aecclesie quibuslibet servitoribus quicquam beneficiare presumant.'

[215] Matthäi (1877) 53 and Metz (1976) 198.

connection between the abbatial property holdings and the *servitium regis*. Whereas the abbot, if he reacquired some of the confiscated or enfeoffed land, had to begin anew to pay *ad servitium regale*, the land designated as the conventual endowment (*ad prebendas fratrum*) received perpetual freedom from any kind of royal service.[216] The burden of the *servitium regis* most clearly fell upon the abbot and his properties. When the abbot, either realistically or theoretically, no longer had a substantial amount of supplementary property at his disposal, the *servitium regis* fell away. This left only the abbatial and conventual *mensae*, which provided the upkeep of the abbot and the congregation. Thus, the sole royal obligation remaining to the congregation was to pray for the salvation of the king and the realm.[217]

These examples demonstrate the very narrow connection between royal service and the division of monastic properties. Although conventual properties may have been called upon to supply (or more correctly to assist the abbot or abbess in supplying) the *servitium regis* in isolated instances, the sources examined demonstrate clearly that it was customary under normal circumstances for the abbot or abbess to pay the *servitium regis* of the royal monasteries and convents from that property over which they had unlimited disposal. The fact that abbots and abbesses paid the *servitium regis* of their monasteries primarily from abbatial property helps to explain why 'on the monastic estates, the estates forming part of the *mensa abbatialis* seem to have suffered worse from enfeoffments, and hence to have undergone greater losses, than those of the *mensa conventualis*'.[218] Moreover, kings made a conscious effort to ensure that the conventual prebend remained free from the burdens of the *servitium regis* and that abbots and abbesses did not unscrupulously seize lands set aside for the upkeep of the congregation to pay the debts that they owed the king.

The evidence thus demonstrates the existence of property divisions in many German royal monasteries by the middle of the

---

[216] *DH II* 500 p. 638, 11. 40–2: 'quo ab expeditione pariter et a curia nec non ab omni regali servitio hac nostra imperiali preceptione liberos eos et absolutos esse constituimus atque firmamus'.

[217] *DH II* 500 p. 638, 11. 39–40: 'pro statu regni nostri et imperii ac successorum nostrorum misericordiam domini eo valeant exorare liberius'.

[218] With this statement, Ganshof and Verhulst (1966) 307 provide a general acknowledgement of what I have shown in my analysis of abbatial property and *servitium regis*, and my analysis, in turn, gives further support to their expression of 'accepted' wisdom.

eleventh century.[219] From these beginnings, the development of monastic property divisions progressed and became more sharply defined in the late eleventh, twelfth and thirteenth centuries, especially in regard to the administration of the conventual *mensa* by the congregation itself or by an official appointed by them, usually the provost (or female provost).[220] The emergence of monastic property divisions comprised a whole series of economic, political, religious and legal processes. Owing to various circumstances this progressed more slowly and less clearly in the areas east of the Rhine than in those west of the Rhine. Whereas the development in the west occurred primarily in connection with events of the ninth century, it did not proliferate in Germany until the late tenth and eleventh centuries. Formal property divisions, comparable to those of the ninth-century west Frankish realm, were first instituted in the German royal monasteries under Henry II and Conrad II. Likewise, they arose when the demands of the state on church property had increased, monasteries and their property had become more secularized, and the monarchy actively supported a programme of monastic reform. To be sure, the establishment of monastic property divisions progressed somewhat in accordance with the general developmental pattern of monastic tenurial arrangements, but the process, within spatial and temporal variations, occurred or was finalized in response to an increased threat of property secularization and in apparent harmony with the political and ecclesiastical principles of the Carolingian and the later Gorzean reform movements.[221]

---

[219] R. Schieffer (1976) 246–9, 281–3 has substantiated a nearly parallel development for the cathedral chapters at the same time. Similar developments also continued in France. For example, Devroey (1984), in the introduction (pp. xciv–cii) to his edition of the polyptych of St Remi, states that it was compiled and put together in the eleventh century from many earlier parts in connection with the monastic reform and the separation of episcopal and monastic property.

[220] Although we cannot prove the same degree of administrative control by the monastic congregations over their prebend as in the cathedral chapters of this time (n. 219 above), many of the monastic congregations or their representatives did administer their *mensa*, such as St Maximin, Essen, Hersfeld and possibly Fulda and Niederaltaich. See Werner-Hasselbach (1942) 137–9 and n. 162 above. In the later eleventh and twelfth centuries, the administration of monastic properties, both conventual and abbatial, most definitely became more specialized. See Bikel (1914) 177–212 esp. 177–9 and *RU* 4.2.235–9. In the nunneries and female convents the situation appears somewhat different. Here a formal unity of the administration generally seems to have prevailed, although the administration was internally specialized. See: Pöschl (1908–12) 2.40 and Weigel (1960) 57–9.

[221] R. Schieffer (1976) 284–9 came to similar conclusions concerning property development in the German cathedral chapters.

Chapter 4

MONASTERIES IN THE SAXON HEARTLAND

DEFINITION AND DELINEATION

Eastern Saxony, the Harz region and northern Thuringia formed an area containing the bases of the Saxon kings' personal and political power.[1] From these areas the kings normally began their continual peregrinations through the realm, that is the *series itionis*.[2] After these journeys they normally returned to this same area to rest, renew their strength, celebrate important religious feasts, or hunt in one of their favourite forests or game preserves.[3] Only gradually, beginning with Henry II, the last Saxon king, and continuing under the first three Salian kings, did Saxony's dominant place in the royal itinerary begin to diminish, and then only slightly. Not until after the revolt of the Saxon nobility in 1073 did the amount and duration of royal presence in Saxony, the intensity of royal government there and Saxony's predominance in the royal itinerary decline to a point approaching the norm in other *regna* of the realm.[4]

The particular political and economic structure of the Saxon heartlands along with a small number of direct references to the *servitium regis* in the tenth- and eleventh-century sources for this region complicates any discussion of the obligation of the royal monasteries in Saxony to provide accommodation for the king or to pay an economic *servitium* for the upkeep of the royal court. This area contained the rich patrimony of the royal family, the

---

[1] Müller-Mertens (1980) 143–8 defines these areas as part of the *Basislandschaft* or the heartlands of the king.   [2] *Ann. Alt. s.a.* 1048 p. 44, 1046 p. 42.

[3] Klewitz (1939a) 75–96; Brühl (1968) 120; Müller-Mertens (1980) 148–58. K. Hauck (1963) esp. 50–7 examines the evidence that the Saxon and Salian kings, as did their Carolingian predecessors and their Byzantine contemporaries, kept game preserves, which included exotic animals, at certain palaces or residences.

[4] Rieckenberg (1941/1965) 89–95, 113–17 and Leyser (1981) 746. On the revolt of the Saxon nobility and its complex background, now see Leyser (1983a). For a discussion of the practice of other regions of the realm being referred to as *regna*, see Reuter (1991a) 91–2.

Liudolfings, the Carolingian fiscal properties granted to them in the late ninth century or taken over by them upon their entrance to the kingship, and many familial, royal and aristocratic monastic foundations. The Liudolfings' patrimony extended from north of Magdeburg, which they apparently acquired from the Carolingians in the later ninth century, to Merseburg on the Saale, which Henry I acquired in his first marriage with Hatheburg. To the west the area comprised the region of the Harz mountains and the upper Leine Valley containing large tracts of royal forest (see Maps 5 and 6).[5]

The proximity of Saxon *curtes*,[6] royal *palatia* and ecclesiastical institutions all obligated with royal service makes it difficult to discern the specific part that each played in the upkeep of the king, the royal family and the court during their long stays in the Saxon homeland. Thus, in this richly endowed area, as Lampert of Hersfeld indicated in the 1060s, one must point to an intricate interworking of familial, royal, episcopal and monastic property as well as numerous markets to provide the daily needs of the court.[7] Although Carlrichard Brühl claimed initially that the Ottonian kings lived predominantly, if not exclusively, off personal and royal property (*curtes* and *palatia*), especially when in Saxony, he then, momentarily at least, entertained the idea that monasteries played a larger role in royal accommodation and upkeep, before retreating to his previous position, but with a marked uncertainty.[8] Soon thereafter, when examining the numerous sources from which Henry IV drew his upkeep, Brühl indicated that one must assume a much greater interworking of various elements in providing for the daily needs of the travelling court.[9] Wolfgang Metz has demonstrated convincingly that the

---

[5] In the Slavic wars of the tenth century, Henry I and Otto I expanded this area considerably beyond the Elbe and Saale Rivers, but the majority of these gains were lost in the great Slavic uprising of 983. See Leyser (1979) 2–3, 12–13, (1981) 734–5.

[6] In general, a *curtis* is the centre of a great manorial estate. The property is usually agricultural in nature, that is, a socage farm, closely connected with a royal palace or frequent stopping place and assigned to provide goods in kind or the general upkeep of a specific person, usually the king, a nobleman or woman, or churchman, abbot or abbess. On this definition and concept, see Gauert (1984).

[7] Lampert, *Annales s.a.* 1066, p. 100: 'Nam preter pauca, quae ex reditibus regalis fisci veniebant, vel quae abbates coacticio famulatu ministrabant, caetera omnia in quottidianos usus eius quottidianis impensis emebantur.' In this instance, the king was forced to extremes because those owing the 'consueta regi servicia' were withholding them in protest at Henry IV's conferring of extraordinary powers on Archbishop Adalbert of Bremen. Concerning the daily needs of the court, see Chapter 2 above at nn. 151, 152.   [8] Brühl (1968) 118–27.   [9] Ibid. 210–11.

Saxon and Salian kings consciously furthered the foundation of markets, especially in places favourably located on the royal roads, and that products (and later, incomes) from these markets helped supply the needs of the court.[10] In addition, as we shall see, the monasteries played a larger role in the overall upkeep of the royal court and the sacral representation of kingship than scholars have previously acknowledged. On the basis of examples such as Quedlinburg and Fulda, it appears that where monasteries and royal residences, and sometimes royal fortresses, stood side by side, the functions and the use of the two were integrated and cannot be separated: rather, one has to think of a double proprietary right or at least of a double function of the various buildings and property.[11] Clearly, in Saxony, the number of female religious institutions of canonesses and nuns,[12] and the part they played in support of the royal court and government, was greater than in the other central regions of kingship (see Map 5). This becomes clear from the charters and other sources for the Saxon convents and monasteries. Moreover, the close connections of these religious institutions to the Saxon royal family (and in some instances to the later Salian royal family), and their position on, or in close proximity to, the routes most frequently used by the royal entourage demonstrate their importance to the Ottonian and Salian kings.

QUEDLINBURG (WALBECK)

The first five charters that Otto I granted after he returned to Saxony in the autumn of 936 favoured powerful royal monasteries.[13] With the first of these, he founded and richly endowed a convent on the burial site of his father, Henry I, in his *urbem*,[14] that is, his fortress, at Quedlinburg. Otto's grant placed the convent for all time under the dominion and protection of the

---

[10] Metz (1971) 280–9, (1972b) 38–9, 50–4 and (1978b) 20.

[11] Streich (1984) 152–3 and 311.

[12] Concerning the differences between institutions of nuns and of canonesses, see Parisse (1978) 109–14, (1990) 319–22, and (1991) 478–83; and Fichtenau (1984) 300–5.

[13] *DO I* 1 (Quedlinburg); *DO I* 2 (Fulda); *DO I* 3 (Corvey); *DO I* 4 (Hersfeld); *DO I* 5 (Werden).

[14] *DO I* 1: 'in urbem in Quidilingoburg supermontem constructam cum curtilibus et cunctis aedificiis inibi constructis'. The word *urbem* in this context means the royal *Burg* or fortress and the *Pfalz* erected on the high ground. See Gauert (1965) 6–8, who gives the pertinent earlier literature, and Niermeyer (1954–76) 1052 (*urbs*, 4th meaning). For a brief summary of Quedlinburg's history in the middle ages, see Fuhrmann (1991).

king. Nevertheless, he maintained the right of advocacy for the Liudolfing family.[15] In addition, in the clause granting the right of free election and immunity to the canonesses, we find a specific mention of the obligation of *servitium* owed by the monastery to the advocate, the diocesan bishop and the king.[16] Obviously, as long as the Liudolfing family acted in the capacities of both advocate and king, the monastery paid this *servitium* to them. Moreover, the size of the initial endowment leaves little doubt as to the convent's ability to meet this obligation. In addition to the *urbem* itself and all appurtenant properties and buildings, the bestowal included the ninth part (*nonam partem*) of all agricultural produce or revenues in Quedlinburg and thirteen other named places, the total produce from five additional places, a tenth part (*decimam partem*) of the total hunt, that is, the game trapped or killed at the royal hunting grounds of Bodfeld and Siptenfelde,[17] and ten wagons of wine and forty large buckets of honey each year from the royal court at Ingelheim.[18] The ten wagons of wine from Ingelheim in the Rhineland were obviously intended to provide the canonesses with an ample supply of wine, and presumably also the king and court when they visited. Moreover, this clause of the grant also provides evidence that a certain amount of long-distance transport occurred to supply particular commodities, especially to the more powerful and prestigious foundations. With this kind of initial endowment for a monastery comprising about sixty members in total (including clerks), of whom many from among the *sanctimoniales* were wealthy noblewomen who came to the foundation with a personal inheritance and prebend – that is,

---

[15] *DO I* 1:

> Et si aliquis generationis nostrae in Francia ac Saxonia regalem potestativa manu possideat sedem, in illius potestate sint ac defensione praenuncupatum monasterium et sanctimoniales inibi in dei servitio congregate; si autem alter e populo eligatur rex, ipse in eis suam regalem teneat potestatem sicut in ceteris catervis in obsequium sanctae trinitatis simili modo congregatis, nostrae namque cognationis qui potentissimus sit, advocatus habeatur et loci praedicit et eiusdem catervae.

[16] *DO I* 1: 'concessimus...ut nulli hominum umquam nisi tantum nobis nostrisque successoribus obtemperet aut quilibet regum aut episcoporum personae aliquod servitium ab ea impendatur'. See Heusinger (1922) 19 [44] n. 6.

[17] The original tithe or produce allotted for the church as it developed in the Carolingian period was a tenth part, and sometimes it was supplemented with a second tithe, or ninth part. See Constable (1960) 246–8. On these royal hunting stations in the Harz mountains, see Nitz (1988) 272–3.

[18] *DO I* 1. Whether or not the stud-farms, *equariciae*, that Henry included in Mathilda's dower (*DH I* 20) now came to the monastery of Quedlinburg remains unclear. See Leyser (1968) 25–6.

a personal income or living stipend[19] – it is little wonder that Otto I made seventeen known halts here during his reign and spent as many as sixty-nine days here![20]

Although on the basis of documented visits no later ruler approached the amount of time that Otto I spent at Quedlinburg,[21] his Ottonian and Salian successors nonetheless did spend ample time at the convent and at other properties owned by it. For instance, Otto III stayed at Quedlinburg in October of 995 for almost two full weeks.[22] Returning from a Slavic campaign, the young king travelled to the convent headed by his aunt Mathilda and received a regal reception. While at Quedlinburg, the king attended the veiling of his sister, Adelheid, as a canoness in the convent – an event which had the aura of an act of state.[23] In addition, Quedlinburg's important position at a crossroads on the eastern border of the Harz mountains surely occasioned numerous royal visits and travel halts that went unrecorded. Quedlinburg lay at the western end of a royal road leading southwest from Magdeburg. At Quedlinburg and Derenburg it joined the important north–south arterial route along the eastern border of the Harz mountains leading from the Saxon residence (*Pfalz*) of Werla and the later Salian stronghold, Goslar, to the royal court at Allstedt (see Map 6).[24] Moreover, although a road did lead through the Harz from around Nordhausen north to Quedlinburg which was used on at least four occasions,[25] Quedlinburg itself normally served as the starting point for the Ottonian kings' autumn hunts at the royal hunting grounds of Bodfeld and Siptenfelde,[26] the latter of which had belonged to Quedlinburg since 961.[27] Calculating very roughly just on the basis of the use of these two roads, one can easily assume forty to fifty royal visits, most likely of short duration, to Quedlinburg or its various properties between 936 and 1046. For instance, given that

---

[19] In general on female religious institutions in Saxony see Leyser (1979) 63–73 and Parisse (1991). On the numbers of members, see Leyser (1979) 71, and on the definition of a noble, female canonry and the style of life in one, see Parisse (1991) 478–81.

[20] Müller-Mertens (1980) 269.   [21] Metz (1978b) 126–7.

[22] DDO III 175, 176, 177.

[23] *Ann. Qued. s.a.* 995. On Adelheid's veiling, see Leyser (1979) 89.

[24] Rieckenberg (1941/1965) 49–51, 97–101.

[25] On this road, see the information contained in *DO III* 155 and discussed at nn. 73, 74 below. Regarding probable use of this road in 961, 965 and 966 by Otto I, and in 980 by Otto II, see *DDO I* 228, 229, 230 (*a.* 961), 302, 303 (*a.* 965), 326, 327, 328, 329 (*a.* 966); *DO II* 226, 227 (*a.* 980); *DDO I* 60, 61, 62, 63 (*a.* 944); and Timm (1941/1943) 464.   [26] Rieckenberg (1941/1965) 50.   [27] *DO I* 228.

Quedlinburg had possessed the *curtis* and the new Benedictine convent at Walbeck since 992, and the *villa* of Siptenfelde since 961, Quedlinburg's property must once again have been considered as one of the sources of royal upkeep when the king or royal family halted in these places. There are five recorded royal stops after 992 (plus another relatively certain stop in 997) at Walbeck, and two after 961 at Siptenfelde, as well as numerous other possible, but unrecorded, halts at both places.[28]

In addition to its favourable location, this convent was not only a site expressly dedicated to the memory of the Ottonian family, built up as it was around a royal tomb, but it also became the traditional place in Saxony for the Ottonian kings to celebrate the feast of Easter.[29] For instance, it is known that Otto I observed the Easter feast at Quedlinburg on five occasions during his reign and it is possible that he celebrated Easter there on ten further occasions.[30] After Otto I's death and his own burial in Magdeburg, the later Ottonians tried to celebrate at least their first Palm Sunday in Magdeburg followed by Easter at Quedlinburg. In this way, the celebration of these two important liturgical feasts became linked with a solemn visit to the most important Ottonian tombs in a kind of 'sacral family reunion'.[31] Indeed, the later Ottonians celebrated Easter seven times at Quedlinburg.[32] Thus, Quedlinburg frequently hosted the highest liturgical feast in the Christian year and thereby was also the site of many important royal assemblies. All of the known dates on which Easter was celebrated in Quedlinburg correspond to known royal assemblies, and some general assemblies of court took place at Quedlinburg at other times during the year.[33] The Easter celebration of 986 offers an excellent example of a joint ceremony. On this occasion, Otto III, although still a boy, solemnly celebrated the Paschal feast at the traditional site and afterward four dukes ministered to the young king in the role of court officials – an echo of the ceremony reported by Widukind after Otto I's coronation in 936.[34] At the same time, this entire royal drama, in which Duke Henry of

---

[28] Rieckenberg (1941/1965) 141–3.

[29] Klewitz (1939a) 79–81; Müller-Mertens (1980) 154–5.

[30] Müller-Mertens (1980) 267–9; Klewitz (1939a) 87–92. In addition to Easter, Otto I celebrated Christmas at Quedlinburg in 937 (*DO I* 18) and possibly on four other occasions. [31] Leyser (1979) 90–1 and, after him, Zotz (1984) 40–1.

[32] Klewitz (1939a) 87–96.

[33] Müller-Mertens (1980) 267–9; Klewitz (1939a) 87–97. On the general practice of 'state' acts occurring on 'holy' days, see Schaller (1974). [34] Thietmar 4 c. 9.

Bavaria played the role of royal servant, also countered his usurpation of the royal Easter rites at Quedlinburg in 984 and thereby symbolized the end of the succession crisis.[35]

The representation of kingship, both sacral and secular, on this scale normally demanded not only resources, but also ceremonial space. At Quedlinburg in 936, upon the foundation of the convent situated on the hilltop site of the old royal fortress with its chapel of St Peter, the small group of canons who had formerly administered the royal chapel were moved down from the hill into a new church of St James and St Wipert located on a royal manor in the valley.[36] There also, by at least the year 1000, a new royal residence was established for which the new canonical church served as a royal chapel to meet the everyday sacral needs of the court. The former royal fortress on the hill was incorporated into the convent as the residence of the female members of the royal house, but occasionally retained its earlier function as a guest house for the king.[37] In addition, Abbess Mathilda, Otto I's daughter, replaced the church on the hill with a greatly enlarged structure, which she had consecrated in March of 997.[38] For the celebration of Easter and the sacral representation of kingship during this feast the new topographical arrangement worked well, as we learn from a report of Otto III's Easter celebration in 1000. Otto spent the *triduum sacrum* and Easter Sunday with his sister Adelheid and the canonesses above at the convent taking part in the solemnities of the feast. Then early on Monday morning, anxiously awaited by princes and the people, he returned to the royal residence (*ad curtem suam*) in the valley to devote himself for the next week to the business of ruling.[39] At Quedlinburg, as at other similar sites, two churches, the small royal chapel and the more prestigious burial church of the convent, served as the two poles of the sacral royal procession.[40]

---

[35] Thietmar 4 c. 2; Leyser (1979) 90.

[36] *DDO I* 1 and 228; *DO II* 10 and JL 3902 contain the evidence for this move.

[37] Concerning the shift of the *Pfalz* from the *Burgberg* to the *curtis* in the plain below, see Erdmann (1941/1943) 24–9. See also Streich (1984) 149–53, 316–18. Wäscher (1959) 35–6 n. 129 has shown that the later church of 1021 appears to have had an extension on the west end or *Westwerk* which contained rooms and a gallery overlooking the nave from which the abbess and probably the royal family could participate in the religious services of the community.

[38] *Ann. Qued. s.a.* 997 p. 74; Streich (1984) 316–17.   [39] *Ann. Qued. s.a.* 1000.

[40] Erdmann (1941/1943) 24–9 and, more recently, Gauert (1965) 5–9 and Streich (1984) 149–53, 315–18 have studied the topology of Quedlinburg and the interconnection between the convent, royal manor and residence, and the new royal chapel in the

Two factors demonstrate the importance of Quedlinburg to the Saxon and Salian kings as a royal bulwark in the Harz region.[41] Firstly, the office of abbess of Quedlinburg was constantly held by a princess of the ruling family.[42] The foundress and dowager queen Mathilda, to whom was entrusted the observance of the Ottonian *memoria*, headed the congregation for its first thirty years.[43] Then in 966, in the presence of a large court assembly, Otto I's daughter, named Mathilda after her grandmother, was elected by the congregation as the first named abbess of Quedlinburg.[44] She had been entrusted to the convent almost from birth and she ruled there until 999. Shortly before the elder Mathilda died in 968, she called her granddaughter to her and entrusted the new abbess with the memorial book of the Liudolfing (Ottonian) and Saxon noble dead whose memory the new abbess and the canonesses had to commemorate with prayers and good works.[45]

Mathilda proved herself to be a formidable abbess and royal princess. Not only did she successfully head this rich and powerful community of women, but she also took an active role in government. In 984, she numbered among the three royal women – together with the two dowager empresses, her mother Adelheid and her sister-in-law Theophanu – who took control of the regency of the young Otto III at Rohr. After this assembly, the three women took the young king to Mathilda's convent at Quedlinburg, where they were greeted with joyous chants of praise for a triumphant kingship.[46] Later, in 997, when Otto III set off to Italy, he chose his aunt, Abbess Mathilda of Quedlinburg, as his regent in Saxony – a position which she exercised actively.[47] Adelheid, daughter of Otto II and sister of Otto III, succeeded Mathilda in 999 and ruled Quedlinburg until 1043.[48] During that time, however, she also became abbess of Gernrode and Vreden in 1014, and abbess of Gandersheim upon her sister Sophie's death in

---

valley. It was customary at sites used for high feasts or frequent processions to have two churches to act as poles of the ceremony. See Gauert (1970) 14–15 on Pöhlde and Claude (1972–5) 2. 293–4 on Magdeburg.

[41] Hörger (1926) 242–9; Feierabend (1913) 188; Goetting (1949) 101; and Parisse (1991) 498–9.   [42] Hörger (1926) 242–9.

[43] Erdmann (1940) 93 and Althoff (1984) 188.

[44] *Ann. Saxo s.a.* 966. On the abbatial elections in these noble canonries, see Parisse (1991) 481–3.

[45] *Vita Math. antiq.* c. 10 p. 578, c. 15 p. 581. See Leyser (1979) 63–73 esp. 72–3 and Althoff (1984) 166–9.   [46] *Ann. Qued. s.a.* 984 p. 66.

[47] *Ann. Hildes. s.a.* 997; Thietmar 4 cc. 41, 42.   [48] Thietmar 4 c. 41.

1039.[49] She was succeeded in turn successively by two daughters from the new Salian ruling house – Beatrix and Adelheid II, both daughters of Henry III from different marriages. The second factor revealing the importance of the convent to the early German kings is the large number of grants of property and rights which Quedlinburg received, especially under the first three Ottos.[50] One cannot say with certainty how much of the monastery's wealth helped to supply the king's upkeep, but the content of some of these grants taken in conjunction with Quedlinburg's favourable geographic position strongly suggests a connection with the accommodation of the royal court. As early as 937 Otto I granted Quedlinburg the right to the tithe paid in cloth garments from two royal fortresses and their appurtenances.[51] Later on 15 July 961, while at Quedlinburg, he granted the monastery the lower court there with the church of St James that served it and eleven other *villas* belonging to it including the one at the hunting palace at Siptenfelde.[52] This lower court, as we have seen, appears to have remained at the full disposal of the royal court, and by the year 1000 a new royal palace had been built there in the area below the monastery on the hill.[53] We have no information about the relation between the convent's obligation of royal *servitium* and the accommodation and upkeep function of the new royal palace and its adjoining court(s). Merely to assume, however, that when the king and his entourage were present they subsisted totally or even predominantly by royal means would not, in my opinion, accurately reflect the situation.[54] We must assume, rather, as in other areas of the realm, an interworking of both royal and monastic incomes for the king's upkeep.[55]

In 974, under Otto II, Quedlinburg acquired four royal *curtes* including one at Duderstadt.[56] Located at the junction of a major north–south route from the Gandersheim area along the western Harz to Heiligenstadt and Mühlhausen/Eschwege in Thuringia, and of a west–east route from the royal *Pfalz* of Grone to Nordhausen and the southern Harz, Duderstadt occupied a geographically strategic position for the travelling court. We have

---

[49] *Ann. Qued. s.a.* 1014 p. 82; *Ann. Hildes. s.a.* 1039 p. 44.

[50] *DDO I* 1, 18, 75, 172, 184, 185, 186, 228; *DDO II* 1, 78; *DDO III* 81, 155, 177.

[51] *DO I* 18. Kirchberg and Dornburg (on the Saale).   [52] *DO I* 228.

[53] *Ann. Qued. s.a.* 1000 p. 77; Gauert (1965) 5–9; Streich (1984) 152 n. 84a.

[54] Brühl (1968) 123–5.

[55] Ibid. 210–11 esp. nn. 394–5 and Streich (1984) 152. See also the corresponding evidence for Gandersheim below, pp. 159–61.   [56] *DO II* 78 (13 May 974).

no documented records of royal stops in Duderstadt, but the frequent use of the two routes by the travelling court and Duderstadt's central location between two royal *Pfalzen*, 25 km from Grone and *c.* 35 km from Mühlhausen, greatly increases the likelihood that Duderstadt may have been used as a place to rest or to stop overnight during a journey. Which properties may have been called upon to provide for the court during such a stop remains unknown, but the former royal *curtis* now held by the royal convent of Quedlinburg would have provided a likely and logical choice (see Map 6).[57]

During the reign of Otto III, Quedlinburg acquired two further grants of importance, a new monastery and a valuable grant of sovereign rights. At a royal assembly in 992 at the residence of Grone, Otto III granted the *curtem* at Walbeck (near Aschersleben) and twenty-four other *villas* in the Halberstadt/Mansfeld area to Quedlinburg on the condition that the abbess (Mathilda) establish a Benedictine convent in honour of St Andrew there which would remain subject to Quedlinburg.[58] The court at Walbeck, an old Liudolfing family possession, formerly belonged to the dower of the empress Adelheid,[59] and the remaining properties probably also derived from private possessions of the Liudolfing family. The Liudolfing origin of these properties, along with the event of a Saxon court assembly, probably accounted for the huge intervention of bishops and Saxon nobility contained in the charter.[60]

As a whole, these properties formed an extensive and significant holding in the southeastern Harz region. Walbeck lay strategically situated on the royal road along the eastern border of the Harz mountains about 25 km – an easy day's march – southeast of Quedlinburg. Walbeck thus provided the royal entourage with another station along this route at which to stop overnight or for a pause during a day's march and be assured of accommodation and sustenance.[61] In fact, the royal entourage appeared at Walbeck

---

[57] See below pp. 157–8 esp. n. 127; Patze (1962) 40 nos. 33, 36; and the lists by Rieckenberg (1941/1965) 141–52.

[58] *DO III* 81; BU 1047; *Ann. Magd. s.a.* 992 p. 158; *Ann. Saxo s.a.* 992 pp. 137–8. See Leyser (1979) 66 concerning the foundation of nunneries by houses of aristocratic canonesses.

[59] Early in his reign (5 February 985) Otto III, at Adelheid's request, granted part of her dower to her daughter, Abbess Mathilda: *DDO III* 7a, 7b. See Uhlirz (1954) 41–2, 444–9 about this grant.   [60] BU 1047; Uhlirz (1954) 151.

[61] Rieckenberg (1941/1965) 49, 76. As with so many other monasteries in Saxony founded on royal or former Liudolfing family property, royal property probably

on several occasions and celebrated numerous religious feasts there. In 997, before starting out on a planned campaign against the Liutizi, Otto III appears to have celebrated the Feast of the Ascension there (6 May 997) and on the next day to have participated, with other members of the Liudolfing family, in the dedication of the new monastic church.[62] Otto's successor, Henry II, stopped at Walbeck on 12 May 1003 and issued a charter there on his way to Quedlinburg to celebrate the feast of St Servitius with his second cousin Abbess Adelheid.[63] Moreover, Henry II customarily celebrated Palm Sunday at Walbeck when he observed the Easter feast at his favourite residence in Merseburg.[64] After 1015, Henry II no longer celebrated Easter at Quedlinburg when in Saxony like his predecessors, but transferred the site of the feast to Merseburg. Thus, in 1015, 1019 and 1021, and very probably in 1023, Henry celebrated Palm Sunday in Walbeck.[65] Also, as at Quedlinburg, numerous unrecorded stops or overnight stays must have occurred owing to the frequent use of this route. Although we do not have any information pertaining to the *servitium regis* at Walbeck, one must assume that the monastery at least provided the upkeep, if not the total accommodation, of the court from the incomes and produce of its extensive properties. At present, there is no evidence to suggest that Walbeck's obligations to the royal court remained separate and independent from those of Quedlinburg. As a proprietary monastery of Quedlinburg, moreover, Walbeck remained firmly within the sphere of royal influence. It may well have been founded with the intention of enhancing and assuring the Liudolfing presence in this region, situated so dangerously close to the eastern frontier. It may also have had auxiliary tasks in the furthering of missionary activity in the area.[66]

In November of 994, Otto III bestowed upon the monastery *in metropoli Quidiliggaburhc* the right to establish a market, a mint and

existed at Walbeck as well after the grant to Quedlinburg and the foundation of the monastery, and the upkeep of the king and royal court came from both sources. If no royal property remained after this grant, the king surely maintained a right of usufruct over the property when he came there. See Brühl (1965) 509–10, cf. Brühl (1968) 124 and see Claude (1978).   [62] Benz (1975) 71–5.

[63] See *DH II* 48, and BG 1541, 1541a. See also Claude (1978) 18–20.

[64] Benz (1975) 70 n. 16, 73 n. 27. *Ann. Qued. s.a.* 1021 states quite succinctly 'Iterim procurrente tempore, cum Saxoniam properatet revisere, palmisque Walbekae iterato rite peracturus, festaque veneratione.'

[65] *Ann. Qued. s.a.* 1015, 1019 and 1021; Rieckenberg (1941/1965) 76 nn. 8, 9.

[66] Benz (1975) 70, 74. See also Leyser (1979) 66.

a toll station, and granted it the same market laws (that is, the royal sanction, protection and ban) as the markets at Cologne, Mainz and Magdeburg, and assigned all the proceeds from these rights to the use of the monastery.[67] This particular charter offers us numerous insights into the trade and economic activity in the area between the Harz, the Elbe and the Saale as well as indicating a general interest in and a need on the part of the travelling court for articles of trade.[68] The charter designated a specifically bounded area, within which no one but Quedlinburg's advocate, whom the congregation chose with the consent of the abbess, could hold any market;[69] it excluded six places, Eisleben, Wallhausen, Rottleberode, Harzgerode, Halberstadt and Osterwiek (Seligenstadt) which earlier had already obtained market privileges; it forbade attendance at any unofficial, that is, not royally sanctioned, market. Considering that the advocate of Quedlinburg had to come from the Liudolfing family, as did the abbesses until the mid-eleventh century when Salian princesses took over, the prescriptions in this charter effectively excluded all powers but those of the king from this market district.[70] We do not know the precise location of the market-place at Quedlinburg, but it surely served the needs of the royal court when it stopped there, in addition to those of the monastery itself. Consequently, the market was very probably located in the area below the monastery in the vicinity of the new royal residence by the church of St James and St Wipert.[71] Most probably the proceeds accruing from the market, toll and mint, and perhaps some trade articles themselves, formed a part of the monastery's economic *servitium regis*.[72]

The information in this charter concerning existing market-places provides us with some additional evidence about the trade routes (and possibly the royal roads) of the time. The charter specifically mentions markets at both Harzgerode and Rottleberode. When one examines the geographical location of these places it quickly becomes clear that neither place would have had much claim as a market town unless a trade route connected them

---

[67] *DO III* 155. [68] Metz (1971) 280–4 and (1972b) 38.

[69] *DO III* 155: '...infra hos terminos: ab orientali plaga ad occidentalem, a Sala dico usque Oueccaram, in australi latere ad aquilonare de Vnstrod et Helmana usque Badam fluvios et paludem quae ex Oscheresleuo tendit usque Hornaburha'.

[70] *DO III* 155; BU 1125. [71] Metz (1971) 283. See above at nn. 36, 39.

[72] Although the evidence indicating these types of income as a part of the *servitium* comes first from the twelfth century, the development most probably occurred some time in the eleventh century. See Metz (1978b) 19–20, 51, 95–115; *MGH Const.* I.144 (a. 1111).

one to the other. Without a connecting route both would stand at best at dead ends in the middle of the Harz mountains. From this it appears evident that a road led from Quedlinburg (with connections to the Harz hunting palaces of Bodfeld and Siptenfelde) via the convent of Gernrode south through the Harz to Wallhausen or Nordhausen. In fact, two contemporaneous sources from the early eleventh century, Thietmar's *Chronicle* and the *Younger Life of Mathilda*, both confirm the existence of a road leading south through the Harz mountains from Quedlinburg via Rottleberode to Nordhausen or to the Nordhausen–Wallhausen road. Both accounts concern the visit of Archbishop William of Mainz to the dowager Mathilda at Quedlinburg in late February 968. William departed from Quedlinburg travelling south (presumably returning to Mainz) and a few days later suddenly fell ill and died at Rottleberode.[73] Moreover, modern maps depict roads running along this same course. The German kings surely made use of this road also. For instance, as reported by the Saxon Annalist, Henry V obviously used one of the routes or parts of several of them when he travelled in 1105 from Erfurt, where he celebrated Palm Sunday, to Gernrode to celebrate Maundy Thursday, and finally on Good Friday, when he walked barefoot to Quedlinburg for the Easter festivities.[74]

This charter of 994 demonstrates clearly the definite relationship between the royal roads and the major centres of trade. It indicates, as would be expected, a growing amount of, and an incentive for, commercial activity in the heartland of the Saxon kings to help supply the needs of the court during its long stays in the region.[75] The Saxon kings did not arbitrarily grant market rights, and the minting and toll rights which so often accompanied them, especially in this area of intensive royal dominion. The grant to Quedlinburg and the information in it concerning commercial activity and existing markets provides some insights into royal

---

[73] *DO III* 155. Thietmar 2 c. 18(12): 'Insuper Willehelmus, sanctae archipresul Magonciae...cum egrotantis reginae finem Mathildis expectaret, in Redulwerothe [Rottleberode] VI. Non. Marci moritur.' *Vita Math. post.* c. 25: 'Episcopus [William] autem inde in Radulveroth [Rottleberode] pergens, ibique medicinalem accipiens potionem, subitanea morte defungitur.'

[74] *Ann. Saxo s.a.* 1105. The information contained in these three sources confirms the existence of a road through the Harz. See also Lorenz (1922) 87; Timm (1941/1943) 464–7; and Metz (1971) 283. The northern section of one of the roads indicated by Timm corresponds exactly to a section of the road running from Quedlinburg via Gernrode to Harzgerode which I have deduced from the information in *DO III* 155.

[75] Metz (1971) 282–3 and (1972b) 37–9; Stein (1922) 9–11, 75–83.

market policies. The kings, at least in Saxony, conferred these grants of royal rights with regard to several factors: the general economic development of the area; the specific location of the place on a trade route or, more importantly, on a royal road; the amount of royal dominion over the community or the institution situated there; and the economic importance of the place, either to the area in general, or specifically to the king.[76]

With grants of market, toll and minting rights the Saxon kings did not alienate valuable royal rights, but rather sanctioned commercial development in an area. In the case of the royal monasteries, they granted these profitable rights to institutions tied closely to the king, who then could turn to them for material support. Indeed, the royal court enjoyed the benefits of this development when visiting the towns, churches and monasteries so favoured.[77] Quedlinburg, with its very close royal connections and large number of royal visits, provides an excellent point in fact. A charter of Henry III in 1042 granting the merchants at Quedlinburg royal protection and the right to conduct business freely and peaceably in all the markets of the realm, just like the merchants of Goslar and Magdeburg, provides a good indication of the quick growth of economic activity at Quedlinburg and its importance as a market city.[78] Quedlinburg's close connections to the royal family and the material support it provided to the kingship with its economic *servitium regis* appears to have been unbroken until the twelfth century.

GANDERSHEIM (ESCHWEGE)

Gandersheim was the second powerful convent of canonesses in Saxony which provided firm support to the Saxon and Salian kings. During the Saxon and Salian periods, Gandersheim resembled Quedlinburg in that it too had close personal links to the Ottonian and Salian ruling families and also possessed a very advantageous location. An old Liudolfing family foundation, Gandersheim achieved royal status in 877 when the Liudolfing counts and brothers, Brun and Otto, gave the monastery to the east Frankish king, Louis the Younger.[79] In return for this *traditio*

---

[76] Metz (1972b) 38–9; BU 1125.
[77] Keller (1985a) 27–8. For a similar development in the west Frankish realm of Charles the Bald, see Nelson (1979) 112–17.   [78] *DH III* 93.   [79] *DLJ* 3.

the monastery received royal protection and immunity, but the Liudolfing family was granted the right to provide the abbess as long as an eligible and suitable member of the family was available,[80] and the convent retained its memorial function of commemorating the dead of the Liudolfing family.[81] Beginning in about 949–50 we know that the abbess of Gandersheim was Gerberga, a niece of Otto I, who ruled the convent until her death in 1001. Her successor was Sophie, the eldest daughter of Otto II and Theophanu. Sophie, who had been reared and educated in the convent since she was four or five and who had taken the veil of a canoness by 987 or 989, appears to have been regarded early on as Gerberga's successor.[82] During her early years in Gandersheim and during her years as a canoness, Gandersheim and Sophie herself were favoured with many grants of property and rights from her father, Otto II, and her younger brother, Otto III. Sophie's grants eventually came to the convent.[83] This dynamic young princess actually spent two years, 995–7, outside the convent, accompanying her brother and the royal court and taking part in royal assemblies and business. For these two years she acted almost as the consort of her brother.[84] Upon the death of Gerberga, Sophie, who had returned to Gandersheim, was the obvious successor but, owing to her brother's death, her election and consecration did not officially take place until 1002 under Henry II. In the meantime, Sophie and her younger sister Adelheid, abbess of Quedlinburg, had played an important role in the election of Henry II as king.[85] These 'imperial' sisters and abbesses also played a role in legitimizing the first Salian king in

---

[80] Ibid.:

> eo videlicet rationis tenore ut praefatum monasterium regio sublevaretur munimine et sanctimoniales feminae ibidem deo famulantes in nostro consisterent patrocinio; et quamdiu in illorum progenie aliqua sanctimonialis femina, quam vite religio et sanctarum scripturarum instructio et omnium bonorum morum commendet compositio, absque ullius personae contradictione sanctimonialibus feminis esset praelata, et si aliter, quod absit, eveniret, quod talis in illa progenie inventa non esset, quae praefatis scilicet virtutibus non ornata videretur, caeterae sanctimoniales femine dignam dei servitio quamcumque vellent eligere inter illas potestatem haberent.

[81] See Althoff (1976) and (1984) 175–6, 213–14.

[82] For the most detailed and balanced study of Sophie of Gandersheim, see Perst (1957); here pp. 8–10.

[83] *DDO II* 35, 36, 119, 201, 214; *DDO III* 66, 67, 146, 150. In addition, some of the properties granted by Otto II to his wife, Theophanu, found their way through Sophie to Gandersheim: *DDO II* 76, 202a, 202b. [84] Perst (1957) 13–23.

[85] *Ann. Qued. s.a.* 1002; Thietmar 5 cc. 3–4.

1024, when he visited them in Vreden and again in Quedlinburg on his initial royal progression.[86] Sophie proved to be a capable and formidable abbess. She ruled Gandersheim successfully until her death in 1039, during which time she also became abbess of Essen in 1011 and acted as abbess in Eschwege perhaps from as early as 997. After Sophie died in 1039 Gandersheim followed the same 'royal' path in its abbesses as Quedlinburg. Adelheid of Quedlinburg took over from her sister until her death in 1044, and she was in turn followed successively by the two daughters of Henry III, Beatrix and Adelheid II, who jointly held Quedlinburg and Gandersheim and ruled the two convents from 1044 until 1096. Thus, Gandersheim's personal connections to the two royal houses could not have been stronger.

Whereas Quedlinburg was located on the northeastern border of the Harz mountains with access to the west–east roads on the northern boundary and the roads leading south around the eastern side of the Harz mountains, Gandersheim was located to the northwest of the Harz mountains and had access to the same east–west roads as well as the roads on the western side of the Harz. The monastery lay near a crossroads of two major routes used frequently by the German kings (see Map 6). A road from the south led from the middle Rhine region through Hesse, or from Bavaria through Thuringia, via the royal palace at Grone, and via Northeim to Gandersheim and Seesen, and then north in the direction of Hildesheim. This artery met near Gandersheim with an old trade route running from the lower Rhine along the Hellweg and then northeast to the Elbe in the vicinity of Magdeburg.[87] With the possible exception of Otto I, the Saxon and Salian kings do not appear to have used the section of this route from Corvey/Höxter on the Weser River north and east via Holzminden to the Gandersheim area.[88] Instead they normally travelled from Corvey southeast to Grone and then north to Gandersheim where they joined the road leading east to Magdeburg and the Elbe River.[89]

---

[86] *Ann. Qued. s.a.* 1024, 1025 p. 90.

[87] *DO I* 180: 'deinde concessit omnes mercatores a Reno usque ad Albiam et Sale transeuntes ad usus sanctimonialium ibi degentium censum thelonei persolvere'. Lechner, in BM² p. 850 (Verlorene Urkunden no. 174). Rieckenberg (1941/1965) 48–9 and Goetting (1973) 76–7.

[88] Rieckenberg (1941/1965) 49, 80–1. For possible uses of this route by Otto I, see Müller-Mertens (1980) 270–83, Table 4 nos. 22 (938), 35 (941), 69 (965), 201? (961) and 228 (965).   [89] Rieckenberg (1941/1965) 48–9 esp. 48 n. 9.

This Liudolfing family monastery, therefore, benefiting from its royal connections and favourably located on a major royal route from the lower and middle Rhine and from east Franconia and Bavaria via the royal palaces of Grone, Werla, and later at Goslar,[90] to Magdeburg, provided the Saxon kings and their successors, the Salians, with a major source of political and material support in Saxony north of the Harz. Although Gandersheim does not have as many records of royal visits as Quedlinburg, we have records of three visits there by Otto III, in 990, 995 and 997, and Conrad II visited Gandersheim in 1025.[91] Otto III was also present in Gandersheim with his mother, Theophanu, and the notables of the realm for his sister Sophie's veiling ceremony on 18 October, most probably in 989.[92] During his visit in 995, the king appears to have held a synod or royal assembly.[93] Moreover, on the basis of the itinerary one can estimate at least twenty-six royal visits,[94] and even more when one considers Gandersheim's later property acquisitions at Bodfeld, Dahlum and Derenburg and its close proximity to Goslar,[95] the Salian kings' favourite royal palace in Saxony. Owing to the proximity of Goslar, royal stays of long duration probably did not occur at Gandersheim. On the other hand, Goslar's rise to importance as a royal palace under Henry II and Conrad II, and the preference shown to it by Henry III and Henry IV, presupposed a sizeable increase in royal traffic to and from Goslar. Consequently, the royal convent of Gandersheim situated *c.* 35 km (a normal day's march) southwest of Goslar on the main route to the south and west provided a convenient and logical place at which to receive overnight lodging or to make short stays on trips to and from Goslar.[96] Thus, in the light of the itinerary and Gandersheim's very close association with both the Saxon and Salian ruling houses, one can conclude that the court stopped often in Gandersheim.[97] In fact, unlike Quedlinburg, at Gandersheim the monastery itself appears to have functioned as the royal palace

---

[90] Ibid. 46–9, 66–70.
[91] *DDO III* 66, 169, 248; Wolfher, *Vita Godehardi prior* c. 26 p. 187.
[92] Thangmar, *Vita Bernwardi* c. 13; BU 1017e. On the date, see Perst (1957) 9–10 n. 26.
[93] Wolfher, *Vita Godehardi prior* c. 20; Perst (1957) 15 n. 51.
[94] Rieckenberg (1941/1965) 141–2.   [95] *DDH II* 205, 206.
[96] Cf. Metz (1976) 207–8, who seems to conclude exactly the opposite. It is not absolutely clear whether Metz at this point refers exclusively to Henry V or more generally to the Salians when he states that royal visits to Gandersheim occurred infrequently owing to the closeness of the large royal palace at Goslar.   [97] Goetting (1973) 88.

during visits from the king, who had his own special room(s) there.[98] As with so many churches with royal connections, the monastic church at Gandersheim had a western extension or *Westwerk*, which contained a royal gallery overlooking the church nave from which the king participated in religious services.[99] Moreover, a private royal chapel may have existed in the upper storey of the *Westwerk* where the king could hear mass alone, though it is possible that the chapter may have participated in the rites.[100] Obviously, when the king stopped at Gandersheim the monastery provided his accommodation and his upkeep and offered several religious alternatives – for royal sacral representation or for private worship.

A single document from Gandersheim itself and royal charters for the convent supply information concerning Gandersheim's obligation to provide economic support for the royal court. The most unequivocal statement that such an obligation existed at Gandersheim comes from an early twelfth-century petition sent by the canonesses of Gandersheim to Pope Paschal II between 1107 and 1110, complaining that their abbess had granted part of their prebend to her *milites*.[101] Referring back to a papal charter of protection granted to Gandersheim under Pope John XIII (965–72) in the presence of Otto I and Otto II,[102] the canonesses explicitly mentioned the convent's historic obligation to provide hospitality for the king when he required it during the royal *iter*.[103] This firm recognition of the monastery's *servitium regis*, coupled with Gandersheim's important position on a royal road of frequent use, leaves us in no doubt that the monastery provided the king's upkeep when he visited it or merely stopped overnight during a journey.[104]

On the basis of the itinerary, moreover, two charters of Otto I for Gandersheim and three of Otto II strongly suggest that the

---

[98] Ibid. 21, 88–9; Streich (1984) 318–19; *Cont. Vitae Bernwardi* p. 167: 'Inde rediit [Conrad II] ad Gandesheim...Post missarum sollemnia dum rex cum episcopis praesentibus sua peteret cubilia...'; Wolfher, *Vita Godehardi prior* c. 26 p. 187: 'hinc rex [Conrad II] Gandesheim adiit...Cum autem rex post missam cubiculum repetivit...'

[99] Goetting (1973) 19–23; Metz (1984) 10–11; Streich (1984) 318–19. For the concept of and the extensive literature on the 'Westwerk', see Streich (1984) 49–66.

[100] Goetting (1973) 88–9.

[101] Goetting (1949) 120–2, which contains an edition of the petition.

[102] JL 3721 (1 January 968); BZ 435; PU 184.

[103] Goetting (1949) 121: 'ut non amplius ullus homo haberet potestatem inde aliquid accipere nisi advocatus quem abatissa eligeret, excepto Romano imperatore, quando itinerio indigeret hospicio'.   [104] Brühl (1968) 124.

respective kings may have stopped at Gandersheim just before their bestowal. In this connection one can possibly consider the grants as a reward or gift of appreciation for accommodating the king.[105] A further charter of Otto II appears to have been granted during a visit to Gandersheim and subsequently formalized.[106] Later, when Otto III granted the monastery some valuable rights during a stay there in 990, the charter specifically mentioned the *servitium* that was often rendered to his father and to him.[107] In this diploma Otto III bestowed upon Gandersheim the right to establish a market there with accompanying minting and toll rights, and to dispose of the proceeds from these rights. Gandersheim's right to coin money must be considered in connection with the discovery around 968 of valuable silver reserves at nearby Rammelsberg.[108] In addition, Otto granted to the abbess and her advocate the royal ban at Gandersheim and conceded to the merchants and inhabitants there the same legal rights as were enjoyed by those in Dortmund.[109] With this grant Otto III again sanctioned commercial development at a royal monastery on an important royal road. Thus, he greatly strengthened the financial position of the monastery and, as a consequence, improved its ability to provide the 'Roman emperors with accommodation when they required it on their itinerary' or generally to pay the *servitia*.[110]

Gandersheim's enrichment at the hands of the Saxon kings continued and reached its apex under Henry II. On 3 September 1009 Henry II, in conjunction with the endowment of the new bishopric at Bamberg, engineered two sizeable property exchanges involving Gandersheim. In the first, Gandersheim ceded three properties in Franconia (Gaukönigshofen, Sonderhofen and Baldersheim)[111] to the king in return for the three royal *curtes* respectively at Derenburg, at Bodfeld (with accompanying rights to the forest and hunting there) and at Reddebar.[112] Apparently, neither at Derenburg nor at Bodfeld did Gandersheim acquire the

[105] *DDO I* 89, 180; *DDO II* 35, 36, 119.

[106] *DDO II* 201; Ficker (1877–8) 1.131.

[107] *DO III* 66: 'simul etiam propter pium interventum dilectae neptis nostrae Gerbirgae Gandersheimensis ecclesiae venerabilis abbatissae quae genitori nostro beatae memoriae Ottoni imperatori augusto et nobis saepius devotum servitium exhibuit...'

[108] Hillebrand (1967).　　　　　　　　　　[109] *DO III* 66; Metz (1972b) 33.

[110] Goetting (1949) 121: 'excepto Romano imperatore, quando itinero indigeret hospicio'. See Reuter (1982) 359 n. 73.

[111] Henry II had granted these properties already on 6 July 1009 to the bishopric of Bamberg. See *DDH II* 200, 201, 202.　　　　[112] *DH II* 205.

actual royal *Pfalz*, but the manors, farms and properties that supported these palaces economically.[113] With regard to Gandersheim's economic *servitium regis* this fact is of significance. Obviously, from this time forward these properties of Gandersheim supported the royal court economically whenever it halted at these *Pfalzen*.[114]

The second of these exchange transactions proved even more profitable for Gandersheim. In this exchange Gandersheim surrendered a former royal property in Belecke,[115] and received in return the nearby royal palace (*curtem*) at Königsdahlum and in addition the sizeable yearly tax of 500 rams paid by the free men (*liberi homines*) of the Ambergau to the royal *curtis* of Dahlum.[116] This grant increased Gandersheim's holdings and yearly income significantly, and it stands to reason that the monastery used the rams to augment or supplement the *servitia* it supplied to accommodate the royal court.[117] Finally, on 28 July 1021 Gandersheim reached the pinnacle of its power and property holdings under the Saxon and Salian kings when Henry II granted the monastery a sizeable county and appurtenant properties in the Flenithigau, Sülbergau and Ambergau to the west and north of Gandersheim.[118] These comital rights encompassed the old Liudolfing endowment to the west and the royal property complex in the north around Königsdahlum acquired eleven years earlier. Coupled with the *Burgbann* or right of castlework that the monastery had acquired under Otto II for Gandersheim, Greene and Seesen,[119] the comital rights made Gandersheim and its

---

[113] Goetting (1973) 266–7.

[114] We possess only a single witness during the reign of Conrad II for a visit to the hunting palace of Bodfeld (*DK II* 46), but his son Henry III visited Bodfeld at least six times during his rule, often spending long periods there: *DDH III* 8, 9, 135, 144, 145, 147, 222, 378, 379, 380, 381, 382. In 1056 Henry III died at Bodfeld after having received the Pope there in September for the autumn hunt. On this visit Henry III spent at least twenty-one days at Bodfeld. See Höfer (1896) 341–3.

[115] Otto II granted this royal property to his wife Theophanu in 979 and it apparently came to Gandersheim after her death. See *DO II* 202a–b.

[116] *DH II* 206. As stated in the introductory remarks to the charter, Otto III had granted the castle, its appurtenances and the accompanying tax to the bishopric of Hildesheim in 1001 (*DO III* 390) and later Henry II repossessed it. On (Königs-)Dahlum, see Goetting (1973) 268–70 and especially Leyser (1983a) 428–9. The yearly tax of 500 rams was very probably the remnant of a former Carolingian tribute paid by the Saxon inhabitants of the area, which later came to the Saxon duke, then to the king, and then to Hildesheim, and finally to Gandersheim. I thank Timothy Reuter for this indication. For a similar tribute from the same general area, see Reuter (1991a) 65, and for Carolingian tribute in general, Reuter (1984). [117] Leyser (1981) 738–9.

[118] *DH II* 444. [119] *DO II* 214; Petke (1974).

advocate one of the most powerful administrators of royal interests from the Leine Valley to Goslar.[120]

Although no charters of Conrad II or Henry III (the first two kings from the Salian family) for Gandersheim have come down to us, there is good reason to believe, without knowing any details, that these two kings also favoured Gandersheim with property grants, probably from the Werla–Goslar complex of royal properties.[121] This would fit well both with the build-up of Goslar as a royal seat, begun already under Henry II and intensified by the Salians,[122] and with the growing need for the 'foreign' Salians, especially under Henry III, to secure bases of royal support in the Harz region to counter a growing Saxon opposition.[123]

In connection with Goslar's fast growth and its rising status as one of the most important royal palaces in the realm, let us once again consider the economic *servitium regis* of Gandersheim. Certainly with the new popularity of the palace at Goslar one has to assume a corresponding increased incidence of the royal entourage travelling the routes to and from Goslar (see Map 6). Thus, whether the royal court travelled east to Goslar along the northern road, or west and south from Goslar to the royal residence at Grone and the connection to the Hellweg, the most likely places for the king to stop overnight or for a few days and claim his hospitality, that is the *servitium*, due to him[124] would be either Gandersheim, which lay a good day's march (*c.* 35 km) from Goslar, or Seesen, which had belonged to Gandersheim since 974 and lay *c.* 20 km from Goslar.[125] Moreover, if the royal *iter* led southeast from Goslar to Quedlinburg (where another monastic *servitium* awaited), to Halberstadt via the palace at Derenburg, or to the hunting lodge at Bodfeld, the Gandersheim possessions there probably provided sustenance for the court.

---

[120] Goetting (1973) 270–1. Regarding the complexity and manifold problems surrounding royal grants of counties to bishops and abbots in the Ottonian and Salian period see Hoffmann (1990) esp. 393–401, where he treats Gandersheim and Fulda, and 456–80, where he deals analytically with the political definitions of counties and discusses the problems regarding their possession and the exercising of the rights encompassed in them. [121] Goetting (1973) 270–1; Petke (1974) 14–15.

[122] Rieckenberg (1941/1965) 77–81, 98–101. Weinfurter (1986) 281–3 discusses the foundation of Goslar as part of Henry II's new concept of ruling.

[123] Goetting (1949) 100–2 and (1973) 94–6; see also Boshof (1979), the very important article by Leyser (1983a), and Parisse (1991) 498–9.

[124] The same of course would apply to the Ottonians travelling to and from the palace at Werla, except perhaps under Otto I when he came via Brüggen and Dahlum. See n. 88 above. [125] *DO II* 36; Petke (1974); see also Roth (1974) 34–5.

On the other hand, when the *iter* led southwest from Goslar and then south on the royal route along the western border of the Harz that led from Seesen and from Gandersheim to Thuringia, via the royal residence and the priory of the archbishop of Magdeburg at Pöhlde,[126] Gandersheim owned properties conveniently situated along these routes also.[127] In fact, in this general area significant royal properties came to royal churches in the late tenth and eleventh centuries. Although administered by ecclesiastical institutions, the properties nevertheless remained at the king's disposal through his claim to *servitium regis* and to the use of royal churches in general.[128] In 990 Otto III endowed his sister Sophie with numerous properties in this general area – west of the Harz mountains and on both sides of the Leine River – for her personal use; these most probably came later to Gandersheim after she became abbess there.[129] Later, in 994, Otto gave Sophie the fiscal district of Eschwege,[130] which had formerly belonged to her mother's dower,[131] and on which Sophie founded a convent some time between 997 and 1002.[132] The convent and properties at Eschwege became Sophie's sole property after a repossession clause contained in the original charter became null and void on Otto III's death in 1002.[133] Later, during Sophie's abbacy at Gandersheim (1002–39), and probably shortly before her death, the convent at Eschwege and the properties appurtenant to it and any of her remaining possessions, that is, the whole fiscal district, became the property of Gandersheim.[134] In addition, during Otto

---

[126] On Pöhlde see Gauert (1970); Claus (1970); and Streich (1984) 162–5.

[127] K. Heinemeyer (1970) 4–5. Two roads apparently came together at Gieboldehausen, which lay on one of the roads indirectly connecting the royal residences of Grone and Pöhlde. The road leading south from Seesen apparently traversed through Gittelde, Badenhausen and Osterode to Pöhlde, from where it continued south to Duderstadt or turned west towards Gieboldehausen. Of the routes south from Gandersheim one led through Förste to Osterode where it joined the road from Seesen south, one went via Förste to Gieboldehausen, and the third went via Northeim and the Katlenburg to Gieboldehausen. See Herbst (1926) 28.   [128] Petke (1974) 10–15.

[129] *DO III* 67; Goetting (1973) 88, 264–5; Petke (1974) 11–12. Cf. K.-A. Eckhardt (1964) 168 n. 14.   [130] *DO III* 146; K. Heinemeyer (1970) 45.   [131] *DO II* 76.

[132] K.-A. Eckhardt (1957) 73–8 and (1964) 190–4.

[133] *DO III* 146: 'si iam dicta soror nostra ante quam nos naturae concedens universae carnis iter arripat, predium quod mancipavimus ad nos hereditario iure recurrat, sin autem nobis superstes existat, commutandi sive vendendi seu magis sibi retinendi vel quicquid libuerit inde faciendi liberam potestatem habeat'; K.-A. Eckhardt (1957) 31–2.

[134] Goetting (1973) 272–3, based on the astute argumentation of K.-A. Eckhardt (1957) 73–8, where he summarizes the results of his research and restates his thesis. K. Heinemeyer (1970) 50–60 argues unconvincingly against K.-A. Eckhardt (1957) that Sophie never founded an actual convent of canonesses at Eschwege, but only a kind of

III's reign, Gandersheim probably acquired the vill of Gieboldehausen, with its sixty *mansi* of land and a church dedicated to St Laurentius. This possession may well have served as an intermediary property or resting place connecting Sophie and later the convent of Gandersheim with their possessions in the former fiscal district of Eschwege.[135]

The routes to and from Goslar and Gandersheim via Mühlhausen or, more importantly, via Eschwege to Thuringia received occasional use by the late Saxon and early Salian kings. On these journeys, at least six in number, the kings very probably claimed hospitality from the possessions of Gandersheim, especially at Eschwege and Gieboldehausen, where stops are confirmed in charters. In 997, Otto III travelled with his sister Sophie from Gandersheim[136] to Eschwege and spent three or more days there. It is likely that on this occasion his sister founded the convent of canonesses at Eschwege.[137] In May 1003 Henry travelled south from Gandersheim, probably to Mühlhausen or Eschwege, and stopped on the way at a Gandersheim vill at Gieboldehausen and issued a charter there.[138] Henry III and Henry IV, on the other hand, stopped several times at Eschwege on their way to or from Goslar or the near vicinity. Henry III spent at least two days at Eschwege in July 1040 on his way south from Goslar to Bavaria.[139] Henry IV went to Eschwege at least three times, in 1057, in 1060 and on his flight from the Harzburg, when Eschwege still belonged to Gandersheim.[140] He also went there in July 1075, the year in which he received the convent and its property at Eschwege back from Gandersheim in a legal exchange.[141] Finally, later in the same year, he granted Eschwege to the bishopric of Speyer.[142] Seen in this light, we cannot correctly speak in terms of a 'fixed' *servitium regis* at this time for Gandersheim, but of one that the king claimed on demand when he stopped at Gandersheim or its various properties.[143]

---

association of canonesses ('verbundene Vereinigung'), and that the fiscal district of Eschwege never came to Gandersheim upon Sophie's death, but reverted immediately to the realm. See also Wolfgang Petke's review (*DA* 28 [1972] 311–12) of Heinemeyer's book, which raises similar doubts about Heinemeyer's thesis.

[135] Goetting (1973) 265. See also n. 127 above concerning Gieboldehausen's strategic location.   [136] *DO III* 248.   [137] *DDO III* 249, 250.
[138] Goetting (1973) 265; *DH II* 50.   [139] *DDH III* 61, 62, 63.
[140] *DH IV* 30; *Vita Gebehardi* p. 35; Lampert, *Annales s.a.* 1073 p. 155.
[141] Lampert, *Annales* p. 225; K.-A. Eckhardt (1957) 41–2, 65–6.
[142] *DH IV* 277; See also K. Heinemeyer (1970) 48–50.
[143] So also Metz (1976) 208.

Still with regard to the new palace at Goslar, there remains the question of whether or not Gandersheim, as a part of its *servitium*, may have made deliveries of foodstuffs or other necessities to Goslar to help support the court during its frequent and often lengthy stays there.[144] Although the Gandersheim sources make no mention of such deliveries, some pertinent inferences can be made from the scattered reports that we do possess. First of all, sources for other monasteries during both the Carolingian and Hohenstaufen periods inform us that deliveries of *servitia* to favoured palaces or episcopal cities occurred commonly, often over considerable distances.[145] Moreover, according to a report by Lampert of Hersfeld from 1065, not only fiscal incomes, but also the *servitium regis* of the abbeys contributed to the king's upkeep in Goslar.[146] Although Lampert often proves not to be a totally trustworthy source (and even in this instance some of his details are incorrect),[147] this does not alter the fact that he, a contemporary witness, regarded it as normal at Goslar (as at Worms)[148] for several sources of supply, notably the royal fisc and the royal church, to share the burden of accommodating the king and his court.[149] In addition, the bishopric of Hildesheim appears to have participated in supplying provisions or services to the court at Goslar;[150] the monastery of Corvey may also have contributed either directly or indirectly.[151] Considering that

---

[144] Henry II – seven times; Conrad II – six times; Henry III – twenty-one times; Henry IV – thirty-two times.

[145] Matthäi (1877) 40–5 first indicated a delivery of obligatory *servitia*. Brühl (1968) 72–5, 205–6, 210–11, provides more detailed information on this topic.

[146] Lampert, *Annales s.a.* 1066 (but in 1065), p. 100: 'sumptus habens regiae magnificentiae multum impares. Nam preter pauca, quae ex reditibus regalis fisci veniebant, vel quae abbates coacticio famulatu ministrabant, caetera omnia in quottidianos usus eius quottidianis impensis emebantur.'

[147] Henry IV celebrated Christmas of 1065 at Mainz, not Goslar.

[148] Lampert, *Annales s.a.* 1074 (25 December 1073), p. 173: 'Rex natalem Domini Wormaciae celebravit, longe aliter ibi victitans, quam regiam magnificentiam deceret. Nam neque ex fiscis regalibus quicquam servicii ei exhibebatur, neque episcopi aut abbates vel aliae publicae dignitates consueta ei obsequia prebebant, sed in sumptus quottidianos necessaria ei vili precio coemebantur.'

[149] Brühl (1968) 210–11 and Metz (1978b) 26–7, 48–9.

[150] Metz (1978b) 3–4, 27; *DH II* 256b: 'Proinde quotiens in expeditionem seu ad palatium vel in aliud quodlibet nostrum servitium ire debeat, quorumlibet hominum suorum ad hoc iter potestatem habeat...'

[151] Metz (1978b) 27 and Kaminsky (1972) 151, 224. In Section 1 of Kaminsky's edition of the so-called 'Registrum Ekenberti' concerning the yearly payments to Corvey of twelve dependent *Smurden* it states: 'Quatuor ex illis [*Smurden*] dant...et 1^m (nummum) pro itinere, quod debet Goslariam facere...' Although Metz implies on the

Gandersheim, like the bishopric of Hildesheim, had substantial property holdings in and around Goslar,[152] it appears justified to assume that Gandersheim, the largest and most powerful monastery in the vicinity of Goslar, also helped to supply the court there with the delivery of a part of its *servitium regis*.

Wolfgang Metz, on the other hand, rejects the idea of a delivery of Gandersheim's *servitium regis* to the royal palace at Goslar.[153] Metz uses the Gandersheim petition of the early twelfth century as his support, claiming that the canonesses would certainly have complained about such deliveries had they occurred. Although the *Gandersheimer Supplik* (petition) is an excellent source for various aspects of Gandersheim's *servitium regis*, it does not really support Metz's position. As in so many other royal monasteries – especially those with close royal connections and sizeable obligations *vis-à-vis* the king and realm – either a formal or, more probably, an informal internal separation of property existed in Gandersheim between the abbess and the congregation of canonesses at least by the twelfth century if not before. Since the abbot or abbess paid the *servitium regis* from his or her part of the monastery's property, the canonesses would have had no reason to complain about deliveries of provisions to the palace at Goslar as part of the overall *servitium regis* unless the abbess acquired such provisions unjustly from the property of the canonesses. Just because the abbess confiscated conventual property to grant in benefice to the monastery's *milites* – a group which at this time was increasing in size, largely by an infusion of 'foreign' Salian vassals having little or no land in the area – this does not necessarily imply that she needed to confiscate conventual property to pay the customary economic *servitium regis* of the monastery. Even if one accepts that there was an increased claim by the court in respect of Gandersheim's economic *servitium regis* on the basis of the expanded use of the palace at Goslar and the roads leading to it, the huge grants of lands, taxes and profitable rights made by the Saxon kings, especially Henry II, to

basis of this passage that Corvey took a direct part in the provisioning of the king at Goslar (which it may well have done), a strict rendering of the passage allows us only to state definitely that this payment supported the cost or provision of the abbot (or provost?) when he travelled to or attended the royal court at Goslar.

[152] Goetting (1973) 270–1; Heinemann (1968) 38–41; and Wilke (1970) 21–4.
[153] Metz (1976) 208.

Gandersheim (e.g. the yearly tax of 500 rams paid by the inhabitants of Ammergau) probably went a long way to cover this increase.[154]

The suggestions that Gandersheim sent provisions, especially agricultural goods, to the palace at Goslar, and that the general upkeep of the court there came from diverse sources, gain additional support when one examines the types of royal incomes at Goslar, especially in its peak years as a royal palace under the Salians after its foundation by Henry II. As the most significant market-place in Saxony in the eleventh century, Goslar provided the king with sizeable incomes from tolls and money-changing; and the silver mining operations at Rammelsberg near Goslar with the consequent minting incomes supplied huge profits. In addition, the king disposed of the proceeds from the nearby royal forest and game rights, and the yields from the *curtes* at Werla and Goslar.[155] From a purely agrarian standpoint, however, Goslar's location, bordering directly on the Harz mountains, was not particularly advantageous and the types of royal incomes available would hardly suffice to provide all the foodstuffs needed to supply the court for the long and frequent sojourns of the Salian kings at Goslar.[156] The nature of the royal incomes at Goslar thus lends new credence to Lampert's remark that the court was forced to buy provisions at the market there when other customary *servitia* remained outstanding.[157] When one considers all of this evidence as a whole, it appears that part of Gandersheim's economic *servitium regis*, especially under the Salian kings, also consisted of the delivery of provisions to help supply the court at Goslar. Combined with its obligation to accommodate the king in the monastery during his *iter*, the economic *servitium regis* of the convent of Gandersheim reveals itself as a sizeable charge and one upon which the Saxon and especially the Salian kings heavily depended and, consequently, furthered and guarded actively.

---

[154] Goetting (1949) 101–2 appears to support this opinion. Concerning monastic property separations and the payment of *servitium regis* from the abbatial property, see Chapter 3. For the example of Corvey, see Kaminsky (1972) 147.

[155] Metz (1978b) 26–7, 50 and Wilke (1970) 20–4.

[156] Wilke (1970) 19–20, 24. Metz (1976) 208, in arguing his position on the *Gandersheimer Supplik*, overlooked the overall economic situation of the Goslar *Pfalz*, which greatly increases the likelihood of such deliveries of provisions from Gandersheim (and other places) to Goslar.

[157] Lampert, *Annales s.a.* 1066 p. 100.

ST MAURICE AT MAGDEBURG

An examination of the economic obligations of the royal monastery of St Maurice presents several inherent difficulties. As elsewhere in Saxony, but especially in Magdeburg, the problem of establishing clear-cut distinctions between royal property and church property, or, more exactly, property of the realm which came to be held by royal churches, is a troublesome one. This in turn makes it difficult to determine exactly from what sources the king received his accommodation and upkeep when in Magdeburg. Moreover, an analysis of the charters granted to St Maurice with regard to their possible relation to the monastery's *servitium regis* is conditioned by another important factor. Although St Maurice technically remained a royal monastery from its foundation in 937 until 968, when it became the seat of a new archbishopric, Otto I envisaged the creation of an arch-bishopric there as early as 955,[158] and by at least 962 (and presumably earlier in 960), had begun actively to further his intentions by granting to St Maurice at Magdeburg property and rights on a scale befitting the elevated stature and increased duties of a future archbishopric.[159] Thus, with regard to St Maurice's economic *servitium regis* as a function of accommodating and providing for the king's upkeep when he visited Magdeburg, one must consider St Maurice technically as a royal monastery until 968 when it legally changed its status. On the other hand, to the extent that the royal charters can provide us with information about a monastery's *servitium regis*, especially its ability to pay or provide such economic support, we can consider only those charters for St Maurice before 955 or 960 as being mostly unaffected by Otto's later designs for the monastery. Since the great majority of Otto's visits to Magdeburg fall before 955,[160] however, his future intentions for the monastery do not really affect an evaluation of the monastery's ability to feed and house the royal entourage in this period or diminish the existence of this burden on the monastery.

On 21 September 937, Otto I founded the royal monastery at Magdeburg, dedicated it to saints Maurice and Innocent, and lavishly endowed it with Liudolfing family properties, primarily

---

[158] Claude (1972–5) 1.63–96 esp. 69–80 deals in depth with the evolution of Otto's plans for an archbishopric in Magdeburg.　　[159] Claude (1972–5) 1.55–8.
[160] Ibid. 57–8.

from the marriage settlement of his wife Edith.[161] As with so many monasteries in the Ottonian period, however, we have little information pertaining specifically to the economic obligations of St Maurice. The sole reference we have regarding any specific service or payment due from St Maurice to the king occurs in Otto's foundation charter of 937.[162] In this charter, Otto stipulated that the congregation of monks should serve no one except God and the saints, and that as recognition of their legal status, that is, a royal monastery under the king's protection, they should give the king a horse, a shield, and a lance, or two fur garments, yearly.[163] Rather than an assessment of the *servitium regis*, however, this requirement appears to be a token levy in recognition of royal protection and immunity, which has several precedents from the Carolingian period and is probably a remnant of the Carolingian *dona annua*.[164]

Far more important with regard to St Maurice's economic *servitium* and its ability to fulfil this obligation are the extensive gifts in land, dependants and profitable rights that Otto I granted to the monastery in order to provide for its material needs. In the foundation charter, Otto granted the monastery his residence at Magdeburg and the manor supporting it (*curtem nostram cum aedificio*), and the entire cultivated area (*territorium*) belonging to this residence.[165] This comprised over thirty localities and their populations west of the Elbe in Nordthüringau that belonged to or owed services to the *curtis* regardless of who might at that time

---

[161] *DO I* 14 (= *UBM* 1): 'coniugis nostrae, et praedictus locus dos fuit' See also *Ann. Magd. s.a.* 929 p. 142: 'Otto magnus Edith…matrimonio sibi iungendam Saxoniae advexit, eique urbem Magdeburg, quae nunc metropolis est Saxoniae, tunc vero Halberstadensi diocesi subiecta fuit, inter ceteras opes pro dote optulit.' Concerning this marriage settlement, see Schmid (1964/1971b) 442–6 with nn. 94–107 and now Leyser (1983b) 80–9. The provisions in the foundation charter concerning the legal status of the new monastery and the report contained in the Magdeburg Annals (*Ann. Magd. s.a.* 938 p. 143: 'Eadem tempore praedictus rex instinctu et peticione pie coniugis suae Edith regine abbaciam regalem intra urbem Magdeburg fundavit.') confirm that St Maurice was a royal monastery from the start.   [162] *DO I* 14 (= *UBM* 1).

[163] Ibid.: 'ut familiae…nulli nisi eidem congregationi serviant et illa nisi deo et sanctis, nisi singulis anni tantum regi unum cavallum, scutum et lanceam vel duas crusinas dent, ut sciant in mundiburdio regis se esse'.

[164] Cf. *DLD* 70, *DArn* 146 and *DZ* 18. On this formulation as a remnant of the *dona annua*, see Lesne (1910–43) vol. 2.2 pp. 416–19. *DKD* 125 (St Evre) and *DArn* 165 (St Magnus) contain similar stipulations. Otto I's charter confirming the restoration of the regular life in St Evre (*DO I* 92) provides a contemporary parallel for the St Maurice charter where it states (*DO I* 92): 'Praeterea statuimus ut servitium…nullus deinceps episcoporum praesumat exigere, nisi tantum quod ipse causa demonstrandae subiectionis instituit…'   [165] For this interpretation, see Schlesinger (1968) 5–6.

hold them as a fief.[166] The charter also spoke of *census* or rents, the tithe – or tenth part – of sales and acquisitions, and the rights to use forests and pastures and of pannage – that is, to pasture pigs in the forest – in three Slavic districts east of the Elbe River.[167] Two additional charters written shortly thereafter completed St Maurice's initial endowment by granting the monastery the tolls or trade duties in Magdeburg (already a busy centre of trade), numerous families of Slavs (*liti, coloni* and *servi*) along with the rights to all dues and services they owed, and finally a second royal residence (*curtis*) in Magdeburg and the estates supporting it.[168] Here we have an endowment on an even larger scale than that of Quedlinburg in the previous year[169] and the first three of over forty charters granted by Otto I to the monastery of St Maurice before it formally became an archbishopric in 968. Moreover, these three charters show that Magdeburg formed the centre of a large district which already had active trade, a nascent fiscal system and military organization.[170]

In the years that followed, until 960 when a significant increase in the number of charters for St Maurice clearly tie it with Otto's plan to create an archbishopric,[171] the monastery of St Maurice received an additional seventeen royal grants.[172] These grants comprised primarily large gifts of land, often by means of exchanges with other ecclesiastical or secular nobles,[173] a huge number of new dependent peoples,[174] and various grants of tithe incomes.[175] Of particular interest with regard to the increase in the

---

[166] *DO I* 14 (= *UBM* 1): 'in Magdeburg curtem nostram cum aedificio et territorium illuc pertinens cum omnibus locis ex occidentali parte Albis fluminis ad eandem civitatem pertinentibus vel servientibus, cuiuscunque sint modo beneficia, hoc est…'

[167] Ibid.: 'et omnis census et venundationis adquisitionis que decimam in Mortsani et Ligzice et Heueldun praefatae congregationi concedimus, et liceat, ut in eis et ligna et herbe in usus sint et porci saginentur'. Carr (unpub. diss. 1986) 59–73 has analysed the types of estates and revenues granted in the charters for St Maurice in order to evaluate the material basis of the monastery (and by extension its ability to provide for the king).

[168] *DDO I* 15, 16 (= *UBM* 2, 3).

[169] *DO I* 1. Also in Quedlinburg, Otto founded both the monastery of St Dyonisius and St Servatius and that of St James and St Wipert on former house or royal property. *DO I* 1: 'urbem in Quidilingoburg supra montem constructam … habuimus'; *Ann. Magd.* c. 32 *s.a.* 988: 'coenobium sanctorum confessorum Dionisii et Servatii in monte Quidilingburgensi situm, alterum in eadem civitate sub honore sanctorum Iacobi apostoli et Wicberti confessoris in curte regia'. [170] Leyser (1979) 1–3.

[171] Claude (1972–5) 1.57.

[172] Claude (1972–5) 1.45–55 provides a very useful summary of the property acquisitions of St Maurice.

[173] *DDO I* 37, 43, 63, 79, 97, 165 (= *UBM* 5, 8, 10, 13, 14, 17).

[174] *DDO I* 16, 21 (= *UBM* 3, 4). [175] *DDO I* 37, 79 (= *UBM* 5, 13).

monastery's economic power is the royal charter of 28 March 942 in which Otto granted the monks of St Maurice all tolls paid in Magdeburg and the profits from the minting of coins there.[176] Normally, a grant of these two valuable rights presupposes that the monastery already had the right to hold a market.[177] This is one of the first charters granting the royal privilege of minting coins to an ecclesiastical institution in Saxony. Considering that Magdeburg numbered among the most active trading centres in the realm, known especially for its trade in honey, fur and slaves, the incomes concerned represent considerable sums.

By and large the great majority of the monastery's possessions, dependants and profitable rights lay in and around Magdeburg. This facilitated both the management and supervision of its cultivated and settled lands, and the collection of dues and taxes. Moreover, within the growing endowment there existed a perceptible and desirable balance between natural and money incomes.[178] Thus, the gifts bestowed upon the monastery prior to 960 provided a relatively compact block of estates in the region and a solid basis of revenues upon which Otto built further, between 960 and 967, to complete the endowment of his future archbishopric. The extensive grants of property, secular and ecclesiastical tithes, tolls and taxes of this period came technically to the monastery, and thus greatly enriched its economic strength but, owing to their close connection with the development and completion of an archepiscopal endowment, I have chosen to disregard royal gifts after 960 in my attempt to evaluate the historical sources concerning the monastery's economic obligations to the king.[179] From this brief summary of the history of property acquisition at St Maurice, however, one cannot deny that even before the substantial royal gifts in the years 960–7, the monastery of St Maurice disposed of a huge amount of properties and incomes in the eastern part of the realm and

---

[176] *DO I* 46 (= *UBM* 9): 'totum, quod a vectigali, id est teloneo vel moneta eiusdem loci utilita venire poterit, ex hoc in antea in usus illorum hoc inperiali regie auctoritatis precepto iure perenni in proprium concessimus'.

[177] Stein (1922) 26–30 and Borchers (unpub. diss. 1952) 62. In fact, Otto's charter of 9 July 965 (*DO I* 301 = *UBM* 39) granting St Maurice the market, minting and toll rights in Magdeburg appears actually to confirm an already existing set of rights. Claude (1972–5) 1.46 also interprets the charter in this way.

[178] Claude (1972–5) 1.53–6.

[179] Almost half of the charters granted by Otto I for St Maurice in Magdeburg were issued between 960 and 968.

obviously had the means to provide the king with considerable economic support.

St Maurice's acquisition of the royal residence in Magdeburg and its supporting estates in 937 reveals the exact nature of that support[180] – to feed and house, at least in part, the king and royal court in Magdeburg. On the basis of a charter of Otto II for the archbishopric of Magdeburg in 981, some scholars have argued that the king lived predominantly off his own property when in Magdeburg.[181] The narration of Otto II's charter states that Otto I had conceded certain of his properties (*sui iuris*) both within and outside of Magdeburg to St Maurice after its elevation to an archbishopric, and that these properties pertained to or formerly pertained to his own uses (*suis usibus*). To be sure, this charter leaves little doubt that some royal property (how much cannot be determined) still existed after the creation of the archbishopric at Magdeburg and therefore also after the foundation of its predecessor, the royal monastery of St Maurice. Indeed, a later clause in the same charter indicates that the king used these retained properties to some degree *morandi gratia*, that is, to stay or reside there.[182] To conclude, however, from this single charter reference 'that the king lived predominantly off his own property when in Magdeburg' ignores numerous indications to the contrary.[183] Otto's grants of 937 for St Maurice indicate that he had, in essence, united his recently built residence there with the newly created monastery.[184] Otto had thus instituted an organizational alteration – royal property became property of a royal monastery which, however, with all of its appurtenances, remained property of the realm. The new holder of the property, the monastery of St Maurice, assumed the administration and the use of the properties, which nonetheless retained some of their former functions

---

[180] *DO I* 14.

[181] *DO II* 258; Brühl (1968) 123–6 following, but expanding upon, Heusinger (1922) 41–2 [66–7].

[182] *DO I* 258 'et quedam loca supradictorum inibi morandi gratia sibimet pro benefitio retinuerat'.

[183] Brühl (1968) 124. Even as late as 1208–9, the obligation of accommodation of the king formed a part of Magdeburg's *servitium regis*: see Metz (1978a) 239–40, 281. And indeed Brühl himself retreats somewhat from this statement in his next paragraph (p. 124) when he once again opts for a more reasonable interworking of royal and church property to provision and accommodate the court. He even goes so far as to restate the often quoted observation of Matthäi (1877) 64, that the tenth century was the 'golden age' of the royal monasteries, and appends to it the royal bishoprics as well!

[184] *DDO I* 14, 15, 16 (= *UBM* 1, 2, 3); Schlesinger (1968) 24–5.

and obligations to the king. For the king, as ultimate lord over the property, held a claim to the property of royal churches and to the use of it upon necessity or demand; from this proprietary right and his position as royal protector of the monastery derived in part his claim to *servitium regis*.[185] Thus, after St Maurice acquired the royal residence and appurtenant property in Magdeburg, Otto, claiming his right to accommodation and provision, apparently used the monastery itself as his royal palace.[186]

During the reign of Otto I this was no easy burden! More visits by Otto to Magdeburg are recorded than to any other place in the realm. In the years prior to St Maurice's elevation to an archbishopric in 968, Otto visited Magdeburg twenty-one times and spent approximately one hundred days there.[187] Of these, seventeen visits occurred before 955 when we have our first evidence indicating Otto's intention to create an archbishopric in Magdeburg. Thus, in the first eighteen years of Otto's reign he averaged nearly one visit a year to the monastery of St Maurice, and in at least four years he visited St Maurice and Magdeburg more than once.[188] Consequently, at least on these occasions, Otto's right to accommodation must be considered unequivocally as a monastic *servitium*.

Although Magdeburg was not among the customary places in Saxony where the German kings celebrated one of the three high church feasts, Easter, Christmas or Pentecost,[189] Otto may have

---

[185] Schlesinger (1962) 1.246–8 and (1968) 13–18.

[186] Schlesinger (1968) 24–5. Using the similar example of St Emmeram in Regensburg, where a royal residence and a monastery stood in close proximity, and the Ottonian foundations of convents of canonesses on old royal *Pfalzen* (Quedlinburg, Walbeck [OSB], Nordhausen, Eschwege and Hilwartshausen), Streich (1984) 311–12 and also 315–16 n. 921 sees the royal residence as being integrated into the monastery, and warns against either a topological or a legal separation of the two. He also sees this as the case for episcopal cities.

[187] Müller-Mertens (1980) 269 Table 3. Although Magdeburg documents more royal visits under Otto I than any other place in the realm, according to Müller-Mertens's calculation of actual time spent in one place Magdeburg with 105 days falls far behind Frankfurt with 226 days.

[188] One of these seventeen documented visits (14 October 936) fell before the foundation of the royal monastery of St Maurice. Moreover, not every visit or sojourn in a place is attested by the issuance of a charter or finds expression in a narrative source. Thus, there is a very high likelihood of numerous undocumented stops in Magdeburg, especially considering its high status, Otto's preference for it and its location in the heartland of the realm. See Schlesinger (1968) 16–18 and Claude (1972–5) 1.58.

[189] Klewitz (1939a) 78–94; Rieckenberg (1941/1965) 43–4.

held his Easter court there in 952.[190] He certainly celebrated the feast of Palm Sunday at St Maurice in 948.[191] This was an extremely important feast because the king's entry into the city liturgically re-enacted the triumphal entry of Christ as king into Jerusalem.[192] After Magdeburg and St Maurice had become an archbishopric in 968, and just prior to his death in 973, Otto once again celebrated Palm Sunday at Magdeburg, after which he proceeded to Quedlinburg to observe Easter in its traditional Saxon setting.[193] It should be borne in mind that this practice, after his burial there, became linked by later rulers with the Easter celebration at Quedlinburg and visits to the tombs at both places.[194] We also find Otto present at the monastery for the feast of St Maurice (22 September) in 937.[195] Otto may well have observed the feast of St Maurice, with its special connection both with the Saxon rulers and with Magdeburg, more frequently in Magdeburg than the sources allow us to determine.[196] On the basis of his itinerary, Otto could have celebrated the feast of St Maurice in Magdeburg as many as eleven times between 938 and 966.[197] In conjunction with the celebration of St Maurice's feast day in 937, Otto held a secular assembly in Magdeburg. Also, in October of 948 – on the foundation of the bishopric of Brandenburg – and in June of 965 assemblies of the royal court took place there.[198] Aside from these documented visits and sojourns in Magdeburg, gaps in the itinerary leave us room to conjecture additional unrecorded visits to Magdeburg, especially prior to 960.[199]

The sources and evidence we have examined reveal that before

---

[190] BO 211a; Claude (1972–5) 1.58; cf. Klewitz (1939a) 90–1.

[191] Based on the evidence of *DO I* 98, which Otto issued in Quedlinburg on 1 April 948, Otto celebrated the Easter feast on the following day (2 April) also in Quedlinburg, as was customary when in Saxony. On the preceding Monday (27 March) Otto granted a charter in Magdeburg to the monastery of Hersfeld and thereby confirmed his presence in Magdeburg on the day following Palm Sunday. Therefore, one cannot doubt that Otto observed Palm Sunday in Magdeburg at St Maurice. Palm Sunday of 973 appears to be the only church feast that Otto ever celebrated in Magdeburg after its elevation to an archbishopric.

[192] See Kantorowicz (1944/1965) 42–3. I thank Karl Leyser for drawing my attention to the high significance of this feast for Ottonian kingship.

[193] Thietmar 2 cc. 30(20), 31.   [194] Leyser (1979) 90.

[195] *DDO I* 14, 15 (= *UBM* 1, 2).

[196] Concerning Magdeburg and the cult of St Maurice, see Brackmann (1937), Beumann (1962) 553–61 and Warner (unpub. diss. 1989) 100–14.

[197] Claude (1972–5) 1.58 n. 294; Schlesinger (1968) 16–18; and Klewitz (1939a) 70 n. 1.

[198] Müller-Mertens (1980) 267–9; BO 69b, 169, 394a.

[199] Schlesinger (1968) 16–18.

the creation of the archbishopric in Magdeburg its predecessor, the royal monastery of St Maurice, provided the king and the court with a substantial *servitium regis* in the form of frequent accommodation and provision. Through the acquisition of the royal residence in Magdeburg and a large complex of royal property appurtenant to it, the monastery had the means to house and feed the court, and the monastery's control of the royal market, tolls and coining rights in Magdeburg further enabled it to supply the various needs of the large royal entourage.[200] When the king came to Magdeburg, he resided in the monastery in his former residence, which after 937 probably also served as the abbot's residence, and the monks and the monastic church functioned in the capacity of a palace chapter and chapel respectively.[201] With the creation of the archbishopric in 968, the properties, duties and functions of the royal monastery were transferred to the fledgling archbishopric and the general *servitium regis* continued and even grew, bolstered by the rich gifts of property and rights granted by Otto I from 960 onwards, and the continued generosity of his son Otto II. The king's right to accommodation and provision, now at the hands of the archbishop, continued throughout the Ottonian period and appears, with the other aspects of the overall *servitium regis*, to have lasted well into the twelfth century.[202] But at this point the *servitium regis* of St Maurice became an episcopal *servitium* and no longer concerns us within the framework of this study.

[200] Following many of the various insights and observations of Stein (1922) 75–81, Metz (1971) 279–91 has concisely indicated the preference of the Ottonian rulers for places having markets and trade activity, and the importance of these early market foundations in supplying the sundry needs and wants of the royal court.

[201] Schlesinger (1968) 24–5. If the *Pfalz* or royal residence granted to St Maurice in 937 later became the archbishop's residence, which he put at the king's disposal or shared with him when he came to Magdeburg, the same residence more than likely served exactly the same function for the abbot of St Maurice prior to 968.

[202] Claude (1972–5) 2.229–43; and Metz (1978a) 239–40, 281.

MINOR ROYAL MONASTERIES AND CONVENTS OF SAXONY:
BERGE, NIENBURG, ALSLEBEN, DRÜBECK, GERNRODE
(FROSE) AND NORDHAUSEN[203]

Concerning the economic obligations to the king of the remaining royal monasteries in Saxony (see Maps 5 and 6) during the Ottonian and early Salian periods we possess far less information either of a specific or of an indicative nature. From the monastery of Berge in Magdeburg, which Otto I founded shortly before 968 to house the monks of St Maurice after it was converted into the archbishopric,[204] there is no mention or indication at all of any economic *servitium*. Although the monastery was a royal foundation, some time in the first half of the eleventh century the archbishop of Magdeburg took possession of it.[205] Especially in light of the royal *servitium* of the archbishop, Berge probably paid little or no service to the king.[206]

The monastery of Nienburg on the Saale River, on the other hand, appears to have paid an economic *servitium* in the form of accommodation and upkeep of the royal court.[207] On 29 August 970, Archbishop Gero of Cologne and his brother Margrave Thietmar, both sons of Margrave Christian, founded a monastery at Thankmarsfeld,[208] which soon became a royal monastery, probably in 971 and certainly before 975.[209] In 975, this foundation was moved to Nienburg on the Saale River near the mouth of the Bode River.[210] Nienburg also belonged to the family of the

---

[203] Any economic obligations of the monastery of Memleben, which was an Ottonian cult site and located on the Unstrut River in northern Thuringia, will be considered in connection with those of Hersfeld, which later came to possess it, and the monasteries of Thuringia and Hesse.   [204] Claude (1972–5) 2.291–4.   [205] Ibid.

[206] Römer (1970) 17–18, 187 and 198 has incorrectly translated *DO I* 382 to make it refer to the monastery's military obligation. As it stands, *DO I* 382 provides absolutely no information about Berge's military obligation.   [207] Claude (1972–5) 2.341.

[208] K. Müller (1933) gives a detailed commentary on this private charter and his appendix (pp. 50–2) provides the most recent edition of the charter. For the older edition, see *CDA* 1 no. 47 pp. 36–7.

[209] Claude (1972–5) 2.321–2 esp. 322 n. 13. A papal charter granted by Pope John XIII on Christmas Day of 971 (*CDA* 1 no. 49 pp. 38–9; *BZ* 489; *PU* 213) for Thankmarsfeld already implied that the monastery had royal status when it stated that Thankmarsfeld should have the emperor as its protector, that is, it stood under the royal *mundiburdium*. Also in Otto II's charter of 975 (*DO II* 114) authorizing the transfer of the monastery from Thankmarsfeld to Nienburg (which he issued before the transfer), he stated that the two brothers 'nostro mundiburdio perpetim imperiali nostra potestate tutandum tradiderant'. The charter also stipulated that the advocacy over the monastery would remain within the founding family.

[210] *DO II* 114; *Chronicon Montis Sereni* s.a. 1171 p. 154.

original founders,[211] and the shift of location appears primarily connected with assigning the monastery a role in the evangelization of recently won Slavic areas.[212] In addition, however, the shift placed the new royal monastery in a strategic location on a royal route and busy trade road, which ran along the Saale and the Elbe, and connected Magdeburg and Merseburg.[213]

Around the time of the transfer, Gero and Thietmar made further property grants in the area to the monastery,[214] but after these grants the accumulation of additional properties and profitable rights derived primarily, if not exclusively, from the hands of the royal family.[215] Two sizeable property grants from Otto II in 978 and 979 appear to have placed the monastery on a firm footing in its new location.[216] All subsequent land grants by the Ottonians were located in Slavic regions.[217] In 993, under Otto III, Nienburg acquired the profitable right to hold a market, collect tolls and mint coins at Hagenrode, and Otto strengthened these rights by appending the royal ban at Hagenrode to the grant. All proceeds from these rights went to the monastery at Nienburg.[218] Later, under Conrad II, the monastery attained the very advantageous right of transferring its mint at Hagenrode, and its market at Staßfurt, and uniting them at Nienburg.[219] These two early markets of the monastery appear to have derived their initial importance from mining activities at Hagenrode and the

---

[211] *Chronicon Montis Sereni s.a.* 1171 p. 154; Claude (1972–5) 2.325. One cannot determine exactly when the monastery acquired Nienburg itself. A royal charter of 961 (*DO II* 3) mentions Nienburg as a possession of Gernrode, another foundation of the same family; and then a papal charter of 983 for Nienburg (*CDA* I no. 71 pp. 55–6; *BZ* 614; *PU* 278) lists the same property among the endowment granted to the transferred monastery. According to a sixteenth-century land register of Gernrode, Nienburg was exchanged shortly after Gernrode's foundation against the four villages of Poley (Groß and Klein Poley, Ysepoley and Kirchpoley) *c.* 6 km south of Bernburg. See Schulze (1965) 180–1, 184. [212] Claude (1972–5) 2.323–31.

[213] Stein (1922) 114–15; Metz (1971) 283. [214] *CDA* I no. 71 pp. 55–6.

[215] *DDO II* 174, 185; *DDO III* 135, 244, 359; *DH II* 83; *DK II* 223.

[216] *DDO III* 174, 185. [217] *DDO III* 244, 359; *DH II* 83.

[218] *DO III* 135. The market of Hagenrode lay near Harzgerode, which also had a market (see *DO III* 155), in the vicinity of the original location of the monastery at Thankmarsfeld (between Gernrode and Harzgerode). It was situated on the road that led from Quedlinburg south through the lower Harz toward Wallhausen and Nordhausen. See above n. 25 and at nn. 73, 74. According to a report in the *Chronicon Montis Sereni* (*s.a.* 1171 p. 154), an early thirteenth-century source of often questionable reliability, a public market may have existed at Nienburg prior to that of the monastery. If this indeed were so, then the monastery may have taken over the existing market instead of establishing a new one. In any case the monastery's possessions in the Harz region still proved profitable. Concerning identification of the various places in this area, see Weyhe (1907). [219] *DK II* 223.

extraction of salt at Staßfurt. Conrad II's privilege facilitated the monastery's control of the market and the mint, and at the same time increased the economic significance of the monastery at Nienburg.[220]

The royal monastery of Nienburg appears to have had a definite significance for the Saxon and Salian kings owing to its geographical location on the main royal road along the Saale between Magdeburg and Merseburg. Nienburg lay one day's march (*c.* 35 km) south of Magdeburg providing an important stopping place for the travelling royal entourage. Apparently the monastery also lay on an auxiliary route from Magdeburg to Allstedt. For somewhere near Nienburg, a road led due west or southwest joining the Elbe–Saale route with the royal road running along the eastern border of the Harz.[221] Thus, Nienburg fulfilled its obligation or *servitium* as a royal monastery to accommodate and provision the king on his *iter*. Although we have only three documented visits by Henry II to Nienburg,[222] a further six visits of Ottonian and Salian monarchs appear not only possible, but very likely.[223] The known itinerary makes all of these six visits possible. Their likelihood increases significantly, however, when one considers not only the frequent use of certain routes, but also the fact that either just before or shortly after all of these possible visits the respective ruler issued a charter for Nienburg. For example, Otto II in 978 may well have used this route travelling from Magdeburg via Nienburg to Allstedt, where on 17 April he granted thirty royal *mansi* in the *Burg* of Grimschleben to Nienburg.[224] Thus, in response to an abbatial request made either in Magdeburg or at Nienburg itself, or possibly in appreciation of accommodation and provision at the monastery, the king repaid the *servitium* with a grant. Also, Otto III issued the monastery two grants, one just shortly after, and one immediately before, travelling the Saale–Elbe route from Merseburg to Magdeburg, most probably via Nienburg.[225] In 1003, Henry II had a charter drawn up for Nienburg and one for nearby Alsleben on the day after he celebrated Palm Sunday at

---

[220] Schwineköper (1977) 14–18.
[221] In the spring of 1024 (March/April), Henry II travelled this route. See *Ann. Qued. s.a.* 1024.
[222] *DH II* 83 (6 August 1004); *DH II* 102 (13 August 1005); BG 2059b.
[223] *DO II* 174; *DDO III* 135, 244; *DDH II* 43, 44; *DK II* 20; *DH III* 258.
[224] *DO II* 174. See n. 229 below for a similar route. [225] *DDO III* 135 and 244.

Magdeburg.[226] Henry kept the Easter feast six days later in Quedlinburg, and although a route to Quedlinburg via Nienburg was not normal, the time span of the itinerary does not exclude such a diversion. In this case, however, it appears more likely that the abbot attended the Palm Sunday feast at Magdeburg along with other nobles and ecclesiastics of the realm, and requested the charter then, especially since it may have been his first opportunity to have the monastery's rights confirmed under the new king. Later, on 6 August 1004, Henry II participated in the dedication of the monastic church at Nienburg,[227] and he issued a charter there in August 1005.[228] Finally, in 1024, Henry celebrated Palm Sunday at Allstedt, and then on account of sickness he stopped and celebrated Maundy Thursday and Good Friday at Nienburg before proceeding to Magdeburg for the Easter feast.[229]

Henry's Salian successors also appear to have stopped occasionally in Nienburg. Conrad II issued a charter for Nienburg after a quick trip from Magdeburg to Merseburg and he very probably stopped at Nienburg overnight along the route.[230] According to a report of a sixteenth-century source, Henry III may also have visited Nienburg some time in 1050 and as a result issued *DH III* 258.[231] Moreover, the *Annals of Niederaltaich* from the mid-eleventh century provide us with additional, although indirect, evidence of Nienburg's obligation and ability to provide the king with a *servitium* in the form of accommodation and provisions. For the year 1069, the *Annals* report that during the Thuringian revolt of that year against Henry IV, led by Margrave Dedi and his ally Count Albrecht of Ballenstedt, Albrecht seized the royal monastery of Nienburg and the royal properties around it. He then 'forced [them] (i.e. the monastery and the royal properties) to serve him', that is, to pay him a *servitium* or provide him with food and accommodation.[232] It is clear from the context that during this rebellion the Count of Ballenstedt had usurped the king's right to

[226] *DDH II* 43, 44.
[227] *DH II* 83. Concerning the consecration and dedication of the monastic church at Nienburg in 1004 and Henry's participation, see Benz (1975) 92–105.
[228] *DH II* 102.   [229] *Ann. Qued. s.a.* 1024; BG 2059b.
[230] *DK II* 20. See Hirsch (1862–75) 1.52.
[231] *Series abbatum Nienburgensium* p. 114. Although this source originated in the sixteenth century and is often unreliable, such a visit could fit into the itinerary of 1050 and other circumstances may give the report additional credibility. See Claude (1972–5) 2.331–2.
[232] *Ann. Alt. s.a.* 1069 p. 77: 'Adalbertus autem regiam abbatiam, Nienburg dictam, invasit et praedia regis, quae in circuitu erant, sibi servire coegit.' Niermeyer (1954–76) 963 reads the same sense in this passage and uses it as an example of the word 'servire'.

hospitality and *servitium* (*servire*), and that the royal properties around the monastery were probably those properties of the realm granted to and administered by Nienburg, and used to provide the royal *servitium*. Later, when Albrecht fled Nienburg, the *Annals* call Nienburg a *civitas* which, like *urbs*, implies a fortified site, that is, a monastery and/or town enclosed within walls. Apparently, the monastery could provide a *servitium* to support and ac-commodate a moderately sized retinue for at least a few days. On the whole, Ottonian and Salian rulers seem to have used Nienburg repeatedly for overnight stays and short visits.

No known evidence has come down to us concerning an economic *servitium* of the royal convent at Alsleben. However, the convent was situated advantageously about 25 km south of Nienburg on the Saale River. Several accounts confirm the existence of river traffic on the Saale, at least downstream, and Alsleben, about 30 km along the Saale from Giebichenstein, would have provided a logical stopping point for such river traffic.[233] Whether or not Alsleben may also have played a role as a stopping place for overland travel cannot be determined on the basis of extant information. It was founded and initially given into royal protection in 979 by Count Gero and his wife, Adala. According to the charter surrendering the convent to the king, Count Gero founded Alsleben in his *civitas*, that is, a fortified town or residence, and intended it for thirty-four or more canonesses.[234] The monastery was situated in the northern part of the *civitas*. The remaining area most probably afforded ample space and the monastery had sufficient provisions at its disposal to accommodate any river traffic stopping there. As Karl Leyser has indicated, the ruin of Count Gero by his enemies, Archbishop Adalbert of Magdeburg and Margrave Dietrich of the Northern March, and his subsequent beheading as a result of a judgement of Otto II and the princes, left his female survivors in need of royal protection

---

[233] In June 981, when Bishop Adalbert of Magdeburg died suddenly west of Halle on a trip to Freckleben (near Sandersleben), his entourage took the body back to Giebichenstein, clothed it in the episcopal *regalia* and then returned with it to Magdeburg by boat, that is, along the Saale and the Elbe. See Thietmar 3 c. 11(8). Similarly, Thietmar 6 c. 84 reports that in 1012 Henry II left Merseburg and went by boat (via the Saale and the Elbe) to Arneburg north of Magdeburg.

[234] *DO II* 190 (20 May 979): 'in civitate sua quae dicitur Eleslebo ... ecclesiam construens triginta quatuor et eo amplius sanctimoniales'. See also the papal privilege of Pope Benedict VII of 22 June 979 (BZ 572; PU 256). Concerning the foundation, see Schölkopf (1957).

against any claims by his kinsmen or enemies.[235] Perhaps as a result of royal protection, the realm appears by 1003 to have secured the better right to the convent, which Henry II confirmed and further strengthened, to the exclusion of the kinsmen of the founding family.[236]

Likewise, the convents of Drübeck and Gernrode became royal convents over time. Drübeck was originally a noble foundation, in which Margrave Dietrich of the Northern March and Margrave Wigger of the March of Zeitz had proprietary interests, but which nevertheless came to the realm as holder of a better although obscure hereditary right.[237] In 1058, however, the regency government of Henry IV granted Drübeck, regardless of its legal status as a royal convent, to the bishopric of Halberstadt.[238] Unfortunately, although located on a royal route frequently used by the Saxon and Salian kings (about 25 km from Goslar, 15 km from Derenburg and 35 km from Quedlinburg), Drübeck provides us with no information or evidence relating to *servitium regis*. With regard to the royal convent of Gernrode, the sources furnish us with a little more information. Originally a noble foundation,[239] Gernrode lay in the Harz region about 14 km south of Quedlinburg on the road leading through the Harz in the direction of Wallhausen and Nordhausen.[240] Owing to its close proximity to Quedlinburg, however, the Saxon and Salian kings probably did not often lay claim to their right of *servitium* or accommodation at Gernrode. The obligation did exist, however, and both the Salian king Henry V in 1105 and later Frederick I in 1188 spent time there.[241] Moreover, in 1004, after Henry II had left Augsburg for his Italian campaign, Queen Kunigunda, accompanied by Archbishop Tagino of Magdeburg and Thietmar (later bishop of Merseburg), found accommodation at Gernrode and celebrated Palm Sunday there on their way to Magdeburg.[242] In addition,

---

[235] Leyser (1979) 45, 69 n. 36 and 99 n. 6; Thietmar 3 cc. 9–10.

[236] *DH II* 44 (22 March 1003).

[237] *DO I* 217 and *DO II* 225. See Leyser (1979) 68–9 esp. 68 n. 30.

[238] *DH IV* 32.   [239] *DO I* 229; Thietmar 2 c. 19(13); and Schulze (1965) 3–5.

[240] See above n. 25 and at nn. 73, 74.

[241] *Ann. Patherbrunn. s.a.* 1105 p. 109. Concerning the origin of these annals in Corvey and not Paderborn, see Schmale (1974) and Wattenbuch and Schmale (1976) 22–7; *Ann. Saxo* 739 *s.a.* 1105. On this occasion Henry V celebrated Maundy Thursday at Gernrode before walking penitent to Quedlinburg on Good Friday and celebrating Easter there. Fredrick I stayed for at least six days at Gernrode and held a *Hoftag* there. See *DDF I* 983, 984, 985 and Stumpf 4507; and Schulze (1965) 9.

[242] Thietmar 6.4.

immediately upon receiving royal status in 961, Otto II granted Gernrode another one of Margrave Gero's foundations, the monastery of Frose, to possess as a proprietary convent; Frose too was taken under royal protection.[243] Frose, near Aschersleben, lay on the royal road along the eastern border of the Harz between Quedlinburg and Walbeck, and thus may have provided the king with another resting place along this route.[244]

Although Nordhausen formed a part of Queen Mathilda's dower,[245] and later a part of Theophanu's marriage settlement,[246] and Mathilda had established a convent there,[247] the Saxon, Salian and Hohenstaufen kings retained the *Königsburg* and *Königshof* there until the mid-twelfth century.[248] Thus, the canonry appears to have been founded in and integrated into the royal residence. If the convent paid a *servitium regis* – and here we have no evidence one way or the other – it would be to supplement the supplies already at hand for the upkeep of the court.[249] Moreover, since the convent had received market, toll and coining rights in Nord-hausen under Otto II (*DO II* 5), it is conceivable, and would be logical, to suppose that the wares and proceeds from those rights could have helped to supply the supplemental needs of the court when it stayed at Nordhausen, but this supposition cannot be proven for lack of evidence.

---

[243] *DO II* 4. Margrave Gero founded a monastery at Frose around 950 dedicated to St Cyriacus (*DO I* 130), but the text of *DO II* 4 specifically mentions 'monasterium puellarum' and later 'que puelle subsunt ecclesie in Gerenrode ab ipso Gerone similiter constructe'. Thus, the monastery was obviously at some time transformed into a convent. See Shulze (1965) 4.

[244] Rieckenberg (1941/1965) 49, 97. This monastery/convent is not to be confused with Frohse on the Elbe, where not only St Maurice (and later, the archbishopric of Magdeburg) and Quedlinburg had possessions, but where also a royal residence and much royal property existed.

[245] *DH I* 20.   [246] *DO II* 21.
[247] *DO I* 393; Hörger (1926) 200 n. 6.   [248] *DF I* 211.
[249] Brühl (1968) 124.

Chapter 5

MONASTERIES IN WESTPHALIA

WESTPHALIA AS A TRANSIT ZONE – THE 'HELLWEG'

The main corridor for travellers running from east to west and connecting the Harz region to the lower Rhine comprised several roads that ran roughly between the Lippe and the Ruhr rivers (see Map 7).[1] Although not the only road through this region, the most important road, called the Hellweg,[2] bore the great majority of the traffic and was the preferred route of the Saxon and Salian kings.[3] This road, which appears to have had a pre-Carolingian, but not a Roman origin, gained significantly in importance as a military road for Charlemagne during the Saxon wars and later, after Saxony became a part of the realm, as a connecting route from the Rhineland to Saxony.[4] But its period of greatest use and highest importance by far came in the tenth and eleventh centuries under the Ottonian and Salian emperors, who traversed it again and again travelling from Saxony to Aachen and the lower Rhine. In fact, during the greater part of the Ottonian and early Salian period, from the reign of Otto I until approximately the Saxon uprising under Henry IV, these rulers made at least a yearly use of this east–west corridor when they were not in Italy or on a foreign campaign.[5] Therefore, the Ottonians took over and completed a

---

[1] In general regarding this area in the early middle ages, see the recent article, Goetz (1990).   [2] Hömberg (1960) 1–3 and (1967a) 204–5.

[3] Rieckenberg (1941/1965) 51; Hömberg (1960) 1–3 and (1967a) 200–1; and Goetz (1990) 129–35.

[4] Hömberg (1967a) 198, on the basis of coin and burial finds at Dortmund and Soest, argued against Karl Rübel (1901) that the Hellweg existed prior to Charlemagne's advances into Saxony. While not denying that the route acquired a much greater significance than it held previously through Charlemagne's measures to organize and fortify it for his Saxon wars, he saw its prior existence as a factor in the Carolingian organizational effort. See now Goetz (1990) 125–9.

[5] Up until the last twenty-five years scholars underestimated the frequency of royal use of the Hellweg. See: Hömberg (1967a) 200 and (1960) 1–3; Deus (1960); Kaminsky (1972) 26 n. 89, 29 n. 121, 54, 59, 65, 71, 78; Metz (1976) 225–7; and most recently, Goetz (1990) 129–35.

system of Carolingian fortresses in southern Westphalia and along the Hellweg itself, and in time established, in conjunction with the royal churches and with their loyal vassals in the region, a stable system of stopping places and provision centres along this road.[6]

Early in his reign, in 938, Otto I held an assembly of the realm (*universalis populi conventio*) in Westphalia at Steele, a vill of the convent of Essen, to conduct a judicial inquiry in response to general unrest in the area caused by the feud between Duke Eberhard of Franconia, a member of the Conradine family, and some of his Saxon vassals.[7] This local dispute, however, soon fuelled the complicated series of internal succession crises (937–9), pitting Otto against his half-brother Thankmar and his brother Henry, who both, at different times, managed to recruit Duke Eberhard to their cause against the king.[8] During these rebellions, the indigenous Westphalian counts of Werl appear to have sided with the Conradines, but finally Otto managed to put down the insurgents and take nominal control of the area. Indeed, these civil disturbances may actually have served Otto by affording him an opportunity to secure the Hellweg and the royal fortresses and other roads in the region, and to diminish substantially the influence of the Conradine family in the area. In fact, after Eberhard's death in 939, Otto did not regrant the dukedom of Franconia just south of the Hellweg, but retained it in his own hands. After this crisis early in his reign Otto appears consciously to have embarked on a policy of supporting the royal churches in the region, especially the bishoprics, and a few loyal vassals, against the powerful counts of Werl. Hahold, a loyal vassal and the chamberlain of Otto I, appears to have achieved the political ascent of his family through supporting Otto during these crises. The Hahold family moved into part of the political vacuum left by the defeat of the Conradine family, and the Haholdian power centre at the family convent of Geseke on the Hellweg probably formed an effective counterweight for Otto against the neighbouring, and not always reliable, counts of Werl. Later, Henry II energetically continued and even furthered Otto's policy of supporting his ecclesiastical vassals in the region to the detriment of the secular lords; and once again we find the counts of Werl in rebellion

---

[6] Hömberg (1967a) 198–201 and (1960) 20–1, and Goetz (1990) 129–35.

[7] Jahn (1938) provides a detailed discussion of this assembly.

[8] Leyser (1979) 1–22, Althoff (1982b) and Erkens (1982) provide the most recent discussions of the insurrections of the nobility during Otto's reign.

against the king, this time in league with the duke of Saxony and other Saxon nobles.[9]

The actual course of the Hellweg progressed along a line of old Carolingian fortresses and mission and parish centres spaced approximately 17 km apart.[10] In regard to the most important stopping places for the accommodation and provision of the royal court, the road ran from the important royal *Pfalz* at Duisburg on the Rhine via the royal convent of Essen,[11] where it joined with the important road coming from Cologne that crossed the Rhine at Neuß and continued northeast crossing the Ruhr on the stone bridge at the royal monastery of Werden (see Map 7).[12] It continued then to the *Königshof* at Dortmund near which, a little further east, a road forked off to the northeast via Beckum, Bielefeld and the royal convent of Herford to the episcopal city of Minden. From Dortmund the Hellweg continued east via the fortress at Werl, Soest, Erwitte and the Haholdian convent at Geseke to Paderborn. Of these towns, Soest had belonged since at least the middle of the tenth century to the archbishopric of Cologne,[13] and the often-visited royal residence at Erwitte came in 1027, under Conrad II, to the bishopric of Paderborn.[14] Geseke, on the other hand, belonged to the Haholdian comital family, who founded a convent there in 950 and had it placed under royal protection and immunity.[15] Later in 1014 they granted the convent to the archbishopric of Cologne.[16]

At Paderborn the road forked once again. One road led northeast via Schieder to the ford over the Weser at Hameln,[17] and

---

[9] For the above see: BO 75b, 76a–e; Diefenbach (unpub. diss. 1952) 131–5; Hömberg (1967d) 63–5; Leidinger (1965) 75, 91–2; Bannasch (1972) 20–2, 31–2, 52–5; Leyser (1979) 13–14, 17–18; Erkens (1982) 346–53; and J. Prinz (1983) 356–7.

[10] Hömberg (1967a) 198–9.

[11] On the early history of the convent of Essen and the nearby monastery of Werden, see Goetz (1990) 135–46.

[12] A charter of Henry IV in 1065 (*DH IV* 172) mentions this road and the bridge over the Ruhr at Werden linking the two monasteries and Cologne with the Hellweg. The main crossing point of the Rhine south of the Lippe River was located at Neuß and another road ran along the east bank of the Rhine from Neuß north via Duisburg to Nijmegen and Utrecht. Concerning the course of these roads and the Rhine crossing at Neuß, see Bömmels (1961) 35–43 and pp. 185–7.

[13] Bannasch (1972) 23; *REK* nos. 458, 476.   [14] *DK II* 82 (7 April 1027).

[15] *DO I* 158. Otto I may well have granted this charter in return for Hahold's loyal service in the crises of 938–9 and to secure a loyal royal vassal on the Hellweg near the less dependable counts of Werl.

[16] *REK* 1 no. 630 and *UB Westfalen* 25 no. 23 (3 February 1014).

[17] Corvey owned thirty *mansi* (*Hufen*) in and around Schieder, the middle point of this road (*c.* 35 km from Paderborn and Hameln) where there was also a royal *curtis* that

another ran south toward Marsberg and Korbach,[18] where it joined the road coming north from Frankfurt. The Hellweg itself continued east via Driburg (Ilburg), Brakel[19] and finally to the royal monastery of Corvey which commanded the ford over the Weser and lay situated at the junction of several north–south roads.[20] Thus, along this all-important artery we begin at a royal residence on the Rhine and then encounter three royal monasteries and a dynastic monastery under royal protection, one royal palace and two royal manors, one of which came in 1027 to Paderborn, and numerous possessions of the archbishopric of Cologne and the bishopric of Paderborn. Here once again we see an interworking of royal property and church property for the accommodation and provision of the royal court, but by the early eleventh century very little royal property remained and the Hellweg lay almost entirely in the hands of royal churches or religious institutions with very strong royal connections.[21]

An evaluation of the economic *servitium regis* of the royal monasteries and convents along and in the vicinity of the Hellweg necessitates using several kinds of sources and information (see Map 5). Although the extant royal charters for both secular and ecclesiastical recipients provide us with little information either about the extent of royal property in the region[22] or about the ecclesiastical (especially the monastic) *servitium regis*, they do supply important evidence concerning the royal itinerary. From this information one can calculate with reasonable accuracy how

Otto III in 997 granted to the archepiscopal church at Magdeburg. See *DArn* 60, *DO III* 245 and *DDH II* 100, 210. Corvey also owned twenty to thirty *mansi* of property in Hastenbeck directly south of Hameln. See Honselmann (1982) 93 no. 61; *Traditiones Corbeienses* no. 277; and Kaminsky (1972) 142, 234 (*RE* §35). Moreover, since the end of the eighth or early ninth century, Fulda possessed a large amount of property in and around Hameln and founded there a proprietary monastery of canons. See Weczerka (1966) 194; *TAF* c. 13 no. 1, c. 43 no. 64, c. 45 no. 13, p. 182 cap. 9; *FUB* 140–7 n. 78 esp. p. 143.

18 Corvey held numerous properties in the general area around both places. Marsberg, Corvey's power and property centre on the Diemel, played a large role in the power struggle of the late tenth and early eleventh centuries between Corvey and the bishops of Paderborn, who also held property in the area and managed, under Henry II and Bishop Meinwerk, substantially to diminish Corvey's influence and holdings in the area. See: Kaminsky (1972) 18, 20, 23 n. 57, 24–5, 33, 64 n. 53 and Bannasch (1972) 33.

19 Corvey possessed a vill in Erkeln just south of Brakel that in the early twelfth century paid towards the *servitium regis*, and the bishopric of Paderborn held a vill in Brakel itself. See: Kaminsky (1972) 139, 147 n. 105 and 226 (*RE* §9); Wigand (1826–8) 1.4 p. 52 and 2.1 pp. 2, 5; and Bannasch (1972) 33 n. 116, 290.

20 Concerning Corvey's advantageous location, see below at nn. 106–8.

21 Metz (1971) 269 and Bannasch (1972) 20–2.   22 Hömberg (1960) 3–7.

often the Saxon and Salian kings traversed the Hellweg and, by extension, how frequently they made use of the monastic *servitium* owed to them.[23] By far the most profitable sources at our disposal regarding the *servitium regis* of the royal monasteries along the Hellweg are the monastic land registers.

The monastery of Werden provides us with extensive and very informative estate surveys containing specific information about payments made from several of the monastery's vills toward the monastery's debt of *servitium regis* during the Ottonian and Salian periods.[24] For any specific evidence regarding payments to the king from the convent of Essen one must rely upon the land registers and other information, primarily from the fourteenth century, but which arguably reflect the development in an earlier period.[25] Although a land register and account book exists for Corvey, similar to the one from Werden and from approximately the same date, it gives us nevertheless no specific information about the monastery's *servitium regis*. Here one must rely upon indirect indications of such payments in the earlier period, similar payments of abbatial *servitium*, and the few notices that we do have from the twelfth and thirteenth centuries, which make several specific declarations about payments owed from several manors or estates of the monastery towards various types of *servitia* including the *servitium regis*, *ad curiam* and *in expeditionum*.[26]

WERDEN

The land and income registers of the monastery of Werden, especially those of the eleventh and twelfth centuries, furnish us with the most detailed data about the monastic *servitium regis* of any royal monastery.[27] Nevertheless, even these, the best of our sources, never reveal the total amount of *servitium* that the abbot had to pay to the king from the monastery's incomes. They do indicate, however, that, from the renders paid to the abbot for his upkeep by the stewards of eleven different abbatial vills or domains of the monastery, predominantly in Westphalia, a certain

---

[23] Metz (1976) 225–7 and n. 5 above.   [24] See below n. 27.
[25] Weigel (1960) 15 and Metz (1976) 192, 247–9.   [26] See below at n. 104.
[27] Rudolf Kötzschke (1906–58) published and commented extensively upon the *Urbare* or land and income registers of the royal monastery of Werden. Also on these *Urbare* and Werden's *servitium regis*, see Heusinger (1922) 127–8 [152–3] and Metz (1976) 191–4. On the economic and developmental changes from the tenth through to the twelfth centuries affecting the structure and the type of productivity of Werden's scattered vills, see Rösener (1985) esp. 188–96.

portion was designated for the royal *servitium*.[28] The majority of
the renders were for the abbot. For instance in the land registers
from *c.* 1031–8,[29] the stewards or local administrators from nine of
the eleven vills each had to provide the abbot a yearly payment of
one cow, five pigs, one piglet, five suckling pigs, one pheasant, ten
chickens, ten cheeses, sixty eggs, five *maldaria* of bread, ten *modii* of
oats, eighteen *amphorae* of beer, thirty dishes (bowls or pans) and
fifteen drinking vessels (cups or bowls).[30] The vill comprising
Friemersheim, Rumeln and Borg paid twenty-five suckling pigs
(*laterales porces*), ten chickens, 300 eggs, one *maldarium* of cheeses,
200 bowls and pots (*olus?*), table dishes and other necessary utensils
for the royal kitchen. In addition, the presbyter of Friemersheim
had to pay ten *solidi* annually to the steward (*villicus*) of Borg[31] to
buy the bowls which pertained to the king's and the abbot's
servitium.[32] The vill of Bögge owed approximately one half of a
'normal' *servitium* for the king, that is, one half of the produce paid
by each of the first nine vills of the monastery.[33] The yearly totals
from the eleven vills comprise: eight cows, forty-three pigs, ten
piglets, thirty suckling pigs, eight pheasants, 195 chickens, ninety-
five cheeses plus one *maldarium* of cheeses, 870 eggs, forty-seven
and a half *maldaria* of bread, ninety-five *modii* of oats, 172 *amphorae*
of beer, 485 bowls, 147 drinking vessels and the ten *solidi* and other
sundry payments from Friemersheim.[34]

The land registers from the twelfth century supply similar
information concerning the same vills, although the individual
payments in kind have often diminished in relation to those of the

---

[28] Metz (1976) 193 and (1978b) 76–7, in contradiction to Heusinger (1922) 19 [45],
correctly pointed out that the contributions of the various Werden vills to the *servitium
regis* do not represent the totality of the abbot's or monastery's *servitium* for the king,
but only subsidies to the abbot towards the total debt.

[29] On the dating of this document, see above Chapter 3, n. 180.

[30] *RU* 2.133 (§44), 137–47 (§§ 1, 4–8, 10, 11, 12, 14) and Heusinger (1922) 127–8 [152–3].

[31] *RU* 2.147 n. 1. Borg and Friemersheim had one and the same *villicus*.

[32] Ibid. 146–7 (§16). It should be borne in mind that the extensive estate of Friemersheim
had been divided between the abbot and the brothers, with the abbot receiving the vills
of Friemersheim and Borg, and the brothers receiving the vill of Asterlagen. Once
again in the eleventh century, when we have some information about the *servitium regis*,
the abbatial properties pay it. See Kötzschke (1901) 19–25; Ganshof and Verhulst (1966)
307–8; and Stüwer (1980) 250–1, 253 and 256–7.   [33] *RU* 2.144 (§11).

[34] These totals come from *Urbar* C of *c.* 1031–8. On the other hand, not included are the
totals from *Urbar* B from around the same time or a little earlier. They comprise ten
piglets or lambs, fifty suckling pigs, 100 chickens, 100 cheeses, 1000 eggs, fifty *maldaria*
of bread, 100 *modii* of oats, 250 eating bowls and 120 drinking cups. When one
compares the payments in *Urbar* B to those of *Urbar* C as compiled by Heusinger (1922)
127–8 [152–3], it appears that *Urbar* C updated *Urbar* B.

assessment lists from the mid-eleventh century. But the twelfth-century lists also include payments in money of eighty-seven *denarii* from the taxes of dependants on three of the vills. In the course of the twelfth and thirteenth centuries a yearly monetary payment progressively replaced the payment in kind to the king for the *servitium regis*, although payments in kind from the vills never ceased entirely.[35] On the other hand, although one can detect a fairly well-developed system of vills under named stewards in the earliest land register of the monastery from the late ninth century or the beginning of the tenth, it made no specific mention of a payment for the *servitium regis*.[36] When we compare the various land registers with one another, or when we combine the detailed information contained in the Werden land registers with the knowledge we have about royal roads or the royal itinerary, we can draw several pertinent conclusions and a few justified inferences about the *servitium regis* of the royal monastery of Werden.

Comparing the land register of the ninth century or early tenth (*Urbar* A) with those of the mid-eleventh century (*Urbare* B and C) and the twelfth century (*Urbare* E and F), certain features become clear. Although land register A depicts a well-developed system of vills paying incomes to the abbot, one does not find any specific reference to the *servitium regis*. On the basis of the section of *Urbar* A pertaining to one Werden vill – Friemersheim – however, Erich Wisplinghoff has argued convincingly that, already in the late eighth and early ninth century, it regularly supported the Carolingian royal court and thus acted as a royal *villa* without any specific mention of this function or of *servitium*.[37] Only this could explain the extent and the nature of the payments and services demanded of the peasant populations holding and working the plots of this vill. Roughly calculated, these included about 7000 Carolingian pennies (an equivalent value of 600–750 pigs), enough beer for between 100 and 200 people depending on consumption, 2800 loaves of rye bread (*c.* 9000 kg), 240 bushels of wheatmeal, and 7000 kg of rye meal to feed large packs of dogs.[38] Thus, according to Wisplinghoff, Friemersheim probably acted as a staging point which provided accommodation and upkeep for Charlemagne and the Frankish army during the almost yearly

[35] Metz (1976) 193, 223, 230–1 and (1978b) 76–7.
[36] *RU* 2.3–87 (*Urbar* A) and Metz (1976) 192–3.   [37] Wisplinghoff (1983) 155.
[38] Ibid. 152–5. On these quantities, see also Kötzschke (1901) 11–19.

campaigns against the Saxons. We have no information to what use these payments might have been devoted in the ninth century or even if they were still collected at the rate given in *Urbar* A (late ninth century), a rate which by then could have been anachronistic. The later assessment rolls (B, C and E, F) from Werden, on the other hand, specifically mention payments for the *servitium regis*. Also, in the ninth- to eleventh-century registers (A, B and C), the debts due from the various vills comprise exclusively payments in kind, but the twelfth-century registers (E and F) show a slight decrease in payments in kind and an increase in money payments.

These data from the assessment rolls correspond very closely both to historical and economic developments in the German realm of the Saxons, the Salians, and later, the Hohenstaufens, and to the growth in Werden's obligation as a royal monastery to provide accommodation and upkeep for the royal court on its travels. Although the Hellweg already formed the most important east–west travel connection between the lower Rhine and Saxony when Charlemagne secured it as a military road and used it during his Saxon wars, royal use of the road diminished dramatically during the ninth century and early tenth. With the accession of the Ottonian kings its greatest period of use began and this continued, only somewhat diminished after about 1073, into the twelfth century.[39] Thus, it is not surprising that we find no mention of payments for *servitium regis* in the earliest register (*Urbar* A) and regular mention of such payments in those registers from the eleventh and twelfth centuries. During the Ottonian and early Salian periods we can assume an almost yearly use of the Hellweg, and it is precisely during this period that we find the heaviest payments required to support the king and his court.[40] Similarly, the increasing monetary payments to *servitium regis* reveal not only the gradual growth of a money economy in the twelfth century, but also the decreasing use of the Hellweg by the Hohenstaufen kings and the consequent redemption of the payments in kind by a yearly tax in money when payments in kind no longer proved as advantageous to the monarchy.[41]

The notices concerning the *servitium regis* in the estate surveys or

[39] Hömberg (1967a) 200–1; Deus (1960) 22–7; Metz (1976) 193, 197, 225, 227 and Goetz (1990) 129–35.

[40] Hömberg (1960) 1–3; Kaminsky (1972) 26 esp. n. 89, 29 n. 121, 54, 59, 65, 71, 78; Goetz (1990) 131–3 and also n. 37 above.

[41] Deus (1960) 22–7 and Metz (1976) 193 and (1978b) 76–7.

polyptychs of the eleventh and twelfth centuries indicate that the abbot apportioned a sizeable part of his monastery's debt to the king among several of the abbatial domains under his disposition.[42] As Wolfgang Metz has pointed out, however, the total of these individual payments most probably does not represent the abbot's (or the monastery's) total debt of *servitium regis*, but only specific subsidies remitted toward it.[43] Especially in the tenth and eleventh centuries, during those periods of the most frequent use of the Hellweg, the total debt of service to the king must have been considerably higher. Consequently, the abbot must also have had to seize upon other abbatial revenues to satisfy the burden.[44] Unfortunately, for the tenth and eleventh centuries we do not possess any specific information indicating the possible source of these other revenues, but some fragmentary evidence from the Ottonian and Salian periods together with some twelfth-century evidence allows us to make some tentative deductions.

The monastery of Werden lay favourably situated on the Ruhr River about 10 km south of Essen and the Hellweg on the main road connecting the Hellweg and Cologne; a charter of Henry IV in 1065 mentions it by name.[45] Henry II most probably used this road in 1017 when he came from Cologne to Werden, where he solemnly celebrated the feast of Pentecost and the abbot Heithanrich provided him with an abundant service.[46] It appears likely that the Ottonian and Salian kings used this road frequently when they travelled to or from Cologne and Aachen to the Hellweg, unless they specifically intended to hold a court day or spend some time at the royal palace at Duisburg on the Rhine, or if they wanted to continue north to Nijmegen or Utrecht via the road along the east bank of the Rhine.[47] An examination of the confirmed royal stops in Duisburg from 936 to 1056 appears to support this opinion. During this time period we have thirteen documented stops of the Saxon or Salian kings in Duisburg. Of these, five times kings came to Duisburg, often to hold a royal

---

[42] Heusinger (1922) 19–20 [44–5] and Metz (1976) 192.

[43] Metz (1976) 193 and (1978b) 76–7 in contradiction to Heusinger (1922) 20 [45].

[44] Metz (1976) 193 and (1978b) 76–7.

[45] *DH IV* 172. Bömmels (1961) 42–3 delineated the course of this road.

[46] BG 1903a, 1903b; Thietmar 7 c. 56 (41): 'Inperator autem audiens contectalem suam levius haberi et votum Domino fecisse, grates Christo persolvit ex animo et pentecosten in Wirthunu ... venerabiliter celebravit, abbate Hethenrico sibi pleniter ibidem servienti.'

[47] Concerning the road along the east bank of the Rhine see Bömmels (1961) 38.

assembly or a royal court of justice, and then immediately returned to Saxony via the Hellweg.[48] Four times the stop in Duisburg occurred immediately before or after a trip to Nijmegen on the lower Rhine.[49] One visit came before a trip to Liège and one after a sojourn in Aachen, before an unplanned meeting with the French king;[50] and finally the king appeared twice at Duisburg travelling to or from Frankfurt. Moreover, in these last four instances the king would have travelled from Duisburg via Kaiserswerth to Neuß because the Rhine crossing was there and not at Duisburg. Also, travelling to Frankfurt the king would most probably use the land roads because they were quicker than travelling upstream by boat.[51] In no instance do we have a confirmed stop in Duisburg followed immediately by a stay in Cologne; and only on three occasions did the king travel to or from Duisburg from the Aachen and Maas River area, and all of these occurred under Otto III. Although the extant evidence in itself is by no means exhaustive and does not exclude visits to Duisburg before or after ones to Cologne, it does, on the basis of the witnessed stops, strongly indicate that the Saxon and Salian kings normally travelled another route to and from the Hellweg to Cologne and the Aachen and Maas region.

Usually, these kings appear to have left the Hellweg proper at Essen and travelled via Werden where the road crossed the Ruhr (see Map 7).[52] From there the road continued via either Kaiserswerth or the toll station at Gerresheim[53] to the Rhine crossing at Düsseldorf (Hamm)-Neuß.[54] Main roads then continued from Neuß south along the Rhine to Cologne, west to Venlo and Flanders, and southwest to Aachen and Maastricht.[55] Frequent use of this route to Cologne from the Hellweg via Werden or vice versa goes a long way towards explaining the considerable sums paid by vills of Werden to the *servitium regis*, despite the monastery's location just south of the royal convent of Essen on the Hellweg and the few recorded stops at the monastery by the kings. Although the Saxon and Salian kings could occasionally have made a diversion of 8–10 km from the Hellweg to the *Pfalz* at Duisburg in order to make use of their *servitium regis*

---

[48] BO 123a, BMik 780, BU 968e, 969, 984b, 985, BG 1604.
[49] BO 427 [BMik 586 k], BMik 644, 728, BG 1498, 1498b.
[50] BU 1083, 1084; BU 1059, 1059a; BU 1059b.   [51] Bömmels (1961) 25–6, 34–8.
[52] Ibid. 41–3.   [53] *DO II* 153, *DH II* 415 and Weidenhaupt (1954) 42.
[54] Bömmels (1961) 34–8 esp. 36.   [55] Ibid. 29–33.

at Werden, simple logic dictates that this practice would not have been the rule at a time when the daily distance covered by the royal retinue averaged about 25–35 km. On the other hand, one could also assume that Werden delivered its *servitium regis* to Essen or perhaps via the Ruhr, which was navigable from the Rhine to Werden, to the royal *Pfalz* at Duisburg or to some other point on the Hellweg, along which Werden owned numerous properties. This may well have been the case during Otto I's *Reichstag* at the Essen vill at Steele when Essen apparently accommodated the royal court, but a joint *servitium* from both Essen and Werden seems very likely.[56] Moreover, numerous other monasteries and convents made such deliveries of *servitium regis*.[57] But by far the least problematic solution (without, of course, excluding the others) is to assume a more frequent use of the Cologne road mentioned in the royal charter of 1065 and of Werden as a stopping point on that road during trips from the Hellweg to Cologne, the Aachen and Maas region, and the middle Rhine area in general.

The royal charter of 1065 also specifically mentioned that one of the few bridges at this time stood at Werden; although we do not have any further information about this bridge, there can be little doubt that the abbot collected a toll, especially from travelling merchants.[58] It is possible in any case that the abbot may have employed some of the income from this toll to supply or, more probably, to supplement the payments in kind of the vills for *servitium regis*. Wolfgang Metz has demonstrated that, at least in the mid-twelfth century, according to *Urbare* D and E, tolls formed a part of the *servitium* that the steward of Werden's east Saxon vill at Helmstedt had to pay to the travelling abbot.[59] In addition, other sources from the early twelfth century also indicate that income from tolls formed a part of monastic and episcopal *servitium*.[60]

In the middle ages, moreover, in settlements where a bridge stood on an important connecting route, trading activity and an ensuing market often developed. Indeed this appears to have been the case with Werden, which benefited from several factors. Firstly, it held a very advantageous geographical position, for it

---

[56] Brühl (1968) 211 n. 397 and cf. Jahn (1938) 86.   [57] Brühl (1968) 205–6.
[58] *DH IV* 172: 'usque ad pontem Wirdinensem' and Stein (1922) 64–5.
[59] Metz (1978b) 19–20 and *RU* 2.90–1 (*Urbar B* §1 from twelfth century), 180 (*Urbar* D §10).   [60] Metz (1978b) 95, 103–5.

was located on a major road which connected the Hellweg and Cologne, and which crossed the Ruhr over a bridge there. The river was also navigable at least to Werden.[61] Secondly, Werden functioned as the centre and collecting depot for the domainial levies in kind of a large supraregional system of manorial estates.[62] Thirdly, as a cult centre for pilgrims travelling to the grave of St Liudger, who was buried there in 809, Werden enjoyed a lively pilgrimage traffic, from which trade inevitably developed and provided the basis for a market.[63] Thus, although scholars have demonstrated that a charter attributed to Otto II in 974 granting market and minting rights to Werden and Lüdingshausen – one of its most important possessions north of the Lippe River – is, at least in regard to Werden itself, a forgery of the twelfth century,[64] other evidence indicates that a market did exist at Werden by the mid-eleventh century at the latest; probably earlier. Although the inclusion of a market and mint at Werden itself in this charter is forged, Otto II's charter is an eleventh-century copy of an authentic exemplar granting a market and minting right to the abbot of Werden in Lüdingshausen and possibly Dülmen. The erasure of the second location (Dülmen?) and the insertion of Werden itself in the twelfth century probably represented an attempt to legitimize a previously existing market (and possibly a mint) at Werden itself.[65] This claim is supported by coins from Werden from around 1130 and evidence from the twelfth-century *Urbar* indicating both *monitor* and *mercator* in Werden.[66] In fact, a sizeable settlement and a market (and possibly also a mint) had probably developed at Werden already by the eleventh century.[67]

---

[61] *DK II* 187 granting the inhabitants and dependants of Werden the right of unhindered ship travel on the Ruhr from its influx into the Rhine up to Werden demonstrates that the Ruhr was navigable to Werden, and the confirmation of this charter in 1147 by Conrad III (*DK III* 187) indicates that ship traffic extended even beyond the monastery. See also Kötzschke (1906–58) vol. 4.2 p. CCXLVII.

[62] Concerning the extent, location, structure and delivery centres of Werden's extensive network of properties, see Rösener (1985) 181–96.

[63] On Werden as a cult centre and the pilgrimage trade, see Flink (1982) 176 and Goetz (1990) 141–4.

[64] *DO II* 88; Bendel (1908) 26–9. Concerning Bendel's work in general and specifically in regard to this charter (*DO II* 88) see the criticism of Hans Wibel (1910–11) esp. 104–5 and Otto Oppermann (1922) 104–40 esp. 125–8.

[65] Wibel (1910–11) esp. 104–5 and Oppermann (1922) 104–40 esp. 125–8.

[66] *Rheinisches Städtebuch* p. 169 and *RU* 2.188 (*Urbar* E §2). See also n. 69 below.

[67] Wibel (1910–11) 82 n. 1 and 104 n. 1 soon raised strong objections to Bendel (1908) 97–100, who claimed that no sizeable settlement arose around the monastery of Werden until after the twelfth century and excluded the possibility of a market in

For instance, the chapel of St Nicholas was built under Abbot Gerold (1031–50) and consecrated by Archbishop Hermann of Cologne,[68] and a charter of 1160 confirms that it was located in the market-place at Werden.[69] Moreover, Werden's location at a bridge on an important road gives additional support to the likelihood of this development which probably occurred around the same time that Essen received a market right from Henry III.[70] Thus, the markets at Lüdingshausen, Werden and possibly at Dülmen, as well as the minting right at Lüdingshausen, formed other sources from which the abbot may have extracted incomes or products to satisfy Werden's debt of *servitium regis*. Evidence from the early twelfth century indicates that market incomes formed a part of the *servitium regis*; and the Werden vill of Helmstedt in the mid-twelfth century paid part of the travelling abbot's *servitium* both from market incomes and products.[71] In addition, the payments toward the king's *servitium* from the vill of Friemersheim around 1031–8 include a yearly payment of ten *solidi* from the presbyter of Friemersheim to the steward of Borg in order to buy the bowls (dishes) pertaining to the abbot's and king's *servitium*.[72] In this instance an eleventh-century witness also indicates that market products formed a part of the *servitium regis*.

Thus, when one examines the extensive information in Werden's land and assessment rolls in conjunction with information about royal roads, trade routes and our increasing knowledge of trade and the development of towns, the royal monastery of Werden emerges as a major source of economic support for the king in the lower Rhine region. Owing to their frequent use of the Hellweg and the connecting route to Cologne, the Saxon and Salian kings called upon Werden more and more to accommodate them during their journeys. Also, as with so many churches having strong royal connections and experiencing royal visits, this may explain the existence of a full *Westwerk* at Werden, which could be used during the sacral representation of the king or royal participation in the religious rites when he was present.[73] This may well have occurred, for instance, in 1017, when Henry

Werden in the eleventh century. Wibel's opinion has found wide acceptance in the recent scholarship. See Stüwer (1980) 198, 201, 208–9 and Flink (1982) 176–7.

[68] *REK* 1 no. 814.   [69] *UBGNR* 277–8 no. 402: 'in foro Werdinensi'.
[70] *DH III* 82.   [71] Metz (1978b) 19–20 and *RU* 2.180 (*Urbar* D § 10).
[72] *RU* 2.147 (*Urbar* C § 16).
[73] Metz (1984) 14–15 and Streich (1984) 310–13, 403.

II celebrated Pentecost at Werden.[74] Even if these stays were of relatively short duration – perhaps one to three days – nevertheless they hold considerable significance in relation to the overall accommodation of the royal court in areas in which the king did not have large tracts of royal property at his disposal.[75] The extensive payments by Werden's vills towards the *servitium regis* in the mid-eleventh century confirm and underline the monastery's role in the support of the king and royal court. Werden's extensive system of estates, moreover, which extended along the Rhine from the Ahr River north into the Netherlands, and from Flanders to the Weser River in western Saxony, and continuing as far east as Helmstedt, may also have provided the king accommodation in isolated instances.[76] For example, Henry II very probably received his accommodation and *servitium* from Werden's proprietary monastery at Helmstedt when he celebrated the feast of All Souls there in 1012.[77]

ESSEN

The convent of Essen resembled those of Quedlinburg and Gandersheim in several ways. All three were noble royal canonries holding the highest legal status or 'liberty' (*libertas*) granted to a royal convent, they were all Ottonian 'family' convents and thus maintained very close ties to the Ottonian family, and they all enjoyed advantageous locations on highly travelled royal roads. In fact, when granting this royal legal status to other convents, royal charters often use these three female religious institutions as examples of 'model' royal convents which already held the coveted legal status.[78] Moreover, as in the cases of Quedlinburg and Gandersheim, the abbesses of Essen for much of the period from the early tenth until the mid-eleventh century appear to have been members of, or very closely connected to, the Liudolfing/

---

[74] BG 1903a, 1903b; Thietmar 7 c. 56 (41).   [75] Metz (1976) 227.
[76] Alberts (1983) 33.
[77] Thietmar 7 c. 84. Although we have no specific information concerning Henry II's accommodation in Helmstedt, we do know that numerous properties in Helmstedt belonged to the abbot of Werden and paid a sizeable *servitium* to him. See *RU* 2.90–1 (*Urbar* B §1), 149 (*Urbar* C §22) and 180 (*Urbar* D §10). One would probably not go too far astray in assuming that during a royal visit, the abbot, at least, would place his *servitium* at the king's disposal.
[78] *DO II* 67; *DDO III* 32, 235, 326, 363; *DH II* 40. On this concept of model institutions, see Hörger (1926) 207 and Semmler (1959) 27.

Ottonian family; and the convent participated in the memorial commemorations of the Ottonian family.[79]

It appears that two early abbesses, Adalwif and Wigburg, had some connection to the Liudolfing family as did their successors, Hathwig and Ida, in the middle of the tenth century, although our knowledge of the order of the abbesses of Essen is incomplete.[80] Thereafter, our information becomes more certain. The next abbess, Mathilda, the daughter of Duke Liudolf of Swabia and his wife, Ida, ruled Essen from 973–1011 and was followed in 1012 by Sophie, abbess of Gandersheim. When Sophie died in 1039, Theophanu, Otto II's granddaughter and Sophie's niece, took over as abbess and ruled until 1056.[81] Essen's close ties with the royal family and its high prestige within the realm increase the likelihood of visits by the king and royal entourage. Thus, not surprisingly, as at Quedlinburg and Gandersheim, the church at Essen was architecturally suited for the liturgical representation of kingship and royal participation in religious services. It appears already in the tenth century to have had a *Westwerk*, a characteristic of monastic churches with strong royal connections.[82] Under Abbess Theophanu, the *Westwerk* underwent extensive expansion and restructuring. The result was a six-storey structure, with three towers on the west wall and a royal loge or gallery on the third level, which was modelled in part on the royal chapel at Aachen.[83]

In addition, Essen enjoyed an advantageous location directly on the Hellweg, about 18 km east of the royal *Pfalz* at Duisburg and 34 km west of the royal residence in Dortmund. Moreover, at Essen the important road from Cologne via Neuß (Deutz) and Werden joined the Hellweg.[84] In fact, farmers from Essen also may well have used this road when they brought the yearly payment of wine to the convent from its vineyard properties on the Ahr and the Erft Rivers via Düsseldorf or Neuß.[85] Thus, Essen's particular location on the much-travelled Hellweg put the

---

[79] On the connections of these abbesses to the Liudolfing/Ottonian family and Essen's role in the Ottonian *memoria*, see Althoff (1976) and (1984) 133–6, 213–14.

[80] Althoff (1976) 403 nn. 14, 17 and (1984) 202–3, 213–14, 350–1, who cites further literature on this problem. Goetz (1990) 140 identifies both Hadwig and a Gerberga, whom he sees as Hadwig's predecessor, as sisters of King Henry I, but without citing any evidence.

[81] *DO II* 49 and *DO III* 114; *Ann. Qued. s.a.* 1011, 1012; Perst (1957) 37; *DH III* 82; Hörger (1926) 243–4.   [82] Perst (1957) 40 and Metz (1984) esp. 10–11.

[83] Streich (1984) 51–4, 320–1, 403. See also Zimmermann (1956), which was unavailable to me.   [84] *DH IV* 172. See above pp. 185–7.

[85] *DZ* 22 (898); Weigel (1960) 61–2.

convent in a position to be visited by, and thus to provide accommodation for, the royal court almost yearly during the period 936–1066, regardless of whether the king continued on to Duisburg or turned south onto the road to Cologne.[86] From the almost yearly royal stops at Essen, calculated solely on the basis of the frequency of royal travel on the Hellweg, only three royal visits can be documented, and charter evidence raises two further possible visits to relative certainty.

In 938, Otto I held a royal assembly or a royal judicial session at the Essen vill of Steele. On this occasion, Essen and perhaps Werden bore the burden of the royal accommodation.[87] Also, in 966 while at Duisburg, just after a probable stop at Essen, Otto granted the canonesses at Essen a court at Ehrenzell that he had formerly given to his granddaughter Mathilda, the future abbess.[88] Otto III appears to have spent several days at Essen in February 993 possibly for the marriage of his sister Mathilda – whom his (half-) cousin Mathilda, abbess of Essen, had raised – to Count Ezzo, the future count palatine.[89] Otto III, like his grandfather, also made a grant to the convent just after a probable stop at Essen. While he broke his journey at Dortmund travelling from Aachen in 997, he granted Essen the royal property of Brüggen.[90] Similarly, in 1028, Conrad II may also have stopped at Essen *en route* from Aachen to Dortmund, where he issued a charter at the request of Abbess Sophie confirming Essen's property holdings and legal status.[91] Finally, in June 1041, Henry III visited the convent and granted Abbess Theophanu the right to hold a market.[92]

Thus, having to meet the varied needs of the king's entourage, as was the case in so many places frequented often by the royal court, Essen under Abbess Theophanu acquired the right to establish a six-day yearly market at Essen and to keep all proceeds from the market for the use of the monastery.[93] With this grant of a market right, Henry III probably recognized and confirmed, and possibly extended, a right that existed in Essen by at least 1039 and

---

[86] See above nn. 47–51.

[87] Robert Jahn (1938) 86 believes the convent of Essen to have been the sole supplier of the king's accommodation and upkeep at Steele, while Brühl (1968) 211 n. 397 makes the plausible suggestion that Werden may also have played a part in supplying the *servitium regis* on this occasion.   [88] *DO I* 325.   [89] *DO III* 114; BU 1081a, 1082.

[90] *DO III* 242 (Dortmund, 18 April 997).   [91] *DK II* 121.   [92] *DH III* 82.

[93] Ibid. Metz (1971) 280–6 does not mention the market at Essen, which was located on the Hellweg, nor does he mention that a market most probably existed at Werden around the same time. See above at nn. 64, 65.

that may have dated even further back to the late tenth century. On the basis of the oldest existing coin from Essen, an Essen *denarius* found in Russia and coined during the abbacy of Sophie and in the reign of Conrad II, it appears that the convent had a coining right at least by 1039 if not earlier, around 1030. The coining right in turn presupposes the existence of a market. Considering Essen's advantageous location, its prestige and its royal ties, it is plausible that the convent may well have acquired the right to coin money (and the presupposed market) at the end of the tenth century when Herford (973), Gandersheim (990) and Quedlinburg acquired similar rights.[94]

Unfortunately, the extant sources for the royal convent of Essen do not provide us with much definitive information about its *servitium regis* in the tenth and eleventh centuries. It is possible, however, using some information from a later period (the early fourteenth century) and certain pertinent comparisons with nearby Werden, to develop a plausible notion of the extent of Essen's obligation for royal service. On the basis of its position on the Hellweg and its nearness (*c.* 10 km) to Werden, one might conjecture a certain degree of similarity in the *servitium* as well. In fact, information from Essen in the early fourteenth century appears to suggest such a similarity. From the fourteenth-century conveyance register (*Kettenbuch*) of the convent of Essen,[95] one learns that eight specific Westphalian vills near the convent provided the weekly *servitium* to the convent and also made money payments to the 'konynxstope', or *Königsstufe* (royal contribution).[96] The same eight possessions and one additional vill designated 'auf dem Dren' (Van Drēne), southwest of Beckum, appear already in a ninth-century assessment register as owing duties to the brewery of the convent, and this payment remained at exactly the same amount in the fourteenth century.[97] The *Königsstufe* must certainly also have had older origins.[98] In fact,

---

[94] Lehnhäuser (1931) 11–13. See also Metz (1971) 279–91. Flink (1982) 193 attributes a mint to Essen by 1040. [95] Arens (1912).

[96] The vills in question are: Viehof, Eickenscheidt, Ringeldorf, Huckarde (near Dortmund), Brockhausen, Hordel-Ückendorf, Neinhausen and Borbeck. See Weigel (1960) 15–16, 60–1, and Metz (1976) 192. Concerning the 'konynxstope' or *Königsstufe*, see Minnigerode (1928) 40–4 and E. Müller (1930).

[97] Jahn (1938) 73–6; Weigel (1960) 54–5; and Metz (1976) 192.

[98] Jahn (1938) 76 concerning Essen in particular and Hömberg (1967d) 54–5 concerning Westphalia in general have both commented on the extremely conservative nature of the Westphalian land registers. Thus, since very little changed on these vills over the centuries, they owed the same services and payments in kind (or later, their equivalent

they probably represent the monetary redemption of the former economic *servitium regis* of the monastery.[99] In similar manner to the abbot of Werden, the abbess of Essen obviously obtained part of her royal obligation by assessing those vills normally responsible for providing a *servitium* for the convent itself. In regard to which vills the abbot (Werden) or the abbess (Essen) assessed to help pay the *servitium regis*, a difference appears to exist between the monastery and the convent. The abbot of Werden assessed ten vills that, according to the property separation in the monastery, belonged to the abbatial properties,[100] whereas in Essen those vills burdened with payment bore the provision of the convent itself. This is only an apparent difference, however, and stems from the specific kind of property separation in Werden as opposed to that in Essen. In Werden the abbot and the congregation each received specific properties to provide only for their provisions or upkeep; whereas in Essen, within the oldest group of vills or possessions provisioning the convent, the original organization remained and only the incomes themselves were divided up between those designated for the abbess and those for the convent.[101] When one calculates the total payment to the 'konynxstope' from the Essen vills in the fourteenth century, moreover, it comes to between $20\frac{1}{2}$ and $22\frac{1}{2}$ marks.[102] This amount corresponds roughly to the *debitum* of 25 marks that Emperors Frederick I and Henry VI exacted from Werden in the late twelfth century, probably as a monetary redemption of the monastery's *servitium regis*.[103] Considering the manifold similarities between Essen and Werden in location, economic structure and development, and in their status in the realm, one can with reasonable assurance conclude that in the tenth and eleventh centuries the royal convent of Essen owed the king an economic *servitium* nearly equal to that paid by the neighbouring royal monastery of Werden.

value in money) year after year, century after century as the example in the text demonstrates. Presumably the same general conservatism existed in regard to payment made to the realm also.

[99] E. Müller (1930) 433–4 and Weigel (1960) 15–16.

[100] See Chapter 3 above, pp. 126–7.

[101] See Weigel (1960) 54–63 esp. 57 and Metz (1976) 192.

[102] E. Müller (1930) 433–4.

[103] Heusinger (1922) 109–10 [134–5] and Metz (1976) 193. Concerning the annual levy of 25 marks by Frederick I and Henry VI see the charter of Otto IV of 1198 absolving the monastery from the payment. Bendel (1908) 76–8 no. 22 and BF 201.

CORVEY

As in the case of the royal convent of Essen, the tenth- and eleventh-century sources for the royal monastery of Corvey do not provide us with any specific information about the abbey's *servitium regis* in the Saxon and early Salian periods. Therefore, one can at best make various inferences about this powerful monastery's *servitium regis* only on the basis of various kinds of related, but indirect information. The sources for Corvey's economic service to the king prove very meagre and it is difficult, even for later centuries, to calculate the extent of the royal support provided by Corvey; nevertheless, Wibald of Stavelot and Corvey, in a letter to Bishop Bernhard of Hildesheim in 1146 concerning the obligations of the Corvey *ministeriales*, said that 'they should be just as abundant in [their] royal service, in making military expeditions, in attending the royal court and in providing hospitality'.[104] This letter provides evidence that, in the twelfth century, Corvey supplied the king with all forms of *servitium regis*, and if one considers the power and prestige of this monastery on the Weser during the tenth and eleventh centuries, its royal service must also have been substantial.

Already from its foundation in the years 822 and 823[105] Corvey occupied an extremely advantageous location strategically and economically. The monastery was situated on a navigable river, the Weser, at the extreme eastern end of the Westphalian Hellweg. After the foundation of the monastery, the Hellweg was apparently diverted from a river-crossing at Höxter, a former royal *villa* which belonged to the foundation endowment of the monastery,[106] to cross the Weser at Corvey using a ford and a ferry. The *Translatio Sancti Viti* provides evidence that this ferry over the Weser existed already in 836.[107] This remained the primary ford and ferry crossing until the twelfth century, when

---

[104] Jaffé, *Bibl.* 1.239 no. 150: 'servitium regis tam in expeditione quam in curia adeunde et in hospiciis procurandis'. See also below, pp. 202–3.

[105] In general, see Kaminsky (1972) 17–19 with further literature and McKitterick (1983) 118.

[106] On the question of ownership of this property, see Hömberg (1967b) 192, (1960) 5, and (1940) 41. Regarding the specific location of Corvey and Höxter, see Krüger (1931) esp. 115–56.

[107] *Translatio Sancti Viti* c. 30 p. 64. As early as 1115 a charter of Abbot Erkenbert documented a bridge at Höxter. Kaminsky (1972) 250–1 provides the best edition of the charter.

the river-crossing shifted once again to Höxter (about 2 km west of Corvey), where a bridge had been built.[108] From Corvey–Höxter a road continued towards the Harz region via Holzminden and Gandersheim to Magdeburg or via Sohlingen and the royal *Pfalz* at Grone towards Merseburg. In addition, near Corvey–Höxter two important roads merged coming from the south – one from Frankfurt via Korbach and Marsberg (the fortress of the Eresburg), and the second from Italy through Bavaria and eastern Franconia via Fulda and Hersfeld – and then continued north along the Weser via Minden and Verden. Thus Corvey, holding a key position on the upper Weser in western Saxony, furnished the later Carolingians with firm support and a principal base from which to exert influence in the Saxon region, provided a missionary centre to the Saxons and the Danes, and established a stronghold of Benedictine monasticism in this area.[109]

Although the monastery did not enjoy as close a bond with the Ottonian and later Salian kings and emperors as it had with its Carolingian founders,[110] Corvey found itself physically in close proximity to the new dynasty as a result of the establishment of the Saxon kingship in 919. Moreover, the monastery was situated on the main route connecting the power centres of the Liudolfing royal family in eastern Saxony with their inherited power centres in the Rhineland and Lotharingia. Consequently, Corvey received frequent royal visits, and by virtue of this almost yearly royal presence the monastery maintained a finger on the political pulse of the realm.[111] Although we have only a single recorded visit of Otto I to Corvey in 940,[112] the king and later emperor very probably visited the Weser monastery as many as twenty-eight times between 936 and 966.[113] Of all the Saxon and Salian monarchs, Otto I also proved to be the most munificent in granting Corvey rights, privileges and new properties.[114] Corvey may not have stood in the foreground of Otto I's royal policies,[115] but the king indicated early in his reign that he expected Corvey's support and general service to the realm. In 940, Otto granted the abbot of Corvey and his advocate the royal ban or right of enforcement over the castlework (*Burgbann*) of those populations

---

[108] Hömberg (1940) esp. 47–50 and also (1967b) 194. Cf. Krüger (1931) esp. 115–56.
[109] Kaminsky (1972) 18 and 24–5; and Semmler (1970).
[110] Beumann (1966) 151–2.   [111] Kaminsky (1972) 25.
[112] DO I 35.   [113] Kaminsky (1972) 26 esp. n. 89.
[114] DDO I 27, 48, 73, 77, 292.   [115] Kaminsky (1972) 26.

living in three areas or *pagi* and located within the jurisdiction of four different counts. These people were obligated to maintain the fortifications at the monastery and the city (*civitas*) surrounding it, in which they had the right of refuge. This grant, the first of its kind in Saxony, enhanced the existing immunity of the monastery by abrogating the *Burgbann* of the counts and shifting that power to the abbot and his advocate.[116] In the arenga of the charter granting this right, Otto explicitly stated that 'not only the customary royal favour of religious institutions occasioned the grant, but also that he [the king] might cause those requesting his favour to be more ready and willing [to perform] royal service'.[117] The issuance of this charter may have had some connection with Otto's wars against his rebelling brothers, Thankmar and Henry, and their Conradine allies in 938–9, during which the Eresburg, a hub of numerous Corvey possessions, played a significant role. Otto I appeared there in July of 938.[118] In this connection, one could regard this grant of an important governmental right in this area, which 'cut across the ordinary competence of counts',[119] in the sense of an overall strengthening of the royal and Liudolfinger position in Engern and Westphalia *vis-à-vis* the Conradine family.[120]

Otto II did not make any recorded stops in Corvey, but during his ten-year reign he travelled the Hellweg almost yearly.[121] In addition he appeared twice at Sohlingen, which was located in the Solling forest between Corvey and the royal residence at Grone.[122] This was a royal hunting area, and Sohlingen appears to have been a forest vill belonging to Corvey which hosted several royal assemblies of note.[123] On the basis of Otto II's stop at Sohlingen in 978, it is likely that Otto celebrated Pentecost at Corvey immediately thereafter.[124] Otto III issued a charter at Corvey in 987,[125] and on the basis of travel on the Hellweg, he may have

---

[116] Concerning this grant and these types of governmental rights in general, see Leyser (1981) 734–5.

[117] *DO I* 27: 'Si petitionibus que pro utilitatibus sanctorum nobis suggeruntur locorum, adsensum prebuerimus, non solum regium morem decentre implemus, sed eosdem qui precantur ad servitium nostrum promtiores efficimus.' In this specific instance, although the charter primarily addressed military and judicial matters, the phrase *ad servitium nostrum* seems to have a quite general meaning.   [118] BO 76b–c.

[119] Leyser (1981) 735.   [120] See above at n. 9.

[121] Deus (1960) 14–15 and Metz (1976) 225.   [122] *DDO II* 6, 7, 178.

[123] Metz (1971) 269 with n. 73 and (1976) 225; and Kaminsky (1972) 126 with n. 72. Concerning Sohlingen's location and its connection to Grone, see Zotz (1984) 21–9.

[124] Zotz (1984) 22–4.   [125] *DO III* 37.

stopped six further times at the monastery.[126] He also held the first royal assembly (*Reichstag*) of his majority in September of 994 at Sohlingen.[127]

The reign of Henry II affords us even better information. Documentary evidence witnesses to six visits by Henry II to Corvey.[128] At least two of the visits of this last Saxon king to Corvey were connected with his reform of the monastery, begun in 1014 and completed in 1015.[129] Although the royal itinerary between 29 July and 17 September 1014 is not totally clear, Bishop Meinwerk of Paderborn came to the king some time in August or early September of 1014, possibly when Henry stopped at Corvey's vill of Sohlingen where he issued a charter, and requested him to institute reform at Corvey.[130] After this meeting, Henry visited Corvey, found the monastic life being practised there displeasing, and forcibly began a reform of the monastery against the wishes of much of the congregation.[131] In the following year, Henry returned to Corvey in June after another meeting with Bishop Meinwerk to complete the reform and at the same time the king may have celebrated the feast of Corvey's patron saint, St Vitus (15 June).[132] Based on his itinerary, Henry may also have celebrated the feast of St Vitus at Corvey in 1017, as he definitely did in 1019.[133] Moreover, his frequent use of the Hellweg provides at least eleven additional occasions when he may have stayed at Corvey.[134] Thus, the last Ottonian king had ample reason and opportunity to visit the monastery on the Weser.

The use of the Hellweg and the stations along it by no means ceased with the Saxon kings. When Conrad II travelled through-

---

[126] Deus (1960) 14–15 and Metz (1976) 225.

[127] *DDO III* 147, 148, 150; BU 1117a; Zotz (1984) 25–8.

[128] (1) 18 July 1005 – *DH II* 101, BG 953; (2) 24 October 1006 – *DH II* 121; (3) February 1011 – *Ann. Hildes. s.a.* 1011; (4) August/September 1014 – Hirsch (1862–75) 3.8 n. 1, *Ann. Qued. s.a.* 1014; (5) June? 1015 – *Ann. Qued. s.a.* 1015, and see Bannasch (1972) 221–2 with n. 59; (6) 15 June 1019 – *Ann. Corb. s.a.* 1019.

[129] Concerning Henry II's reform of Corvey, see Matthäi (1877) 74–6; Kaminsky (1972) 47–58; and Bannasch (1972) 218–28.

[130] *Vita Meinwerci* c. 145 pp. 76–7; *DH II* 321.

[131] *Ann. Qued. s.a.* 1014 p. 82; BG 1849a.

[132] *Ann. Qued. s.a.* 1015 p. 83; *Ann. Corb. s.a.* 1014 (instead of 1015); Thietmar 7 c. 13; BG 1866c.   [133] BG 1903b, *DDH II* 368, 369; *Ann. Corb. s.a.* 1019.

[134] (1) August 1002; (2) spring 1005; (3–4) November 1005; (5) March 1009; (6) February 1012; (7) November 1015; (8) December 1016; (9) January/February 1021; (10) June 1021; (11) December 1023. In addition there are three further possible, but uncertain, uses of the Hellweg: (1) April 1006; (2) January? 1016; (3) December 1023. Cf. Deus (1960) 15–17 and Kaminsky (1972) 29 with n. 121, and 54.

out his realm receiving the homage and allegiance of his vassals and subjects several months after his election as king in September 1024, he stopped for at least six days in Corvey, where he celebrated the feast of Epiphany and issued several charters.[135] Although no further documented visits of Conrad II to Corvey have come down to us, his use of the Hellweg permits one to posit at least eight additional stops at Corvey or at monastic estates administered by Corvey.[136] On at least two of these occasions, in 1028 and 1033, Conrad's itinerary suggests that he would have been ideally positioned to celebrate St Vitus's feast day at Corvey.[137] Similarly, Conrad's son and successor Henry III almost certainly visited Corvey in 1039 on his peregrination through the realm soon after succeeding to the kingship,[138] and he has two additional recorded visits to Corvey, in 1040, when he stopped there to celebrate the feast of St Michael (29 September), and later in 1046.[139] In 1046, the king, in connection with new reform activity in the monastery, supervised the election of the new abbot and resided in the quarters (*conventus*) of the brothers.[140] Travelling the Hellweg from the Rhineland to Goslar, his favourite residence in Saxony, Henry III presumably made ten further visits to the abbey on the Weser; and between 1056 and 1072 Henry IV appears to have travelled along the Hellweg via Corvey fifteen times.[141] In total, during the Ottonian and early Salian period (936–1075), the German monarchs made at least eighteen documented visits and an additional eighty-five to ninety-two probable visits to Corvey; each visit was between one and at least six days in duration.[142] When one subtracts the time these rulers spent in Italy or on campaign outside of the realm during this period of

---

[135] *DDK II* 10–15; BA 9a–15.

[136] Deus (1960) 17–18; Kaminsky (1972) 59; and Metz (1976) 227. Several of Corvey's vills may have been called upon to provide *servitium regis* when Conrad II travelled in May/June 1028 from Dortmund to Paderborn and on to Fritzlar. See Metz (1971) 285 and n. 192, and also below, n. 163.

[137] In June of both years the itinerary and the constellation of charters around that date make this a plausible suggestion. See *DDK II* 122, 123, 124 and 190.

[138] *DH III* 5; E. Müller (1901) 19; Kaminsky (1972) 65.

[139] *Ann. Saxo s.a.* 1040 p. 684; *Ann. Corb. s.a.* 1046 p. 39.

[140] Kaminsky (1972) 67; *Ann. Corb. s.a.* 1046 p. 39. Concerning Henry III's reform activity in Corvey, see Freise (1983) and Vogtherr (1991) 436–8, for an overview.

[141] Kaminsky (1972) 71, 78.

[142] Ibid. 80. My totals vary slightly from Kaminsky's depending on the degree of certainty one wants to place on several uses of the Hellweg. I calculated my totals using both Kaminsky's and Deus's research on the itineraries and my own research on the itinerary using the royal charters and the *Regesta Imperii*.

nearly a century and a half, it becomes clear that Corvey probably accommodated the king and his retinue on a yearly basis when he resided within the boundaries of the German kingdom proper.

Once again, it no longer should be surprising that the church at Corvey, like those at other monasteries and convents in Westphalia and Saxony which had strong royal connections and which were visited frequently by the court, had a full *Westwerk*. From the royal loge in the upper storey of this structure, the king could participate in the religious services of the congregation and take his symbolic place for the staging of any liturgical celebrations of kingship. Corvey's *Westwerk* was Carolingian in origin (*c.* 885) and became a model for this type of sacral structure. Its greatest period of use by kings and emperors, however, came not under the late Carolingians, but under the Ottonian and Salian kings with their frequent visits to Corvey when travelling the Hellweg.[143]

In spite of the information we have examined regarding royal visits in Corvey, no tenth- or eleventh-century source provides any specific information about the payments made for the accommodation and upkeep of the king and the royal court. In connection with Henry II's reform of Corvey along Gorzean lines, an extensive property and accounts book was produced at Corvey, probably during the abbacy of Druthmar.[144] Corvey's land and income register provides much more extensive information about the monastery's land holdings, its dependent populations and the labour services owed from them than anything that we find in the registers of Werden, with the possible exception of Werden's *Urbar* for Friemersheim and the monastery's holdings west of the Rhine.[145] Unfortunately, however, also in contrast to the land registers of Werden, Corvey's land and assessment roll does not mention any payments specifically designated for the *servitium regis*, which makes it difficult to estimate the extent of the burden on the monastery.[146] This lack of fixed or specialized incomes for the *servitium regis* in Corvey's account book, however, does not in any way prove that the burden did not exist at Corvey also. In fact,

---

[143] Metz (1984) 14 and Streich (1984) 51–3, 58, 403, who cites the extensive archaeological and art historical literature on Corvey and on the *Westwerk* in general.

[144] Kaminsky (1972) 52–3 and 193–222, where the author provides a new edition of the eleventh-century *Heberolle*.

[145] Rösener (1985) has analysed and compared the land and income registers of Werden and Corvey to demonstrate the different types of monastic property structures in Westphalia and Saxony in the tenth century and to trace subsequent changes in monastic property structure.   [146] Metz (1976) 209.

Wolfgang Metz has observed that although the land and income registers of Corvey do not provide amounts owed for the *servitium regis*, they do indicate the abbatial *servitium* owed by various vills of the monastery. When Metz compared the type and extent of payments from Corvey's vills for the abbatial *servitium* with the payments in Werden's registers designated for the *servitium regis* in the eleventh and twelfth centuries, they showed a remarkable similarity on all accounts.[147] Considering the general similarity of payments owed in Corvey's and Werden's land registers, one can more accurately assess the lack of specific payments in Corvey's income registers merely as a variation in the internal organization or financial structure of the abbey. The abbot had the freedom to employ the total abbatial incomes of the monastery at his own discretion. Thus, whereas the abbot of Werden chose to designate specific incomes from his vills for partial payment of the *servitium regis*, the abbot of Corvey at this time merely supplied the king his *servitium* from the totality of the abbatial incomes.[148] This interpretation gains additional support when one takes into account the documented evidence from a later period to the effect that Corvey and its vills did make payments towards the *servitium regis*.[149]

The land registers of the early eleventh century and the twelfth-century *Registrum* of Abbot Erkenbert thus provide an excellent indication of Corvey's extensive land holdings and the vast amount of income paid to the monastery. Thereby they give a good indication of the abbey's ability to provide the king with an ample *servitium*.[150] Moreover, Corvey had other types of income to supplement those in the land registers. Already in 833 Louis the Pious had granted Corvey one of the earliest known coining rights (with the market right implied) east of the Rhine,[151] and later, under Louis the Child in 900, Corvey acquired the market, minting and toll rights in the *villa* of Horhusen (Niedermarsberg), the settlement at the base of the Eresburg.[152] When Otto I granted

---

[147] Metz (1985) 289–90.

[148] Heusinger (1922) 20 [45] has made similar observations. See also Kaminsky (1972) 147.

[149] See Metz (1985) 283–8 and below pp. 202–3.

[150] Kaminsky (1972) 31–9, 138–58 gives an analysis of both land registers, indicating the extent of Corvey's possessions and incomes in the early eleventh and the early twelfth centuries, and provides new editions (pp. 193–239) of both texts.

[151] BM² 992; *Kaiserurkunden ... Westfalen* 1.40–2 no. 13.

[152] *DLK* 6. See Kaminsky (1972) 20, 23–4, 29–30 and Metz (1990) 27–30. With regard to an early eleventh-century forgery in the name of Otto I (*DO I* sp. 444) granting the citizens of Horhusen (Niedermarsberg) the same law or right as the merchants at

Corvey market and coining rights for its possessions in Meppen,[153] moreover, the abbey then possessed the right to hold markets and mint coins in the three areas in which it possessed the largest amount of its property. As Karl Leyser has pointed out, the market and minting privileges, which Otto I granted to Corvey, must be seen as a part of the general development under Otto and his successors of the newly discovered silver deposits in the Harz mountains. The expansion of mining operations necessitated an increase in facilities for the minting of coins.[154] Moreover, Corvey's minting and market rights, seen in conjunction with coin finds from the early eleventh century, demonstrate that Corvey actively made use of these rights and took part in the brisk trade of the period.[155] The incomes accruing to the abbot from these rights and the actual existence of a market at Corvey increased both the abbot's ability to provide a sufficient and varied *servitium* for the king and Corvey's desirability as a stopping point for the royal entourage.[156] A charter from the mid-twelfth century provides us with an excellent indication that the incomes from such external sovereign rights granted to Corvey (and in general to other monasteries) heightened the monastery's ability to provide services for the king. In 1150, when Conrad III granted Corvey the mining rights to the Eresburg, he concluded the grant saying 'so that the church of Corvey may be able so much better to serve in divine as well as in royal matters'.[157]

In addition, several notices from the twelfth and early thirteenth centuries make specific mention of Corvey's obligation to pay a *servitium regis*, without, however, indicating the total sum assessed from the monastery. After Conrad III had enriched the Weser monastery by granting it the former royal convent of Kemnade, Corvey had to pay a sum of six marks 'ad debitum regis servitium' for the new possession.[158] Wibald of Stavelot and Corvey, in his letter to Bishop Bernhard of Hildesheim, remember, mentioned

---

Dortmund, see Kaminsky (1972) 55–6 and Stoob (1970) 118–19. Cf. Hömberg (1955) 95 n. 117.   [153] *DDO I* 73, 77.   [154] Leyser (1981) 742–3.

[155] Kaminsky (1972) 54.

[156] Metz (1971) 280–2 indicated the desirability of market towns as stopping points for the king and royal retinue.

[157] *DK III* 232: '... ut tanto melius possit Corbeiensis ecclesia tam divinis quam regni rebus subservire'. See also Metz (1976) 250–1 no. 2.142a, who provides an excerpt from the charter.

[158] *DK III* 245 ('towards the obligation of royal service'); Metz (1976) 208–9, 250 no. 2.142. Concerning the event see: Lübeck (1953); Stephan-Kühn (unpub. diss. 1973) 96–132; and Jakobi (1979).

the various obligations of the Corvey *ministeriales* from their vills for the *servitium regis*.[159] A fragmentary property and assessment list from around 1200 describes six *curiae* or vills of Corvey: one near Brakel on the Hellweg, one near Holzminden, three in Waldeck near and south of Warburg, and one in Waldeck south of Medebach, that made payments 'for military expeditions and for the royal service, and for the abbot [to go] to the court'.[160] Later, in 1250, when Abbot Hermann and the chapter at Corvey sold their domain at Scherfede near Warburg to the Cistercian monastery of Hardehausen, the resulting charter designated the property concerned thus: 'We sell our entire domain in Scherfede with all its appurtenances, either for the service of the abbot, for the itinerary of the king, or to whatever right they might pertain.'[161] This vill of the monastery and three others in the general area of Warburg (Pappenheim, now deserted, Vorst near Külte, and Lütersheim east of Arolsen), all have documented payments to the *servitium regis* in the thirteenth century.[162] Conceivably, they may have been used to accommodate or provide upkeep for the king on at least two occasions in 1019 and 1028 when the German monarchs travelled through this area from Paderborn respectively to Kaufungen and to Fritzlar.[163]

ROYAL CONVENTS IN WESTPHALIA AND ENGERN

Little or no information concerning the payment of *servitium regis* by the remaining monastic and canonical institutions standing under royal protection in Westphalia and the areas bordering the Hellweg survives (see Map 5). These institutions consisted exclusively of royal convents, which were not located on the most frequently used royal roads and consequently were seldom called upon to accommodate the king. In this regard, Geseke, situated directly on the Hellweg, provides the sole exception. Although Geseke stood under royal protection, and it enjoyed the royal right to elect its abbess,[164] the convent nevertheless remained a dynastic

---

[159] Jaffé, *Bibl.* 1.238 no. 150 ('servitium regis tam in expeditione quam in curia adeunda et in hospiciis procurandis exuberare'). See above, Chapter 2, at n. 154.

[160] Wigand (1826–8) 1.4 p. 52 ('ad expeditionem et servitium regis et tunc abbatis ad curiam') and 2.1. Excerpts provided by Metz (1976) 209 and 251 no. 2.144. See also Metz (1985) 284–7.

[161] *Westfälisches Urkundenbuch 4.1* no. 417 p. 268: '...totum officium nostrum in Scerve cum omnibus pertinentiis suis sive ad servitium abbatis sive ad iter regis seu ad quod cumque ius pertineant...vendidimus'.　　　　　[162] See n. 160 above.

[163] Metz (1971) 279 n. 147 and 285 with nn. 191, 192.　　　[164] DO I 158; DO III 29.

convent of the Haholdian family, whose proprietary rights were never effectively shut out by its royal connections.[165] The royal protection and the election right were probably granted in connection with Otto I's alliance with the Haholdian family and possibly on account of Geseke's strategic location on the Hellweg. All stipulations concerning the election of the abbess and the appointment and constitution of the advocate, however, were tied to the founding family. In fact, since the descendants of the founding family gave the convent to the archbishop of Cologne in 1014 without any royal involvement, the Haholdian family appears to have retained the sole right of disposition over the convent, which would not have been the case had Geseke become a royal convent.[166] Although, because of its location between Paderborn and Erwitte, Geseke frequently witnessed the progress of the royal court on its many trips along the Hellweg, we have no compelling evidence pointing to its providing regular accommodation for the king. Not only do we have no mention of Geseke ever making any payments to the king, but two further considerations weigh against it. As Albert Hömberg pointed out, the convent was relatively poor and therefore probably could not have afforded to accommodate the entire royal retinue. Its location between two major royal stopping points, Paderborn and Erwitte, made frequent stops even less likely. Under normal conditions the royal court could easily cover the distance from Paderborn to Erwitte in a single day with little need to remain at Geseke. Thus, it is more likely that Geseke merely provided a normal rest stop on the journey between the two more customary and comfortable points of accommodation and does not appear to have been a regular accommodation point, especially for the full retinue.[167]

Likewise, although the royal convent of Meschede lay somewhat south of the Hellweg and was located at a fork on an important road leading north through the Sauerland to Soest and Paderborn, the Saxon and Salian kings rarely if ever visited this region and we have no information from it concerning any payments towards the *servitium regis*.

[165] Semmler (1959) 17.
[166] *REK* 1 no. 630 and *UB Westfalen* 25 no. 23 (3 February 1014).
[167] Hömberg (1967c) 163–4. Cf. BU 986, where Uhlirz, without evidence or compelling argument, contends that Otto III's confirmation of Geseke's immunity, the granting of the right of free abbatial election, and his added concession of electing the advocate, were bestowed possibly in gratitude for accommodation on a trip from Grone to Dortmund.

Several royal convents north of the Hellweg remain to be mentioned. In the region around Münster lay the convents of Vreden and Metelen. The sources tell us nothing about any *servitium* paid by Metelen and very little about Vreden. We know that Conrad II received accommodation at Vreden in November 1024 from the daughters of Otto II, the abbesses Sophie of Gandersheim and Essen, and Adelheid of Quedlinburg, Gernrode and Vreden, on his journey from the lower Rhine to Dortmund during his initial royal progress throughout the realm.[168] Vreden appears to have become a royal convent under Henry II when he installed Adelheid in 1014 as its abbess.[169] It is conceivable that Henry II may have stopped there already in the winter of 1003 on his way from Nijmegen to Saxony and Magdeburg,[170] but we have no evidence stating that he did so. In any case, although Vreden was located on an old trade route from Utrecht and Deventer to Münster,[171] its location nonetheless did not place it on a road frequently travelled by the royal court. Thus, the king had little opportunity to claim his *servitium* there; however, this does not mean that the obligation did not exist. This fact finds an echo and confirmation in two sources from Cologne, of the fourteenth and fifteenth centuries respectively, long after the archbishop of Cologne had acquired Vreden in the twelfth century. According to these sources, each full *mansus* from Vreden's property had to pay twelve *denarii* and each half *mansus* six *denarii* to the archbishop of Cologne to satisfy their debt to the king, called the 'koeningescult' ('coninxschult'). The total payment amounted to thirty marks to be paid once every ten years on the feast of St Valentine.[172] As we have seen from similar sources from Essen and Werden, this obligation probably originated in an earlier time and corresponded to the convent's debt of *servitium regis*.[173] The ten-yearly payment most probably reflected the very irregular collection of this debt owing to Vreden's location.[174]

---

[168] *Ann. Qued. s.a.* 1024 p. 90; BA 7, 8a–c.

[169] Ficker (1861) 1.349; Metz (1976) 208; *Ann. Qued. s.a.* 1014 p. 82.

[170] *DDH II* 42, 43, 44; BG 1534, 1535, 1535a–b, 1536. [171] Kohl (1980) 116.

[172] Wilmans (1874) 152–3 n. 8 and *UB Westfalen* 639 n. 657. Metz (1976) 249–50 no. 2.131 and 2.132 excerpts the pertinent passages from both sources. The total amount of the debt, although paid only once every ten years, corresponds approximately to the twelfth-century payments of Werden, Essen and Stavelot-Malmédy (twenty-five, *c.* twenty-two and twenty or thirty marks respectively).

[173] E. Müller (1930) 433 and Brons (1907) 36–7. Whether this debt of *servitium regis* arose first in the eleventh century or in the twelfth cannot be determined from the sources.

[174] See also Metz (1976) 208.

In Engern, between the Teutoburgerwald and the Weserberg-land, lay the royal convents of Schildesche and Herford. Both lay on the main route coming north from Dortmund to Minden, with Herford situated at the site of fords over the Aa and the Werre rivers. Schildesche, which achieved royal status in 940,[175] appears to have developed entirely in the shadow of its older and more powerful neighbour Herford, and finally in 1019 Henry II gave the convent to the bishop of Paderborn.[176] We have no information or indication about the payment of any kind of *servitium regis* from Schildesche.[177] Herford too offers us scanty information, but a few conclusions can be drawn. It was founded about the same time as Corvey and was closely associated with it.[178] Under the Ottonian kings it was considered along with Quedlinburg, Gandersheim and Essen as one of the model royal convents in regard to its legal status.[179] It possessed a very large endowment, primarily out of royal property, and along with Corvey had already been granted market, toll and coining rights under Louis the Pious. Later, in 973, Otto I confirmed the monastery's possession of market, toll and minting rights in Odenhausen (a district or area of Hersfeld, today called Radewig) along with the royal ban and the guarantee of royal peace for the market there.[180] The convent certainly appears to have had ample means to accommodate or pay *servitium* to the king, but owing to its location it received relatively few visits. On the few occasions, however, when the Ottonian and Salian kings did find themselves in this area, usually on the way to or from Minden, they must have received their accommodation at Herford, which lay a day's march to the southwest. For instance, we find that Henry III issued a charter at Herford in December 1040,[181] and he may also have stopped there on two further occasions in 1051 and 1053.[182] On

---

[175] *DO I* 35; *DO II* 75 confirmed and strengthened its legal status.

[176] *DH II* 403.

[177] In general concerning Schildesche see Bannasch (1972) 43–6, 217.

[178] In general concerning Herford's early history, see Jäschke (1963–4) 234–7, Semmler (1970) and Lobbedey (1970) 335–40. [179] Semmler (1959) 27.

[180] Sandow (1970). The arenga of Otto's 973 charter (*DO I* 430) made a reference to the earlier charter: 'qualiter quaedam venerabilis abbatissa Herfordensi monasterii nomina Imma nobis scripta Hluthuuuici regis de quodam mercato cum omnibus inde exigendi usibus, id est moneta teloneo vel quicquid ad publicum videtur pertinere mercatum'.

[181] *DH III* 67. Henry III came to Herford from Allstedt where he issued a charter on 5 December (*DH III* 66) and continued on to Münster where he celebrated Christmas: E. Müller (1901) 30.

[182] In June 1051 Henry III travelled from Dortmund to Minden and almost certainly stopped at Herford: *DDH III* 270, 271. In 1053, Henry III travelled from Goslar to

two earlier occasions, in 1003 and 1024, Henry II and Conrad II may have visited Herford.[183] On the basis of the itinerary, therefore, it seems very likely that the German kings visited Herford and took advantage of their right to accommodation and upkeep. Thus, although we have no specific information about Herford's *servitium regis*, Conrad II's royal charter confirming Herford's rights (which were originally based in part on interpolations contained in a charter of Louis the German) provided specific provisions concerning the amount of *servitium* Herford had to pay the bishop on his yearly visit.[184] Surely if the royal convent paid an episcopal *servitium* it would also pay the king a *servitium* when he came to visit or merely stop overnight. Owing to the low frequency of the royal presence in this area until the eleventh century, one has to assume that the convent merely paid the *servitium* upon royal demand.

There remain to be mentioned the two royal convents located on the middle Weser, Fischbeck and Kemnade. Fischbeck was located slightly northwest of Hameln on the east bank of the Weser river. A noble Saxon matron named Helmburg founded the convent on property that she had first granted over to Otto I. The king held the highest advocacy over the convent and he granted it both the royal immunity and the right to select its own abbess. Thus, Fischbeck became a royal convent immediately upon its foundation.[185] Kemnade lay midway between Corvey and Hameln on the west bank of the Weser. Kemnade was founded by two Saxon noble sisters, Friderun and Countess Imma, daughters of Count Wichmann the Younger, with the intervention of Count Gero and the permission of Otto I. The nunnery

---

Minden and then on to Paderborn. The route from Minden to Paderborn would have taken him via Herford: *DDH III* 306–9.

[183] In the winter of 1003, Henry II travelled from Nijmegen on the lower Rhine via Minden and Hildesheim to Magdeburg. Along this route he could very probably have stopped at Herford. See *DDH II* 42, 43; *BG* 1534, 1535, 1535a–b, 1536. Later, in December of 1024, Conrad II went from Dortmund to Minden with a probable stop in Herford: *BA* 8a–b.   [184] *DK II* 10; *DLD* 178.

[185] *DO I* 174. Krumwiede (1955) 92–7, 112–15 and 127–8 builds a thought-provoking, but unconvincing, argument that Fischbeck never really achieved the status of a royal abbey. He claims that it merely held a 'special royal protection' conditioned by the specific circumstances of the convent's foundation. In spite of his argument, it is difficult to ignore the legal language of the various charters for Fischbeck (*DO I* 174, *DH II* 81, *DK II* 15) stating 'nullius seculari dominio subiecte, excepto nostro, qui earum defensor deo annuente esse volumus' and the fact that Fischbeck possessed all the hallmarks of a royal convent. See Leyser (1979) 69; Lübeck (1941) 8–15; and especially K. Heinemeyer (1974) 132 n. 125.

appears to have been founded on lands which had been confiscated by Otto I from the rebel Wichmann the Younger, but which had formed part of his daughters' inheritance and which they, through royal grace, could use during their lifetimes.[186] A charter of Henry II in 1004 states that after the deaths of the two sisters the nunnery would revert to full ownership of the realm,[187] and its royal status was confirmed in 1017.[188] Again, we do not know anything specific with regard to any *servitium regis* of the two convents during the Ottonian and Salian periods, but their location suggests that they may have served as stopping points for the royal retinue, albeit seldom. Henry III, in particular, may have stopped at one or the other, or both, of these convents on several occasions during trips from Goslar or Hildesheim to Minden or vice versa.[189]

Aside from several charters for both convents granting or confirming their legal status,[190] we know very little about them from the time of their respective foundations until 1147 when they both appear enmeshed in a power struggle with King Conrad III and Wibald, abbot of Corvey, over their legal status in the realm. The grant of both convents to Abbot Wibald of Corvey under Conrad III provides some indirect information concerning the *servitium regis*.[191] In January 1147, when Wibald originally convinced Conrad III to grant the two convents to him, we hear that in return for the royal grant, Corvey had to pay an additional ten pounds of silver, either in money or goods of equivalent worth, every time it was called upon to serve the king.[192] Later,

---

[186] *Ann. Saxo s.a.* 967, 970 pp. 621, 624 claims that Otto I endowed the monastery with half of the lands that he had confiscated from the rebel Wichmann the Younger. Concerning these problems see Leyser (1979) 55–6 with n. 55 and 68–9 with n. 34.

[187] *DH II* 87: 'Ad hec statuimus, ut in prefate abbatisse sueque sororis comitisse potestate predictum monasterium et abbacia nostro persistat concessu diebus vite earum, post obitum vero utrarumque earum ad nostrum publicum eadem abbacia ius in perpetuum pertineat.' [188] *DH II* 362.

[189] Henry III's trip from Speyer to Minden in July 1048 may have occasioned stops at both Kemnade and Fischbeck (*DDH III* 220, 221) as might have his journeys in May/June 1049 (Goslar–Minden–Hildesheim: *DDH III* 234–6), in June 1051 (Dortmund–Minden–Kaufungen: *DDH III* 270–1) and in July 1053 (Goslar–Minden–Paderborn–Goslar: *DDH III* 306–9). In addition, Henry II travelled from Nijmegen via Minden and Hildesheim to Magdeburg in March 1003, making likely a stop in Fischbeck (*DDH II* 41–3; *BG* 1534, 1535, 1535a–b, 1536) and Henry IV as a child travelled from Goslar to Minden and on to Augsburg (*DDH IV* 32–4).

[190] Fischbeck: *DH II* 81 and *DK II* 15. Kemnade: *DH II* 362, *DK II* 19, *DH III* 7.
[191] See below p. 202.
[192] Jaffé, *Bibl.* 1.55 (*Chronographus Corbeiensis*):

> Rex autem, quamquam non facile acquiesceret...et ecclesie nostre abbaciolas duas Kymenaden et ei vicinam Visbike concessit, ac per anulum gemario lapide

however, at the *Reichstag* in March of 1147 when Conrad made the official transfer, and also in a letter to Pope Eugene III, Conrad stated that neither convent owed the king or the realm anything towards the *militia* or the *servitium (regis)*.[193] In 1151, Conrad at last issued the charter (which by then concerned only Kemnade) that settled the longstanding dispute.[194] He granted Kemnade to Corvey and at the same time raised Corvey's debt of *servitium regis* by six *marce* in return for enriching Corvey.[195] In the initial form of the transaction concerning both convents, Corvey's debt to the king was to be increased by ten pounds of silver for the acquisition of both convents, and in the end Corvey realized an increase of six *marce* for obtaining Kemnade only. This increase upon acquisition must have corresponded in some way to the estimated value of the *servitium regis* that the king could originally collect from the two convents. Since we have no information about the amount of the *servitium* the convents paid or were liable for in an earlier time, it is not possible to determine how the ten pounds or six marks corresponded to any former debt of *servitium*. Considering that abbess Judith of Kemnade depleted a large amount of the convent's wealth, the final increase realized by Corvey may not correspond at all to any former debt, but could be based on the remaining properties and incomes of Kemnade. The fact that Corvey's debt did increase upon acquisition of one or both convents does, however, seem to indicate that they previously had some liability to the king for the overall *servitium regis*. As Wolfgang Metz has pointed out, one can resolve the apparent contradiction created by the king's statement that no payments towards the *militia* or the

condecorosum ad nos transmisit…Nam ne minus et rex hinc regno prospiceret, quocienscumque serviri sibi de loco nostro legis debito et priorum longe dierum instituto contingeret: si argento anticipanda foret, denae appenderentur librae, sin autem pastibus, aucmentarentur tanti precii pro temporis qualitate ac comparationis commoditate.

[193] *DK III* 182: 'Sane ad prefata duo loca neque militia neque ullum servitium nobis aut regno debebatur.' Jaffé, *Bibl.* 1.113 no. 34: 'Erant in propinquo duae abbatiolae feminarum, quae nullum regno et nobis vel in milicia vel in alio servicio prebebant supplementum.'

[194] *DK III* 245. Concerning Corvey's long and complicated struggle to acquire Kemnade and Fischbeck see: Lübeck (1941); Krumwiede (1955) 98–115; and Lübeck (1953). Krumwiede contends that Fischbeck was able to prevail against being granted to Corvey because it was not a royal convent (see above, n. 185), whereas Lübeck (1953) 422–3 offers the more plausible suggestion of a compromise between Conrad III and Pope Eugene over the two convents.

[195] *DK III* 245 p. 429: 'ut pro augmento prefati monasterii, quod ecclesie Corbeiensi in perpetuam possessionem tradidimus, ad debitum regis servitium VI marce aut servitium VI marcarum regno de abbatia Corbeiensi persolvantur'.

servitium regis were collected from the two convents by considering their location in relation to the historical situation under the Hohenstaufen kings. Because the Hohenstaufen kings rarely, if ever, travelled to the middle Weser region, the *servitium regis* of the two convents was essentially worthless to them, but if one or both were subordinate to Corvey their incomes could be used to increase Corvey's ability to serve the realm and thus its *servitium regis*.[196]

[196] Metz (1976) 208–9.

Chapter 6

MONASTERIES IN THE SAXON–HESSIAN
BORDER REGION

RIVER BASINS AS A GEOPOLITICAL SETTING

In the late tenth and early eleventh centuries, one can discern a general Ottonian policy of securing the approaches and the river crossings along the upper Weser and the lower Fulda and Werra Rivers which led to the main routes connecting Saxony to the middle Rhine and to eastern Franconia, Bavaria and Italy through Thuringia. The Ottonian rulers gradually brought these approaches and fords directly or indirectly within royal influence. The foundation of several abbeys, Helmarshausen – a royal monastery – and three royal convents – Hilwartshausen, Kaufungen and Eschwege – can be linked to this general policy. All of these royal abbeys were located in an area containing large royal forests and some royal property, considerable parts of which the Carolingian royal monasteries of Fulda, Hersfeld and Corvey, administered for the realm.[1] In the same area, however, the indigenous nobility also owned considerable amounts of allodial property interspersed between these large complexes of royal forest and scattered royal properties. For example, the foundation endowment and later property grants for Hilwartshausen, and grants for Helmarshausen, originated almost exclusively from the allodial possessions of the Saxon nobility.[2] However, the noble founders of both abbeys quickly turned to the king to protect their religious foundations from the property claims of their kinsfolk. Consequently, both Hilwartshausen and Helmarshausen offered a method for the Ottonian kings to strengthen and extend their influence in an area already containing substantial royal holdings without initially granting royal property to the new foundations.[3]

---

[1] Goetting (1980) 152. For a succinct overview of the early medieval pattern of property-holding in this area, see K. Heinemeyer (1973) 156–67.

[2] Kroeschell (1957) 9–14 and K. Heinemeyer (1974) 111–46.

[3] Kroeschell (1957) 8–9; K. Heinemeyer (1974) 149; and Goetting (1980) 152–3.

These royal abbeys, along with the later ones at Eschwege and Kaufungen, whose properties immediately before the foundation of the religious communities on them had belonged to Otto III's sister, Abbess Sophie of Gandersheim, and Queen Kunigunda respectively, enabled the Ottonian rulers to keep the great majority of royal possessions in the area intact and directly or indirectly in royal hands. At the same time, the kings were able to acquire influence or control over numerous parcels of property throughout the region, which formerly had belonged to the indigenous nobility, and also encourage economic development in the area. Royal initiatives in the upper Weser region culminated under Henry II as part of his programme to enhance royal power in the centre of the realm and to create a core of property there belonging directly to the realm or to royal churches.[4] Later, the Salians, who needed to secure their access to the Harz region in an increasingly hostile Saxony, also benefited from these policies. As we shall see, the locations of these royal abbeys and the various properties under their control held strategic and economic importance for the travelling royal court. In fact, the locations of these monasteries and their properties on royal roads, and their control of important river fords and of the areas traversed by the main roads to the royal residences in the Leine valley and the southern Harz region, proved as important as their actual ability to accommodate the royal court or provide it with the *servitium regis*.

HELMARSHAUSEN

The northernmost of these royal institutions, Helmarshausen, held great promise and potential upon its foundation in 997 and during the early years of its existence. Helmarshausen held a potentially advantageous position in regard to travel and trade (see Map 8). Although not located specifically on a royal road, it was situated on an important ford of the lower Diemel River, at the intersection of major north–south and east–west roads. North–south arteries ran from Frankfurt or from Bavaria and eastern Franconia via Fulda and/or Hersfeld to Kassel. From there a road continued through a large royal forest, the Reinhardswald, to Helmarshausen where it crossed the Diemel. Leaving Helmarshausen the road ran

---

[4] Concerning these designs of Henry II, only partially realized before his death in 1024, see Diefenbach (unpub. diss. 1952) 127–35 and the end of Chapter 1 above.

north crossing the Weser at Herstelle, an old royal possession,[5] and continued downstream along the river to Bremen. Another road coming from the west connected Helmarshausen to the major route running from Cologne east to Erfurt and to the one coming from Münster southeast to Northeim. This road also crossed the Diemel at Helmarshausen and then continued east, crossing the Weser at Lippoldsberg and running via Uslar to Northeim and the Leine valley. Moreover, river traffic from the Weser could navigate the Diemel up to the monastery. Thus, owing to the confluence of these land routes at Helmarshausen with a navigable stretch of the Diemel, Helmarshausen must have been a rather important point of trans-shipment from wagon to ship and probably a site of early trade.[6]

The foundation of Helmarshausen took place in 997.[7] A nobleman and his wife, Count Eckhard and Mathilde, transferred their possession of a church and an estate at Helmarshausen to King Otto III with the request that he found a monastery. Otto III founded the monastery as a royal monastery by granting it royal immunity and the same legal status as Corvey. As in many monasteries founded on lands donated by noble families, the advocacy of the monastery remained in the hands of the founding family. Otto III appointed Count Eckhard as advocate and stipulated that after Eckhard's death, the eldest of his offspring should follow him. If his family died out, however, selection of the advocate reverted to the abbot acting in accordance with the will of the community. Apparently, when the only son of the founding pair died young, they approached first Pope Sylvester II in 999 and then Otto III again in April 1000 to request a change in the stipulations governing the advocacy. Thereafter a second royal charter was issued. It reaffirmed the full royal status of the monastery and granted to the abbot and the brothers the right to select their own advocate after Count Eckhard's death.[8] In addition to special royal protection, Helmarshausen also enjoyed papal sanctions containing a *poena* formula recognizing the foundation

---

[5] In 797 Charlemagne celebrated the winter feast here. For the various sources see Abel and Simson (1865–83) 2.139–40.

[6] W. Heinemeyer (1963–4) 301–2 provides a convenient summary of the literature discussing Helmarshausen's geographical location and its relation to travel and trade. Pfaff (1910) 197–8, writing earlier, does not consider Helmarshausen's location to have been advantageous as do Heinemeyer and others.

[7] *DO III* 256 (Kehr no. 1). Kehr (1932) 102–4 provides the best edition of the Helmarshausen charters.   [8] *DO III* 356 (Kehr no. 2).

as a royal abbey and granting the right freely to select its
advocate.[9] With these requests, however, Count Eckhard and his
wife effectively disinherited their family in favour of the monastery and Helmarshausen found itself plunged into a long and
bitter struggle with the count's powerful relatives over its
independence.[10] The struggle with Eckhard's family sapped much
of the monastery's energy and assets and, more importantly, it
effectively closed off a source of valuable property grants and of
support by the Saxon nobility during the normal early period of
a newly-endowed foundation's growth. Perhaps in an attempt to
counter these difficulties and in general accordance with late
Ottonian economic policies, Otto III granted the monastery the
important and profitable commercial rights to establish and hold
a market with the royal ban, to collect tolls and to coin money.[11]
To facilitate these rights, the charter granted the king's peace to the
merchants doing business there and tied this peace to the royal
ban.[12] However, without active royal support in the form of royal
property grants, without real and immediate protection, and in
the face of the opposition of the powerful indigenous nobility, the
young abbey had little chance to grow and develop its commercial
advantages effectively. Thus, Helmarshausen's status as a royal
monastery did not correspond to the political or economic reality
of its situation;[13] in short, the monastery appears to have become
more of a liability than an asset to the realm.

Despite the fact that the foundation of Helmarshausen as a royal
monastery in 997 fits in well with Ottonian designs in this area to

---

[9] Kehr nos. 7, 8.

[10] Pfaff (1910) 194–203 and W. Heinemeyer (1963–4) 350–6 provide the most detailed
accounts of the monastery's early history, but also see Bannasch (1972) 110–14, who
views events within the broader perspective of royal politics.

[11] *DO III* 357 (Kehr no. 3). The partially forged foundation charter of 997 (*DO III* 256,
Kehr no. 1) for Helmarshausen also contained these rights to hold a market, coin money
and collect tolls. Although Kehr (1932) 90–1 originally entertained doubts as to the
authenticity of these rights in the charter of 997, he finally accepted them as a part of
the original core of the charter. W. Heinemeyer (1963–4) 329–30 has built a good
argument countering Kehr, but it is by no means conclusive, since, as Kehr himself
indicated, it is very difficult to separate the interpolations from the core text in this
charter.

[12] *DO III* 357 (Kehr no. 3): 'ut omnes negociatores caeterique mercatum excolentes
commorantes euntes et redeuntes talem pacem talemque iusticiam obtineant, qualem
illi detinent, qui Mogunciae, Coloniae, Trutmanniae negotium exercent, talemque
bannum persolvant, qui idem mercatum inquietare aut infringere praesumant'. On the
early history and significance of grants protecting merchants and thus encouraging
commercial development, see Metz (1972b) esp. 33–4, 42–4.

[13] Pfaff (1910) 200–2; *Translatio s. Modoaldi* c. 3 p. 291.

maintain points of indirect royal control and to encourage economic development,[14] we know little about its royal service owing to its short and turbulent existence as a royal monastery. In the partially forged foundation charter of 997,[15] the immunity clause expressly prohibits anyone from making any exactions from or demands upon the monastery that pertain to the *servitium regale*.[16] A similar prohibition appears in the later charters of 1107[17] and 1144,[18] but as with so many monasteries, nowhere do we find information specifically defining Helmarshausen's obligations to the king or the frequency of payment. Since it was a royal abbey, however, and especially in light of the foundation charter, one must assume that Helmarshausen, like other royal monasteries, initially had an obligation to serve the king.[19] On the other hand, considering the early history of the monastery, one realistically has to conclude that Helmarshausen's obligations to the king probably existed more in theory than in practice.

Consequently, in 1017 after an assembly of princes had adjudged the monastery's royal status against the claims of Eckhard's heirs, Henry II, on the counsel and intervention of the assembled princes and bishops, granted Helmarshausen as a proprietary monastery to Bishop Meinwerk of Paderborn and his bishopric.[20] The three

[14] W. Heinemeyer (1963–4) 354.

[15] *DO III* 256. (Kehr no. 1); W. Heinemeyer (1963–4) 321–42 esp. 329–33, where he deals in depth with the forgeries and partial forgeries among the Helmarshausen charters.

[16] Kehr no. 1:

'...ut nullus iudex aut aliqua iudiciaria potestas vel publica magna aut parva persona ⟨cuiuscunque sit conditionis vel dignitatis⟩ in iam dicto monasterio vel locis eidem monasterio subditis vel pertinentibus placitum tenere, districtum facere, parafredos aut aliquam functionem vel pensionem publicam ad nostrum servicium regale vel servitii redemptionem exigere nullusque in eius domibus sine eiusdem loci abbatis aut congregationis assensu et voluntate mansionaticum habere presumat.

(The Latin text here from Kehr no. 1 differs slightly from *DO III* 256.) Heusinger (1922) 25 [50] n. 4 sees the entire mention of *servitium regale* as a forgery or interpolation, but several of Otto III's other charters imply a similar concept without specifically stating *servitium regale*. See, for example, *DDO III* 32, 115, 235, 318. Concerning this passage see Metz (1976) 210, who in my opinion correctly interprets the passage and concedes to Heusinger's position only that the 'vel servitii redemptionem' of the passage is a twelfth-century interpolation.

[17] Stumpf 3017; *Inventar...Paderborn* 9 no. 13. [18] *DK III* 117.

[19] *DO III* 256 (Kehr no. 1) specifically mentions the *servitium regale* and *DO III* 356 (Kehr no. 2) in confirming Helmarshausen's rights states: '...tali libertate quali Corbeya caeteraque monachorum nostri imperii monasteria publica nostrae speciali providentiae sunt subdita'. This notion of *libertate* and *monasteria publica nostri speciali providentiae* carries the reciprocal obligation of *servitium*.

[20] *Vita Meinwerci* c. 144 p. 76.

sources reporting the event all give different reasons for the *traditio* and they all appear to hold a kernel of truth.[21] In fact, a composite of the three seems to shed the most light on the situation.[22] Since Helmarshausen did lie in the diocese of Paderborn, Meinwerk's possession of the abbey would indeed have facilitated his episcopal duties *vis-à-vis* the monastery. More importantly, however, Helmarshausen was a poor relative to most royal abbeys and, consequently, it did not have the means to provide the realm with the obligatory economic or military *servitium* of a royal monastery. Thus, whether the monastery by means of a special dispensation did not owe any *servitium* to the realm[23] or whether it was merely too poor to supply the king a *servitium*, the fact remains that when the abbey no longer paid a *servitium regis* it held marginal value for the realm and was granted away. Moreover, as Henry, the assembly of secular and ecclesiastical princes, and even the abbot and monks at Helmarshausen must have perceived, the *traditio* to the bishop of Paderborn provided the best possible solution for all parties involved. Since Meinwerk was a powerful lord in the area, he could provide the monastery with real protection against encroachments from the indigenous nobility. At the same time, as a proprietary monastery of the bishop of Paderborn, who was a leading member of the royal church, Helmarshausen remained indirectly under royal influence, and thereby could be used to further royal interests in the area or as a part of an overall royal design.[24]

HILWARTSHAUSEN

In 960, Otto I, in co-operation with Aeddila, a noble Saxon matron, authorized the founding of Hilwartshausen, a convent of canonesses.[25] The convent was located on the extreme upper Weser just north of the confluence of the Fulda and the Werra Rivers, about 30 km south of the future site of Helmarshausen and in the immediate vicinity of two large royal forests and scattered royal properties. Hilwartshausen's initial endowment, however, came primarily from property of the indigenous nobility, that is, Aeddila's inheritance. Although Aeddila made the property

---

[21] *DH II* 371; *Translatio s. Modoaldi* cc. 3, 4; *Vita Meinwerci* c. 144.
[22] Pfaff (1910) 200–1.   [23] *Translatio s. Modoaldi* c. 1.
[24] W. Heinemeyer (1963–4) 356 also points out that the *traditio* of Helmarshausen to Paderborn corresponded to overall church policy under Henry II and may have formed part of a larger design in the area.   [25] *DO I* 206.

transfer 'with the consent of her co-heirs and her advocate',[26] she nonetheless turned to the king to issue the foundation charter and give royal confirmation to her intentions. Moreover, Otto's foundation charter granted the canonesses of Hilwartshausen the right to free election of their abbess and implied a similar legal status to the royal convents of Gandersheim and Herford.[27] Thereby, from its beginning, the convent entered the sphere of those royal monasteries and convents enjoying the king's special protection.[28] Nevertheless, after Aeddila's death (soon after 960) the hereditary claims of other family members threatened the intended foundation and caused her daughters and the later abbesses, Berthildis and Hemma, to turn anew to the king for protection.[29]

Thus in July 963, when Otto I was on campaign in Italy, Berthildis and Hemma went to his son king Otto II, who at that time had stopped in the nearby royal residence at Sohlingen, and requested his aid to protect the fledgling convent from the property claims of their relatives. The charter resulting from this encounter placed Hilwartshausen exclusively under the same royal protection as other royal abbeys and expressly excluded all claims to the convent and its property from any of the sisters' relations.[30] In general, the purpose of a *traditio* to the king of the kind initiated by Aeddila, or of royal interventions and royal diplomas of protection and immunity for noble foundations, frequently was to favour the institution over the hereditary claims of the relatives of the founders or foundresses by permanently alienating the lands

---

[26] *DO I* 206: 'cum consensu coeredum ipsius ac patronis.'

[27] *DO I* 206: 'Concessimus etiam prescriptis virginibus...abbatissam sibi quam-cumque...voluerint eligere et in omnibus talibus ordinibus perfruere sicuti cetera monasteria virginum que ex nostro regimine potestatem habent elegendi sibi abbatissam, id est Heriford et Gandresheim'.

[28] Stengel (1910) 409–10 and K. Heinemeyer (1974) 135 n. 145. See above, Chapter 2, on the legal status of royal monasteries and convents.

[29] On the sons of Aeddila, a member of the Esiconian family, and her husband Bunico, a member of the Ricdag kindred, and their *coheredes*, see K. Heinemeyer (1974) 136–7 nn. 150, 156 and Goetting (1980) 152–62.

[30] *DO II* 6 (20 July 963):

Nos vero piam illarum peticionem non parvi pendendam iudicantes cum consilio archiepiscopi Uuillihelmi fratris scilicet nostri, ad cuius diocesim idem locus pertinere videtur, nostrae sublimitatis aures accommodavimus et privilegium illis a domino nostro impetore collatum per nos nihilominus roborare decrevimus, ea siquidem racione ut prescriptus locus sub nostro nostrorumque successorum videlicet regum mundiburdio vel defensione sicut cetere regales abbatie consistat nec alicui parentum vel proheredum earundem sororum debitor vel possidendus existat.

and property of the institution from the *coheredes*.[31] Unlike the later situation in Helmarshausen, where the conflict with the founders had stunted the growth and sapped the strength of the new monastery, Aeddila's heirs and relatives appear to have accepted the royal proclamation concerning Hilwartshausen without any trace of conflict. The apparent lack of opposition from Aeddila's heirs to the formal proclamation of Hilwartshausen as a royal convent may have resulted from stipulations concerning the convent's advocate. Otto II did not grant the abbess and canonesses of Hilwartshausen the right to elect their own advocate. Instead, this right remained with the king who appears to have appointed the position within Aeddila's circle of relatives. Not only was the first advocate of Hilwartshausen, Count Palatine Adelbero/Bern, a noble of high standing in the realm and a close royal advisor, but he also appears to have had a close familial relationship to Aeddila, probably on the maternal side.[32]

Hilwartshausen's natural location combined with the numerous properties it acquired in the first hundred years of its existence gave it a formidable position in the upper Weser River valley near the confluence of the Fulda and Werra Rivers and in the area east and northeast of it leading to the Leine valley (see Map 8). Prior to the foundation of the city of Münden in the mid-twelfth century, which eventually became the convergence point of the main roads traversing these valleys, Hilwartshausen, located about three miles north of Münden, provided the first opportunity to cross the Weser. Until one reached the wider and flatter ground at Hilwartshausen on the west bank of the Weser or at Gimte on the east bank (later a possession of Hilwartshausen) the narrow, winding and steep valleys of the Fulda and the Werra Rivers near their confluence did not offer particularly advantageous crossing places.[33]

Before the establishment of Münden between the Fulda and the Werra at their confluence, the main routes to the northeast and north crossed the Fulda River further south at either Wolfsanger or Spiekershausen, just north of Kassel. One road led on high

---

[31] Goetting (1980) 152 and Leyser (1979) 68–70.

[32] Goetting (1980) 166–8 and K. Heinemeyer (1974) 139–46.

[33] Uhl (1907) provides an in-depth study of the geographical conditions and the roads in this area. Beuermann (1951) 12, 16 and 58–65, and K. Heinemeyer (1973) 145–52 offer more succinct and accessible treatments. Heinemeyer's notes provide the most recent literature on the subject and Beuermann provides the best map of the medieval roads around Münden.

ground through the middle of the Kaufunger Forest to the Werra ford at Hedemünden. A second road, after similarly crossing the Fulda, ran due north along the western ridge of the Kaufunger Forest and crossed the Fulda again in a northerly direction at Bonafort, thus avoiding the low marshlands in the triangle between the two rivers. This road continued on to Ratten where it joined the road west from Holzhausen and across the southern tip of the Reinhard Forest. From Ratten it followed the Fulda and the Weser along the eastern slopes of the Reinhard Forest to the ford over the Weser at Hilwartshausen. A third road followed the same path as the second to Lutterberg, but then continued due north towards Münden in a steep and difficult descent and finally crossed the Werra at the Kattenbühl. From there it picked up the high roads via Wiershausen, Meensen and Jühnde or via Scheden and Dransfeld to the Leine valley. Thus, the roads coming from Immenhausen and Holzhausen in the west, or from Kassel in the south on the west bank of the Fulda, forded the Weser at Hilwartshausen and then linked up with the major routes to the northeast and east.[34] Also, owing to its location at a frequently used ford, Hilwartshausen must have served, in the tenth and eleventh centuries, as a point of trans-shipment of goods from land transport to the river traffic on the Weser to and from Bremen, and thereby it had some economic importance.[35]

Over and above its advantageous location, Hilwartshausen's importance in the area and to the Ottonian–Salian kings increased dramatically as a result of its property acquisitions. In addition to the *curtis* at Hilwartshausen, Aeddila's foundation endowment included properties (*curtes*) in Jühnde, Dransfeld and the now defunct Fredershausen, east of Dransfeld (see Map 8).[36] All of these places are located north and east of Münden on the high ground between the Werra–Weser valley and the Leine valley.[37] Later, presumably in 965 or 966,[38] a noblewoman, Helmburg,[39] upon

---

[34] Goetting (1980) 151–2.

[35] Ibid. 152. See also Beuermann (1951) 64 and K. Heinemeyer (1973) 150–2.

[36] *DO I* 206. For the location of these places, see Goetting (1980) 154, who cites the older literature. Kroeschell (1957) 6 provides a map giving their approximate locations.

[37] K. Heinemeyer (1973) 159.

[38] Concerning the dating of this grant, which is known only from a later private charter, a *Chirograph*, of 1004, see Starke (1955) 25–6; K. Heinemeyer (1974) 142–3 nn. 183, 188; and especially Goetting (1979) 39 n. 11.

[39] Goetting (1980) 162–6 and 173–80 has convincingly and masterfully demonstrated that this Helmburg was neither a later abbess of Hilwartshausen nor the same Helmburg

the entrance of two of her daughters as canonesses in Hilwarts-hausen, granted the convent three additional possessions in the Leine valley and two west of the Weser, as well as Vaake, just north of Hilwartshausen, where Corvey also owned property, and the now deserted site, Gauze, on the western boundary of the Reinhard Forest near Carlsdorf.[40]

Several years thereafter Hilwartshausen received the first of its royal grants. In 970, Otto I and his son Otto II, obviously at the request of the advocate of Hilwartshausen and their loyal retainer, Count Palatine Bern, granted the religious house, which stood under Abbess 'Helmburg' (= Hemma),[41] six families and six *mansi* with fruit trees and appurtenances in Gimte, just south of Hilwartshausen on the opposite bank of the Weser.[42] In 973, Otto II granted the convent under Abbess 'Hemma' (= Helmburg) several vineyards on the Rhine and the Moselle. One of these vineyards alone was to supply the convent with at least fourteen wagons of wine for its normal use and the grant included three additional vineyards without any stipulation of the amount of wine.[43] As we have seen before, royal monasteries and convents distant from wine-growing regions often received property holdings in these regions to provide them with allotments of wine to supply their needs.[44] In two separate charters of Otto III,[45] Abbess Hemma and the canonesses received royal confirmation of several properties that a noble matron, Ida, had granted to the convent before her death in 986. Ida was the former daughter-in-law of Otto I, mother of Mathilda, abbess of Essen, and was later the wife of Count Palatine Bern until his death in 982.[46] The properties granted comprised three *villae*, all of which were at one time royal property: the now deserted site of Ratten on the north bank of the Fulda river above Bonafort, and Wiershausen and Meensen, both located northeast of Münden on the important

---

who founded the monastery of canonesses at Fischbeck in 955. By doing so he has provided some solutions to a confusing problem of identification and prosopography that has plagued many scholars. Cf. Krumwiede (1955) 52; K. Heinemeyer (1974) 126–35, 146–7; and Leyser (1979) 56.

[40] For identification of the properties, see Goetting (1980) 158 nn. 54–5.

[41] Goetting (1980) 162–6 has demonstrated convincingly that Abbess Helmburg and Abbess Hemma are one and the same person – Hemma being a nickname or shortened version of the name Helmburg.

[42] *DO I* 395 and *DO II* 20; Goetting (1980) 162 n. 86.   [43] *DO II* 60.

[44] E.g. Quedlinburg, Gandersheim, St Maurice (Magdeburg), Werden, Essen and Corvey, to mention only a few.   [45] *DDO III* 59, 60.

[46] In general concerning Ida, see K. Heinemeyer (1974) 148 and Goetting (1980) 168.

road leading to the *Pfalz* of Grone and the Leine valley (see Map 8).[47]

In the early eleventh century, Hilwartshausen lost and regained its status as a royal convent, having become briefly a proprietary convent of Bishop Bernward of Hildesheim. Bishop Bernward was a grandchild of Count Palatine Adelbero/Bern and a nephew of his daughter Hrotgard, abbess of Hilwartshausen. He appears to have acquired Hilwartshausen, possibly in 1001 from Otto III on the basis of his heredity, but most probably as a close friend and advisor of the king and as part of the machinations of the first phase of the struggle between Hildesheim and Mainz over the diocesan rights to the convent of Gandersheim. Hilwartshausen seems to have reverted to its royal status as early as 1007, but certainly by 1017.[48] Thereafter, Henry II, during a stop at the nearby nunnery of Kaufungen in 1017, substantially increased Hilwartshausen's possessions in Gimte by sixty-six *iugera* with appurtenances.[49] Then in January 1032, Hilwartshausen received the only recorded royal visit of its early history when Conrad II stopped there *en route* from Paderborn to Fritzlar. Obviously, the convent supplied the food and lodging for the king and his retinue.[50] In 1046, Henry III granted the convent the royal properties in the *villa* of Scheden which lay across from Hilwartshausen in the Schede valley and which was situated at the junction of the roads leading north to Dransfeld and east to Jühnde.[51] Thus, by the mid-eleventh century the royal convent of Hilwartshausen had acquired a substantial concentration of important properties on both sides of the Weser extending east and north to the Leine valley and controlled the access to important royal *Pfalzen*.

Seen in the context of overall property-holding and royal influence in this area, the foundation and build-up of Hilwartshausen appears to have been a crucial part of an overall royal

---

[47] Kroeschell (1957) 4 (map p. 10) first made the correct identification of the now abandoned village of Ratten. It is not at all clear exactly how Ida came to possess these properties. For a short history of Ratten, see K. Heinemeyer (1974) 122–6, 147–8. Kroeschell (1957) 11, 13 and 22 surmises that Wiershausen and Meensen were former Carolingian royal property. Beuermann (1951) 15–16 and K. Heinemeyer (1973) 160 n. 102 appear to follow him. Cf. Dietrich (1953) 78, who considers these properties as former possessions of the Conradine family.

[48] Goetting (1980) 168–73 gives a concise summary and analysis of this phase of Hilwartshausen's history. [49] *DH II* 363.

[50] *DK II* 177. [51] *DH III* 163.

design for this region. The royal convent held an almost unbroken chain of possessions from the former Ratten on the northwest bank of the Fulda to Vaake on the Weser, thus controlling the property up to the boundary of the huge royal forest behind it to the west, the Reinhardswald. Immediately east of the Weser, the convent's possessions were bordered to the north by another extensive royal forest, the Bramwald, and to the south by the Werra River and the royal Kaufungen Forest, extending from the Werra–Fulda confluence south to Witzenhausen, Kaufungen and Kassel. More importantly, with the possession of Gimte, Wiershausen, Scheden, Meensen, Jühnde and Dransfeld, the royal convent of Hilwartshausen held and controlled the main routes to the Leine valley and to the royal residences in Saxony.[52] Thus, Hilwartshausen's possessions filled the gaps between the three large tracts of royal forest immediately bordering on them and significantly increased royal influence and presence in the area. Although we have only a single recorded instance when the convent accommodated the king and no further evidence about the convent's *servitium regis*, there is little doubt that it was an important base of royal support and served the Ottonian and early Salian kings by securing the roads in the region, if in no other way.[53] For it can hardly be mere coincidence that within the first hundred years of its existence it acquired property on every major road in the area as well as an important ford on the Weser.

KAUFUNGEN

Twenty years after the foundation of Helmarshausen on the Diemel River, Henry II and Queen Kunigunda in 1017 began the foundation of a Benedictine convent in the recently relocated royal residence at Kaufungen (see Map 8). Like the foundation of so many other noble and royal religious houses during the Saxon era, the actual establishment of the convent appears to have occurred over an extended period of time, from the first royal grants in December 1017 until the first mention of an abbess in June 1019.[54] As with Helmarshausen and Hilwartshausen,

---

[52] K. Heinemeyer (1973) 158–67 and Goetting (1980) 150–3, 173.

[53] Although we have no mention of the convent paying or delivering a *servitium regis* to the royal residence at Grone, Hilwartshausen's location and that of the majority of its properties, within 20–30 km of Grone, certainly does not rule out such a possibility.

[54] K. Heinemeyer (1971) 181–2.

Kaufungen by virtue of its location and the location of many of its properties possessed a position favourable to travel and trade; furthermore, as one of a line of royal monasteries extending from Fulda on the Fulda River and Eschwege on the Werra River north to Corvey on the eastern end of the Hellweg, it was of strategic importance politically. With regard to its original endowment, however, Kaufungen resembled the convent in Eschwege more than the two religious establishments further north, because the royal house alone initiated the foundation of the convent and gave it a rich endowment of almost exclusively royal property.

From the beginning, the redevelopment of this area around the old royal *Pfalz* at Kassel and the eventual foundation of the convent at Kaufungen had close connections with Queen Kunigunda, and also with Henry's attempts to create an integrated core of properties in the centre of the kingdom belonging to the realm or to royal churches and extending from the Rhine to the eastern borderlands. An examination of Kaufungen's early history and of the royal grants lavished upon it reveals that Henry II had a twofold purpose in founding a royal convent at Kaufungen. On the one hand, this convent, founded on a part of Queen Kunigunda's dower, would provide her with a residence and material security for her later years should she outlive her husband. On the other hand, the new foundation would afford the realm an economically promising new centre in this border region between Hesse, Saxony and Thuringia. From Kaufungen, the abbess and the nunnery's advocate could administer the extensive royal properties and forests that it came to hold, could oversee the roads and river fords in the area, and could further develop trade and markets in the region. Thus, both personal and political motives worked jointly in the creation of this Benedictine convent.[55]

The creation of a suitable dower for Queen Kunigunda greatly influenced Henry's designs in this area, and the queen herself participated decisively and directly in the foundation of the nunnery at Kaufungen. Narrative and diplomatic sources reveal the background to and the process of Henry's and Kunigunda's actions. At a synod held on 1 November 1007 in Frankfurt, Henry II had realized his long-standing plan to create a bishopric at Bamberg. Reporting this event, Thietmar of Merseburg said that

---

[55] Ibid. 173, 191–2.

Henry, with the consent of his wife, Kunigunda, and of his brother
and co-heir, Bruno, founded the new bishopric on hereditary
properties which he had formerly bequeathed to his wife as a
marriage gift; and that Henry promised both Bruno and
Kunigunda suitable compensation.[56] Henry and his brother Bruno
had inherited the properties which Otto II had granted in 973 to
their father, Duke Henry the Quarrelsome.[57] Henry, the later
king, gave his share of the inheritance to Kunigunda upon their
marriage. Other sources further substantiate Thietmar's report. In
the protocol to the Frankfurt synod, the only one to give his
consent to the proceedings, aside from the appropriate metropolitan, the archbishop of Mainz, was Henry's brother and co-
heir, Bishop Bruno.[58] Likewise, one of the many endowment
charters for Bamberg expressly mentions Queen Kunigunda's
consent to the grant.[59] Later, Sigebert of Gembloux reported that
Kunigunda's brother, Bishop Dietrich of Metz, rebelled against
the king because he feared that his sister's 'dotem et patrimonium'
would be used to found the new bishopric.[60]

Several months after the Frankfurt synod, on 24 May 1008,
Queen Kunigunda began to receive her compensation for the
properties she had forfeited at Bamberg. Henry II granted her the
old royal *Pfalz* at Kassel and presumably the whole fiscal district
centred upon it.[61] Then, some time between 1008 and 1011, in
conjunction with this grant and with the establishment of a
complex of properties and facilities, suitable for Kunigunda's
dower and comparable to those at Bamberg, Henry II transferred
the centre of the fiscal district from Kassel to Kaufungen and built
a new *Pfalz* there. This new residence must have already existed by
August 1011 when Henry and his retinue spent ten days there.
Thietmar referred to the transfer of the *Pfalz* when he reported the
events of Henry's next stay there, for nine days in 1015.[62] Most
probably, an estate or vill existed at Kaufungen already in the

---

[56] Thietmar 6 cc. 30 and 31. [57] *DO II* 44.
[58] See K. Heinemeyer (1971) 169 n. 167. [59] *DH II* 168.
[60] Sigebert, *Chronica* p. 354, incorrectly placed under 1004.
[61] *DH II* 182. Concerning the connection between Queen Kunigunda, the founding of
Bamberg, her acquisition of the fiscal district centred upon Kassel, and its redevelopment as her dower, see K. Heinemeyer (1971) 169–73 and W. Eckhardt (1961)
29–32. Similarly, in 994 Otto III appears to have granted his sister Sophie the entire
fiscal district with his grant of Eschwege. See Chapter 4 above.
[62] *DDH II* 236, 237. Thietmar 7 c. 13 p. 412: 'Haec inperator agnoscens a nobis discessit
et proximos rogationum dies in Capungen fuit, quo ipse curtem suam de civitate
Cassalun dicta transtulit.'

ninth century, which was subordinate to the *Pfalz* at Kassel and from which the large royal forest east of the Fulda was administered. Henry appears to have expanded and developed this vill in line with his new plans and made it the centre of the entire fiscal district with Kassel subordinate to it. Since Henry could just as easily have modernized and even expanded the *Pfalz* at Kassel, it appears that other factors and intentions beyond just the personal influenced his actions. Unlike the *civitas* of Kassel, the site at Kaufungen appears to have been a large unfortified royal manor, but one that was easily defensible owing to its location.[63] Nevertheless, it had facilities extensive enough to support a sizeable royal entourage. A contemporary *notitia* recording a property exchange documented in a charter issued at Kaufungen in 1015 (*DH II* 335) contains a witness list naming over thirty prelates, nobles and knights; and court assemblies carried out other royal ecclesiastical business there as well. Moreover, as later sources indicate, one can assume the early presence of a royal chapel or a small church. In 1011, it is highly probable that the court celebrated the Assumption of the Virgin (15 August) and possibly also the Feast of St Lawrence (10 August) at Kaufungen, and later, in 1015 Henry and his court celebrated the Rogation Days and most probably Ascension Day there.

In April 1017, the king and queen and their retinue made a short stop at the *curtis* of Kaufungen *en route* from Goslar to Mainz and Ingelheim, where they celebrated Palm Sunday and Easter respectively.[64] After a visit to the *Pfalz* in Frankfurt, the royal couple departed in different directions some time after 9 May. Henry travelled to Aachen for an assembly of the realm and then on to Werden where he celebrated Pentecost. Kunigunda headed northeast, presumably toward Saxony.[65] While still *en route*, Kunigunda became ill on her arrival at Kaufungen and made a vow to God that she would found a monastery.[66] She recovered

---

[63] K. Heinemeyer (1971) 192; cf. Streich (1984) 324–5. In general, in the following I summarize the research of K. Heinemeyer (1971) 170–6, 196–7, who provides a thorough analysis of the transfer from Kassel to Kaufungen, making many pertinent observations and commenting on the probable facilities there.

[64] *DH II* 363; BG 1898, 1898a–b.   [65] BG 1903, 1903a–b; Thietmar 7 c. 54.

[66] Thietmar 7 c. 54 p. 466: 'Regina autem a Froncanavordi a cesare discedens, cum ad locum, qui Capungun dicitur, veniret, infirmatur et ibi tunc Deo promisit, se laudem eius unum facturam monasterium.' The Corvey revision of Thietmar from the mid-twelfth century by adding *ibidem* in the last clause made the intent agree with the historical reality. Thietmar 7 c. 54 p. 467: 'Regina ... infirmatur promisitque, se Deo ad laudem eius ibidem facturam unum monasterium.'

from her illness at Kaufungen and later joined the king at Paderborn.[67] There Henry and Kunigunda endowed two prebends for themselves in the cathedral chapter of canons. Thereby, they were granted full participation in the chapter and accepted into the community of prayer.[68] On 6 December 1017, King Henry II issued the first of ten charters for the nunnery and it expressly mentioned that the empress founded the convent and established the first nuns there.[69] Thus, some time between mid–May and December – most probably during her recovery there and in conjunction with her vow – Kunigunda founded a Benedictine nunnery at Kaufungen.

A brief survey of Henry II's grants for Kaufungen affords us some insight into the foundation of the nunnery and into Henry's designs for the new convent. In his first two charters for the new foundation, Henry granted Kaufungen the royal *curtis* of Hedemünden,[70] which was an important ford on the Werra River on a frequently used route to the Leine valley,[71] and Heroldis-hausen, a royal manor in Thuringia.[72] In June of 1018, the king gave the convent Leidenhofen, a property near Marburg, located on or near the route called the 'long Hessian' road which the Ottonian and Salian kings frequently travelled.[73] Shortly after this grant, while Henry led an army to Burgundy, Kunigunda made her second visit without her husband to Kaufungen and continued the foundation of the monastery.[74]

The year 1019 proved decisive for the new nunnery. Between Henry's visit to the convent on 9 January,[75] and the issuance of a

---

[67] Henry received the news of Kunigunda's recovery while at Werden for Pentecost. See Thietmar 7 c. 56.

[68] Thietmar 7 c. 57; *DH II* 368. K. Heinemeyer (1971) 183 with n. 279 points out that this endowment may also be connected with Kunigunda's recovery and her vow at Kaufungen. On the entire topic of kings (and queens) participating in cathedral chapters, see Fleckenstein (1964), Groten (1983) and Fuhrmann (1984), who all cite the older literature.

[69] *DH II* 375: 'quod dilecta contectalis nostra Cvnigvnda videlicet imperatrix augusta monasterium ... in loco qui dicitur Cofunga construxit, in quo virgines sub regula sancti Bendicti ordinavit'. [70] *DH II* 375.

[71] Uhl (1907) 9, 25; Beuermann (1951) 60–1. [72] *DH II* 376.

[73] *DH II* 394.

[74] Thietmar 8 c. 18 pp. 515–16: 'Imperatrix autem ad dilectam sibi Capungam veniens, monachicam [sic!] ibi vitam ordinavit.' As K. Heinemeyer (1971) 178 correctly pointed out, Thietmar's report does not necessarily contradict the foundation of the convent in the previous year, but should be construed as part of the establishment of the nunnery. Moreover, Thietmar's words demonstrate the closeness of the foundation to Kunigunda as does the fact that she appeared at Kaufungen for a second time without Henry. [75] *DH II* 398.

charter for Kaufungen on the last day of the same year,[76] the new nunnery received six of its ten grants from Henry II. Thus, the foundation process, materially and religiously, reached its official completion, and Henry had created the basis for Kunigunda's later security as well as for the further development of the area under royal auspices.

Henry celebrated Christmas of 1018 at Paderborn and journeyed to Kaufungen in early January, possibly for Epiphany, before spending the following Lenten season in Goslar. His visit appears to have initiated the final phase of Kaufungen's foundation, especially in light of Kaufungen's acquisitions later that spring.[77] For in May and June of 1019, Henry II granted the new nunnery the largest and most significant portion of its foundation endowment. The first of these charters comprised the royal *villae* of Upper and Lower Kaufungen as well as Vollmarshausen and Uschlag nearby.[78] On the same day the convent acquired all of the royal properties in Escheberg and Meiser, which were located west of the Fulda River between Kassel and Warburg in the Hessengau.[79] A few weeks later, on 20 May, Henry gave the convent five properties (*loca*) in the Moselle region with vineyards, obviously intended to supply the nunnery with wine.[80] Soon thereafter, probably in the last half of June, Henry, at Kunigunda's request, bequeathed one of her hereditary properties, Herleshausen on the Werra, to the new foundation.[81] This charter and the one following it contain the first references to an abbess of the nunnery and therefore may signify the completion of the religious ordering of the convent. While in Paderborn, King Henry bestowed upon Kaufungen some of its most valuable properties and rights. He granted to the new foundation the church in Wolfsanger with its entire endowment and the right to hold a weekly market there on Saturdays and a three-day market on the feast of its patron saint, John the Baptist (24 June). In the same charter, the king entitled the nunnery to hold another three-day annual market in Kaufungen itself on the feast of the Exaltation of the Holy Cross (14 September). This included rights to the possession of the income

---

[76] *DH II* 420.

[77] K. Heinemeyer (1971) 178. It is also conceivable that Henry and his retinue may have celebrated Epiphany at Kaufungen.

[78] *DH II* 406a (4 May 1019). As K. Heinemeyer (1971) 179–80 with n. 247 has demonstrated, the grant of Upper Kaufungen must have included the royal demesne (*Königshof*) as well as the older settlement of the same name next to it. Cf. W. Eckhardt (1961) 22.   [79] *DH II* 407.   [80] *DH II* 409.   [81] *DH II* 411.

resulting from the jurisdiction over those markets (*districtum*) and from the tolls exacted at them.[82] With these two charters Henry and Kunigunda appear to have completed the material endowment and the religious ordering of the nunnery of Kaufungen. Henry's remaining charter of 1019 and one from 1023 merely served to increase Kaufungen's property holdings in outlying areas.[83]

Over and above merely determining what properties the nunnery actually received, a careful analysis of the royal charters for Kaufungen provides further information about the interplay of personal, political and economic motives in the foundation of the convent. The wording of the charters confirms the personal nature of the foundation and Kunigunda's active participation in creating it; but at the same time these diplomas reveal the influence and interests of the realm on various levels. All of the charters for Kaufungen mention Queen Kunigunda in some aspect. The first five diplomas all name her as foundress of the convent[84] and three later charters refer to 'her Kaufungen'.[85] Moreover, from its beginning Kaufungen had very close ties to Kunigunda's family. In 1019, Henry named Kunigunda's niece, Uta, as the first abbess of the nunnery[86] and it appears very probable that Kunigunda's brother, Frederick, was simultaneously the ruling count in the immediate area and the monastery's first advocate.[87] Even after the

---

[82] *DH II* 412. It appears that the *dos* and appurtenances of the church at Wolfsanger included sizeable properties and tithing rights in nearby Sandershausen and Ihringshausen as well. In addition, Kaufungen seems to have acquired significant properties and tithes in Niederzwehren, south of Kassel, as a part of its foundation endowment in 1019. See K. Heinemeyer (1971) 65–9, 72–5 and 112–13.

[83] *DDH II* 420, 487; K. Heinemeyer (1971) 180–1. A seventh charter, possibly from the year 1019, appears to have been totally erased and written over in the twelfth century with a forged charter. Its original contents remain a mystery. See the introduction to *DH II* 521.

[84] *DDH II* 375, 376, 394, 406a, 407. *DH II* 375 served as the model for the four succeeding charters.   [85] *DDH II* 411, 412 and 420: 'monasterio suo Chuofunga'.

[86] *DH II* 411; K. Heinemeyer (1971) 184.

[87] Frederick appears as count in Lower Hesse (in Frankish Hessengau and in Phirnihgau) as early as 1008 and held that position until his death in 1019 (*Ann. Qued. s.a.* 1019). Both Kassel and Kaufungen were in his county: *DDH II* 178, 182, 406a, 412. Although we have no direct witness to him as advocate of Kaufungen, later evidence demonstrates the plausibility of this assertion. Frederick did not succeed in making his countship hereditary and the first Salian king, Conrad II, granted the countship to Count Werner I. In 1040 (*DH III* 61), Werner also appears as advocate of Kaufungen. One can reasonably assume therefore that Werner not only succeeded Frederick as count, but also as advocate of Kaufungen. Concerning Frederick, his county in Hesse, and the later counts Werner, see: Renn (1941) 106–8; Demandt (1972) 161–2, 166–7; and Bannasch (1972) 181–2, 330–1.

advocacy had passed to Count Werner under the Salian kings, Kunigunda's other brother, Bishop Dietrich of Metz, still maintained a special relationship with the convent.[88] Dietrich's exact legal position cannot be determined from the evidence. The charter states that Henry III granted him the position of *senior* or lord to the entire *familia* of the nunnery of Kaufungen. Because of the inexact terminology of the charter, however, it remains unclear whether Henry III actually granted the nunnery to Bishop Dietrich or whether he, owing to his familial connection as Kunigunda's heir, merely held an honorary position in regard to the nunnery. In any case, even if Dietrich had actually been granted the nunnery, he obviously had the usufruct over it only during his lifetime because the monastery was once again in royal possession in 1086 when Henry IV granted it to the bishop of Speyer. Moreover, even during Dietrich's lifetime, Henry III still used the nunnery, like other royal property, for stopovers during his itinerary.

In spite of Kaufungen's personal connection to Queen Kunigunda, the nunnery was founded on fiscal property and most of the properties which made up its endowment likewise proceeded from the realm. Although some of Kaufungen's property, such as Herleshausen on the Werra (*DH II* 411), proceeded from hereditary properties of Kunigunda, Kaufungen itself, the properties granted with it, and possibly also Wolfsanger, belonged to the greater fiscal district of Kassel which Henry II granted to Kunigunda in 1008 as her dower. As dower, Kunigunda had usufruct and right of disposition over the properties during her lifetime. Unlike a morning gift (*Morgengabe*), such as Kunigunda's former properties at Bamberg, however, a queen's dower legally remained royal property and reverted to the realm upon her death. Consequently, properties comprising the dower needed a separate royal charter to be permanently granted to the nunnery.[89] Kaufungen therefore was a royal nunnery from the

---

[88] *DH III* 61. For the various interpretations of this charter and Bishop Dietrich's legal position, see: Stengel (1935b) 177; W. Eckhardt (1961) 32–7; and K. Heinemeyer (1971) 184–6.

[89] See Schröder (1871) 2.2.214–34 and W. Eckhardt (1961) 31–7. Using Kassel as an example and on the basis of a charter of exchange between Archbishop Bardo of Mainz, Bishop Dietrich of Metz and Abbess Hildegard of Kaufungen (*DH III* 61), W. Eckhardt demonstrated that this portion of Kunigunda's dower reverted to the realm, was later granted to her brother, Dietrich of Metz, and was in turn granted by him to the nunnery of Kaufungen. See n. 106 below regarding the 'morning gift'.

beginning and the language of the charters reveals this fact.[90] The clause, 'whom we [that is, Henry II] appointed to that place' modifies the first reference to an abbess of the nunnery named Uta.[91] A subsequent diploma makes an oblique reference to the king's participation in the foundation,[92] and Henry's last grant to the nunnery blatantly affirms Kaufungen's legal status when he designates it as 'monasterio nostro Cofunga nominato'.[93] Thus, although Henry had a definite personal motive in founding the nunnery, the charters demonstrate that the royal prerogative progressively received more and more emphasis.

In addition, the economic and political motives of the king become clear when one carefully considers not only the properties and rights which the king granted to the nunnery, but also their location. The largest part of Kaufungen's endowment consisted of an extensive, coherent complex of properties east of the Fulda River and south of the Fulda–Werra confluence – in essence, the eastern half of the old fiscal district formerly centred on the old royal *Pfalz* at Kassel.[94] The nunnery also came to possess certain important properties and rights in the western half of the fiscal district.[95] The possession of these properties alone gave the convent an extremely favourable position in regard to travel and trade, for no less than ten long-distance roads from all directions, including several royal routes, came together in this region.[96] With the exception of its possessions on the Moselle, the remaining properties that Henry II granted to Kaufungen were relatively far apart, but they were all connected to the nunnery by their location on or near roads leading out from the general vicinity of Kaufungen. These roads included important fords over the Fulda River at Niederzwehren and at Wolfsanger, and over the Werra River at Hedemünden.[97]

---

[90] Eisenträger and Krug (1935) 176 n. 26 and K. Heinemeyer (1971) 182.

[91] *DDH II* 411, 412.

[92] *DH II* 420. It is difficult to understand this reference completely since the clause beginning with *quod nos* has no predicate and the writer or the scribe appears to have lost his train of thought. [93] *DH II* 487.

[94] *DH II* 406a; K. Heinemeyer (1971) 122–4, 186–7. It remains unclear how much of the huge royal forest complex the nunnery possessed or had the right to use. By and large the forest remained in royal possession, but the nunnery without doubt owned some of it, probably in the southwestern section later called the Stiftswald.

[95] *DDH II* 407, 412; K. Heinemeyer (1971) 76, 187–8.

[96] For a summary of the roads in this area see especially K. Heinemeyer (1971) 18–21 and Beuermann (1951) 58–64 (with map) for the northeastern part of this region.

[97] *DH II* 375; K. Heinemeyer (1971) 189–90.

The picture of economic intent on the part of the king becomes even clearer when one considers the profitable rights of holding markets, and of collecting tolls and juridical fees at Wolfsanger and Kaufungen, that Henry II granted to the nunnery.[98] Seen in conjunction with the advantageous location of the nunnery and its properties for trade and travel, Henry's further design for the new religious community becomes evident: to create a new centre for travel and economic activity in this strategic area of extensive royal property and interests.[99] Later evidence, indeed, indicates that Kaufungen, at least in the eleventh century, began to realize the economic potential that Henry II had envisioned for it. In 1040, Henry III granted the nunnery the right to hold two further markets at Kaufungen, a second three-day annual market on the feast of St Margaret (13 July) and a weekly market on Wednesdays. The yearly market on the feast day of St Margaret held additional significance for the nunnery in that it fell on the anniversary of Henry II's death in 1024 and of the consecration of the monastic church at Kaufungen in 1025. In addition, he conceded the tolls and other proceeds from the markets to the nunnery.[100] This charter specifically mentioned the traders visiting the markets at Kaufungen (and presumably also its markets at Wolfsanger) and granted them the right of unimpeded access to these markets. Thus, it confirmed Kaufungen as a place active in long-distance trade.[101] Later in 1081, when Kaufungen served as the site for a meeting between princes loyal to Henry IV and those opposing him, Bruno, the historian of the Saxon rebellion, even designated Kaufungen as a city.[102] This designation could refer both to a fortified site and to a regional centre of travel and trade.

---

[98] *DH II* 412.

[99] In general, concerning the economic development of Kaufungen and Henry II's designs for it, see K. Heinemeyer (1971) 189–91. Especially in regard to economic development, K. Heinemeyer (pp. 191–3) demonstrates the close parallel between the transfer of the royal *Pfalz* from Kassel to Kaufungen and the foundation of the nunnery there, and the shifting of the royal *Pfalz* in Saxony from Werla to the newly established Goslar and the eventual establishment of a royal canonry there. [100] *DH III* 85.

[101] *DH III* 85: 'omnium hominum contradictione remota, negotiatoribus ceterisque hominibus ad ipsum mercatum venientibus eundi et redeundi liberam facultatem tribuimus'. Concerning the granting of the 'royal peace' for traders visiting certain markets, see Metz (1972b) 33–9, 45–6. In this instance instead of 'pax' or 'licentia' the charter reads 'liberam facultatem', but obviously with the same intent.

[102] Bruno, *Sax. Bellum* c. 126 p. 119: 'in silva, quae inde Capuana vocatur, quia ad urbem, quae Capua nominatur...' As K. Heinemeyer (1971) 201–3, points out, in spite of Bruno's actual words, there can be little doubt that the meeting took place in the nunnery, which, as a royal monastery, had the ability to accommodate the participants.

The diverse evidence about the foundation of the nunnery of Kaufungen indicates that King Henry II had specific personal, political and economic reasons for establishing and royally supporting this foundation. The history of the foundation in the eleventh century confirms that essentially he had achieved his objectives. His original and primary intention of establishing material support and a religious community for Queen Kunigunda in her later years came to fruition in 1025. After directing the government since Henry's death (13 July 1024), formally transferring the royal *regalia* to Conrad upon his election, and arranging other secular business,[103] Kunigunda withdrew to Kaufungen, where on 13 July 1025 she participated in the dedication of the new church and entered the community of nuns there.[104] She lived in Kaufungen as a nun until her death in 1033.[105] Moreover, by means of this foundation for Kunigunda, Henry appears to have achieved the auxiliary personal and political goal of attaining peace and a new alliance with Kunigunda's brothers, members of the newly powerful comital house of Luxembourg. The foundation of Bamberg in 1007 on properties formerly belonging to Kunigunda's marriage gift had met with strong resistance from Kunigunda's brothers, especially Bishop Dietrich of Metz, and had caused a long-standing disaffection between the queen's family and King Henry. This resulted both from a desire to protect their sister against any questionable alienation of her properties and from the realization that they no longer could make a claim to her inheritance. The provision of a suitable dower for Kunigunda and the close personal connections between the convent and the queen's family appear to have mollified the former causes of enmity.[106]

From the standpoint of the realm, the royal nunnery provided the king with a new basis of political and economic support in the important border region between Hesse, Thuringia and Saxony, through which the king and his entourage travelled frequently. Already in Saxony and Westphalia we have seen how the later Ottonian and early Salian kings began to institute markets along

---

[103] Wipo, *Gesta Chuonradi* c. 1 p. 9, c. 2 p. 19; *DDKunig* 2, 3; BA 25a, 27.
[104] *Vita s. Cunegundis* c. 5 pp. 822–3. [105] Ibid. c. 9 p. 824.
[106] K. Heinemeyer (1971) 183–6. The properties of a marriage or morning gift (*Morgengabe*) could be inherited by the bride's surviving heirs, but a dower (*Wittum*), especially one composed of royal property, reverted to the husband or his heirs, or to the realm, upon the death of the appointed recipient. See above at n. 89 and Schröder (1871) 2.2.242–50.

their customary routes and to favour places with market activity as their stopping places even if only in transit. Kaufungen also fits into this pattern. After the finalization of its foundation in 1019, Henry II stopped at Kaufungen when travelling from Fulda to Allstedt in 1020, and he appears intentionally to have visited the nunnery once again in December 1022.[107] Of the first three Salian kings we have documented visits only by King Henry III.[108] It appears likely that Henry III stopped at Kaufungen in 1040 *en route* from Fritzlar to Goslar,[109] and his charters confirm his presence at the nunnery again in 1042,[110] 1044[111] and 1051.[112] In fact, it is reasonable to consider that these Salian monarchs may have stopped at the nunnery more often than the sources indicate. As a former royal *curtis*, Kaufungen had the physical ability to accommodate the king and his retinue even during the winter months.[113] Moreover, its advantageous location near several important routes and royal grants of sovereign rights had created favourable economic conditions, enhancing its own economy and its ability to accommodate the court. Finally, the existence of two churches at Kaufungen equipped with galleries made the nunnery a suitable venue to celebrate the sacrality of kingship and it provided the king and the royal family with the opportunity to participate in the liturgical celebrations of the community.[114] It is probably no accident therefore that in 1086 Henry IV, when attempting to regain royal bases of support for the Salians in a then largely hostile Saxony, granted the royal nunnery of Kaufungen to one of his staunchest supporters in the realm, the bishop of

---

[107] *DH II* 430. K. Heinemeyer (1971) 221–2 and (1983a) 92 provides the supporting evidence for Henry's probable visit at Kaufungen in December 1022.

[108] Bresslau (1879–84) 2.79 conjectures that Conrad visited Kaufungen in 1033 shortly after Kunigunda's death, but there is no hard evidence upon which to base the conjecture although, of course, it is possible. Cf. Rieckenberg (1941/1965) 104.

[109] E. Müller (1901) 28 and *DH III* 61 with its introduction. In light of the itinerary and of the contents of this charter – the settlement in Fritzlar of a dispute between Kaufungen and the archdiocese of Mainz – it seems logical and likely that Henry III would have stopped at Kaufungen in transit from Fritzlar to Goslar, possibly while accompanying the abbess and her entourage back to the nunnery.

[110] *DDH III* 94, 95.   [111] *DH III* 119.

[112] *DDH III* 271, 272, 273. This visit on 17 and 18 July 1051 as well as Henry's assumed stop at the nunnery between 4 and 20 July 1040 could both have coincided with the anniversary of Henry II's death (13 July 1024) and of the consecration of the monastic church (13 July 1025).

[113] Henry II was at Kaufungen in January 1019 and very probably in December 1022, and Henry III visited Kaufungen in January 1044.

[114] K. Heinemeyer (1971) 194–7 and Streich (1984) 325–7.

Speyer.[115] Kaufungen remained a possession of the bishopric of Speyer until the early thirteenth century when it regained its royal status under Frederick II.[116]

[115] *DH IV* 384. One can see a definite parallel to this situation in regard to another former royal convent in this area, Eschwege. Although Henry granted it to the bishopric of Speyer in 1075 (*DH IV* 277), an entry in the necrology of Speyer from the thirteenth century implies that Henry IV reconfirmed this grant upon the death of his wife Bertha in 1087. At that time the power balance in this area had once again shifted in favour of the king, and the bishop of Speyer could realistically take possession of his possessions there. See Metz (1972a).

[116] K. Heinemeyer (1971) 203–4 esp. nn. 430, 431.

Chapter 7

MONASTERIES IN HESSE AND THURINGIA

GEOPOLITICAL STRUCTURE OF HESSE AND THURINGIA

With the accession of the Ottonian kings from Saxony to the German throne, the strategic importance of Thuringia and Hesse increased dramatically. Located in the centre and on the east-central border of the German realm, Hesse and Thuringia lay between the familial power base of the Ottonian kings in the Harz region and the valuable crown properties in the Rhine–Main basin (see Maps 1 and 4). Thus, the Ottonian kings and the early Salians, who assumed control of the crown properties in Saxony in succession to the Ottonians, continually had to cross these regions when travelling between their centres of kingship in Saxony and those in the middle Rhineland. Moreover, because these two areas were likewise situated between Saxony and the southernmost duchies of the realm, their strategic importance actually increased in the early eleventh century when Henry II and the first two Salian kings began to integrate Bavaria and Swabia more fully into the royal itinerary. Therefore, the structure of the realm and political necessity demanded that the early German kings have secure passage through the centre of their realm. This meant that they had to control Hesse and Thuringia politically or at least decentralize the local power structure there sufficiently, so that no indigenous power could grow strong enough to block royal access to the other regions of the realm. In addition, since these two areas did not abound in royal property, the Ottonian and Salian monarchs had to assure the accommodation and upkeep of the royal retinue during its passage. Both in their quest to gain political control of these areas and to assure the subsistence of the royal court there, the early German kings relied heavily on the royal churches situated and landed in these regions, especially on two royal monasteries, Hersfeld and Fulda.

The political situation in Thuringia in the tenth and early

eleventh centuries was generally favourable to the Ottonian and
early Salian kings.[1] Already before their ascent to the kingship the
Liudolfing family had acquired a large number of former
Carolingian royal possessions in northern Thuringia. When Duke
Otto the Illustrious had served as lay abbot at Hersfeld, the family
came to hold or control many properties of the monastery in
northern Thuringia. Upon becoming kings of the German realm
in 919, the Liudolfing family took possession of the former
Carolingian royal properties remaining in this area. Thus, from
their beginning as German kings, the Liudolfing or Ottonian
family controlled much of northern Thuringia. Moreover, at the
time of the Liudolfing ascent to the throne, no one duke ruled over
all of Thuringia. The counts in central Thuringia, for instance, did
not recognize the Saxon duke as their own, but claimed allegiance
only to the king. Thus, no unified power structure existed in
Thuringia. This decentralization proved advantageous for the
Ottonians. The political leadership of Thuringia fell to five
predominant comital families: the counts of Merseburg, the
Ekkehardine counts in eastern Thuringia, the counts of Bilstein in
western Thuringia, the counts of Weimar in east-central Thuringia
and the Ludowing counts in west-central Thuringia.[2] Apart from
a few lapses of allegiance, these comital houses remained loyal to
the Ottonian and early Salian kings.[3] Indeed, they tended to vie
with and counterbalance each other in such a way that no unified
power emerged in Thuringia with sufficient resources or the desire
to challenge the royal suzerainty effectively until the mid-twelfth
century.

A similar situation developed in Hesse, the former duchy of
Franconia, but there the German kings, especially Otto I and
Henry II, had to intervene actively to establish a political structure
favourable to the kingship. Since the political situation in Hesse
was more complex and the royal intervention more intense, it
demands a more detailed description.[4] During the rulership of the

---

[1] In general concerning the political structure of Thuringia and the individual comital
families of Thuringia during this period, see Patze (1974) 1–10, 12–13, 211–12.

[2] For a detailed prosopographical study of the Thuringian comital families, especially
those in western Thuringia, see K.-A. Eckhardt (1964) 26–165 *passim*.

[3] See Schölkopf (1957) 57.

[4] For the following overview of the political development in Hesse as it affected the use
of Hesse as a transit zone, I generally follow Demandt (1972) 144–68. On the nobility,
counts and ecclesiastical advocates in Hesse from the late tenth into the twelfth century,
see now Metz (1991) esp. 337–49.

later Carolingians, the Conradine family, led by Conrad the Elder, had solidified their position in Hesse and created a territorial and hereditary basis of power. They united all of the Hessian countships, some of which extended beyond Franconia into southwestern Thuringia and southeastern Saxony, into Conradine hands and provided Hesse with a unified political structure. It was from this that the duchy of Franconia developed after the demise of the last Carolingian kings in the east Frankish realm. These lordships in the centre of the realm, familial and political relations with the later Carolingians, and the support of Archbishop Hatto of Mainz all helped Conrad (the Younger) of Franconia secure the election as king in 911. When Conrad designated Duke Henry of Saxony to succeed him in 919, Conrad's brother Eberhard remained the head of the Conradine family and their lands in Hesse, became the duke of Franconia, and loyally supported the new monarch from Saxony.

As we have seen earlier, however, Eberhard's loyalty did not continue under Henry's successor, Otto I. Eberhard became involved in the rebellion of Otto's brother and step-brother, Henry and Thankmar, took up arms against the king and against those Conradine family members who supported the king, and fell in battle at Andernach in 939. After Eberhard's death, Otto retained the former duchy of Franconia as a royal possession, but he did not eliminate the power and influence of the Conradine house from Hesse. Initially, he allowed the loyal Conradine nobles to retain both their property and control of their counties but, at the same time, he granted a large amount of property and political control in Hesse to his loyal Conradine supporter, Duke Hermann of Swabia, with whom he forged an alliance by means of a marriage between his eldest son and heir-apparent, Liudolf, and Hermann's daughter, Ida, whom Hermann had endowed with Conradine property in Hesse. With this strategy, Otto protected the interests and even rewarded the loyal members of the Conradine family, while at the same time arranging for his son to inherit the duchy of Swabia and large amounts of Conradine property (a kind of 'super-county') in Hesse upon Hermann's death.[5] Thus, Otto devised a plan whereby he could eventually incorporate this important transit zone between Saxony and the middle Rhine–Main region into the royal sphere of power. He

---

[5] See Chapter 1 above, pp. 20–1.

hoped thereby to be able gradually to re-establish the sovereign and proprietary rights within the region formerly held by Carolingian kings.[6]

The revolt of Liudolf, Conrad the Red, and their supporters in 953-4 appears to have caused an alteration in Otto's plans for Franconia. Aside from the primary causes for this rebellion,[7] a possible contributing factor may have been a perception on the part of Liudolf that his father's ambitious plans and actions to reinstate royal rights in Hesse, which began in northeastern Hesse, threatened his own position there.[8] After the failure of Liudolf's rebellion, Otto I appears to have rejected the concept of a few politically unified Hessian counties held by specific comital families, which had been maintained to a certain degree under the Conradines, Hermann, and Liudolf. He decentralized the political structure in Hesse and based it on many individual countships, whose counts were appointed by the king. Moreover, the new countships were not held exclusively by indigenous families, but were also granted to loyal vassals from outside Hesse. Thus, from the north and east, Saxon noble families carried Saxon influence into the border regions of Hesse and acquired countships there, gradually winning and securing the region for the king. New comital families such as the counts of Reinhausen, the Haholdian counts, the counts of Bilstein, and those of Northeim appeared in the border areas of Hesse and gradually established themselves in the central territories of the region. Later, under Henry II and the early Salian kings, other noble families from outside Hesse, the Gleiberg clan (formed from a marriage of noble families in Luxembourg and the Wetterau) and the powerful Werner family (brought from Swabia into Hesse by the Salian kings), acquired counties in Hesse. In central and southern Hesse the same policy prevailed, namely to retard the movement towards the inheritability of countships, to appoint loyal vassals as counts, and to prevent the consolidation of power by any indigenous comital families.[9]

In addition, the Ottonian kings made use of the bishoprics, in

---

[6] McKitterick (1983) 182-3 discusses Charles the Bald's similar policy of amalgamating many counties into the hands of a trusted vassal in order to safeguard royal authority.

[7] On the revolt of 953-4, see Chapter 1 above, pp. 23-5.

[8] Demandt (1972) 148-9 offers this interpretation. See also Keller (1982) 105-8 esp. n. 144.

[9] Demandt (1972) 144-68 provides a general overview of all of the various comital families in Hesse during this period. Now see also Metz (1991) esp. 337-49.

and bordering on Hesse, and the royal monasteries in Hesse. Through extensive grants of royal property and royal bans over hunting and large areas of forest region, the bishops and abbots of these institutions became in effect administrators of the realm and guardians of royal interests. This policy culminated under Henry II and the first two Salian rulers. They continued the earlier Ottonian policy of making grants of property and royal bans to the royal churches, but extended these policies by granting additional sovereign rights – such as the right to hold markets and mint coins, and even the right to govern entire counties – to favoured bishoprics and royal monasteries. At least eight Hessian counties were granted to bishoprics or royal monasteries, thereby bringing these counties both more closely under royal influence and blocking the growth of powerful comital families. The bishopric of Paderborn and the royal monastery of Fulda alone accounted for the possession of six counties.[10] Thus, the Ottonian and early Salian kings managed to exert considerable influence and control over the political structure of Hesse, in both the secular and the ecclesiastical spheres, and encouraged and furthered economic development in Hesse. They were able thereby to secure this crucial transit zone for the realm and facilitate their passages through it.

Unlike the great east–west transit zone across Saxony and Westphalia, where the Ottonian and Salian kings travelled continually and almost exclusively on one major route, the Hellweg, the Thuringian–Hessian transit zone through the centre of the realm offered the German kings a large number of different routes depending upon their preferences and destination. Various roads criss-crossed Thuringia and Hesse in all directions, offering the royal *iter* numerous possibilities for alternative routes. Consequently, it is not possible to establish the same overwhelming pattern of usage for any single road in the central transit zone as we did for the Hellweg in the east–west corridor further north.

---

[10] Paderborn received the following counties: in 1011, the Westphalian and Waldeck county of the Haholdian counts (*DH II* 225); in 1021, the Diemel county of Count Dodiko of Warburg (*DH II* 439 and *DK II* 198); and in 1032, the county of Hermann of Reinhausen in the Reinhard Forest (*DK II* 178). Fulda acquired the following counties: in 1024, the county of Stockstadt near Aschaffenburg (*DH II* 509); in 1025, the county of Netra, south of Eschwege (*DK II* 23); and in 1043, the county of Maelstat in the Wetterau (*DH III* 101). On the granting of counties to ecclesiastical institutions, see Hoffmann (1990) esp. 393–6 where he discusses Fulda's counties. Also on Henry III's grant of the county of Maelstat to Fulda, see Franke (1987) 145.

Although I shall discuss specific roads in conjunction with the individual royal monasteries and their properties in these regions, it is useful here to give the general course of the major roads used by the Ottonian and Salian kings when crossing the central transit zone from Saxony to the middle Rhine–Main region and to Bavaria. Basically three major royal routes (and their various offshoots) crossed Hesse from the Mainz or Frankfurt area in a northeasterly direction (see Maps 6 and 9). The 'long Hessian' road ran from Frankfurt via the Amöneburg basin to Treysa, where it split into two branches. One continued to Fritzlar and Kassel (Kaufungen) and then northeast to the *Pfalz* of Grone near Göttingen or east via Heiligenstadt to Nordhausen; the other led east via Homberg to the ford over the Fulda at Melsungen/Malsfeld and on to Wichmannshausen or Reichensachsen (east of Waldkappel), whence it could divert east to Thuringia via Creuzburg and Eisenach, north and northeast to Saxony via Eschwege and Grone or Wanfried and Mühlhausen, or join with a route south to Bavaria. The 'short Hessian' road also originated near Frankfurt and traversed Hesse via Berstadt, Hungen and Alsfeld to Hersfeld, where it could connect with the northern road to Saxony via the ford over the Fulda at Breitenbach/Bebra or with the roads east to central Thuringia over the Werra fords either at Gerstungen or Heimboldshausen to Eisenach. A third road, having various strands, led from Frankfurt to Fulda and from there east to Thuringia via Hünfeld and the Werra fords east of Vacha, at Salzungen or at Breitungen. Between Hesse and Thuringia there were two major north–south roads from Bavaria and eastern Franconia to Saxony (see Maps 9 and 10). The westernmost road left Würzburg and ran via Hammelburg and Fulda to Hersfeld. From there it continued north to Saxony via the Werra fords at Wanfried, Eschwege or Wahlhausen near Sooden-Allendorf. The easternmost road led from Bavaria via Nuremberg and Bamberg in eastern Franconia and then followed the valley of the Werra River via Meiningen and Barchfeld to the ford at Berka. It continued north via Wichmannshausen and Reichensachsen to the Werra fords in the region around Eschwege.

Thuringia, on the other hand, had one major west–east road that cut through the centre of the region with several north–south roads crossing it (see Map 9). This main artery through Thuringia began in western Thuringia at Eisenach, where all the roads converged coming from Hesse via the major fords over the Werra

River (Breitungen, Salzungen, Heimboldshausen, Berka, Ger-
stungen and Creuzburg). From Eisenach it traversed the region via
Gotha, Erfurt and Weimar and then continued northeast to
Merseburg or Naumburg. Coming from Bavaria and eastern
Franconia, a road with several branches crossed the Thuringian
Forest via the Rennsteig to Gotha and Erfurt. The main trunk of
this road ran from Meiningen via the *Pfalz* of Rohr to Suhl and the
pass at Oberhof. From there it continued via Ohrdruf to Gotha or
Erfurt, or via Crawinkel and Arnstadt to Erfurt. From Erfurt two
roads led to eastern Saxony. One ran via the ford over the Gera at
Gebesee and the ford over the Unstrut at Straußfurt, and from
there either to Sonderhausen or to Allstedt, Sangerhausen and
eastern Saxony. The second ran via Schloßvippach, Sömmerda
and Kölleda to the Unstrut valley and the royal *Pfalzen* in southern
Saxony. In addition to these roads, three other roads led
respectively from Eisenach, Gotha and Erfurt in a generally
northern direction via Bad Langensalza to Mühlhausen, where
they connected with the roads to western Saxony.[11]

HERSFELD AND FULDA: BACKGROUND AND DEVELOPMENT

Already in the Carolingian period, both monasteries rose to great
prominence. Fulda and Hersfeld were founded as ascetic centres on
the eastern boundaries of the Frankish realm by ecclesiastical
proprietary lords, Bishop Boniface and his student Bishop Lull.
From about 736, Hersfeld was the site of a hermitage, where
Sturm and a few companions lived before Boniface sent Sturm in
search of a more secure site further away from the Saxon border
on which to found a new monastery, the later Fulda. In 744,
Boniface founded Fulda in a sparsely settled forest region on the
site of a deserted Merovingian fortress, to which he had directed
his disciple Sturm and which the Frankish mayor of the palace,

[11] In general concerning the roads through Hesse and Thuringia used by the royal court,
see Rieckenberg (1941/1965) 59–61, 104–7 and Metz (1971), 269–71, 284–5, who
primarily follows Rieckenberg. For more detailed discussions of the specific roads
through Hesse and Thuringia, see the following studies: Görich (1955); Berger (1957);
and Patze (1962) 30–41. Aside from Patze, the best detailed delineations of the actual
courses of the individual roads in Hesse and Thuringia are found in DKP Rep. (1983,
1984, 1986 and 1988), vols. 1.1, 2.1–2, in the articles on specific royal and royal church
properties. See: Gockel (1983a) 2–3 and (1983b) 45; K. Heinemeyer (1983a) 85–6 and
(1983b); Gockel (1984a) 2, (1984b) 71–3, (1984d) 104–5, (1984e) 149, (1984f) 156–8,
(1984g) 170, (1984h) 179–81, (1984i) 197, (1984j) 226.

Carloman, granted to Boniface to establish his monastery.[12] After Sturm settled at Fulda and later became its abbot, Hersfeld appears to have remained a tiny hermitage until Boniface's student and successor to the bishopric of Mainz, Lull, founded a proprietary monastery there, some time between 765, when he lost lordship over Fulda, and 775, the first mention of Hersfeld as a monastery.[13] Both came under royal influence at an early stage of their existence. Hersfeld became a royal monastery in 775 when Bishop Lull personally placed the monastery under royal protection.[14] Fulda, on the other hand, became a royal monastery in gradual stages.[15] Boniface himself was under mayoral protection from the early days of his missionary activity, when the Carolingians were still mayors of the palace. Carolingian patronage, as we have seen, extended to the grant of land on which to found Fulda.[16] Pope Zacharias granted Boniface a papal exemption from normal ecclesiastical jurisdiction in 751,[17] and Pippin III took the monastery under royal protection and again recognized Fulda's papal exemption in 765 upon the reinstatement of Sturm as abbot and the revocation of Lull's proprietary claims to Fulda as Boniface's heir and episcopal successor.[18] In 774, Charlemagne issued Fulda a charter granting it the right to free abbatial election and another granting it royal immunity.[19] All of these grants came together in 816 under Louis the Pious and formally finalized Fulda's constitutional status.[20]

As royal monasteries, Fulda and Hersfeld came to play a role in the economic, military and religious designs of the Carolingian rulers, especially Charlemagne, for the eastern regions of the realm. Their tasks included continued colonization, military organization and some brief missionary activities in Saxony and northern Thuringia.[21] The missionary activity of these monasteries

---

[12] On the foundation and earliest history of Fulda, see Eigil's *Vita Sturmi*, Boniface, *Ep.* no. 86, K. Heinemeyer (1980), Semmler (1980), and Hussong (1985) 1–108, who provides an extensive review of the primary and secondary literature on Fulda. Parsons (1983) provides an important functional analysis of monastic sites in Hesse from an archaeological perspective.

[13] On Hersfeld's foundation and early history, see K. Heinemeyer (1980) 39–45 and Jäschke (1971).   [14] *HUB* no. 5.

[15] On Fulda's constitutional development, see Franke (1987) 58–84 for a focussed summary, and Hussong (1985) 24–156 for a more discursive treatment.

[16] Boniface *Ep.* no. 22; Willibald c. 6 p. 30; Eigil c. 12.   [17] Boniface *Ep.* no. 89.

[18] Eigil c. 20.   [19] *FUB* nos. 68, 67 (= *DDKar* 86, 85).   [20] *CDF* no. 322.

[21] In general, on Charlemagne's Saxon mission, see Büttner (1965) 467–87 and Semmler (1965) 268–9, 281–7.

east of the Rhine was not as significant as their participation in economic development and colonization. The former, however, was often a prerequisite for the latter.[22] The monasteries themselves were well positioned for such activities. They were both situated on a navigable river and on main roads connecting Saxony with Regensburg and Bamberg in Bavaria and eastern Franconia and, more importantly, connecting Saxony with Frankfurt and Mainz, the centres of royal power and politics in the Rhine–Main basin. They also came to hold numerous properties along these crucial corridors. Thus, both of these Hessian monasteries held strategic locations for the continued expansion and consolidation of the Carolingian realm and key central positions in the later German realm.

Although founded initially as a centre of asceticism,[23] Fulda took part in opening up lands and in colonization in Buchonia (the area around the monastery itself), eastern Franconia (around Hammelburg), and eventually in western Thuringia.[24] This activity gradually helped to extend Frankish domains to the east along the early road from Mainz via Fulda to the east, the Antsanvia,[25] and gradually reduced the area between Fulda and Thuringia that was not under royal influence.[26] In the Wetterau region it took part in similar activities as well as in the ecclesiastical organization of the area.[27] Both Fulda and Hersfeld became involved in evangelizing activity as a result of Charlemagne's invasion of Saxony in 772,[28] his decision in 775 to subdue and Christianize Saxony at all costs,[29] and his later decisions at royal assemblies held at Paderborn in 777 and 780, which divided spheres of missionary activity among the bishops and abbots called to participate and issued general guidelines for the Christianization of Saxony.[30] Fulda under Abbot Sturm appears to have been responsible for a sizeable area on the middle Weser and the Leine Rivers stretching from the Solling Forest to the Harz and possibly

---

[22] Semmler (1965) 280.

[23] Eigil c. 2; Boniface *Ep.* no. 86; K. Heinemeyer (1980) 31; Hussong (1985) 39–43.

[24] *FUB* nos. 77, 145a–b, 146, 167.

[25] Concerning this road and other early roads in the area of Fulda, see Görich (1955) and Berger (1957).

[26] Diefenbach (unpub. diss. 1952) 30–2. On the use of forest rights to further colonization, see Metz (1956).   [27] Büttner (1989).   [28] *Ann. reg. Franc. s.a.* 772.

[29] *Ibid. s.a.* 775.

[30] *Ann. Laur. s.a.* 777, 780; see also the *Capitulatio de partibus Saxoniae* of 775–80 in *MGH Capit.* 1 no. 26, esp. cc. 1, 5, 8, 10, 15–17.

later around Minden.[31] Charlemagne also assigned Sturm the task
of defending the Eresburg during one of his campaigns.[32] After
Sturm's death in 779, Erkanbert, brother of Baugulf (the new
abbot of Fulda) and later bishop of Minden, assumed the task of
Fulda's mission in Saxony,[33] but Fulda's role appears to have
diminished greatly as the diocesan organization of Saxony
advanced and tasks initially assigned to monasteries were gradually
taken over by the secular clergy centred on new bishoprics.[34] The
area of Hersfeld's missionizing and colonizing tasks, on the other
hand, fell much further to the north and east along the
Saxon–Slavic borders and south of the Harz to Quedlinburg.
While we have no specific reports of Hersfeld's missionary
activity, on the basis of the massive grants of property and tithe
incomes granted to Hersfeld in southern Saxony and northern
Thuringia by Charlemagne[35] and the frequency of churches
dedicated to St Wigbert, Hersfeld's patron saint,[36] scholars have
built strong arguments for Hersfeld's active and long-lasting
missionary and colonizing activity in Saxony.[37]

Early in their history Fulda and Hersfeld also acquired
substantial property and tithes, both secular and ecclesiastical, in
Thuringia, which provided them with the means to carry out
various tasks in these regions. Whereas Fulda's holdings were
predominantly in western and southern Thuringia,[38] the majority
of Hersfeld's properties were located further to the north and east
just south of the Harz mountains along the Unstrut and Saale
Rivers, in the area known as the Hochseegau or Hassegau and the
Friesenfeld. Additionally, Hersfeld had acquired numerous properties throughout central and western Thuringia located strategically along two routes leading to its most northerly and easterly

---

[31] Eigil cc. 22–3. On Fulda's role in the Saxon mission, see Semmler (1965) 281–2, Wehlt
(1970) 260–1 and Hussong (1986) 129–41.   [32] Eigil c. 24.

[33] Earlier, scholars such as Büttner (1965) 471–2, Semmler (1965) 281–6 and Hussong
(1986) 133–6, traditionally regarded Hameln on the Weser as an early proprietary
missionary church or priory belonging to Fulda and the centre of Fulda's missionary
activity in Saxony; but Nass (1986) 36–72, 149–50 has argued convincingly that: the
area of Fulda's missionary activity was much smaller than previously thought; it was
centred on the region around Minden not on Hameln and Brunshausen, both of which
were founded later; and that Fulda's missionary activity can be proven first with
Erkanbert (lasting from 785 until about 830), not with Sturm. See also Freise (1978)
1130–4, 1208–11.   [34] Semmler (1965) 284–7.

[35] *HUB* nos. 14, 38; Hörle (1960) 31–4.

[36] *Ex Miraculis s. Wigberhti* p. 227; Erdmann (1941/1943) 15–19; Hörle (1960) 30–1.

[37] Hörle (1960); Semmler (1965) 267–8; Wehlt (1970) 162–72; and Reuter (1991a) 105.

[38] Diefenbach (unpub. diss. 1952) 31–2; Patze (1962) 49–57.

properties.[39] Apparently, Hersfeld also had defensive military responsibilities. The oldest land register of the monastery lists 1095 *hufen* and 698 *mansi* of property of which approximately four-fifths lay in Thuringia, with the greatest concentration occurring in the Hochseegau and the Friesenfeld (see Map 9).[40] In addition, Hersfeld received secular tithes from 239 villages and from nineteen burgwards located along this border, that is, three lines of *Burgen* or citadels one behind the other with their pertinent properties. Obviously, these were part of a Frankish fortification system protecting this important frontier.[41] Thus, both monasteries had extensive holdings in Thuringia, many of which they retained into the twelfth century.[42] By virtue of their location on important roads leading from the centre of the realm to Thuringia and of the considerable properties they held there, Hersfeld and Fulda had good connections with Thuringia and manifold interests there. This is especially true of Hersfeld in light of the position assigned to it in northern Thuringia and southern Saxony, where it was apparently called upon by the Carolingian rulers to undertake tasks related to colonization, military defence and missionary work. Thus, in order to understand fully the economic and political importance of Hersfeld and Fulda in the tenth and eleventh centuries, it is necessary to sketch briefly developments in Thuringia under the Ottonian kings as they relate to these two monasteries.

Hersfeld's large property holdings in northeastern Thuringia had several inherent disadvantages. Owing to their being far from the monastery and its direct influence, the properties were difficult to oversee and administer. Thus, after Saxony was incorporated into the realm, they became enviable targets for seizure by a variety of powers in Saxony – the dukes and later kings, as well as newly founded ecclesiastical institutions. With the cessation of effective Carolingian rule in the east Frankish realm in the early tenth century, powerful families in Saxony began slowly but steadily to force Hersfeld out of this increasingly Saxon area of influence.[43] Some time before 908, Otto the Illustrious, the

---

[39] Hörle (1960).   [40] *HUB* no. 38.

[41] Schlesinger (1937/1961) wrote the seminal article on the development of a system of fortifications along the Slavic borders in the northeast. See also Baaken (1961) 39–51 and Nitz (1988).   [42] Lampert, *Annales s.a.* 1073 pp. 141–4.

[43] For a detailed discussion of the developments in Thuringia during this period and the supporting literature, see Patze (1962) 41–96 and his more recent summary, Patze

Liudolfing Duke of Saxony (880–912), became the lay abbot of Hersfeld. Apparently, he used this position to seize additional properties of the monastery north of the Unstrut, such as Tilleda and Memleben, which after the Liudolfing accession to the throne appear as favourite royal residences. A late ninth-century register of Hersfeld's tithe incomes from the Friesenfeld includes a mention of specific monastic properties that the emperor (either Charles the Fat or Arnulf) and Duke Otto had confiscated.[44] These confiscations probably represent a military strengthening of the realm against the Slavs on the important Saale frontier. This becomes especially evident when one considers the location of the confiscated properties: the majority comprise the easternmost of Hersfeld's burgwards. After the conquest of the Saxons in the late eighth century and their assimilation into the east Frankish realm in the ninth, the military importance of the burgwards along the Unstrut west of Merseburg as a front against the Saxons lessened considerably. Later, when Duke Otto's son Henry became king in 919, he inherited the burgwards formerly held by his father as royal or imperial burgwards. Before he became king, Henry had exploited the opportunity presented by his short-lived marriage to Hatheburg, a daughter of Count Erwin of Merseburg, and significantly strengthened the Liudolfings' position and property holdings in northern Thuringia, where Hersfeld had its highest concentration of property holdings.[45] All of these actions document a substantial push by the Liudolfings to the east and into northern and central Thuringia, which later became firm policy.

After Henry became king in 919, the royal demands upon Hersfeld and its properties increased dramatically. Henry and his Ottonian successors untiringly took measures to protect the realm from the incursions of the pagan Slavic and Hungarian peoples from the east. At the same time they consciously pushed further east themselves, conquering, colonizing and evangelizing. This created a series of buffer zones and spheres of influence beyond the Elbe–Saale line. In his efforts further to secure the Thuringian frontier, and probably to strengthen his own position in northern Thuringia, Henry I entered into a series of property exchanges

(1974) 1–10. Concerning Henry II's later shift away from Ottonian policy in the east and how it affected Hersfeld, Fulda and the constellation of power in Thuringia, see Diefenbach (unpub. diss. 1952) and Hörle (1960) 44–8, where he summarizes the thesis of Diefenbach's rather inaccessible dissertation.

[44] *HUB* no. 37.   [45] Patze (1962) 70.

with Hersfeld which were not particularly advantageous to the monastery. These had the effect of easing Hersfeld out of the area and diminishing its role on the eastern frontier. In return for the properties exchanged, Hersfeld enlarged its possessions in western and central Thuringia.[46] Henry also exchanged properties with Fulda to increase royal holdings in this area. In return for properties in the Wipper–Unstrut–Helme basin and in Merseburg, Fulda received a sizeable property, Abenheim, in the Wormsgau west of Worms.[47] The pattern was always the same – possessions of the two monasteries in the northeast were exchanged for properties further south and west. The greatest proprietary forfeitures that Hersfeld endured in this area occurred under Henry's successors Otto I and Otto II.

In conjunction with their foreign policy on the Slavic frontier, the Ottonian kings called upon Hersfeld and Fulda in differing degrees for political support and economic assistance, often in the form of substantial sacrifices. These two Hessian monasteries and their abbots provided Otto I with major political and diplomatic support in his struggle with Archbishop William of Mainz regarding the creation of an archbishopric at Magdeburg.[48] Of these two monasteries Hersfeld alone had to make great economic sacrifices, however, in the interest of the protracted endowing of Magdeburg and the foundation of Memleben. In an exchange charter of 948, Otto I obtained the *villa* of Wormsleben and the churches at Wormsleben and Oberwiederstadt with all the tithes pertaining to them.[49] This tithing district encompassed the entire northern half of Hersfeld's tithes in the Hochseegau. Three days later Otto granted these same properties and incomes to the church of St Maurice at Magdeburg.[50] In return, Hersfeld received nineteen properties scattered in eastern and western Hesse and in Thuringia. Thus, the monastery was compelled to exchange a closed and income-intensive complex of properties for relatively dispersed properties. Although this exchange was not entirely disadvantageous for Hersfeld because some of the properties it

---

[46] *HUB* nos. 44, 45, 46.   [47] *DH I* 34.

[48] In general, concerning this struggle and the parts played by the abbots of Fulda and Hersfeld, see Demandt (1972) 333, 351. For more specific information, see Wehlt (1970) 173–4, 276–8, Jakobi (1978) 845–50 and Hussong (1986) 257–65.

[49] *HUB* no. 48 (= *DO I* 96).

[50] *HUB* no. 49 (= *DO I* 97 or *UBM* 14). In a later property transaction concerning the establishment of the archbishopric at Magdeburg, these properties and incomes came in 968 into the possession of the bishopric of Halberstadt (*UBM* 61 p. 85).

received enabled it to enlarge its sizeable holdings in south-central Thuringia around Arnstadt,[51] nevertheless the Liudolfings had once again pushed Hersfeld further out of eastern Saxony.[52]

By far the most devastating blow to Hersfeld's position in the northeast, however, occurred under Otto II in connection with the foundation of the new royal monastery of Memleben in 979.[53] Memleben, located exactly on the boundary between southern Saxony and Thuringia, lay directly in the middle of Hersfeld's most valuable complex of properties and incomes. The fledgling monastery was founded as a memorial church on the site of the royal *Pfalz* where Henry I and Otto I died. In one sense, then, Memleben functioned as a tomb where the king went to die as part of the ritualistic way that the Germanic nobility lived their lives.[54] Thus, Memleben was founded initially as a new Ottonian cult site as well as a royal monastery (*libera abbacia*).[55] It appears, from a copy of a papal charter of Benedict VII for Memleben and on King Henry II's charter of 1003, that Memleben received a charter from Otto II, which is now lost, designating its royal status.[56] In order to endow it in a fitting manner as a cult site and as a royal monastery, and to equip it materially for the tasks of colonization and evangelization he envisaged, Otto II prevailed upon Hersfeld to forfeit its sizeable interests in southern Saxony and northern Thuringia. Hersfeld relinquished its three chapels in Allstedt, Osterhausen and Riestedt, as well as the monastery's tithe incomes in the Friesenfeld and those remaining in the Hochseegau. Otto II then granted the chapels and the tithes to Memleben as a part of its foundation endowment.[57] In exchange, Hersfeld received only fifty medium-sized *mansi* in four different locations in the Hochseegau and the royal *villa* of Moffendorf in the Rhineland east of Bonn.[58] The tithing district that Hersfeld had to abandon comprised the same eighteen burgwards (*civitates* or *Burgen*) that

---

[51] See Gockel (1984b) 78–9.

[52] Although Fulda also exchanged some of its properties in eastern Saxony in and around Eisleben, Mansfeld and Bernburg with Magdeburg in 972 (*UBM* 78) in return for numerous properties in southwestern Thuringia, this exchange, in contrast to Hersfeld's, appears to have benefited both parties significantly, allowing them both to consolidate their respective holdings.

[53] In general, concerning Memleben, see Schubert (1969) and Leopold and Schubert (1990).

[54] I thank the late Karl Leyser for the private conversation in which he pointed out the importance of this aspect of Memleben's foundation.   [55] Thietmar 3 c. 1.

[56] See *HUB* no. 65, pp. 121–7; *DH II* 25; Weirich (1936).   [57] Thietmar 3 c. 1.

[58] *HUB* no. 60 (= *DO II* 191).

paid tithes to the monastery in the late ninth century.[59] With this forfeiture the Ottonians had ousted Hersfeld totally from its position as a Carolingian bulwark on the Saxon border. Thereby, they materially anchored Memleben in northeastern Thuringia and transferred Hersfeld's original missionary and colonizing mandate to the new Liudolfing foundation, now directed not to Saxony, but to the Slavs east of the Elbe and the Saale Rivers.

This new arrangement stood solidly in line with the eastern policy and the Slavic mission as it developed under the Ottonians. Three massive grants of property and burgwards, east of the Elbe and Mulde Rivers, to Memleben in 979 show clearly that the Ottonian king intended this new royal monastery to play an integral role in the Christianization and colonization of the Slavic lands. Memleben's properties and burgwards in the east were located in the region of the Hevelli tribe, on the middle Elbe beyond the confluence with the Mulde, and around Meißen in the region of the Daleminzi (see Map 2).[60] The dissolution of the bishopric of Merseburg shortly thereafter, in 981, gives further credence to Memleben's new role as bearer of the mission to the Slavs between the bishoprics of Magdeburg and Meißen. Otto III likewise continued to favour Memleben and he strengthened its position significantly. He granted it further properties east of the Elbe,[61] and the valuable sovereign rights to collects tolls, hold a market and mint coins at Memleben, all with the royal ban.[62] Later, he gave to the monastery the royal *civitas* of Wiehe,[63] which Henry I had acquired in an exchange with Hersfeld in 933.[64] Thus, in Hersfeld's stead, the last two Ottonian kings had founded and richly endowed their own new royal monastery, located near the Slavic frontier, in order to propagate the Slavic mission.[65] However, the great Slavic uprising of 983 and its continuing repercussions in the years following, and the incursions and conquests of Boleslav Chrobry around Meißen in the early eleventh century, nullified Memleben's acquisitions and incomes

---

[59] *HUB* no. 37.

[60] *HUB* nos. 66, 67, 68 (= *DDO II* 194, 195, 196). Although the royal charters for these grants are dated 981, the transactions occurred earlier in 979. See Weirich's introduction to *HUB* no. 66.

[61] *HUB* no. 71 (= *DO III* 106).   [62] *HUB* no. 73 (= *DO III* 142).

[63] *HUB* no. 74 (= *DO III* 305).   [64] *HUB* no. 46 (= *DH I* 35).

[65] Baaken (1961) 70–1 provides a concise statement concerning the foundation of Memleben, its connection with the Ottonian fortification system in this area and its role in the Slavic mission.

in the east and doomed its part in the Slavic mission to failure.[66] Under these altered conditions and in response to the dissolution of Otto III's Polish alliance,[67] Henry II began his revision of the Ottonian 'eastern' policy, and this revision greatly affected Memleben, Hersfeld and Fulda.

Having already reinstated the bishopric of Merseburg in 1004 and founded the new bishopric of Bamberg in 1007, Henry II implemented his last major change on the eastern frontier early in 1015 through a series of interrelated property transactions. At the request of Abbot Arnolf of Hersfeld, who came to petition the king with his entire congregation of monks and the monastery's retainers (*milites*), the king issued Hersfeld a charter revoking Otto II's charter of 979. It confiscated the tithes in the Hochseegau and the Friensenfeld from the monastery of Memleben, and the three chapels to which they pertained, and restored them all to Hersfeld.[68] By expropriating a fundamental part of the incomes remaining to the Ottonian royal monastery, after most of its incomes and possessions in the east had been lost in the Slavic uprising of 983 and the almost unbroken chain of conflicts on the eastern frontier thereafter, Henry had further impoverished it. Ten days later, in spite of the fact that he had confirmed Memleben's royal status in 1002 before launching his new programmes,[69] Henry II granted all of the monastery's remaining possessions to Hersfeld.[70] Memleben thus became a proprietary monastery of Hersfeld. Obviously, the Frankfurt *Weistum* of 951, which forbade giving a monastery holding a royally granted right of free abbatial election to another monastery, did not constrain Henry in his action.[71] The contemporary chronicler Thietmar of Merseburg, however, did report and bemoan the suppression of Memleben with strong language, commenting that Memleben had to exchange its constitutional freedom (*libertas*) for servitude (*servitudo*).[72]

Contrary to many widely held opinions, no single factor – not

[66] Wehlt (1970) 178 and Schlesinger (1962) 1.149–50. A good treatment of the Slavic uprising of 983 and the continuing problems in the east in the years following can be found in Claude (1972–5) 1.153–73, 1.202–5.

[67] Beumann and Schlesinger (1955) 226–36 and Reuter (1991b) 25–7.

[68] *HUB* no. 81 (= *DH II* 330) and *HUB* no. 60 (= *DO II* 191).

[69] *HUB* no. 75 (= *DH II* 25).   [70] *HUB* no. 82 (= *DH II* 331).

[71] *MGH Const.* 1 no. 8 p. 17. On the Frankfurt *Weistum*, see above, Chapter 2, pp. 73–4. This happened once again in 1017, when Henry granted the royal monastery of Helmarshausen to Bishop Meinwerk of Paderborn. See above, Chapter 6, pp. 215–16.

[72] Thietmar 7 c. 31.

the foundation and continuing endowment of Bamberg,[73] nor the impoverishment of Memleben,[74] nor Henry's plans to strengthen royal interests by having a centrally-based royal monastery as the representative of royal power in the area[75] – alone appears to have moved the king to take this action; but rather it was the multiplicity of important factors merging at one time that brought the king to subjugate one richly endowed and significant royal monastery to another.[76] The *narratio* of the charter granting Memleben to Hersfeld stated that Henry intended to relieve the desperate impoverishment of the monastery by granting it to the much richer Hersfeld.[77] Although this *narratio* expressed the king's intentions in only the noblest terms, it nevertheless did have a basis in fact and cannot be dismissed merely as a collection of empty phrases.[78] For the *narratio*, of course, failed to mention that, by restoring the three chapels and their pertinent tithes to Hersfeld, Henry had confiscated the substance of Memleben's remaining incomes. In the Slavic uprising of 983 and the numerous Slavic and Polish wars following it, the young royal monastery of Memleben had lost virtually all of its properties and incomes east of the Saale and the Elbe. Thus, it had lost much of its total basis of subsistence and had failed in its tasks of Christianizing and colonizing areas in the east.

Seen in this light one can view the subjection of Memleben to Hersfeld as Henry's final renunciation of Ottonian plans in the east.[79] In a weakened economic state and without further prospects of a royal mission in the east, Memleben could better serve the realm by enhancing Hersfeld's ability to provide service to the king.[80] The reinstatement of Hersfeld in this area as a representative and a supporter of royal power complemented both the re-foundation of Merseburg and the foundation of Bamberg on the

---

[73] Weirich's introduction to *HUB* no. 81 and Patze (1962) 85, 88–90.

[74] Wehlt (1970) 177–9.   [75] Diefenbach (unpub. diss. 1952) 136–8.

[76] Hirsch (1862–75) 3.5–7 (very probably with insight from Bresslau).

[77] *HUB* no. 82 (= *DH II* 331): '...qualiter nos divini amoris instinctu pro remedio animae nostrae cuiusdam abbatiae Mimeleua dictae inopiam considerantes fratrumque ibi deo famulantium penuriam inspicientes hoc modo eis providere decrevimus, ut eandem abbatiam Heroluesueldensi abbatiae tradamus, ea videlicet ratione, uti ex Arnoldi eiusdem abbatiae abbatis suorumque successorum industria ac eiusdem abbatiae copia iam dictorum fratrum relevetur inopia'.

[78] As does Patze (1962) 85. On the other hand, Wehlt (1970) 178 perhaps over-emphasizes the importance that the monastery's weakened economic state played in the overall process. Hoffmann (1988) demonstrates very clearly that in the arengas of Henry II's charters one often hears a true echo of the king himself, not merely formulaic rhetoric.

[79] Schlesinger (1962) 1.149–50.   [80] Wehlt (1970) 178.

eastern frontier. With the exception of the burgward of Merseburg, the majority of Merseburg's properties lay east of the Saale. Another exchange between Henry and Hersfeld in 1015 helped further to enrich Bamberg and to reinforce its political power.[81] In return for restoring to Hersfeld its former tithes and chapels, Henry II had received the properties of Moffendorf and Klobikau and several other possessions. A week later he engineered a three-party exchange between Hersfeld, Bamberg and the realm. Henry granted Klobikau (west of Merseburg) once again to Hersfeld as well as other properties in west-central Thuringia near Wanfried, which he had acquired from a certain landholder named Sigfried. In return, Hersfeld transferred four properties, which were situated in the Main region between Bamberg and Würzburg, to the bishopric of Bamberg. This allowed Bamberg to consolidate its properties in Franconia and gave Hersfeld additional lands around its new proprietary monastery and on roads between Hersfeld and its easternmost holdings. The king now had three royal church institutions, all of which were especially indebted to him, as royal representatives on the eastern frontier; and two of these were firmly anchored in the centre of the realm, Henry's newly emerging core of royal power.[82] The whole process appears to have been expedited by a new affinity between Hersfeld and the king that resulted from the royally initiated reform of the monastery (1005–12) by Henry's friend and confidant, Godehard, and the election of Godehard's student, Arnolf, to succeed him as abbot of Hersfeld. In addition, it corresponded to the new conception of rulership which Henry II had been developing since the beginning of his reign. Royal power should be total and undiminished, the royal church should be controlled, but allowed to retain some political muscle, and weaker members of the church (*membra*) should be hierarchically subordinated to the stronger with the king as the head (*caput*) of both the church and the government.[83]

HERSFELD AND FULDA

Without a doubt the monasteries of Hersfeld and Fulda were two of the major pillars of the royal itinerary in the central transit zone.

[81] *HUB* no. 83 (= *DH II* 332a).   [82] See above, Chapter 1, pp. 42–4.
[83] Seibert (1991) 507–16, who discusses the classical head–body–members terminology in reference to the arenga in *DH II* 277 for the bishop of Strasbourg. See also Weinfurter (1986) and T. Schieffer (1951).

They were located on the Fulda River a long day's march from each other (that is, 35 or 40 km apart) and they provide another clear and compelling example of the crucial contribution made by royal monasteries to German itinerant kingship. This statement requires some explanation. The traditional method of establishing the king's itinerary consists of using the royal charters as the evidentiary basis and determining the *iter* according to where and when the charters were issued. By that method, Hersfeld received only four royal visits, and Fulda six in the years from 920 to approximately 1075. Adding information from the narrative sources, the total royal visits for the two monasteries increases only by about six. Even attempts to supplement these documented visits by calculations based on travel patterns or the monasteries' *servitium regis* help only marginally. The large number of roads that the Ottonian and Salian kings used when traversing Thuringia and Hesse, and the location of both monasteries on or in the vicinity of several of these roads, complicate and limit our ability to establish (as we did with Corvey, Werden and Essen on the Hellweg) even approximately how often the king may have called upon Hersfeld or Fulda to provide accommodation and provisions for himself and his retinue. In addition, as with most religious houses in the tenth and eleventh centuries, these two monasteries on the Fulda River do not provide us with any specific information about their obligations to the economic *servitium regis*. Consequently, based on the traditional approaches to researching and evaluating royal visits, scholars have concluded that these two monasteries played only a very minor role in the accommodation and upkeep of the royal court.[84] Sixteen royal visits in 155 years hardly supports the contention about the importance of these monasteries for the itinerary; nor, however, does it correspond to the traditional reverence accorded these two Hessian royal monasteries in German history.

The apparent contradiction between my contention and the traditional reverence of these monasteries on the one hand, and our lack of specific information regarding royal visits and the *servitium regis* on the other, highlights problems inherent in the traditional methods of analysis. When one uses the royal charters to establish a chronological and geographical window for the general movements of the royal court in addition to the specific time and

---

[84] Most recently, Hussong (1986) 284–98.

place of their issue,[85] and when one applies evidence from multiple sources, such as property holdings, grants of sovereign rights, and the archaeological record, to the relationship between royal monasteries and the king's itinerary, the role of these monasteries appears significantly altered. This approach reveals that the real significance of Hersfeld and Fulda for the royal itinerary and the *servitium regis* does not lie merely in the fact that the monasteries themselves provided stopping places for the royal court much more frequently than the extant sources attest. For example, Otto I travelled fifteen times from Saxony to the middle Rhine and thirteen times in the reverse direction, made twenty-one trips from the northeast to southern Germany (eleven to and ten in return), and journeyed six or seven times to Thuringia or Hesse and then back to Saxony.[86] Likewise, calculations based on his itinerary show that Otto III crossed Hesse at least twelve times between 989 and 1000. Rough estimates for the other Ottonian and early Salian kings confirm the pattern. In addition, the attested royal itinerary through these central regions of the realm reveals that the king and his retinue very frequently took their accommodation and *servitium* on the many vills of the two monasteries scattered along virtually all of the major roads traversing Thuringia and Hesse (see Map 11).

HERSFELD (MEMLEBEN)

For the Ottonian and Salian kings, the royal monastery of Hersfeld held a strategically important position (see Map 9). Located in east-central Hesse on the west bank of the Fulda River, the monastery controlled three nearby fords over the Fulda. Two fords over the river lay in the immediate vicinity of the monastery and later town, just northwest and south of it, and the third was located at Bebra/Breitenbach where two major roads from the north joined. The monastery was also situated at the junction of two major routes.[87] The first, known in the sixteenth century as the 'short

---

[85] These new methods were used already by Metz (1971), but without the full methodological foundation established by Müller-Mertens (1980).

[86] Müller-Mertens (1980) 141.

[87] The earliest roads in this area were high roads that circumvented the low-lying and somewhat marshy basin where the monastery was founded. By erecting plank or pile roads, Hersfeld was able to draw these high roads down into the valley, thus bringing itself economic and strategic advantages. See Görich (1953), with a map of the immediate vicinity, and Wehlt (1970) 149–50.

Hessian' road, led from Frankfurt via Friedberg, Berstadt, Hungen, Grünberg and Alsfeld, to Hersfeld, where it crossed the Fulda. The road then separated into two strands which continued into Thuringia via fords over the Werra respectively at Berka (Gerstungen) or Heimboldshausen near Vacha.[88] From these fords one could continue east to Erfurt and Leipzig or connect with several main roads leading north to Saxony or south to the Main valley and Bavaria.[89] The second road transecting Hersfeld was the major north–south artery. It ran from Würzburg via the river ford at Hammelburg to Fulda and then via Michelsrombach and the ford across the Fulda River at Wegfurth to Hersfeld.[90] From here the road continued north to the monastery's properties at Breitenbach/Bebra where it again crossed the Fulda.[91] In Bebra the road joined with two main routes coming out of northern Germany: one from Minden, Paderborn and Kassel (then following the Fulda River), and the other from the western and eastern Harz region via Grone and Eschwege.[92] Thus, the monastery's location near Saxony and Thuringia, and at a major crossroads connecting Saxony with Franconia and the Rhineland with Thuringia, made it a frequent stopping point on the royal progress.

Although the great majority of recorded royal stops in Hersfeld occurred under Henry IV, strong evidence indicates that the previous Ottonian and Salian kings used the monastery for a halting point much more frequently than scholars have recognized.[93] Otto I visited the monastery some time during the second

---

[88] Demandt (1972) 24–5 (with map) and Wehlt (1970) 149–50. Both Hersfeld and Fulda possessed property in Berka and it was included in Hersfeld's *Wildbann* of 1016 (*HUB* no. 85 = *DH II* 350). See 'Berka', in Patze (1968) 47–8; *HUB* no. 38 [2] p. 72; *TAF* c. 38 no. 303; and *FUB* no. 442 p. 476 n. 1. Gerstungen was the administrative centre for several of Fulda's vills. Concerning the Werra ford at Heimboldshausen (not at Vacha!), see Patze (1962) 31 no. 2 and Küther (1971) 4–6. Both monasteries appear to have held property in and around Vacha. See 'Vacha', in Patze (1968) 447–8; *HUB* nos. 20 (= *DKar* 153), 46 (= *DH I* 35) and 85 (= *DH II* 350); and Küther (1971) 8–23.

[89] Concerning these roads see above pp. 240–1.

[90] Berger (1957) 186 n. 56. There also appears to have been a high road between Hersfeld and Fulda east of the river which this road followed until it turned towards Wegfurth around Michelsrombach. See Wehlt (1970) 150.

[91] Hörle (1960) 27, 50 (Table 2b, D nos. 153–6); Gockel (1983b).

[92] Roads frequently travelled by the royal court from eastern Saxony and northern Thuringia via Nordhausen and Mühlhausen led into the latter road between Grone and Eschwege.

[93] For instance, Brühl (1983) 621–3 drew attention to this fact and thereby even revised some of his earlier opinions on stops by the court at royal monasteries.

year of his reign (937)[94] and his son, Otto II, came to Hersfeld in the autumn of 975 after a campaign to Bohemia.[95] Medieval sources then remain silent concerning any royal visits until the mid-eleventh century. A twelfth-century source states that Empress Gisela was present at the monastery some time in 1034 when Abbot Adalhard of St Trond died there.[96] In the summer of 1040, Henry III, along with Archbishop Hunfried of Magdeburg and Bishops Kadeloh of Naumburg and Hunold of Merseburg, participated in the consecration of the crypt and the newly rebuilt church at Hersfeld.[97] In addition to these stops, the royal itinerary suggests another six royal visits with a high degree of certainty. Henry II may have visited Fulda on 16 December 1012,[98] and then travelled northeast via Hersfeld to Pöhlde, where he issued a charter on 29 December for Fulda.[99] Considering that it was winter, the route via Hersfeld would have presented fewer difficulties than the Thuringian Forest in that season. In 1020, after spending at least three days with Pope Benedict VIII at Fulda (1–3 May),[100] Henry II appeared on 22 May in Kaufungen.[101] The major and the logical route between these two points undoubtedly took him through Hersfeld.[102] Henry's successor, Conrad II, during his royal progress through all regions of the realm following his election, appeared on 29 March 1025 at Fulda. The known itinerary does not allow one to determine accurately whether he came from Wallhausen or from Grone, which of course, could alter his route. When one considers, however, that on this progress the newly elected king stopped in nearly every major power centre of the realm, including the royal monasteries and convents of Vreden, Corvey, Gandersheim, Quedlinburg, possibly Nienburg, and Fulda, it appears highly likely, if not compelling, that he also stopped at Hersfeld on his way to Fulda.[103] In 1047, Henry III's trip from his Christmas court at Pöhlde via Fulda to Würzburg and Ulm undoubtedly took him by way of Hersfeld, which lay on this north–south route approximately a day's march from Fulda.[104] A few years later in

---

[94] *Ann. Hildes.* and *Ann. Weissenburg. s.a.* 936 (937); *Ann. Alt.* and Lampert, *Annales s.a.* 936; Wehlt (1970) 152.
[95] *Ann. Weissenburg.* and *Ann. Alt. s.a.* 975; Wehlt (1970) 152.
[96] *Gesta abbatum Trodonensium* p. 232; Bresslau (1879–84) 2.117 n. 1; Wehlt (1970) 152.
[97] Lampert, *Libelli* p. 351.   [98] Wehlt (1970) 293.   [99] *DH II* 253.
[100] *DDH II* 427, 428 and 429.   [101] *DH II* 430.   [102] See Wehlt (1970) 239.
[103] See *DK II* 23; *Vita Bardonis Maior* p. 534; BA nos. n-23.
[104] See E. Müller (1901) 68–9 and Wehlt (1970) 240.

July of 1051, Henry III appears to have stopped at Hersfeld and probably Fulda on his way from Kaufungen[105] up the Fulda River through Hesse and Franconia to Nuremberg, where he issued a charter granting Hersfeld a vineyard in Ingelheim.[106] Finally, Henry III travelled in July of 1056 from Worms via Berstadt,[107] a vill of Fulda, to Goslar, where he received the pope, and then on to Bodfeld. Based on the charter that Henry issued for Fulda at Bodfeld, it is possible that the king's journey took him via the monastery itself.[108] Although it is impossible to determine Henry's route from Berstadt to Goslar, the three major routes available to him would have taken him by way of Fulda and Hersfeld, or just via Hersfeld, or, if he travelled the 'long Hessian' road, via Hersfeld's properties. In any case, Hersfeld or its properties appear to have provided the king and his retinue with some sort of accommodation or upkeep on this trip, as did Fulda's vill of Berstadt and possibly Fulda itself.[109] As we have seen elsewhere, the charters issued for Hersfeld in 1051 and 1056 both occurred immediately after probable visits to the monastery or its properties, possibly as compensation for hospitality.

By far the greatest concentration of recorded royal visits to Hersfeld in the Ottonian and early Salian period occurred between 1062 and 1074 during the regency and early reign of King Henry IV. Within this period contemporary sources place the king and the royal retinue at Hersfeld seven times. The young king issued a charter there in 1062 on his way to Mainz[110] and four years later, in 1066, he celebrated the feast of Pentecost at Hersfeld just after recovering from a serious illness that had confined him for several weeks at Fritzlar.[111] Then, beginning in 1070, he appeared at least once a year at the monastery for the next five years.[112] In 1070, Henry IV appears to have stopped overnight in Hersfeld on a hasty trip to Mainz via the 'short Hessian' road.[113] Likewise, a year later he travelled the same route to a synod in Mainz (15 August), stopped overnight at the monastery, and hastily returned the next day (30 July) after a trusted vassal had a fatal accident at

---

[105] *DDH III* 271, 272 and 273.
[106] *DH III* 274; E. Müller (1901) 89–91; Wehlt (1970) 153.
[107] *DDH III* 376 and 377.   [108] *DH III* 380; E. Müller (1901) 117 n. 4.
[109] See Gockel (1983a) and Wehlt (1970) 240.
[110] *DH IV* 88; Meyer von Knonau (1890–1909) 1.290.
[111] Lampert, *Annales s.a.* 1066 p. 103; *DH IV* 179; Meyer von Knonau (1890–1909) 1.525.
[112] In general concerning these visits, see Wehlt (1970) 153–5.   [113] Ibid. 153.

Udenhausen, where the retinue had stopped to eat.[114] In December 1072, Henry came to the monastery to direct the abbatial election and to install the successor to Abbot Ruthard, who had resigned because of sickness.[115] After the uprising of the Saxon nobility in 1073, Hersfeld and its nearby properties became the centre of operations for the king's campaigns and negotiations in Thuringia and Saxony. After fleeing the beleaguered Harzburg with a small retinue in August 1073, Henry IV rested and regrouped for four days at Hersfeld.[116] Several months later, in January 1074, the king asked Abbot Hartwig to bring his pregnant wife, Queen Bertha, from the fortress of Volkenroda near Mühlhausen to Hersfeld where she spent the final weeks of her pregnancy and bore him a son on 12 February.[117] Around the same time, at the end of January, Henry marched with his troops from Worms to Hersfeld, where he paused briefly before continuing on the same day to the monastery's property at Breitenbach, a ford over the Fulda River, where they made their encampment.[118]

Our knowledge of these visits rests primarily, but not solely, on the fortunate circumstance that Lampert, a monk at Hersfeld during this time, dutifully recorded five of them in his *Annals*, which cover the years up to 1077.[119] Consequently, for this short period, using Lampert and other contemporary sources, historians have been able to record numerous royal visits to the monastery, unlike the earlier years on which our meagre sources remain silent. Yet, not only did Lampert himself fail to mention two of the royal visits about which we have other witnesses, but the itinerary indicates that Henry IV may possibly have visited Hersfeld briefly on three additional occasions. The king appears to have visited Fulda in 1060, between his stop in Bamberg on 8 February and the celebration of the Easter feast in Halberstadt at the end of March, to install the monk Widerad as abbot.[120] If so, the court may very well have continued north towards Saxony via Hersfeld. In August 1065, Henry IV travelled in ten days from Trebur to the

[114] Lampert, *Annales s.a.* 1071 pp. 129–30; *DH IV* 243; Meyer von Knonau (1890–1909) 2.75–7.

[115] Lampert, *Libelli* p. 354; Lampert, *Annales s.a.* 1072 p. 139; Meyer von Knonau (1890–1909) 2.173.

[116] Lampert, *Annales s.a.* 1073 p. 156; Meyer von Knonau (1890–1909) 2.254–5.

[117] Lampert, *Annales s.a.* 1074 p. 174; Meyer von Knonau (1890–1909) 2.310, 327.

[118] Lampert, *Annales s.a.* 1074 pp. 175–7; *DDH IV* 268, 269; Meyer von Knonau (1890–1909) 2.315–7; Gockel (1983b) 46–7.   [119] Brühl (1983) 621–3.

[120] *Ann. Alt. s.a.* 1060; Meyer von Knonau (1890–1909) 1.175.

Fulda vill of Gerstungen on the Werra.[121] The most customary and, perhaps, quickest route between these two points was the 'short Hessian' road from Frankfurt via Hersfeld. Finally, in August 1068, the court journeyed from Goslar to the Fulda vill of Berstadt.[122] Since Berstadt lay both on the 'short Hessian' road and a branch of the 'long Hessian' road, we cannot determine exactly which route was chosen. But, in either instance, the king and his retinue either touched Hersfeld itself or one of its properties on the 'long Hessian' road. The chance survival of Lampert's detailed account of this brief period, and the fact that the established royal routes, itinerary and patterns of accommodation remained relatively constant until after the great Saxon uprising of 1073,[123] lead one to conclude that Henry IV's Ottonian and Salian predecessors, like Henry himself, certainly frequented Hersfeld much more often than we are able to document from the existing sources.

Recent archaeological evidence also appears to confirm a more frequent royal presence at Hersfeld than formerly assumed, especially under the Salian kings. In 1975, excavations at Hersfeld unearthed the remains of an extensive palace or fortified residence. The structure appears to date from the Salian period – according to a coin find probably from the mid-eleventh century – but it apparently had its origins as a Carolingian fortification. This hall-like structure, approximately 60 m in length and 13 m wide, had an adjoining chapel and probably consisted of two storeys. With an estimated internal area of 535 square metres (= 5756 sq. ft), this structure measured about three quarters of the size of the royal *Pfalz* at Goslar, the largest known in Germany. The building was located about 100 m east of the monastic church on the grounds of the later hospital.[124] This recently discovered structure, therefore, appears to have served as the residence of the king and his immediate retinue on the numerous visits of the royal court to Hersfeld.[125] One hopes that continuing excavations at Hersfeld will shed further light on the specific design and function of this structure. This royal residence at Hersfeld may have been built in connection with the recently begun construction of a new and larger church, which replaced the one destroyed in the fire of 1038.

---

[121] *DDH IV* 163 and 164.   [122] *DDH IV* 207 and 208.
[123] Zielinski (1984) 211 n. 69 and Müller-Mertens (1991) 147–8.
[124] Helberg (1977), Gensen (1979) 80, 88 and Streich (1984) 312.
[125] Streich (1984) 312.

Only after this fire did Hersfeld build a church as large as the one at Fulda.[126] The crypt was dedicated in 1040 in the presence of Henry III, but the dedication of the completed church did not take place until a century later under Conrad III.[127]

Hersfeld's obligation to provide the king with accommodation and provisions did not cease, however, at the walls of the monastery. A comparison of Hersfeld's known properties with the recorded stopping places of the royal itinerary and with the roads customarily travelled by the king through Hesse and Thuringia reveal that infrequently mentioned and obscure halting points of the royal court were often manors or estates of the monastery. Since medieval sources mention royal stops on individual properties even less often than sojourns at actual monasteries, which themselves appear to have been more frequent than reported, it is impossible to determine precisely how frequently the king and his entourage may have halted on a particular property or called upon it for some kind of service. Nevertheless, regardless of their limitations, the documented instances we have of royal visits to monastic properties confirm that royal monasteries also had to provide the king with accommodation and *servitium* beyond the confines of their abbey when he chose to halt on one of their properties. Thus, the king on his continual progresses through the realm frequently made stops of short duration at larger monastic estates, especially in areas where fiscal property did not abound, that is in Hesse and Thuringia.[128]

In fact, whichever route the king may have chosen to travel through the transit zone in the centre of the realm, it would have been difficult to avoid the property of Hersfeld.[129] In Hesse, Hersfeld had acquired, from Archbishop Lull, numerous properties in the Wetterau on the 'short Hessian' road. Likewise, Charlemagne's grant to the monastery of forty *hubae* and twenty-eight *mansi* at Hungen, near the Fulda vill of Berstadt, and of several other properties near Hersfeld itself (Niederjossa and Niederaula) significantly increased Hersfeld's holdings along this road.[130] The monastery also held property in at least one major

---

[126] Lampert, *Libelli* p. 350; Binding (1971).
[127] Lampert, *Libelli* p. 350; *DDK III* 115, 116, 117.
[128] In general, see Metz (1971) 269–72, 279–86, (1978b) 69–71 and (1976) 226–8. Metz first called attention, in a systematic fashion, to the accommodation of the royal court on monastic estates distant from the monastery.   [129] Metz (1976) 227–8.
[130] Hörle (1960) 28, 33–4, 40; *HUB* no. 17 (= *DKar* 44) and no. 38 [1] p. 72 [= Hörle (1960) 49 Table 1C nos. 64, 71, 72].

station, Treysa, on one of the various strands of the 'long Hessian' road, and at several points along the Antsanvia to Thuringia via Fulda (see Map 9).[131] To the north of the monastery, Hersfeld held a somewhat closed complex of properties around Rotenburg (Breitingen) and Breitenbach/Bebra at important river fords, on which Henry IV encamped his army in 1074 and 1075.[132] Thus, whenever the king travelled any of the major roads through Hesse, properties of Hersfeld could provide rest stops, accommodation or provisions to the court. Along with Hersfeld and Fulda, Fritzlar was also one of the preferred stopping places in Hesse for the Ottonian and Salian kings during their passages. During the period 936–1073 there are at least ten documented royal visits to Fritzlar. Since the great majority of stops at Fritzlar presupposed use of the 'long Hessian' road, one may consider the halts at Fritzlar as a further indication of how often the properties of Hersfeld and Fulda situated on this route may have been pressed into service by the travelling court.[133]

Similarly, Hersfeld had amassed a huge amount of property throughout Thuringia, much of which was located at strategic points on important roads. It held one large complex of properties and rights around the bend in the middle Werra River near (Bad) Salzungen and Dorndorf. Charlemagne granted Hersfeld the secular tithe, ten *hubae* and ten *mansi* in (Bad) Salzungen, as well as the entire *villa* or *Mark* of Dorndorf with fourteen *hubae* and fourteen *mansi*.[134] In 933, Hersfeld acquired Barchfeld and Breitungen, with its river ford and the pertinent parish territory, in an exchange charter with Henry I.[135] Then, in 1016, Henry II included practically all of these properties and areas within the forest and hunting ban that he granted Hersfeld over an extensive area (*c.* 33 km × 37 km) centred on these former holdings.[136]

---

[131] Hörle (1960) 28, 50 (Table 2b, F no. 161); *HUB* no. 38 [2] p. 73. Hersfeld also held several properties around Mardorf and Fritzlar along the 'long Hessian' road, but it is not entirely clear whether these remained in Hersfeld's possession in the tenth and eleventh centuries, or if they had already been absorbed into Fritzlar's sphere of influence before Henry IV gave Fritzlar to the archbishop of Mainz in 1066. See Hörle (1960) 34–9.

[132] Hörle (1960) 50 (Table 2b, D nos. 153–6); *HUB* no. 38 [2] p. 73; Lampert, *Annales s.a.* 1074 pp. 175–7, 1075 pp. 210, 214–17; Gockel (1983b) 46–7, (1983c).

[133] See Karl Wenck (1907) esp. 145 n. 1 and Demandt (1939) 5–9 esp. 6 n. 31.

[134] *HUB* nos. 7, 20 (= *DDKar* 90, 153), 38 [1] p. 71 (= Hörle (1960) 49 [Tafel IA nos. 4, 6]).   [135] *HUB* no. 46 (= *DH I* 35).

[136] *HUB* no. 85 (= *DH II* 350). The forest and hunting ban of 1016 did not include the easternmost part of the Breitungen parish territory or *Mark*. See Gockel (1984j) 229 and Ziegler (1939) 9. Cf. Küther (1974) 200–1, 204.

Breitungen was an important ford over the Werra located on the road leading from Fulda via Hünfeld, Rasdorf and Roßdorf to Thuringia, and on a road along the Werra that led to Barchfeld from the Franconian Saale region (royal residence of Salz) and from Bamberg via Meiningen and the nearby *Pfalz* of Rohr. Breitungen's location on a north–south route along the Werra is indicated by Henry V's stop there in 1122 coming from Würzburg to Saxony. Moreover, the importance of its location on the east–west road received confirmation in 1114 when Henry V granted Abbot Adelmann of Hersfeld the right to hold a weekly and a yearly market there (that is, at Frauenbreitungen just west of the Werra).[137] Numerous roads branched off this route and led over the Rennsteig to Eisenach, Gotha and Erfurt.[138] Hersfeld held sizeable amounts of property along the two major roads over the Rennsteig, notably around Ohrdruf (Wolfis), Arnstadt (Oberndorf) and Wechmar, all just south of Gotha and Erfurt.[139] These two major north–south roads across Thuringia with their numerous alternate strands corresponded to the Hersfeld 'eastern route' and the old Thuringian road coming from Mainz through eastern Franconia. Interestingly enough, Ohrdruf, Arnstadt and Wechmar make isolated appearances in the royal itinerary. Otto I made a five-day stop at Ohrdruf in 961,[140] and in December 954 he held an important *Reichstag* at Arnstadt,[141] where the abbot of Hersfeld appears to have established a market by the middle of the eleventh century.[142] In 1086, Henry IV stopped at Wechmar, although strictly speaking this does not fall chronologically within the timespan of the generally homogeneous pattern exhibited by the itinerary (approximately 936–1075).[143]

Moving north of the *via regia*, the great west–east road (Eisenach–Erfurt–Jena–Leipzig) cutting through the middle of Thuringia, we continue to find Hersfeld properties conveniently situated on the north–south roads traversing Thuringia, which occasionally received royal visits. Coming either from Allstedt or

---

[137] Gockel (1984j) 226; Patze (1962) 31 no. 3, 32 no. 5, 33–4 nos. 10, 11; and Metz (1971) 270. Although a documented royal stop at Breitungen by Henry III in 1049 appears to be a twelfth-century fabrication of Eberhard of Fulda, Henry's route from Würzburg via Geltersheim to Pöhlde for Christmas certainly does not disallow such a visit. See Gockel (1984j) 229, 231 and E. Müller (1901) 80; cf. Kehr, intro. to *DH III* 24.

[138] Patze (1962) 31–4.   [139] See Hörle (1960) 32–3, 40–4.

[140] *DDO I* 230–2. For the northern section of Otto's trip through Thuringia, see Patze (1962) 36–7 no. 22.   [141] BO 239b.   [142] Gockel (1984b) 73 and 77–81.

[143] *DH IV* 386.

Mühlhausen on his way to Bamberg and Frankfurt,[144] Henry II stopped in December 1017 at Gottern,[145] where Hersfeld, the archbishopric of Mainz, and the collegiate chapter of St Victor in Mainz all held properties.[146] The king's accommodation and provisioning in Gottern could have fallen on any or, more probably, on all of the ecclesiastical institutions holding property there.[147] Although Gottern does not appear to have been situated on a major road, it was located on a regionally important road from Mühlhausen to Langensalza and very near the road from Allstedt and Sangerhausen via (Bad) Tennstedt and (Bad) Langensalza to Eisenach.[148] Also situated on this latter road was Hersfeld's property of (Groß-)Behringen,[149] where Henry IV and the royal troops made their camp in 1075 before entering battle with the Saxons and Thuringians, who were camped nearby at Lupnitz (Nägelstedt).[150]

From Erfurt a road led north through the Gera valley on the east bank of the river to Gebesee, where it forded the Gera, and then continued to the Unstrut, crossing it at Vehra (= German, *Fähre*, or English, ferry) about 5 km northeast of Gebesee. Just north of the Unstrut at Straußfurt the road forked into a northwestern and a northeastern branch. The former led via Greußen and Sonderhausen to Nordhausen, and the latter followed the valley of the Unstrut and the Helme via Weißensee and Kindelbrück to Sandershausen and southeastern Saxony.[151] Also from Gotha, a road led northeast via Molschleben and Fahner to Gebesee, where it joined the road from Erfurt.[152] This section of road from Gotha to Gebesee corresponded exactly to a section of Hersfeld's 'eastern road' or 'Wigbert's' road. Finally, another route left Erfurt and travelled in a northeasterly direction via Schloßvippach, Vogelsberg and Kölleda to the lower Unstrut.[153] From all of these roads there was easy access to various royal residences and strongholds at Tilleda, Wallhausen, Wiehe, Memleben and Allstedt.

These various roads corresponded almost exactly to those that the abbots and monks of Hersfeld used to travel to their numerous properties around Allstedt and along the Unstrut River, which the

---

[144] *DDH II* 372, 373, 374, 375, 376, 377, 378; BG 1909–17; Hirsch (1862–75) 3.60–5.
[145] *DDH II* 375, 376.   [146] Gockel (1984g) 172–7.   [147] Ibid. 168, 171, 177.
[148] Ibid. 170 and Hörle (1960) 29–30.
[149] *HUB* no. 38 [2] p. 73; Hörle (1960) 30, 50 (Table 2a no. 106).
[150] Lampert, *Annales s.a.* 1075 pp. 217, 214; Bruno, *Sax. Bellum* c. 46.
[151] Gockel (1984e) 149; Patze (1962) 36–7 no. 22.   [152] See Hörle (1960) 32, 41–2.
[153] Patze (1962) 37 no. 24.

monastery had acquired under Charlemagne. Consequently, the monastery owned properties on virtually all of these routes (see Maps 9 and 11).[154] With the increased use of Thuringia as a transit zone by the Ottonian and Salian kings, these properties as well were called upon to serve as stations along the royal itinerary. For instance, at Gebesee, which stood at the junction of the roads coming from Gotha and Erfurt, Hersfeld held its most extensive single property in Thuringia, comprising seventy *hubae* and forty-four *mansi*. It was strategically placed at the confluence of the Gera and the Unstrut and controlled the ford over the Gera.[155] Here we have one of the few documented royal stops on monastic estates. In March 1004, Henry II halted at Gebesee and issued a charter there on his way south through Thuringia from Wallhausen to Regensburg.[156] Undoubtedly, the king found his accommodation at the central manor of Hersfeld's large vill there.[157]

We also find royal visits to Hersfeld properties along the Unstrut. Both Henry III and Henry IV made documented stops at the former royal *civitas* of Wiehe. Hersfeld acquired Wiehe from Charlemagne, but exchanged it with King Henry in 933.[158] Later, in 998, Otto III granted the *civitas* of Wiehe and all its appurtenances to the royal monastery of Memleben but, in 1015, when Henry II granted Memleben to Hersfeld as a priory, Wiehe reverted to Hersfeld's possession.[159] Henry III visited Wiehe in 1053 and issued a charter for its owner, Hersfeld, during his visit.[160] He appears to have come from Merseburg, where he celebrated Easter and held a *Hoftag*.[161] In 1067, Henry IV stopped at Wiehe presumably on his way from Regensburg to Goslar to celebrate Easter.[162] Finally, Memleben, the former royal *Pfalz* and royal monastery, and after 1015 priory of Hersfeld, also figures in the itinerary of the Ottonian and Salian kings. As we have seen above, Memleben had been a favourite royal residence under Henry I and Otto I and, during its existence as an independent royal monastery, it had received several royals visits.[163] In 980, Otto II visited Memleben on his way from Wallhausen to Dornberg on the Saale.[164] Otto III stopped at Memleben twice, in

---

[154] Hörle (1960) 32, 41–2.
[155] *HUB* no. 38 [1] p. 71; Hörle (1960) 41, 49 (Table 1A no. 1); Gockel (1984e).
[156] *DH II* 66.   [157] Gockel (1984e) 152, 155.
[158] *HUB* no. 38 [1] p. 72; *HUB* no. 46 (= *DH I* 35).
[159] *DO III* 305; *DH II* 331.   [160] *DH III* 302.   [161] E. Müller (1901) 96.
[162] *DDH IV* 190, 191; Meyer von Knonau (1890–1909) 1.563 n. 27.
[163] See above, pp. 245–9.   [164] *DO II* 213.

August 987 coming from Frankfurt,[165] and in October 994 before setting out for the middle Rhine region and the royal *Pfalz* at Ingelheim.[166] After Henry II had returned Memleben to Hersfeld's possession in 1015 as a priory, Conrad II, travelling from Merseburg across Thuringia via Haina on the Nesse to the middle Rhine region, stopped for three days at the former royal monastery of Memleben.[167] No further royal visits to the priory of Memleben are known.

FULDA

The royal monastery of Fulda was located approximately 40 km south of Hersfeld on the east bank of the Fulda River. Like its northern monastic neighbour, Fulda also enjoyed an advantageous location in regard to early medieval travel and trade (see Map 10). Three ridge roads, leading in an easterly–northeasterly direction from the Rhine–Main area, crossed the Fulda River in the immediate vicinity of the monastery.[168] The first was an old trade route connecting Mainz with Thuringia.[169] It forded the river about 5 km north of Fulda at Kämmerzell and then continued via the Fulda vills of Hünfeld, Rasdorf and Geisa towards the Werra, which it forded either at Heimboldshausen or near Röhringshof, about 4 km west of Vacha.[170] The second road, designated as the *Ortesvecha* in Eigil's *Life of Saint Sturm*, crossed the river 4 km south of the monastery, at Bronnzell, and connected the Wetterau district with that of the Grabfeld.[171] The third and last early road joined the first road about 9 km west of Fulda, at the point where

---

[165] *DO III* 39. [166] *DO III* 152. [167] *DDK II* 194, 195, 196.

[168] In general, see Wehlt (1970) 234–5. For a detailed discussion and delineation of all the early roads around Fulda, see Görich (1955) esp. 74–83, where Görich, citing the previous literature, reviews the older scholarship on these roads and then re-evaluates and revises it on the basis of his own research.

[169] Eigil, *Vita S. Sturmi* 369 c. 7: '...viam, quae a Turingorum regione mercandi causa ad Magontiam pergentes ducit'.

[170] For the course of this road west of Kämmerzell, see Görich (1955) 76–8 and esp. his maps on 77 and at 80–1. For its delineation from Kämmerzell to the Werra, see Küther (1971) 5–6, 19, 28 and his map no. 1 for the exact location of the Werra ford. At Geisa, on the eastern stretch of this route, a road branched off to the east via Wiesenthal and Roßdorf to the Werra ford at Breitungen, and from this road another appears to have led to the ford at Bad Salzungen. See Gockel (1984j) 226.

[171] Eigil, *Vita S. Sturmi* 369 c. 8: '...ubi semita fuit quae antiquo vocabulo Ortessveca dicebatur...Cumque eum homo Dei interrogasset, unde venire; respondit se de Wedereiba venire...et statim vir saecularis ad Grabfeld per viam suam pergere coepit.' The eastern and southeastern extensions of this road appear to have led via Hilders to Meiningen (with Rohr – royal *Pfalz* and Fulda vill – nearby) and via Lütter or Dietges to Steinach or (Bad) Neustadt (royal *Pfalz* of Salz) on the Frankish Saale River. See Görich (1955) 80–1 (map).

it turned north towards Kämmerzell. This last road, on the other hand, continued due east towards Fulda, where it crossed the river over an early wooden bridge, which was later rebuilt in stone and called the 'long bridge'. Designated the 'semita antiqua' east of the river, this road continued east a short way, crossed the main north–south road to Saxony, and then continued northeast to rejoin the old Mainz–Thuringian trade route.[172] This road's local importance to Fulda was significant. It diverted all local traffic to the monastery by connecting it with the main trade route to Thuringia as well as with one of the strands of the 'short Hessian' road further west (by the Taufstein).[173] The importance of this road undoubtedly increased after 1019, when Fulda obtained the rights to hold a market, coin money and collect tolls and all proceeds from those rights.[174] Not only did Fulda enjoy an advantageous position between Thuringia and the central Rhineland by virtue of these roads, but it was also located on the major north–south road connecting Würzburg and Bavaria to Saxony via Fulda and Hersfeld.[175] In addition, the Fulda River was navigable up to Fulda and thus provided another north–south artery of travel.[176]

Considering Fulda's favourable location, its prestige and the reverence given to its founder, St Boniface, it is not surprising that kings, emperors and popes visited it.[177] In fact, unlike most royal monasteries, Fulda, with its relatively constant history of royal visits under the Carolingian, Ottonian and Salian kings, even attained a new and increased significance under the Hohenstaufen kings which lasted until the fourteenth century.[178] On the other

---

[172] Wehlt (1970) 234–5; Görich (1955) 76–8, 85–7. In my brief description of these roads, I have refrained from giving the roads specific names to avoid a general confusion that exists in the literature. In a seminal article, Görich (1955) provided a comprehensive treatment of the roads around Fulda and addressed many of the problems of the previous literature. Görich (1952) 481–2 n. 2 has succinctly summarized his findings regarding these early medieval roads in Hesse.

[173] Gockel (1983a) 2–3; Wehlt (1970) 235; and Görich (1955) 76–9.

[174] *DH II* 413; Görich (1955) 85–7.

[175] For the course of this road see above, pp. 240, 255. One strand of this north–south road forded the Fulda River at Wegfurth, where Fulda held a central manor of a larger multiple estate. Thus, the monastery must have controlled this important ford. See *TAF* c. 43 nos. 32, 44. On Fulda's extensive holdings in Hesse and western Thuringia in regard to these roads, see also Hussong (1986) 211–15.   [176] Eigil c. 5.

[177] Wehlt (1970) 251.

[178] Ibid. 241–50. Just prior to this newly attained significance under the Hohenstaufen, there is a noticeable gap during the Investiture Struggle and the Saxon uprisings (1066–1126), when Fulda has only one recorded visit (in 1014).

hand, we have no source for Fulda that provides us with anything like the detail that Lampert, for instance, gives for Hersfeld in the Salian period. In addition, the seemingly endless forging activity in the mid-twelfth century by the Fulda monk Eberhard injected chaos into the extant charters and land registers of Fulda, and these formerly valid sources must always be used and interpreted with utmost caution. Consequently, our record of documented royal visits in Fulda does not compare in number to what one would expect. Although reasonable (if not certain) conjectures based on the royal itinerary significantly supplement the documented visits, it is very difficult to press this evidence too hard owing to the great number of roads used by the royal court when travelling through Hesse and Thuringia and to large gaps in the known royal itinerary. Thus, as with Hersfeld, one gets at best a diminished view of Fulda's importance as a stopping place on the royal *iter*.

The first Saxon king, Henry I, has two known visits to Fulda, both specified as *orationis causa*.[179] The second of these visits resulted in a charter which, although issued at Wallhausen and not at Fulda, was written for Fulda and contains evidence of a visit made to Fulda shortly before. Henry's predecessor, Conrad I, had celebrated Easter there in 912 and designated the monastery as his burial site.[180] Our next documented royal visitor to Fulda was Otto II. After celebrating the feast of Pentecost at Frankfurt in May 975, the king stopped at Fulda on 27 May *en route* to Weimar in Thuringia.[181] Almost exactly two years later, Otto II appears to have halted again at Fulda on his way from the middle Rhine region to Saxony.[182] The next recorded visit of a king at Fulda ranks as one of the most glorious. In May of 1020, Henry II came to Fulda from Bamberg accompanied by Pope Benedict VIII and a large retinue. They spent at least three days at Fulda, during which time the Pope said a public mass at the altar of St Boniface and Henry issued two charters.[183] It could also have been at Fulda, if not earlier at Bamberg, that Henry had the *Ottonianum* of Otto

---

179 *DDH I* 1 (3 April 920), 4 (22 June 922): '…qualiter nos ad venerabile coenobium quod dicitur Fulta causa orationis venientes'. See Wehlt (1970) 238 and Hussong (1986) 241–5. 180 *DDK I* 6, 7; *Cont. Reg. s.a.* 919; Wehlt (1970) 238.

181 *DDO II* 103, 104.

182 *DO II* 160; Wehlt (1970) 238–9. The king was in Diedenhofen (near Thionville north of Metz) on the Moselle River in early May. After his stop at Fulda (27 May) he is next witnessed on 30 July in Magdeburg.

183 *BG* 1962a–1970; *Mariani Scotti Chronicon s.a.* 1020; *Annales Necrologici Fuldenses s.a.* 1020; *DDH II* 428, 429; Wehlt (1970) 239.

I (*DO I* 275) renewed and extended to include the commendation of Fulda and Bamberg to papal protection.[184] While it is not possible without further evidence to determine whether the renewed *Ottonianum* was issued at Bamberg or at Fulda, if indeed the *Ottonianum* was renewed at Fulda, then its extensive witness list of ecclesiastical and secular dignitaries would give some insight into the size and the composition of the retinue that accompanied Henry II and the Pope to Fulda.[185] Benedict departed from Fulda on his journey back to Rome and Henry II, with his retinue, travelled north and east to Saxony, probably via Hersfeld and then to Kaufungen, where we find him on 22 May.[186] Later, the first Salian king, Conrad II, came to Fulda in 1025 on his way from Saxony to Bavaria (Augsburg) and granted the monastery a small county, Netra, in the Ringgau south of Eschwege, an area in which Fulda held other properties.[187] This occurred during his first royal progression through the realm following his election, when he visited all the major regions or *regna* of his realm as well as the major churches and royal monasteries.

In addition to these visits, specific aspects of the royal itinerary allow us to assume with good reason at least another nine royal stops at Fulda. In 948, after a church synod in Trier, Otto I's chaplain Liudolf led the visiting papal legate Marin to Otto's court in Saxony. During his stay, presumably on 1 November, Marin consecrated the newly completed monastic church at Fulda, which Abbot Hadamar had had erected with splendour to replace the church consumed by fire in 937.[188] Although it cannot be proven, it appears almost certain that Otto himself also would have been present at the consecration of such an important royal monastery, especially when one considers that his honoured guest performed the consecration, and that Abbot Hadamar was a trusted supporter of the king.[189] Several factors indicate that Henry II most probably visited Fulda in December 1012.[190] One of Eberhard's forged Fulda charters places Henry at the monastery on 16 December

[184] *DH II* 427; BG 1968; Wehlt (1970) 239.
[185] For a similar charter issued at Kaufungen in 1015 (*DH II* 335) that also provides valuable insights into the size of the group of dignitaries that travelled with the king on certain occasions, see K. Heinemeyer (1971) 174–6 and above, Chapter 6, p. 225.
[186] *DDH II* 429, 430.
[187] Wipo, *Gesta Chuonradi* c. 6; *DK II* 23; *Vita Bardonis Maior* c. 7 pp. 325–6. On Netra, see Hoffmann (1990) 394–5.   [188] Thietmar 2 c. 42; Widukind 2 c. 38.
[189] Flodoard *s.a.* 948, p. 120; Köpke and Dümmler (1876) 166 n. 1; Wehlt (1970) 238, 274–7, cf. Hussong (1986) 254–5.   [190] Wehlt (1970) 239.

1012.[191] Not only does this placement fit in well with Henry's itinerary in 1012 – he was in Mainz at the beginning of December and celebrated Christmas at Pöhlde[192] – but Eberhard's forgery contains other elements from an authentic charter of Henry II, and the king did issue a valid charter for Fulda on 29 December while at Pöhlde.[193] Henry III came to Fulda in December 1047.[194] The king celebrated Christmas at Pöhlde and then travelled to Ulm via Würzburg. He almost certainly used the north–south road via Hersfeld and Fulda to Würzburg. Moreover, during the same time the king named Egbert as abbot of Fulda to replace Rohing, who had died on 29 November. Considering Henry's most logical route, this installation probably took place in the monastery.[195] In addition, Henry III's itinerary easily points to the likelihood of three further visits to Fulda. In July/August 1040 Henry travelled from Eschwege, probably via Hersfeld, to Regensburg. Presuming a stop at Hersfeld for the consecration of the new crypt, Henry had two major routes at his disposal for the trip to Regensburg; either via Fulda and Würzburg, or southeast along the Werra. A similar situation existed in 1051 when the king travelled from Kaufungen to Nuremberg.[196] And finally, in 1056, coming from the Rhineland, Henry III stopped in the Wetterau, at the Fulda vill of Berstadt, on his way to Goslar and the hunting residence at Bodfeld. Since Berstadt is located on the 'short Hessian' road before the road to Fulda branches off it, however, one can only conjecture whether the king travelled through Fulda, or over the 'short Hessian' road via Hersfeld and on to Saxony. On the basis of a charter which the king issued for the monastery of Fulda while at Bodfeld, however, it is possible that Henry negotiated the provisions of the charter while at Fulda on the trip through Hesse.[197] Indeed, he could have stopped at both Fulda and Hersfeld. Even were one to view the charter as a 'thank you' or some kind of compensation for monastic hospitality, since Fulda had a sizeable vill at Berstadt – where the king did indeed stop – the monastery might have received such a reward regardless of

---

[191] *DH II* 518.   [192] BG 1764d, 1767a.
[193] *DH II* 253; Franke (1987) 105 n. 260.   [194] Wehlt (1970) 240.
[195] *Ann. Alt. s.a.* 1048; Steindorff (1874–81) 2.30; E. Müller (1901) 68 n. 2; Stumpf no. 2343. Although the date of 30 December 1047 cannot be exact, a forgery bearing that date issued for Margrave Frederick of Saxony may also correspond to an actual visit.
[196] See Wehlt (1970) 152–3; *DDH III* 63, 271–4; and E. Müller (1901) 27–8, 89–90.
[197] *DH III* 380; E. Müller (1901) 117 (with n. 4) to 118.

whether the king had taken hospitality at the monastery or on one of its properties.

Where the details of the *iter* of Henry IV allow us to make any reasonable inferences, we find at least three possible instances of the king stopping at Fulda. During his regency, in the winter of 1060, Henry and the royal retinue, led by Henry's mother and regent, Empress Agnes, appear to have stopped at Fulda *en route* from Bamberg to Halberstadt and personally installed the monk, Widerad, as abbot, replacing Abbot Siegfried, who had recently acquired the archbishopric of Mainz.[198] Later, we find Henry IV travelling the road south from Hersfeld to Würzburg, on which Fulda was a logical and customary stopping point, both in 1066 and 1072.[199] Thus, although it is supported by even fewer sources than was the case for Hersfeld, Fulda nevertheless appears to have had a consistent, although sporadically reported, history of providing the royal retinue with accommodation on its journeys through Hesse.

Other evidence from the late tenth and early eleventh centuries, indeed, supports this claim. Both literary and archaeological evidence complement and confirm each other to demonstrate that a complex of rooms existed at Fulda designated for the accommodation of the king and his immediate retinue at least by the late tenth century. These were integrated topographically into the overall structure of the monastery and its church as a part of a large east atrium added onto the basilica under Abbot Werner (968–82).[200] Two royal chapels, recorded in contemporary sources, were connected with this royal residential complex. A late tenth-century sacramentary from Fulda mentions a royal chapel dedicated to Saints Paul and Barnabas among the places to pray

---

[198] *Ann. Alt. s.a.* 1060 p. 55; Meyer von Knonau (1890–1909) 1.175; Wehlt (1970) 154; BS 188.

[199] 1066: *DDH IV* 179, 180; Lampert, *Annales s.a.* 1066 p. 103; Meyer von Knonau (1890–1909) 1.525; Wehlt (1970) 153. 1072: Lampert, *Libelli s.a.* 1072 p. 354; Lampert, *Annales s.a.* 1072 p. 139; Meyer von Knonau (1890–1909) 2.173 n. 107; Wehlt (1970) 154.

[200] Concerning the literary and archaeological evidence indicating the existence of royal residential rooms at Fulda and other rooms specifically used for the liturgical display of kingship, which together probably constituted a royal *Pfalz*, see: Hahn (1954); Meyer-Barkhausen (1956) 32–8, (1958), (1960); Wehlt (1970) 253–6; and Streich (1984) 59–63, who provides an excellent summary and analysis of the previous research. Hussong (1986) 292–8 also reviews this literary and archaeological evidence, but remains sceptical of it owing to his conviction – based solely on documented stops and not on the totality of the itinerary and royal relations – that the Ottonian kings did not visit Fulda frequently.

during prayer-rounds in the monastery,[201] and an old inscription, known in the early seventeenth century, records the dedication in 973 of a second royal chapel (*regale sacellum*) to John the Baptist by Bishop Udalrich of Augsburg (923–73).[202] The latter chapel appears to have been located in the easternmost choir of the double-choired apsis on the second floor of the east atrium, whereas the other royal chapel may have been located opposite it in the western choir.[203] Moreover, when describing the visit of Henry II and Pope Benedict VIII to Fulda in 1020, the *Annales Necrologici Fuldenses* referred to the royal *Pfalz* there, stating that the Pope, after he had performed the Mass at the altar of St Boniface, proceeded to the throne room (*arces Romani imperii*) and gave his blessing to all present there.[204]

The archaeological excavations of the site have uncovered remains of the Ottonian east atrium at Fulda, and the analysis and interpretation of these findings, especially when compared to other similar Ottonian structures, strongly support the existence of a royal palace or palace-like complex at Fulda. This appears to have been located in the two-storey northern wing of the east atrium, which was twice as wide as the southern wing, and also in the wide eastern wing on both sides flanking the double choir. The building seems to have contained not only the royal chapels and living apartments, but also official rooms. These included a formal reception hall for the royal *adventus* and for the symbolic and liturgical display of kingship, a site for a court of justice and other legal proceedings and, probably, a throne room (*arces Romani imperii*).[205] Presumably, whatever arrangements had existed previously for the accommodation of the king, they had been destroyed or severely damaged in the fire of 937. Although Abbot Hadamar had replaced and extended Fulda's sacral space with the elaborate new church consecrated in 948,[206] a new space for royal

---

[201] *Sacramentium Fuldense Saeculi X*, 377 no. 2846. This sacramentary has consistently been dated to around 975. See Meyer-Barkhausen (1956) 32 n. 32.

[202] *Fuldensium Antiquitatum Libri IIII*, p. 123: 'Dedicatum est hoc regale sacellum IIII. Non. Jun. a beato Uodalrico Augustae civitatis episcopo ... in honorem Christi domini sanctice baptistae Johannis rogatu reverendi abbatis Werinharii ...' A more accessible reprint of this dedication notice appears in the *Notae Dedicationum Fuldenses*.

[203] Concerning these chapels, see Meyer-Barkhausen (1956) 32–4, (1958) 34–5 with n. 134, (1960) 8 n. 15; and Streich (1984) 61–3.

[204] *Annales Necrologici Fuldenses s.a.* 1020: 'Sicque aliis secundum ordinem finitis omnibusque ad hunc locum pertinentibus sibi adsignatis, arces Romani imperii requisivit cunctosque istic morantes, apostolica benedictione data, vivo et vero Domino commendavit.' [205] See n. 200 above. [206] Hussong (1986) 255–6.

accommodation and the display of kingship appears to have been constructed first along with the new atrium under Abbot Werner (968–82).[207] Considering the monastery's close ties to the Ottonians, its prestige, and its location, the construction of a building or complex of rooms for the use of the king and his retinue is highly appropriate and not at all surprising.

The royal monastery of Fulda, in common with its Hessian neighbour Hersfeld, also had to provide the king and royal retinue with provisions and accommodation beyond the boundaries of the monastery on its many estates and properties throughout Hesse and Thuringia (see Map 11).[208] Fulda owned numerous properties in central Hesse along branches of the 'short' as well as the 'long Hessian' roads. Besides a large conglomeration of properties comprising the monastery and the area immediately around it, Fulda held a dense concentration of properties in the Wetterau district of Hesse.[209] Although the sources remain silent until the later period of our investigation, we do find documented visits by the royal retinue to two properties of Fulda in Hesse. One of these, Berstadt, was the administrative centre of an extensive domain of Fulda in the Wetterau.[210] Obviously, it owed its place in the royal itinerary to its very advantageous location. Not only was Berstadt located approximately 45 km from Frankfurt on one of the branches of the 'short Hessian' road connecting the Rhine–Main basin with Thuringia, but it was also situated on this road south of the points where the road to Fulda and the connector road to the 'long Hessian' route branched off.[211] Consequently, Berstadt could be used as a stopping point when travelling any of these three routes and was most probably used more frequently by the Ottonian and Salian kings than our four attested royal stops indicate. Henry III issued two charters at Berstadt in 1056 when travelling from Worms to Goslar, possibly via Fulda,[212] and his successor, Henry IV, made three visits there. The first took place on 12 August 1068 *en route* from Goslar to Frankfurt(?);[213] the second on 7 June 1070 when the king travelled from Merseburg to Mainz, most probably via Hersfeld on the 'short Hessian' road;[214]

[207] Wehlt (1970) 253 and Streich (1984) 63.   [208] See above, pp. 261–5.

[209] Kropat (1965) 122–34 and Büttner (1989).

[210] *TAF* c. 43 no. 37. Gockel (1983a) 5–7 gives a convenient summary and history of Fulda's possessions in Berstadt.   [211] Gockel (1983a) 2–3.

[212] *DDH III* 376, 377; Steindorff (1874–81) 2.350; Gockel (1983a) 4.

[213] *DH IV* 208; Meyer von Knonau (1890–1909) 1.597–8; Gockel (1983a) 5.

[214] *DH IV* 232; Meyer von Knonau (1890–1909) 2.8; Gockel (1983a) 5; Wehlt (1970) 153.

and the third, in August of 1073 after Henry IV's flight from the Harzburg, which brought the king via Eschwege to Hersfeld and again along the 'short Hessian' road through Grebenau (Kappel) to Berstadt and then on to Trebur.[215]

Approximately 25 km south–southeast of Berstadt and 30 km northeast of Frankfurt one finds Rommelshausen, the other property of Fulda in the Wetterau, regarding which we have a documented royal visit.[216] Rommelshausen was situated on the main high road running in a northeasterly direction through the Wetterau along the watershed between the Kinzig and the Nidder Rivers. Thus, it was located before the junctions of the three main roads crossing the Fulda River near Fulda and it had an auxiliary connection to the 'short' and 'long Hessian' roads via Echzell, Hungen and Grünberg.[217] Henry IV stopped at Rommelshausen in 1074, apparently when travelling a branch of the 'long Hessian' road from Fritzlar to Worms.[218] Thus, in spite of the small number of documented royal visits to Berstadt and Rommelshausen, the particular location of these Fulda properties places one or the other of them on virtually every major road travelled by the Saxon and Salian kings through Hesse, and correspondingly increases the likelihood of their use as royal stopping places.

Unfortunately, our information for northern Hesse is even more vague. There are indications, however, that properties of Fulda between Gießen and Kirchhain on the 'long Hessian' road may have contributed to the king's upkeep in this area, but the evidence allows little more than a conjecture. In November 920, King Henry I held a *regale placitum* at (Groß)seelheim, where Fulda possessed several properties and, by the early eleventh century, a substantial vill.[219] Likewise, Fulda, several other ecclesiastical institutions, and the Salian house all appear to have held property

---

[215] *DH IV* 262b (esp. von Gladiss's introduction); Meyer von Knonau (1890–1909) 2.54–5; Lampert, *Annales s.a.* 1073 p. 156; Gockel (1983a) 5.

[216] Concerning Fulda's possessions at Rommelshausen, see *CDF* 313 no. 677, 369 no. 762 and Kropat (1965) 123–4.   [217] Kropat (1965) 7 and Görich (1955) 80–1 (map).

[218] *DH IV* 272; Meyer von Knonau (1890–1909) 2.335–6, where the author (p. 335 n. 37) argues in addition that the royal visit at Berstadt in August 1073 should be placed in 1074 between those at Fritzlar and Rommelshausen. Cf. von Gladiss's introduction to *DH IV* 262b and Gockel (1983a) 5.

[219] *DH I* 2; BO 1b, 2. Concerning Fulda's holdings in (Groß)seelheim, see *FUB* nos. 116, 427, 428 and *TAF* c. 6 nos. 12, 31, 150, c. 43 nos. 28, 31, 32. The monastery also had sizeable holdings in Roßdorf (*c.* 5 km SW): see *TAF* c. 6 nos. 2, 11, 17, 19, 30, 36, 42, 59, 60, 100 and 142.

around Ebsdorf,[220] where Henry III stopped in 1054 and Henry IV in 1057 and 1066.[221] Both (Groß)seelheim and Ebsdorf are conveniently located halting points for the royal *iter* on the 'long Hessian' road about a day's march from Treysa and two days from Fritzlar. Although we have no information about the king's accommodation or upkeep in these locations, considering the known circumstances of property holdings in the area and the relatively frequent use of this route,[222] one might suppose that, as in some areas of Saxony, the king's *servitium* was drawn from the various royal and church properties at his immediate disposal.[223]

Fulda also possessed several sizeable and important properties along the Hessian–Thuringian border and in western Thuringia that appear sporadically or in isolated instances in the royal itinerary. One such property, Ermschwerd, located on the Werra River between the important fords at Hedemünden and Witzenhausen, was the administrative centre of a group of Fulda's estates.[224] As in many locations in this area of the former Frankish–Saxon–Thuringian border, as well as in other areas of Hesse, royal, church and private property existed side by side. Archaeological evidence has shown that a Frankish fortress (presumably with a supporting agricultural manor) existed at Ermschwerd, which dated to the mid–eighth century and apparently had the task of securing the important river fords and highland passes of the roads leading from Frankish territory into Saxony. In the early ninth century, Fulda received a large grant at Ermschwerd from the indigenous nobility,[225] which apparently formed the core of its extensive holdings there in the early eleventh century.[226] Although Ermschwerd hardly seems to have

---

[220] For Fulda's possessions in Ebsdorf, see *FUB* nos. 113, 116, 118, 422 and *TAF* c. 6 nos. 9, 11, 16, 25. Concerning the royal possessions and those of Hersfeld, Kaufungen and the collegiate chapter of St Stephen's at Mainz in and around Ebsdorf, see the summary provided by Gockel (1983d) 80–1.

[221] *DH III* 321; *DDH IV* 29, 182. The first two of these visits appear to have occurred while using the 'long Hessian' road from the middle Rhine region to Saxony and the last during a west–east journey from Lotharingia to Thuringia.

[222] See above at n. 133. For the general course of the 'long Hessian' road, see Patze (1962) 39 no. 26 and Metz (1971) 284–5.

[223] A similar situation may have existed further south in Hesse at Rommelshausen, where Fulda owned property that was immediately bordered by a large royal vill. See Kropat (1965) 187.

[224] Concerning Ermschwerd, see K. Heinemeyer (1971) 218–36 esp. 220–3, 235–6 and (1983a). [225] *TAF* c. 38 no. 40.

[226] *TAF* c. 43 no. 60. By the late twelfth or thirteenth century, Fulda was the sole possessor of an undivided property complex there.

been a regular stopping point on the royal itinerary,[227] Henry II and a sizeable retinue came there from Grone in early December 1022 and decided a case tried before the royal court of justice.[228] Among those present were one archbishop, three bishops, two counts, a relative of another count and many others. The *Vita Meinwerci* does not identify the exact site at Ermschwerd of this court process, nor does it offer any information about the accommodation of the retinue on this occasion. On the basis of the property holding at Ermschwerd, however, one must assume that the judicial procedure as well as the accommodation of the entourage occurred either at the former royal fortress and its supporting manor, or on the central manor of the Fulda vill. Even if royal and monastic property still existed side by side at Ermschwerd in 1022, other similar situations would indicate an interworking of all properties to accommodate and provision the king and his court. Whatever the case, it appears likely on this occasion that Fulda either contributed to the royal upkeep or bore the entire burden itself.[229]

Further south along the Werra, in an area of extensive Fulda property holdings, we encounter Gerstungen, one of Fulda's largest and most important properties.[230] It was the administrative centre of a large domain of Fulda in the early eleventh century, comprising five *territoria*, sixty *hubae* of *liti* or semi-free tenants, eighty-two *hubae* of serfs, 173 Slavs, forty-three *coloni* or free tenants, seven mills and two churches.[231] At Gerstungen, Fulda controlled an important and strategic ford over the Werra River on the 'short Hessian' road from Mainz to Erfurt. Gerstungen also lay on a main north–south road along the Werra. Owing to its location, the Saxon and Salian kings must have passed through Gerstungen on numerous occasions. In addition, during the Saxon wars its location on the Hessian–Thuringian border brought it additional significance as an important staging area for the royal army and the site of various negotiations between the warring factions.[232] Henry IV issued a charter there on 18 August 1065 on his way from Trebur to Goslar,[233] and in February 1074, the king travelled from Breitenbach on the Fulda to Gerstungen to sign a

---

[227] Metz (1971) 285.   [228] *Vita Meinwerci* c. 173 p. 96; BG no. 2031a.

[229] See K. Heinemeyer (1971) 222–3 and (1983a) 93–6.

[230] Concerning Gerstungen, see Gockel (1984f) 164.   [231] *TAF* c. 43 no. 23.

[232] Gockel (1984f) 156, 159–61, 166.

[233] *DH IV* 164; Meyer von Knonau (1890–1909) 1.466.

peace agreement with the rebellious Saxons.[234] Later the next year, Henry IV again came to Gerstungen in October for at least three days, when it functioned as the point of assembly for the royal army.[235] On another occasion, in 1073, Gerstungen served as the site of a peace council between the noble vassals of the king and the Saxon princes.[236] On all of these occasions, and whenever else the royal court may have stopped at Gerstungen travelling to or from Thuringia and the Rhineland, the royal monastery of Fulda must have provided the accommodation and upkeep for the king and at least his immediate retinue on the central manor of the vill.[237] On the basis of the money rents at Gerstungen mentioned in the eleventh-century Fulda land register and the triangular form of the market-place there, which corresponds to other early Hessian and Thuringian markets, it is likely that an early market existed at Gerstungen.[238] In addition, the two enfeoffed *oppidia* mentioned in the Gerstungen entry of the Fulda land register may designate a market-place or a river port.[239] Thus, as in many other places frequented by the court and situated on regularly travelled royal roads, Gerstungen also appears to have had some kind of market in the early eleventh century, which may have served in part to facilitate the upkeep and other needs of the royal retinue.[240]

Northeast of Gerstungen in western Thuringia, between Eisenach, Gotha and (Bad) Langensalza, was another area of extensive properties belonging to the royal monastery of Fulda.[241] In this region the monastery held three of its largest vills, centred on (Bad) Langensalza, (Großen)Lupnitz and Haina.[242] Since 1014, Fulda had possessed the royal ban over the forests and hunting in an extensive area, whose eastern reaches encompassed two of these vills, Lupnitz and Haina.[243] One of these, Haina, appears twice in

---

[234] Lampert, *Annales s.a.* 1074 pp. 180, 212 (at *a.* 1075); *Annales Patherbrunn.* p. 95; Meyer von Knonau (1890–1909) 2.326.

[235] Lampert, *Annales s.a.* 1075 pp. 229–30, 234–5 (22 October 1075); Meyer von Knonau (1890–1909) 2.519, 527–9, 830–2.

[236] 20 October 1073. Lampert, *Annales s.a.* 1073 pp. 162–6; Meyer von Knonau (1890–1909) 2.271, 286–8, 820–2. See also Gockel (1984f) 161–3 on assemblies in 1084 and 1085.   [237] Gockel (1984f) 159.

[238] *TAF* c. 43 no. 23; Hess (1974a) 313, 326–7.

[239] *TAF* c. 42 no. 23; Metz (1971) 286, with support from Schlesinger (1954) 119–21.

[240] Metz (1971) 279–86 esp. 284–6.

[241] Hersfeld, as well as Fulda, owned a large amount of property in this area. See Küther (1974) 189–99 with map (p. 195).   [242] *TAF* c. 43 nos. 11, 12, 18.

[243] *DH II* 327. The area of the ban extended from just north of Gerstungen along the Werra River to just south of Mihla, east to modern-day Route 84 near Reichenbach,

the royal itinerary.[244] Haina was located on an auxiliary branch of the main route from the middle Rhine to eastern Thuringia and, in addition, it was accessible through tributary roads to traffic coming from Mühlhausen, north from the Unstrut valley and the eastern Harz region, and from Bavaria and Hesse through the Thuringian Forest via the Rennsteig.[245] Like Gerstungen, Haina was the administrative centre of a large group of estates and dependent populations, and it appears to have been the centre of Fulda's domains here already in the late tenth century. It consisted of six *territoria* with seventy-five *hubae* held by semi-free tenants, 133 *hubae* held by serfs, twenty-seven free tenants and 120 Slavs. In addition, there were six mills and eight chapels belonging to the abbatial court there, and a workshop employing twelve shield-makers. A later land register from the twelfth century lists, in addition, fishermen, masons, fullers and cooks at Haina.[246] Haina also resembled Gerstungen in that it appears to have had one of the early markets in Thuringia.[247] Consequently, Haina was large enough and well-equipped to provide royal accommodation. In the summer of 1033, Conrad II visited there and issued a charter on his journey across Thuringia from Memleben to the middle Rhineland,[248] and Henry IV came to Haina in December 1069 on a journey from Allstedt to Freising.[249] During these visits and any others that may have occurred, the king and his entourage apparently resided in the *curia abbatis* mentioned in the eleventh-century land register, and the burden of the royal *hospitium* fell upon the royal monastery of Fulda.[250]

Before leaving Fulda's Thuringian properties, the monastery's holdings at Rohr near Meiningen deserve mention.[251] Both the king and the monastery of Fulda appear to have had sizeable holdings in and around Rohr from the early ninth century.[252] By 824 a nunnery existed there that was founded on former royal

---

then southeast to the Krahnberg near Gotha. From here the boundary ran west to Sättelstädt and then southwest beyond Ruhla, from where it partly followed the old Rennsteig in a northwesterly direction back to the Werra. See Küther (1974) 191 (map), 202 and Knaus (1937) 56.   [244] Gockel (1984h).

[245] Gockel (1984h) 179–81. For a map delineating some of these roads (on which, unfortunately, Haina is not designated!), see Küther (1974) 191.

[246] *TAF* c. 43 no. 12. See Gockel (1984h) 185–8, 194.

[247] Hess (1963) 33 n. 88 and Gockel (1984h) 181.   [248] *DK II* 197; BA no. 204.

[249] *DH IV* 228; Meyer von Knonau (1890–1909) 1.630.

[250] Gockel (1984h) 184–8.

[251] In general concerning Rohr, see Patze (1968) 352–3.

[252] Ibid. *DLD* 135; *CDF* nos. 323, 453, 577 and 598.

property and appears to have been a priory of Fulda.[253] In 975, Otto II gave a church and a royal manor at Rohr to the church of St Peter at Aschaffenburg.[254] Fulda's eleventh-century land register indicates that the monastery still held properties and collected rents from a large and socially diverse population at Rohr. Fulda's dependent populations at Rohr included eight *lidi* or half-free tenants, seventy-eight serfs, eighteen Saxons, seventy-five Slavs, thirty *coloni* or hereditary tenants and thirty-nine *tributorii* or rent-paying tenants.[255] Rohr possessed an advantageous location near the junction that connected the numerous routes out of Saxony and Thuringia to the main roads into the Rhine–Main basin, and into Bavaria via Bamberg to Regensburg or Augsburg.[256] The five documented royal visits to Rohr all occurred under the Saxon kings and appear to have been influenced by Rohr's favourable location. Three took place in the normal transit of the court from one region to another[257] and twice, probably owing to its somewhat central location, Rohr was the site of royal assemblies. In 959, Otto I came from Saxony to Rohr for an assembly with the Bavarian princes and spent at least five days there.[258] Afterwards he returned immediately to Saxony. Later, on 29 June 975, Rohr was the site of a large assembly attended by the regency government of Otto III and many princes from all parts and territories of the empire. At this royal assembly, Henry the Quarrelsome, Duke of Bavaria, returned the young Otto III, whom he had abducted, to the empresses Adelheid and Theophanu, his grandmother and mother, and preliminary considerations were made on the question of Henry's now questionable position as Duke of Bavaria.[259] Thus, under the Ottonian kings, who did not spend much time in Bavaria (except at Regensburg), Rohr, owing to its somewhat centralized location in eastern Franconia, appears to have served as a site for assemblies that dealt with matters particularly concerning Bavaria.[260] Since

---

[253] See *CDF* nos. 452 and 598; *DLD* 135; and Uhlirz (1954) 430–1.

[254] *DO II* 98: 'unam ecclesiam et unum curtem cum integris eorum pertinenciis in villa Rora sitas in orientali Francia'.   [255] *TAF* c. 13 no. 1 and c. 43 nos. 32 and 50.

[256] Rieckenberg (1941/1965) 59–60; Uhlirz (1954) 430–1.

[257] 11 August 926: *DH I* 10, BO 13; 7 June 941: *DO I* 40, BO 98, when Otto I must also have celebrated the Feast of Pentecost on 6 June – see Müller-Mertens (1980) 141; and 30 May 1003: *DH II* 51, BG 1544. In 941 Otto was travelling from the middle Rhine to Saxony and in 1003 Henry II was journeying from Saxony to Bavaria.

[258] *DDO I* 202, 203, 204 and BO 269, 270, 271, 272.

[259] *Ann. Qued. s.a.* 975 p. 66; Thietmar 4 c. 8 p. 140; BU 956q/2.

[260] See Rieckenberg (1941/1965) 59–60 and Müller-Mertens (1980) 140–1.

we have only these scattered references to Rohr in the sources, and no detailed study of the pattern of property holding there has been completed to date,[261] we can only speculate about the king's upkeep when the court was present at Rohr. However, the meagre evidence we do have regarding property holding in the area suggests at least that the provisioning of the royal court at Rohr may have been, as in other places, a joint function of royal property and church property. In spite of a sizeable amount of royal property in the area,[262] the continuity of Fulda's holdings and the large dependent populations paying duties both to the abbot and the brothers of the monastery in the eleventh century prompt one to consider that Fulda may well have contributed to the king's upkeep at Rohr and to his travels throughout this area.[263]

The evidence and indications offered about the accommodation and upkeep of the king and his retinue both at Fulda and on various of the monastery's properties receive additional support from several sources. These specify dues in kind and the tithes (*decimationes*) paid from numerous monastic properties to the porter of the monastery, who organized and administered the provision of food and shelter for visitors to the monastery, including royal visitors. A section of a Fulda land register begins as following: 'from Borsch seventy-six units (*modii*) are given to the *kunigesphuter*' (or *Königsfutter*).[264] Immediately following the entry for Borsch sixteen more properties appear with the amount they owed to *dez futar*.[265] Moreover, the following section of this land register contains the payments to this same debt (*ad hoc idem debitum*) from an additional sixteen properties, which formerly (*olim*) pertained to the incomes of the porter.[266] This land register (*TAF* c. 45) was transmitted by Eberhard of Fulda (*fl.* 1150) and

---

[261] A detailed analysis of Rohr's status as a royal *curtis* and/or a monastic property claiming royal visits is expected in the series, *Die deutschen Königspfalzen: Repertorium*.

[262] In general, the realm disposed of a large amount of property around Rohr, especially in and around Meiningen. Henry II granted much of this to the bishopric of Würzburg in 1008 (*DDH II* 174, 175) as partial compensation for territory it lost when he founded the bishopric of Bamberg. By 1020 this whole area and the roads traversing it were in the hands of royal churches. See Diefenbach (unpub. diss. 1952) 101–2.

[263] Uhlirz (1954) 431; and Metz (1971) 270–1 and (1978b) 70–1.

[264] *TAF* c. 45 no. 25 p. 131: 'De Borsaha LXXVI modii dantur ad kunigesphuter.'

[265] *TAF* c. 45 no. 25 p. 131. Section 25 of c. 45 also appears in its entirety in Metz (1976) 253.

[266] *TAF* c. 45 no. 26 p. 131. Metz (1976) 253 has also reproduced this section entirely.

has been dated to the early twelfth century.[267] But the wealth of the properties in sections 25 and 26 and the archaic German words (*dez futar, phortam*) suggest an earlier date, perhaps in the first half of the eleventh century.[268]

Another document, a charter of Abbot Erlolf from 1116, contains Erlolf's decree about a reduction of the income paid to the porter, obviously in response to pleas about the difficulty of paying the former dues.[269] It mentions far fewer properties than are contained in the two entries of the land register, but it does have six properties in common with it.[270] In addition, a charter forged by Eberhard in the name of Hatto I for the year 852 contains an authentic register of thirty-four properties pertaining to the monastic porter that appears to date from the eleventh century.[271] Here again numerous of the named properties overlap with those designated in Abbot Erlolf's charter of 1116.[272] The overlap of properties in the land registers contained in *TAF* c. 45 nos. 25 and 26 with those of c. 36 attest to the authenticity of the contents and give absolute confirmation that sixteen of the properties of c. 36 actually pertained to the office of the porter in the eleventh century. Moreover, the charter from 1116 documents that seven of these properties still paid dues to the porter's office in the early twelfth century, at a time when the monastery was impoverished in relation to its former holdings.[273]

The Old High German term 'kunigesphuter' and the close connection of sections 25 and 26 of *TAF* c. 45 present several difficulties. At face value one would assume that 'kunigesphuter' or *Königsfutter* merely referred to the old Frankish *fodrum*, a duty of providing fodder to feed the horses and pack animals of the king and his retinue.[274] The composition of the duties in section 25 – exclusively payments of grain – moreover, appears to support this

---

[267] Werner-Hasselbach (1942) 44–5.   [268] Metz (1976) 254.

[269] Schannat (1729), *Codex probationum* no. 52; Metz (1976) 254–5 provides the essential portions of this charter in a more accessible publication.

[270] Metz (1976) 211–12, 253 (with map) and Werner-Hasselbach (1942) n. 96, who confirmed the authenticity of the charter. The six properties appearing both in Erlolf's charter of 1116 and sections 25 and 26 of c. 45 are: Lauterbach, (Ober-)Aula, Wegfurt, Borsch, Spahl and Bimbach.

[271] *TAF* c. 36 pp. 66–7. For the dating, see Werner-Hasselbach (1942) 58–75 esp. 73–5 and Metz (1976) 211.

[272] For the properties overlapping in the three documents, see Werner-Hasselbach (1942) 72 and 73 n. 104.

[273] Ibid. Concerning the monastery's impoverishment in the mid- and late eleventh century, see ibid. 139–42.   [274] See Brühl (1959).

notion. But the structure and nature of the section immediately following it, section 26, suggest a very close connection to the previous section and probably an actual continuation of it.[275] Two particular indications of this are the 'ad hoc idem debitum' following one property's dues that does not have any apparent antecedent except the previous section, and the concluding sentence, 'Hec omnia olim ad Phortam pertinebant', which suggests that these properties formerly pertained to the porter's office in general and now pertained specifically to the 'kunigesphuter'.

If one accepts these indications that section 26 is a continuation of section 25, then another interpretation of the documents becomes possible. The tithes and payments from the individual properties and demesne land 'ad kunigesphuter' thus would no longer consist merely of grain fodder, but would also include the pigs, cloths or tunics, money rents (*uncias*) and sheep of section 26; in short, items for the full upkeep of the king and his retinue, not only of his horses. Seen in this light, the named payments appear to correspond to the *servitium regis*[276] of the monastic properties similar to those we have seen already in the mid-eleventh century at the royal monastery of Werden.[277] This Germanic term 'kunigesphuter' could possibly be an isolated instance outside of Italy of the Latinized *fodrum regis*, which the Ottonians instituted in Italy, in a form that corresponded not to the old Frankish *fodrum*, but to the concept of *servitium regis* in Germany.[278] Although to my knowledge we have no instances of the *fodrum regis* or *regale* in charters or documents from the regions of Germany where *servitium regis* or *regale* and later *küneges stiure* (royal tax) are used exclusively, the indications of the present documents appear so close to the Italian concept of *fodrum regis* that the possibility should at least be left open. In the light of the information presented regarding the royal upkeep and accommodation both at Fulda and on its properties, moreover, it hardly seems mere chance that the properties paying dues to the 'kunigesphuter' in section 25 and those paying similarly in section

[275] Werner-Hasselbach (1942) 42–5, 72–3 and Metz (1976) 211–12.
[276] Metz (1976) 211–12 assumes that the properties of both sections 25 and 26 apply to the 'kunigesphuter' and has pointed out the connection of these duties to the *servitium regis*.
[277] See above, Chapter 5, pp. 181–5.
[278] On the *fodrum regis* in Italy and its correspondence to the German *servitium regis*, see Brühl (1968) 445–6, 534–48; however cf. Fleckenstein's review of Brühl in *HZ* 212 (1971) 123.

26 were located in the three main areas – around Fulda itself, in the Wetterau, and in the Grabfeld, east of Fulda – where we have numerous documented royal visits or where, owing to the location of the properties, the likelihood of such stops is high.[279] The monastery itself was the site of many recorded visits and apparently many more unrecorded visits. Likewise, the properties in the Wetterau bordered on Fulda's ban-forest near Echzell[280] and included Berstadt, which has documentary evidence of stops made by Henry III and Henry IV, and which had a most advantageous location, accessible to a majority of the royal routes through Hesse.[281] The group of properties in the Grabfeld, although we have no records of stops at them by Saxon or Salian kings, were located on the main road from Fulda to Thuringia about one day's march from the monastery. This increases the likelihood that the royal retinue may have made overnight stops at or in the vicinity of these properties. Thus, known aspects of the royal *iter* with regard to Fulda appear to support the payments in sections 25 and 26 of *TAF* c. 45 for the royal upkeep both at the monastery and on monastic estates. Although these payments were apparently allocated to the office of the porter, who was charged with organizing the king's provisions and accommodation at the monastery, one must assume that the same dues could be used to support the king when he stopped at or near the various properties themselves.

HERSFELD AND FULDA: GRANTS OF SOVEREIGN RIGHTS

In order to evaluate fully the role played by these two powerful monasteries in the centre of the realm, it is instructive, at the risk of some repetition to review as a whole the various grants of sovereign rights which Hersfeld and Fulda received from the Ottonian and Salian kings. These grants document the enrichment of both monasteries through jurisdictional and income-producing rights and through participation in the economic development of Hesse and Thuringia. Such grants also often provided the foundation from which Hersfeld or Fulda could consolidate their existing territorial holdings or expand their dominion over new

---

[279] Metz (1976) 253 provides a map generally depicting the location of these three groups of properties.   [280] *DO I* 131 (19 January 951); Hussong (1985) 145–6.
[281] See above, pp. 272–3.

areas. While many of these grants were connected with Henry II's attempt to build up the central regions of the realm through the support of royal churches and monasteries and with the continuation of these plans under the early Salians, Fulda and Hersfeld had already begun to consolidate and expand their rights by means of earlier royal grants.

In 951, Otto I granted Fulda the *Wildbann* or the right to regulate hunting in a delineated area in the Wetterau,[282] which was an appurtenance of Fulda's manor at Echzell. This area lay near Fulda's domains around Berstadt and the old royal domains at Bingenheim and Dauerheim, which also appear to have come to Fulda in the ninth century.[283] The domain over which Fulda had the right to oversee the hunt included some property not owned by the monastery. This further strengthened Fulda's influence in the region and provided a corner-stone for the development of a monastic territory in the Wetterau, which Fulda continued to pursue until the twelfth century.[284] Later, in 980, Fulda acquired a hunting and 'forest' right from Otto II in the Bram Forest, a prescribed area – not all wooded – immediately to the northeast of the monastery comprising the watershed of the Haune River.[285] This grant not only gave the abbot of Fulda the right to regulate hunting in the Bram Forest, but also to oversee every other use of the 'forest', such as rights of pannage, gathering timber or clearing. Although Fulda already possessed the area included in the ban, it nevertheless enhanced Fulda's rights and provided it with a closed area of jurisdiction between the monastery itself and its holdings around Hünfeld and Rasdorf.[286]

In the early eleventh century, Henry II granted valuable concessions to Hersfeld and to Fulda in areas near the monasteries. These grants continued the consolidation of this area in monastic hands. In 1003, Hersfeld received the right to exclusive use, including the right of chase, of the Eherin Forest surrounding the monastery and bordering on Fulda's Bram Forest in the south.[287] With this grant all of the area between the two monasteries had in effect been brought under their control. Shortly after a brief visit

---

[282] *DO I* 131. On the legal concept of enforestation, that is, establishing a 'forest' right over an area, and its correlation with the *Wildbann*, or ban over hunting in the area, see Knaus (1936) 97–109, 113–18, (1937) 15–16.
[283] *FUB* no. 149 (with the introduction); Büttner (1989) 84.
[284] Knaus (1936) 118–27; Büttner (1989) 85–8.   [285] *DO II* 221.
[286] Knaus (1937) 11–16; Diefenbach (unpub. diss. 1952) 31; Hussong (1985) 145–6.
[287] *HUB* no. 76 (= *DH II* 51); Knaus (1937) 11–12.

to Fulda almost a decade later, in December 1012,[288] Henry II conceded to the monastery the sovereign rights in another large forest. By that date, the grant probably stood in conjunction with Henry's general plan to create a central core of 'royal' properties. The king gave the abbot of Fulda dominion over the Zundernhart Forest, which surrounded the monastery's core property on three sides and extended to the Rhön in the southeast and the Vogelsberg in the west.[289] The charter included the royal forest ban, that is, the right to exercise the king's legal jurisdiction over the forest, and to collect and enjoy all fines accruing from that jurisdiction, and it designated the specific boundaries of the grant, which began and ended on the boundaries of the Bram Forest, where Fulda already possessed the exclusive right of the chase.[290] The combination of Fulda's forest jurisdictions in the Bram and Zundernhart Forests with Fulda's property holdings at the monastery and in the surrounding area created a large complex of property and jurisdiction on the upper Fulda River, which was roughly 45 km in diameter with the monastery at its centre. In 1059, the monastery of Fulda received a further extension of its rights to the south, which was linked to these two previous 'forest' grants. The regency government under Empress Agnes granted Abbot Siegfried of Fulda the hunting ban or 'forest' rights over a large area bordering on the Zundernhart and the Bram Forests in the north and extending south to Fulda's properties in Hammelburg.[291] As was the case with the hunting ban of 951 near Echzell, this right extended over some areas not owned by Fulda. Thus, the charter contains the consent of the Bishop of Würzburg, of several counts, and of other owners of property in the designated area, who also agreed to allow the abbot of Fulda to hunt and fish on their private property. Once again Fulda received jurisdictional rights in areas linking its various properties. Moreover, it bears repeating that all of the areas in which Fulda received 'forest' rights had major royal roads running through them.

In conjunction with his planned consolidation and centralization of the royal domain, Henry II also granted Fulda and Hersfeld

---

[288] See at n. 193 above.

[289] *DH II* 253. On the grant of the Zundernhart Forest and its interlocking boundaries, see Knaus (1937) 36–46 and Diefenbach (unpub. diss. 1952) 104.   [290] *DO II* 221.

[291] *DH IV* 61. On Fulda's holdings at Hammelburg and its environs, see *FUB* no. 77 (= *DKar* 116) and the ninth-century boundary delineation contained in *FUB* no. 83 with addenda on pp. 525–7.

valuable concessions in western and central Thuringia. For instance in 1014, after Henry had imposed reform on Fulda during the previous year, he granted the monastery the royal hunting ban in a precisely delineated territory (Gerstungen–Eisenach–Behringen) in western Thuringia, centred on Lupnitz,[292] an area in which Hersfeld already held secular tithing rights.[293] Hersfeld also played a significant role in Henry's designs. Two years after granting Fulda the 'forest' rights around Lupnitz, Henry granted Hersfeld the royal ban over hunting in a large forest area[294] lying between the Ulster and the Werra Rivers and bordering on the area of Fulda's rights in the northeast. This encompassed older properties of Hersfeld, those at Dorndorf as well as part of the parish of Breitungen, which the monastery had obtained from Henry I.[295] Some properties of Fulda as well were included within Hersfeld's new banal district. This meant that the monastery controlled the forest and exercised the king's rights there in his stead. Thus, Hersfeld had the exclusive right to use the forest and its proceeds, to regulate hunting there, and to exercise the king's legal jurisdiction over the forest. Together these formed a closed territory of sovereign rights on the upper Fulda and lower Werra Rivers along the boundary of Hesse and Thuringia. In the areas comprising the *Mark* or fisc of Lupnitz and Hersfeld's *Wildbann*, various ecclesiastical and secular powers held rights, properties and other interests. Thus, Henry II's grant of the *Wildbann* in the *Mark* of Lupnitz,[296] and his later grant to Hersfeld of the *Wildbann* between the Ulster and the Werra,[297] both contain the consent and recognition of the various parties having property and rights in the prescribed areas. Hersfeld and Fulda already had a history of conflict in this area. A charter of Otto II from 979 documents royal intervention in a dispute between the abbots of Hersfeld and Fulda to ensure that boats from both monasteries had the right of passage on the Hörsel River.[298] Fulda's acquisition of the *Wildbann* in 1014 appears to have intensified the general rivalry between the two monasteries in the area and, consequently, to have led to further conflict. Finally, in 1024, Henry II had to issue an edict

---

[292] *DH II* 327; Knaus (1937) 54–7.
[293] *HUB* no. 12 (= *DKar* 121). Specifically concerning Lupnitz, see Küther (1974).
[294] *HUB* no. 85 (= *DH II* 350).
[295] *HUB* no. 40 (= *DH I* 35). Concerning Hersfeld's acquisition of the parish centred on Breitungen, see Stengel (1935a).　　[296] *DH II* 327.
[297] *DH II* 350.　　[298] *HUB* no. 63 (= *DO II* 209).

condemning the fighting between the *familiae* of the two monasteries and designating specific penalties to punish any further incidents.[299] By means of these grants of forest and hunting bans to Hersfeld and Fulda, Henry had substantially extended their sphere of influence in the middle Hessian–Thuringian border lands, had inserted them as royal supports between the property complexes of Bamberg and Würzburg to their south and that of Mainz (around Eschwege) in the north, and had given them a basis from which to develop territorial claims. Together these formed a closed territory of sovereign rights on the upper Fulda and lower Werra Rivers along the boundary of Hesse and Thuringia. The royal monasteries of Hersfeld and Fulda thus had control over the roads running in all directions through these areas in the middle of the realm stretching from central Hesse to central Thuringia.[300]

In the wake of Henry II's efforts to centralize the royal domain and further to secure this crucial transit zone between Saxony, Bavaria and the Rhine–Main basin, Hesse and Thuringia also experienced an upsurge of economic development that continued under the Salian kings. In 1019, soon after granting two markets to the nearby royal nunnery of Kaufungen – one at Wolfsanger (near Kassel) and one at Kaufungen itself[301] – Henry granted Fulda the right to hold a market and establish a mint. Once again these rights came with the full royal ban. Thus, the monastery could collect the king's revenues from the market and the mint, collect the tolls and customs dues, and enjoy any fines resulting from exercise of the royal jurisdiction.[302] Hersfeld appears to have had a mint at about the same time and an even earlier market.[303] Thus, by the early eleventh century there was a line of markets along the Fulda and the Weser extending from Würzburg to Corvey – at Würzburg, Fulda, Hersfeld, Kaufungen/Wolfsanger, Helmarshausen and Corvey. Income from money taxes reported in a Fulda land register from Gerstungen in the early eleventh century,[304] moreover, implies that another north–south chain of markets – Westera (Sooden-Allendorf), Creuzburg, Gerstungen and Salzungen – existed along the Werra in western Thuringia.[305] Although we cannot determine precisely who was the lord of these predominantly local markets, the large amount of property

---

[299] *DH II* 507a.   [300] Diefenbach (unpub. diss. 1952) 103–7.   [301] *DH II* 412.
[302] *DH II* 413.   [303] Hess (1963) 26–8 and (1954) 87–91, 116.
[304] *TAF* c. 43 (pp. 115–25) nos. 10, 21, 22, 23. For the dating, see Werner-Hasselbach (1942) 9–22 esp. 14–17.   [305] Hess (1974a) 313.

owned by Fulda in these settlements and the fact that, already under Charlemagne, Fulda possessed Westera, its saltworks, and the market and tolls there, strongly suggest that the abbot of Fulda probably controlled the other markets as well.[306]

In central Thuringia too, markets and mints developed and expanded under royal and ecclesiastical auspices.[307] At Erfurt, which had a Carolingian market and was the oldest trading centre in Thuringia, lively new episcopal minting activity began under Archbishop Aribo of Mainz (1021–31). It overshadowed the intermittent royal coin production and introduced a new phase of economic development. The market expanded greatly and the coinage from Erfurt became the standard and model for other Thuringian mints.[308] Fulda and Hersfeld took part in the general economic upswing there also. Money taxes paid by Fulda's dependants and tenants at Haina on the Nesse indicate that the monastery most probably had a market there in the early eleventh century, and archaeological evidence further supports this notion.[309] Considering Fulda's huge concentration of properties at Haina, there is little reason to doubt that the abbot of Fulda was lord of the market there, and a statement in a mandate of King Rudolf from 1295 concerning the market at Haina reinforces this attribution, when it mentions the antiquity of the market.[310] The existence of a market on an obscure site which has two documented stops by the royal court is no mere coincidence. Likewise, the existence of a royal mint at Arnstadt under King Henry III presupposes trading activity there and suggests that the abbot of Hersfeld established a market in the early eleventh century at Arnstadt in conjunction with the monastery's manor there and its numerous properties in the immediate area.[311] Let us also not forget that after 1015 the market, toll and minting rights at Memleben and the royal ban over them reverted to Hersfeld along with the other possessions of the former royal abbey. Thereafter, Hersfeld administered the sovereign rights at Memleben from the

---

[306] *FUB* 140 (= *DKar* 290). Although the charter itself is a forgery, its contents are based on earlier authentic charters. Also, see Hess (1963) 36.   [307] Hess (1974a) 316.

[308] Ibid. 313–14 and Gockel (1984d) 105–6. For a more detailed, but also more discursive account of Erfurt's development, see Hess (1963) 29–35.

[309] Hess (1963) 33 n. 88 and Gockel (1984h) 181.

[310] *CDF* no. 845: 'Abbates fuldenses eodem foro, iuribus, condicionibus et attinentiis omnibus et singulis ab antiquo et a tempore, quo non extat memoria, sunt gauisi.'

[311] Gockel (1984b) 73 and 77–81 gives a detailed summary of the proprietary history of Arnstadt and the surrounding area, from which it would be hard to imagine anyone other than the abbot of Hersfeld as lord over the market and the town.

centre of the realm. In all, starting with Henry II an economic upsurge occurred throughout Thuringia and the monasteries of Hersfeld and Fulda played major roles in this growth.

Whereas grants of the *Wildbann* or 'forest' rights were increasingly used to help churches and monasteries consolidate the areas around their institutions and even to establish them in areas outside of their main holdings – where they often exercised these rights as guardians of royal interests – the most obvious example of churches exercising sovereign rights in the ruler's stead occurred with the grant of a county.[312] Although the Ottonian and Salian rulers granted counties to numerous bishoprics, they bequeathed counties to monastic institutions on only five occasions. Four of the five went to monastic institutions discussed in this study.[313] The powerful Saxon convent of Gandersheim received the county of Boto from Henry II in 1021,[314] and Fulda was granted three counties, one each from Henry II, Conrad II and Henry III.[315] Unfortunately very little is known about Fulda's counties and they were not as important in the long run to the monastery in terms of expanding its territorial claims as were its grants of *Wildbann*.[316] All of the counties given to Fulda, however, were located in areas where the monastery had substantial property.[317] Henry II's grant of the county of Stoddenstat in the Maingau (Stockstadt, west of Aschaffenburg) could possibly have served as a barrier to further expansion of the archbishopric of Mainz, which had acquired the canonry of Aschaffenburg as a collegiate chapter.[318] Likewise, Henry III's grant of the county of Maelstat in the Wetterau may have served a similar purpose as well as helping Fulda consolidate control over its holdings in the area.[319] Later historical developments in the Wetterau, however, show that the local nobility came to hold the better right. Finally, the county of Netra, south of Eschwege, gave Fulda stronger judicial control over its property in that area. In each of these cases the judicial power of the countship appears to have formed the core of the grant. The abbot of Fulda or his advocate gained the right to exercise high and low justice in the respective areas as an agent of the king. To the extent that the

---

[312] Keller (1982) 86.
[313] Henry III's grant of a county to St Ghislain in 1040 (*DH III* 48) has not been examined in the context of this work.   [314] *DH II* 444. See above, Chapter 4, at n. 118.
[315] *DH II* 509 (Stoddenstat); *DK II* 23 (Netra); and *DH III* 101 (Maelstat).
[316] Knaus (1936) and (1937).
[317] On Fulda's counties, see Hoffmann (1990) 393–6.
[318] Franke (1987) 128–9.   [319] Franke (1987) 145.

abbot was able to realize this power, the monastery had another source of income – the fines accruing from exercising royal justice. Just like other incomes from markets or the exercise of royal banal rights, these incomes also would enhance the monastery's economic ability to serve the realm.

CONCLUSION

During the tenth and eleventh centuries in Germany, the Ottonian and Salian monarchs drew much of their political and economic support from the royal churches of their realm. In fact, during the Ottonian period royal churches increasingly became the most important economic bases for the accommodation of the royal presence in the realm, as well as the venues for the liturgical representation of sacral kingship.[1] One can see this particularly well in the numerous royal palaces that these kings gave fully or in part to ecclesiastical institutions. For instance, Otto I founded St Maurice and later the archbishopric at Magdeburg on his *Pfalz* at Magdeburg, and the archbishopric later acquired the monastery and a large part of the palace complex at Pöhlde, where the Ottonians traditionally celebrated Christmas. The monastery of canons that Queen Mathilda had founded at Pöhlde became a proprietary Benedictine monastery when Magdeburg acquired it in 981.[2] The royal convent of Quedlinburg was established on a former royal residence and later was granted the former *Pfalz* of Walbeck as well as revenues and holdings at the hunting palace at Siptenfelde. Gandersheim, originally a Liudolfing family convent, received the royal residence at Dahlum, the convent founded by Sophie at Eschwege and its extensive holdings there, and a *curtis* at the hunting palace of Bodfeld with forest and hunting rights. The royal *Pfalz* at Nordhausen was granted to Queen Mathilda, who founded her favourite convent of canonesses there. In northern Thuringia, Otto II used the royal palace of Memleben with its large church to establish a royal monastery, which in 1015 became a priory of Hersfeld. Finally, in the early eleventh century Henry II gave his wife, Queen Kunigunda, the royal palace and fiscal district of Kassel, and founded a new *Pfalz* at Kaufungen. This in turn was used by

[1] Keller (1985a) 19–20 and Streich (1984).
[2] On Pöhlde see Gauert (1970); Claus (1970); and Streich (1984) 162–5.

Queen Kunigunda in 1017 to found the Benedictine nunnery there.

Previous research on the economic, religious and political support of German itinerant kingship by royal churches has concentrated primarily on bishops and on episcopal cities,[3] while consistently underestimating the contribution made by royal monasteries.[4] As we have seen, however, the monasteries and convents located in the Saxon heartlands and in the transit zones of the German realm played an important, even crucial, role in support of the German monarchy (see Map 5). Throughout the core region of royal power in Saxony and in the crucial transit zones of the realm, royal monasteries, convents and monastic properties were strategically located along routes of the royal itinerary. These religious communities maintained close connections with the king, and they came to possess and administer large estates, forests, even counties, and to hold jurisdiction over these. In addition, they shared in the economic development of their respective areas through royal grants of markets and the valuable income-producing rights associated with them – tolls, coining rights and revenues, and judicial fines. Thus, they had the landed wealth and the financial ability to support royal power and they helped make possible the Ottonian and Salian kings' intinerant method of governing by supplying accommodation and food for the king and his court on their travels throughout the realm.

As we have seen, Saxony, more specifically the Harz region, was the heartland of the early German kings. Thus, in Saxony we found the largest concentration of royal property, the greatest amount of time spent there by the king, and the most intense hands-on royal government. Owing to the extraordinary amount of time that the Ottonians and early Salians spent in this region, we have also seen the greatest amount of interaction between royal property (*curtes* and *Pfalzen*) and church property in support of the king and the royal court. The Harz region fell within the ecclesiastical jurisdiction of the four Saxon bishoprics which surrounded it to the north and east – Hildesheim, Halberstadt, Magdeburg and Merseburg – and the massive diocese of Mainz, which extended into the western and southwestern area of Saxony.

---

[3] See R. Schieffer (1989), who provides a summary of recent research; Engels (1989); Finck von Finckenstein (1989); Zielinski (1984); and Reuter (1982).

[4] The main exceptions to this are the many works by Wolfgang Metz, especially Metz (1971), (1976), and (1984); Wehlt (1970); and Streich (1984).

Along with these four episcopal cities in the region, numerous royal convents and monasteries dotted the area – Gandersheim, Drübeck, Quedlinburg, Gernrode, St Maurice at Magdeburg, Nienburg, Alsleben, Nordhausen and Memleben (in northern Thuringia). In addition, three ecclesiastical proprietary monasteries – Walbeck (Quedlinburg), Frose (Gernrode) and Pöhlde (Magdeburg) – increased the number of royally-allied monastic institutions.

Obviously, not all of these monastic institutions supported or were able to support the royal court equally owing to differences in size and wealth; and often when they did offer accommodation and upkeep to the court, church property and royal property may have shared the burden jointly. Several characteristics emerge, however, that are striking and certainly not accidental. All of these monasteries lay either on trade routes or on one of the several roads ringing the Harz mountains; they were usually located about a day's march from another stopping point on the known itinerary; and a few owned large estates at other locations on these roads. In addition, all of these convents and monasteries either were connected very closely to the Liudolfing/Ottonian family, or they were originally foundations of the Saxon nobility which were protected and given patronage by the German monarchs and thereby finally became royal institutions. Quedlinburg and its Benedictine priory of Walbeck, Gandersheim, and St Maurice at Magdeburg (before it became the site of an archbishopric) were the monastic jewels in the crown of the early German monarchs. Drübeck, Gernrode, Nienburg, Alsleben and Nordhausen, on the other hand, appear to have functioned as stations of support on the itinerary, but they did not approach the others in wealth, royal use or prestige. Pöhlde received extensive use as a Christmas palace, but since it was a proprietary monastery of the archbishop of Magdeburg, any *servitium* it paid to supplement the separate royal palace there was an obligation of its proprietary lord, the archbishop of Magdeburg, and not that of an independent royal monastery. Memleben began as a royal *Pfalz* at the extreme southeastern edge of Saxony with access to Merseburg and the roads through Thuringia, and after Henry I and Otto I died there, it became a royal monastery and an Ottonian cult site to their memory.

St Maurice at Magdeburg, Quedlinburg and Gandersheim had special and enduring relations with the royal family. The first two became Ottonian cult sites, Quedlinburg upon its foundation on the location of Henry I's grave, and St Maurice after it became the burial place for Otto I's wife Edith and later for the emperor himself. Gandersheim traditionally was a centre for the perpetuation of the Liudolfing family *memoria*.[5] The importance and prestige of Quedlinburg and Gandersheim are mirrored in their abbesses – all members or princesses of the royal family throughout the duration of our study. The royal connections of these institutions as well as their location occasioned many royal visits during which these institutions supplied and accommodated the court. Otto I visited his new foundation of St Maurice many times; even before it became an archbishopric, he celebrated St Maurice's feast-day and Palm Sunday there, and held at least one royal assembly there. Quedlinburg became the traditional place in Saxony for the Ottonians to celebrate Easter; and both Quedlinburg and Gandersheim functioned as meeting-places for church synods or royal assemblies and as normal stopping places on the royal *iter*. Consequently, they served as venues for the sacral representation of the kingship, which included the royal *adventus* ceremony, crown-wearings during religious feasts and assemblies of state, and the participation of the king and the royal family in religious solemnities. The general development of both convents reflects the impact of royal connections and royal visits. Both convents expanded their churches substantially in the Ottonian period. Thereby, they created the sacral and the physical space necessary to host and venerate their royal visitors properly and to include them in the religious services of the community. Moreover, in addition to receiving large and numerous grants of property from the German kings, Quedlinburg and Gandersheim were granted the right to hold markets, mint coins and collect tolls in their localities. These grants heightened the convents' abilities to provide for the royal court by increasing their revenues and expanding the availability of goods. Early grants of coining rights and toll revenues to St Maurice presuppose a market there also. Although Quedlinburg ceased in the early eleventh century to be the primary place to celebrate Easter in Saxony, it retained its traditional reverence, and since the roads travelled and the pattern of the *iter* in Saxony did not change dramatically, it continued to be a frequent stopping point. Moreover, when Henry II began to

---

[5] Althoff (1976) 372–81.

celebrate Easter in Saxony more frequently at Merseburg, Quedlinburg's Benedictine priory of Walbeck became Henry's Palm Sunday feast-site, occasioning festival stops of the court there in addition to any other halts connected with general travel.

The other royal convents and monasteries in Saxony offer us exiguous information about actual stops or contributions to the upkeep of the court. Although most were located at logical halting-points on roads used by the German kings, they appear to have served normally only as overnight halting points or for stops of a short duration. Four of these institutions, Nienburg, Drübeck, Gernrode and Alsleben, were originally noble foundations. In regard to these foundations, one can perhaps see a concerted effort by the German monarchs to use royal protection and patronage to gain and secure new centres of support, allied to the realm and located on important roads in the Saxon heartlands. The transfer of the monastery at Thankmarsfeld to Nienburg on the Saale and the foundation of the royal monastery of Memleben around the same time, both located very near the eastern frontier, and the grants of property they received in Slavic areas, suggest that Otto II may have had some missionary goal in mind for these institutions. If that were so, these hopes were dashed with the Slavic incursion of 983 and the continuing unrest in the 990s, for neither institution appears to have played much of a role in evangelizing in Slavic regions. It is also significant that the three institutions about which we have definite information on royal visits – the royal monasteries of Nienburg and Memleben, and the convent at Nordhausen – not surprisingly were also sites of early markets. As with the other royal monastic institutions in Saxony, the acquisition of market, coining and toll rights appear connected with the royal *iter*, royal visits and general support for the monarchy. The Ottonian and Salian kings engaged in a general effort to increase economic development in Saxony under royal auspices.[6] Although they did not directly control the revenues from the income-producing rights granted to convents and monasteries, they established the principle that such rights derived from the king, they created personal bonds of patronage, and they could expect to reap the benefits either materially in the form of their *servitium* or hospitality when present, or politically in the form of greater loyalty.[7]

---

[6] On Ottonian and Salian market policy in Saxony, see Metz (1971); Schlesinger (1973); and Schwineköper (1977) esp. 11–20, 138–59. [7] Keller (1985a) 26–8.

Finally, it is important to note that throughout the period of this study the general structure of the royal *iter* within Saxony and the roads travelled there remained constant, as did the customary pattern of the king's accommodation. To be sure, outside the framework of the visits occasioned merely by the specific route travelled, the frequency and duration of visits to one place or another within Saxony changed according to the will and the whims of the individual ruler and in regard to changing political circumstances. For instance, no ruler spent as much time in Magdeburg as Otto I, and Otto I and Otto III spent more time in Quedlinburg than later kings. Otto III appears to have frequented Gandersheim by personal choice more often than other rulers owing to his close relationship with his sister Sophie. Henry II celebrated Easter at Merseburg rather than at Quedlinburg, and Palm Sunday at Walbeck rather than at Magdeburg. He also founded a new palace at Goslar to replace the indigenous Saxon stem seat at Werla. His Salian successors continued and greatly heightened the royal presence at Goslar and increased the number of visits to this new palace, which became their favourite *Pfalz* in Saxony. At the same time, the increased use of the *Pfalz* at Goslar probably increased the occasional use of or short-duration visits at Gandersheim *en route* to Goslar. This may also be the case with Drübeck and Quedlinburg, but we will understand this better when Gerald Beyreuther's structural study of the realm under Henry II has been published.

What apparently did not happen, however, was the supposed shift in the pattern of royal accommodation beginning around 1000 whereby the early German kings stayed longer and more frequently in Saxon episcopal cities and less frequently in the royal *Pfalzen*, convents and monasteries. In a preliminary study of the structure of the realm under Conrad II, Eckhard Müller-Mertens has offered compelling data which demonstrate that this commonplace of scholarship since Bruno Heusinger and Carlrichard Brühl does not apply to the Saxon central region when it is separated from the accommodation patterns in the new *Nahzonen*, which emerged because of the expansion of royal government around the millennium.[8] In these new areas of royal property, power and influence, royal stays at episcopal cities surpassed all other forms of hospitality by a margin of nine to one and thereby

---

[8] On these regions, see above, Chapter 2.

skewed the data for the other regions of the realm. In fact, in Saxony and the other central regions of kingship, royal stays in the *Pfalzen* actually outnumber those in episcopal cities.[9] Since we have so little hard data on royal accommodation in convents and monasteries, since the line between *Pfalzen* and monastic *Pfalzen* is not always clear, and since Müller-Mertens does not provide a separate category for monastic hospitality, this of course does not tell us anything specific about an increase or a decrease in royal accommodation in the convents and monasteries of Saxony. However, even before this new study, Wolfgang Metz indicated that it is false to assume the rigid construct that after Otto III, and especially after Henry II, the economic obligations of the episcopal cities and their properties to the king increased dramatically and those of the monasteries remained essentially constant.[10] What did change was that kings tended more often to frequent centres which had the sacral space necessary for a proper liturgical celebration of kingship and which had an increasing economic activity to supply the needs of the court. At the end of the tenth century and the beginning of the eleventh, examples from our Saxon convents and monasteries show exactly these characteristics – new and larger churches, such as at Quedlinburg, Gandersheim, Walbeck and Memleben, and newly developing markets, such as at Quedlinburg, Gandersheim, Nienburg, Nordhausen and Memleben. Thus, not only did Saxony remain the paramount region of royal hospitality into the 1070s, as Karl Leyser and others have shown, but the traditional pattern of royal hospitality in Saxony – a balance of the royal *Pfalzen*, the episcopal sees, and the royal convents and monasteries – also remained largely constant, with a few variations among particular places. Monastic hospitality in Saxony appears therefore to have remained constant as well and may have increased in the case of monastic institutions which took part in the economic development of the area. Thus, the royal convents and monasteries of Saxony must be seen as one of the crucial elements providing economic and political support to the German kings in Saxony.

As we have seen already, after the accession of the Ottonian kings of Saxony to the east Frankish/German throne the importance of the transit zones of the realm, which contained the main roads connecting the three central regions of kingship,

---

[9] Müller-Mertens (1991) 152–5.   [10] Metz (1971) 276–8.

increased sharply as they became the strategic links between these three political and economic centres. In order to govern as effectively as possible without a capital or a central bureaucracy, the German kings required unimpeded access to the three central zones of their political power. Consequently, they had to ensure that they could travel again and again through the transit zones safely and with adequate provision and accommodation. As in Saxony, so also in the transit zones do we find that royal *Pfalzen*, bishoprics and royal monastic institutions all provided the kings' accommodation and provision; but in the transit zones a greater share of the burden fell on royal churches and their properties since the German kings did not have extensive personal property there and much former royal property came through royal grants to ecclesiastical institutions.

In western Saxony (Engern) and Westphalia – the main east–west transit corridor of the realm through which the Hellweg was the main route – royal monasteries and convents helped to provide political and economic support for the early German monarchs as had their counterparts in Saxony. On the basis of the royal itinerary and several individual studies, it has become clear that the early German monarchs used the Hellweg for transit almost every year when they were not in Italy. Royal visits in Westphalia and in the transit zones, while frequent, usually were not of long duration, although Otto III did spend several days at Essen in 993 and Conrad II spent almost a week at Corvey in 1025. Not surprisingly, the convents and monasteries for which we found the best indications of royal visits and payments towards the *servitium regis* were all located directly on the Hellweg. While we have no annalist source for monastic institutions of this area which provides us with the kind of detailed information about royal visits as do the *Annals of Quedlinburg* for Quedlinburg or Lampert's *Annals* for Hersfeld, the land registers of Essen, Werden and Corvey provide us either with some definite information about payments of these institutions toward the *servitium regis*, or give us the basis, through comparison of the registers, to make reasoned judgements about such payments. In addition, information contained in royal charters and archaeological reports enables us to draw further conclusions about the ability of these institutions to host the royal court on its travels.

In spite of a lack of annalistic sources, all three of these monastic institutions have records of visits by the royal court. Whereas the great majority of visits to Corvey, Werden or Essen – that is, those occurring in the normal course of transit – went unrecorded, those for which we do have some information are usually known for a specific reason. Either the king celebrated a religious feast or saint's day there (for instance, Pentecost at Werden in 1017, Epiphany at Corvey in 1025, or St Vitus's feast-day at Corvey several times under Henry II and Conrad II), or he went there in connection with monastic reform or an abbatial election (Henry II and Henry III at Corvey), or the visit occurred for purely personal reasons, such as Otto III's visit to Essen for the marriage of his sister Mathilda. While all three of these institutions benefited from royal patronage, only the convent of Essen had strong familial connections with the royal house. As is the case with the abbesses of Quedlinburg and Gandersheim in Saxony, all of the abbesses known at Essen until 1056 appear to have been related to the Liudolfing/Ottonian family, and the convent frequently received mention as one of the 'model' royal convents in the realm. Two other important similarities between these three royal monastic institutions located on the Hellweg and those which provided the monarchy with political, religious and economic support in Saxony deserve another mention. Firstly, Corvey, Werden and Essen all had the sacral space necessary to entertain the king and participate in the cult of kingship. Corvey's *Westwerk* had a late Carolingian origin, but undoubtedly received its greatest use by the Ottonian and Salian kings, and the expansion of the churches at Werden and Essen occurred in the tenth and early eleventh centuries respectively. Secondly, as with other monastic institutions which received frequent royal visits, Corvey, Werden and Essen were all granted the right to hold markets and to mint coins at the monastery or convent, or at one of their settlements on a distant estate. These royal grants of sovereign rights helped these institutions develop economically and thereby increased their ability to supply the court when requested. The extensive payments to the *servitium regis* contained in Werden's eleventh-century land registers provide us with an indication of amounts and kinds of payments involved in this obligation, and a comparative analysis of land registers from Corvey and Essen suggest that they made similar payments as well. In addition, Otto I's grant of the royal ban over the castlework of several dependent populations imply political functions for Corvey as well.

The remaining royal convents in Engern and Westphalia offer us very little information concerning royal visits and even less about payments made towards the *servitium regis*. Yet even our lack of information and the little that we do have allow us to draw some tentative conclusions. With the exception of Geseke – which appears to have remained in the hands of its founding family, the Haholdian counts, who were loyal vassals of the Ottonians – none of the other royal convents was located on the Hellweg, which the German monarchs used over ninety per cent of the time. This most probably accounts for the lack of information and lack of royal visits. Yet, the little information that we do have about royal visits concerns precisely those convents located on roads, but roads used only infrequently and mostly in the eleventh century. Thus, Vreden and Herford have documentary evidence of royal visits, and Kemnade and Fischbeck may, on the basis of their location, have received royal visits. Moreover, visits to all of these convents occurred in the eleventh century when Henry II and the Salians began to expand royal power within the transit zones and former remote zones. In this process, Minden became one of the centres of royal patronage in one of the new *Nahzonen* of kingship. Consequently, Herford, which was situated between the Hellweg and Minden and held market, coining and toll rights dating back to the Carolingians and confirmed by Otto I, received royal visits. Kemnade and Fischbeck, originally noble foundations where the realm eventually prevailed, lay on routes from Goslar and Hildesheim to Minden and thereby may have been visited. In the case of Vreden, which became a royal convent under Henry II, it lay on a route from the extreme lower Rhine area to Minden or Dortmund on the Hellweg, which was infrequently used by the German kings. When it was visited by Conrad II, its abbess was a royal princess. Prior to the eleventh century the existence of these royal convents in Engern and Westphalia may have served only to ensure a small royal presence in an area controlled predominantly by the Billung family. In any case, by the mid-eleventh century, with the exception of the royal *Pfalzen* at Dortmund and Duisburg, the main east–west corridor of transit in the realm lay in the hands of the royal convents, monasteries or bishoprics which supplied the king's accommodation and support.

In the river basins of the Weser, the Werra and the Fulda Rivers, the Ottonian and Salian kings also made good use of monastic institutions. This region contained the main access routes from Saxony to the roads through the central transit zone of the realm. While these institutions (especially Kaufungen) played a role in the accommodation and upkeep of the court, the Ottonian kings appear to have had additional designs for these foundations. They used them to increase the royal presence and to consolidate royal property holdings in an area of mixed ownership, to maintain loyal control of the large network of roads, river fords and royal forests in the region, and eventually to stimulate economic development. Helmarshausen and Hilwartshausen were both founded on private property by members of the Saxon nobility and were given over immediately to the king to protect the integrity of the religious foundations from any claims of kinsfolk. Both also happened to be located on important river fords over the Diemel and the Weser respectively and were separated by the Reinhardswald, a large royal forest. Thus, through the acquisition of these foundations, the realm had increased royal property along the Weser, gained control of two important fords, and had royal monastic institutions situated on the northern and eastern borders of an extensive royal forest. Despite its royal status and the acquisition of market, minting and toll rights with the royal ban, Helmarshausen could not survive conflicts with the founders' heirs as an independent institution and Henry granted it to the bishop of Paderborn in 1017. Nevertheless, the realm did not forfeit its gains because a loyal bishop became proprietary lord of the monastery. Apparently, owing to arrangements made by Aeddila, the Saxon noblewoman who founded the convent of Hilwartshausen, and the vigilance of its first two abbesses – her daughters – Hilwartshausen maintained its status as an independent royal convent. Unfortunately, we have only a single record of a visit by a German king to Hilwartshausen and no information concerning the *servitium regis*. Nevertheless, this royal convent still appears to have played a role in support of the monarchy. It can be no accident that all of its grants of property from the realm were located on the roads leading from Hilwartshausen's ford over the Weser to the royal *Pfalzen* in Saxony, and all were in or bordered on large royal forests, the Reinhardswald, the Bramwald and the Kaufunger-wald. Even if Hilwartshausen played only a minor role in the accommodation of the king, its property grants show it to be a guardian of royal interests in the area and a valuable addition to existing royal property complexes there.

The royal nunnery of Kaufungen played an even greater role. Upon its foundation in 1019, this royal nunnery came to possess the entire fiscal district of Kassel, which Henry II had granted to Queen Kunigunda as her dower, as well as the new royal *Pfalz* that Henry had established at Kaufungen after relinquishing Kassel. These grants, this foundation, and subsequent grants to Kaufungen served multiple purposes. They provided the Queen with a new dower to replace Bamberg, soothed political relations with her brothers, and formed part of Henry's larger attempt to create a core of royal property and power in the centre of the realm. Kaufungen has records of royal visits both as a *Pfalz* and after the foundation of the nunnery. It was apparently a large complex of buildings and property situated in the middle of a huge royal forest, which could accommodate the court all the year round, and the existence of two churches with royal galleries marked it as particularly suited to host royal visitors and to provide a home for a dowager queen. Royal grants of property and sovereign rights by Henry II and Henry III to Kaufungen not only complemented its role as a convenient halting point on the royal *iter*, but revealed other royal designs for the nunnery as well. Kaufungen came to possess and control all of the river fords over the Fulda and the Werra south of the confluence of the Fulda, the Werra and the Weser, virtually all of the roads traversing the region, and the entire royal forest surrounding the nunnery. Moreover, the royal rights to hold four different markets and to collect tolls, and the royal ban over these rights, increased the nunnery's wealth and its ability to accommodate royal visits, and it initiated the economic development of the entire area. With Kaufungen, Hilwartshausen, Helmarshausen (later to Paderborn), and Eschwege (which was mentioned with Saxony), the Ottonian kings had consolidated and increased royal property in the Saxon, Thuringian and Hessian river basins, had gained oversight of all the roads and fords through the region, and began to stimulate economic growth.[11]

One striking feature should not go unnoticed about the monastic institutions supporting the king and the royal itinerary in Saxony and Westphalia, and in the Weser, Werra and Fulda river basins. A large number of these monastic institutions were religious communities of women, that is, canonesses or nuns. Moreover, the

---

[11] See also W. Heinemeyer (1963–4) 354 and Bannasch (1972) 178.

abbesses who presided over these communities were very frequently members or relatives of the royal family. In these regions
of the realm, where royal convents outnumbered royal
monasteries by over two to one,[12] female religious institutions
bore a large share of the monastic contribution to the accommodation and to the political and religious underpinning of the
Ottonian and Salian kings. These facts, in the context of this study,
provide us with some new insights regarding the role of royal and
aristocratic women and their convents in Ottonian and Salian
Germany. These insights in turn complement other recent research
on Ottonian and Salian religious women and female religious
communities.

Karl Leyser indicated the manifold social importance of Saxon
convents. They provided shelter for unmarried daughters of the
nobility from the advances of their kinsmen in order to avoid the
social complications or possible feuds arising from such unwanted
advances or illegitimate issue. The endowment of new religious
communities coupled with charters of royal protection helped to
secure the inheritances of many women from the claims of their
kinsmen and at the same time helped the king, another competing
nobleman, by diminishing the property holding of the nobility
and increasing the royal sphere of influence. Leyser also elucidated
the crucial role that foundresses and canonesses alike played in
giving alms and saying prayers to assure the *fortuna* of their
kinsmen and in perpetuating the *memoria* of their noble dead.[13]
Other studies have focussed on the hagiography of the period to
examine the complexities and manifestations of female sanctity –
the tensions between the private and public roles of the female
saint and, specifically in regard to Ottonian female saints, the
relationship between their private or personal piety and their royal
status.[14] Michel Parisse has examined the diversity and flexibility
of the canonical life for noble women in terms of noble social
needs and values and in regard to the religious desires and
sensibilities of these women.[15] Finally, Rosamond McKitterick's
study of the depictions of women in Ottonian iconography
reveals that women appeared frequently in Ottonian illustra-

---

[12] On the spate of religious foundations for women in Saxony in the ninth and tenth
centuries, see A. Hauck (1952) 3. 1011; Schäfer (1907); and Parisse (1991) 466–74. On
their constitutional and legal status, see Hörger (1926).

[13] Leyser (1979) 63–73.

[14] Schulenburg (1988) and Corbet (1986).   [15] Parisse (1978) and (1990).

tions, even in Christian and biblical books, and that they were portrayed in 'positive and visible' roles, whether in a pious religious setting or in the context of a royal or aristocratic household.[16]

This visible, pious and noble characterization of Ottonian women accurately reflects the role they played in the royal convents and nunneries of the realm. Rather than solely performing good works and playing the important but passive role of guardians of the *memoria* or prayer-commemoration of noble and royal families, these women, as the foundresses, patrons and abbesses of female religious foundations, had an active and central function in support of royal government. These convents and their abbesses kept and administered hostels for the court on the routes of the royal itinerary and maintained spheres of influence for the king in areas of less frequent royal presence. They politically supported royal government by administering large property holdings, even counties, controlling important roads and river fords in their areas, and exercising important sovereign rights, such as the right to hold markets, mint coins and exercise the jurisdiction of royal banal rights through their advocates.[17] The wealthiest and most prestigious of these convents, whose abbesses were members of the royal family, were located on the most frequently travelled routes of the royal *iter*. Consequently, they hosted royal assemblies, in which their abbesses participated, and they provided venues for the king's observance of major and minor feast-days of the church and for the liturgical celebration of kingship, which greeted royal visits and was a part of the great festivals of the church. While we have no evidence that the needs of the *iter* and the possibilities of *servitium regis* actually occasioned the foundation of a royal convent – although one might entertain this notion in the case of Kaufungen and possibly Walbeck – there is little doubt that the early German monarchs consciously made use of the manifold possibilities for support that existing convents or new foundations presented. Moreover, in the case of the most strategically located and increasingly powerful royal convents, it appears likely that in addition to the social and religious reasons for encouraging royal dowagers, princesses, sisters and cousins to head

---

[16] McKitterick (1990).
[17] On the possibilities of the abbatial office for noble women to exercise active and real power, see also Parisse (1990) 322–4.

convents,[18] the German monarchs also had very concrete political and economic reasons – to secure and maintain crucial support of their itinerant mode of governance.

Moving to the large and important central transit zone of the realm, where the early German monarchs had little or no patrimonial property and there were no episcopal cities, we found that the royal monasteries of Hersfeld and Fulda provided the essential political and economic support for the Ottonian and Salian kings. From the investigation of the interworking of Hersfeld and Fulda in the larger policies of the Ottonian and Salian monarchs and of the property holdings of both monasteries, these two Hessian monasteries emerged as two of the premier royal monasteries in the realm. Hersfeld and Fulda frequently provided accommodation and upkeep for the royal itinerary as did their widespread properties throughout Hesse and Thuringia. Moreover, their acquisitions of property and sovereign rights, especially under Henry II, reveal that they played a key role in Henry's plans to create a core of royal property and power in the centre of the realm.

In the crucial transit zone through central Hesse, which connected the crown properties in Saxony with those in the Main–Rhine region and in which there were only meagre royal holdings, these two royal monasteries held property on virtually every major road crossing the area. Consequently, they appear to have borne a major portion of the king's accommodation and upkeep. Indeed, when one makes a thorough and careful analysis of the known royal itineraries for the Saxon and early Salian periods, and estimates how often, year after year, these kings crossed and recrossed this region, it becomes even more evident how many times it went totally unreported that the royal retinue must have stopped, if only overnight or for a short time, at these Hessian monasteries or their properties. For instance, we have only one recorded visit of Otto I to Hersfeld and one likely visit to Fulda. Yet, travelling to the middle Rhine region or to Bavaria or to Hesse itself, Otto I made at least sixty trips across or into Hesse.[19] Similarly, we have no recorded or conjectured stops of

---

[18] Leyser (1979) 89 suggested that Adelheid's entrance into the community of canonesses at Quedlinburg in 995 at age eighteen, after two years of climatic abnormalities and natural calamities, may have been a 'propitiatory offering, a sacrifice in Christian form ... to ensure better times, continuity, stability and peace'. See *Ann. Qued. s.a.* 995.

[19] Müller-Mertens (1980) 141.

Otto III at Fulda, Hersfeld, or any of their properties. Nevertheless, a rough calculation based on his itinerary shows that he crossed Hesse at least twelve times in twelve years, from 989–1000. In addition, archaeological information has indicated the existence of palace or palace-like complexes at both monasteries in the eleventh century and possibly earlier, and both expanded or rebuilt their churches in the tenth and eleventh centuries, giving them the sacral as well as the physical space necessary to host the king (and, in the case of Fulda, the Pope). Also, as with other monasteries and convents receiving frequent royal visits, Hersfeld and Fulda held markets at their localities and minted coins there.

Likewise, in the transit zone through Thuringia which connected Saxony to eastern Franconia and Bavaria, Hersfeld and Fulda played a significant role. Their estates in central and western Thuringia contributed to the provisioning and accommodation of the king.[20] In the Thuringian–Hessian border regions, these two monasteries controlled large tracts of land. In addition to those holdings acquired under the Ottonian kings in this area, Conrad II granted Fulda the small county of Netra, near Eschwege, and in 1059, Henry IV, under the regency government, granted Fulda the royal hunting and forest ban in an extensive forest region in the Saalegau between the monastery and the Fränkische Saale River.[21] Moreover, these monasteries held or controlled a majority of the river fords over the Werra, the Fulda, and their tributaries. Hersfeld held the fords over the Fulda River at Hersfeld and at Breitenbach/Bebra. Along the Werra it controlled the fords at Wanfried (east of Eschwege), Barchfeld near Salzungen, and (Herren-, Frauen-) Breitungen. Fulda controlled the fords over the Fulda River at the monastery itself, at Kämmerzell and Bronnzell (respectively just north and south of the monastery), and at Wegfurth on the road to Hersfeld. On the Werra River, Fulda held the important river crossings at Creuzburg and Gerstungen, and in addition possessed the Haune ford at Hünfeld, the Ulster ford at Geisa, and the important north–south crossing of the Fränkische Saale River at Hammelburg. Moreover, both monasteries had sizeable holdings at the Werra river-crossings at

---

[20] Metz (1976) 226 provides a very general map depicting the properties of Hersfeld, Fulda and Mainz in Hesse and Thuringia that appear as stopping points on the royal itinerary. Unfortunately, Metz's map must be used with caution as it contains several errors and incorrect attributions of property.

[21] *DK II* 23; see Knaus (1937) 57–64.

Berka and (Bad) Salzungen. Consequently, the roads of this crucial border region lay predominantly in royal monastic hands.[22] The eleventh-century markets at both monasteries, coupled with Kaufungen's markets further north, the string of local markets under Fulda's auspices along the Werra, and the markets at Haina (Fulda) and Arnstadt (Hersfeld) in Thuringia provided additional opportunities for the royal court to supply its needs and to procure particular goods and services while in transit and distant from large centres of commerce.[23] Thus, the Ottonian and Salian kings made effective use of the royal monasteries in the Hessian–Thuringian borderland. Through extensive grants of royal property and royal bans over large forests, these monastic institutions became guardians of royal interests in eastern Hesse and western Thuringia. Hersfeld, Fulda and Kaufungen controlled the majority of roads in all directions, as well as a great number of river fords from the Bavarian–Hessian border to central and northern Thuringia.[24] Moreover, incomes from their markets and mints must have greatly increased their ability to serve the king and the realm, and the mere existence of the markets must have greatly facilitated royal travel. In fact, when travelling through Hesse and Thuringia proper, whatever route the king chose, it would have been difficult for him to avoid the property of Hersfeld or Fulda, one of their fords, or one of their markets (see Maps 9 and 11).

Therefore, when Lampert in 1063 talks of a repeated exaction of royal services that depleted his monastery's wealth,[25] and later, in 1075, when he relates that contenders for the abbacy of Fulda promised Henry IV greater *servitia* than before,[26] his remarks, in spite of his blatantly anti-royal point of view, probably do not fall far from the truth.[27] Nevertheless, the monk of Hersfeld was speaking about a time of contention and conflict between various political and military factions, during which the customary *servitia* of these monasteries became an abnormal and unbearable burden.[28] The increased royal demands upon these two Hessian

---

[22] Diefenbach (unpub. diss. 1952) 101–2, 108–9.   [23] Metz (1971) 282–6, 289.

[24] Diefenbach (unpub. diss. 1952) 103–7.

[25] Lampert, *Annales s.a.* 1063 p. 89: 'Et primo quidem predia monasteriorum fautoribus suis, prout libitum erat, distribuebant, et quod reliquum erat crebra regalium serviciorum exactione usque ad feces ultimas exhauriebant.'

[26] Ibid., *s.a.* 1075 p. 240: 'Postera die cum ad eligendum Fuldensem abbatem rex cum principibus assedisset...alius solito impensiora in rem publicam servicia promittebant, nec prorsus in promittendo modum aut modestiam ullam servabant.'

[27] Metz (1971) 272.   [28] Wehlt (1970) 158, 294–5.

monasteries to provide service for the realm, however, should not be attributed solely to Henry IV. Owing to their location and their wealth of properties in transit zones crucial to the Ottonians, these monasteries were already experiencing a high degree of royal presence under the Ottonians and were called upon to provide a greater degree of royal service than many other royal monasteries. The relationship between the German monarchs and these Hessian monasteries peaked in the eleventh century. It should be borne in mind, for example, that in the early eleventh century both monasteries played central roles when Henry II began to make more systematic demands of royal *servitium* on the bishoprics and royal monasteries of the realm.[29] Thus, in particular with Hersfeld and Fulda, the establishment of these new conditions can be seen in Henry's forceful reform interventions in these two monasteries,[30] the use of Hersfeld and Fulda in his plan to create a unified core of royal and royal church properties in the centre of the realm, and increased incidence of royal visits to the monasteries and their properties. As we have seen with Saxony, it is an error to assume that after Otto III and Henry II the economic obligations to the king of only the episcopal cities and their properties increased dramatically, while those of the monasteries remained essentially constant. For Hersfeld and Fulda, these new conditions produced greater wealth and greater power; but they also produced increased royal visits to the monasteries and their properties, and greater demands to serve the realm.

Using the examples of Hersfeld and Fulda, in areas having little royal property and no episcopal cities, and on account of certain historical events (like Henry IV's Saxon wars), the burdens of accommodation, provision and general aid that fell on the royal monasteries increased substantially. Likewise, the burdens of those monasteries along the Hellweg in Westphalia and others in Saxony probably increased or at least remained constant and substantial throughout the Saxon and Salian periods. In fact, Hans Conrad Peyer implies that the early attempts to limit or record the servitial renders for royal residences and monasteries, as for example at Werden, may well indicate that they were the most drawn upon for *servitium regis* and most affected by this demand from an early period.[31] A statement from a charter of Henry II granting Fulda a county best expresses his concept of the

---

[29] Matthäi (1877) 68–73; T. Schieffer (1951) 397–402; and Diefenbach (unpub. diss. 1952) 103–45.   [30] See above, Chapter 3, pp. 122–6.   [31] Peyer (1987) 160.

relationship between monastery and monarch: 'to whom much is entrusted, from them much is demanded' (*Cui plus committitur, plus ab eo exigitur*).[32]

This investigation of the royal monasteries and convents in the Saxon heartlands and the main transit zones of the realm and their role in support of the king and itinerant kingship has led to some significant findings. In general, royal monastic institutions provided early German kingship with extensive religious, political and economic support. In terms of supplying goods, revenues and accommodation, they played a crucial role in supporting and facilitating the itinerant kingship of the Ottonian and early Salian rulers. Moreover, within the context of this overall monastic support for kingship, religious communities of women emerge as active and important participants. Finally, the German rulers' use of their monasteries appears to be part of a long developmental process and, to a certain degree, a product of plan and policy. The cumulative weight of the evidence indicates that not only did the monasteries play a very important role in the support of German kings and their itinerant method of government, but that their role remained constant and even increased over time in the case of the monastic institutions which developed markets and which were located on frequently used roads or in locations distant from episcopal cities. Although one cannot point to a predetermined 'system' in the modern sense, the early German kings appear to have combined tradition, conscious choice, the use of available opportunities and their response to new situations to achieve a monastic 'policy' that, while not 'systematic', reveals a consistent set of responses. As Timothy Reuter has indicated, the relationship and policies of Ottonian and Salian kings and emperors with the higher churches in their realm, especially in respect to controlling episcopal and abbatial elections, did not approach a 'Church system' in the modern sense.[33] However, in regard to the monasteries in the central and the transit zones of the realm, one

---

[32] *DH II* 509. As Hoffmann (1986) 24–5 n. 40 has indicated, this quote is derived from Isidor, *Synonyma* 2.89, PL 83.865, where he talks about the rights and obligations of kings, or from Augustine, *Epistolae* 194.24, CSEL 57.195.9, not from Luke 12.48. Moreover, although this charter was partially forged in the twelfth century by Eberhard of Fulda, the use of this passage probably derives from an authentic charter of Henry II for Fulda and not the other charter of Henry II (*DH II* 433) where it appeared, because it is highly unlikely that Eberhard would have known that charter. Cf. Franke (1987) 113 n. 303.   [33] Reuter (1982).

can see at least a consistent and coherent set of responses and policy decisions, which enriched royal monasteries and expanded their jurisdictions. Thereby, the early German monarchs increased the ability of their monastic institutions to support their kingship and to serve the realm.

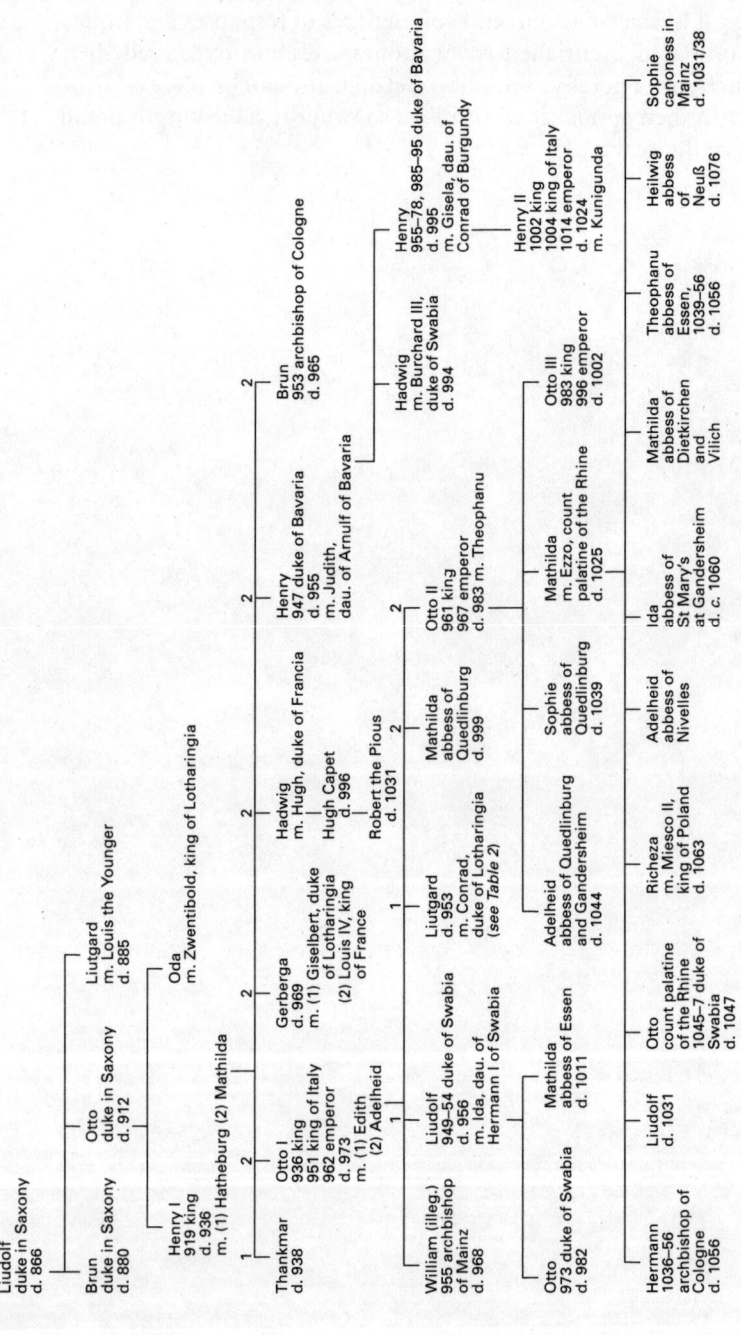

Genealogical Table I The Ottonians

Source: Adapted from Reuter, Germany in the Early Middle Ages, p. 337.

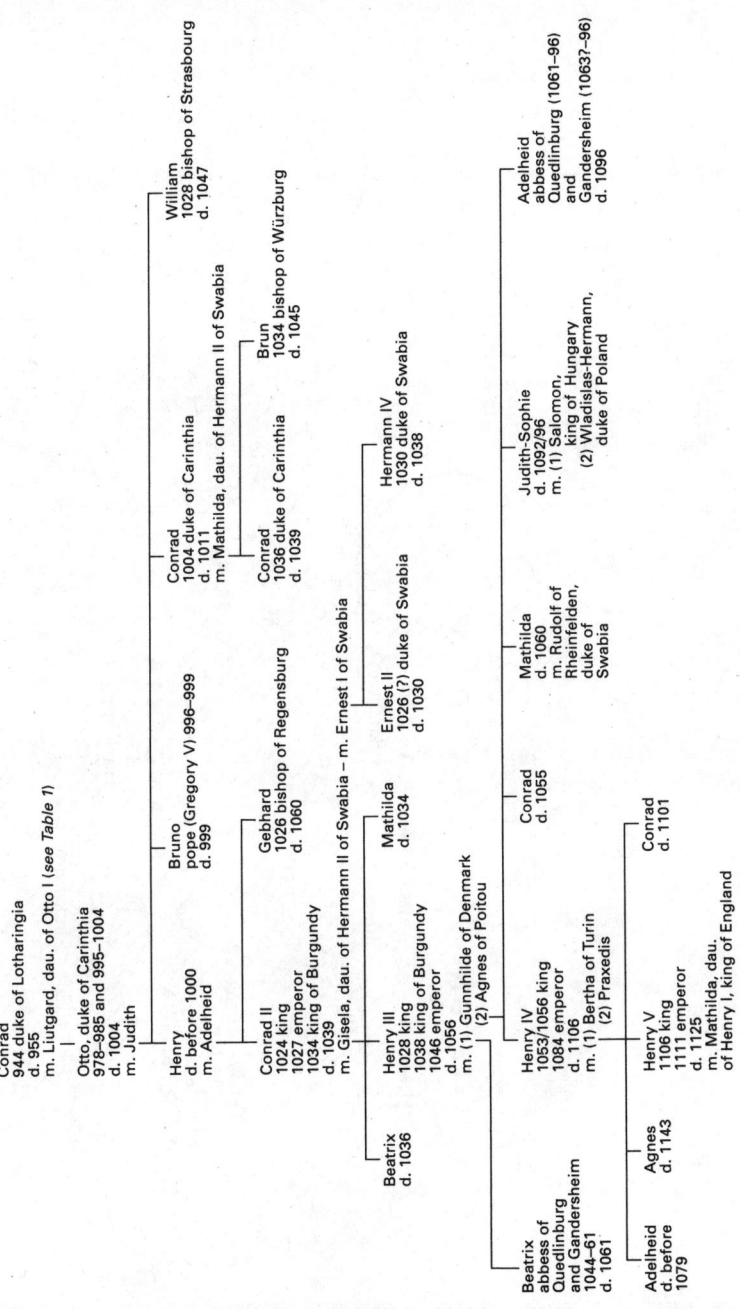

Genealogical Table 2   The Salians

Source: Adapted from Reuter, *Germany in the Early Middle Ages*, p. 338.

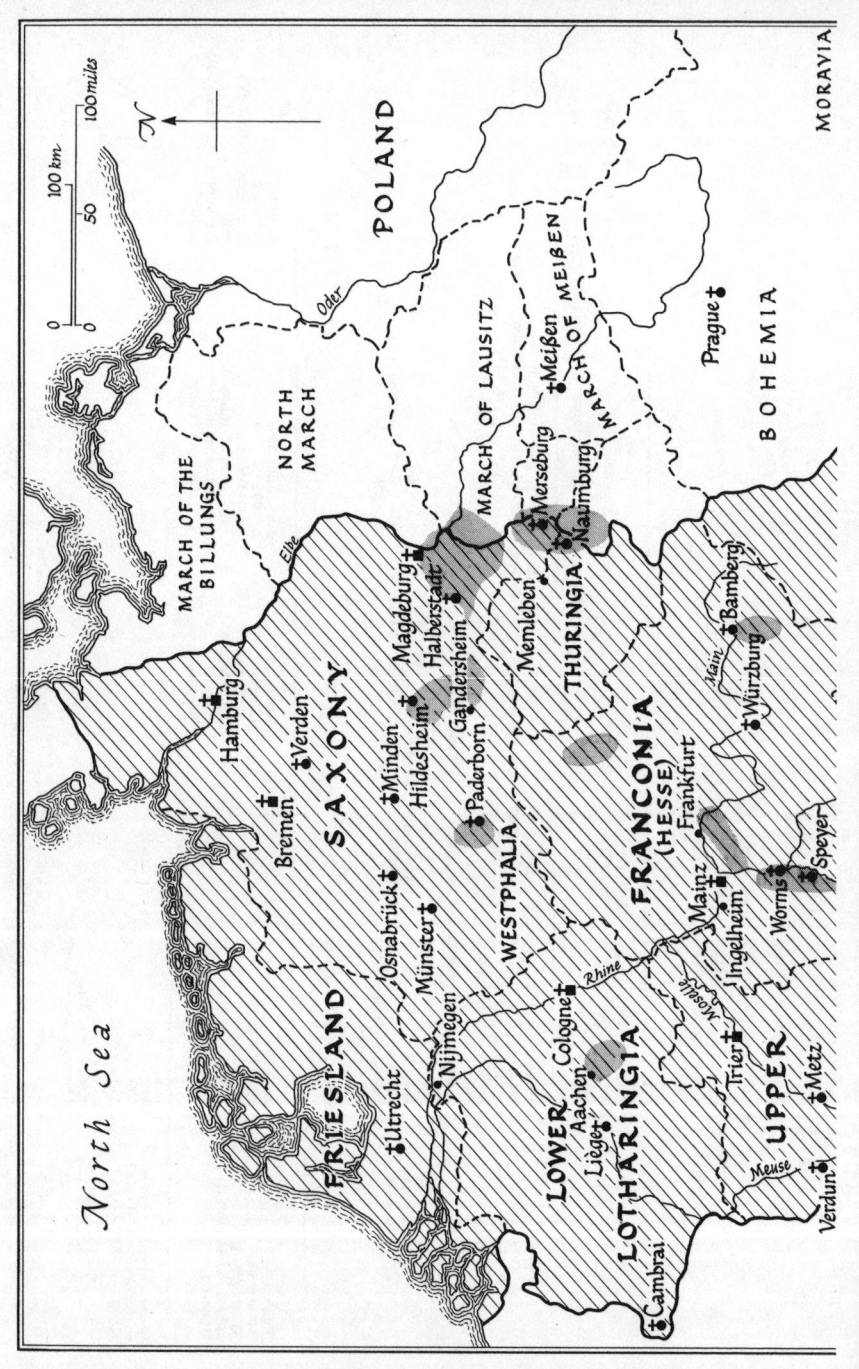

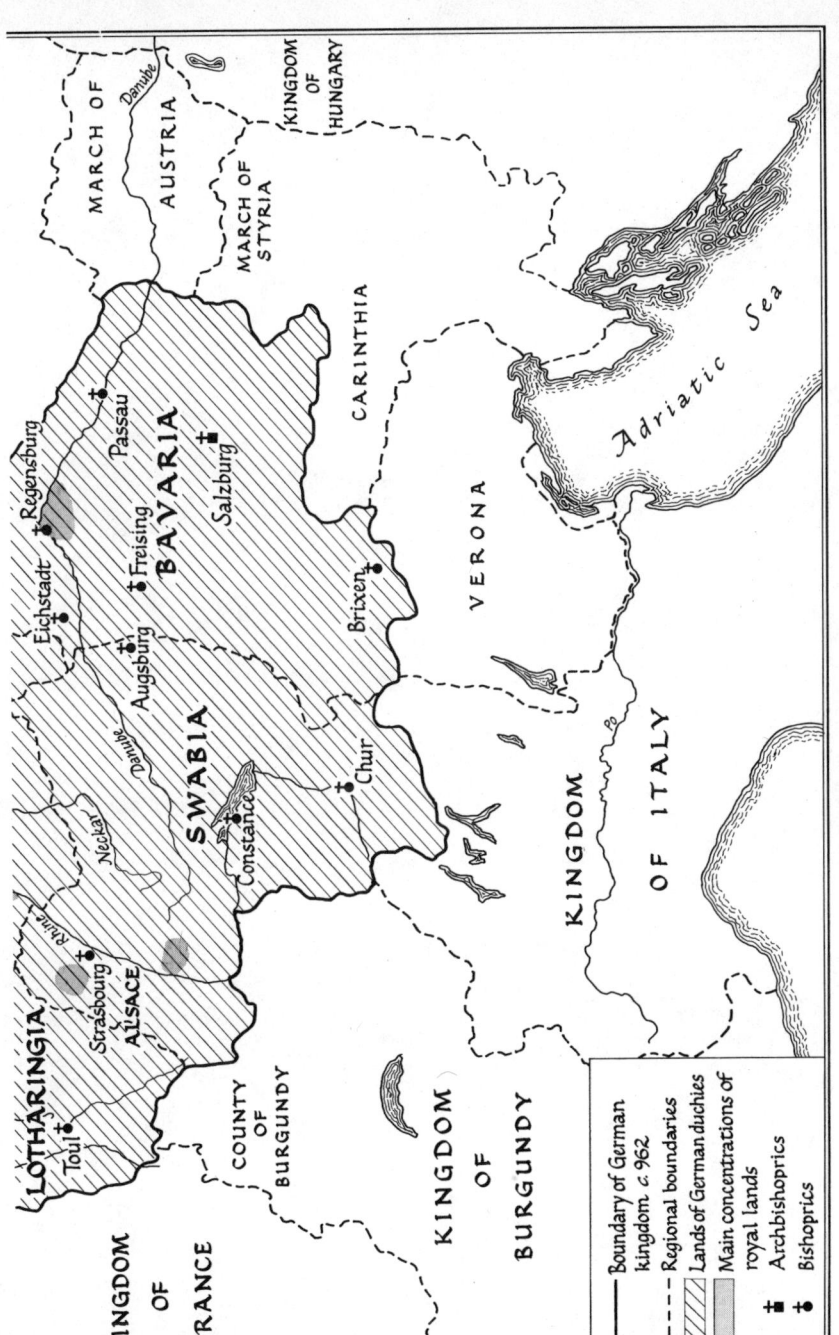

Map 1 Ottonian–Salian Germany: political

Source: Adapted from George Holmes, ed., Oxford Illustrated History of Medieval Europe (Oxford 1988), p. 151.

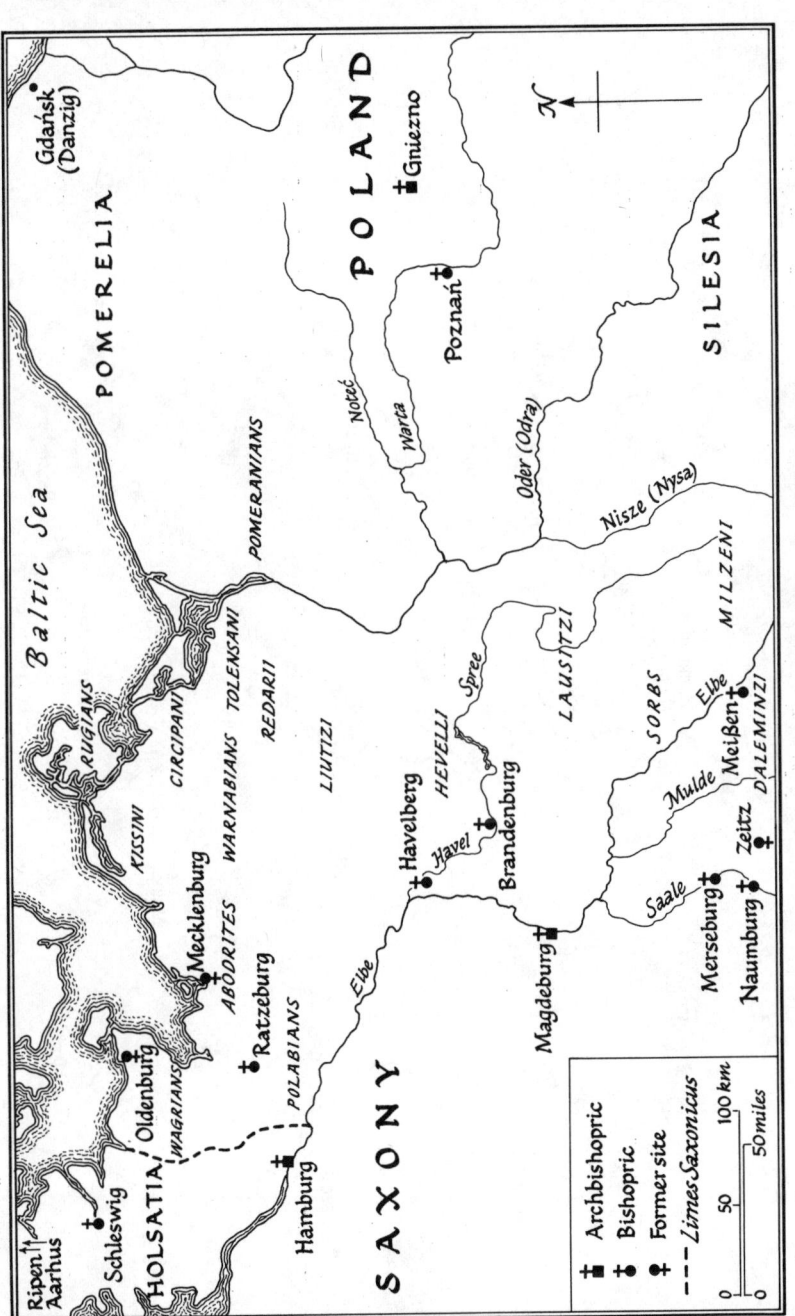

Map 2   Northeastern frontier: Slavic peoples and territories

Source: Adapted from Friedrich Lotter, 'The crusading idea and the conquest of the region east of the Elbe', in Robert Bartlett and Angus MacKay, eds., *Medieval Frontier Societies* (Oxford 1989). p. 268.

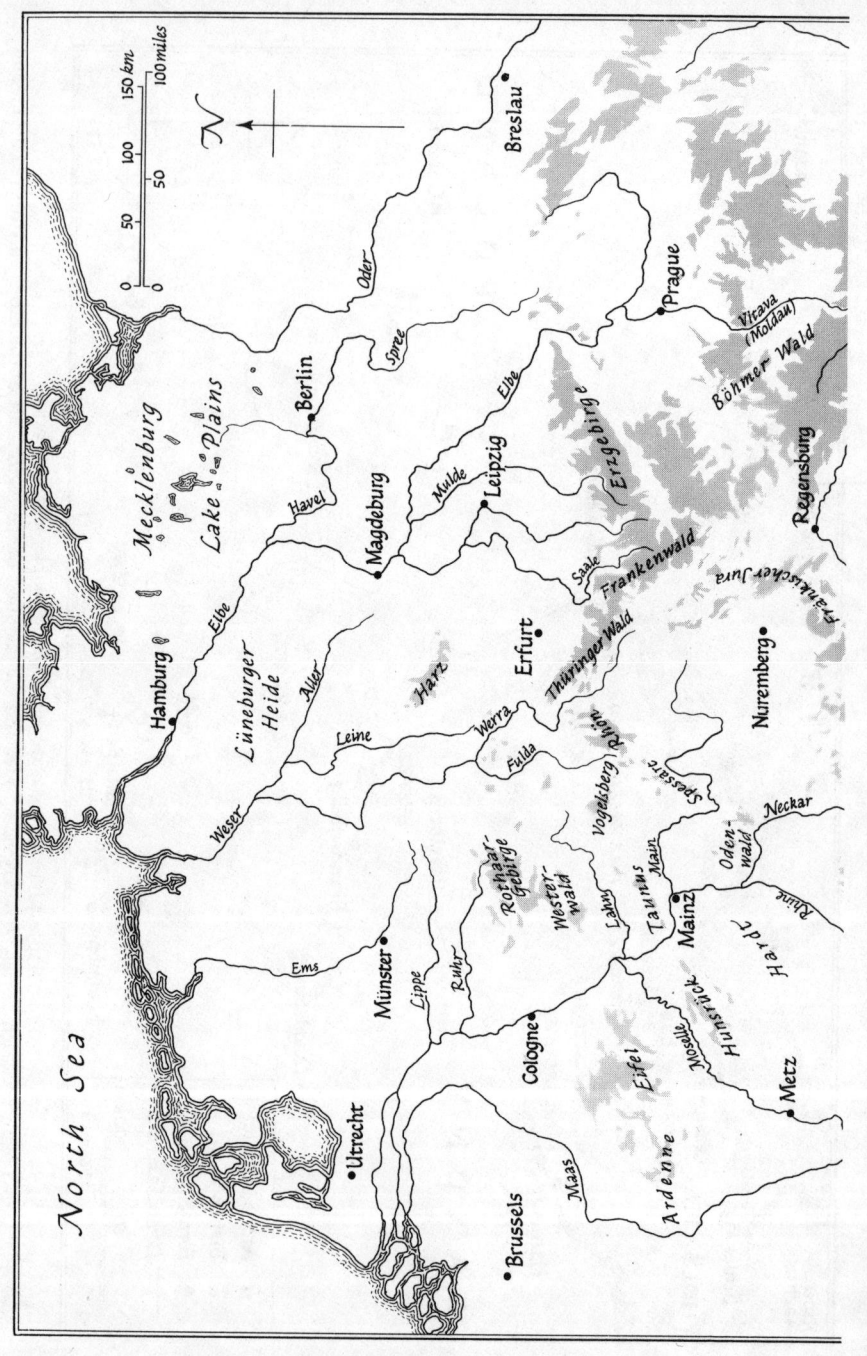

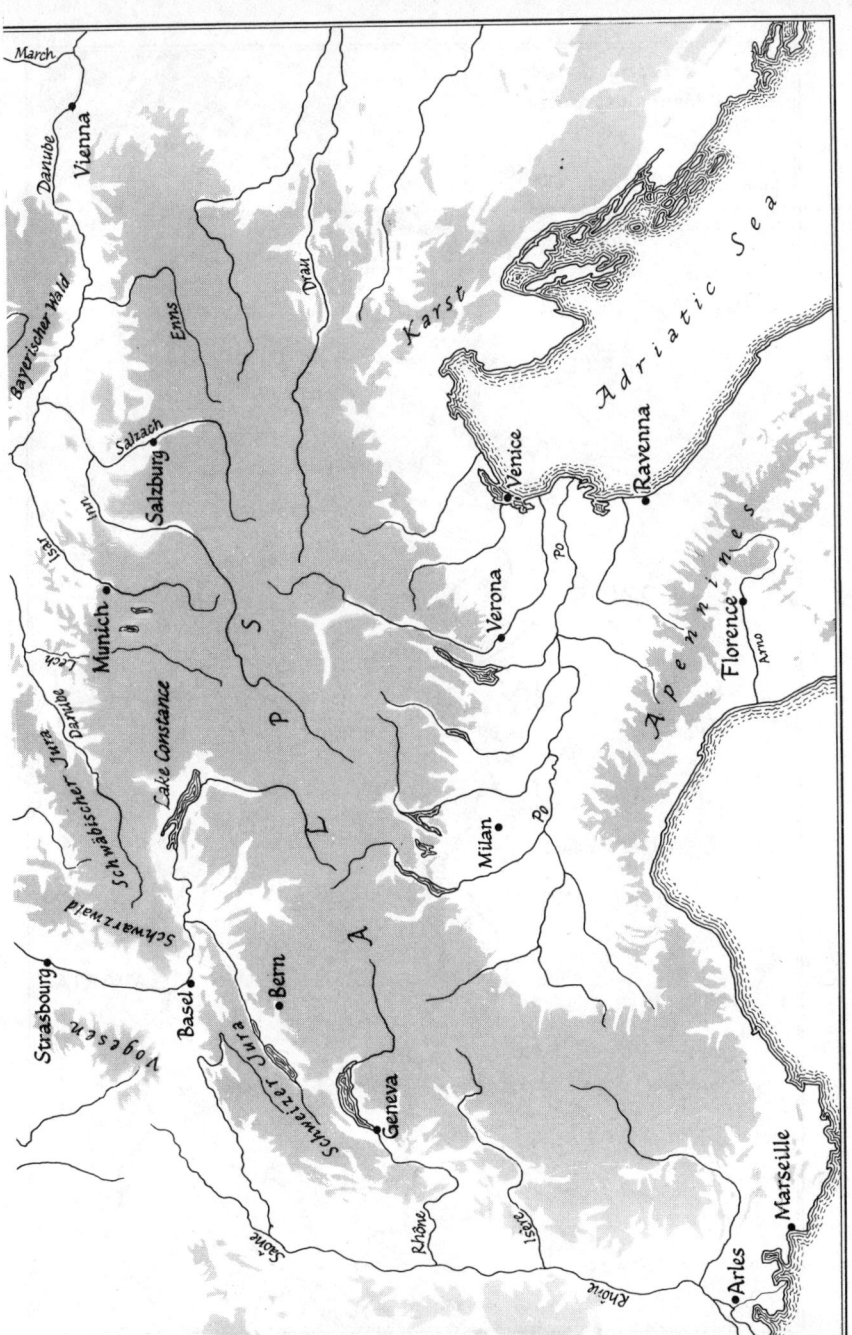

Map 3   Ottonian–Salian Germany: physical

Source: Adapted from Hans K. Schulze, *Das Reich und die Deutschen 3: Hegemoniales Kaisertum. Ottonen und Salier* (Berlin 1991), frontispiece.

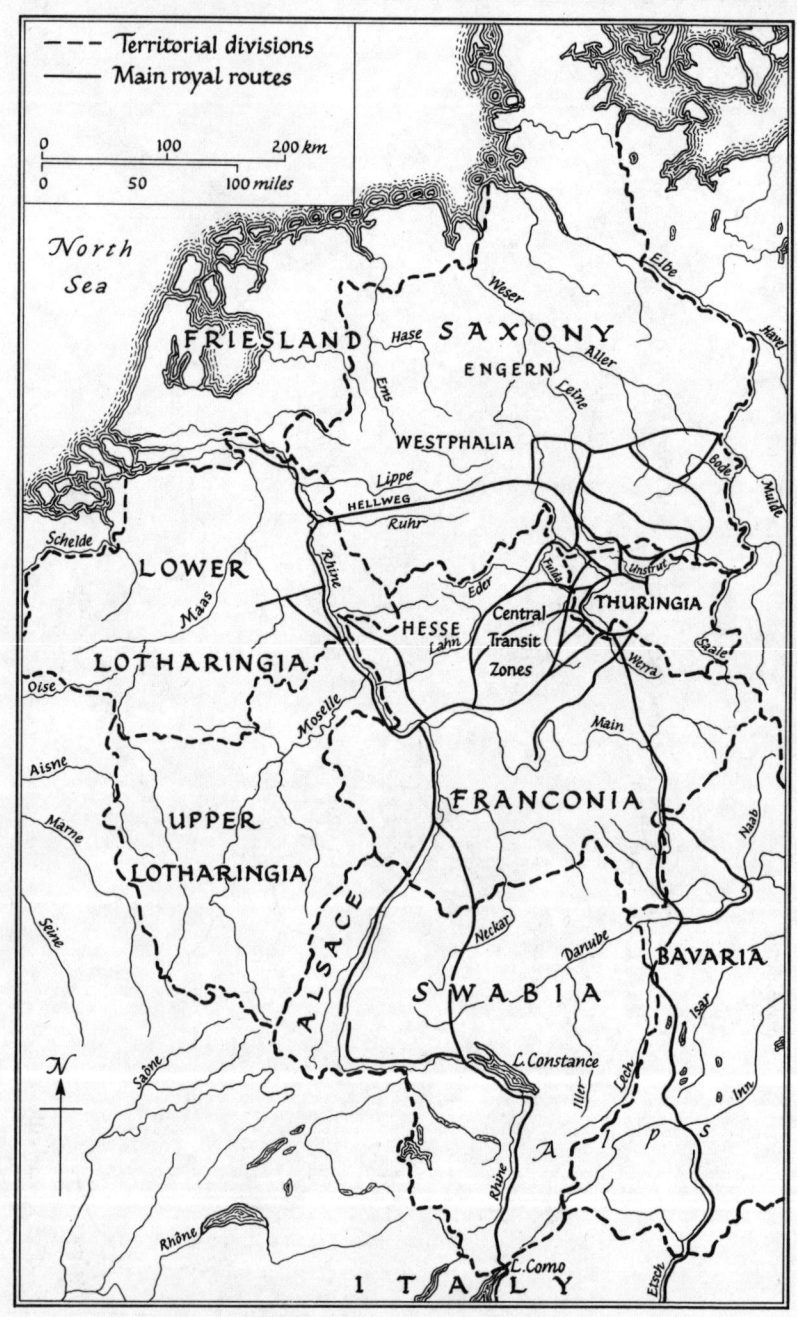

Map 4   Main royal routes and transit zones
Source: Adapted from Müller-Mertens, *Die Reichsstruktur*, map entitled 'Die deutschen Reichsteile bzw. die politischen Bezugsräume der Darstellung und des Itinerarkalenders'.

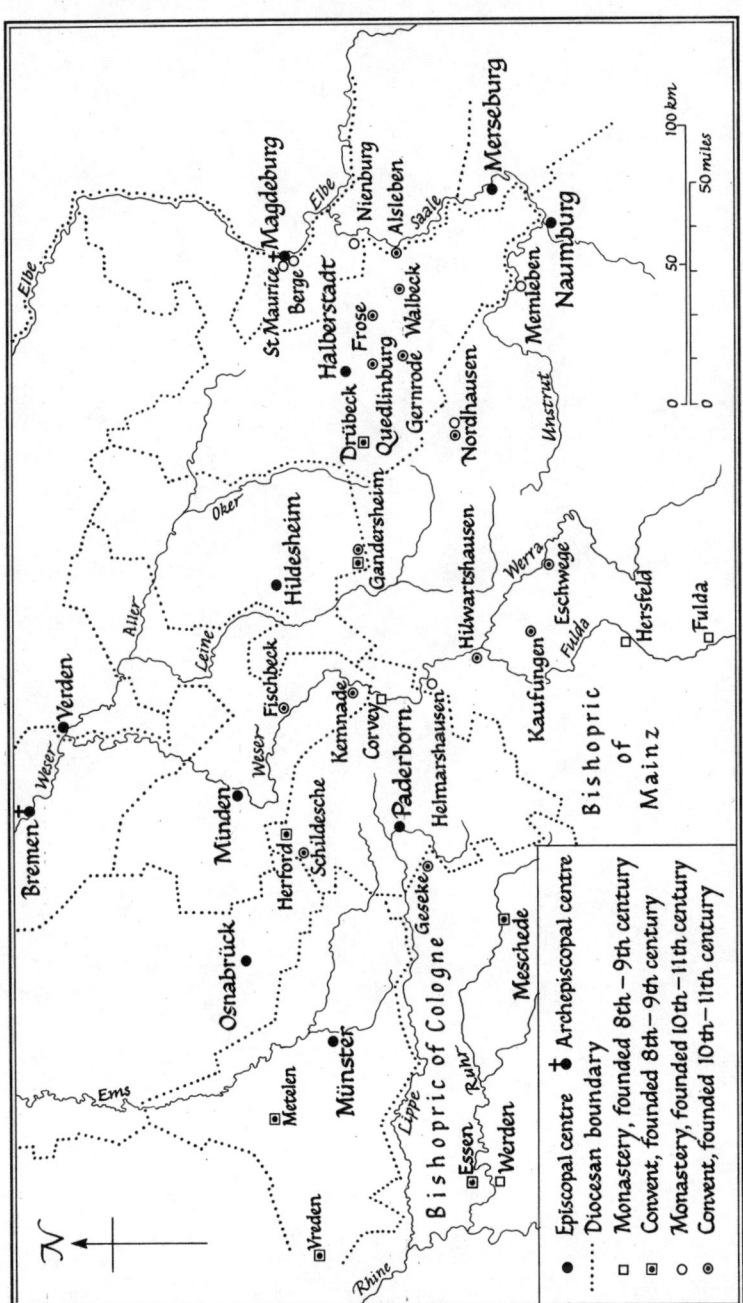

Map 5 Royal convents and monasteries in Saxony, Westphalia, Hesse and Thuringia
Source: Adapted from Parisse, 'Die Frauenstifte und Frauenklöster in Sachsen', p. 477.

Legend:

- Episcopal centre
- † Archepiscopal centre
- ..... Diocesan boundary
- ▢ Monastery, founded 8th–9th century
- ▣ Convent, founded 8th–9th century
- ○ Monastery, founded 10th–11th century
- ◎ Convent, founded 10th–11th century

Places:

Bremen, Verden, Magdeburg, St Maurice, Berge, Halberstadt, Elbe, Nienburg, Alsleben, Merseburg, Naumburg, Saale, Memleben, Drübeck, Frose, Quedlinburg, Gernrode, Walbeck, Nordhausen, Unstrut, Oker, Hildesheim, Gandersheim, Hilwartshausen, Werra, Eschwege, Hersfeld, Fulda, Kaufungen, Leine, Aller, Weser, Fischbeck, Kemnade, Corvey, Paderborn, Helmarshausen, Bishopric of Mainz, Minden, Herford, Schildesche, Geseke, Meschede, Osnabrück, Münster, Ems, Metelen, Vreden, Essen, Werden, Ruhr, Lippe, Rhine, Bishopric of Cologne

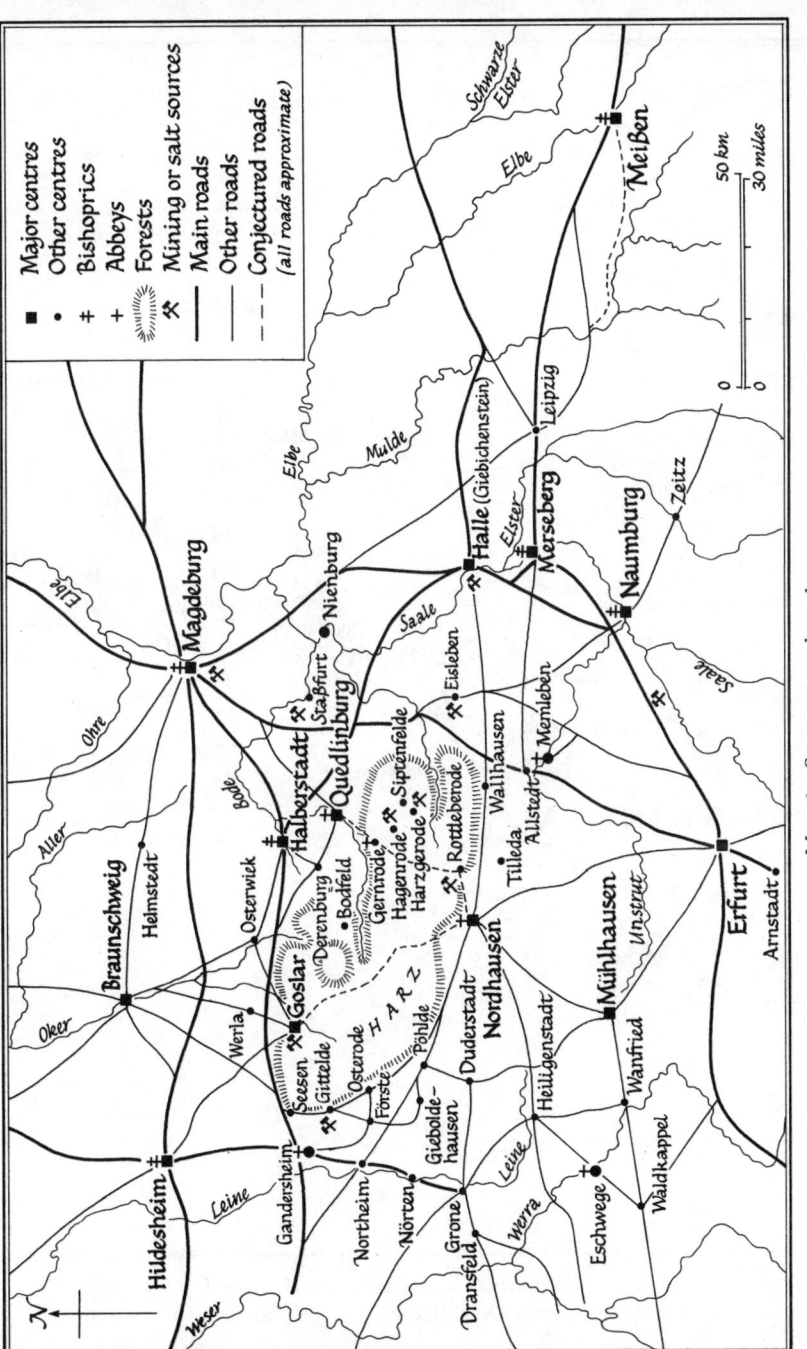

Map 6 Saxony: roads and centres

Source: Adapted from Schwineköper, *Königtum und Städte*, p. 13.

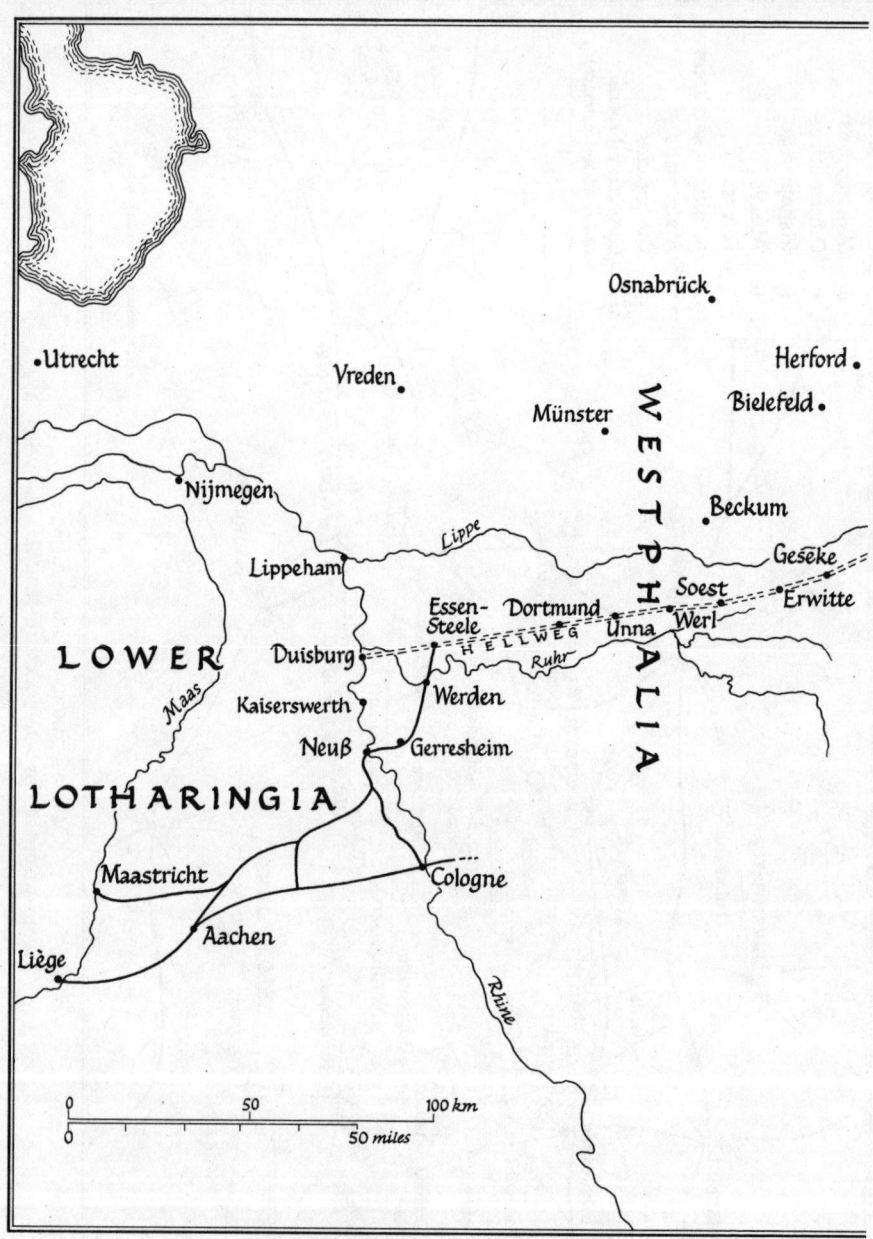

Map 7 Westphalian transit zone: the Hellweg
Source: Adapted from Deus, 'Kaiserbesuche in Soest', p. 6.

S A X O N Y

Minden

Weser

Hameln

Leine

Braunschweig

Hildesheim

Brüggen

Werla

Magdeburg

Elbe

Dahlum

Goslar

Halberstadt

Gandersheim

Derenburg

Nienburg

Harz

Bodfeld

Quedlinburg

Driburg

Corvey

Höxter

Hasselfelde

Paderborn

Brakel

Solling

Herstelle

Diemel

Pöhlde

Saale

Eresburg

Grone

Nordhausen

Marsberg

Warburg

Allstedt

Merseburg

T H U R I N G I A

Werra

Mühlhausen

Fritzlar

Fulda

H E S S E

Hersfeld

N

Fulda

E N G R E Z

===== Hellweg
——— Other roads
Forests

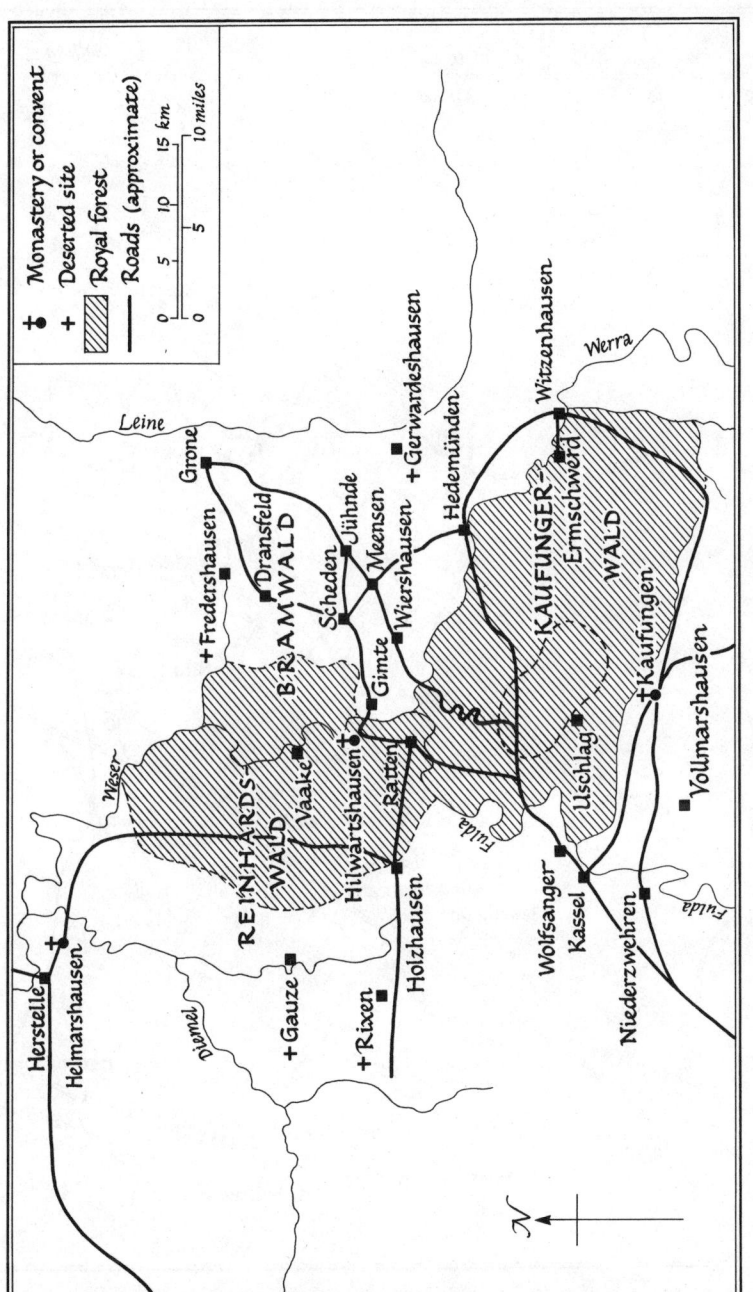

Map 8   Saxon–Hessian river basins

Source: Adapted from Kroeschell, 'Zur älteren Geschichte', pp. 6, 10.

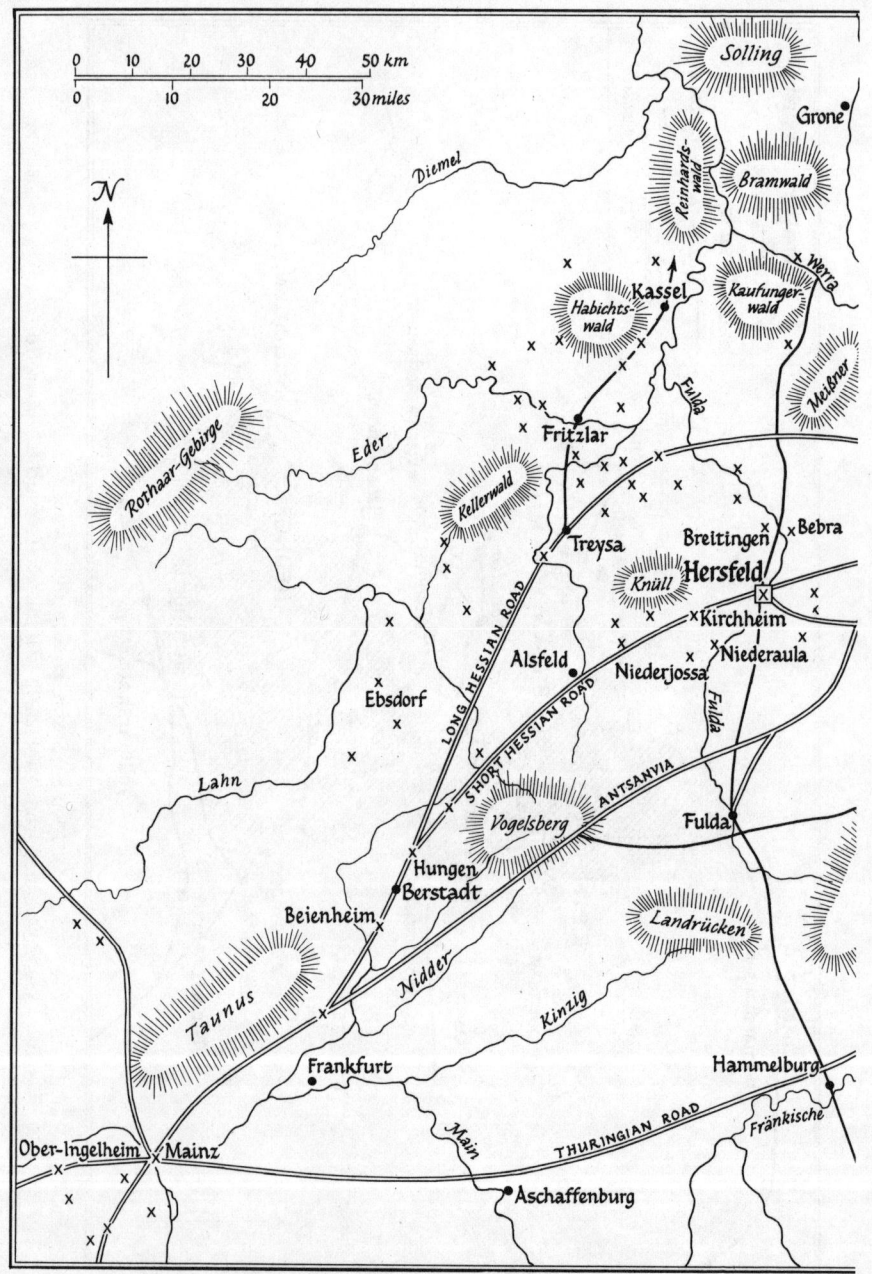

Map 9   Central transit zone: main routes and Hersfeld's properties
Source: Adapted from Hörle, '*Breviarum Sancti Lulli*', p. 53, and Wehlt,
Reichsabtei und König.

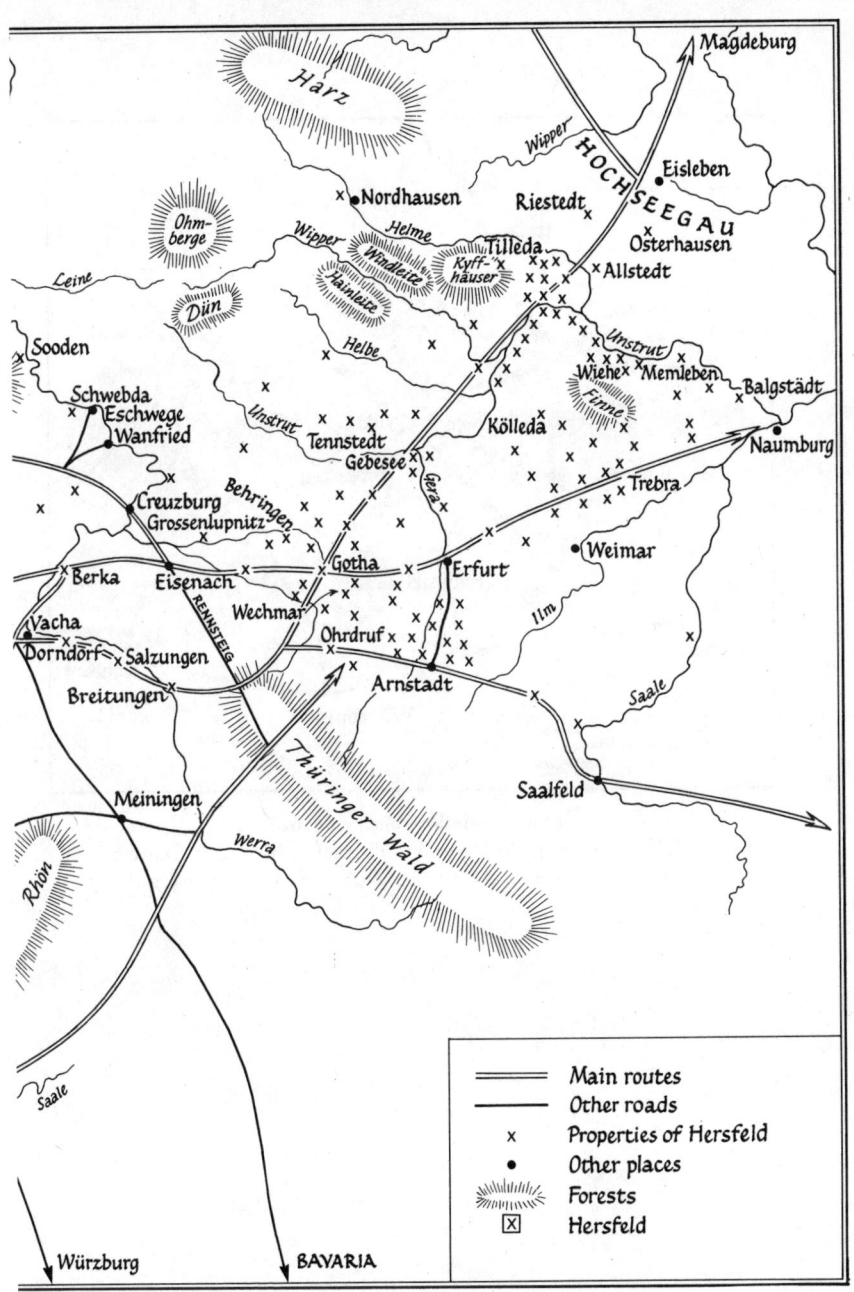

		Main routes
		Other roads
	x	Properties of Hersfeld
	•	Other places
	⋤⋤⋤	Forests
	⊠	Hersfeld

Magdeburg

Harz

Wipper · HOCHSEEGAU

Eisleben

Nordhausen

Riestedt

Ohm-berge

Wipper · Helme · Tilleda · Osterhausen

Kyff-häuser · Allstedt

Leine

Windleite · Hainleite

Dün

Unstrut

Sooden

Helbe

Wiehe · Memleben · Balgstädt

Schwebda · Eschwege

Wanfried

Unstrut · Tennstedt · Kölleda

Naumburg

Gebesee · Gera · Finne

Creuzburg · Behringen

Grossenlupnitz

Trebra

Berka · Eisenach · Gotha · Erfurt

Weimar

Wechmar

Vacha · Dorndorf · Salzungen

Ohrdruf · Ilm

Breitungen · Arnstadt

Saale

RENNSTEIG

Thüringer Wald

Meiningen · Werra

Saalfeld

Rhön

Saale

Würzburg · BAVARIA

327

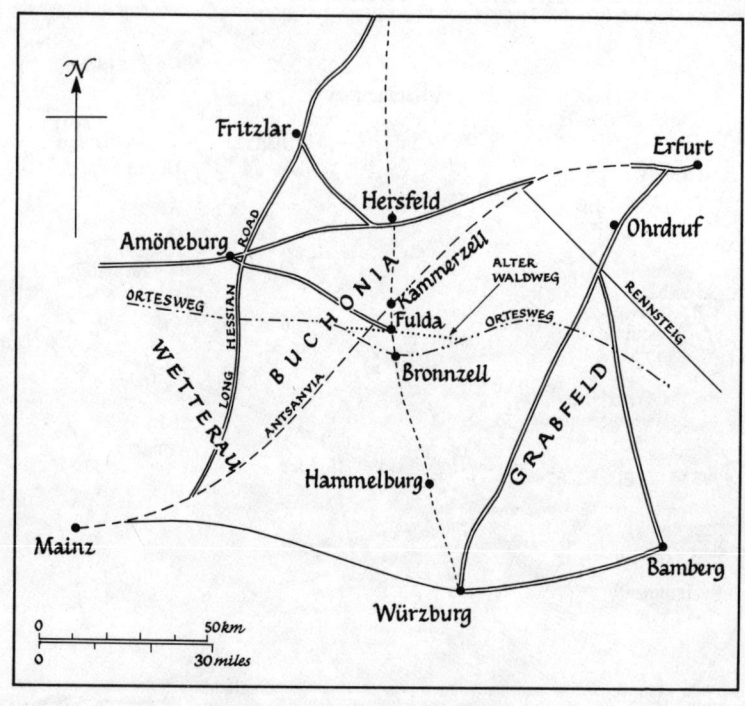

Map 10   Fulda: pertinent roads
Source: Adapted from J. Vonderau and J. Schalkenbach, *Die Gründung des Klosters Fulda und seine Bauten bis zum Tode Sturms* (Fulda 1944), Fig. 5.

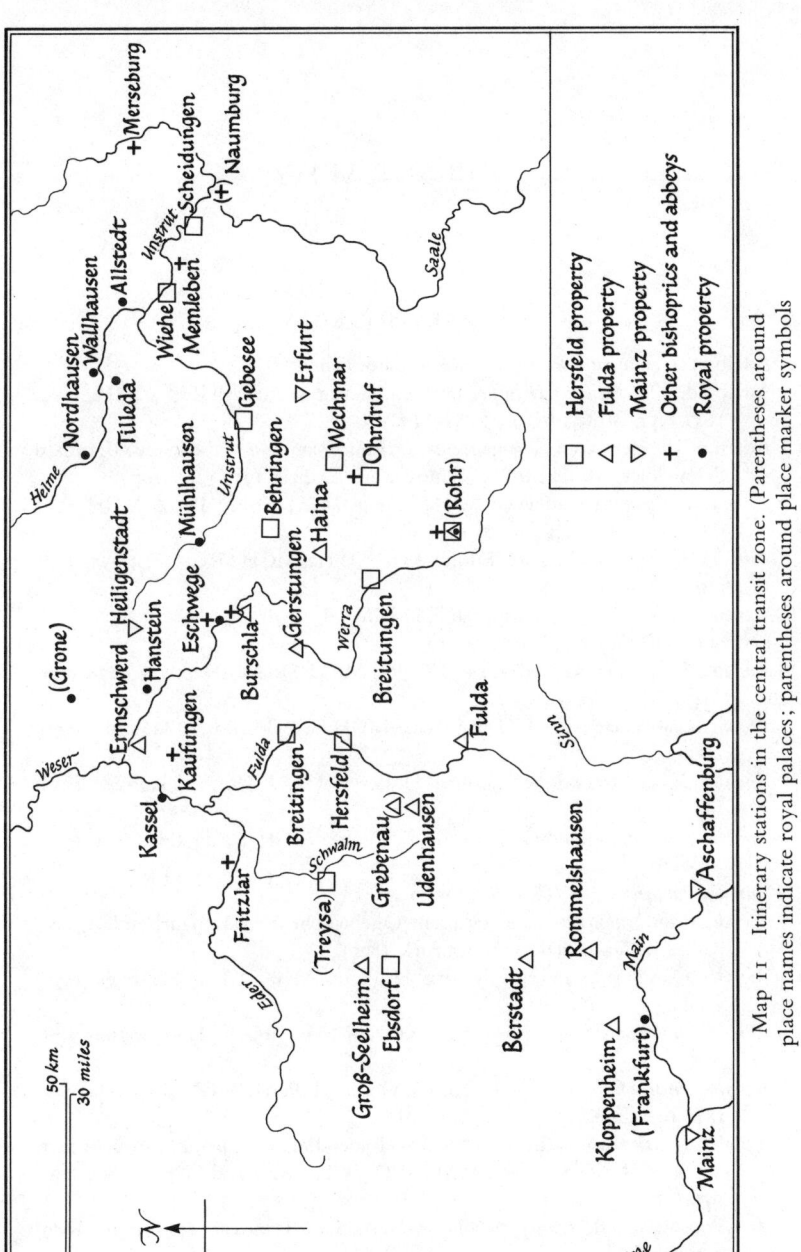

Map 11 Itinerary stations in the central transit zone. (Parentheses around place names indicate royal palaces; parentheses around place marker symbols indicate palaces of episcopal, abbatial or unknown type.)

Source: Adapted from Metz, 'Quellenstudien zum *Servitium regis*, I', p. 226.

BIBLIOGRAPHY

PRIMARY SOURCES

Adalbert, *Continuatio Reginonis*. See Regino, *Chronicon*.

Adalbold, *Vita Heinrici II imperatoris*, ed. Georg Waitz, MGH SS 4 (Hanover 1841 repr. Stuttgart 1982) 787–814.

Adam of Bremen, *Gesta Hamburgensis Ecclesiae Pontificum* 3rd edn, ed. Bernhard Schmeidler, MGH SRG 2 (Hanover and Leipzig 1917 repr. 1977).

Annales Alamannici continuatio Sangallensis tertia, ed. Georg Pertz, MGH SS 1 (Hanover 1826 repr. 1976) 19–60.

Annales Altahensis maiores, ed. Edmund von Oefele, MGH SRG 4 (Hanover 1891 repr. 1979).

Annales Corbeienses, ed. Philipp Jaffé, in Jaffé, ed., *Bibl.* 1. 33–44.

Les Annales de Flodoard. See Flodoard.

Annales Hildesheimenses, ed. Georg Waitz, MGH SRG 8 (Hanover 1878 repr. 1947).

Annales Laureshamenses, ed. Georg Pertz, MGH SS 1 (Hanover 1826 repr. 1976) 22–39.

Annales Magdeburgenses, ed. Georg H. Pertz, MGH SS 16 (Hanover 1859) 105–96.

Annales Necrologici Fuldenses, ed. Georg Waitz, MGH SS 13 (Hanover 1881) 161–216.

Annales Palidenses. See Theodor, the monk.

Annales Patherbrunnenses (eine verlorene Quellenschrift des 12. Jahrhunderts), ed. Paul Scheffer-Boichorst (Innsbruck 1870).

Annales Quedlinburgenses, ed. Georg H. Pertz, MGH SS 3 (Hanover 1839) 22–90.

Annales regni Francorum, ed. Friedrich Kurze, MGH SRG 6 (Hanover 1895 repr. 1950).

Annales sancti Maximini Trevirensis, ed. Georg H. Pertz, MGH SS 4 (Hanover 1841 repr. 1982) 5–7.

Annales Weissenburgenses, ed. Oswald Holder-Egger, appendix to Lampert, monk of Hersfeld, *Opera*, MGH SRG 38 (Hanover and Leipzig 1894 repr. 1984).

Annalista Saxo, ed. Georg Waitz, MGH SS 6 (Hanover 1844 repr. 1980) 542–777.

Ardo, *Vita Benedicti Abbatis*, ed. Georg Waitz, MGH SS 15.1 (Hanover 1887 repr. 1963) 198–220.

Primary sources

Arnold, *Ex libris de sancto Emmeramo*, ed. Georg Waitz, MGH SS 4 (Hanover 1841 repr. 1982) 543–74.

Böhmer, Johann Friedrich, *Regesta Imperii 1. Die Regesten des Kaiserreiches unter den Karolingern 751–918*, new edn by Engelbert Mühlbacher, 2nd edn completed by J. Lechner (Innsbruck 1908 repr. with new introduction and additions by Hans H. Kaminsky, Hildesheim 1966). [Abbreviated to BM².]

Regesta Imperii 2 (Sächsisches Haus 919–1024)/1: Die Regesten des Kaiserreiches unter Heinrich I. und Otto I. 919–973, new edn by Emil von Ottenthal (Innsbruck 1893 repr. with additions by Hans H. Kaminsky, Hildesheim 1967). [Abbreviated to BO.]

Regesta Imperii 2 (Sächsisches Haus 919–1024)/2: Die Regesten des Kaiserreiches unter Otto II. 955 (973)–983, new edn by Hans L. Mikoletzky (Graz 1950). [Abbreviated to BMik.]

Regesta Imperii 2 (Sächsisches Haus 919–1024)/3: Die Regesten des Kaiserreiches unter Otto III. 980 (983)–1002, new edn by Mathilde Uhlirz (Graz and Cologne 1956–7). [Abbreviated to BU.]

Regesta Imperii 2 (Sächsisches Haus 919–1024)/4: Die Regesten des Kaiserreiches unter Heinrich II. 1002–1024, new edn by Theodor Graff (Vienna, Cologne and Graz 1971). [Abbreviated to BG.]

Regesta Imperii 2 (Sächsisches Haus 919–1024)/5: Papstregesten 911–1024, ed. Harald Zimmermann (Vienna, Cologne and Graz 1969). [Abbreviated to BZ.]

Regesta Imperii 3 (Salisches Haus 1024–1125)/1.1: Die Regesten des Kaiserreiches unter Konrad II. 1024–1039, new edn by Heinrich Appelt (Graz 1951). [Abbreviated to BA.]

Regesta Imperii 3 (Salisches Haus 1024–1125)/2.3: Die Regesten des Kaiserreiches unter Heinrich IV.1056 (1050)–1106 pt. 1: 1056 (1050)–1065, new edn by Tilman Struve (Cologne and Vienna 1984). [Abbreviated to BS.]

Regesta Imperii 5 (Jüngere Staufer 1198–1272): Die Regesten des Kaiserreiches unter Philipp...und Richard (1198–1272), new rev. edn by Julius Ficker and Eduard Winckelmann (Innsbruck 1881–1901 repr. Hildesheim 1969). [Abbreviated to BF.]

Boniface, *S. Bonifatii et Lulli epistolae (Die Briefe des heiligen Bonifatius und Lulllus)*, ed. Michael Tangl, MGH Epis. Select. 1 (Berlin 1916 repr. Munich 1989).

Bouquet, Martin, ed., *Recueil des historiens des Gaules et de la France*, Rerum Gallicarum et Franciarum Scriptores, 8 vols., 2nd new edn by Léopold Delisle in 6 vols. (Paris 1870 repr. 1967). [Pagination in the two edns is identical.] [Abbreviated to Bouq. or *DLF*.]

Brun of Querfurt, 'Letter to King Henry II (1008)', in Giesebrecht (1885) 702–5.

Bruno, *Saxonicum Bellum (Brunos Buch vom Sachsenkrieg)*, ed. Hans-Eberhard Lohmann, MGH Deutsches Mittelalter 2 (Leipzig 1937).

Cartulaire de l'Abbaye de Gorze, ms. 826 de la Bibliothèque de Metz, ed. A. d'Herbomez, Mettensia 2, Mémoires et documents publiés par la Société Nationale des Antiquaires de France (Paris 1898).

Cartulaire de l'Abbaye de Saint-Bertin, ed. Benjamin Guérard, Collection de documents inédits sur l'histoire de France (Paris 1841).

Bibliography

Casus s. Galli continuatio II, ed. Georg H. Pertz, MGH SS 2 (Hanover 1829 repr. 1976) 148–63.

Chronicon Benedictoburanum, ed. Wilhelm Wattenbach, MGH SS 9 (Hanover 1851 repr. 1983) 210–38.

Chronicon Montis Sereni, ed. Georg H. Pertz, MGH SS 23 (Hanover 1874) 138–226.

Codex Diplomaticus Anhaltinus 1, ed. Otto von Heinemann (Dessau 1867). [Abbreviated to *CDA*.]

Codex Diplomaticus Fuldensis, ed. Ernst F. J. Dronke (Kassel 1850 repr. Aalen 1962). [Abbreviated to *CDF*.]

Codex Laureshamensis, 3 vols., ed. Karl Glöckner (Darmstadt 1929–36). [Abbreviated to *CL*.]

Constantine, *Vita Adalberonis II Mettensis Episcopi*, ed. Georg H. Pertz, MGH SS 4 (Hanover 1841 repr. 1982) 658–72.

Continuatio Vitae Bernwardi, Georg H. Pertz, MGH SS 11 (Hanover 1854) 165–7.

Corpus Consuetudinum Monasticarum 1: Initia Consuetudinis Benedictiae. Consuetudines Saeculi Octavi et Noni, ed. Kassius Hallinger OSB (Siegburg 1963). [Abbreviated to *CCM*.]

Een Diplomatisch Oonderzoek van de oudste particuliere Oorkonden van Werden, ed. Dirk Peter Blok (Assen 1960).

Eigil, *Vita Sancti Sturmi*, ed. Georg H. Pertz, MGH SS 2 (Hanover 1829 repr. 1976) 365–77. [Also published as *Die Vita Sturmi des Eigil von Fulda*, ed. Pius Engelbert, Veröffentlichungen der Historischen Kommission für Hessen und Waldeck 29 (Marburg 1968) 129–70.] [Chapter numbers in the two editions coincide. Page references are to the edition by Pertz in MGH.]

Ekkehard IV, *Casus Sancti Galli*, ed. Hans Haefele, Ausgewählte Quellen zur Deutschen Geschichte des Mittelalters 10 (Darmstadt 1980).

Everhelm, *Vita Popponis Abbatis Stabulensis*, ed. Wilhelm Wattenbach, MGH SS 11 (Hanover 1854) 291–316.

Ex Miraculis s. Wigberhti, ed. Georg Waitz, MGH SS 4 (Hanover 1841 repr. 1982) 224–8.

Flodoard, *Les Annales de Flodoard*, ed. Philip Lauer, Collection de textes pour servir à l'étude de l'enseignement de l'histoire 39 (Paris 1905).

Folcwin, the Deacon, *Gesta Abbatum s. Bertini Sithiensium*, ed. Oswald Holder-Egger, MGH SS 13 (Hanover 1881) 600–35.

Froumund, *Codex Epistolarum Tegernseensium (Die Tegernseer Briefsammlung)*, ed. Karl Strecker, MGH Epis. Select. 3 (Berlin 1925 repr. Munich 1964).

Fuldensium Antiquitatum Libri IIII, ed. Christoph Brower (Antwerp 1612).

Gerhard, *Vita s. Oudalrici episcopi Augustani*, ed. Georg Waitz, MGH SS 4 (Hanover 1841 repr. Stuttgart 1982) 377–419.

Gesta abbatum Trudonensium, ed. Rudolf Koepke, MGH SS 10 (Hanover 1852) 211–448.

Gesta archiepiscoporum Magdeburgensium, ed. W. Schum, MGH SS 14 (Hanover 1883 repr. Stuttgart 1988) 374–489.

Hrotsvitha, *Gesta Ottonis*, in *Hrotsvithae Opera*, ed. Paul von Winterfeld, MGH SRG 34 (Berlin 1902 repr. 1965) 201–28.

Primary sources

Inventar des Archivs des Bishöflichen Generalvikariats zu Paderborn [= Inventare der nichtsstaatlichen Archive der Provinz Westfalen, Beiband 2.1], ed. Johannes Linneborn (Münster 1920).

Jaffé, Philipp, *Regesta pontificum Romanorum ab condita ecclesia ad annum post Christum natum MCXCVIII*, 2nd edn rev. F. Kaltenbrunner (to 590), P. Ewald (590–882), S. Loewenfeld (882–1198), 2 vols. (Berlin 1885–8). [Abbreviated to JL.]

Jaffé, Philipp, ed., *Bibliotheca rerum Germanicarum*, 6 vols., (Berlin 1864 repr. Aalen 1964).

Die Kaiserurkunden der Provinz Westfalen (777–1284), ed. Roger Wilmans and Friedrich Philippi, 2 vols. (Münster 1867–81).

Kehr, Paul (1932), 'Die älteren Urkunden für Helmarshausen', *NA* 49 (1932) 86–114.

Lampert, monk of Hersfeld, *Annales*, in Lampert, *Opera* pp. 1–304.

Libelli de institutione Herveldensis ecclesiae, in Lampert, *Opera* pp. 341–54.

Opera, ed. Oswald Holder-Egger, MGH SRG 38 (Hanover and Leipzig 1894 repr. 1956).

Liudprand of Cremona, *Die Werke Liudprands von Cremona*, 3rd edn, ed. Joseph Becker, MGH SRG 41 (Hanover 1915 repr. 1977).

Mariani Scotti Chronicon, ed. Georg H. Pertz, MGH SS 5 (Hanover 1844) 485–562.

MGH Capitularia regum Francorum, vol. 1, ed. Alfred Boretius (Hanover 1883 repr. 1984).

MGH Concilia 2.1–2: Concilia aevi Karolini (742–842), ed. Albert Werminghoff (Hanover 1906–8 repr. 1979).

MGH Concilia 6: Concilia aevi Saxonici (916–1001) Pars I DCCCCXVI–DCCCCLX, Die Konzilien Deutschlands und Reichsitaliens 916–1001: Teil 1: 919–960, ed. Ernst-Dieter Hehl (with the assistance of Horst Fuhrmann) (Hanover 1987).

MGH Constitutiones et acta publica imperatorum et regum inde ab a. DCCCCXI usque ad. a. MCXCVII 911–1197, ed. Ludwig Weiland (Hanover 1893 repr. 1963).

MGH Diplomata Karolinorum 1: Pippini, Carlomanni, Caroli Magni Diplomata, ed. Engelbert Mühlbacher (Berlin 1906 repr. Munich 1980). [Abbreviated to *DPep III, DKarl, DKar*.]

MGH Diplomata Karolinorum 3: Lotharii I. et Lotharii II. Diplomata, ed. Theodor Schieffer (Berlin and Zürich 1966 repr. Munich 1980). [Abbreviated to *DLoth I, DLoth II*.]

MGH Diplomata regum Germaniae ex stirpe Karolinorum 1: Ludowici Germanici, Karolmanni, Ludowici Iunioris Diplomata, ed. Paul Kehr (Berlin 1932–4 repr. Munich 1980). [Abbreviated to *DLD, DKarlo, DLJ*.]

MGH Diplomata regum Germaniae ex stirpe Karolinorum 2: Karoli III. Diplomata, ed. Paul Kehr (Berlin 1936–7 repr. Munich 1984). [Abbreviated to *DKD*.]

MGH Diplomata regum Germaniae ex stirpe Karolinorum 3: Arnolfi Diplomata, ed. Paul Kehr (Berlin 1940 repr. Munich 1988). [Abbreviated to *DArn*.]

MGH Diplomata regum Germaniae ex stirpe Karolinorum 4: Zwentiboldi et Ludowici

Bibliography

Infantis Diplomata, ed. Theodor Schieffer (Berlin 1960 repr. Munich 1982). [Abbreviated to *DZ, DLK*.]

MGH Regum Burgundiae e stirpe Rudolfina Diplomata et Acta, ed. Theodor Schieffer and Hans Eberhard Mayer (Munich 1977 repr. 1983). [Abbreviated to *DKo*.]

MGH Diplomata regum et imperatorum Germaniae 1: Conradii I., Heinrici I. et Ottonis I. Diplomata, ed. Theodor Sickel (Hanover 1879–84 repr. Munich 1980). [Abbreviated to *DK I, DH I, DO I.*]

MGH Diplomata regum et imperatorum Germaniae 2.1: Ottonis II. Diplomata, ed. Theodor Sickel (Hanover 1888 repr. Munich 1980). [Abbreviated to *DO II.*]

MGH Diplomata regum et imperatorum Germaniae 2.2: Ottonis III. Diplomata, ed. Theodor Sickel (Hanover 1926–31 repr. Munich 1980). [Abbreviated to *DO III.*]

MGH Diplomata regum et imperatorum Germaniae 3: Heinrici II. et Arduini Diplomata, ed. Harry Bresslau, Hermann Bloch and Robert Holtzmann (Hanover 1900–3 repr. Munich 1980). [Volume contains the charters of Kunigunda.] [Abbreviated to *DH II, DKunig.*]

MGH Diplomata regum et imperatorum Germaniae 4: Conradi II. Diplomata, ed. Harry Bresslau (Hanover 1909 repr. Munich 1980). [Abbreviated to *DK II.*]

MGH Diplomata regum et imperatorum Germaniae 5: Heinrici III. Diplomata, ed. Harry Bresslau and Paul Kehr (Hanover 1926–31 repr. Munich 1980). [Abbreviated to *DH III.*]

MGH Diplomata regum et imperatorum Germaniae 6.1–3: Heinrici IV. Diplomata, ed. Dietrich von Gladiss and Alfred Gawlick (Hanover 1941–78 repr. Munich 1978). [Abbreviated to *DH IV.*]

MGH Diplomata regum et imperatorum Germaniae 9: Conradi III Diplomata, ed. Freidrich Hausmann (Vienna 1969 repr. Munich 1987). [Abbreviated to *DK III.*]

MGH Diplomata regum et imperatorum Germaniae 10: Friderici I. Diplomata, ed. Heinrich Appelt *et al.* (Hanover 1975–91). [Abbreviated to *DF I.*]

MGH Epistolae 5: Epistolae Karolini aevi 3, ed. Ernst Dümmler, Karl Hampe *et al.* (Berlin 1898–9 repr. Munich 1978).

MGH Epistolae 6: Epistolae Karolini aevi 4, ed. Ernst Dümmler, Ernst Perels *et al.* (Berlin 1902–25 repr. Munich 1978).

MGH Formulae Merowingici et Karolini aevi, ed. Karl Zeumer (Hanover 1882–6 repr. 1963). [Pagination in the two edns is identical.]

Notae Dedicationum Fuldenses, ed. Oswald Holder-Egger, MGH SS 15.2 (Hanover 1888 repr. 1963) 1287–8.

Notitia de servitio monasteriorum, ed. D. P. Becker OSB, in *CCM* 1 pp. 483–99.

Papsturkunden, 896–1046, ed. Harald Zimmermann, 2 vols., Österreichische Akademie der Wissenschaften, Phil.-Hist. Kl., Denkschriften 174, 177. [Abbreviated to *PU.*]

Le Polyptyque de l'abbaye de Saint-Bertin (844–859): Edition critique et commentaire, ed. François-Louis Ganshof *et al.*, Académie des Inscriptions et Belles-Lettres (Paris 1975).

Primary sources

Poupardin, René, ed., *Recueil des chartes de l'abbaye de Saint-Germain-des-Prés* 1 (Paris 1909).

Recueil des actes de Charles II le Chauve, roi de France (840–877), ed. Georges Tessier, Chartes et diplômes relatifs à l'histoire de France 9, 3 vols. (Paris 1943–55). [Abbreviated to *DKK*.]

Recueil des actes de Charles III le Simple, roi de France (893–923), ed. Philippe Lauer (Paris 1949). [Abbreviated to *DKE*.]

Recueil des chartes de l'abbaye de Stavelot-Malmédy, ed. Joseph Halkin and C. G. Roland, 2 vols. (Brussels 1909–30).

Die Regesten der Erzbischöfe von Köln im Mittelalter 1: *313–1099*, ed. F. W. Oediger, Publikationen der Gesellschaft für Rheinische Geschichtskunde 21 (Bonn 1954–61). [Abbreviated to *REK*.]

Regino, abbot of Prüm, *Chronicon cum continuatione Treverensi*, ed. Friedrich Kurze, MGH SRG 50 (Hanover 1890 repr. 1978) [the 'continuatio' by Adalbert].

Registrum Erkenberti Corbeiensis Abbatis, ed. Hans H. Kaminsky, in Kaminsky (1972) 223–39. [Abbreviated to *RE*.]

Rheinisches Städtebuch, ed. E. Keyser (Stuttgart 1956).

Rheinische Urbare, vols. 2, 3, 4.1–2: *Die Urbare der Abtei Werden an der Ruhr*, ed. Rudolf Kötzschke (Bonn 1906–58). [Abbreviated to *RU*.]

Ruotger, *Vita Brunonis Archiepiscopi Coloniensis*, ed. Irene Ott, MGH SRG NS 10 (Weimar 1951).

Sacramentium Fuldense Saeculi X, ed. Gregor Richter and Albert Schönfelder, Quellen und Abhandlungen zur Geschichte der Abtei und der Diözese Fulda 9 (Fulda 1912).

Saint Bertin. See *Le Polyptyque*.

Series abbatum Nienburgensium, ed. F. Winter, *Magdeburger Geschichtsblätter* 2 (1867) 111–21.

Sigebert, monk of Gembloux, *Chronica*, ed. Ludwig C. Bethmann, MGH SS 6 (Hanover 1844 repr. 1980) 268–374.

Sigehard, *Ex miraculis s. Maximini*, ed. Georg Waitz, MGH SS 4 (Hanover 1841 repr. 1982) 228–34. [Pagination in the two edns is identical.]

Stumpf, Karl Friedrich, *Die Reichskanzler vornehmlich des X., XI. und XII. Jahrhunderts* 2: *Die Kaiserurkunden des X., XI. und XII. Jahrhunderts* (Innsbruck 1865–83 repr. Aalen 1960).

Supplex libellus monachorum fuldensium Carolo imperatori porrectus, ed. Josef Semmler, in *CCM* 1 pp. 320–7.

Thangmar of Hildesheim, *Vita Bernwardi Episcopi Hildesheimensis*, ed. Georg H. Pertz, MGH SS 4 (Hanover 1841 repr. Stuttgart 1981) 757–82.

Theodor, the monk, *Annales Palidenses*, ed. Georg H. Pertz, MGH SS 16 (Hanover 1859) 48–98.

Thietmar, bishop of Merseburg, *Chronicon*, ed. Robert Holtzmann, MGH SRG NS 9 (Berlin 1955).

Die Traditionen des Hochstifts Regensburg und des Klosters S. Emmeram, ed. Josef Widemann, Quellen und Erorterungen zur bayerischen und deutschen Geschichte, NF 8 (Munich 1943).

335

Bibliography

Traditiones Corbeienses, ed. Paul Wigand (Leipzig 1843).

Traditiones et Antiquitates Fuldenses, ed. Ernst F. J. Dronke (Fulda 1844 repr. Osnabruck 1966). [Abbreviated to *TAF*.] [Pagination in the two edns is identical.]

Translatio Sancti Modoaldi, ed. Philipp Jaffé, MGH SS 12 (Hanover 1856) 284–315.

Translatio Sancti Viti Martyris, ed./trans. Irene Schmale-Ott, *Fontes minores* 1, Veröffentlichungen der Historische Kommission für Westfalen 41.1 (Münster 1979).

Urkundenbuch der Abtei Sanct Gallen, ed. Hermann Wartmann, 3 vols. (Zürich 1863–82). [Abbreviated to *UBSG*.]

Urkundenbuch des Erzstiftes Magdeburg 1 (937–1192), ed. Friedrich Israël and Walter Möllenberg, Geschichtsquellen der Provinz Sachsen und des Freistaates Anhalt 18 (Magdeburg 1937). [Abbreviated to *UBM*.]

Urkundenbuch des Klosters Fulda, ed. Edmund E. Stengel, Veröffentlichung der Historischen Kommission für Hessen und Waldeck 10.1 (Marburg 1958). [Abbreviated to *FUB*.]

Urkundenbuch der Reichsabtei Hersfeld, ed. Hans Weirich, Veröffentlichung der Historischen Kommission für Hessen und Waldeck 19 (Marburg 1936). [Abbreviated to *HUB*.]

Urkundenbuch für die Geschichte des Niederrheins 1, ed. Theodor Josef Lacomblet (Düsseldorf 1840). [Abbreviated to *UBGNR*.]

Urkundenbuch zur Geschichte der jetzt die Preussischen Regierungsbezirke Coblenz und Trier bildenen mittelrheinischen Territorien 1, ed. Heinrich Beyer (Coblenz 1860 repr. Hildesheim and New York 1974). [Abbreviated to *MRUB*.]

Urkundenbuch zur Landes- und Rechtsgeschichte des Herzogthums Westfalen 1 (799–1300), ed. Johannes S. Seibertz, in Seibertz, *Landes- und Rechtsgeschichte des Herzogthums Westfalen 2* (Arnsberg 1839). [Abbreviated to *UB Westfalen*.]

Vita Adalberonis. See Constantine.

Vita Bardonis Maior, ed. Wilhelm Wattenbach, MGH SS 11 (Hanover 1854) 321–42 [also in Jaffé, ed., *Bibl*. 3. 529–64].

Vita Bernwardi. See Thangmar.

Vita Bonifatii. See Willibald.

Vita Brunonis. See Ruotger.

Vita Burchardi Episcopi, ed. Georg Waitz, MGH SS 4 (Hanover 1841 repr. Stuttgart 1981) 829–46.

Vita Gebehardi Archiepiscopi, ed. Georg H. Pertz, MGH SS 11 (Hanover 1854) 33–50.

Vita Godehardi. See Wolfher.

Vita Heinrici II. See Adalbold.

Vita Mahthildis reginae antiquior, ed. Rudolf Koepke, MGH SS 10 (Hanover 1852 repr. 1987) 573–82.

Vita Mahthildis reginae (= posterior), ed. Georg H. Pertz, MGH SS 4 (Hanover 1841 repr. 1981) 282–302.

Secondary works

Vita Meinwerci episcopi Patherbrunnensis (*Das Leben des Bischofs Meinwerk von Paderborn*), ed. Franz Tenckhoff, MGH SRG 59 (Hanover 1921 repr. 1983).

Vita Popponis. See Everhelm.

Vita Sanctae Cunegundis, ed. Georg Waitz, MGH SS 4 (Hanover 1841 repr. 1982) 821–8.

Vita s. Oudalrici episcopi Augustani. See Gerhard.

Vita Sancti Sturmi. See Eigil.

Westfälisches Urkundenbuch 4: Die Urkunden des Bistums Paderborn von Jahren 1201–1300, ed. Roger Wilmans and Heinrich Finke (Münster 1877–94).

Widukind, monk of Corvey, *Rerum Gestarum Saxonicarum Libri Tres* (*Die Sachsengeschichte des Widukind von Korvei*), 5th edn, ed. Hans-Eberhard Lohmann and Paul Hirsch, MGH SRG 60 (Hanover 1935 repr. 1977).

Willibald, *Vita Bonifatii archiepiscopi Moguntini*, ed. Wilhelm Levison, MGH SRG 57 (Hanover 1905 repr. 1977).

Wipo, *Gesta Chuonradi*, in *Wiponis Opera* pp. 1–62.

'Tetralogus', in *Wiponis Opera* pp. 75–82.

Wiponis Opera, 3rd edn, ed. Harry Bresslau, MGH SRG 61 (Hanover 1915 repr. 1977).

Wolfher, *Vita Godehardi Episcopi prior*, ed. Georg H. Pertz, MGH SS 11 (Hanover 1854) 167–96.

SECONDARY WORKS

Abel, Sigurd and Simson, Bernhard (1865–83), *Jahrbücher des fränkischen Reiches unter Karl dem Großen*, Jahrbücher der Deutschen Geschichte, 2 vols. (Berlin [vol. 1, 2nd edn 1888] repr. 1969). [Page references are to reprint of 1969.]

Alberts, Wybe Jappe (1983), 'Die Reisen der deutschen Könige in die Niederlande im Mittelalter', in *Niederlande und Nordwestdeutschland: Studien zur Regional- und Stadtgeschichte Nordwestkontinentaleuropas im Mittelalter und in der Neuzeit, FS Franz Petri*, ed. Wilfried Ehbrecht and Heinz Schilling, Städteforschung A/15 (Cologne) 18–35.

Althoff, Gerd (1976), 'Unerkannte Zeugnisse zum Totengedenken der Liudolfinger', *DA* 32 (1976) 370–404.

(1978), 'Die Beziehungen zwischen Fulda und Prüm im 11. Jahrhundert', in Schmid (1978) vol. 2.2, pp. 888–930.

(1982a), 'Das Bett des Königs in Magdeburg', in *FS für Berent Schwineköper zu seinem siebzigsten Geburtstag*, ed. Helmut Maurer and Hans Patze (Sigmaringen) 141–54.

(1982b), 'Zur Frage nach der Organisation sächsischer *coniurationes* in der Ottonenzeit', *FMS* 16 (1982) 129–42.

(1984), *Adels- und Königsfamilien im Spiegel ihrer Memorialüberlieferung. Studien zum Totengedenken der Billiger und Ottonen*, Münstersche Mittelalter Schriften 47 (Munich).

(1986), 'Unerforschte Quellen aus quellenarme Zeit (IV): Zur Verflechtung der Führungschichte in den Gedenkquellen des frühen 10. Jahrhunderts', in *Medieval Lives and the Historian*, ed. N. Bulst and J.-P. Genet (Kalamazoo) 37–71.

Bibliography

(1990), *Verwandte, Freunde und Getreue. Zum politischen Stellenwert der Gruppenbildungen im früheren Mittelalter* (Darmstadt).

Althoff, Gerd and Keller, Hagen (1985), *Heinrich I. und Otto der Grosse: Neubeginn und karolingisches Erbe*, Persönlichkeit und Geschichte, vols. 122/123 and 124/125 (Göttingen). [The two volumes have continuous pagination.]

Angenendt, Arnold (1982), '*Rex et sacerdos*. Zur Genese der Königssalbung', in *Tradition als historische Kraft. FS Karl Hauck*, ed. Norbert Kamp and Joachim Wollasch (Berlin) 100–18.

Arens, Franz (1912), 'Das Heberegister des Stiftes Essen', *EB* 34 (1912) 3–111.

Auer, Leopold (1971), 'Der Kriegsdienst des Klerus unter den sächsischen Kaisern, Erster Teil: Der Kreis der Teilnehmer', *MIÖG* 79 (1971) 316–407.

(1972), 'Der Kriegsdienst des Klerus unter den sächsischen Kaisern, Zweiter Teil: Verfassungsgeschichtliche Probleme', *MIÖG* 80 (1972) 48–70.

Baaken, Gerhard (1961), *Königtum, Burgen und Königsfreie*, VF 6 (Stuttgart) 7–95.

Bannasch, Hermann (1972), *Das Bistum Paderborn unter den Bischöfen Rethar und Meinwerk 983–1036*, Studien und Quellen zur Westfälischen Geschichte 12 (Paderborn).

Barraclough, Geoffrey (1938), *Mediaeval Germany, 911–1250: Essays by German Historians*, 2 vols. (1938).

Beattie, John Hugh Marshall (1960), *Bunyoro, An African Kingdom* (New York).

Bendel, Franz Josef (1908), *Die älteren Urkunden der deutschen Herrscher für die ehemalige Benediktinerabtei Werden a.d. Ruhr*, Beiträge zur Geschichte des Stiftes Werden, Ergänzungsheft 1 (Bonn).

Benz, Karl J. (1975), *Untersuchungen zur politischen Bedeutung der Kirchweihe unter Teilnahme der deutschen Herrscher im hohen Mittelalter. Ein Beitrag zum Studium des Verhältnisses zwischen weltlicher Macht und kirchliche Wirklichkeit unter Otto III. und Heinrich II.*, Regensburger historische Forschungen 4 (1975).

Berger, Dieter (1957), 'Alte Wege und Straßen zwischen Mosel, Rhein und Fulda', *RVJB* 22 (1957) 176–92.

Beuermann, Arnold (1951), *Hann. Münden: Das Lebensbild einer Stadt*, Göttinger geographische Abhandlungen 9 (Göttingen).

Beumann, Helmut (1948), 'Die sakrale Legitimierung des Herrschers im Denken der ottonischen Zeit', *ZRG GA* 66 (1948) 1–45. [Also with a supplement of 1970 in *Königswahl und Thronfolge in ottonisch-frühdeutscher Zeit*, ed. Eduard Hlawitschka, WdF 247 (Darmstadt 1975) 148–98.]

(1962), 'Das Kaisertum Ottos des Großen. Ein Rückblick nach tausend Jahren', *HZ* 195 (1962) 529–73.

(1966), 'Die Stellung des Weserraumes im geistigen Leben des Früh- und Hochmittelalters', in *Kunst und Kulter im Weserraum (800–1600)*, vol. 1: *Beiträge zu Geschichte und Kunst*, ed. Bernard Korzus (Münster) 144–60.

(1973), '*Regnum Teutonicorum* und *rex Teutonicorum* in ottonischer und salischer Zeit', *AKG* 55 (1973) 215–23.

(1978), 'Die Bedeutung des Kaisertums für die Entstehung der deutschen Nation im Spiegel der Bezeichnungen für Reich und Herrscher', in *Aspekte der Nationenbildung im Mittelalter*, ed. Helmut Beumann and Werner Schröder [= Nationes 1] (Sigmaringen) 317–65.

Secondary works

(1981), '*Unitas ecclesiae – unitas imperii – unitas regni*. Von der imperialen Reichseinheitsidee zur Einheit der *Regna*', in *Nascita dell'Europe ed d'Europa Carolingia: Un'equazione da verificare*, Settimane 27 (1981) 531–71 (with discussion 573–82).

(1991), *Die Ottonen*, 2nd rev. edn (Stuttgart).

Beumann, Helmut and Schlesinger, Walter (1955), 'Urkundenstudien zur deutschen Ostpolitik unter Otto III.', *AD* 1 (1955) 132–256.

Beyerle, Konrad (1925), 'Zur Einführung in die Geschichte des Klosters 1: Von der Gründung bis zum Ende des freiherrlichen Klosters (724–1427)', in *Die Kulter der Abtei Reichenau. Erinnerungsschrift zur zwölfhundertsten Wiederkehr des Gründungsjahres des Inselklosters 724–1924*, 2 vols., ed. Konrad Beyerle (Munich) 1.155–212.

Bikel, Hermann (1914), *Die Wirtschaftsverhältnisse des Klosters St. Gallen von der Gründung bis zum Ende des 13. Jahrhunderts* (Freiburg).

Binding, Günther (1971), 'Die karolingisch-salische Klosterkirche Hersfeld', *Aachener Kunstblätter* 41 (1971) 189–201.

Blume, Karl (1914), *Abbatia: Ein Beitrag zur Geschichte der kirchlichen Rechtssprache*, Kirchenrechtliche Abhandlungen 83 (Stuttgart).

Boegl, Johann (1949), 'Das älteste Urbar der bayerischen Besitzungen des Hochstifts Freising', *Oberbayerisches Archiv für vaterländische Geschichte* 75 (1949) 85–96.

Bömmels, Nicholas (1961), *Wirtschaftsleben in Neuß von den Anfängen bis 1794*, FS zum hundertjährigen Bestehen der Industrie- und Handelskammer zu Neuß 1861–1961 (Neuß).

Boshof, Egon (1979), 'Das Reich in der Krise. Uberlegungen zum Regierungsausgang Heinrichs III.', *HZ* 228 (1979) 265–87.

Bosl, Karl (1966), 'Die Sozialstruktur der mittelalterlichen Residenz- und Ferhandelsstadt Regensburg', *Untersuchungen zur gesellschaftlichen Struktur der mittelalterlichen Städte in Europa*, VF 11 (Reichenau) 93–213. [Orig. in *Abhandlungen der Bayerische Akademie der Wissenschaften. Phil.- hist. Klasse* NF 63 (Munich 1966).]

(1980), *Europa im Aufbruch. Herrschaft, Gesellschaft, Kultur vom 10. bis zum 14. Jahrhundert* (Munich).

Brackmann, Albert (1937), 'Die politische Bedeutung der Mauritiusverehrung im frühen Mittelalter', *SB Leipzig* 30 (1937) 279–305. [Also in *Gesammelte Aufsätze* (Weimar 1941) 211–41.]

Bresslau, Harry (1879–84), *Jahrbücher des deutschen Reichs unter Konrad II.*, Jahrbücher der deutschen Geschichte 2 vols. (Berlin repr. Darmstadt 1967). [Pagination in the two edns is identical.]

(1886), 'Über die Älteren Königs- und Papsturkunden für das Kloster St. Maximin bei Trier', *Westdeutsche Zeitschrift für Geschichte und Kunst* 5 (1886) 20–65.

Brons, Berhard (1907/1976), *Geschichte der wirtschaftlichen Verfassung und Verwaltung des Stiftes Vreden im Mittelalter*, Münstersche Beiträge zur Geschichtsforschung 25 [= NF 13] (Münster). [Repr. as Beiträge des

Bibliography

Heimatvereins Vreden zur Landes- und Volkskunde, Beiheft 2 (Vreden 1976).] [Pagination in the two editions is identical.]

Brühl, Carlrichard (1957), 'Diplomatische Miszellen zur Geschichte des ausgehenden 9. Jahrhunderts', *AD* 3 (1957) 1–19.

(1958), 'Königspfalz und Bishofsstadt in fränkischer Zeit', *RVJB* 23 (1958) 161–274.

(1959), 'Die fränkische *Fodrum*', *ZRG GA* 76 (1959) 53–81.

(1965), 'Die Wirtschaftliche Bedeutung der Pfalzen für die Versorgung des Hofes von der fränkischen bis zur Stauferzeit', *GWU* 16 (1965) 505–15.

(1967), 'Remarques sur les notions de "Capitale" et de "Résidence" pendant le haut Moyen Age', *Journal des Savants* (1967) 193–215.

(1968), *Fodrum, Gistum, Servitium Regis*, 2 vols. (Cologne). [Page references are to vol. 1.]

(1972), *Die Anfänge der deutschen Geschichte*, SB der Wissenschaftlichen Gesellschaft an der Johann Wolfgang Goethe-Universität Frankfurt/Main 10.5 (Wiesbaden) 147–81.

(1983), 'Die Herrscheritinerare', in *Popoli e paesi nella cultura altomedievale*, Settimane 29.2 (1983) 615–39.

(1990), *Deutschland – Frankreich. Die Geburt zweier Völker* (Cologne).

(1991), 'Die Geburt des modernen Europa nach 1000', in *Il seccolo di ferro : mito e realtà del secolo X*, Settimane 38.2 (1991) 1085–1106.

Brüske, Wolfgang (1955), *Untersuchungen zur Geschichte des Liutizenbundes*, Mitteldeutsche Forschungen 3 (Münster).

Budde, Rudolf (1914), 'Die rechtliche Stellung des Klosters St. Emmeram in Regensburg', *AUF* 5 (1914) 153–238.

Bullough, Donald (1985), '*Aula renovata*: The Carolingian court before the Aachen palace', *Proceedings of the British Academy* 71 (1985) 267–301.

Bulst, Walter (1941), '*Susceptacula regum*. Zur Kunde deutscher Reichsaltertümer', in *Corona quernea. Festgabe K. Strecker*, ed. Edmund E. Stengel, MGH Schriften 6 (1941) 97–135.

Büttner, Heinrich (1964), *Heinrichs I. Südwest- und Westpolitik* (Stuttgart).

(1965), 'Mission und Kirchenorganisation des Frankenreiches bis zum Tode Karl der Großen', in *Karl der Große. Lebenswerk und Nachleben*, ed. Wolfgang Braunfels, vol. 1: *Persönlichkeit und Geschichte*, ed. Helmut Beumann (Düsseldorf) 454–87.

(1989), 'Fulda und Wetterau', in *Mittelrhein und Hessen. Nachgelassene Studien von Heinrich Büttner*, ed. Alois Gerlich, Geschichtliche Landeskunde 33 (1989) 83–8.

Classen, Peter (1973), 'Das Wormser Konkordat in der deutschen Verfassungsgeschichte', in *Investiturstreit und Reichsverfassung*, ed. Josef Fleckenstein, VF 17 (Sigmaringen) 411–60.

Claude, Dietrich (1972–5), *Geschichte des Erzbistums Madgeburg bis in das 12. Jahrhundert*, 2 vols., Mitteldeutsche Forschungen 67/1–2 (Cologne).

(1978), 'Der Königshof Walbeck', *Jahrbuch für die Geschichte Mitteldeutschlands* 27 (1978) 1–27.

Claus, Martin (1970), 'Die Pfalz Pöhlde (Palithi)', in *Führer zu vor- und*

Secondary works

frühgeschichtlichen Denkmälern 17: *Northeim–Südwestliches Harzvorland–Duderstadt*, ed. Römisch-Germanischen Zentralmuseum Mainz, (Mainz) 115–39.

Constable, Giles (1960), '*Nona et decima*', *Speculum* 35 (1960) 224–50.

Corbet, Patrick (1986), *Les Saints Ottoniens*, Beihefte der Francia 15 (Sigmaringen).

Demandt, Karl E. (1939), *Quellen zur Rechtsgeschichte der Stadt Fritzlar im Mittelalter*, Veröffentlichungen der Historischen Kommission für Hessen und Waldeck 13.3: Quellen zur Rechtsgeschichte der Hessischen Städte (Marburg/Lahn).

(1972), *Geschichte des Lands Hessen*, 2nd rev. edn (Kassel).

Denecke, Dietrich (1969), *Methodische Untersuchungen zur historischgeographischen Wegeforschung im Raum zwischen Solling und Harz. Ein Beitrag zur Rekonstruktion der mittelalterlichen Kulturlandschaft*, Göttinger Geographische Abhandlungen 54 (Göttingen).

(1970), 'Wüstungs- und Wegeforschung im Südniedersachsen: hohes Mittelalter bis frühe Neuzeit', in *Führer zu vor- und frühgeschichtlichen Denkmälern* 17: *Northeim–Südwestliches Harzvorland–Duderstadt*, ed. Römisch-Germanischen Zentralmuseum Mainz (Mainz) 17–33.

Deus, Wolf Herbert (1960), 'Kaiserbesuche in Soest', *SZ* 73 (1960) 6–27.

Deutsche Königspfalzen (1963, 1965, 1979), *Deutsche Königspfalzen. Beiträge zu ihrer historischen und archäologischen Forschungen*, 3 vols., VMPIG 11.1–3 (Göttingen).

[Die] Deutschen Königspfalzen: Repertorium (1983, 1984, 1986 and 1988), *Die deutschen Königspfalzen: Repertorium der Pfalzen, Königshöfe und übrigen Aufenthaltsorten der Könige im deutschen Reich des Mittelalters*, vols. 1.1–3 (Hessen); 2.1–2, 2.3 (Thüringen); 3.1 (Baden-Württemberg), ed. Thomas Zotz (Göttingen). [Abbreviated to DKP Rep.]

Devroey, Jean-Pierre (1984) ed., *Le Polyptyque et les listes de cens de l'abbaye de Saint-Remi de Reims (IXe–XIe siècles)*, Travaux de l'Académie Nationale de Reims 163 (Reims).

(1986) ed., *Le Polyptyque et les listes de biens de l'abbaye de Saint-Pierre de Lobbes (IXe–XIe siècles)* (Brussels).

Dietrich, Irmgard (1953), 'Die Konradiner im fränkisch-sächsischen Grenzraum von Thüringen und Hessen', *HJBLG* 3 (1953) 57–95.

Dollinger, Philippe (1982), *Der bayerische Bauernstand vom 9. bis zum 13. Jahrhundert*, ed. Franz Irsigler and trans. Ursula Irsigler [from the original French with an updated bibliography] (Munich). [Orig. published as *L'Evolution des classes rurales en Bavière depuis la fin de l'époque carolingienne jusqu'au milieu du XIII siècle* (Paris 1949).]

Droege, Georg (1970), 'Fränkische Siedlung in Westfalen', *FMS* 4 (1970) 271–88.

Duby, Georges (1968), *Rural Economy and Country Life in the Medieval West*, trans. Cynthia Postan (London).

(1974), *The Early Growth of the European Economy: Warriors and Peasants from the Seventh to the Twelfth Century*, trans. Howard B. Clarke (Ithaca, NY).

341

Bibliography

Eckhardt, Karl-August (1957), 'Domina Sophia *constructrix et procuratrix monasterii sanctimonialium Aeskinewag*', *AD* 3 (1957) 29–78.

(1964), *Eschwege als Brennpunkt thüringisch-hessischer Geschichte*, Beiträge zur hessischen Geschichte 1 (Marburg).

Eckhardt, Wilhelm (1961), 'Kaufungen und Kassel. Pfalz – Kloster – Stift', in *FS zum 60. Geburtstag von Karl August Eckhardt*, ed. Otto Perst, Beiträge zur Geschichte der Werralandschaft 12 (Marburg) 21–53.

Eisenträger, Margaret and Krug, Eberhard (1935) (with contributions from Edmund E. Stengel), *Territorialgeschichte der Kasseler Landschaft*, Schriften des Instituts für geschichtliche Landeskunde von Hessen und Nassau 10 (Marburg).

Engels, Odilo (1989), 'Der Reichsbischof in ottonischen und frühsalischen Zeit', in *Beiträge zur Geschichte und Struktur der mittelalterliche Germania Sacra*, ed. Irene Crusius, Studien zur Germania Sacra 17 (1989) 135–76.

Erdmann, Carl (1938), 'Der ungesalbte König', *DA* 2 (1938) 311–40.

(1940), 'Beiträge zur Geschichte Heinrichs I. (I.–III.)', *SA* 16 (1940) 77–106.

(1941/1943), 'Beiträge zur Geschichte Heinrichs I. (IV.–VI.)', *SA* 17 (1941/1943) 14–61.

Erkens, Franz-Reiner (1982), 'Fürstliche Opposition in ottonisch-salischer Zeit', *AKG* 64 (1982) 307–70.

Ewig, Eugen (1963), 'Résidence et capitale pendant le haut moyen âge', *Revue Historique* 230 (1963) 25–72.

(1982a), 'Der Gebetsdienst der Kirchen in den Urkunden der späteren Karolinger', in *FS für Berent Schwineköper zu seinem siebzigsten Geburtstag*, ed. Helmut Maurer and Hans Patze (Sigmaringen) 45–86.

(1982b), 'Die Gebetsklausel für König und Reich in den merowingischen Königsurkunden', in *Tradition als historische Kraft: Interdisziplinäre Forschungen zur Geschichte des früheren Mittelalters*, ed. Norbert Kamp and Joachim Wollasch (Berlin) 87–99.

Feierabend, Hans (1913), *Die politische Stellung der deutschen Reichsabteien während des Investiturstreites*, Historische Untersuchungen 3 (Breslau repr. Aalen 1971). [Pagination in the two edns is identical.]

Feine, Hans Erich (1972), *Kirchliche Rechtsgeschichte*, 5th edn (Cologne).

Felten, Franz J. (1974), 'Laienäbte in der Karolingerzeit. Ein Beitrag zum Problem der Adelsherrschaft über die Kirche', in *Mönchtum, Episkopat und Adel zur Gründungszeit des Klosters Reichenau*, ed. Arno Borst, VF 20 (Sigmaringen) 397–431.

(1980), *Äbte und Laienäbte in Frankenreich*, Monographien zur Geschichte des Mittelalters 20 (Stuttgart).

Fenske, Lutz, Rösener, Werner and Zotz, Thomas (1984) eds., *Institutionen, Kultur und Gesellschaft im Mittelalter: FS für Josef Fleckenstein* (Sigmaringen).

Fichtenau, Heinrich (1984), *Lebensordnungen des 10. Jahrhunderts: Studien über Denkart und Existenz im einstigen Karolingerreich*, 2 vols., Monographien zur Geschichte des Mittelalters 30.1–2 (Stuttgart). [Trans. by Patrick Geary as *Living in the Tenth Century: Mentalities and Social Orders* (Chicago 1991).]

[Page references are to 1984 edn unless stated otherwise; the two vols. have continuous pagination.]

Ficker, Julius (1861), *Vom Reichsfürstenstand*, 4 vols. (in two) (Innsbruck repr. Aalen 1961).

(1872), 'Über das Eigentum des Reiches am Reichskirchengute', *SB Wien* 72 (1872) 55–146, 381–450.

(1877–8), *Beiträge zur Urkundenlehre*, 2 vols. (Innsbruck).

Finckenstein, Albrecht Graf Finck von (1989), *Bischof und Reich: Untersuchungen zum Integrationsprozeß des ottonisch-frühsalischen Reiches (919–1056)* (Sigmaringen).

Flach, Dietmar (1976), *Untersuchungen zur Verfassung und Verwaltung des Aachener Reichsgutes*, VMPIG 46 (Göttingen).

Fleckenstein, Josef (1956), 'Königshof und Bischofschule unter Otto der Grosse', *AKG* 38 (1956) 38–62.

(1959), *Die Hofkapelle der deutschen Könige. 1. Teil: Grundlegungen. Die karolingische Hofkapelle*, MGH Schriften 16.1 (Stuttgart).

(1964), '*Rex Canonicus*. Über Entstehung und Bedeutung des mittelalterlichen Königskanonikats', in *FS für Percy Ernst Schramm*, ed. Peter Classen, vol. 1 (Wiesbaden) 57–71.

(1966), *Die Hofkapelle der deutschen Könige. 2. Teil: Die Hofkapelle im Rahmen der ottonisch-salischen Reichskirche*, MGH Schriften 16.2 (Stuttgart).

(1974), 'Zum Begriff der ottonisch-salischen Reichskirche', in *Geschichte – Wirtschaft – Gesellschaft: FS für Clemens Bauer*, ed. Erich Hassinger, J. Heinz Müller and Hugo Ott (Berlin) 61–71.

(1985), 'Problem und Gestalt der ottonisch-salischen Reichskirchen', in *Reich und Kirche vor dem Investiturstreit: Gerd Tellenbach zum achtzigsten Geburtstag*, ed. Karl Schmid (Sigmaringen) 83–98.

Flink, Klaus (1982), 'Stand und Ansätze städtischer Entwicklung zwischen Rhein und Maas in salischer Zeit', in *Beiträge zum Hochmittelalterlichen Städtewesen*, ed. Bernhard Diestelkamp, Städteforschung A/11 (Cologne) 170–95.

Foltz, Karl (1877–8), 'Die Siegel der deutschen Könige and Kaiser aus dem sächsischen Hause 911–1024', *NA* 3 (1877–8) 9–45.

Folz, Robert (1950), *Le Souvenir et la légende de Charlemagne dans l'Empire germanique médiéval*, Publications de l'Université de Dijon 7 (Paris).

Fossier, Robert (1978), *Polyptyques et censiers*, Typologie des Sources du Moyen Age Occidental, ed. L. Genicot, Fasc. 28 (Turnhout).

Franke, Thomas (1987), 'Studien zur Geschichte der Fuldaer Äbte im 11. und frühen 12. Jahrhundert', *AD* 33 (1987) 55–238.

Freise, Eckhard (1978), 'Studien zum Einzugsbereich der Klostergemeinschaft von Fulda', in Schmid (1978) vol. 2.3, pp. 1003–1269.

(1983), 'Corvey in hochmittelalterliche Reformmönchtum', in Schmid and Wollasch (1983) 87–106.

Fried, Johannes (1982), 'Die Karolingische Herrschaftsband im 9. Jh. zwischen "Kirche" und "Königshaus"', *HZ* 235 (1982) 1–43.

(1987), 'Bemerkungen zu einigen neuen Gesamtdarstellungen', *HZ* 245 (1987) 626–59.

Bibliography

(1989), *Otto III. und Boleslaw Chrobry: Das Widmungsbild des Aachener Evangeliars, der 'Akt von Gnesen' und das frühe polnische und ungarische Königtum*, Frankfurter Historische Abhandlungen 30 (Stuttgart).

Fritze, Wolfgang, H. (1954), 'Die fränkische Schwurfreundschaft der Merowingerzeit. Ihr Wesen und ihre politische Funktion', *ZRG GA* 71 (1954) 74–125.

(1973), *Papst und Frankenkönig. Studien zu den päpstlich-fränkischen Rechtsbeziehungen von 754 bis 824*, VF Sonderband 10 (Sigmaringen).

(1984), 'Der slawische Aufstand von 983: Eine Schicksalswende in der Geschichte Europas', in *FS der Landesgeschichtlichen Vereinigung für die Mark Brandenburg zu ihrem hundertjährige Bestehen 1884–1984*, ed. Eckart Henning and Walter Vogel (Berlin) 9–55.

Fry, Timothy, OSB (1981) ed., *RB 1980: The Rule of St. Benedict* (Collegeville, MN).

Fuhrmann, Horst (1964), 'Die Synoden von Ingelheim', in *Forschungen und Studien zur Geschichte Ingelheims*, ed. Johanne Autenrieth (Stuttgart) 147–73.

(1984), '*Rex canonicus – Rex clericus?*', in Fenske, Rösener and Zotz (1984) 321–6.

(1986), *Germany in the High Middle Ages, 1050–1200*, trans. Timothy Reuter (Cambridge).

(1991), 'Vom einstigen Glanz Quedlinburgs', in *Das Quedlinburger Evangeliar. Das Samuhel-Evangeliar aus dem Quedlinburger Dom*, ed. Florentine Mütherich and Karl Dachs (Munich 1991) 13–22.

Ganshof, François L. (1951), 'Charlemagne et l'usage de l'écrit en matière administrative', *Le Moyen Age* 57 (1951) 1–25.

Ganshof, François L. and Verhulst, Adriaan (1966), 'Medieval agrarian society in its prime 1: France, the Low Countries and Western Germany', in *Cambridge Economic History of Europe 1: The Agrarian Life of the Middle Ages*, 2nd edn, ed. M. M. Postan (Cambridge) 290–339.

Gast, Franz Georg (1965), '*Stipendium* und Unterhaltsvertrag im fränkisch-kirchlichen Recht', *ZRG KA* 51 (1965) 24–138.

Gauert, Adolf (1965), 'Zur Struktur und Topographie der Königspfalzen', in *Deutsche Königspfalzen* (1965) 1–60.

(1970), 'Königspfalzen im südlichen Niedersachsen', in *Führer zu vor- und frühgeschichtlichen Denkmälern 17: Northeim–Südwestliches Harzvorland–Duderstadt*, ed. Römisch-Germanischen Zentralmuseum Mainz (Mainz) 10–16.

(1984), '*curtis*', in *Reallexicon der germanischen Altertumskunde* 5 (Berlin) 105–12.

Geertz, Clifford (1977), 'Centers, kings, and charisma: Reflections on the symbolics of power', in *Culture and its Creators*, ed. Joseph Ben-David and Terry Nichols Clark (Chicago) 150–71.

Gensen, Rolf (1979), *Althessens Frühzeit. Frühgeschichtliche Fundstätten und Funde in Nordhessen*, Führer zur hessischen Vor- und Frühgeschichte 1 (Wiesbaden).

Giese, Wolfgang (1982), 'Zur Bautätigkeit von Bischöfen und Äbten des 10. bis 12. Jahrhunderts', *DA* 38 (1982) 388–438.

Secondary works

Giesebrecht, Wilhelm (1885), *Geschichte der deutschen Kaiserzeit*, vol. 2, 5th edn (Leipzig).

Gillingham, John B. (1971), *The Kingdom of Germany in the High Middle Ages (900–1200)*, Historical Association Pamphlet 77 (London).

Gockel, Michael (1983a), 'Berstadt', in DKP Rep. (1983) vol. 1.1 (Hessen) 1–7.

(1983b), 'Breitenbach', in DKP Rep. (1983) vol. 1.1 (Hessen) 45–9.

(1983c), 'Breitingen', in DKP Rep. (1983) vol. 1.1 (Hessen) 50–4.

(1983d), 'Ebsdorf', in DKP Rep. (1983) vol. 1.1 (Hessen) 74–82.

(1984a), 'Allstedt', in DKP Rep. (1984) vol. 2.1 (Thüringen) 1–38.

(1984b), 'Arnstadt', in DKP Rep. (1984) vol. 2.1 (Thüringen) 71–82.

(1984c), 'Dornburg', in DKP Rep. (1984) vol. 2.1 (Thüringen) 83–102.

(1984d), 'Erfurt', in DKP Rep. (1984) vol. 2.1 (Thüringen) 103–12 and vol. 2.2 (Thüringen) 113–48.

(1984e), 'Gebesee', in DKP Rep. (1984) vol. 2.2 (Thüringen) 149–55.

(1984f), 'Gerstungen', in DKP Rep. (1984) vol. 2.2 (Thüringen) 156–67.

(1984g), 'Gottern', in DKP Rep. (1984) vol. 2.2 (Thüringen) 168–79.

(1984h), 'Haina', in DKP Rep. (1984) vol. 2.2 (Thüringen) 179–95.

(1984i), 'Heiligenstadt', in DKP Rep. (1984) vol. 2.2 (Thüringen) 196–223.

(1984j), 'Herrenbreitungen', in DKP Rep. (1984) vol. 2.2 (Thüringen) 224–33.

Goetting, Hans (1949), 'Die Gandersheimer Originalsupplik an Papst Paschalis II. als Quelle für eine unbekannte Legation Hildebrands nach Sachsen', *NSJBLG* 21 (1949) 93–122.

(1973), *Das Bistum Hildesheim 1: Das Reichsunmittelbare Kanonissenstift Gandersheim*, Germania Sacra NF 7 (Berlin).

(1979), 'Das Hilwartshäuser Chirograph von 1004', *AD* 25 (1979) 37–58.

(1980), 'Gründung und Anfänge des Reichsstifts Hilwartshausen an der Weser', *NSJBLG* 52 (1980) 145–80.

Goetz, Hans-Werner (1990), 'Das Ruhrgebiet im frühen Mittelalter. Zur Erschliessung einer Randlandschaft', *BDLG* 126 (1990) 123–60.

Görich, Willi (1952), 'Rast-Orte an alter Straße?', in *FS Edmund E. Stengel zum 70. Geburtstag*, ed. Erika Kunz (Münster) 473–94.

(1953), 'Nochmals: Hersfeld. Der Stadtgrundriß als Geschichtsquelle', *ZHG* 64 (1953) 136–40.

(1955), 'Ortesweg, Antsanvia und Fulda in neuer Sicht. Zur Heimatführung des Bonifatius vor 1200 Jahren', *Germania* 33 (1955) 68–88.

Görlitz, Siegfried (1936), *Beiträge zur Geschichte der königlichen Hofkapelle im Zeitalter der Ottonen und Salier bis zum Beginn des Investiturstreites*, Historisch-diplomatische Forschungen 1 (Weimar).

Groten, Manfred (1983), 'Von der Gebetsverbrüderung zum Königskanonikat: Zu Vorgeschichte und Entwicklung der Königskanonikat an den Dom- und Stiftskirchen des deutschen Reiches', *HJB* 103 (1983) 1–34.

Hahn, Heinrich (1954), 'Ausgrabungen am Fuldaer Domplatz im Jahre 1953', in *Sankt Bonifatius: Gedenkgabe zum Zwölfhundertsten Todestag*, ed. Stadt Fulda, 2nd rev. edn (Fulda) 641–86.

Hallinger, Kassius (1950), *Gorze–Kluny: Studien zu den monastischen Lebensformen und Gegensätzen im Hochmittelalter*, 2 vols. (Rome).

Bibliography

Hardt-Friedrichs, Friederun (1980), 'Markt, Münze und Zoll im ostfränkischen-Reich bis zum Ende der Ottonen', *BDLG* 116 (1980) 1–31.

Hauck, Albert (1952), *Kirchengeschichte Deutschlands*, vols. 1–3, 6th edn (Berlin).

Hauck, Karl (1963), 'Tiergärten im Pfalzbereich', in Deutsche Königspfalzen (1963) 30–74.

(1967), 'Die Ottonen und Aachen', in *Karl der Große. Lebenswerk und Nachleben 4: Das Nachleben*, ed. Wolfgang Braunfels and Percy Ernst Schramm (Düsseldorf) 39–53.

Haverkamp, Alfred (1968), 'Königsgastung und Reichssteuer', *ZBLG* 31 (1968) 768–821.

Heinemann, Wolfgang (1968), *Das Bistum Hildesheim im Kräftespiel der Reichs- und Territorialpolitik* (Hildesheim).

Heinemeyer, Karl (1970), *Der Königshof Eschwege in der Germar-Mark*, Schriften des Hessischen Landesamtes für geschichtliche Landeskunde 34 (Marburg).

(1971), *Königshöfe und Königsgut im Raum Kassel*, VMPIG 33 (Göttingen).

(1973), 'Die Gründung der Stadt Münden: Ein Beitrag zur Geschichte des hessisch-sächsischen Grenzgebiets im hohen Mittelalter', *HJBLG* 23 (1973) 141–230.

(1974), 'Adel, Kirche und Königtum an der oberen Weser', in *Historische Forschungen für Walter Schlesinger*, ed. Helmut Beumann (Cologne) 111–49.

(1980), 'Die Gründung des Klosters Fulda im Rahmen der bonifatianischen Kirchenorganisation', *HJBLG* 30 (1980) 1–45.

(1983a), 'Ermschwerd', in DKP Rep. (1983) vol. 1.1 (Hessen) 83–97.

(1983b), 'Eschwege', in DKP Rep. (1983) vol. 1.1 (Hessen) 98–112.

Heinemeyer, Walter (1963–4), 'Ältere Urkunden und ältere Geschichte der Abtei Helmarshausen', *AD* 9/10 (1963–4) 299–368.

Helberg, Til (1977), 'Einer der größten Pfalz-Saale Deutschlands im Hersfelder Stiftsbereich gefunden. Entdeckung beim Altenheimbau. 900 Jahre alter Königspalast', *Fuldaer Zeitung* 98 (1 Dec. 1977) No. 279, p. 12. [Illustrations by Ubbo Mozer, excavation director.]

Herbst, Alfred (1926), *Die alten Heer und Handelsstraßen Südhannovers und angrenzender Gebiet* (Göttingen).

Herrmann, Joachim (1982) ed. et al., *Deutsche Geschichte 1: Von den Anfangen bis zur Ausbildung des Feudalismus Mitte des 11. Jahrhunderts* (Cologne).

Hess, Wolfgang (1954), 'Der Hersfelder Marktplatz, Ursprung und Bedeutung der Ebenheit für die Entwicklung der Stadt', *HJBLG* 4 (1954) 81–116.

(1963), 'Hersfeld, Fulda, und Erfurt als frühe Handelsniederlassungen', in *FS für Harald Keller*, ed. Hans Martin Freiherrn von Erffa and Elisabeth Herget (Darmstadt) 23–43.

(1974a), 'Anfänge des Stadtewesens. Markte, Münzstätten und Städte bis *ca.* 1330/40', in Patze (1974) 310–30.

(1974b), 'Zoll, Markt und Munze im 11. Jahrhundert. Der älteste Koblenzer Zolltariff im Lichte der numismatischen Quellen', in *Historische Forschungen für Walter Schlesinger*, ed. Helmut Beumann (Cologne) 171–93.

Heusinger, Bruno (1922), Servitium Regis *in der deutschen Kaiserzeit* (Berlin).

Secondary works

[Also appeared under the same title in *AUF* 8 (1923) 26–159 – page numbers in square brackets refer to *AUF*.]

HHSD (1964–75), *Handbuch der Historischen Stätten Deutschlands*, 11 vols., Kröners Taschenausgabe 271–77; 311–14 (Stuttgart).

Hillebrand, Werner (1967), 'Von den Anfängen des Erzbergbaus am Rammelsberg bei Goslar', *NSJBLG* 39 (1967) 103–14.

Hilsch, Peter (1972), 'Der Bischof von Prag und das Reich in sächsischer Zeit', *DA* 28 (1972) 1–41.

Hirsch, Siegfried (1862–75) with Hermann Pabst and Harry Bresslau, *Jahrbücher des Deutschen Reiches unter Heinrich II.*, 3 vols., Jahrbücher der Deutschen Geschichte (Berlin repr. 1975). [Pagination in the two edns is identical.]

Hlawitschka, Eduard (1968), *Lotharingen und das Reich an der Schwelle der deutschen Geschichte*, MGH Schriften 21 (Stuttgart).

(1986), *Vom Frankenreich zur Formierung der europäischen Staaten- und Völkergemeinschaft, 840–1046* (Darmstadt).

(1988), *Von der großfränkischen zur deutschen Geschichte* (Munich).

Hoebaux, Jean J. (1952), *L'Abbaye de Nivelles des origines au 14ᵉ siècle* (Brussels).

Höfer, Paul (1896), 'Der Königshof Bodenfeld', *Harz Zeitschrift* 29 (1896) 341–415.

Hoffmann, Hartmut (1972), 'Zur Geschichte Ottos des Großen', *DA* 28 (1972) 42–73.

(1986), *Buchkunst und Königtum im ottonischen und frühsalischen Reich*, MGH Schriften 30.1–2 (Stuttgart).

(1988), 'Eigendiktat in den Urkunden Ottos III. und Heinrichs II.', *DA* 44 (1988) 390–423.

(1990), 'Grafschaften in Bischofshand', *DA* 46 (1990) 375–480.

Holtzmann, Robert (1955), *Geschichte der sächsischen Kaiserzeit (900–1024)* 3rd rev. edn (Darmstadt).

Hömberg, Albert K. (1940), 'Höxter und Corvey', *Westfalen* 25 (1940) 41–51.

(1943–52), 'Studien zur Entstehung der mittelalterlichen Kirchenorganisation in Westfalen', *Westfälische Forschungen* 6 (1943–52) 46–108.

(1955), 'Die karolingisch-ottonischen Wallburgen des Sauerlands in historischer Sicht (1955)', in Hömberg, *Zwischen Rhein und Weser* (1955) 80–113, 253–68 (notes).

(1960), 'Probleme der Reichsgutforschung in Westfalen', *BDLG* 96 (1960) 1–21.

(1965), *Kirchliche und weltliche Landesorganisation in südlichen Westfalen*, Veröffentlichungen der Historischen Kommission Westfalens 22 (Münster).

(1967a), 'Der Hellweg – sein Werden und seine Bedeutung', in Hömberg (1967e) 196–207.

(1967b), 'Höxter und Corvey', in Hömberg (1967e) 191–5.

(1967c), 'Lippstadt–Geseke–Rüthen, Ein historischer Vergleich', in Hömberg (1967e) 159–73.

(1967d), *Westfälische Landesgeschichte* (Münster).

(1967e), *Zwischen Rhein und Weser: Aufsätze und Vorträge zur Geschichte Westfalens*, Schriften der Historischen Kommission Westfalens 7 (Münster).

Bibliography

Honselmann, Klemens (1982) ed., *Die alten Mönchslisten und die Traditionen von Corvey, Teil 1*, Abhandlungen zur Corveyer Geschichtsschreibung 6.1 (Paderborn).

Hörger, Karl (1926), 'Die Reichsrechtliche Stellung der Fürstäbtissinnen', *AUF* 9 (1926) 195–270.

Hörle, Josef (1960), '*Breviarum Sancti Lulli* – Gestalt und Gehalt', *AMRKG* 12 (1960) 18–53.

Horvath, Ronald J. (1969), 'The wandering capitals of Ethiopia', *Journal of African History* 10 (1969) 205–19.

Howell, Margaret (1982), 'Abbatial vacancies in medieval England', *JEH* 33 (1982) 173–92.

Hussong, Ulrich (1985), 'Studien zur Geschichte der Reichsabtei Fulda bis zur Jahrtausendwende. Erster Teil', *AD* 31 (1985) 1–226.

(1986), 'Studien zur Geschichte der Reichsabtei Fulda bis zur Jahrtausendwende. Zweiter Teil', *AD* 32 (1986) 129–304.

Jahn, Robert (1938), 'Der Hoftag König Ottos I. bei Steele im Mai 938', *EB* 56 (1938) 9–90.

Jakobi, Franz-Josef (1978), 'Die geistlichen und weltlichen Magnaten in den Fuldaer Totenannalen', in Schmid (1978) vol. 2.2, pp. 792–887.

(1979), *Wibald von Stablo und Corvey (1098–1158) Benediktinischer Abt in der frühen Stauferzeit*, Abhandlungen zur Corveyer Geschichtsschreibung 5 (Münster) 83–104.

Jäschke, Kurt-Ulrich (1963–4), 'Studien zur Quellen und Geschichte des Osnabrücker Zehnstreits unter Heinrich IV.', *AD* 9–10 (1963–4) 112–285.

(1971), 'Zu schriftlichen Zeugnissen für die Anfänge der Reichsabtei Hersfeld', *BDLG* 107 (1971) 94–135.

Jedin, Hubert and Dolan, John (1969) eds., *Handbook of Church History*, vol. 3: *The Church in the Age of Feudalism*, by Hans Georg Beck, Josef A. Jungmann, Friedrich Kempf and Hans Wolter, trans. Anselm Biggs (London).

John, Eric (1955), 'The division of the *mensa* in early monasteries', *JEH* 6 (1955) 143–55.

Kaiser, Reinhold (1976), 'Münzprivilegien und bischöfliche Münzprägung in Frankreich, Deutschland und Burgund im 9.-12. Jahrhundert', *VSWG* 63 (1976) 289–338.

Kallen, Gerhard (1924), 'Der Säkularisationsgedanke in seiner Auswirkung auf die Entwicklung der mittelalterlichen Kirchenverfassung', *HJB* 44 (1924) 197–210.

Kaminsky, Hans Heinrich (1972), *Studien zur Reichsabtei Corvey in der Salierzeit* (Cologne).

Kantorowicz, Ernst H. (1944/1965), 'The "king's advent" and the enigmatic panels in the doors of Santa Sabina', *The Art Bulletin* 26 (1944) 207–31. [Repr. in Kantorowicz, Ernst H., *Selected Studies* (Locust Valley, NY 1965) 37–75.] [Page references are to 1965 edn.]

(1958), *Laudes regiae* (Berkeley).

Karpf, Ernst (1984), 'Königserhebung ohne Salbung', *HJBLG* 34 (1984) 1–24.

Secondary works

Kehr, Paul (1932), 'Die älteren Urkunden für Helmarshausen', *NA* 49 (1932) 86–114.

Keller, Hagen (1964), *Kloster Einsiedeln im ottonischen Schwaben* (Freiburg).

(1982), 'Reichsstruktur und Herrschaftsauffassung in ottonisch-frühsalischer Zeit', *FMS* 16 (1982) 74–128.

(1985a), 'Grundlagen ottonischer Königsherrschaft', in Schmid (1985a) 17–34.

(1985b), 'Herrscherbild und Herrschaftslegitimation. Zur Deutung der ottonischen Denkmäler (Taf. XXIII–XXIX)', *FMS* 19 (1985) 290–311.

(1986), *Zwischen regionaler Begrenzung und universalem Horizont: Deutschland im Imperium der Salier und Staufer, 1024 bis 1250*, Propyläen Geschichte Deutschlands 2 (Berlin).

Kempf, Friedrich (1969), 'Rural Churches', in Jedin and Dolan (1969) 258–64.

Klein, Peter (1984), 'Zu einigen Reichenauer Handschriften Heinrichs II. für Bamberg', *Bericht des Historischen Vereins Bamberg (FS Gerd Zimmermann)* 120 (1984) 417–22 with plates.

Klewitz, Hans-Walter (1937), '*Cancellaria*. Ein Beitrag zur Geschichte des geistlichen Hofdienstes', *DA* 1 (1937) 44–79.

(1939a), 'Die Festkrönungen der deutschen Könige', *ZRG KA* 28 (1939) 48–97.

(1939b), 'Königtum, Hofkapelle und Domkapitel im 10. und 11. Jahrhundert', *AUF* 16 (1939) 102–56.

Klocke, Friedrich von and Bauermann, Johannes (1970) eds., *Handbuch der historischen Stätten Deutschlands. Nordrhein-Westfalen*, 2nd edn (Stuttgart).

Knaus, Hermann (1936), 'Die königliche Forstprivilegien für die Abtei Fulda', *Fuldaer Geschichtsblätter* 28 (1936) 97–109, 113–27.

(1937), 'Die königliche Forstprivilegien für die Abtei Fulda', *Fuldaer Geschichtsblätter* 29 (1937) 11–16, 36–46, 54–64.

Kohl, Wilhelm (1980), 'Bemerkungen zur Typologie der Frauenklöster des 9. Jahrhunderts im westlichen Sachsen', in *Untersuchungen zu Kloster und Stift*, ed. Max Planck Institut, VMPIG 68 (Göttingen) 112–39.

Köhler, Oskar (1968), 'Die ottonische Reichskirche. Ein Forschungsbericht', in *Adel und Kirche: FS Gerd Tellenbach*, ed. Josef Fleckenstein and Karl Schmid (Freiburg) 141–204.

Kölzer, Theo (1989), *Studien zu den Urkundenfälschungen des Klosters St. Maximin vor Trier (10.–12. Jahrhundert)*, VF Sonderband 36 (Sigmaringen).

Köpke, Rudolf and Dümmler, Ernst (1876), *Kaiser Otto der Große*, Jahrbücher der Deutschen Geschichte (Leipzig).

Kötzschke, Rudolf (1901), *Studien zur Verwaltungsgeschichte der Großgrundherrschaft Werden an der Ruhr* (Leipzig).

(1906–58), *Rheinische Urbare*, vols. 2, 3, 4.1–2: *Die Urbare der Abtei Werden an der Ruhr* (Bonn).

Kroeschell, Karl A. (1957), 'Zur älteren Geschichte des Reichsklosters Hilwartshausen und des Reichsguts an der oberen Weser', *NSJBLG* 29 (1957) 1–23.

Kropat, Wolf-Arno (1965), *Reich, Adel und Kirche in der Wetterau von der Karolinger- bis zur Stauferzeit* (Marburg).

Bibliography

Krüger, Herbert (1931), *Höxter und Corvey: Ein Beitrag zur Stadtgeographie* (Münster). [Also in *WZ* 87/2 (1930) 1–108 and 88/2 (1931) 1–93.]

Krumwiede, Hans-Walter (1955), *Das Stift Fischbeck an der Weser: Untersuchungen zur Frühgeschichte 955–1158* (Göttingen).

Küther, Waldemar (1971), *Vacha und sein Servitienkloster im Mittelalter*, Mitteldeutsche Forschungen 64 (Cologne).

— (1974), 'Lupnitz. Fiskus – Villa – Gau – Mark – Wildbann', in *FS für Walter Schlesinger*, 2 vols., ed. Helmut Beumann, Mitteldeutsche Forschungen 74/1–2 (Cologne) 2.162–237.

Leclercq, Jean (1957), 'Cluny, fut-il ennemi de la culture?', *Revue Mabbillon* 47 (1957) 172–82.

Lehnhäuser, Anton (1931), 'Die Münzen des Hochstiftes Essen', *EB* 49 (1931) 1–48.

Leidinger, Paul (1965), *Untersuchungen zur Geschichte der Grafen von Werl*, Studien und Quellen zur Westfälischen Geschichte 5 (Paderborn).

Leopold, Gerhard, and Schubert, Ernst (1990), 'Otto III. und die Sachsen. Die ottonische Kirche im Memleben. Geschichte und Gestalt', in *Kaiserin Theophanu: Begegnung des Ostens und Westens um die Wende des ersten Jahrtausends*, 2 vols., ed. Anton von Euw and Peter Schreiner, Gedenkschrift des Kölner Schnütgen-Museums zum 1000. Todesjahr der Kaiserin (Cologne) 1.371–82.

Lesne, Emil (1910), *L'Origine des Menses dans le temporel des églises et des monastères en France au IXᵉ siècle*, Mémoires et travaux publiés par des professeurs des Facultés Catholiques de Lille 7 (Lille).

— (1910–43), *Histoire de la propriété ecclésiastique en France*, 6 vols. in 8 parts, Mémoires et Travaux des Facultés Catholiques de Lille 6, 19, 30, 34, 44, 46, 50, 53 (Lille).

— (1914), 'Évêché et abbaye: les origines du bénéfice ecclésiastique', *RHEF* 5 (1914) 15–50.

— (1920), 'Les Ordonnances monastiques de Louis le Pieux et la *Notitia de servitio monasteriorum*', *RHEF* 6 (1920) 161–75, 321–38 and 449–93.

Leyser, Karl (1968), 'Henry I and the beginnings of the Saxon empire', *EHR* 83 (1968) 1–32.

— (1979), *Rule and Conflict in an Early Medieval Society* (London).

— (1981), 'Ottonian government', *EHR* 96 (1981) 721–53.

— (1983a), 'The crisis of medieval Germany' (Raleigh Lecture on History), *Proceedings of the British Academy* 69 (1983) 409–43.

— (1983b), 'Die Ottonen und Wessex', *FMS* 17 (1983) 73–97.

Lintzel, Martin (1953/1971), 'Miszellen zur Geschichte des zehnten Jahrhunderts', *Berichte Leipzig* 100.2 (Leipzig) 1–85. [Also in *Königswahl und Thronfolge in Ottonisch-Frühsalischer Zeit*, ed. Eduard Hlawitschka, WdF 178 (Darmstadt 1971) 309–88.] [Page references to 1971 edn.]

— (1955/1961b), 'Heinrich I. und die fränkische Königssalbung', *Berichte Leipzig* 102.3 (Leipzig) 1–56. [Also in Lintzel (1961b) 583–612.]

— (1961a, 1961b), *Ausgewählte Schriften*, 2 vols. (Berlin).

Lobbedey, Uwe (1970), 'Zur archäologischen Erforschung westfälischer

Secondary works

Frauenklöster des 9. Jahrhunderts (Freckenhorst, Vreden, Meschede, Herford)', *FMS* 4 (1970) 320–40.

Lorenz, Hermann (1922), *Werdegang von Stift und Stadt Quedlinburg*, Quedlinburgische Geschichte zur Tausendjahrfeier der Stadt Quedlinburg 1 (Quedlinburg).

Loyn, Henry R. (1984), *The Governance of Anglo-Saxon England, 500–1087* (Stanford).

Lübeck, Konrad (1941), 'Aus der Frühzeit des Stiftes Fischbeck', *NSJBLG* 18 (1941) 1–38.

(1953), 'Korvey's Kampf um das Stift Kemnade', *WZ* 101/102. (1953) 401–28.

Ludat, Herbert (1971), *An Elbe und Oder um das Jahr 1000. Skizzen zur politik des Ottonenreiches und der slavischen Mächte in Mitteleuropa* (Cologne).

Lütge, Friedrich (1963), *Geschichte der deutschen Agrarverfassung vom frühen Mittelalter bis zum 12. Jahrhundert* (Stuttgart).

McKitterick, Rosamond (1979), 'Town and monastery in the Carolingian period', in *The Church in Town and Countryside*, ed. Derek Baker, Studies in Church History 16 (Oxford) 93–102.

(1983), *The Frankish Kingdoms under the Carolingians, 751–987* (New York).

(1989), *The Carolingians and the Written Word* (Cambridge).

(1990), 'Women in the Ottonian church: an iconographical perspective,' in *Women in the Church*, ed. Diana Wood, Studies in Church History 27 (Oxford) 79–100.

(1991), 'Frauen und Schriftlichkeit im frühen Mittelalter', in *Weibliche Lebensgestaltung im frühen Mittelalter*, ed. Hans-Werner Goetz (Weimar 1991) 65–118.

Matthäi, Georg (1877), 'Die Klosterpolitik Kaiser Heinrichs II.: Ein Beitrag zur Geschichte der Reichsabteien' (Grünberg).

Maurer, Helmut (1978), *Der Herzog von Schwaben: Grundlagen, Wirkungen und Wesen seiner Herrschaft im ottonischer, salischer und staufischer Zeit* (Sigmaringen).

Mayer, Johann (1900–2), 'Die Klosterpolitik Ottos I.', *Program des K. K. deutschen Staats-Obergymnasiums zu Ungarish-Hradisch* (1900/1901) 1–17 and (1901/ 1902) 3–21.

Mayer, Theodor (1941/1959), 'Das deutsche Königstum und sein Wirkungsbereich', in *Das Reich und Europa*, ed. Fritz Hartung *et al.* (Leipzig) 52–75. [Also in Mayer, *Mittelalterliche Studien* (Konstanz 1959) 28–44.]

(1950), *Fürsten und Staat* (Weimar).

(1958), 'Der Wandel unseres Bild vom Mittelalter. Stand und Aufgaben der mittelalterlichen Geschichtsforschung', *BDLG* 94 (1958) 1–37.

Mayr-Harting, Henry (1991), *Ottonian Book Illuminations: An Historical Study*, 2 vols. (London).

Metz, Wolfgang (1956), 'Die Fuldaer Bramforsturkunden', *FGB* 32 (1956) 1–7.

(1970), 'Die mittelalterliche Königsgastung und ihre Organisation im Bereich der späteren Pfalz', *Mitteilungen des Historischen Vereins der Pfalz* 68 (1970) 183–93.

Bibliography

(1971), 'Tafelgut, Königstrasse und *Servitium Regis* in Deutschland vornehmlich im 10. und 11. Jahrhundert', *HJB* 91 (1971) 257–91.

(1972a), 'Eschwege im Nekrolog des Speyerer Domstifts', *HJBLG* 22 (1972) 343–6.

(1972b), 'Marktrechtfamilie und Kaufmannsfriede in ottonisch-salischer Zeit', *BDLG* 108 (1972) 28–56.

(1976), 'Quellenstudien zum *Servitium regis* (900–1250), Erster Teil', *AD* 22 (1976) 187–272.

(1978a), 'Quellenstudien zum *Servitium regis* (900–1250), Zweiter Teil', *AD* 24 (1978) 203–91.

(1978b), *Das* Servitium Regis (Darmstadt).

(1981), 'Zu Wesen und Struktur der geistlichen Grundherrschaft', in *Nascita dell'Europe ed d'Europa Carolingia: Un'equazione de verificare*, Settimane 27 (1981) 147–74.

(1984), 'Königshaus, Königsgut und Königskirchen', *BDLG* 120 (1984) 1–19.

(1985), 'Quellenstudien zum *Servitium regis* (900–1250), Dritter Teil', *AD* 31 (1985) 273–327.

(1989), 'Corveyer Studien. Die jüngeren Traditionen und das Wohltäter-verzeichnis. Zweiter Teil', *AD* 35 (1989) 255–96.

(1990), 'Corveyer Studien. Dritter Teil', *AD* 36 (1990) 11–43.

(1991), 'Wesen und Struktur des Adels Althessens in der Salierzeit', in *Die Salier und das Reich 1: Salier, Adel und Reichsverfassung*, ed. Stefan Weinfurter (Sigmaringen) 331–66.

Meyer, Marc Anthony (1981), 'Patronage of the West Saxon royal nunneries in late Anglo-Saxon England', *RB* 91 (1981) 333–58.

Meyer von Knonau, Gerold (1890–1909), *Jahrbücher des deutschen Reiches unter Heinrich IV. und Heinrich V.*, 7 vols. (Leipzig repr. Berlin 1964–5).

Meyer-Barkhausen, Werner (1956), 'Die Ausgrabungen auf dem Fuldaer Domplatz 1953 in neuer Sicht', *ZHG* 67 (1956) 23–38.

(1958), 'Die frühmittelalter Vorbauten am Atrium von Alt St. Peter in Rom, zweitürmige Atrien, Westwerke und karolingisch-ottonische Königs-kapellen', *Wallraf-Richartz-JB* 20 (1958) 7–40.

(1960), 'Die karolingische Klosterkirche zu Fulda in ihren baugeschichtlichen Beziehungen zu Rom', *HJBLG* 10 (1960) 1–15.

Minnigerode, Heinrich Freiherr von (1928), *Königszins, Königsgericht, Königs-gastung im altsächsischen Freidingrechte* (Göttingen).

Minninger, Monika (1978), *Von Clermont zum Wormser Konkordat: Die Auseinandersetzung um den Lehnsnexus zwischen König und Episkopat*, Beihefte zu J. F. Böhmer, Regesta Imperii 2 (Cologne).

Müller, Ernst (1901), *Das Itinerar Kaiser Heinrichs III. (1039–56)*, Historische Studien 26 (Berlin).

(1930), '"kuningstoph" 1282 and "koningesstope" 1308 u. ff.', *AUF* 11 (1930) 423–34.

Müller, Kurt (1933), 'Die Schenkungs-Urkunde des Erzbischofs Gero von Köln und des Markgrafen Thietmar für Kloster Thankmarsfelde vom 29. August 970', in *Kritische Beiträge zur Geschichte des Mittelalters: FS für Robert*

Secondary works

Holtmann zum 60. Geburtstag, ed. Walter Mollenberg and Martin Lintzel, Historische Studien 238 (Berlin) 43–52.

Müller-Kehlen, Helga (1973), *Die Ardennen im Frühmittelalter*, VMPIG 38 (Göttingen).

Müller-Mertens, Eckhard (1970), *Regnum Teutonicum. Aufkommen und Verbreitung der deutschen Reichs- und Königsauffassung im früheren Mittelalter*, Forschungen und mittelalterlichen Geschichte 15 (Berlin).

—— (1980), *Die Reichsstruktur im Spiegel der Herrschaftspraxis Ottos des Großen* (Berlin).

—— (1990), '*Romanum imperium* und *regnum Teutonicorum*. Der hochmittelalterliche Reichsverband im Verhältnis zum Karolingerreich', *JB für Geschichte des Feudalismus* 14 (1990) 47–54.

—— (1991), 'Reich und Hauptorte der Salier: Probleme und Fragen', in *Die Salier und das Reich 1: Salier, Adel und Reichsverfassung*, ed. Stefan Weinfurter (Sigmaringen) 139–58.

Nass, Klaus (1986), *Untersuchungen zur Geschichte des Bonifatiusstifts Hameln. Von den monastischen Anfängen bis zum Hochmittelalter*, VMPIG 83, Studien zu Germania Sacra 16 (Göttingen).

Nelson, Janet (1973), 'Royal saints and early medieval kingship', in *Sanctity and Secularity*, ed. D. Baker, Studies in Church History 10 (Oxford) 39–44. [Also in Nelson (1986) 69–74.]

—— (1979), 'Charles the Bald and the church in town and countryside', in *The Church in Town and Countryside*, ed. Derek Baker, Studies in Church History 16 (Oxford) 103–18. [Also in Nelson (1986) 75–90.] [Page references are to 1979 edn.]

—— (1986), *Politics and Ritual in Early Medieval Europe*, History series 42 (London).

—— (1990), 'Literacy in Carolingian government', in *The Uses of Literacy in Early Medieval Europe*, ed. Rosamond McKitterick (Cambridge) 258–96.

Neuman, Ronald (1978), 'Die Arengen der Urkunden Ottos des Grosses', *AD* 24 (1978) 292–358.

Niermeyer, Jan F. (1954–76), *Mediae Latinitatis Lexicon Minus* (Leiden).

Nitz, Hans-Jürgen (1988), 'Settlement structures and settlement systems of the Frankish central state in Carolingian and Ottonian times', in *Anglo-Saxon Settlements*, ed. Della Hooke (Oxford) 249–73.

Oppermann, Otto (1922), *Rheinische Urkundenstudien 1: Die kölnisch-niederrheinischen Urkunden*, Publikationen der Gesellschaft für Rheinische Geschichtskunde 32 (Bonn).

Otto, Eberhard Friedrich (1933), *Die Entwicklung der deutschen Kirchenvogtei im 10. Jahrhundert*, Abhandlungen zur mittleren und neueren Geschichte 72 (Berlin).

Parisse, Michel (1978), 'Les Chanoinesses dans l'Empire germanique (IXᵉ–XIᵉ siècles)', *Francia* 6 (1978) 107–26.

—— (1990), 'Les Femmes au monastère dans le nord de l'Allemagne du IXᵉ au XIᵉ siècle. Conditions sociales et religieuses', in *Frauen im Spätantik und Frühmittelalter. Lebensbedingungen – Lebensnorm – Lebensformen*, ed. Werner Affelt (Sigmaringen) 311–24.

Bibliography

(1991), 'Die Frauenstifte und Frauenklöster in Sachsen vom 10. bis zur Mitte des 12. Jahrhunderts', in *Die Salier und das Reich 2: Die Reichskirche in der Salierzeit*, ed. Stefan Weinfurter (Sigmaringen) 465–501.

Parsons, David (1983), 'Sites and monuments of the Anglo-Saxon mission in central Germany', *The Archaeological Journal* 140 (1983) 280–321.

Patze, Hans (1962), *Die Entstehung der Landesherrschaft in Thüringen* 1 (Cologne).
   (1968), *Thüringen*, vol. 9 of HHSD (1964–75).
   (1974), *Geschichte Thüringens 2.1: Hohes und Spätes Mittelalter*, Mitteldeutsche Forschungen 48/2.1 (Cologne).

Pätzold, Barbara (1979), '"Francia et Saxonia" – Vorstufe einer sächsischen Reichsauffassung', *JB für Geschichte des Feudalismus* 3 (1979) 19–49.

Pauler, Roland (1982), *Das Regnum Italiae in ottonischer Zeit: Markgrafen, Grafen und Bischöfe als politische Kräfte*, Bibliothek des Deutschen Historischen Instituts in Rom 54 (Tübingen).

Perst, Otto (1957), 'Die Kaisertochter Sophie Äbtissin von Gandersheim und Essen (975–1039)', *Braunschweigisches Jahrbuch* 38 (1957) 5–46.

Petke, Wolfgang (1974), 'Die Schenkung des Reichsgutes Seesen an das Stift Gandersheim im Jahre 974', *Tausend Jahre Seesen 974–1974: Beiträge zur Geschichte der Stadt Seesen am Harz* (Seesen) 1–16.

Peyer, Hans Conrad (1964/1982), 'Das Reisekönigtum des Mittelalters', *VSWG* 51 (1964) 1–21. [Also in *Könige, Stadt und Kapital: Aufsätze zur Wirtschafts- und Sozialgeschichte des Mittelalters*, ed. Ludwig Schmugge *et al.* (Zürich) 98–115, 286–90.] [Page references are to 1982 edn.]
   (1987), *Von der Gastfreundschaft zum Gasthaus: Studien zur Gastlichkeit im Mittelalter*, MGH Schriften 31 (Hanover).

Pfaff, Friedrich (1910), 'Die Abtei Helmarshausen. Ein Beitrag zur älteren Geschichte der Landschaft an der unteren Diemel', *ZHG* 44 (1910) 188–286.
   (1911), 'Die Abtei Helmarshausen. Ein Beitrag zur älteren Geschichte der Landschaft an der unteren Diemel', *ZHG* 45 (1911) 1–80.

Pöschl, Arnold (1908–12), *Bischofsgut und Mensa Episcopalis*, 3 vols. (Bonn).
   (1928), *Die Regalien der mittelalterlichen Kirchen* (Graz).

Prinz, Friedrich (1971), *Klerus und Krieg im früheren Mittelalter: Untersuchungen zur Rolle der Kirche beim Aufbau der Königsherrschaft*, Monographien zur Geschichte des Mittelalters 2 (Stuttgart).
   (1985), *Grundlagen und Anfänge: Deutschland bis 1056*, Die Neue Deutsche Geschichte 1 (Munich).

Prinz, Joseph (1983), 'Das hohe Mittelalter vom Vertrag von Verdun (843) bis zur Schlacht von Worringen (1288)', in *Westfälischen Geschichte 1: Von den Anfängen bis zum Ende des alten Reiches*, ed. Wilhelm Kohl (Düsseldorf) 337–401.

Reindel, Kurt (1953), *Die bayerischen Liutpoldinger, 893–989*, QEBG NF 11 (Munich).

Renn, Heinz (1941), *Das erste Luxemburger Grafenhaus*, Rheinisches Archiv 39 (Bonn).

Reuter, Timothy (1981), 'Review article: A new history of medieval Germany', *History* 66 (1981) 440–3.

Secondary works

(1982), 'The "imperial church system" of the Ottonian and Salian rulers: A reconsideration', *JEH* 33 (1982) 347–74.

(1985), 'Plunder and tribute in the Carolingian Empire', *Transactions of the Royal Historical Society*, 5th ser. 35 (1985) 75–94.

(1990), 'The end of Carolingian military expansion', in *Charlemagne's Heir: New Perspectives on the Reign of Louis the Pious (814–840)*, ed. Peter Godman and Roger Collins (Oxford) 391–405.

(1991a), *Germany in the Early Middle Ages (800–1056)* (London).

(1991b), 'Otto III and the historians', *History Today* 41 (1991) 21–7.

Rieckenberg, Hans Jürgen (1941/1965), 'Königsstrasse und Königsgut in liudolfingischer und frühsalischer Zeit (919–1056)', *AUF* 17 (1941) 32–154. [Also published separately with double pagination as *Königsstrasse und Königsgut in liudolfingischer und frühsalischer Zeit (919–1056)* (Darmstadt 1965).]

Römer, Christof (1970), *Das Kloster Berge bei Magdeburg und seine Dörfer 968–1565*, Studien zur Germania Sacra 10 (Göttingen).

Rösener, Werner (1980), 'Strukturformen der älteren Agrarverfassung im sächsischen Raum', *NSJBLG* 52 (1980) 107–43.

(1985), 'Zur Struktur und Entwicklungen der Grundherrschaft in Sachsen in karolingischer und ottonischer Zeit', in Verhulst (1985) 173–207.

(1989) ed., *Strukturen der Grundherrschaft im frühen Mittelalter*, VMPIG 92 (Göttingen).

Roth, Otto (1974), 'Die Entwicklung Seesens von den Anfängen bis zum dreissigjahrigen Krieg', in *Tausend Jahre Seesen 974–1974: Beiträge zur Geschichte der Stadt Seesen am Harz* (Seesen) 25–88.

Rübel, Karl (1901), *Reichshöfe im Lippe-, Ruhr- und Diemelgebiet und am Hellweg*, Beiträge zur Geschichte Dortmunds und der Grafschaft Mark 10 (Dortmund).

Sandow, Erich (1970), 'Herford', in Klocke and Bauermann (1970) 312–16.

Santifaller, Leo (1964), *Zur Geschichte des ottonischen-salischen Reichskirchensystems*, SB Vienna 229.1, 2nd expanded edn (Vienna).

Schäfer, Karl Heinrich (1907), *Die Kanonissenstifter im deutschen Mittelalter*, Kirchrechtliche Abhandlungen 43/44 (Stuttgart).

Schaller, Hans Martin (1974), 'Der heilige Tag also Termin mittelalterlicher Staatsakte', *DA* 30 (1974) 1–25.

Schalles-Fischer, Marianne (1969), *Pfalz und Fiskus Frankfurst*, VMPIG 20 (Göttingen).

Schannat, Johann Friedrich (1729), *Historia Fuldensis* (Frankfurt).

Scheibelreiter, Georg (1983), *Der Bischof in merowingischer Zeit*, Veröffentlichungen des Instituts für österreichische Geschichtsforschung 27 (Vienna).

Scheyhing, Robert (1960), *Eide, Amtsgewalt und Bannleihe: Eine Untersuchung zur Bannleihe im hohen und späten Mittelalter*, Forschungen zur deutschen Rechtsgeschichte 2 (Cologne).

Schieffer, Rudolf (1976), *Die Entstehung von Domkapiteln in Deutschland*, Bonner Historische Forschungen 43 (Bonn).

Bibliography

(1989), 'Der ottonische Reichsepiskopat zwischen Königtum und Adel', *FMS* 23 (1989) 291–301.

Schieffer, Theodor (1951), 'Heinrich II. und Konrad II.', *DA* 8 (1951) 384–437.

(1952), 'Cluniazensische oder gorzische Reformbewegung?', *AMRKG* 4 (1952) 24–44.

Schlesinger, Walter (1937/1961), 'Burgen und Burgbezirke, Beobachtungen im mitteldeutschen Osten', in *Von Land und Kultur. FS für Ruldolf Kötzschke*, ed. Werner Emmerich (Leipzig) 77–105. [Repr. in Walter Schlesinger, *Mitteldeutsche Beiträge zur deutschen Verfassungsgeschichte des Mittelalters* (Göttingen 1961) 158–87.]

(1948), 'Die Anfänge der deutschen Königswahl', *ZRG GA* 66 (1948) 381–440.

(1954), 'Burg und Stadt', in *Aus Verfassungs- und Landesgeschichte: FS für Theodor Mayer*, ed. Heinrich Büttner, Otto Feger and Bruno Meyer, vol. 1 (Constance) 97–150. [Also in Schlesinger (1963) 2. 92–147; page references are to the latter edn of 1963.]

(1962), *Kirchengeschichte Sachsens im Mittelalter*, 2 vols., Mitteldeutsche Forschungen 27/1–2 (Cologne).

(1963), 'Verfassungsgeschichte und Landesgeschichte', in *Beiträge zur deutschen Verfassungsgeschichte des Mittelalters*, ed. W. Schlesinger, vol. 2. (Göttingen) 9–41, 254–61.

(1968), 'Zur Geschichte der Magdeburger Königspfalz', *BDLG* 104 (1968) 1–31.

(1973), 'Der Markt als Frühform der deutschen Stadt', in *Vor- und Frühformen der europäischen Stadt im Mittelalter*, ed. Herbert Jankuhn, W. Schlesinger and Heiko Steuer, Abhandlungen Göttingen, Phil.-Hist. Kl. ser. 3, vol. 83 (Göttingen) 262–93.

Schmale, Franz-Josef (1974), '"Paderborner" oder "Korveyer" Annalen?', *DA* 30 (1974) 205–27.

Schmid, Karl (1960/1971a), 'Neue Quellen zum Verständnis des Adels im 10. Jahrhundert', *ZGOR* 108 NF 69 (1960) 185–202. [Section 1 with addenda also in *Königswahl und Thronfolge in Ottonisch-Frühsalischer Zeit*, ed. Eduard Hlawitschka, WdF 178 (Darmstadt 1971) 389–416]. [Page references are to 1971 edn.]

(1964/1971b), 'Die Thronfolge Ottos des Großen', *ZRG GA* 81 (1964) 80–163. [Also with addenda in *Königswahl und Thronfolge in Ottonisch-Frühsalischer Zeit*, ed. Eduard Hlawitschka, WdF 178 (Darmstadt 1971) 417–508]. [Page references are to 1971 edn.]

(1978) ed., *Die Klostergemeinschaft von Fulda im früheren Mittelalter*, 5 vols. [= vols. 1, 2.1–3, 3], Münstersche Mittelalter Schriften 8.1, 8.2.1–3, 8.3 (Munich).

(1985a) ed., *Reich und Kirche vor dem Investiturstreit: Gerd Tellenbach zum achtzigsten Geburtstag* (Sigmaringen).

(1985b), 'Das Problem der "Unteilbarkeit des Reiches"', in Schmid (1985a) 1–15.

Schmid, Karl and Wollasch, Joachim (1983), *Die Liber Vitae der Abtei Corvey*,

Secondary works

Veröffentlichungen der historischen Kommission für Westfalen 40, Westfälische Gedenkbücher und Nekrologien 2 (Wiesbaden).

Schmidt, Roderich (1961), *Königsumritt und Huldigung in ottonisch-salischer Zeit*, VF 6 (Stuttgart) 7–8, 97–233.

Schmitt, Ursula (1974), *Villa Regalis Ulm und Kloster Reichenau: Untersuchungen zur Pfalzfunktion des Reichsklostergutes im Alemannien (9.–12. Jahrhundert)*, VMPIG 42 (Göttingen).

Schneider, Reinhard (1964), *Brüdergemeine und Schwurfreundschaft. Der Auflösungsprozeß des Karolingerreiches im Spiegel der* caritas-*Terminologie in den Verträgen der karolingischen Teilkönige des 9. Jahrhunderts*, Historische Studien 388 (Lübeck).

Schölkopf, Ruth (1957), *Die Sächsischen Grafen [919–1024]*, Studien und Vorarbeiten zum historischen Atlas Niedersachsens 22 (Göttingen).

Schramm, Percy Ernst (1928), *Die deutschen Kaiser und Könige in Bildnissen ihrer Zeit, 1: 751–1152 (Text)* (Leipzig).

Schramm, Percy Ernst and Mütherich, Florintine (1981), *Denkmale der deutschen Könige und Kaiser 1: Von Karl dem Großen bis Friedrich II.*, 2nd rev. edn (Munich).

Schröder, Richard (1871), *Geschichte des ehelichen Güterrechts*, 2 vols. (Stettin repr. Aalen 1967). [Pagination in the two edns is identical.]

Schubert, Ernst (1969), 'Zur Datierung der ottonischen Kirche zu Memleben', in *Siedlung, Burg und Stadt*, ed. Karl-Heinz Otto and Joachim Hermann, Deutsche Akademie der Wissenschaften zu Berlin, Schriften der Sektion für Vor- und Frühgeschichte 25 (Berlin) 515–24.

Schulenberg, Jane Tibbetts (1988), 'Female sanctity: Public and private roles, ca. 500–1100', in *Women and Power in the Middle Ages*, ed. Mary Erler and Maryanne Kowaleski (Athens, GA) 102–25.

Schulze, Hans K. (1965) with Specht, Reinhold and Vorbrodt, Günter Wilhelm, *Das Stift Gernrode*, Mitteldeutsche Forschungen 38 (Cologne).

(1973), *Die Grafschaftsverfassung der Karolingerzeit in den Gebieten östlich des Rheins*, Studien zur Verfassungsgeschichte 19 (Berlin).

(1991), *Hegemoniales Kaisertum: Ottonen und Salier*, Siedler Deutsche Geschichte (Berlin).

Schwarz, George M. (1985), 'Village populations according to the polyptyque of the abbey of St Bertin', *Journal of Medieval History* 11 (1985) 31–41.

Schwineköper, Berent (1977), *Königtum und Städte bis zum Ende des Investiturstreits: Die Politik der Ottonen und Salier gegenüber den werdenden Städten im östlichen Sachsen und Nordthüringen*, VF Sonderband 11 (Sigmaringen).

Seibert, Hubertus (1991), '*Libertas* und Reichsabtei. Zur Klosterpolitik der salischen Herrscher', in *Die Salier und das Reich 2: Die Reichskirche in der Salierzeit*, ed. Stefan Weinfurter (Sigmaringen) 505–69.

Semmler, Josef (1958), 'Studien zum *Supplex Libellus* und zur anaianischen Reform in Fulda', *ZKG* 69 (1958) 268–98.

(1959), '*Traditio* und Königsschutz. Studien zur Geschichte der königlichen *monasteria*', *ZRG KA* 45 (1959) 1–33.

Bibliography

(1963), 'Die Beschlüsse des Aachener Konzils im Jahre 816', *ZKG* 74 (1963) 15–82.

(1965), 'Karl der Große und das fränkische Mönchtum', in *Karl der Große. Lebenswerk und Nachleben*, ed. Wolfgang Braunfels, vol. 2: *Das Geistige Leben*, ed. Bernhard Bischoff (Düsseldorf) 255–89.

(1970), 'Corvey und Herford in der benediktinischen Reformbewegung des 9. Jahrhunderts', *FMS* 4 (1970) 289–319.

(1973–7), 'Die Geschichte der Abtei Lorsch von der Gründung bis zum Ende der Salierzeit 764 bis 1125', in *Die Reichsabtei Lorsch: FS zum Gedenken an ihre Stiftung 764*, 2 vols., ed. Friedrich Knöpp (Darmstadt) 1.75–173.

(1980), 'Die Anfänge Fuldas als Benediktiner- und als Königskloster', *Fuldaer Geschichtsblätter* 56 (1980) 181–200.

(1982), '*Iussit ... princeps renovare ... pracepta.* Zur verfassungsrechtlichen Einordnung der Hochstifte und Abteien in die karolingische Reichskirche,' in *Consuetudines Monasticae: Eine Festgabe für Kassius Hallinger aus Anlass seines 70. Geburtstages*, ed. Joachim F. Angerer and Josef Lenzenweger, Studia Anselmiana 85 (Rome) 97–124.

(1983), 'Benedictus II: *Una Regula – Una Consuetudo*', in *Benedictine Culture: 750–1050*, ed. W. Lourdaux and D. Verhelst, Mediaevalia Lovaniensia Ser. 1 Studia 11 (Louvain) 1–50.

(1989), 'Das Erbe der karolingischen Klosterreform im 10. Jahrhundert', in *Monastische Reform im 9. und 10. Jahrhundert*, ed. Raymund Kottje and Helmut Maurer, VF 38 (Sigmaringen) 29–77.

Starke, Heinz-Dieter (1955), 'Die Pfalzgrafen von Sachsen bis zum Jahre 1088', *Braunschweigisches Jahrbuch* 36 (1955) 24–52.

Stein, Walter (1922), *Handels- und Verkehrsgeschichte der deutschen Kaiserzeit* (Berlin repr. Darmstadt 1967). [Pagination in the two edns is identical.]

Steindorff, Ernst (1874–81), *Jahrbücher des Deutschen Reiches unter Heinrichs III.*, 2 vols., Jahrbücher der Deutschen Geschichte (Leipzig repr. Darmstadt 1963).

Stengel, Edmund E. (1910), *Die Immunität in Deutschland bis zum Ende des 11. Jahrhunderts 1: Diplomatik der deutschen Immunitäts-Privilegien vom 9. bis zum Ende des 11. Jahrhunderts* (Innsbruck repr. Aalen 1964).

(1935a), 'Über die Schenkung von Breitungen an die Reichsabtei Hersfeld', *MIÖG* 49 (1935) 439–44.

(1935b), see: Eisenträger and Krug (1935).

Stoob, Heinz (1970), 'Doppelstädte, Gründungsfamilien und Stadtwüstungen im engrischen Westfalen', in *Kunst und Kultur im Weserraum (800–1600)*, vol. 3: *Ostwestfälisch-Weserländische Forschungen zur Geschichtlichen Landeskunde*, ed. H. Stoob (Münster) 113–48.

Störmer, Wilhelm (1966), 'Fernstrasse und Kloster. Zur Verkehrs- und Herrschaftsstruktur des westlichen Altbayern im frühen Mittelalter', *ZBLG* 29 (1966) 299–344.

Streich, Gerhard (1984), *Burg und Kirche während des deutschen Mittelalters. Untersuchungen zur Sakraltopographie von Pfalzen, Burgen und Herrensitzen*, 2 vols., VF Sonderband 29.1–2 (Sigmaringen). [The two volumes have continuous pagination.]

Secondary works

Stutz, Ulrich (1894/1938), 'The proprietary church as an element of mediaeval Germanic ecclesiastical law', in Barraclough (1938) 1.35–70. [First published as *Die Eigenkirche als Element des mittelalterlich-germanisch Kirchenrechts* (Berlin 1894).]

Stüwer, Wilhelm (1980), *Das Erzbistum Köln 3: Die Reichsabtei Werden an der Ruhr*, Germania Sacra NF 12 (Berlin).

Szabo, Thomas (1984), 'Antikes Erbe und karolingisch-ottonische Verkehrspolitik', in Fenske, Rösener and Zotz (1984) 125–45.

Thiele, Augustinius (1976), 'Der "supplex libellus" – soziologisch gesehen', *Erbe und Auftrag* 52 (1976) 220–2.

Thomas, Heinz (1976), '*Regnum Teutonicorum – diutiscono richi*? Bemerkungen zur Doppelwahl des Jahres 919', *RVJB* 40 (1976) 17–45.

Timm, Albrecht (1941/1943), 'Wallhausen, eine vergessene Pfalz am Südharz', *SA* 17 (1941/1943) 455–73.

Uhl, Bernhard (1907), *Die Verkehrswege der Flußtäler um Münden und ihr Einfluß auf Anlage und Entwicklung der Siedlungen*, Forschungen zur Geschichte Niedersachsens 1.4 (Hanover) 1–52.

Uhlirz, Mathilde (1954), *Jahrbücher des Deutschen Reiches unter Otto II. und Otto III. 2: Otto III. 983–1002*, Jahrbücher des Deutsche Geschichte (Berlin).

Verhulst, Adriaan (1966), 'La Genèse du régime domanial classique en France au haut moyen âge', in *Agricoltura e mondo rurale in Occidente nell'alto medioevo*, Settimane 13 (1966) 135–60.

(1983), 'La Diversité du régime domanial entre Loire und Rhin à l'époque carolingienne, Bilan de quinze années de recherches', in *Villa – curtis – grangia. Landwirtschaft zwischen Loire and Rhein von der Römerzeit zum Hochmittelalter*, ed. W. Janssen and D. Lohrmann, Beihefte der Francia 11 (Munich 1983) 133–48.

(1985) ed., *Le Grand Domaine aux époques mérovingienne et carolingienne* [*Die Grundherrschaft im frühen Mittelalter*] (Ghent).

(1989), 'Die Grundherrschaftsentwicklung im östfränkischen Raum vom 8. bis 10. Jahrhundert. Grundzüge und Fragen aus westfränkischer Sicht', in Rösener (1989) 29–46.

Vogel, Cyrille and Elze, Reinhard (1963–72) eds., *Le Pontifical romano-germanique du dixième siècle*, 3 vols., Studi e Testi 226, 227, 269 (Vatican City).

Vogtherr, Thomas (1991), 'Die Reichsklöster Corvey, Fulda und Hersfeld', in *Die Salier und das Reich 2: Die Reichskirche in der Salierzeit*, ed. Stefan Weinfurter (Sigmaringen) 429–64.

Voigt, Karl (1917), *Die Karolingische Klosterpolitik* (Stuttgart repr. Amsterdam 1965). [Pagination in the two edns is identical.]

Voss, Ingrid (1987), *Herrschertreffen im frühen und hohen Mittelalter : Untersuchungen zu den Begegnungen der östfränkischen und westfränkischen Herrscher im 9. und 10. Jahrhundert sowie der deutschen und französischen Könige vom 11, bis 13. Jahrhundert* (Cologne).

Waas, Adolf (1919), *Vogtei und Bede in der deutschen Kaiserzeit. Erster Teil*, Arbeiten zur deutschen Rechts- und Verfassungsgeschichte 1 (Berlin).

Bibliography

Wadle, Elmar (1971), 'Mittelalterliches Münzrecht im Spiegel der *Confoederatiocum principibus ecclesiasticis*', *JBNG* 21 (1971) 187–224.

Waitz, Georg (1893–6), *Deutsche Verfassungsgeschichte*, 8 vols., 2nd edn (Berlin repr. Graz 1955). [Page references are to 1955 edn.]

Wäscher, Hermann (1959), *Der Bergburg in Quedlinburg, Geschichte seiner Bauten bis zum ausgehenden 12. Jahrhundert nach den Ergebnissen der Grabungen von 1938 bis 1942* (Berlin).

Wattenbach, Wilhelm and Schmale, Franz-Josef (1976), *Deutschlands Geschichtsquellen in MA: Vom Tode Kaiser Heinrichs V. bis zum Ende des Interregnums*, vol. 1, (Darmstadt).

Weczerka, Hugo (1966), 'Verkehrsgeschichtliche Grundlagen des Weserraums', in *Kunst und Kultur im Weserraum (800–1600)*, vol. 1 : *Beiträge zu Geschichte und Kunst*, ed. Bernard Korzus (Münster) 192–202.

Wehlt, Hans Peter (1970), *Reichsabtei und König*, VMPIG 28 (Göttingen).

Weidenhaupt, Hugo (1954), 'Das Kanonissenstift Gerresheim von seiner Gründung bis zum Ende des 14. Jahrhunderts', *Düsseldorfer Jahrbuch* 46 (1954) 1–120.

Weidinger, Ulrich (1989), 'Untersuchungen zur Grundherrschaft des Klosters Fulda in der Karolingerzeit', in Rösener (1989) 247–65.

Weigel, Helmut (1960), *Die Grundherrschaft des Frauenstiftes Essen : Studien zur Verfassung und Verwaltung des Grundbesitzes des Frauenstiftes Essen (852–1803)*, Beiträge zur Geschichte von Stadt und Stift Essen 76 (Essen).

Weinfurter, Stefan (1986), 'Die Zentralizierung der Herrschaftsgewalt im Reich durch Kaiser Heinrich II.', *HJB* 106 (1986) 241–97.

Weirich, Hans (1936), 'Das Privileg Benedikt VII. für Memleben', *SA* 12 (1936) 83–94.

Wenck, Karl (1907), 'Deutsche Kaiser and Könige in Hessen', *ZHG* 40 (1907) 139–57.

Werner, Karl Ferdinand (1968), 'Heeresorganisation und Kriegführung im deutschen Königsreich des 10. und 11. Jahrhunderts', in *Ordinamenti militari in Occidente nell'alto medioevo*, Settimane 15.2 (Spoleto 1968) 791–843.

Werner-Hasselbach, Traut (1942), *Die älteren Güterverzeichnisse der Reichsabtei Fulda*, Marburger Studien zur älteren deutschen Geschichte 2.7 (Marburg).

Weyhe, Emil (1907), *Landeskunde des Herzogtums Anhalt*, 2 vols. (Dessau).

Wibel, Hans (1910–11), 'Zur Kritik der älteren Kaiserurkunden für das Kloster Werden an der Ruhr', *AUF* 3 (1910–11) 81–113.

Wigand, Paul (1826–8), 'Verzeichnisse Corvey'-scher Güter und Einkünfte aus dem 12. und 13. Jahrhundert', *Archiv für Geschichte und Altertumskunde Westphalens* 1.4 (Hamm 1826) 48–55 and 2.1 (Hamm 1828) 1–6.

Wilke, Sabine (1970), *Das Goslarer Reichsgebiet und seine Beziehungen zu den territorialen Nachbargewalten*, VMPIG 32 (Göttingen).

Willmes, Peter (1976), *Der Herrscher-'Adventus' im Kloster des Frühmittelalters*, Münstersche Mittelalter Schriften 22 (Munich).

Wilmans, Roger (1874), 'Studien zur Geschichte der Abtei Vreden', *WZ* [formerly *Zeitschrift für vaterländische Geschichte und Altertumskunde*] 32.1 (1874) 111–59.

Unpublished dissertations

Wisplinghoff, Erich (1970), *Untersuchungen zur früheren Geschichte der Abtei S. Maximin bei Trier von den Anfangen bis etwa 1150*, Quellen und Abhandlungen zur mittelrheinischen Kirchengeschichte 12 (Mainz).

(1983), 'Bauerliches Leben am Niederrhein im Rahmen der benediktinischen Grundherrschafte', in Villa – curtis – grangia. *Landwirtschaft zwischen Loire and Rhein von der Römerzeit zum Hochmittelalter*, ed. W. Janssen and D. Lohrmann, Beihefte der Francia 11 (Munich 1983) 149–63.

Wolf, Gunther (1983), 'Das sogenannte "Gegenkönigtum" Arnulfs von Bayern 919', *MIÖG* 91 (1983) 375–400.

Wolff, P. Carl (1930), 'Die Gorzer Reform in ihrem Verhältnis zu deutschen Klöster: Ein Beitrag zu lothringisch-deutschen Klosterbeziehungen des Mittelalters', *Elsass-Lothringisches Jahrbuch* 9 (1930) 95–111.

Wollasch, Joachim (1977), 'Neue Methoden der Erforschung des Mönchtums im Mittelalter', *HZ* 225 (1977) 529–71.

(1978), 'Die Necrologien in der Edition der Gedenküberlieferung von Fulda', in Schmid (1978) vol. 2.2 pp. 931–52.

Wühr, Wilhelm (1948), 'Die Wiedergeburt Montecassinos unter seinem ersten Reformabt Richer von Niederaltaich', *Studi Gregoriani* 3 (1948) 369–450.

Ziegler, Elisabeth (1939), *Das Territorium der Reichsabtei Hersfeld von seinen Anfängen bis 1821*, Schriften des Instituts für geschichtliche Landeskunde von Hessen und Nassau 7 (Marburg).

Zielinski, Herbert (1984), *Der Reichsepiskopat in spätottonischer und salischer Zeit 1 (1002–1125)* (Stuttgart).

Zimmermann, Walter (1956), *Das Münster zu Essen*, Die Kunstdenkmäler des Rheinlandes, Beihefte 3 (1956).

Zotz, Thomas (1984), 'Königspfalz und Herrschaftspraxis im 10. und frühen 11. Jahrhundert', *BDLG* 120 (1984) 19–47.

(1989), '*Amicitia* und *Discordia*. Zu einer Neuerscheinung über das Verhältnis von Königtum und Adel in frühottonischer Zeit', *Francia* 16.1 (1989) 169–75.

UNPUBLISHED DISSERTATIONS

Borchers, Herta (1952), 'Untersuchungen zur Handels- und Verkehrsgeschichte am Mittel- und Oberrhein bis zum Ende des 12. Jahrhunderts' (Ph.D. Marburg).

Carr, Amnon (1986), 'Otto I and the church of S. Mauricius at Magdeburg: A survey of the evidence of the charters' (BA Diss. Cambridge).

Diefenbach, Hans Jörg (1952), 'Die "*Renovatio Regni Francorum*" durch Kaiser Heinrich II.' (Ph.D. Cologne).

Eibl, Elfie-Marie (1982), 'Studien zur Reichsstruktur anhand der Herrschaftspraxis Arnulfs von Kärnten' (Ph.D. Berlin).

Huschner, Wolfgang (1986), 'Studien zur Reichsstruktur unter Konrad II. (1024–1039)' (Ph.D. Berlin).

Kallen, Gerhard (1924), 'Der rechtliche Charakter der frühmittelalterlichen sogenannten Güterteilung zwischen Bischof und Kapitel' (Dr. Jur. Bonn).

Bibliography

Oehler, Hans (1957), 'Das Itinerar des Königs, seine Ordnung und seine Beziehungen zur Regierungstätigkeit in der Zeit Kaiser Lothars III.' (Ph.D. Freiburg).

Ribbeck, Konrad (1883), 'Die sogennante *divisio* des fränkischen Kirchengutes' (Ph.D. Leipzig).

Scherff, Bruno (1985), 'Studien zum Heer der Ottonen und der ersten Salier (919–1056)' (Ph.D. Bonn).

Seelig, Friedrich (1919), 'Verleihungen Ottos I. an Bistümer und Klöster' (Ph.D. Cologne).

Stephan-Kühn, Freya (1973), 'Wibald als Abt von Stablo und Corvey im Dienst Konrads III.' (Ph.D. Cologne).

Stüllein, Hans-Jochen (1971), 'Das Itinerar Heinrichs V. in Deutschland' (Ph.D. Munich).

Volz, Peter (1967), 'Königliche Münzheit und Münzprivilegien im Karolingischen Reich und die Entwicklung in der sächsischen und fränkischen Zeit' (Dr. Jur. Heidelberg).

Warner, David A. (1989), 'The cult of Saint Maurice: Ritual politics and political symbolism in Ottonian Germany' (Ph.D [University of California] Los Angeles).

INDEX

Aachen, 9, 21, 22, 39, 48, 185–6, 225
  coronation of 936, 4
Aarhus, 38
abbots (abbesses), secular obligations,
  85–6, 119
Abodrites, 37, 40
Adalard, abbot of St Bertin, 128, 129
Adalbert, archbishop of Bremen, 53, 74,
  137n
Adalbert, bishop of Metz, 129
Adalbert, bishop of Prague and martyr,
  41
Adalbert of St Maximin, continuator of
  Regino of Prüm, first archbishop of
  Magdeburg, 54, 59, 174
Adalbold, royal chaplain, bishop of
  Utrecht and Henry II's biographer,
  53
Adalhard, abbot of St Trond, 256
Adalwif, abbess of Essen, 191
Adelbero/Bern, count palatine and
  advocate of Hilwartshausen, 218, 220
Adelheid, daughter of Otto II
  abbess of Gernrode, Vreden, and
    Gandersheim, 143–4, 151, 205
  abbess of Quedlinburg, 140, 142, 143,
    151
  role in royal elections, 69n, 150–1
Adelheid, wife of Otto I and empress,
  24–5, 26, 59, 143, 145, 278
Adelheid II, abbess of Quedlinburg, 144,
  151
Adelmann, abbot of Hersfeld, 262
advent (adventus), royal, 20n, 49n, 140,
  143, 168, 271, 293
advocacy, 29, 139
advocate, 7, 34, 73, 288, 302
Aeddila, Saxon noblewoman, 216–18,
  300
Aethelstan, king of Wessex, 14
Agnes, empress, 270, 284
agriculture, structure of estates, 81–2
Aiterhofen, 100, 102–4, 105

Alberada, daughter of Giselbert, duke of
  Lotharingia and Gerberga, sister of
  Otto I, 22
Albrecht, count of Ballenstedt, 173, 174
Allstedt, royal residence, 140, 173, 248,
  263
Alsleben, convent, 172, 174–5, 292, 294
Altfrid, bishop of Hildesheim, 114
Ambergau, 155
amicitia, 11, 12, 16, 17, 38, 41
  as a diplomatic device, 12, 13, 16, 17,
    38
Andernach, battle of (939), 19, 21, 237
Annales Necrologici Fuldenses, 271
Annalista Saxo: see Saxon Annalist
Annals of Niederaltaich, 173
Annals of Quedlinburg, 297
anointing, anointment, of kings, 4–5, 48,
  49
Antsanvia, 243, 261
Aquileia, 24
arces Romani imperii, 271
Ardo, biographer of Benedict of Aniane,
  93
Aribo, archbishop of Mainz, 287
Arnold, monk of St Emmeram, 102
Arnolf, abbot of Hersfeld, 250, 252
Arnstadt, 248, 262, 287, 306
Arnulf, duke of Bavaria, 11, 17
Arnulf of Bavaria, count palatine, 25
Arnulf of Carinthia, emperor, 86, 109
Aschaffenburg, 278, 288
assemblies, royal, 209
  at Arnstadt, 262
  at Duisburg, 185–6
  at Erfurt, 3
  at Merseburg, 264
  at Quedlinburg, 141
  at Rohr, 143
  at Sohlingen, 197, 198
  at Steele, 178, 187, 192
  at Worms, 12
Autlandus, abbot of Tours, 107

Index

Bad Langensalza, 241
Baldiuc, 97
Bamberg, bishopric, 68, 252, 258, 262, 267
  foundation of, 43, 43n, 223–4, 232, 250, 251
  ban, royal, definition of, 31, 284
  grants of, 147, 154, 171, 214, 227–8, 239, 249, 261, 266, 283, 284–6
bad immunity: see under immunity
Barchfeld, 261, 262, 305
Bardo, abbot of Werden, 127
Basislandschaft, 62–3, 65
  see also Saxony
Baugulf, abbot of Fulda, 244
Bavaria, Bavarians, 62, 278
  as a Fernzone of the realm, 62, 69
Beatrix, abbess of Quedlinburg, 144, 151
Bebra/Breitenbach: see Breitenbach/Bebra
Behringen (Groß-), 263, 285
Benedict VII, pope, 248
Benedict VIII, pope, 256, 267, 271
Benedict of Aniane, 92–3
Berengar II, king of Italy, 24–5, 36
Berge, monastery, 170
Berka, 240, 241, 255, 306
Bern: see Adelbero/Bern
Bernard, bishop of Halberstadt, 38
Bernhard, bishop of Hildesheim, 79, 202
Bernward, bishop of Hildesheim, 221
Berstadt, 240, 255, 257, 259, 260, 269, 272–3, 282, 283
Bertha, queen, 258
Berthildis, abbess of Hilwartshausen, 217
Berthold, duke of Bavaria, 17, 21
Bertram, abbot of Stavelot-Malmédy, 124
Billungs, 25n, 53, 65, 70, 299
Bilstein, counts of, 236, 238
Bodfeld, 139, 140, 148, 154, 155n, 156, 257, 269, 290
Bohemia, Bohemians, 14, 37–8, 39–40
Boleslav Chrobry, ruler of Poland, 41–2, 249
Boniface, St, bishop of Mainz, 241–2, 266
book production, 76
Bram Forest, 283–4
Bramwald, 222, 300
Brandenburg, 38, 39, 40, 168
Breitenbach/Bebra, 240, 254, 255, 258, 261, 275, 306
Breitungen, 240, 241, 261, 305
Bronnzell, 265, 305
Brühl, Carlrichard, 79, 137, 295

Brun, brother of Otto I, archbishop of Cologne, 3, 26, 27
  called archidux, 27
Brun, Liudolfing count, 149
Bruning, vassal of duke Eberhard (937), 18
Bruno, bishop of Augsburg, brother of Henry II, 102–3, 224
Bruno, historian of Saxon War, 231
Burchard, bishop of Worms, 59
Burchard II, duke of Swabia, 11, 13, 26, 57
Burchard III, duke of Swabia, 26
Burgbann, 57, 155, 196–7
burgward, burgwards, 38, 245, 246, 248–9, 252

capellani, 32
Capetians, 36
capitularies, 92n, 94n, 128
Carloman, Frankish mayor of the palace, 241–2
Carolingians, 4, 8, 10, 12, 36
  marriage connections with east Frankish nobility, 9–10
castlework: see Burgbann
cathedral chapters, 33
cathedral schools, 32, 33
centres of royal power
  Carolingian, 7, 9, 22, 39, 62, 67
  Saxon, 7, 9, 22–3, 38, 40, 62, 67
  see also fisc, Carolingian
chancery, royal, 31
chapel, court, 15, 27, 31–3
chaplains, 32–3
Charlemagne, Carolingian emperor, 48, 89, 90, 92, 177, 183, 184, 242–4, 287
  as a model king (and emperor), 4–5, 36, 39
  as a monastic benefactor, 96, 107, 242, 260, 261
  wars against Saxony, 177, 183–4, 243–5
Charles the Bald, west Frankish Carolingian king, 121
  as a monastic benefactor, 107–8, 109
Charles (III) the Fat, Carolingian emperor, 97
Charles the Simple, west Frankish Carolingian king, 5n, 11, 12
  as a monastic benefactor, 86, 109
charters, 53
  kinds of formulae, 95, 99–100, 102, 104, 106
  repossession clauses in, 97–8, 99–101, 102–5, 157

Index

used to determine royal itinerary, 180–1, 253–4
used to institute monastic property divisions, 106–10, 113, 132–3
used to limit abbatial or episcopal disposition of monastic property, 95–7, 102–3, 106, 108, 113, 128
Christian, margrave, 170
Christianization: see mission
church building, 50
church property: see property, monastic
churches
  mediatized in west Frankish realm, 30
  providing *servitium regis*, 67–8, 69–70
  royal control of, 30–1
coining rights: see minting rights
Cologne, archbishopric of, 179, 185, 186, 204, 205
colonization, 242–5
Conrad, king of Burgundy, 35, 74n
Conrad I, king, 5n, 11, 237
Conrad II, king and emperor, 36, 41, 51, 131, 135, 198–9, 205
  celebration of Epiphany at Corvey, 199, 298
  celebration of St Vitus day at Corvey, 199, 298
  charters of: for Essen, 192; for Fulda, 288; for Herford, 207; for Hilwartshausen, 221; for Nienburg, 171, 172, 173; for Werden, 188n
  expansion of the royal itinerary under, 55, 66, 235, 295–6, 299
  favoured itinerary halting points, 152
  itinerary of, 60–1, 65, 256, 268
Conrad III, king and emperor, 202, 208–9
Conrad the Elder, 237
Conrad the Red, duke of Lotharingia, 22, 24–5, 26, 238
Conradines, 10, 13n, 19, 21–2, 178, 197, 237–8
consuetudo (custom, custumal): see custumal, monastic
contingents, military: see *indiculus loricatorum* and, under *servitium regis*, obligation to provide troops and weapons
Corvey, monastery, 43, 67, 68, 83, 159n, 180, 180n, 195–203, 211, 286, 297
  acquisition of Kemnade, 202, 208–10
  church at, 200, 298
  foundation of, 195
  granted to Adalbert of Hamburg, 74
  grants of property and rights for, 196

grants of sovereign rights to, 201–2
location of, 195–6
market(s) at or of, 201–2, 286, 298
missionary activity from, 39–40, 196
property division in, 123–4
reform of, 123–4, 198, 199, 200
royal visits to, 196–200, 256, 297–8
counts, 236, 238
county, counties, 237–8
  grants of to ecclesiastical institutions, 155, 156n, 239n
court, royal, daily needs of, 78
court chapel: see chapel, court
Creuzburg, 286, 305
curtis, curtes, definition of, 137n
custumal, monastic, 119, 120, 124

Dahlum, 155, 290
Daleminzi, 249
Danes, Denmark, 16, 39, 40, 54
Dedi, margrave, 173
Denecke, Dietrich, 80
Derenburg, 140, 154, 156
Deus, Wolf, 80
Diemel River, ford of, 212–13, 300
Dietrich, bishop of Metz, 224, 229, 232
Dietrich, margrave of the Northern March, 174, 175
Dobrava, Bohemian princess, 38
dona annualia (annua), 77, 78, 163, 163n
Dorndorf, 261
Dortmund, 59, 179, 299
dos, 6
dower, 7, 14–15, 157, 176, 223, 224, 229, 232
Dransfeld, 219, 221, 222
Droge, Georg, 83
Drübeck, convent, 175, 292, 294
Druthmar, abbot of Corvey, 123, 124, 200
duchies, dukes, 5, 20n, 23, 25–7
  quasi-royal or vice-regal status of, 10, 11–12, 26–7
  royal appointment of, 13, 17
Duderstadt, 144–5
Duisburg, 179, 185–7, 191, 299
Durchzugsgebiete (transit zones), 61, 66–8, 299–300
  function of in itinerary, 66–7, 297, 304–9
  lengths of visits in, 67

Easter, sites of celebration, 7
  at Magdeburg (952), 25, 168

365

at Merseburg, 43
at Quedlinburg (941), 19
eastern policy, Ottonian, 9, 14, 37–44
Eberhard, abbot of Tegernsee, 56
Eberhard, duke of Bavaria, 16–17, 25
Eberhard, duke of Franconia, 11, 13,
    17–18, 19, 178, 237
Eberhard, monk of Fulda, 267, 268,
    279–80
Ebsdorf, 274
Echternach, monastery, 109
Echzell, 282, 283, 284
Eckhard, count, 213–14
economy, 78, 81
Edith, wife of Otto I, 6, 14
    death of (946), 21, 24, 25
    property in Magdeburg, 6, 163
Egbert, abbot of Fulda, 269
Eherin Forest, 283
Ehrenzell, 115–16
Eigil, 265
Eisenach, 240–1, 262, 263, 276, 285
Ekkehard I, margrave of Meißen, 41
Ekkehardine, comital family, 236
Elbe River, as frontier, 4, 41, 42
election
    abbatial, 7; freedom of granted, 73–4,
        139, 191n, 192n, 214, 217, 242; royal
        influence upon, 28, 29, 73
    episcopal, royal influence upon, 28, 29,
        32
    royal: of 919, 5, 11; of 936, 5
empire, emperor, 25, 36, 37, 39
Eresburg, 197, 201, 244
Erfurt, 241, 262–3, 287
    royal assembly at, 3, 16
    synod of (932), 15
Erkanbert, bishop of Minden, 244
Erkenbert, abbot of Corvey, 201
Erlolf, abbot of Fulda, 280
Ermschwerd, 274–5
Ernest II, duke of Swabia, 74
Erwin, count of Merseburg, 246
Erwitte, 179
Eschwege, royal *curtis* and convent, 151,
        157–8, 211, 223, 234n, 240, 255, 290
    royal visits at, 158, 269, 273
Essen, convent, 67, 178, 179, 186, 187,
        190–4, 297
    as a 'model' convent, 190, 298
    connections to royal family, 190–2, 298
    expansion of the church at, 191, 298
    grants of property and rights for, 191n,
        192

grants of sovereign rights to, 192
location of, 191–2, 193
market at, 192, 298
property division at, 114–16
royal visits to, 192, 297–8
estate organization, 81–3, 181–5
Eugene, pope, 209
Ezzo, count palatine, 192

feasting: *see* meals, ceremonial
Felten, Franz, 91, 111
Fernzonen (remote areas), 61, 65–6
feud, 6n, 18n, 25
fisc, Carolingian, 9, 20–1, 22
Fischbeck, 207–8, 299
fishing rights (privileges), 31
Flavigny, monastery, 90, 107
Fleckenstein, Josef, 70, 71
fodrum, 75, 86, 280–1
Folcwin of St Bertin, 128, 129
foreign policy: *see under* government
forest rights, 31, 161, 239, 282
    defined, 283
    granted, 154, 164, 261, 283–4
forests, 137, 216, 219, 222, 225, 300
Fortunatus, patriarch of Grado, 93
Franconia, duchy and region, 20, 236–8
    duchy suppressed, 20, 178, 237
Frankfurt, 15n, 20, 22, 225, 240, 255, 267
    celebration of Christmas at, 19
    council of (951), 73
    synod of (1007), 223–4
    Weistum of (951), 73–4, 250
Franks and Saxons, as dominant people,
        9–10, 13n, 20–3, 64
Frederick I (Barbarossa), 175, 194
Frederick of Luxembourg, brother of
        Kunigunda, 228n
Friderun, foundress of Kemnade, 207
Friemersheim, 83, 126, 131, 182, 183, 189
friendship: *see amicitia*
Friesenfeld, 244–5, 246, 248, 250
Fritzlar, 240, 257, 261, 274
frontier, 8–9
    eastern, 37, 39–44
    western, 12, 14, 35–6
Frose, convent, 176, 292
Frotharius, bishop of Toul, 93–4
Fulda, monastery, 43, 90, 92, 211, 241–54
    passim, 265–82, 282–9 *passim*, 304–6
    bridge at, 265
    celebration of Easter at, 267
    church (chapels) at, 268, 269, 270–2
    foundation of, 241–2

Index

grants of comital rights, 239, 288–9,
  307–8
grants of property and rights for,
  242
grants of sovereign rights to, 266, 268,
  282–9
location of, 243, 253, 265–6
market(s) at or of, 276, 286–8, 306
military responsibilities of, 243–4
missionary activity from, 242–4
property division in, 112, 122–3
property exchanges with the Ottonians,
  247, 248n
property holdings of, 244–7, 272–9
reception of royal grants, 96
reform of, 122–3
royal protection of, 242
royal residence at, 270–2
royal visits to (and to its properties),
  256–8, 266–70, 272–9, 284, 304–6
Fulda River, 218–19, 265–6, 286
  fords over, 219, 220, 230, 240, 254–5,
    258, 261, 265–6, 266n, 273, 301,
    305

Gandersheim, convent, 62, 69, 72, 149–61,
  290, 295
as a 'model' convent, 190
connections to royal family, 150–1,
  152, 293
expansion of the church at, 153, 296
foundation of, 149–50
Gandersheimer Supplik, 160, 161n
grants of property and rights for,
  154–6, 157–8
grants of sovereign rights to, 154–5,
  288
location of, 151–2, 156–7
market at, 154, 193, 296
royal assemblies at, 152, 293
royal protection of, 150
royal residence at, 152–3
royal visits to, 152–4, 256, 295
struggle with bishopric of Hildesheim,
  221
Gebesee, 241, 263, 264
Gebhard I, bishop of Regensburg, 101–2
geneaologies, royal, 310–11
Gera River, 264
  ford over, 241, 263, 264
Gerberga, abbess of Gandersheim and
  daughter of Duke Henry I, of
  Bavaria, 150
Gerberga, daughter of King Henry I, 22

Geresheim, 186
Gernrode, convent, 69, 175–6, 292, 294
Gero, archbishop of Cologne, 170, 171
Gero, count, 174
Gero, margrave (d. 965), 18, 37, 38, 176
Gerstungen, 241, 255, 259, 275–7, 285,
  286, 305
Gertrude, abbess of Niedermünster, 131
Geseke, convent, 73, 178, 179, 203–4, 299
Giebichenstein, 174
Gieboldehausen, 158
Gimte, 218, 220, 221, 222
Gisela, abbess of Nivelles, 109
Gisela, empress, 256
Giselbert, duke of Lotharingia, 13, 19, 22
Glieberg, clan, 238
Gniezno, 41
Godehard, abbot and reformer, 120, 126,
  252
Gorze, monastery, 120, 129
Goslar, 62, 140, 152, 156–61, 227, 257,
  259, 269, 295
  celebration of Easter at, 264
Göss, convent, 103
Gotha, 240–1, 262–3, 276
Gottern, 263
government
  co-operation between kings and
    ecclesiastical institutions, 28–31,
    34–5, 48, 290–1
  foreign policy, 12, 14, 35–42
  see also itinerary, support of by
    monastic institutions
Gozpert, abbot of Tegernsee, 55
Grabfeld, 265, 282
Grone, royal palace (Pfalz, curtis), 144–5,
  151, 152, 156, 221, 240, 255
  assembly at, 145
(Groß)seelheim, 273–4
(Großen)Lupnitz, 263, 276, 285
Grundherr, Grundherrschaft: see seigneur,
  seigneurie grande

Hadamar, abbot of Fulda, 268, 271
Hadwig, daughter of Duke Henry I of
  Bavaria, 26
Hagenrode, 171
Hahold, Haholds, 73, 178, 204, 238, 299
Haina, 265, 276–7, 287, 306
Halberstadt, bishopric, 38, 43, 175, 258
Hamburg–Bremen, archbishopric, 38
Hameln, 179, 244n
Hammelburg, 240, 255, 284, 305
Harald Bluetooth, 38–9

Hardehausen, monastery, 203
Harz mountains, 140, 148, 151, 161, 244
  mining of silver in, 154
Harzburg, 258, 273
Harzgerode, 147
Hassegau, 244
Hatheburg, first wife of Henry I
  (marriage repudiated), 137, 246
Hathwig, abbess of Essen, 191
Hatto, archbishop of Mainz, 237
Havelberg, 38, 39, 40
Heberolle, 83
Hedemünden, 219, 226, 230, 274
hegemony, 36, 41, 42
Heiligenstadt, 240
Heimboldshausen, 241, 255, 265
Heimpel, Hermann, 68
Heitanrich, abbot of Werden, 127, 185
Hellweg, 68, 69, 80, 151, 156, 177–81,
  184, 186, 297, 299
  course of, 179–80, 185, 239, 307
Helmarshausen, monastery, 68, 211,
  212–16, 300
  foundation of, 212–14
  granted to Paderborn, 74, 215–16, 300
  grants of property and rights for,
  213–14
  grants of sovereign rights to, 214
  location of, 212–13
  market at, 214, 286
  royal protection of, 213
Helmburg, foundress of Fischbeck, 207
Helmburg, Saxon noblewoman, 117,
  219–20
Helmstedt, 187
Hemma, abbess of Hilwartshausen (also
  named 'Helmburg'), 217, 220
Henry I, duke of Saxony and king, 3, 5,
  11–16, 47, 104, 237, 246
  charters of, for Kempten, 104–5
  foreign policy of, 14–16, 246–7
  house ordering of (929), 14–15
  western policy of, 12, 14
Henry II, king and emperor, 36, 53, 56,
  59, 101, 102–3, 120–2, 132–5, 172–3,
  190, 198, 215–16, 223–8 *passim*,
  250–2, 267–8, 275
  accession crisis, 40, 41
  celebration of Pentecost at Werden,
  185, 189–90, 225, 298
  celebration of St Vitus day at Corvey,
  198, 298
  charters of: for Alsleben, 172, 175; for
  Fulda, 256, 284–6; for Gandersheim,
  154–5; for Göss, 103; for Hersfeld,

250–2, 261, 264, 283–7; for
  Hilwartshausen, 221; for Kaufungen,
  226–31, 301; for Kemnade, 208; for
  Kunigunda, 224; for Memleben,
  250; for Niedermünster, 132; for
  Nienburg, 172, 173; for
  Obermünster, 132; for Prüm, 122;
  for St Emmeram, 104; for St
  Maximin, 132–3
  expansion of the royal itinerary under,
  42, 55, 66, 235, 299
  favoured itinerary halting points, 146
  founder of Bamberg, 43, 43n, 223–4
  founder of convents, 223
  governmental programme, 42–4,
  120–1, 178–9, 212, 223, 239, 246n,
  250–2, 284, 301, 304, 307
  intercessor for St Emmeram, 102–4
  monastic reform under, 120–7, 198,
  252, 307
  relations with powers in the east, 41–2,
  59
Henry III, king and emperor, 53
  charters of: for Essen, 189, 192; for
  Fulda, 257, 288; for Herford, 206;
  for Hersfeld, 126, 257, 264, 287; for
  Hilwartshausen, 221; for Kaufungen,
  231, 301; for Nienburg, 173; for
  Quedlinburg, 149
  expansion of the royal itinerary, 55, 66,
  235, 299
  favoured itinerary halting points, 152
Henry IV, king and emperor, 74, 131,
  173, 233–4, 257–9, 275–6
  charters of: for Niedermünster, 131;
  for Obermünster, 131
  favoured itinerary halting points, 152,
  257–9
Henry V, king and emperor, 58, 148
Henry VI, king and emperor, 194
Henry I, brother of Otto I, duke of
  Bavaria, 3, 17, 18–19, 22–3, 24–5,
  178, 197
Henry II, the Quarrelsome, duke of
  Bavaria, 26, 105, 141–2, 224, 278
Henry V, duke of Bavaria, 55, 56, 103
Herford, convent, 113, 179, 206–7
  as a 'model' convent, 206
  foundation of, 206
  grants of property and rights for, 207
  grants of sovereign rights to, 206
  location of, 206
  market at, 193, 206, 299
  royal visits to, 206–7, 299
Heririch, 98

Hermann, abbot of Corvey, 203
Hermann I, duke of Swabia, 13, 21, 237
Hermann Billung, margrave and duke in
    Saxony, 18, 24, 25, 37, 53-4
    advent in Magdeburg, 54
Hersfeld, monastery, 43, 68, 74, 90, 112,
    211, 242-54 *passim*, 254-65, 282-9
    passim, 304-6
    celebration of Pentecost at, 257
    church at, 256, 259-60
    'eastern' road of, 244-5, 263-4
    foundation of, 241-2
    grants of property and rights for,
        247-8, 250, 252, 264
    grants of sovereign rights to, 261, 262,
        282-9
    location of, 243, 253, 254-5
    market(s) at or of, 262, 286-8, 306
    military responsibilities of, 245, 258,
        261, 263
    missionary activity from, 242, 244, 245,
        249
    property division in, 126
    property exchanges with the Ottonians,
        246-9, 252, 261, 264
    property holdings of, 244-7, 260-5
    reform of, 122-3, 252
    royal protection of, 242
    royal residence at, 259
    royal visits to (and to its properties),
        255-65, 304-6
Herstelle, 213
Hesse, 62, 304
    geopolitical structure of, 235-41
Heusinger, Bruno, 79, 295
Hevelli, 38, 249
Hildesheim, bishopric, 159-60
Hilduin, abbot of St Germain-des-Prés,
    128
Hilwartshausen, convent, 68, 117, 211,
    216-22, 300
    foundation of, 216-17
    granted to Bernward of Hildesheim,
        221
    grants of property and rights for, 217,
        219-20, 221
    location of, 216, 218-20
    royal protection of, 217-18
    royal visits to, 221
Hitherius, abbot of Tours, 107
Hochseegau, east Saxon *pagus*, 244-5, 247,
    248, 250
Holy Lance, 41
Hömberg, Albert, 80, 204
Hörsel River, 285

hospitality (accommodation and
    provision), 34, 51, 60, 68, 75, 86,
    144, 153
Höxter, 196
Hrotgard, abbess of Hilwartshausen, 221
Hrotsvitha of Gandersheim, 59
Hünfeld, 240, 262, 265, 305
Hunfridings, 10
Hunfried, archbishop of Magdeburg, 256
Hungary, Hungarians: *see* Magyars
Hungen, 240, 255, 260, 273
Hunold, bishop of Merseburg, 256
hunting
    areas, 139, 140, 148, 197
    rights, 288; defined, 283; granted, 154,
        261, 283
Huschner, Wolfgang, 61

Ida, abbess of Essen, 191
Ida, wife of Liudolf, 21, 220, 237
Imma, foundress of Kemnade, 207
immunity (*immunitas*), 29, 31, 72, 73
    ban, 34, 284-5
    definition of, 29
    grants of, 113, 115, 125, 139, 150, 179,
        191n, 192n, 213, 217, 242
income, fiscal, 31
indiculus loricatorum, 34, 118
indivisibility of the realm, 5n, 7n, 13-14,
    18, 20, 23
Ingelheim, 20, 59, 139, 225, 265
    synod of (948), 36
Innocent, St, 8
insignia, royal: *see* regalia
Ismundus, abbot of Moyenmoutier, 94
Italy, Italians, 24-5, 36-7
itinerary (*iter*), itineration, 9, 34, 48, 51,
    52, 68, 252-4
    carefully administered, 53, 56-7, 59-60,
        63
    expansion of, 42, 55, 66, 235
    frequency of, 47
    method of establishment of, 60, 253-4
    nature of, 46-7, 136, 295-6
    of abbots and bishops, 45
    of kings, 15, 45, 254, 260
    outside of Europe, 45-6
    support of by monastic institutions,
        291-4, 296-309

John VIII, pope, 153
Judith, abbess of Kemnade, 209
Judith, daughter of Duke Arnulf of
    Bavaria, wife of Duke Henry I of
    Bavaria, 22, 26, 100, 102-3

Index

Jühnde, 219, 221, 222
justice, jurisdiction, 29, 39, 174, 178, 275
  high justice, 29, 34, 288
  low justice, 29, 288

Kadeloh, bishop of Naumburg, 256
Kämmerzell, 265, 266, 305
Kassel, 218, 240, 255
  Pfalz and fiscal district of, 223–5, 229, 230, 290
Kaufungen, *Pfalz* and convent, 68, 211–12, 222–34, 301, 306
  celebration of religious feasts at, 225, 227
  connections to royal family, 223–8 *passim*
  expansion of church at, 232, 233
  foundation of, 222, 223–8
  granted to Speyer, 229, 233–4
  grants of property and rights for, 226–30, 301
  grants of sovereign rights to, 227, 231, 301
  location of, 223, 230
  market(s) at or of, 227, 231, 286, 301
  royal assemblies at, 225
  royal protection of, 229–30
  royal residence at, 224
  royal visits to, 221, 224–6, 233, 256, 257, 268, 269
Kaufunger Forest (*Wald*), 219, 300
Keller, Hagen, 64
Kemnade, 202, 207–9, 299
Kempten, monastery, 72, 74
Kernlandschaften (central zones), 61, 62–4
kingdom, indivisibility of: see indivisibility
kingship, Carolingian models of, 4, 9, 12, 14, 18n, 20
  core regions of, 62–4
  sacral, 47, 48–50, 298
  sacral representation of, 49, 141–2, 153, 189, 191, 200, 233, 271–2, 290, 293, 303
  see also symbolism of state
Kölleda, 263
Königsfutter: see *kunigesphuter*
Königsklöster, 72
  see also monasteries, royal
Königsstufe (*konynxstope*), 193, 194
Kropat, Wolf-Arno, 80
kunigesphuter, 279–81
Kunigunda, queen and empress, 103, 175, 212, 222–33 *passim*

dower, of 223, 229, 232, 301
foundress of Kaufungen, 223–8, 290–1

Lampert, monk of Hersfeld and annalist, 137, 159, 161, 258, 297, 306
land registers, monastic, 83–4, 122–3, 126–7, 130–1, 181–5, 200–1, 279–81, 286, 297, 298
Langensalza, 241, 263
lauds, 49
Lausanne, Annals of, 15
Lausitzi, 38
lay abbots (abbesses), lay abbacy, 87–8, 91–2, 111–12, 246
Lech, battle of the (955), 16, 25, 36, 38, 52
Lesne, Emil, 86, 87
Leyser, Karl, 9, 63, 174, 202, 248n, 296, 302
libri memoriales, 15, 143, 150, 191
Liudger, St, 188
Liudolf, chaplain, 268
Liudolf, duke of Swabia and son of Otto I
  by Edith, 21, 23, 59, 64, 237
  rebellion of, 24–6, 238
Liudolfings, 3, 10, 63, 67, 137, 139, 145, 149–52, 190–1, 236, 246
  see also Ottonians
Liudprand, bishop of Cremona, historian, 22
Liutgard (d. 953), daughter of Otto I, 22
Liutizi, 38, 40, 41
Liutpoldings, 10, 19
Lorsch, monastery, 43
  given to Adalbert of Hamburg, 74
  reception of grants, 99
Lothar (941–86), king of west Francia, 36
Lothar I, Carolingian emperor, as a monastic benefactor, 107
Lotharingia, Lotharingians, 4, 5n, 11, 12, 21–2, 27, 108–10
  Lower Lotharingia, 27, 62, 64
  Upper Lotharingia, 27, 53, 62, 65
Louis V, king of west Francia, 36
Louis the Child, east Frankish king, 9, 11, 57
Louis the German, Carolingian king, as a monastic benefactor, 96, 113–14
Louis the Pious, Carolingian emperor, 29, 89, 90, 92–4
  as a monastic benefactor, 96, 107, 128, 201
Louis the Younger, east Frankish king, 149
Ludowing, comital family, 236

Index

Lull, bishop of Mainz, 241–2, 260
Lupnitz: see (Großen)Lupnitz
Luxembourg, comital family, 232

McKitterick, Rosamond, 302
Maelstat, 288
Magdeburg, royal *curtis*, fortress, *civitas*
    and district, 6, 8, 9, 22
    burial site of Otto I and Edith, 8, 141,
        293
    centre of trade, 8
    roads leading to, 140, 151–2
Magdeburg, St Maurice, monastery and
    archbishopric, 162–9, 290, 292
    archbishopric, foundation of, 38–40,
        162, 247
    celebration of Easter at, 168, 173
    celebration of Palm Sunday at, 51, 141,
        168, 173, 293
    grants of property and rights for, 163–6
    grants of sovereign rights to, 164–5
    location of, 8–9
    market at, 165, 169
    missionary activity from, 8–9, 37–40
    monastery, foundation of, 8, 37, 39, 40,
        162–3
    royal assemblies at, 168, 293
    royal protection of, 167
    royal residence at, 163, 166–7, 169, 290
    royal visits to, 167–8
Magyars (Hungary, Hungarians), 14,
    15–16, 24, 25, 37
Mainz, 15, 20
    archbishopric of, 38, 43, 225, 257, 263,
        288
maps, text references to
    Map 1: 5, 62, 63, 235
    Map 2: 37, 249
    Map 3: 48
    Map 4: 62, 66, 235
    Map 5: 137, 138, 170, 180, 203, 291
    Map 6: 137, 140, 145, 151, 156, 170,
        240
    Map 7: 177, 179, 186
    Map 8: 212, 218, 221, 222
    Map 9: 240, 245, 254, 261, 264, 306
    Map 10: 240, 265, 306
    Map 11: 264, 272
marches, margraves, 37
Marin, papal legate, 268
market incomes, as a possible element of
    the *servitium regis*, 138, 147, 149, 169,
        189
market rights (privileges), 31, 147, 149,

    154, 214n, 231, 239, 262, 293, 298
    granted, 146–7, 154, 171, 176, 188, 192,
        201–2, 214, 227, 231, 249, 286–7
    markets, 81, 137, 138, 147–9, 169n, 188–9,
        286, 294, 296, 306
marriage alliance, 13, 21–2
Mathilda, abbess of Essen, daughter of
    Liudolf and Ida, 115, 191, 220
Mathilda, daughter of Otto I, abbess of
    Quedlinburg, 140, 142, 143
    as regent in Saxony, 143
Mathilda, daughter of Otto II, 192
Mathilda, wife of Henry I, 6, 14–15, 148,
    176, 290
    foundress of convent at Quedlinburg, 7
Matthäi, Georg, 87
Maurice (Mauritius), St, 8
    feast of, 168, 293
Maximin, St, monastery: see Saint-
    Maximin
Mayer, Theodor, 68, 71, 72
meals, ceremonial, 5, 15, 141–2
Meiningen, 240, 241, 277
Meinwerk, bishop of Paderborn, 198,
    215–16
Meißen, bishopric, 39, 249
Memleben
    death site for kings, 3, 6n, 40, 248, 292
    royal property and residence at, 3, 246,
        263, 290
Memleben, royal monastery of, 40, 170n,
    263, 290, 294, 296
    foundation of, 247–50, 290
    granted to Hersfeld, 74, 250–2, 264,
        290
    grants of property and rights for, 249,
        250, 264
    grants of sovereign rights to, 249
    market at, 287, 296
    missionary and colonizing mandate of,
        249–50, 251, 294
    royal protection of, 248, 250
    royal visits to, 264–5
memoria, of the Ottonian family, 6, 7, 141,
    142, 150, 168, 292–3, 302–3
merchants, 149, 154
Merseburg, bishopric, 39, 40, 42–3, 252
    celebration of Easter at, 43, 59, 146,
        264, 294, 295
    dissolution and re-foundation of, 42,
        249–50, 251
Merseburg, counts of, 236
Meschede, 204
Metelen, 205

Index

Metz, Wolfgang, 58, 79, 80, 132, 137, 185, 187, 201, 209, 296
Miesco I, ruler of Poland, 38
military service, 34
Minden, bishopric, 179, 299
mining
of salt, 172, 287
of silver, 154, 161, 171, 202
minting rights, 31, 169, 239, 293, 298
granted, 146, 154, 165, 171, 176, 188, 193, 201–2, 214, 249, 266, 286–8
missi dominici, 76, 93–4
mission, Christianization, 9, 37–40, 171, 243–5, 249–50
Moffendorf, 248, 252
monasteries (convents), royal
alienation of, 72, 73–4
legal definition of, 70–5
location on royal roads, 140–1
supporting the itinerary, 67–70, 75
use as prisons, 76
monastic reform, 27, 87, 89, 111
Carolingian, 92
Gorzean, 111, 119–27, 252
Moyenmoutier, monastery, 93
Mühlhausen, royal palace (*Pfalz*), 145, 240, 241, 263, 277
Müller-Mertens, Eckhard, 60–1, 63, 80, 295–6
Münden, 218, 220

Nahzonen, 61, 295, 299
Naumburg, bishopric, 39
Netra, 288, 305
Neuß, 179, 186
Niederaltaich, 114
Niedermünster, 70, 131
Nienburg, monastery, 170–4, 292, 294
foundation of, 170–1
grants of property and rights for, 171
grants of sovereign rights to, 171
location of, 170–1, 172
market(s) at or of, 171–2, 296
missionary activity from, 171, 294
royal visits to, 172–3
Nijmegen, 185–6
Nivelles, convent, 109
Nordhausen, 240, 290, 292, 296
convent of, 176, 290, 292, 294
Notitia de servitio monasteriorum, 76n, 77, 93, 112n
Nuremberg, royal residence, 257, 269

Obermünster, 70, 131

Oeren, convent, 74, 130
Ohrdruf, 241, 262
Oldenburg, bishopric, 39
ordeal, judicial, 39, 174
Ortesvecha (*Ortesweg*), 265
Osterhausen, 248
Otbert, 97
Otgar, abbot of Niederaltaich, 114
Otto I, king and emperor, 74, 105, 196–7, 278
as a monastic benefactor, 115, 130
charters of: for Corvey, 196, 201–2; for Drübeck, 175; for Essen, 115–16, 192; for Fischbeck, 207; for Fulda, 283; for Gernrode, 175; for Hilwartshausen, 216–17, 220; for Niedermünster, 132; for Nordhausen, 176; for Oeren, 130; for Quedlinburg, 138–9; for St Emmeram, 105; for St Maurice at Magdeburg, 162–3, 164–5; for Stavelot-Malmédy, 125
coronation, 4–5; imperial, 36
death of, 64
designation as king, 3, 5, 47
early crises, 16–20, 23–6, 178, 197, 237
favoured itinerary halting points, 140, 162
foreign policy of, 35–40; in Italy, 24–5, 36–7
founder of monasteries and convents, 6–7, 8–9, 138–40, 162–3
itinerary of, 60, 254, 304
practice of government, 9, 16–17, 20, 23, 118, 178, 197, 237–9, 246
Otto II, king and emperor, 34, 36, 285
charters of: for Alsleben, 174; for Drübeck, 175; for Fulda, 283, 285; for Gandersheim, 150, 155; for Gernrode, 175; for Hersfeld, 285; for Hilwartshausen, 217, 220; for Magdeburg, 166; for Memleben, 248–9; for Nienburg, 171; for Nordhausen, 176; for Quedlinburg, 144–5; for St Maximin, 110; for Sophie, 150; for Werden, 188
Otto III, king and emperor, 34, 36, 66, 101, 278
accession crisis, 40, 64, 141–2, 278
alliance with Poland, 41, 250
charters of: for Corvey, 197; for Essen, 192; for Gandersheim, 150, 154, 158; for Helmarshausen, 213, 214; for Hilwartshausen, 220, for Memleben,

249, 264; for Nienburg, 171, 172;
for Quedlinburg, 145, 146–9; for
Sophie, 150, 157
favoured itinerary halting points, 140,
152
itinerary of, 305
pilgrimage to Poland (1000), 41
regency of, 64
spends Easter at Quedlinburg, (986)
141, (1000) 142
Otto, duke of Lotharingia, 22
Otto, Liudolfing count, 149
Otto the Illustrious, duke of Saxony, 112,
236, 246
as lay abbot of Hersfeld, 112, 246
Ottonian 'system', 26n, 27–35, 28n, 308
Ottonians (Saxon royal family), 3, 63, 67,
177–8, 190–1, 211–12
cult of the: see memoria
economic and market policies of,
148–9, 154, 171, 212, 214–15, 223,
231–3, 294–5, 301
foreign policy of, 12, 14–16, 24–5,
35–40, 42–3, 247–52, 294
use of marriage alliances, 9, 13, 21–2
use of writing in government, 51–2
Ottonianum, 267

Paderborn, bishopric, 68, 74, 179, 215–16,
226, 239n, 243, 255
celebration of Christmas at, 227
palaces (palatia), royal, 137
granted, 155, 290
Parisse, Michel, 302
Paschal II, pope, 58, 153
Pavia, 24, 36
peace, 14
Peringer, abbot of Tegernsee, 55, 56
Peyer, Hans Conrad, 307
Pfalz, Pfalzen: see residences, royal
Piasts: see Poland
Pippin, Carolingian king, 242
Pöhlde, 157, 292
celebration of Christmas at, 59, 256,
269, 290, 292
Pöhlder Annals, 78
Poland, 38–9, 41
polyptych, 77, 83
Poppo I, reformer and abbot of Stavelot-
Malmédy, 124–5
Poppo II, abbot of Stavelot-Malmédy,
125
Pöschl, Arnold, 86
Poznań, 39

Prague, 39
prebend, monastic (conventual), 88, 97
definition of, 86
development of: in the east Frankish
realm, 110–27; in the west Frankish
realm, 106–10
progress, royal: see itinerary
property, monastic, alienation or
secularization of, 85, 92–5, 98
division of, 86–7, 88–9, 91–2, 106–27
passim
increase of, 89–90
protection
papal: grants of, 153, 174n
royal (mundiburdium), 29, 71, 72, 74, 75,
204; benefits from, 30; grants of,
125, 138, 150, 163n, 170n, 174, 175,
176, 179, 192n, 213, 217, 242
Prüm, monastery, reception of royal
grants, 96, 98
reform of, 121–2
Przemyslids: see Bohemia

Quedlinburg
burial site of Henry I, 4, 6, 138
royal residence at 6, 138
Quedlinburg, convent, 69, 72, 138–49,
295
as a 'model' convent, 190
celebration of Christmas at, 141n
celebration of Easter at, 141, 142, 148,
168, 173, 175n, 293
connections to royal family, 140–1,
143–4, 293
expansion of the church at, 142, 296
foundation of, 6, 138–9, 142
grants of property and rights for, 139,
144–6
grants of sovereign rights to, 146–7,
149
location of, 140
market at, 147, 149, 193
royal assemblies at, 141, 293
royal protection of, 138–9
royal residence at, 142, 144, 147, 290
royal visits to, 140–3, 256

Rammelsberg, 161
discovery of silver at, 41, 154
Ramwold, abbot at St Emmeram, 101
Ratbod, archbishop of Trier, 109
realm, structure of, 9, 45, 60–70
rebellion, noble, 6, 16–20
rebellion, Slavic: see Slavs, uprising

Recknitz, 38
Redarii, 53, 54
regalia, 4, 11, 58, 81
Regensburg, 70, 73
Reginarids, 11
regna, 136, 268
Reichenau, monastery, 15
Reichskirche, 69, 121
Reichsklöster, 72
  see also monasteries, royal
Reichstag: *see* assemblies, royal
Reinhard Forest (*Wald*), 219, 220, 222,
  300
Reinhausen, counts of, 238
Rennsteig, 241, 262
Renovatio imperii Romanorum, 42n
Renovatio regni Francorum, 42, 120
residences, royal, 34, 47–8, 80, 179, 186–7,
  290–1, 295–6
Reuter, Timothy, 35n, 52, 308
rex et sacerdos, 48, 50
Rhön, 284
Riade, battle of, 15–16, 37, 52
Richard of St Vanne, monastic reformer,
  124
Richolf, abbot of St Emmeram, 102
Riestedt, 248
Ripen, 38
river basins, geopolitical setting of,
  211–12
roads
  long Hessian, 240, 257, 259, 260, 261,
    272–4
  research of, 80
  royal: in Hesse and Thuringia, 239–41,
    252–4, 260, 263, 265–6, 277; in
    Saxony, 140, 144, 148, 151, 157n,
    158; in the Weser, Werra, and Fulda
    River basins, 211–13, 218–19, 222,
    226; in Westphalia, 177–81, 185–7,
    195–6, 199
  short Hessian, 240, 254–5, 257, 259–60,
    269, 272–3, 275
  upkeep, 57, 76
Robertines, 36
Rohing, abbot of Fulda, 269
Rohr
  royal *Pfalz*, 143, 241, 262, 277–9
  vill of Fulda, 277–9
Rommelshausen, 273
Rösener, Werner, 83
Rottleberode, 147, 148
royal chapel: *see* chapel, court
Rudolf, king, 287

Rudolf II, king of Burgundy (d. 937), 8,
  12
Rudolf III, king of Burgundy (d. 1032),
  35–6
Ruhr River, 179, 186–7, 188
Rule of St Benedict, 93, 114
Ruotger, biographer of Archbishop Brun
  of Cologne, 27
Ruthard, abbot of Fulda, 258

Saale River, as a frontier, 244–6
Saint-Bertin, monastery, 90, 128–9
Saint-Columbe de Sens, monastery, 93
Saint-Denis, monastery, 90, 107
Saint-Emmeram, monastery, 70, 73,
  100–4, 105, 113–14
Saint-Gall, monastery, 15, 90, 97, 117
Saint-Germain-des-Prés, monastery, 90,
  107, 128
Saint-Maurice, monastery in Magdeburg:
  see Magdeburg
Saint-Maximin, monastery in Trier, 8,
  109, 110, 132–4
  reform of, 133n
Saint-Mihiel, monastery, 108
Saint-Servitius, monastery, 74
Saint-Trond, monastery, 256
Salians, 7, 61, 65, 69
Salzungen, 240, 261, 286, 305, 306
Saxon, nobility, 6, 37, 40, 41, 54, 63, 145,
  211
  uprising of (1073), 258
Saxon Annalist, 78, 148
Saxony, Saxons, 62–3, 65, 136–8
  Carolingian wars against, 177, 183–4,
    243–5, 246
  dominant place in royal itinerary, 62–5,
    136, 291–6
Scheden, 219, 221
Schieffer, Rudolf, 87
Schildesche, 206
Schleswig, 38
Schmid, Karl, 68
Schulze, Hans K., 111
Seesen, 151, 155
seigneur, 29
seigneurie grande, 81–2
Semmler, Josef, 72
servitium regis, servitia (royal service), 30,
  58, 69, 72, 75–81, 215, 254, 274, 281
  definition of, 1, 30, 68, 75–7, 86, 182–3
  effect on church property, 85, 108,
    118–19, 123–7, 134–5, 306–7
  historiography of, 79–80

Index

money payment of, 75, 78–9, 182–3,
194
obligation to pray for the king and
realm, 76, 86
obligation to provide accommodation
and upkeep, 75, 78–9, 81, 138,
153–4, 156–61, 166–7, 169, 170, 172,
173–4, 180–5, 189–90, 192, 193–4,
200–3, 205–6, 253, 259–60, 264,
271–2, 277, 279–82, 296–9, 303–9
obligation to provide troops and
weapons, 34n, 76, 118, 203, 277, 306
paid from abbatial property, 127–35
transport of, 76, 78, 139, 159–61, 187,
189
see also hospitality; market incomes
Siegfried, abbot of Fulda and archbishop
of Mainz, 270, 284
Siegfried, count and margrave? (d. 937),
6, 18
Sigebert of Gembloux, 224
Siptenfelde, 139, 140, 141, 144, 148, 290
Slavs, 246, 249–50
as dependent populations, 163–4
Baltic, 9, 37–8
Elbian, 9, 37–8
uprising (983), 40, 42, 249–50, 251
see also Abodrites; Bohemia; frontier;
Hevelli; Lausitzi; Liutizi; Poland;
Wagrians; Wilzes
Smaragdus, abbot of St Mihiel's at
Mosen, 93–4
Soest, 67, 179
Sohlingen, 197–8, 217
Solling Forest, 197, 243
Sophie, daughter of Otto II and abbess of
Gandersheim and Essen, 150–1,
157–8, 191, 205, 212, 295
as consort of Otto III, 150
role in royal elections, 69n, 150–1
sovereign rights (income producing), 34
granted to monasteries, 146–7
Speyer, bishopric, 158, 233–4
Stavelot-Malmédy, monastery
property division in, 124–5, 130
Steele, 178, 187
Stoddenstat, 288
Sturm, abbot of Fulda, 241–2, 243–4
Supplex libellus, 92
Swabia (Swabians), 11, 13
as a Fernzone of the realm, 62, 65, 69
Sylvester II, pope, 213
symbolism of state, 4, 6, 14–15, 46–7,
49–50, 54, 141–2

Tagino, archbishop of Magdeburg, 101n,
175
Tegernsee, monastery, 55–6
Tellenbach, Gerd, 68
Thankmar, son of Henry I, half-brother
of Otto I, 3, 17, 18–19, 178, 197
Thankmarsfeld, monastery, 170
Theophanu, abbess of Essen, 191
Theophanu, empress, wife of Otto II, 143,
150n, 155n, 176, 278
Thiemo, count in Bavaria, 55
Thietmar, margrave, 170, 171
Thietmar of Merseburg (975–1018),
bishop and author of the Chronicon,
7, 54, 102, 148, 175, 223, 224, 250
Thuringia, 62, 66n, 244–7, 304
geopolitical structure of, 235–41
Thuringian forest, 241, 256, 277
Tilleda, 246
tithes
ecclesiastical, 244–5, 247
secular, 139, 144, 164, 245, 247, 249,
261, 285
toll incomes, as a possible element of the
servitium regis, 187
tolls, 31, 81, 293
rights granted to monasteries and
convents, 147, 157, 165, 169, 171,
176, 187, 201, 206, 214, 228, 231,
249, 266
Tours, monastery (St Martin's), 107
trade, 81, 148
trade routes, 147–8, 151, 205, 265–6
traditiones, 95, 97–8, 102–4
transit zones: see Durchzugsgebiete
Translatio Sancti Viti, 195
Trebur, 258, 273
Treysa, 240, 261, 274
tribute, 14, 15, 155n
paid by German rulers, 14, 15–16
paid to German rulers, 37, 38, 40, 41
Trier, archbishopric
synod of (948), 268

Udalrich, bishop of Augsburg, 25, 74, 271
Udo, brother of Duke Hermann of
Swabia, 21
Ulm, 256, 269
Ulrich, St: see Udalrich
Umritt, 46–7, 64, 65, 69n
unction: see anointing of kings
Unstrut River, 244, 246–7, 263, 264
fords over, 241, 263
Urbar, 83, 126n, 183–4, 200

Index

Uta, abbess of Kaufungen, 228, 230

Vacha, 240, 255, 265
Verona, 24
via regia, 262
Vikings, 90
Villikation, 82, 83
Vitus, St, 39, 198
Vogelsberg, 284
Vogtareuth, 104
Voigt, Karl, 129
Vreden, convent, 143, 151, 205, 256, 299

Wagrians, 39
Walbeck, royal *curtis* and convent, 43, 141, 145, 292, 296
   celebration of Palm Sunday at, 146, 294, 295
   granted to Quedlinburg, 145, 290
   location of, 145
   royal visits at, 146
Walh, abbot of Corvey, 123
Wallhausen, 147, 148, 175, 263
Warmund, count, 104n, 105
Wechmar, 262
Weidinger, Ulrich, 83
Weimar, counts of, 236
Weistum of 951: *see under* Frankfurt
Werden, monastery, 83, 179, 181–90, 297
   as a cult centre, 188
   bridge at, 179, 187–8
   church at, 189, 298
   grants of property and rights for, 188
   grants of sovereign rights to, 188, 189
   location of, 185–7
   market(s) at or of, 188–9, 298
   property division in, 126–7, 130–1, 194
   reform of, 123–4
   royal visits to, 184, 185, 190, 225, 298
Werinhar, count, 99
Werl, 179
   counts of, 178
Werla, 62, 140, 152, 156n
   site of Saxon assemblies, 6, 53, 295
Werner, abbot of Fulda, 270, 272
Werner, count and comital family, 229, 238
Werra River, 218–19, 285–6
   fords over, 226, 230, 240, 255, 261, 265, 274–5, 301, 305–6
Weser River, 218–19
   fords over, 213, 218, 219, 222, 300

west Francia, France, development of monastic property in, 106–10
Westera (Sooden-Allendorf), 286
western policy of Henry I, 12, 14
Westphalia, 62, 297, 299
Westwerk(e), 142, 142n, 153, 189, 191, 200, 298
Wetterau, 243, 260, 265, 269, 272, 282, 283
Wibald, abbot of Corvey and Stavelot-Malmédy, 79, 125, 195, 202–3, 208
Wichmann the Elder (Billung), 17, 19
Wichmann the Younger (Billung), 24, 25, 208
Wichmannshausen, 240
Widerad, abbot of Hersfeld, 258, 270
Widukind, monk of Corvey and author of *Saxon History*, 4, 9, 17, 59, 64
Wiehe, 249, 263, 264
Wigbert, St, 244
Wigburg, abbess of Essen, 191
Wigger, margrave of the March of Zeitz, 175
Wildbann: *see* hunting, rights
William (Wilhelm), archbishop of Mainz, 38, 148, 247
Wilzes, 38
wine, transport of, to monastic institutions, 139, 191, 220, 227, 257
Wipo, royal chaplain, biographer of Conrad II, 51, 53n
Wisplinghoff, Erich, 183
Wissembourg, monastery, 74
Wolfgang, bishop of Regensburg, 101–2, 120
Wolfsanger, 218, 227, 229, 230, 231
women
   religious institutions of, 7, 138, 301–4
   royal, as abbesses, 7, 143
   royal, as regents, 143
Worms, bishopric, 12n, 20, 22, 257, 258
writing
   in government, 46, 51–2
   in monastic institutions, 115n
Würzburg, bishopric, 43, 240, 255, 256, 269, 284, 286

Younger Life of Mathilda, 148

Zacharias, pope, 242
Zeitz, bishopric: *see* Naumburg
Zundernhart Forest, 284
Zwentibold, king of Lotharingia, as a monastic benefactor, 86, 108–9

376

Cambridge studies in medieval life and thought
Fourth series

Titles in the series

1 The Beaumont Twins: The Roots and Branches of Power in the Twelfth Century
   D. B. CROUCH
2 The Thought of Gregory the Great*
   G. R. EVANS
3 The Government of England under Henry I*
   JUDITH A. GREEN
4 Charity and Community in Medieval Cambridge
   MIRI RUBIN
5 Autonomy and Community: The Royal Manor of Havering, 1200–1500
   MARJORIE KENISTON MCINTOSH
6 The Political Thought of Baldus de Ubaldis
   JOSEPH CANNING
7 Land and Power in Late Medieval Ferrara: The Rule of the Este, 1350–1450
   TREVOR DEAN
8 William of Tyre: Historian of the Latin East*
   PETER W. EDBURY AND JOHN GORDON ROWE
9 The Royal Saints of Anglo-Saxon England: A Study of West Saxon and East Anglian Cults
   SUSAN J. RIDYARD
10 John of Wales: A Study of the Works and Ideas of a Thirteenth-Century Friar
   JENNY SWANSON
11 Richard III: A Study of Service*
   ROSEMARY HORROX
12 A Marginal Economy? East Anglian Breckland in the Later Middle Ages
   MARK BAILEY
13 Clement VI: The Pontificate and Ideas of an Avignon Pope
   DIANA WOOD
14 Hagiography and the Cult of Saints: The Diocese of Orléans, 800–1200
   THOMAS HEAD
15 Kings and Lords in Conquest England
   ROBIN FLEMING
16 Council and Hierarchy: The Political Thought of William Durant the Younger
   CONSTANTIN FASOLT
17 Warfare in the Latin East, 1192–1291
   CHRISTOPHER MARSHALL
18 Province and Empire: Brittany and the Carolingians
   JULIA M. H. SMITH

* *Also published as a paperback*

19 A Gentry Community: Leicestershire in the Fifteenth Century, *c.* 1422–*c.* 1485
    ERIC ACHESON
20 Baptism and Change in the Early Middle Ages, *c.* 200–1150
    PETER CRAMER
21 Itinerant Kingship and Royal Monasteries in Early Medieval Germany, *c.* 936–1075
    JOHN W. BERNHARDT